Criminal Procedure

Criminal Procedure

SEVENTH EDITION

JOHN M. SCHEB II, Ph.D.
Professor of Political Science
University of Tennessee, Knoxville

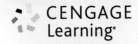

Australia • Brazil • Mexico • Singapore • United Kingdom • United States

Criminal Procedure,
Seventh Edition
John M. Scheb II

Product Director: Marta Lee-Perriard

Product Manager: Carolyn Henderson-Meier

Content Developer: Jeannine Lawless

Product Assistant: Catherine Ryan

Media Developer: Andy Yap

Manufacturing Planner: Judy Inouye

Art & Cover Direction, Production Management, and Composition: Integra Software Services Pvt. Ltd.

Cover Image Credits: © Steve Allen | Dreamstime.com; © Kenny1 | Dreamstime.com; © Steve Lovegrove | Dreamstime.com, Dabarti CGI; iStockphoto/mauro grigollo; iStockphoto/hatman12; copyright iStockphoto/36clicks

For product information and technology assistance, contact us at **Cengage Learning Customer & Sales Support, 1-800-354-9706.**

For permission to use material from this text or product, submit all requests online at **www.cengage.com/permissions.** Further permissions questions can be e-mailed to **permissionrequest@cengage.com.**

Library of Congress Control Number: 2013957913

ISBN-13: 978-1-285-45904-2

ISBN-10: 1-285-45904-0

Cengage Learning
200 First Stamford Place, 4th Floor
Stamford, CT 06902
USA

Cengage Learning is a leading provider of customized learning solutions with office locations around the globe, including Singapore, the United Kingdom, Australia, Mexico, Brazil, and Japan. Locate your local office at **www.cengage.com/global.**

Cengage Learning products are represented in Canada by Nelson Education, Ltd.

To learn more about Cengage Learning Solutions, visit **www.cengage.com.**

Purchase any of our products at your local college store or at our preferred online store **www.cengagebrain.com.**

Printed in the United States of America
1 2 3 4 5 6 7 18 17 16 15 14

DISCLAIMER

In this textbook, the author has attempted to present the general principles of procedural criminal law. However, because of the variance in statutes and court decisions from state to state, it is recommended that students and criminal justice professionals conduct their own research or consult with their legal advisors and not assume that principles of law discussed in the text are applicable in their jurisdictions or apply to specific situations.

DEDICATION

This edition of *Criminal Law and Procedure* is dedicated to **Judge John M. Scheb**, the co-author of previous editions of this textbook, who passed away on November 17, 2010.

During his long and distinguished career, Judge Scheb served as a lawyer, a municipal judge, an appellate judge, a city attorney, a mediator, a law professor, and a reserve officer in the Judge Advocate General's Corps of the United States Air Force. He also was an exemplary husband and father. He is sorely missed by his family and many friends and colleagues.

About the Author

JOHN M. SCHEB II was born in Sarasota, Florida, in 1955. He attended the University of Florida from 1974 to 1982, receiving the B.A., M.A., and Ph.D. in political science. He is now Professor and Head of Political Science at the University of Tennessee, Knoxville, where he specializes in public law, courts, and the judicial process. Professor Scheb has authored numerous articles in professional journals and is coauthor of several other textbooks, including: *An Introduction to the American Legal System*, 3rd ed. (Wolters Kluwer 2013), *Law and the Administrative Process* (Thomson/Wadsworth 2005), and *American Constitutional Law*, 5th ed. (Wadsworth/Cengage 2012).

Brief Contents

Table of Contents

Preface

I am pleased to present the seventh edition of *Criminal Procedure*. While students being exposed to this textbook for the first time will not know this, instructors who have used the book in the past know that previous editions were coauthored with my father, the late Judge John M. Scheb. While I am excited to offer a new edition of the book, doing so in the absence of my long-time coauthor is bittersweet.

Like the previous editions, the seventh edition provides a comprehensive introduction to procedural criminal law. It is designed primarily for students of criminal justice, legal studies, political science, and paralegal studies. It is also an appropriate reference for the criminal justice professional who seeks a better understanding of the functioning of the criminal justice system in the United States.

Criminal procedure is among the most dynamic fields of American law. In preparing the seventh edition, I have endeavored to capture the most significant recent developments, including state and federal statutes, appellate court decisions, and trials. And yet I recognize that what students need to know most are the basic concepts of criminal procedure—concepts rooted in the English common law, the U.S. Constitution, and the fifty state constitutions. Thus I continue to emphasize the common-law background and constitutional foundations of criminal procedure.

An Overview of the Text

Part I furnishes an overview of the criminal process and the criminal justice system. Chapter 1 explains the distinction between substantive and procedural criminal law, constitutional requirements pertaining to criminal procedure, and the stages of the criminal process. Chapter 2 surveys the key agencies involved in the enactment and enforcement of the criminal law as well as the adjudication of criminal cases.

Part II of the text examines law enforcement and criminal procedure and contains separate chapters on search and seizure (Chapter 3) and arrest, interrogation, and identification procedures (Chapter 4). The reader is then taken through the pretrial processes (Chapter 5), the criminal trial (Chapter 6), and sentencing and punishment (Chapter 7). The book concludes with an outline of the appeals process and postconviction relief (Chapter 8). Throughout Part II there are numerous examples of how procedures are regulated by federal and state statutes, court rules, and judicial decisions, as well as by the principles of the federal and state constitutions.

What's New in the Seventh Edition?

In addition to thoroughly updating the book with respect to recent judicial decisions, statutes, and trials, I have attempted to streamline the text to make it more accessible to readers. I have also adopted three new pedagogical features: (1) throughout the book, shaded boxes labeled **Jurisprudence** provide summaries of important Supreme Court decisions pertaining to specific issues of criminal procedure; (2) capsules relating back to these key decisions are placed at the end of each chapter; and (3) key terms are now defined in marginal notes so that students do not have to turn to the end of the chapter or the glossary to see find definitions:

On a more detailed level, the following changes were made to the chapter content:

Chapter 1—Fundamentals of Criminal Procedure

- Changed chapter opening vignette to feature case involving shooting of Trayvon Martin by George Zimmerman
- Added Jurisprudence boxes and capsules on two key Supreme Court decisions: *Duncan v. Louisiana* (1968) and *Roper v. Simmons* (2005)

Chapter 2—Organization of the Criminal Justice System

- Updated chapter opening vignette on the Arizona immigration controversy and lawsuit
- Added Jurisprudence boxes and capsules on six key Supreme Court decisions: *Gideon v. Wainwright* (1963), *Hurtado v. California* (1884), *Williams v. Florida* (1970), *Solorio v. United States* (1987), *Hamdan v. Rumsfeld* (2006), and *In re Gault* (1967)
- Filled in incomplete citations from last edition
- Updated data on FBI and prisons
- Updated material on military tribunals
- Shortened treatment of prison populations
- Eliminated Sidebar features; incorporated important material into main text

Chapter 3—Search and Seizure

- Added material on GPS car tracking case, *United States v. Jones* (2012)
- Added Jurisprudence boxes and capsules for eight key cases: *Katz v. United States* (1967); *California v. Greenwood* (1988); *United States v. Ross* (1982); *Terry v. Ohio* (1968); *United States v. Jones* (2012); *Mapp v. Ohio* (1961); *United States v. Leon* (1984); *Herring v. United States* (2009)
- Updated material on the USA Patriot Act and the Foreign Intelligence Surveillance Act
- Added material on NSA spying controversy

Chapter 4—Arrest, Interrogation, and Identification Procedures

- Added discussion of New York City stop and frisk policy and related court case
- Added discussion of recent confessions case, *Salinas v. Texas* (2012)
- Added mention of South Carolina case on DNA swab of arrested persons, *Maryland v. King* (2013)

- Added Jurisprudence boxes and capsules on 13 key cases: *Dunaway v. New York* (1979); *Tennessee v. Garner* (1985); *Minnesota v. Dickerson* (1993); *Illinois v. Wardlow* (2000); *Whren v. United States* (1996); *United States v. Sokolow* (1989); *City of Indianapolis v. Edmond* (2000); *Hiibel v. Sixth Judicial Dist. Court of Nevada* (2004); *Miranda v. Arizona* (1966); *Nix v. Williams* (1984); *New York v. Quarles* (1984); *Arizona v. Fulminante* (1991); *United States v. Wade* (1967)

Chapter 5—The Pretrial Process

- Expanded chapter opener on the Scottsboro case
- Added Jurisprudence boxes and capsules on seven key cases: *Scott v. Illinois* (1980); *Stack v. Boyle* (1951); *United States v. Salerno* (1987); *United States v. Armstrong* (1996); *United States v. Calandra* (1974); *Bruton v. United States* (1968); *Bordenkircher v. Hayes* (1978)

Chapter 6—The Criminal Trial

- Added Jurisprudence boxes and capsules on six key cases: *Williams v. Florida* (1970); *Batson v. Kentucky* (1986); *Rivera v. Illinois* (2009); *Sheppard v. Maxwell* (1966); *Nebraska Press Association v. Stuart* (1976); *Crawford v. Washington* (2004)

Chapter 7—Sentencing and Punishment

- Replaced chapter opener with new vignette on South Carolina decision in *Miller v. Alabama* (2012)
- Added Jurisprudence boxes and capsules on nine key cases: *Kansas v. Hendricks* (1997); *Furman v. Georgia* (1972); *Gregg v. Georgia* (1976); *Ford v. Wainwright* (1986); *Payne v. Tennessee* (1991); *Bearden v. Georgia* (1983); *Cunningham v. California* (2007); *Ewing v. California* (2003); *Apprendi v. New Jersey* (2000)

Chapter 8—Appeal and Postconviction Relief

- Added Jurisprudence boxes and capsules on five key cases: *Chapman v. California* (1967); *Douglas v. California* (1963); *Felker v. Turpin* (1996); *O'Sullivan v. Boerckel* (1999); *Wiggins v. Smith* (2003)

Other Pedagogical Features

Other pedagogical features are included in the book to help students understand and retain the book's content:

- To enhance student comprehension, each chapter contains an **outline** delineating the major topics covered in the chapter.
- **Learning Objectives** highlight each chapter's key topics and themes.
- **Case-in-Point** boxes provide concise summaries of illustrative state court and lower federal court decisions.

- **Key Terms** are identified in boldface type throughout each chapter and listed at the end of the chapter.
- A comprehensive **Glossary** includes definitions of all key terms.
- **Chapter Summaries** keyed to the learning objectives serve to reinforce key concepts.
- To test understanding and stimulate classroom dialogue, a set of **Questions for Thought and Discussion** is placed at the end of each chapter.
- Commencing with Chapter 3, hypothetical **Problems for Discussion and Solution** stimulate students' analytical skills.
- For students and instructors who wish to venture into the realm of **legal research**, Appendix A, "Access to the Law through Legal Research," includes guidance on researching law through the Internet and computerized services.

Ancillaries

Instructor's Manual with Test Bank

Revised by the author, the manual includes learning objectives, key terms, a detailed chapter outline, a chapter summary, discussion topics, student activities, media tools, and a newly expanded test bank. The learning objectives are correlated with the discussion topics, student activities, and media tools. Each chapter's test bank contains questions in multiple-choice, true/false, completion, essay formats, and critical thinking questions with a full answer key. The test bank is coded to the learning objectives that appear in the main text, and includes the section in the main text where the answers can be found. Finally, each question in the test bank has been carefully reviewed by experienced criminal justice instructors for quality, accuracy, and content coverage.

The manual is available for download on the password-protected website and can also be obtained by emailing your local Cengage Learning representative.

Acknowledgments

At the outset I must acknowledge the team at Cengage—in particular, Carolyn Henderson Meier and Rachel McDonald, for their constant support throughout this project. I must also extend thanks to Jeannine Lawless of KHLowery Consulting for her excellent assistance in preparing the manuscript. As always, I thank my wife, Sherilyn Claytor Scheb, for her steadfast support, without which the project could not have been completed. Finally, I wish to thank the reviewers of this and previous editions for their excellent guidance:

Richard Banahan, St. Louis Community College
Richard Barnhart, Dutchess Community College
John Boston, Austin Community College
Thomas Brennan, Lansing Community College
Stanley Brown, Webster University
Patrick Connolly, MiraCosta College
Christine Corken, Loras College
Jo-Ann Della Giustina, Bridgewater State University
Michael Ferrante, Keuka College

Paul Gormley, University of Massachusetts at Lowell
Thomas Gysegem, Kent State University
Ruth Harrison, Yavapai College
Dr. James Jengeleski, Argosy University Online
David Kirkland, Troy University, Dothan
Philip Lucas, The University of Findlay
Dyan McGuire, Saint Louis University
Nicholas Meier, Kalamazoo Valley Community College
Haley Slade, Delta Community College
Gary Todd, Virginia Intermont College
Jason Waller, Tyler Junior College

I have endeavored to make the seventh edition of *Criminal Procedure* the most complete, yet interesting, textbook in the field. I always welcome comments and suggestions from our readers. Of course, I assume responsibility for any errors contained herein.

John M. Scheb II
scheb@utk.edu
Knoxville, TN
August 16, 2013

Legal Foundations of Criminal Procedure

CHAPTER 1

Fundamentals of Criminal Procedure

CHAPTER OUTLINE

JURISPRUDENCE FEATURE BOXES

Duncan v. Louisiana (1968)

Roper v. Simmons (2005)

LEARNING OBJECTIVES

After reading this chapter, you should be able to explain

1. the difference between substantive and procedural criminal law

2. the basic principles governing the American system of criminal justice

3. why a crime is an offense against society and what this means for the prosecution of criminal cases

4. the relevance of the U.S. Constitution, Bill of Rights, and the constitutions of the fifty states to the criminal justice system

5. how to cite and brief a case

6. the basic procedural steps associated with criminal prosecutions

7. the variety of sanctions imposed on people convicted of crimes and the principal justifications for criminal punishment

CHAPTER OPENING VIGNETTE

On the night of February 26, 2012, an African-American teenager named Trayvon Martin was walking through The Retreat at Twin Lakes, a gated community in Sanford, Florida. Martin had just been to a nearby convenience store where he bought candy and a drink, and was walking back to the townhome where he and his father were staying as guests. He was spotted by George Zimmerman, a 28-year-old neighborhood watch volunteer, who thought that the young African-American man looked out of place and was behaving suspiciously. Zimmerman called police from his truck and reported what he had observed, saying "This guy looks like he is up to no good or he is on drugs or something." Zimmerman exited his vehicle and began to follow Martin while keeping the police dispatcher on the line. The dispatcher asked if Zimmerman was following the young man and when Zimmerman replied in the affirmative, the dispatcher told him, "We don't need you to do that." Zimmerman replied, "Okay," but continued his pursuit anyway. The cell phone call was terminated. When the police arrived a few minutes later, they found Trayvon Martin dead on the ground and George Zimmerman standing near the body with a gun in his hand. Zimmerman told police he shot the unarmed 17-year-old in self-defense after being attacked by him. Zimmerman, who had a permit to carry the weapon, was taken into police custody, was questioned and released.

On March 8, Trayvon Martin's family held a press conference to call attention to the case. Four days later, the chief of police announced that there were no grounds upon which to arrest Zimmerman, as there was no evidence to disprove his claim of self-defense. This touched off a wave of protest as well as intense media coverage. There were claims that Zimmerman had used "racial profiling" in identifying Trayvon Martin as a suspicious person. Many questioned how the killing of an unarmed 17-year old ever could be justified as self-defense. The NAACP wrote a letter to the Attorney General of the United States, expressing "no confidence that, absent federal oversight, the Sanford Police Department will devote the necessary degree of care to its investigation" and requesting that federal authorities investigate the case as a possible hate crime. The Attorney General agreed and dispatched the FBI, who after interviewing thirty people who knew George Zimmerman, found no evidence that the shooting of Trayvon Martin was driven by racial bias or animus. The ongoing uproar persuaded Governor Rick Scott to appoint a special prosecutor to investigate the case. That prosecutor eventually charged Zimmerman with second-degree murder. The nation was riveted as the trial was covered constantly on the news networks. And many were shocked in July 2013 when the jury returned a verdict of not guilty.

The frenzy of public communication via mass media, the blogosphere, and Twitter and Facebook in the George Zimmerman case revealed tremendous variance in people's understandings of the justice system. While there is no legally correct view of whether justice was done in the Trayvon Martin killing, it is important that opinions be informed by good understandings of the legal issues and principles involved. That, of course, is the reason for this textbook. As you navigate through these chapters, you will acquire a better understanding of the legal process that took place in the Zimmerman case and how our rules of criminal procedure are developed and applied.

Introduction

rule of law The idea that law, not the discretion of officials, should govern public affairs.

nullum crimen, nulla poena, sine lege "There is no crime, there is no punishment, without law." Refers to the doctrine that one cannot be found guilty of a crime unless there is a violation of an existing provision of law defining the applicable criminal conduct.

All modern societies have developed complex systems for administering criminal justice. What distinguishes democratic societies from authoritarian ones is a commitment to the **rule of law**. In democratic societies such as ours, a person cannot be convicted of a crime unless he or she has committed a specific offense against a law that provides for a penalty. This principle is expressed in the maxim ***nullum crimen, nulla poena, sine lege***, a Latin phrase meaning, "there is no crime, there is no punishment, without law." This concept, like so many of our legal principles, was inherited from the **English common law** that developed during the medieval era and was transplanted to America by way of the colonies. In the United States, formal law governs every aspect of criminal justice, from the enactment of criminal prohibitions to the imposition of punishment upon those who violate these prohibitions.

Basic Principles of American Criminal Justice

English common law The body of law based largely on custom as declared by English judges beginning in the medieval period.

Our criminal law prescribes both substantive and procedural rules governing the everyday operation of the criminal justice system. **Substantive criminal law** prohibits certain forms of conduct by defining crimes and establishing the parameters of penalties. **Procedural criminal law** regulates the enforcement of the substantive law, the determination of guilt, and the punishment of those found guilty of crimes. For example, although substantive law makes the possession of heroin a crime, the

substantive criminal law That branch of the criminal law that defines criminal offenses and defenses and specifies criminal punishments.

procedural criminal law The branch of the criminal law that deals with the processes by which crimes are investigated, prosecuted, and punished.

constitutional supremacy The doctrine that the Constitution is the supreme law of the land and that all actions and policies of government must be consistent with it.

judicial review The power of courts of law to review governmental acts and declare them null and void if they are found to be unconstitutional.

federalism The constitutional distribution of government power and responsibility between the national government and the states.

procedural law regulates the police search and seizure that produce the incriminating evidence. The substantive law makes premeditated murder a crime and sets the penalty to be imposed for those convicted of the offense whereas the procedural law determines the procedures to be observed at trial and, if a conviction ensues, at sentencing. This book deals with the procedural criminal law. It examines the legal rules that govern the criminal process from investigation through arrest, prosecution and the imposition of punishment. We begin our examination with the fundamental constitutional principles that underlie the criminal justice system.

Figure 1.1 provides an overview of the American criminal justice system. The figure suggests three fundamental constitutional principles at work:

1. **Constitutional supremacy.** In keeping with the ideal of the rule of law, the entire system of criminal law and procedure is subordinate to the principles and provisions of the U.S. Constitution. The Constitution sets forth the powers of government, the limits of those powers, and the rights of individuals. The Constitution thus limits government's power to make and enforce criminal sanctions in several important ways. These limitations are enforced by **judicial review**, which is the power of courts of law to invalidate substantive laws and procedures that are determined to be contrary to the Constitution.

2. **Federalism.** There is a fundamental division of authority between the national government in Washington, D.C., and the fifty state governments. Although both levels of government have authority and responsibility in the realm of criminal justice, most of the day-to-day peacekeeping function is exercised by the states and their political subdivisions (primarily counties and cities). Each of the states has its own machinery of government as well as its own constitution that empowers and limits that government. Each state constitution imposes limits on the criminal justice system within that state. Of course, the provisions of the state constitutions, as well as the statutes adopted by the state legislatures, are subordinate to the provisions of the U.S. Constitution and the laws adopted by Congress.

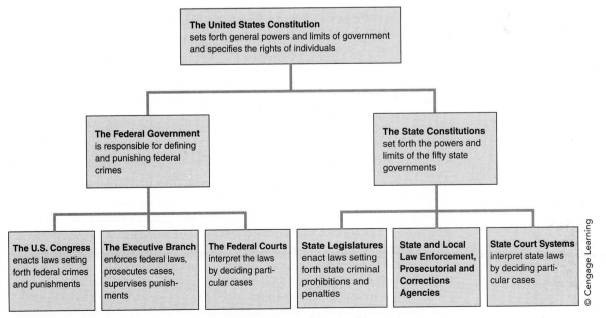

© Cengage Learning

FIGURE 1.1 Overview of the American System of Criminal Law and Procedure.

separation of powers
Constitutional assignment of legislative, executive, and judicial powers to different branches of government.

3. **Separation of powers.** The national government and each of the fifty state governments are constructed on the principle that legislative, executive, and judicial powers must be separated into independent branches of government. Thus, the federal government and the states have their own legislative branches, their own executive branches, and their own systems of courts. The legislative branch is responsible for enacting laws that specify crimes and punishments. The executive branch is responsible for enforcing those prohibitions and for carrying out the punishments imposed by the judicial branch, but it is the judicial branch that interprets the laws and ensures that persons charged with crimes receive fair treatment by the criminal justice system.

The Nature of Criminal Prosecution

actus reus A "wrongful act" which, combined with other necessary elements of crime, constitutes criminal liability.

Every crime involves a wrongful act (*actus reus*) specifically prohibited by the criminal law. For example, in the crime of battery, the *actus reus* is the striking or offensive touching of another person. Even the failure to take action can be considered a wrongful act if the law imposes a duty to take action in a certain situation. For example, a person who fails to file a federal income tax return may be guilty of a federal offense.

mens rea "Guilty mind"; criminal intent.

In most cases, the law requires that the wrongful act be accompanied by criminal intent (*mens rea*). Criminal intent does not refer to a person's motive or reason for acting, but merely refers to having formed a mental purpose to act. To convict a person of a crime, it is not necessary to know why that person committed the crime. It is only necessary to show that the individual intentionally committed a prohibited act. An unintentional act is usually not a crime, although, as we will discover, there are exceptions to this principle. Moreover, in certain instances, one may be held criminally responsible irrespective of intent. Crimes of this latter nature are classified as **strict liability offenses**. A good example of a strict liability offense is selling liquor to a minor.

strict liability offenses
Crimes that do not require proof of the defendant's intent.

Felonies and Misdemeanors

felonies Serious crimes for which a person may be imprisoned for more than one year.

Criminal law distinguishes between serious crimes, known as **felonies**, and less serious offenses, called **misdemeanors**. Generally speaking, felonies are offenses for which the offender can be imprisoned for more than one year; misdemeanors carry jail terms of less than one year. Common examples of felonies include murder, rape, robbery, burglary, aggravated assault, aggravated battery, and grand theft. Typical misdemeanors include petit theft, simple assault and battery, disorderly conduct, prostitution, and driving while intoxicated.

misdemeanors Minor offenses, usually punishable by fine or imprisonment for less than one year.

Crime: An Injury against Society

Our legal system regards crimes not merely as wrongs against particular victims but as offenses against the entire society. Indeed, there does not have to be an individual victim in order for there to be a crime. For example, it is a crime to possess cocaine, even though it is unlikely that a particular individual will claim to have been victimized by another person's use of the drug. This is a crime because society, through its governing institutions, has made a collective judgment that cocaine use is inimical to the public welfare.

Because crime is an injury against society, the government, as society's legal representative, brings charges against persons who are accused of committing crimes. In the United States, we have a federal system—that is, a division of power and responsibility between the national and state governments. Both the national government and the states enact their own criminal laws. Thus, both the national government and the state governments may prosecute persons accused of crimes. The national government initiates a prosecution when a federal (national) law has been violated; a state brings charges against someone who is believed to have violated one of its laws.

The Role of the Crime Victim

victim A person who is the object of a crime or tort.

Because the government prosecutes criminals on behalf of society, the **victim** of a crime is not a party to the criminal prosecution. By filing a complaint with a law enforcement agency, a victim initiates the process that leads to prosecution, but once the prosecution begins, the victim's participation is primarily that of being a witness. Quite often, victims feel lost in the shuffle of the criminal process. They sometimes feel that the system is insensitive or even hostile to their interests in seeing justice done. Most states have taken steps to address victims' concerns, but despite these measures, crime victims remain secondary players in the criminal justice system. The principal parties in a criminal case are the prosecution (that is, the government) and the defendant (that is, the accused person). In some situations, however, the victim may have another remedy: a civil suit to recover damages for losses or injuries suffered.

The Adversarial System

In a very real sense, the prosecution and the defendant are adversaries. While prosecutors may proclaim publicly that their only goals are seeking truth and justice, once criminal charges have been filed the role of the prosecutor is to persuade a court of law that the defendant is guilty of the offense charged. The goal of defense counsel is to find a legal reason why the charges should be dropped or, if the case gets to trial, to persuade a judge or jury that there is reasonable doubt as to the defendant's guilt. Without trivializing the process or in any way diminishing what is at stake, one can look at criminal prosecution as a kind of game. Like any game, the criminal process has rules, and these rules can be referred to collectively as the procedural criminal law.

Sources of Procedural Law

Although the procedural criminal law is rooted in the English common law, it is impacted more profoundly by our federal and state constitutions. It is also determined by legislative bodies through enactment of statutes and by the courts through judicial decisions and the development of rules of court procedure. The U.S. Supreme Court prescribes **rules of procedure** for the federal courts. Generally, the highest court of each state, usually called the state supreme court, is empowered to promulgate rules of procedure for all the courts of that state.

rules of procedure Rules promulgated by courts of law under constitutional or statutory authority governing procedures for trials and other judicial proceedings.

Constitutional Sources of Procedural Law

Bill of Rights A written enumeration of basic rights, usually part of a written constitution—for example, the first ten amendments to the U.S. Constitution.

Many of the most important constitutional provisions relative to criminal justice are found in the **Bill of Rights** (the first ten amendments to the Constitution, adopted by Congress in 1789 and ratified by the states in 1791).

These provisions, which constitute much of the basis of criminal procedure, include the Fourth Amendment prohibition of unreasonable searches and seizures, the Fifth Amendment injunction against compulsory self-incrimination, and the Sixth Amendment right to trial by jury. Finally, the Eighth Amendment prohibition of "cruel and unusual punishments" protects citizens against criminal penalties that are barbaric or excessive.

While this was not the case at the time the Bill of Rights was adopted, nearly all the provisions of the Bill of Rights have been held to apply with equal force to the states and to the national government. See, e.g., *Duncan v. Louisiana,* 391 U.S. 145, 88 S.Ct. 1444, 20 L.Ed.2d 491 (1968). The Supreme Court accomplished this by interpreting the Due Process Clause of the Fourteenth Amendment, which applies specifically to the states, to incorporate most of the protections of the Bill of Rights. Consequently, the Bill of Rights now limits the adoption of criminal laws, whether by Congress, the state legislatures, or the myriad city and county legislative bodies. Thus, the First Amendment prohibits state legislatures, just as it prohibits Congress, from enacting laws abridging the freedoms of speech, press, assembly and religion. The Bill of Rights also limits the actions of police, prosecutors, judges, and corrections officers at the local, state, and national levels. Thus, for example, the Fourth Amendment prohibition of unreasonable searches and seizures applies with equal force to a deputy sheriff in a remote rural area as it does to the FBI.

State legislatures, courts, and law enforcement agencies must also be aware of the limitations contained in their own state constitutions. Although state constitutional provisions are subordinate to provisions of the federal constitution, state constitutions often go beyond the federal constitution in protecting citizens from governmental authorities. For example, in the area of search and seizure, a number of state courts have interpreted their respective state constitutions more stringently than the federal courts have interpreted the Fourth Amendment to the U.S. Constitution.

By far the broadest and most important constitutional principle relating to criminal justice is found in the Due Process Clauses of the Fifth and Fourteenth Amendments to the Constitution. The same principle can be found in similar provisions of every state constitution. Reflecting a legacy that can be traced to the Magna Charta (1215), such provisions forbid the government from taking a person's life, liberty, or property, whether as punishment for a crime or any other reason, without **due process of law**. Due process refers to those procedural safeguards necessary to ensure the fundamental fairness of a legal proceeding. Daniel Webster defined due process to mean "a law which hears before it condemns, which proceeds on inquiry and renders judgment only after trial."

Most fundamentally, due process requires **fair notice** and a **fair hearing**. That is, persons accused of crimes must have ample opportunity to learn of the charges and evidence being brought against them as well as the opportunity to contest those charges and that evidence in open court.

due process of law Procedural and substantive rights of citizens against government actions that threaten the denial of life, liberty, or property.

fair notice The requirement, stemming from due process, that government provide adequate notice to a person before it deprives that person of life, liberty, or property.

fair hearing A hearing in which both parties have a reasonable opportunity to be heard—to present evidence and make arguments.

JURISPRUDENCE

Duncan v. Louisiana, 391 U.S. 145, 88 S.Ct. 1444, 20 L.Ed.2d 491 (1968).

Here the U.S. Supreme Court interpreted the Due Process Clause of the Fourteenth Amendment as incorporating the right to trial by jury recognized by the Sixth Amendment, thus making the right of trial by jury applicable to defendants in state criminal courts. Gary Duncan was convicted of a misdemeanor (simple battery) and under Louisiana law at that time was not entitled to a jury trial. The Supreme Court reversed Duncan's conviction, holding that the right of trial by jury must apply to all serious offenses, including major misdemeanors.

presumption of innocence In a criminal trial, the accused is presumed innocent until proven guilty.

reasonable doubt standard The requirement in a criminal trial that the prosecution prove the defendant's guilt beyond a reasonable doubt.

One of the most basic tenets of due process in criminal cases is the **presumption of innocence**. Unless the defendant pleads guilty, the prosecution must establish the defendant's guilt by evidence produced in court. Everyone accused of a nonpetty offense has the right to a trial by jury (although, we shall see, trials are actually conducted in only a small minority of cases). In a criminal trial, the standard of proof is "beyond a reasonable doubt." The **reasonable doubt standard** differs markedly from the "preponderance of evidence" standard that applies to civil cases. In a civil trial, the judge or jury must find only that the weight of the evidence favors the plaintiff or the defendant. In a criminal case, the fact finder must achieve the "moral certainty" that arises from eliminating "reasonable doubt" as to the defendant's guilt. Of course, it is difficult to define with precision the term "reasonable." Ultimately, this is a judgment call left to the individual judge or juror.

The Role of Courts in Developing the Procedural Law

trial courts Judicial tribunals, usually presided over by one judge, that conduct proceedings and trials in civil and criminal cases with or without a jury.

appellate courts Judicial tribunals that review decisions from lower tribunals.

Courts of law play a crucial role in the development of the procedural criminal law. **Trial courts** exist primarily to make factual determinations, apply settled law to established facts, and impose sanctions on those found guilty of criminal offenses. In so doing, trial courts are bound, as are all courts of law, by relevant constitutional provisions and principles. In reviewing the decisions of trial courts, **appellate courts** must interpret the federal and state constitutions and statutes. The federal and state constitutions are replete with majestic phrases, such as "equal protection of the laws" and "privileges and immunities," that require interpretation. That is, courts must define exactly what these grand phrases mean within the context of particular legal disputes. Likewise, federal and state statutes often use vague language like "affecting commerce" or "reasonable likelihood." Courts must assign meaning to these and a multitude of other terms.

In rendering interpretations of the law, appellate courts generally follow precedent, in keeping with the common-law doctrine of *stare decisis*, which is Latin for "Let the decision stand." In our rapidly changing society, however, courts often encounter situations to which precedent arguably does not or should not apply. In such situations, courts will sometimes deviate from or even overturn precedent. Moreover, there are situations in which there is no applicable precedent. When this occurs, the appellate courts have the opportunity to "make new law." Thus, appellate courts perform an important **lawmaking function** as well as an **error correction function**. Therefore, any serious student of criminal law must follow developments in the **decisional law**—that is, law as developed by courts in deciding cases.

lawmaking function One of the principal functions of an appellate court; often referred to as the law development function.

error correction function The function of appellate courts in reviewing routine appeals and correcting the errors of trial courts.

decisional law Law declared by appellate courts in their written decisions and opinions.

Locating and Citing Judicial Decisions

Throughout this text the reader will find references to decisions of federal and state courts. Court decisions cited in the text are almost always decisions of federal or state appellate courts. For example, *Brandenburg v. Ohio*, 95 U.S. 444; 89 S.Ct. 1827; 23 L.Ed. 2d 430 (1969), indicates the name of the defendant petitioning for review and the state that prosecuted the defendant. Data following the name of the case indicates the name of the court and date of its decision, followed by numbers indicating the volume and page number of the Reporter, a compendium of judicial decisions, where the decision is found. Thus, the decision in *Brandenburg v. Ohio*

"BRIEFING CASES"

Reading judicial decisions, especially the decisions of the U.S. Supreme Court, can be very useful to anyone seeking to understand the criminal law. Quite often instructors will assign cases to be read and frequently will ask their students to "brief" some or all of these cases.

A case brief is simply a summary of a court decision, usually in outline format. Typically, a case brief contains the following elements:

- The name of the case and the date of the decision
- The essential facts of the case
- The key issue(s) of law involved (or those applicable to a point of law being considered)
- The holding (ruling) of the court
- A brief summary of the court's opinion, especially as it relates to key issue(s) in the case
- Summaries of concurring and dissenting opinions, if any
- A statement commenting on the significance of the decision

Here is a sample case brief:

Gideon v. Wainwright
U.S. SUPREME COURT
372 U.S. 335; 83 S.Ct. 792; 9 L.Ed.2d. 799 (1963)

FACTS: Clarence Earl Gideon was convicted of breaking and entering a poolroom with intent to commit a misdemeanor, a felony under Florida law. Unable to afford legal representation, Gideon requested that the trial judge appoint a lawyer to represent him. The judge refused, as Florida law at that time required judges to appoint counsel at public expense to represent indigent defendants only in capital cases.

ISSUE: Whether the Due Process Clause of the Fourteenth Amendment requires state courts to appoint counsel at public expense to represent indigent defendants accused of felonies.

DECISION: The Supreme Court held that this was a denial of the Sixth Amendment right to counsel as applied to the states under the Fourteenth Amendment.

OPINIONS: In his opinion for the Court, Justice Hugo Black reflected on the importance of defense counsel in criminal cases, saying: "The right of one charged with crime to counsel may not be deemed fundamental and essential to fair trials in some countries, but it is in ours."

COMMENT: The *Gideon* decision reflects the Supreme Court's concern for fundamental fairness in the criminal justice system. The decision had a dramatic impact, as many states established public defender offices to deliver defense services to indigent defendants.

© Cengage Learning

was rendered in 1969 by the U.S. Supreme Court and can be found in Volume 95 of the *United States Reports* at page 444, in Volume 89 of the *Supreme Court Reporter* at page 1827, and in Volume 23 of the *Lawyer's Edition*, second series, at page 430. *Whitner v. State*, 482 S.E.2d 777 (S.C. 1997) illustrates a state court decision—in this instance a 1997 decision of the Supreme Court of South Carolina—found in volume 482, page 777 of the second series of the Southeastern Reporter, which encompasses the South Carolina state appellate courts.

The Criminal Process

Certain basic procedural steps are common to all criminal prosecutions, although specific procedures vary greatly among jurisdictions. (Figure 1.2 illustrates the major components of the criminal process.) In every jurisdiction law enforcement agencies make arrests, interrogate persons in custody, and conduct searches and seizures. All of these functions are regulated by the procedural law. In every jurisdiction there are procedures through which persons accused of crimes are formally notified of the charges against them and given an opportunity to answer these charges in court.

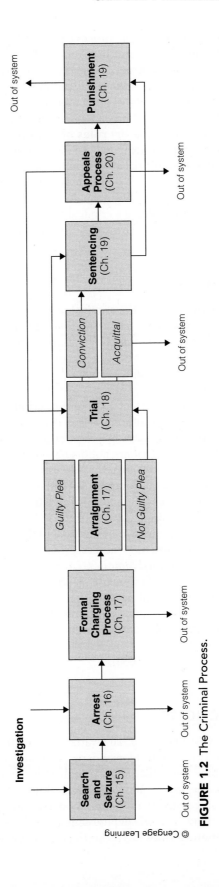

FIGURE 1.2 The Criminal Process.

indictment A formal document handed down by a grand jury accusing one or more persons of the commission of a crime or crimes.

grand jury A group of citizens convened either to conduct an investigation or to determine whether there is sufficient evidence to warrant the prosecution of an accused.

There is a formal charging process, which, depending on the jurisdiction, involves an **indictment** by a **grand jury** or an **information** filed by a prosecutor. In every jurisdiction there is a procedure known as an **arraignment**, in which the defendant enters a plea of guilty or not guilty, or in some instances a plea of *nolo contendere* (no contest). Only a plea of not guilty necessitates a **criminal trial**. The trial is the crown jewel of criminal procedure—an elaborate, highly formal process, governed by **rules of procedure** and **rules of evidence**, for determining guilt or innocence and imposing punishment on those found guilty.

The decisions of trial courts, with respect to pretrial matters as well as the conduct of criminal trials, are subject to review by appellate courts. All court procedures, from the initial appearance of an accused before a magistrate to the decision of an appellate court upholding a criminal conviction and/or sentence, are governed by an elaborate framework of laws, rules, and judicial decisions.

The Sieve Effect

information A document filed by a prosecutor under oath charging one or more persons with commission of a crime.

arraignment An appearance before a court of law for the purpose of pleading to a criminal charge.

criminal trial A trial in a court of law to determine the guilt or innocence of a person charged with a crime.

rules of procedure Rules promulgated by courts of law under constitutional or statutory authority governing procedures for trials and other judicial proceedings.

rules of evidence Legal rules governing the admissibility of evidence at trial.

As cases move through the criminal justice system from arrest through adjudication and, in many instances, toward the imposition of punishment, there is considerable attrition. Of any one hundred felony arrests, perhaps as few as twenty-five will result in convictions. This "sieve effect" occurs for many reasons, including insufficient evidence, police misconduct, procedural errors, and the transfer of young offenders to juvenile courts.

Nationwide, less than 5 percent of criminal cases go to trial. Some cases are dropped by the prosecutor for lack of evidence or because of obvious police misconduct. Others are dismissed by judges at preliminary hearings, usually for similar reasons. In those cases that are not dismissed, defendants usually enter pleas of guilty, very frequently in exchange for concessions from the prosecution. To avoid trial, which is characterized by both delay and uncertainty, the prosecutor may attempt to persuade the defendant to plead guilty, either by reducing the number or severity of charges or by promising not to seek the maximum penalty allowed by law.

The U.S. Supreme Court has upheld the practice of **plea bargaining** against claims that it violates the Due Process Clauses of the Fifth and Fourteenth Amendments. *Brady v. United States,* 397 U.S. 742, 90 S.Ct. 1463, 25 L.Ed.2d 747 (1970); *North Carolina v. Alford,* 400 U.S. 25, 91 S.Ct. 160, 27 L.Ed.2d 162 (1970). However, because there is always a danger of coerced guilty pleas, especially when defendants are ignorant of the law, it is the judge's responsibility to ascertain whether the defendant's guilty plea is voluntarily and knowingly entered and that there is some factual basis for the offense charged. *Boykin v. Alabama,* 395 U.S. 238, 89 S.Ct. 1709, 23 L.Ed.2d 274 (1969).

Criminal Sanctions

plea bargaining Negotiations between a defendant and a prosecutor whereby the defendant agrees to plead guilty in exchange for some concession (such as a reduction in the number of charges brought).

Courts have at their disposal a variety of sanctions to impose on persons convicted of crimes. During the colonial period of American history, and indeed well into the nineteenth century, the **death penalty** was often inflicted for a variety of felonies, including rape, arson, and horse theft. Today, the death penalty is reserved for only the most aggravated forms of murder and is infrequently carried out. **Incarceration** is the conventional mode of punishment prescribed for persons convicted of felonies, while **monetary fines** are by far the most common punishment for those convicted

SIDEBAR — Justifications of Criminal Punishment

- **Retribution**. This is the ancient idea that a wrong-doer must pay his or her debt to society. The biblical phrase "an eye for an eye" is often invoked in this regard. Another oft-used phrase is that criminals must be given their "just deserts." Critics question whether retribution, which they see as little more than legalized vengeance, is a legitimate goal of criminal justice in a civilized society. But defenders of retribution note that it requires proportionality—punishment must fit the crime. In its strictest sense, then, retribution limits the degree of punishment that can be inflicted.

- **Deterrence**. Popularized by the reformers of the eighteenth and early nineteenth centuries, this theory holds that by punishing criminals other potential offenders will be deterred from committing crimes. Today, it is generally assumed that criminal sanctions actually deter potential offenders. This is the idea that punishing persons who commit crimes will prevent other similarly disposed individuals from committing like offenses. This assumes, of course, that potential criminals are rational calculators of costs and benefits associated with particular courses of action. In many cases, this may be basically true, but it certainly does not apply to crimes of passion. Another problem with deterrence theory is that people discount the negative consequences of crime by the improbability of being caught. To be an effective deterrent, punishment would have to be so severe that even those who did not believe that they were going to be caught would not take the risk.

- **Rehabilitation**. Perhaps the loftiest goal of the criminal justice system, rehabilitation means changing the offender to function in civil society without resorting to criminal behavior. On its face, this is the most appealing theory of criminal punishment. We would like to believe that by punishing people we can improve them. Of course, rehabilitation involves more than punishment. It entails various sorts of programs and therapies, each of which is based on its own theory of what causes criminal behavior. Today, high recidivism (repeat offending) rates among those convicted of felonies have made society much less sanguine about its ability to rehabilitate "hardened criminals."

- **Incapacitation**. The idea here is that that punishment should prevent criminals from committing additional crimes. Contemporary American society resorts to imprisonment or, in extreme cases, execution to rid itself of seriously threatening behavior. While nearly everyone favors incapacitation of violent offenders, in practice incapacitation extends beyond the execution or incarceration of violent criminals. For instance, when the state revokes the driver's license of someone convicted of driving while intoxicated, the purpose is primarily incapacitation. Similarly, some states have laws offering convicted rapists the option of taking a drug to render them incapable of committing rape.

---

death penalty Capital punishment; a sentence to death for the commission of a crime.

incarceration Another term for imprisonment.

monetary fines Sums of money that offenders are required to pay as punishment for the commission of crimes.

probation Conditional release of a convicted criminal in lieu of incarceration.

restitution The act of compensating someone for losses suffered.

of misdemeanors. For first-time offenders, especially those convicted of nonviolent crimes, **probation** is a common alternative to incarceration, although probation usually entails a number of restrictions on the offender's freedom.

All criminal sanctions must comport with the Eighth Amendment's prohibition of "cruel and unusual punishments." The Supreme Court has said repeatedly that the Cruel and Unusual Punishments Clause must be interpreted in light of evolving standards of decency in the society. *Trop v. Dulles*, 356 U.S. 86, 78 S.Ct. 590, 2 L.Ed.2d 630 (1958). Thus, in *Roper v. Simmons*, 543 U.S. 551, 125 S.Ct. 1183, 161 L.Ed.2d 1 (2005), the Supreme Court held that the Eighth Amendment prohibits the execution of anyone who was under eighteen at the time of their offense.

As society becomes more cognizant of the rights of crime victims, courts are increasingly likely to require that persons convicted of crimes pay sums of money to their victims by way of **restitution**. Requiring offenders to make restitution and perform community service are common conditions of release on probation. Community

JURISPRUDENCE

Roper v. Simmons, 543 U.S. 551, 125 S.Ct. 1183, 161 L.Ed.2d 1 (2005)

Here the Supreme Court struck down capital punishment for juvenile offenders. The case involved Christopher Simmons, who was seventeen when he kidnapped and murdered a woman after burglarizing her home. Writing for the Court, Justice Anthony Kennedy noted the decreasing frequency with which juvenile offenders were being sentenced to death as evidence of an emerging national consensus against capital punishment for juveniles. Thus, the execution of juvenile offenders, even for the most atrocious crimes, was deemed to be cruel and unusual punishment in violation of the Eighth Amendment.

service is often imposed as a condition as part of a **pretrial diversion** program in which first-time nonviolent offenders are offered the opportunity to avoid prosecution by completing a program of counseling or service. Increasingly, courts are requiring drug offenders to undergo **treatment programs** as conditions of probation.

Conclusion

The American system of criminal justice is rooted in the English common law, but the specifics of criminal procedure have evolved substantially from their rudimentary English origins. Today, criminal cases are governed by complex procedural rules developed by courts based both on legislative enactments and judicial interpretation of relevant constitutional provisions.

One of the more tragic aspects of the crime problem is that many Americans have lost faith in the ability of their government to protect them from criminals, even though crime rates have dropped in recent years. Indeed, in some areas of the country, victims are unlikely even to report crimes to the police. Some victims are unwilling to endure the ordeal of being a witness. Others simply believe that the perpetrator will not be apprehended or, if so, will not be punished. It also must be recognized that in many of the nation's inner cities, many people do not trust the police. Moreover, in certain communities cooperation with the police can be dangerous, as criminal gangs will often retaliate against those who cooperate with the authorities.

Our state and federal governments are severely constrained by both law and economic reality in their efforts to fight crime. Not only is the specter of "a cop on every corner" distasteful to most Americans, but it is also impossible to achieve, given the fiscal constraints on government. Local governments in particular often find it very difficult to provide adequate support to their law enforcement agencies.

pretrial diversion A program in which a first-time offender is afforded the opportunity to avoid criminal prosecution by participating in some specified treatment, counseling, or community service.

For many years the public demanded that more convicted criminals be incarcerated and for longer periods of time. Yet, the public has been unwilling to provide the revenues needed to build the additional prisons necessary to house these inmates. This led to a crisis of overcrowding in the nation's prison system. Increasingly courts are turning to alternatives to incarceration, especially for first-time and nonviolent offenders.

treatment programs Programs designed to rehabilitate offenders. The term is most commonly used in connection with alcohol or drug abuse rehabilitation.

Finally, society must confront the problem of the constitutional limitations on crime definition and law enforcement. Judges do have considerable discretion in interpreting the state and federal constitutions. But if these documents are to be viable protections of our cherished liberties, we must accept that they place significant constraints on our efforts to control crime. For instance, to what degree is the public willing to allow erosion of the constitutional protection against unreasonable searches and seizures? To what degree are we willing to sacrifice our constitutionally protected privacy and liberty to aid the ferreting out of crime? Today the question is amplified by the threat of terrorism and the belief of many that government needs greater powers to address the terrorist threat. These are the fundamental questions of criminal law and procedure in a society that prides itself on preserving the rights of the individual.

Chapter Summary

- LO1

  - Substantive criminal law prohibits certain forms of conduct by defining crimes and establishing the parameters of penalties. Procedural criminal law regulates the enforcement of the substantive law, the determination of guilt, and the punishment of those found guilty of crimes.

- LO2

  - The American system of criminal justice is based on three fundamental constitutional principles: constitutional supremacy, which means that the U.S. Constitution is the supreme law of the land; federalism, the division of authority between the national government and the states; and separation of powers, the division of government into separate legislative, executive, and judicial branches.

- LO3

  - Our legal system regards crimes not merely as wrongs against particular victims but as offenses against the entire society. Because crime is an injury against society, the government, as society's legal representative, brings charges against persons accused of committing crimes. The national government initiates a prosecution when a federal (national) law has been violated; a state brings charges against someone who is believed to have violated one of its laws. The principal parties in a criminal case are the prosecution (that is, the government) and the defendant (that is, the accused person).
  - Because the government prosecutes criminals on behalf of society, the victim of a crime is not a party to the criminal prosecution. By filing a complaint with a law enforcement agency, a victim initiates the process that leads to prosecution; but once the prosecution begins, the victim's participation is primarily that of being a witness.

- LO4

  - The federal and state constitutions impose limitations on the criminal justice system and provide significant rights to persons who are suspected, accused, or convicted of crimes. Many of these protections are found in the Bill of Rights, the first ten amendments to the U.S. Constitution.
  - The most fundamental constitutional principle is the requirement that the government not deprive persons of life, liberty, or property without due process of law.
  - Courts develop procedural rules based on these constitutional pri‍‍‍ples. These rules are essential to the day-to-day administrati‍‍‍ justice system.

- LO5

  - Court decisions cited in the text are almost always decisions of federal or state appellate courts. Data under the name of the case indicates the name of the court and date of its decision, followed by numbers indicating the volume and page number of the Reporter, a compendium of judicial decisions, where the decision is found.
  - A case brief is simply a summary of a court decision, usually in outline format. Typically, a brief includes a summary of the facts and procedural history of the case, a statement of the issue before the court, a statement of the court's decision, and summaries of any opinions produced by the court.

- LO6

  - Before a person can be adjudicated guilty of a crime, the authorities prosecuting a defendant must follow strict guidelines set forth in the in the federal and state constitutions and the substantive and procedural law. There is a certain "sieve effect" in the criminal justice system as cases proceed from arrest through pretrial procedures, trial, and sentencing. Cases that do not merit prosecution are strained out. Others are dismissed after courts exclude key evidence. Negotiated guilty pleas also remove the need for many criminal trials.

- LO7

  - Criminal sanctions include the death penalty, incarceration, monetary fines, and probation. Requiring offenders to make restitution and perform community service are common conditions of release on probation.
  - Increasingly, courts are requiring drug offenders to undergo treatment programs as conditions of probation.
  - Justifications of criminal punishment include retribution, deterrence, incapacitation, and rehabilitation.
  - All criminal penalties are subject to the Eighth Amendment's prohibition against "cruel and unusual punishments."

Key Terms

actus reus	fair notice
appellate courts	federalism
arraignment	felonies
Bill of Rights	grand jury
constitutional supremacy	incarceration
criminal trial	indictment
death penalty	information
decisional law	judicial review
due process of law	lawmaking function
English common law	*mens rea*
error correction function	misdemeanors
fair hearing	monetary fines

nullum crimen, nulla poena, sine lege

plea bargaining

presumption of innocence

pretrial diversion

probation

procedural criminal law

reasonable doubt standard

restitution

rule of law

rules of evidence

rules of procedure

separation of powers

strict liability offense

substantive criminal law

treatment programs

trial courts

victim

Key Court Decisions

Duncan v. Louisiana (1968): The right of trial by jury, like most of the other procedural protections enumerated in the Bill of Rights, is applicable to state criminal cases via the Due Process Clause of the Fourteenth Amendment.

Roper v. Simmons (2005): It is a violation of the Eighth Amendment's Cruel and Unusual Punishments Clause to impose capital punishment for a crime committed when the defendant was under the age of 18.

Questions for Thought and Discussion

1. What is the essential difference between substantive criminal law and procedural criminal law? Can you give examples of each?
2. Why does federalism make the American system of criminal justice more complex?
3. Why is crime viewed by the law as an offense against society rather than a wrong against an individual victim?
4. What does "due process of law" imply in the context of criminal justice?
5. What means of punishment for criminal offenses exist in your state? Is capital punishment available for persons convicted of first-degree murder? Which punishments, if any, do you think are most effective in controlling crime?

CHAPTER 2

Organization of the Criminal Justice System

CHAPTER OUTLINE

JURISPRUDENCE FEATURE BOXES

Gideon v. Wainwright (1963)

Hurtado v. California (1884)

Williams v. Florida (1970)

Solorio v. United States (1987)

Hamdan v. Rumsfeld (2006)

In re Gault (1967)

LEARNING OBJECTIVES

After reading this chapter, you should be able to explain

1. why federalism is such an important concept in understanding the American system of criminal justice

2. the different roles played by legislatures, courts, and law enforcement agencies at the federal, state, and local levels of government

3. the differences and similarities between Congress and the state legislatures with respect to their legislative powers

4. how modern American policing has evolved from its medieval English origins

5. the roles of prosecutor and defense counsel

6. how grand juries differ from trial juries

7. how the federal and state judicial systems are structured

8. how military tribunals differ from civilian criminal courts

9. how the juvenile justice system differs from the criminal justice system for adults

10. how the system of corrections is structured and how criminal punishment has evolved

CHAPTER OPENING VIGNETTE

One of the basic organizing principles of the American system of criminal justice is *federalism*—the constitutional division of power and responsibility between the national government and the fifty states. Our federal system sometimes produces uncertainty and even conflict over what powers reside exclusively in the federal government, what powers are reserved to the states, and what powers may be exercised concurrently. The issue of illegal immigration provides a good example. Frustrated at what it perceived to be an inadequate effort by the federal government to control illegal immigration across the nation's southern border, the state of Arizona enacted a law allowing the state to enforce the federal law prohibiting unauthorized entry into the country. Senate Bill 1070 made it a crime to be in the state of Arizona illegally, banned undocumented immigrants from working in the state, and authorized warrantless arrest of persons believed to have committed deportable offenses. It also required state and local law enforcement agents who have made a lawful stop, detention, or arrest to verify a person's immigration status if they have "reasonable suspicion" that the person is in the United States illegally.

S.B. 1070 set off a firestorm of criticism from immigrants' rights and civil rights groups, who expressed fear that the law would lead to racial profiling. President Barack Obama called the Arizona law "ill-conceived" and said that it was an affront to civil rights to require people to produce proof of citizenship or lawful status based only on the suspicion of a police officer.

In July 2010 the U.S. Department of Justice filed suit in federal court against the state of Arizona, claiming that S.B. 1070 was a usurpation of federal authority. The complaint in *United States v. Arizona* asserted that "the federal government has preeminent authority to regulate immigration matters" and that "a state may not establish its own immigration policy or enforce state laws in a manner that interferes with the federal immigration laws." Several weeks later a federal district judge issued an injunction against enforcement of key provisions of the law and, later, that injunction was upheld by a federal appeals court.

In *Arizona v. United States*, 567 U.S. ____, 132 S.Ct. 2492, 183 L.Ed.2d 351 (2012), the Supreme Court struck down the provisions of the Arizona law that made illegal entry into the country a state offense, banned undocumented immigrants from working in the state, and allowed warrantless arrest of those suspected of deportable offenses. Noting that the U.S. Constitution grants authority over immigration solely to the federal government, the Court held that these provisions were preempted by federal law. However, the Court refused to strike down the most controversial provision of the bill, namely the one requiring police to verify immigration status if they have reasonable suspicion that someone is an illegal immigrant. The Court remanded this issue to the federal district court for a hearing on the constitutionality of the measure. The Court thus postponed to a later day a decision on the most controversial element of the Arizona law.

Introduction

federalism The constitutional distribution of government power and responsibility between the national government and the states.

In every modern country, criminal justice is a complex process involving a plethora of agencies and officials. In the United States, criminal justice is particularly complex, largely because of **federalism,** the constitutional division of authority between the national and state governments. Under our federal scheme the national government operates one criminal justice system to enforce federal criminal laws; additionally, each state has a justice system to apply its own criminal laws. As a result of this structural complexity, it is difficult to provide a coherent overview of criminal justice in America. Each system is to some extent different in both substantive and procedural law.

legislature An elected lawmaking body such as the Congress of the United States or a state assembly.

United States Congress The national legislature of the United States, consisting of the Senate and the House of Representatives.

Despite the differences that exist between federal and state criminal justice systems, there are certain similarities. Like the federal system, all fifty states have legislative bodies, law enforcement agencies, prosecutors, defense attorneys, courts of law, and corrections agencies (see Table 2.1). All follow certain general procedures beginning with arrest and, in some cases, ending in punishment. Finally, all systems are subject to the limitations of the U.S. Constitution, as interpreted by the courts. In this chapter, we present an overview of the roles played by the institutions that make up the criminal justice system in the United States.

Legislatures

statutes Generally applicable laws enacted by legislatures.

The governmental institution with primary responsibility for enacting laws is the **legislature**. Because the United States is organized on the principle of federalism, there are fifty-one legislatures in this country—the **United States Congress** and the fifty state legislatures. Each of these bodies has the power to enact **statutes** that apply within its respective jurisdiction. The U.S. Congress adopts statutes that apply throughout the United States and its territories, whereas the Illinois General Assembly, for example, adopts laws that apply only within the state of Illinois. For the most part, federal and state statutes complement one another. When there is a conflict, the federal statute prevails.

TABLE 2.1	Criminal Justice Agencies and Their Functions
Type of Agency	**Functions**
Legislatures	Enacting Criminal Prohibitions
Law Enforcement Agencies	Enforcing Criminal Prohibitions Maintaining Public Order and Security Conducting Investigations of Crimes Performing Searches and Seizures Making Arrests of Persons Suspected of Crimes Interrogating Suspects
Prosecutorial Agencies	Enforcing Criminal Prohibitions Conducting Investigations Gathering Evidence Initiating Criminal Prosecutions Representing the Government in Court
Public Defenders	Representing Indigent Persons Accused of Crimes
Grand Juries	Reviewing Evidence Obtained by Prosecutors Indicting Persons Accused of Crimes Granting Immunity to Witnesses
Courts of Law	Issuing Search Warrants Issuing Arrest Warrants Conducting Summary Trials in Minor Cases Conducting Initial Appearances Conducting Preliminary Hearings Conducting Arraignments Holding Hearings on Pretrial Motions Conducting Trials Sentencing Persons Convicted of Crimes Conducting Posttrial Hearings Hearing Appeals from Lower Court Rulings
Corrections Agencies	Incarceration of Persons Convicted of Crimes Supervision of Persons on Probation or Parole Carrying out Executions of Persons Sentenced to Death

© Cengage Learning

Legislative Powers of Congress

enumerated powers
Powers explicitly granted to a government by its constitutions.

implied powers Powers not expressly granted to government by a constitution but fairly implied by the document.

Congress's legislative authority may be divided into two broad categories: **enumerated powers** and **implied powers**. Enumerated powers are those that are mentioned specifically in Article I, Section 8 of the Constitution, such as the power to tax and the power to borrow money on the credit of the United States. Among the constitutionally enumerated powers of Congress, there are only two direct references to criminal justice. Congress is explicitly authorized to "provide for the Punishment of counterfeiting the Securities and current Coin of the United States" and to "define and punish Piracies and Felonies committed on the high Seas, and Offenses against the Law of Nations." Of course, Congress's power to define federal crimes is much more extensive than these two clauses suggest.

The enumerated power to "regulate commerce among the states" has provided Congress with a vast reservoir of legislative power. Many of the criminal statutes enacted by Congress in recent decades have been justified on the basis of the Commerce Clause of Article I, Section 8.

Congress's implied powers are those that are deemed to be "necessary and proper for carrying into Execution the foregoing Powers, and all other Powers vested … in the Government of the United States, or in any Department or Officer thereof." As long as Congress's policy goal is permissible, any legislative means that are "plainly adapted" to that goal are likewise permissible. *McCulloch v. Maryland,* 17 U.S. (4 Wheat.) 316, 4 L.Ed. 579 (1819). Under the doctrine of implied powers, scarcely any area exists over which Congress is absolutely barred from legislating, because most social and economic problems have a conceivable relationship to the broad powers and objectives contained in the Constitution.

As the nation expanded and evolved, Congress became more active in passing social and economic legislation. In the twentieth century, and especially the last several decades, Congress established a host of federal crimes. There is now an elaborate body of federal criminal law. Of course, Congress may not enact laws that violate constitutional limitations such as those found in the Bill of Rights.

Publication of Federal Statutes

U.S. Code The comprehensive and systematic collection of federal laws currently in effect.

Federal statutes are published in *United States Statutes at Large,* an annual publication dating from 1789 in which federal statutes are arranged in order of their adoption. Statutes are not arranged by subject matter, nor is there any indication of how they affect existing laws. Because the body of federal statutes is quite voluminous, and because new statutes often repeal or amend their predecessors, it is essential that new statutes be merged into legal codes that systematically arrange the statutes by subject. To find federal law as it currently stands, arranged by subject matter, one must consult the latest edition of the *Official Code of the Laws of the United States,* generally known as the **U.S. Code**. The U.S. Code is broken down into fifty subjects, called "titles." Title 18, "Crimes and Criminal Procedure," contains many of the federal crimes established by Congress.

United States Code Annotated (U.S.C.A.) An annotated version of the United States Code. The annotations include references to court decisions and other legal authorities.

The most popular compilation of the federal law, used by lawyers, judges, and criminal justice professionals, is the ***United States Code Annotated*** (**U.S.C.A.**). Published by West Group, the U.S.C.A. contains the entire current U.S. Code, but each section of statutory law in U.S.C.A. is followed by a series of annotations consisting of court decisions interpreting the particular statute along with historical notes, cross-references, and other editorial features (for more discussion, see Appendix A).

State Legislatures

Each state must have a democratically elected legislature because that is the most fundamental element of a "republican form of government" required by Article IV, Section 4 of the U.S. Constitution. State legislatures for the most part resemble the U.S. Congress. Each is composed of representatives chosen by the citizens of their respective states. All of them are bicameral (i.e., two-house) institutions, with the exception of Nebraska, which has a unicameral legislature. In adopting statutes, they all follow the same basic procedures. When state legislatures adopt statutes, they are published in volumes known as **session laws**. Then statutes are integrated into state codes. Lawyers make frequent use of annotated versions of state codes. These are available at law school libraries, and often at local law libraries, to those who wish to see how state statutes have been interpreted and applied by the state courts.

session laws Collection of laws enacted during a particular legislative session.

After the American Revolution, states adopted the English common law as their own state law to the extent that it did not conflict with their new state constitutions. (Congress, on the other hand, never did.) Eventually, however, state legislatures codified much of the common law by enacting statutes, which in turn have been developed into comprehensive state codes. Periodically, states revise portions of their codes to make sure they remain relevant to a constantly changing society. For example, in 1989 the Tennessee General Assembly undertook a modernization of its criminal code. Old offenses that were no longer being enforced were repealed, other offenses were redefined, and sentencing laws were completely overhauled.

Statutory Interpretation

Statutes are necessarily written in general language, so legislation often requires judicial interpretation. Because legislative bodies have enacted vast numbers of laws defining offenses that are *mala prohibita*, such interpretation assumes an importance largely unknown to the English common law. Courts have responded by developing certain techniques to apply when a statute appears unclear as related to a specific factual scenario. These techniques are generally referred to as **rules of statutory interpretation** and over the years have given rise to reference to legislative history and various maxims that courts apply in attempting to determine the legislature's intention in enacting a statute.

Courts recognize that it is the legislative bodies and not the courts that exercise the power to define crimes and penalties. It follows that the most frequent maxim applied by courts in determining legislative intention is the **plain meaning rule**. As the U.S. Supreme Court observed early in the twentieth century, "Where the language [of a statutory law] is plain and admits of no more than one meaning the duty of interpretation does not arise...." *Caminetti v. United States*, 242 U.S. 470, 37 S.Ct. 192, 61 L.Ed. 442 (1917). The Court's dictum seems self-evident, yet even learned judges often disagree as to whether the language of a given statute is plain. This gives rise to certain **canons of construction** applied by courts to determine the **legislative intent** behind a statutory definition of a crime.

A primary canon of construction is that criminal statutes must be strictly construed. The rule originated at common law, when death was the penalty for committing a felony, but the rule has remained. However, it is now based on the rationale that every criminal statute should be sufficiently precise to give fair warning of its meaning. Today, we see the rule applied most frequently in a constitutional context when courts determine a criminal statute to be **void for vagueness**. We address this aspect in more detail in the following chapter. Another canon of construction provides for an **implied exception** to a statute. For example, courts have ruled that there is an implied exception to a law imposing speed limits on the highway in instances where police or other emergency vehicles violate the literal text of the law. Would a court apply a statute that makes it an offense for any person to sleep in a bus terminal and thereby find a ticketed passenger guilty who fell asleep while waiting for a bus that was overdue? The implied exception doctrine seems to reflect a commonsense approach to determining the meaning of a statute.

Often a statute uses a term that has a definite meaning at common law. In general, courts interpret such terms according to their common-law meaning. But this rule does not always apply when dealing with modern statutes, particularly at the federal level, where there is generally considerable legislative history in the form of committee reports and floor debates recorded in the *Congressional Record* that can aid in determining the true intent of a statute. Thus, in *Perrin v. United States*, 444 U.S. 37, 100 S.Ct. 311, 62 L.Ed.2d 199 (1979), the Supreme Court determined that the word "bribery" in a federal statute was not limited to its common-law definition because the legislative history revealed an intent to deal with bribery in organized crime beyond its common-law definition. In general, there is considerably less

mala prohibita Crimes that are considered wrong because the law makes them wrong, as opposed to inherently evil acts.

rules of statutory interpretation Rules developed by courts to determine the meaning of legislative acts.

plain meaning rule The judicial doctrine holding that if the meaning of a text is plain, a court may not interpret it but must simply apply it as written.

canons of construction Rules governing the judicial interpretation of constitutions, statutes, and other written instruments.

legislative intent The purpose the legislature sought to achieve in enacting a particular provision of law.

void for vagueness Doctrine of constitutional law holding unconstitutional (as a violation of due process) legislation that fails to clearly inform the person of what is required or proscribed.

implied exception An exclusion that can reasonably be inferred or assumed based on the purpose and intent of an ordinance, statute, or contract.

legislative history available at the state legislative level. However, at times state courts seek to determine legislative intent based on available resources.

Law Enforcement Agencies

Law enforcement agencies are charged with enforcing the criminal law. They have the power to investigate suspected criminal activity, to arrest suspected criminals, and to detain arrested persons until their cases come before the appropriate courts of law. Society expects law enforcement agencies not only to arrest those suspected of crimes but also to take steps to prevent crimes from occurring.

Historical Development

Before the Norman Conquest in 1066, there were no organized police in England, but by the thirteenth century constables and justices of the peace came to symbolize enforcement of the rule of law in England. Large communities, somewhat similar to counties in America, were called "shires." The king would send a royal officer called a "reeve" to each shire to keep order and to exercise broad powers within the shire. The onset of the Industrial Revolution led to the development of large cities. Industrialists and merchants began to establish patrols to protect their goods and buildings. But the need for more effective policing became evident. In 1829, Sir Robert Peel, the British Home Secretary, organized a uniformed but unarmed police force for London. The name "Bobbies" is still applied to police officers in England in honor of Peel, and in Ireland police officers were once called "Peelers." In later years, Parliament required counties and boroughs to establish police departments modeled along the lines of the London force.

Colonial America basically followed the English system, with local constables and county sheriffs following the English concept of constables and shire reeves. These early law officers were often aided by local groups of citizens known as "posses." Once America became a nation, states and local communities began to follow the Peel model, and by the mid-1800s, Boston, New York, and Philadelphia had developed professional police departments. By the twentieth century, police were aided by technological developments, and by the 1930s, many departments were equipped with motorcycles and patrol cars. Detectives were soon added to the force, police became equipped with modern communications equipment, and police were trained in ballistics and the scientific analysis of blood samples and handwriting.

Policing in Modern America

sworn officers Law enforcement officers sworn to uphold the Constitution and laws of the United States and of their own states.

In the United States nearly 20,000 federal, state, and local agencies are involved in law enforcement and crime prevention. Collectively, these agencies employ nearly 800,000 **sworn officers**. Increasingly, law enforcement officers are trained professionals who must acquire a good working knowledge of the criminal law. At the local level, the typical police recruit now completes about 1,000 hours of training before being sworn in. Modern police forces are highly mobile and are equipped with computers, sophisticated communications technology, and scientific crime detection equipment.

Federal Bureau of Investigation (FBI) The primary federal agency charged with investigating violations of federal criminal laws.

Policing at the National Level

At the national level, the **Federal Bureau of Investigation** (FBI) is the primary agency empowered to investigate violations of federal criminal laws. Located in the

Department of Justice (DOJ) The department within the executive branch of the federal government that is headed by the Attorney General and staffed by the U.S. Attorneys.

special agents Officers of the FBI with the power to make arrests and use force in the enforcement of federal law.

cybersecurity Security measures designed to protect computers and computer networks from unauthorized access.

United States Marshals Service Law enforcement officers of the U.S. Department of Justice who are responsible for enforcing federal laws, enforcing federal court decisions, and effecting the transfer of federal prisoners.

Department of Justice, the FBI is by far the most powerful of the federal law enforcement agencies, with broad powers to enforce the many criminal laws adopted by the Congress. On April 30, 2012, the FBI employed 13,851 **special agents** and 21,999 support professionals, such as intelligence analysts, language specialists, forensic scientists, information technology specialists, and other professionals. Its personnel are spread out over fifty-six field offices in major cities in the United States and more than sixty international offices in embassies worldwide. The FBI uses the most sophisticated methods in crime prevention and investigation. Its crime laboratory figures prominently in the investigation and prosecution of numerous state and federal crimes. In fiscal year 2012, the FBI's total budget was approximately $8.1 billion, including $119 million in program enhancements for intelligence, counterterrorism, laboratory, information technology, and **cybersecurity**. (See http://www.fbi.gov/quickfacts.htm.)

The **United States Marshals Service** is the oldest unit of federal law enforcement, dating back to 1790. The agency employs nearly 4,000 deputy marshals and criminal investigators. Deputy Marshals provide security for the federal judiciary, execute federal court orders, apprehend federal fugitives, seize property under the federal forfeiture laws, provide security for federal witnesses, and serve as custodians for the transfer of federal prisoners.

Nearly fifty other federal agencies have law enforcement authority in specific areas. Among them are the Bureau of Alcohol, Tobacco, and Firearms; the Internal Revenue Service; the Bureau of Indian Affairs; the Drug Enforcement Administration; the Bureau of Postal Inspection; the Tennessee Valley Authority; the National Park Service; the Forest Service; the U.S. Capitol Police; the U.S. Mint; the Secret Service; and Immigration and Customs Enforcement (ICE) within the Department of Homeland Security.

State and Local Policing

All states have law enforcement agencies that patrol the highways, investigate crimes, and furnish skilled technical support to local law enforcement agencies. Similarly, every state has a number of state agencies responsible for enforcing specific areas of the law, ranging from agricultural importation to food processing and from casino gambling to dispensing alcoholic beverages. Probably among the best known to all citizens are the state highway patrol and the fish and game wardens. Generally, cases developed by state officers are processed through local law enforcement and prosecution agencies.

At the local level, we find both county and municipal law enforcement agencies. Nearly every county in America (more than three thousand of them) has a **sheriff**. In most states, sheriffs are elected to office and exercise broad powers as the chief law enforcement officers of their respective counties. They are usually dependent on funding provided by a local governing body, generally the county commission. In some areas, particularly the urban Northeast, many powers traditionally exercised by sheriffs have been assumed by state or metropolitan police forces. In the rest of the country, however, especially in the rural areas, sheriffs (and their deputies) are the principal law enforcement agents at the county level.

Nearly 15,000 cities and towns have their own **police departments**. Local police are charged with enforcing the criminal laws of their states, as well as of their municipalities. Although the county sheriff usually has jurisdiction within the municipalities of the county, he or she generally concentrates enforcement efforts on those areas outside municipal boundaries.

sheriff The chief law enforcement officer of a county.

police departments Agencies, established by municipalities and sometimes states, whose function is to enforce the criminal laws within their respective jurisdictions.

In addition to city and county law enforcement agencies, there are numerous special districts and authorities that have their own police forces. Most state universities have their own police departments, as do many airports and seaports.

Besides providing law enforcement in the strictest sense of the term, local law enforcement agencies initiate the criminal justice process and assist prosecutors in preparation of cases. Sheriffs in many larger counties and many metropolitan police departments have developed SWAT (special weapons and tactics) teams to assist in the rescue of victims of catastrophes and persons taken hostage. They are also heavily involved in **order maintenance** or "keeping the peace," hence the term "peace officers." Often, keeping the peace involves more of a process of judgment and discretion rather than merely applying the criminal law.

order maintenance The police officer's function of keeping the peace, as distinct from enforcement of the law.

Some of the newer and more innovative policing responsibilities include community relations departments that seek to foster better relations among groups of citizens, especially minorities and juveniles, and to assist social agencies in efforts to rehabilitate drug and alcohol abusers. Finally, the public looks to the police to prevent crime through their presence in the community and through education of the public on crime prevention measures. Under the rubric of **community policing**, police agencies are making an effort to become actively involved in their communities in order to earn the trust and confidence of the citizens they serve. Most police departments in cities of 50,000 people or more now have specialized community policing divisions.

community policing Style of police work that stresses development of close ties between police officers and the communities they serve.

Prosecutorial Agencies

Although law enforcement agencies are the "gatekeepers" of the criminal justice system, prosecutors are central to the administration of criminal justice. It is the **prosecutor** who determines whether to bring charges against suspected criminals. Prosecutors have enormous discretion, not only in determining whether to prosecute but also in determining what charges to file. Moreover, prosecutors frequently set the tone for plea bargaining and have a powerful voice in determining the severity of sanctions imposed on persons convicted of crimes. Accordingly, prosecutors play a crucial role in the criminal justice system.

prosecutor A public official empowered to initiate criminal charges and conduct prosecutions.

Historical Background

The early English common law considered many crimes to be private matters between individuals; however, the role of the public prosecutor evolved as early as the thirteenth century, when the king's counsel would pursue crimes considered to be offenses against the Crown and, in some instances, when injured victims declined to prosecute. Today in England, a public prosecutor prosecutes crimes that have great significance to the government, but the majority of offenses are handled by police agencies that hire barristers to prosecute charges. Unlike American prosecutors, the English barrister may represent the police in one case and in the next case represent the defendant.

The office of public prosecutor in England became the prototype for the office of attorney general in this country at the national and state levels. In colonial days, an attorney general's assistants handled local prosecutions. However, as states became independent, the practice ceased. The state attorneys general assumed the role of chief legal officers, and local governments began electing their own prosecuting attorneys.

Federal Prosecutors

Attorney General The highest legal officer of a state or of the United States.

In the United States, the chief prosecutor at the federal level is the **Attorney General**, who is the head of the Department of Justice. Below the Attorney General are the **United States Attorneys**, each responsible for prosecuting crimes within a particular federal district. The United States Attorneys, in turn, have a number of assistants who handle most of the day-to-day criminal cases brought by the federal government. The president, subject to the consent of the Senate, appoints the Attorney General and the U.S. Attorneys. Assistant U.S. Attorneys are federal civil service employees.

United States Attorneys Lawyers appointed by the president with consent of the U.S. Senate to prosecute federal crimes in federal judicial districts.

In addition to the regular federal prosecutors, Congress has provided for the appointment of **independent counsel** (special prosecutors) in cases involving alleged misconduct by high government officials. By far, the most infamous such case was "Watergate," which resulted in the convictions of several high-ranking officials and led to the resignation of President Richard Nixon in 1974. But there have been numerous cases where, under congressional direction, a special prosecutor has been appointed. A more recent example of this was Kenneth Starr's appointment to investigate the Whitewater scandal, which involved close associates of President Bill Clinton and First Lady Hillary Rodham Clinton. This investigation eventually culminated in President Clinton's impeachment and his subsequent acquittal by the U.S. Senate in February 1999.

independent counsel A special prosecutor appointed to investigate and, if warranted, prosecute official misconduct.

State and Local Prosecutors

Each state likewise has its own attorney general, who acts as the state's chief legal officer, and a number of assistant attorneys general, plus a number of district or **state's attorneys** at the local level. Generally speaking, local prosecutors are elected for set terms of office and have the responsibility for the prosecution of crimes within the jurisdiction for which they are elected. In most states, local prosecutors act autonomously and possess broad discretionary powers. Many local prosecutors function on a part-time basis, but in the larger offices the trend is for the prosecutor and assistant prosecutors to serve on a full-time basis. Larger offices are establishing educational programs and developing specially trained assistants or units to handle specific categories of crime—for example, white-collar crime and governmental corruption, narcotics offenses, and consumer fraud.

state's attorneys State prosecutors.

Cities and counties also have their own attorneys. These attorneys, generally appointed by the governing bodies they represent, sometimes prosecute violations of city and county ordinances, but increasingly their function is limited to representing their cities or counties in civil suits and giving legal advice to local councils and officials.

The Prosecutor's Broad Discretion

Federal and state prosecutors (who may be known as district attorneys, state attorneys, or county prosecutors) play a vital role in the criminal justice system in the United States. As mentioned, a politically appointed U.S. Attorney supervises prosecutors at the federal level, whereas state and local prosecutors generally come into office by election in partisan contests. Thus, prosecutors become sensitive to community norms while exercising the broad discretion that the law vests in prosecutorial decision making.

nolle prosequi A formal entry by a prosecutor who declines to proceed further in the prosecution of an offense; commonly called a *nol pros.*

Prosecutors not only determine the level of offense to be charged; in exercise of their very broad discretion they also exercise the power of **_nolle prosequi,_** usually called *nol pros,* which allows a prosecutor not to proceed in a given case, irrespective of the factual basis for prosecution. Prosecutors sometimes *nol pros* cases to secure cooperation of a defendant in furthering other prosecutions; in other instances, a prosecutor may allow a defendant to participate in some diversionary program of rehabilitation. In recent years, completion of a prescribed program in a drug court has often resulted in a case being *nol prossed* by a prosecutor.

Counsel for the Defense

In American criminal law, individuals accused of any crime, no matter how minor the offense, have the right to employ counsel for their defense. U.S. Const. Amend. VI. Indeed, the U.S. Supreme Court has held that a defendant has the right to be represented by an attorney at all criminal proceedings that may substantially affect the rights of the accused, such as a post-trial probation revocation hearing. *Mempa v. Rhay,* 389 U.S. 128, 88 S.Ct. 254, 19 L.Ed.2d 336 (1967).

In this country, many lawyers specialize in criminal defense work. Of course, defendants are free to employ an attorney of their choice at their own expense. Some well-known attorneys specialize in representing defendants in high-profile trials. However, most criminal defendants are not wealthy, and few people accused of crimes can afford to hire legal "dream teams" to represent them.

Many attorneys are highly skilled in handling criminal cases and are available for employment in federal and state criminal proceedings. In fact, it is not uncommon for attorneys who start their careers as prosecutors eventually to enter private practice in criminal matters. Today some state bar associations grant special recognition to lawyers who qualify by virtue of experience and examination as "certified criminal defense attorneys."

Representation of Indigent Defendants

indigent defendants Persons accused of crimes who cannot afford to retain private legal counsel and are therefore entitled to be represented by a public defender or a court-appointed lawyer.

public defenders Public officials who are attorneys and are responsible for defending indigent persons charged with crimes.

Beginning in the 1960s, the U.S. Supreme Court greatly expanded the right to counsel by requiring states to provide attorneys to **indigent defendants**. *Gideon v. Wainwright,* 372 U.S. 335, 83 S.Ct. 792, 9 L.Ed.2d 799 (1963); *Argersinger v. Hamlin,* 407 U.S. 25, 92 S.Ct. 2006, 32 L.Ed.2d 530 (1972). In some states, courts appoint attorneys from the private bar to represent indigent defendants. However, most states have chosen to handle the problem of indigent defense by establishing the office of public defender. Like public prosecutors, **public defenders** are generally elected to set terms of office. Because of their constant contact with criminal cases, public defenders acquire considerable expertise in representing defendants. Moreover, because they are public officials who, like prosecutors, are provided with budgets, public defenders are often able to hire investigators to aid their staff of assistant public defenders in their representation of indigent defendants.

The Role of Defense Attorneys

defense attorney A lawyer who represents defendants in criminal cases.

The role of the **defense attorney** is perhaps the most misunderstood in the criminal justice system. First and foremost, a defense attorney is charged with zealously representing his or her client and ensuring that the defendant's constitutional rights are fully protected. To anyone who has watched *Law and Order* or a similar television

JURISPRUDENCE

Gideon v. Wainwright, 372 U.S. 335, 83 S.Ct. 792, 9 L.Ed.2d 799 (1963)

Clarence Earl Gideon, a fifty-one-year-old indigent drifter who had been in and out of jails all his adult life, was charged with felonious breaking and entering. At trial, he requested that the court appoint an attorney to represent him. The court refused, citing the Florida law that required appointment of counsel for indigent defendants only in capital cases. While serving his sentence in the Florida State Prison, Gideon unsuccessfully challenged his conviction in the Florida Supreme Court on a writ of habeas corpus. He then obtained review by the U.S. Supreme Court on a writ of certiorari. In a unanimous decision, the Court reversed Gideon's conviction. Writing for the Court, Hugo Black opined that "[t]he right of one charged with a crime to counsel may not be deemed fundamental and essential to fair trials in some countries, but it is in ours." Because *Gideon* was made retroactive, it allowed numerous persons serving time in state prisons to win their freedom by seeking writs of habeas corpus in the federal courts. Without question, *Gideon* was one of the most important decisions of the modern Supreme Court in the field of criminal justice.

program, the defense attorney's most visible role is that of vigorously cross-examining prosecution witnesses and passionately pleading for a client before a jury. However, the defense attorney's role is far greater than being a courtroom advocate. As a counselor, a defense attorney must evaluate the alternative courses of action that may be available to a defendant. The great majority of criminal cases are disposed of through plea bargaining. As part of this process, defense counsel must attempt to gauge the strength of the prosecution's case, advise the client on the feasibility of entering a plea of guilty, and attempt to negotiate a fair and constructive sentence. In instances where a defendant elects to plead not guilty, defense attorneys challenge the police and prosecution. Many observers point out that these efforts by defense attorneys "keep the system honest" by causing police and prosecuting authorities to be scrupulous in their adherence to constitutional standards.

Perhaps the most frequently voiced reservation concerning defense attorneys relates to representation of a defendant who, from all facts available, is believed to be guilty. Defense attorneys are quick to point out that it is not their function to make a judgment of the defendant's guilt or innocence; there are other functionaries in the system charged with that responsibility. The answer does not easily satisfy critics. Nevertheless, in our system of adversarial justice the defense attorney is required to represent a defendant with fidelity, to protect the defendant's constitutional rights, to assert all defenses available under the law of the land, and to make sure before a defendant is found guilty that the prosecution has sustained its burden of proving the defendant guilty beyond a reasonable doubt. A defense attorney must make sufficient objections and other tactical moves to preserve any contention of error for review by a higher court. If the defendant is convicted, the defense attorney's duty continues. He or she must seek a fair sentence, advise as to the right to appeal to a higher court, and, in some instances, seek postconviction relief if an appeal fails.

Juries

jury A group of citizens convened for the purpose of deciding factual questions relevant to a civil or criminal case.

The **jury** is one of the great contributions of the English common law. By the twelfth century, juries had begun to function in England, but not as we know juries today. Rather, these early juries were comprised of men who had knowledge of the disputes they were to decide. However, eventually juries began to hear evidence and make their verdicts accordingly. By the eighteenth century, juries occupied a prominent role in the English common-law system and served as a buffer between the Crown and the citizenry. The colonists brought the concept to the New World. Today, juries composed of both men and women represent an important component of the American system of criminal justice.

grand jury A group of citizens convened either to conduct an investigation or to determine whether there is sufficient evidence to warrant the prosecution of an accused.

petit (trial) jury A trial jury, usually composed of either six or twelve persons.

There are two types of juries: the **grand jury** and the **petit (trial) jury**. The juries derive their names from the number of persons who serve, with the grand jury consisting of a larger number than the petit jury.

Grand Juries

Grand juries essentially serve to consider whether there is sufficient evidence to bring charges against a person; petit or trial juries sit to hear evidence at a trial and render a verdict accordingly. The Fifth Amendment to the U.S. Constitution stipulates that "[n]o person shall be held to answer for a capital, or otherwise infamous crime, unless on a presentment or indictment of a grand jury." The constitutional requirement binds all federal courts; however, the Supreme Court has held that states are not bound to abide by the grand jury requirement. *Hurtado v. California*, 110 U.S. 516, 4 S.Ct. 111, 28 L.Ed.232 (1884).

true bill An indictment handed down by a grand jury in a criminal case.

no bill Decision of a grand jury not to return an indictment.

indictment A formal document handed down by a grand jury accusing one or more persons of the commission of a crime or crimes.

Sixteen to twenty-three persons serve on a federal grand jury. The number varies according to each state but usually consists of between twelve and twenty-three citizens. Grand jurors serve for a limited time to hear evidence and to determine whether to hand down an indictment, sometimes referred to as a **true bill**, or to refuse to indict when the jury determines there is insufficient evidence of a crime by returning a **no bill**. Twelve jurors must vote to return an indictment in federal court, and states usually require at least a majority of grand jurors to return an indictment. Courts have broad authority to call a grand jury into session, and grand juries are authorized to make wide-ranging inquiries and investigations into public matters. Grand juries may make accusations, called *presentments*, independently of a prosecutor.

Although the English common law system gave birth to the grand jury, England abolished grand juries in the 1930s, having found that the return of **indictments** was almost automatic and that the use of grand juries tended to delay the criminal process. Today, critics argue that grand juries are so dominated by the prosecutors

---

JURISPRUDENCE

Hurtado v. California, 110 U.S. 516, 4 S.Ct. 111, 28 L.Ed.232 (1884).

Joseph Hurtado was charged with murder by the state of California by way of an information rather than the traditional grand jury indictment. He was tried, convicted, and sentenced to death. Hurtado claimed that the grand jury procedure required in federal criminal cases by the Fifth Amendment was an essential feature of "due process of law" and thus required in state criminal cases by the Fourteenth Amendment.

Dividing 7–1, the U.S. Supreme Court rejected that argument and sustained his conviction. The Court said that states should be free to design their own criminal justice systems without interference by the federal courts. Today, despite the application of most of the provisions of the Bill of Rights to the states via the Fourteenth Amendment, the *Hurtado* decision remains "good" law. States are not required by the federal constitution to use grand juries to bring criminal charges, although many still do.

information An accusatorial document filed under oath by a prosecutor charging a person with one or more violations of the criminal law; similar to an indictment issued by a grand jury.

who appear before them that they have ceased to serve as an independent body to evaluate evidence. Indeed, many states have eliminated the requirement that a grand jury hand down indictments and have substituted a prosecutor's **information**, an accusatorial document charging a crime. Yet many reformers would retain the grand jury as an institution for investigation of corruption in government.

Trial Juries

speedy and public trial An open and public criminal trial held without unreasonable delay as required by the Sixth Amendment to the U.S. Constitution.

Article III, Section 2 of the U.S. Constitution establishes the right to trial by jury in criminal cases. The Sixth Amendment guarantees "the right to a **speedy and public trial** by an impartial jury." The Seventh Amendment grants a right to a trial by jury in civil suits at common law. All state constitutions confer the right of trial by jury in criminal cases; however, the federal constitutional right to a jury trial applies to the states, thereby guaranteeing a defendant a right to a jury trial in a state criminal prosecution if such a right would exist in a federal prosecution. *Duncan v. Louisiana*, 391 U.S. 145, 88 S.Ct. 1444, 20 L.Ed.2d 491 (1968). However, as we note below, the right to trial by jury does not extend to juvenile delinquency proceedings.

A common-law trial jury consisted of "twelve men good and true." Today, twelve persons are required in federal juries; however, the number varies in states, although all states require twelve-person juries in capital cases. The Supreme Court has approved the use of six-person juries in noncapital felony prosecutions. *Williams v. Florida*, 399 U.S. 78, 90 S.Ct. 1893, 26 L.Ed.2d 446 (1970).

| The Courts

trial courts Judicial tribunals usually presided over by one judge who conducts proceedings and trials in civil and criminal cases with or without a jury.

Courts of law are the centerpieces of the federal and state criminal justice systems. Courts of law are responsible for determining both the factual basis and legal sufficiency of criminal charges and for ensuring that criminal defendants are provided due process of law. Essentially, the federal courts adjudicate criminal cases where defendants are charged with violating federal criminal laws; state courts adjudicate alleged violations of state laws.

Basically, there are two kinds of courts: trial and appellate courts. **Trial courts** conduct criminal trials and various pretrial and posttrial proceedings. **Appellate courts** hear appeals from the decisions of the trial courts. Trial courts are primarily concerned with ascertaining facts, determining guilt or innocence, and imposing

appellate courts Judicial tribunals that review decisions from lower tribunals.

punishments, whereas appellate courts are primarily concerned with matters of law. Appellate courts correct legal errors made by trial courts and develop law when new legal questions arise. In some instances appellate courts must determine whether there is legally sufficient evidence to uphold a conviction.

The first question facing a court in any criminal prosecution is that of **jurisdiction**, the legal authority to hear and decide the case. A court must have jurisdiction over both the subject matter of a case and the parties to a case before it may proceed to adjudicate that controversy. The jurisdiction of the federal courts is determined by both the language of Article III of the Constitution and the statutes enacted by Congress. The respective state constitutions and statutes determine the jurisdiction of the state courts.

The Federal Court System

Article III of the U.S. Constitution provides that "[t]he judicial Power of the United States shall be vested in one supreme Court, and in such inferior Courts as the Congress may from time to time ordain and establish." Under this authority Congress enacted the Judiciary Act of 1789, creating the federal court system. After Congress passed the Judiciary Act of 1801, the Supreme Court justices were required to "ride circuit," a practice that had its roots in English legal history. The circuit courts then consisted of district court judges who heard appeals alongside "circuit-riding" Supreme Court justices. In 1891, Congress created separate appellate courts, and since then Supreme Court justices have remained as reviewing justices.

United States District Courts

United States District Courts handle prosecutions for violations of federal statutes. In addition, federal courts sometimes review convictions from state courts when defendants raise issues arising under the U.S. Constitution. Appeals are heard by United States Courts of Appeals, and, of course, the Supreme Court is at the apex of the judicial system.

The principal trial court in the federal system is the United States District Court. There are district courts in ninety-four federal judicial districts around the country. A criminal trial in the district court is presided over by a judge appointed for life by the president with the consent of the Senate. Federal magistrate judges, who are appointed by federal district judges, often handle pretrial proceedings in the district courts and trials of misdemeanors.

Most of the cases filed in the federal district courts are civil, as distinct from criminal, cases. In 2011, nearly 290,000 civil cases were filed in the district courts. In that year, 70,896 criminal cases were filed involving nearly 103,000 defendants. (Chief Justice's 2011 Year-End Report on the Federal Judiciary, December 31, 2011, p. 14.) The largest categories of criminal filings in the district courts tend to be drug crimes, weapons offenses, and immigration violations.

Congress created the district courts by the Judiciary Act of 1789. Since then, Congress has created specialized courts to handle specific kinds of cases (for example, the United States Court of International Trade and the United States Claims Court).

The United States Courts of Appeals

The **intermediate appellate courts** in the federal system are the **United States Courts of Appeals** (also known as circuit courts). Twelve geographical circuits (and one "federal circuit") cover the United States and its possessions. Figure 2.1 indicates the geographical distribution of the circuit courts. The circuit courts hear

---

jurisdiction The authority of a court to hear and decide certain categories of legal disputes. Jurisdiction relates to the authority of a court over the person, subject matter, and geographical area.

United States District Courts The principal trial courts in the federal judicial system, these courts sit in ninety-four geographical districts throughout the United States.

intermediate appellate courts Judicial tribunals consisting of three or more judges that review decisions of trial courts but that are subordinate to the final appellate tribunals.

United States Courts of Appeals The twelve intermediate appellate courts of appeals in the federal system that sit in specified geographical areas of the United States and in which panels of appellate judges hear appeals in civil and criminal cases, primarily from the U.S. District Courts.

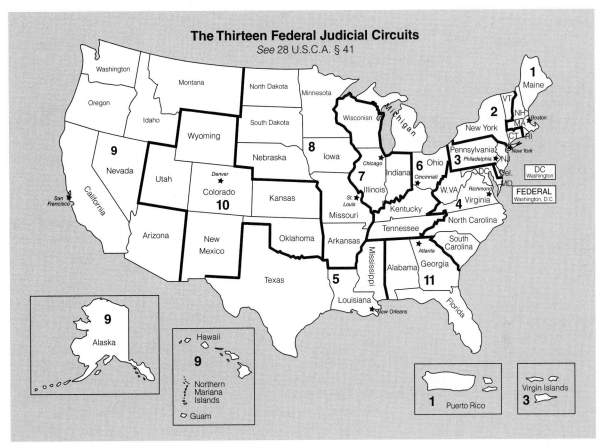

FIGURE 2.1 The Federal Judicial Circuits. Source: *Federal Reporter*, 2nd series (West Publishing Company).

criminal and civil appeals from the district courts and from quasi-judicial tribunals in the independent regulatory agencies. In 2011, 55,126 appeals were commenced in the federal circuit courts (Administrative Office of the United States Courts, *2011 Judicial Business*, online at http://www.uscourts.gov/uscourts/Statistics/JudicialBusiness/2011/JudicialBusiness2011_Summary.pdf).

Generally, decisions of the courts of appeals are rendered by panels of three judges who vote to affirm, reverse, or modify the lower-court decisions under review. There is a procedure by which the circuit courts provide an ***en banc* hearing**, where all judges assigned to the court (or a substantial number of them) participate in a decision. Like their counterparts in the district courts, federal appeals court judges are appointed to life terms by the president with the consent of the Senate.

The United States Supreme Court

The highest appellate court in the federal judicial system is the **United States Supreme Court**. The Supreme Court has jurisdiction to review, either on appeal or by **writ of certiorari** (a form of discretionary review), all the decisions of the lower federal courts and the decisions of the highest state courts involving questions of federal law. Most of the Supreme Court's cases come to it via certiorari, which means that the Court is largely able to set its own agenda. It tends to grant certiorari only in the most important cases or where lower courts are in conflict on a matter of federal law.

en banc **hearing** A hearing in an appellate court in which all or a substantial number of the judges assigned to that court participate.

United States Supreme Court The highest court in the United States, consisting of nine justices, that has jurisdiction to review, by appeal or writ of certiorari, the decisions of lower federal courts and many decisions of the highest courts of each state.

writ of certiorari Order issued by an appellate court to grant discretionary review of a case decided by a lower court.

The Supreme Court is comprised of nine justices who, like district and circuit judges, are appointed for life by the president with the consent of the Senate. These nine individuals have the final word in determining what the U.S. Constitution requires, permits, and prohibits in the areas of law enforcement, prosecution, adjudication, and punishment. The Supreme Court also promulgates **rules of procedure** for the lower federal courts to follow in both criminal and civil cases.

rules of procedure Rules promulgated by courts of law under constitutional or statutory authority governing procedures for trials and other judicial proceedings.

As of June 1, 2011, John Roberts was the chief justice of the Supreme Court, and the associate justices were Antonin Scalia, Anthony Kennedy, Clarence Thomas, Ruth Bader Ginsburg, Stephen Breyer, Samuel Alito, Sonia Sotomayor, and Elena Kagan. During the October 2010 Term (which ended in June 2011), 7,857 cases were filed with the Court. The Court granted review in only eighty-three of these cases, which is just over 1 percent. During its 2010 Term, the Court issued only seventy-five signed opinions (Chief Justice's 2011 Year-End Report on the Federal Judiciary, December 31, 2011, p. 13). Of course, even a small number of Supreme Court opinions can have a major impact on the law, because they settle conflicts among lower courts and resolve salient issues of law and public policy.

Military Tribunals

court-martial A military tribunal convened by a commander of a military unit to try a person subject to the Uniform Code of Military Justice who is accused of violating a provision of that code.

Crimes committed by persons in military service are ordinarily prosecuted in proceedings before **courts-martial**. Article 1, Section 8 of the U.S. Constitution grants Congress the authority to regulate the armed forces. Under this authority, Congress has enacted the **Uniform Code of Military Justice (UCMJ)**, 10 U.S.C.A. §§ 801–940. The UCMJ gives courts-martial jurisdiction to try all offenses under the code committed by military personnel. Notwithstanding this grant of authority, the United States Supreme Court held in 1969 that military jurisdiction was limited to offenses that were service connected. *O'Callahan v. Parker,* 395 U.S. 258, 89 S.Ct. 1683, 23 L.Ed.2d 291 (1969). The *O'Callahan* decision greatly narrowed military jurisdiction over offenses committed by servicepersons. In 1987, the Court overturned *O'Callahan* and said that military jurisdiction depends solely on whether an accused is a military member. *Solorio v. United States,* 483 U.S. 435, 107 S.Ct. 2924, 97 L.Ed.2d 364 (1987). Thus, courts-martial may now try all offenses committed by servicepersons in violation of the UCMJ.

Uniform Code of Military Justice (UCMJ) A code of laws enacted by Congress that governs military service personnel and defines the procedural and evidentiary requirements in military law and the substantive criminal offenses and punishments.

Commanders of various military units convene court-martial proceedings and appoint those who sit similar to a civilian jury. These commanders are called the

---

JURISPRUDENCE

Solorio v. United States, 483 U.S. 435, 107 S.Ct. 2924, 97 L.Ed.2d 364 (1987)

While serving in the Coast Guard, Richard Solorio was accused of sexually abusing children in his private residence. A general court-martial was convened to adjudicate the case. Solorio moved to dismiss the charges on the ground that they were not "service connected." The presiding judge granted the motion and dismissed the charges. The prosecution appealed to the Coast Guard Court of Military

Review, which reversed and reinstated the charges. After the Court of Military Appeals affirmed this ruling, Solorio obtained review by the U.S. Supreme Court. Dividing 5–4, the Court upheld the reinstatement of the charges and overturned its 1969 decision in *O'Callahan v. Parker.* Chief Justice William Rehnquist, writing for the Court, concluded that the "service connection approach" set forth in *O'Callahan* "has proven confusing and difficult for military courts to apply."

convening authorities and are assisted by military lawyers designated as staff judge advocates. Military trial procedures and rules of evidence are similar to the rules applied in federal district courts.

There are three classes of court-martial: summary, special, and general. The summary court-martial is composed of one military officer with jurisdiction to impose minor punishments over enlisted personnel. It is somewhat analogous to trial by a civilian magistrate, whereas special and general courts-martial proceedings are formal military tribunals more analogous to civilian criminal courts of record.

A special court-martial must be composed of three or more members with or without a military judge, or a military judge alone, if requested by the accused. It can impose more serious punishments on both officers and enlisted personnel. A general court-martial tries the most serious offenses and must consist of five or more members and a military judge (or a military judge alone, if requested by the accused). A general court-martial may try any offense made punishable by the UCMJ and may impose any punishment authorized by law against officers and enlisted personnel, including death for a capital offense. Trial by a military judge alone is not permitted in capital cases.

A military judge presides at special and general courts-martial. A trial counsel serves as prosecutor, and a defendant is furnished legal counsel by the government unless the accused chooses to employ private defense counsel. The extent of punishment that may be imposed varies according to the offense and the authority of the type of court-martial convened.

United States Court of Appeals for the Armed Forces The court (formerly known as the Court of Military Appeals), consisting of five civilian judges, that reviews sentences affecting a general or flag officer or imposing the death penalty and cases certified for review by the judge advocate general of a branch of service. It may grant review of convictions and sentences on petitions by service members.

Decisions of courts-martial are reviewed by military courts of review in each branch of the armed forces. In specified instances, appeals are heard by the **United States Court of Appeals for the Armed Forces**. This court is staffed by civilian judges who are appointed to fifteen-year terms by the president with the consent of the Senate.

Only under conditions of martial law do military tribunals have the authority to try American citizens in civilian life who are not connected with the military or naval services. *Ex parte Milligan*, 71 U.S. (4 Wall.) 2, 18 L.Ed. 281 (1866). Historically, the Supreme Court has permitted "enemy aliens" captured during wartime to be tried by military tribunals. See *Ex parte Quirin*, 317 U.S. 1, 63 S.Ct. 2, 87 L.Ed. 7 (1942). Under an executive order issued by President George W. Bush on November 13, 2001, the military established special tribunals to try foreign nationals accused of terrorism against the United States. Several accused terrorists detained at the U.S. Naval Base at Guantanamo Bay, Cuba, were brought to trial, but the proceedings were

JURISPRUDENCE

Hamdan v. Rumsfeld, 548 U.S. 547, 126 S.Ct. 2749, 165 L.Ed.2d 723 (2006)

Salim Ahmed Hamdan, a Yemeni national who was detained at the American naval base at Guantanamo Bay, Cuba, brought suit to challenge the legality of the military tribunal before which he was to be tried for conspiracy to commit terrorism. The Supreme Court held that the federal government's plan to try Guantanamo Bay detainees before military commissions was unauthorized by statute and violated international law. However, the Court indicated that Congress could, through appropriate legislation, provide for the use of military tribunals to try Guantanamo Bay detainees. In announcing the judgment of the Court, Justice John Paul Stevens noted that "in undertaking to try Hamdan and subject him to criminal punishment, the Executive is bound to comply with the Rule of Law that prevails in this jurisdiction."

interrupted by a dramatic decision from the nation's highest court. In *Hamdan v. Rumsfeld*, 548 U.S. 547, 126 S.Ct. 2749, 165 L.Ed.2d 723 (2006), the U.S. Supreme Court ruled that the military tribunals were neither authorized by federal law nor required by military necessity. Moreover, the Court held that they ran afoul of the Geneva Conventions governing the treatment of prisoners of war.

In passing the Military Commissions Act of 2006, Pub. L. No. 109-366, 120 Stat. 2600 (Oct. 17, 2006), Congress provided for "the use of military commissions to try alien unlawful enemy combatants engaged in hostilities against the United States for violations of the law of war and other offenses triable by military commission." After a decade of delay and controversy, five foreign nationals accused of participating in the 9/11 terrorist attacks were arraigned before a military tribunal convened at Guantanamo Bay. When they were brought into the courtroom, Khalid Sheik Mohammed and his fellow defendants refused to speak, so the court entered pleas of not guilty on their behalf. It would be a year, however, before the trial would get underway.

Tribal Courts

Article I, Section 8 of the U.S. Constitution mentions Indian tribes as being subject to Congressional legislation. Congress has provided that federal courts have jurisdiction over specified offenses committed by Native Americans on Indian reservations. 18 U.S.C.A. § 1153. At the same time, Congress has permitted certain states to exercise jurisdiction over such offenses. 18 U.S.C.A. § 1162. Furthermore, offenses committed by one Native American against another on a reservation are generally subject to the jurisdiction of tribal courts, unless the crime charged has been expressly made subject to federal jurisdiction. *Keeble v. United States,* 412 U.S. 205, 93 S.Ct. 1993, 36 L.Ed.2d 844 (1973). Courts of the state where a Native American reservation is located have jurisdiction over crimes on the reservation when the offense is perpetrated by a non-Indian against a non-Indian, but non-Indian defendants charged with committing a crime on a reservation are subject to federal jurisdiction if the victim

CASE-IN-POINT

The Trial of Private Bradley Manning

Private Bradley Manning, an American soldier serving in Iraq as an intelligence analyst, had access to classified information. After becoming disenchanted with the war, Manning leaked thousands of classified documents to Wikileaks, an organization dedicated to exposing government secrets. The leaked documents included more than 250,000 State Department cables involving 271 American embassies and consulates in 180 countries. In May of 2010, after being identified as the source of the leaks, Manning was arrested and charged with numerous offenses under the Uniform Code of Military Justice, including "Aiding the Enemy." He was held in solitary confinement for three years while his case was pending before a military court. The trial by court martial was held at Fort Meade, Maryland,

and lasted eight weeks. Manning opted for a bench trial rather than a trial by jury. He admitted to leaking the classified documents, but denied any intent to aid the enemies of the United States. On July 30, 2013, the military judge, Colonel Denise Lind, delivered her verdict. Manning was acquitted of the most serious charge—aiding the enemy—but was convicted of the remaining charges. Given these convictions, he faced the possibility of being sentenced to 135 years in prison. Had he been convicted of aiding the enemy, he would have faced life in prison with possibility of parole. The Manning case aroused great passions in the country. Many saw his actions as despicable, while others hailed him as a hero. His case became a focal point for the ongoing national conversation about national security, government secrecy, and the public's right to know.

is a member of the tribe. *United States v. Antelope,* 430 U.S. 641, 97 S.Ct. 1395, 51 L.Ed.2d 701 (1977).

State Court Systems

courts of general jurisdiction Courts that conduct trials in felony and major misdemeanor cases. Also refers to courts that have jurisdiction to hear civil as well as criminal cases.

courts of limited jurisdiction Courts that handle pretrial matters and conduct trials in minor misdemeanor cases.

state supreme court The highest appellate court of a state.

juvenile courts Judicial tribunals having jurisdiction over juveniles accused of offenses.

Each state has its own independent judicial system. These courts handle more than 90 percent of criminal prosecutions in the United States. State judicial systems are characterized by variations in structure, jurisdiction, and procedure but have certain commonalities. Every state has one or more levels of trial courts and at least one appellate court. Most states have **courts of general jurisdiction**, which conduct trials in felony and major misdemeanor cases, and **courts of limited jurisdiction**, which handle pretrial matters and conduct trials in minor misdemeanor cases. Most states also have some form of intermediate appellate courts that relieve the **state supreme court** (known as the Court of Appeals in New York and Maryland) from hearing routine appeals. Many states also have separate **juvenile courts**, which operate in ways that differ significantly from the criminal courts for adults.

Some states, like North Carolina, have adopted tidy, streamlined court systems (see Figure 2.2). Other states' court systems are extremely complex, as is the case in Texas (see Figure 2.3). In structural complexity, most states' systems fall somewhere between the two extremes.

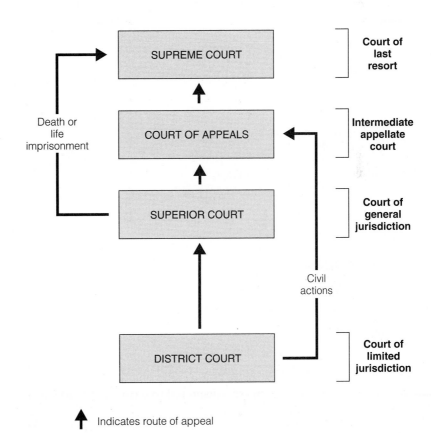

↑ Indicates route of appeal

FIGURE 2.2 The North Carolina Court System. Source: U.S. Department of Justice/ National Center for State Courts.

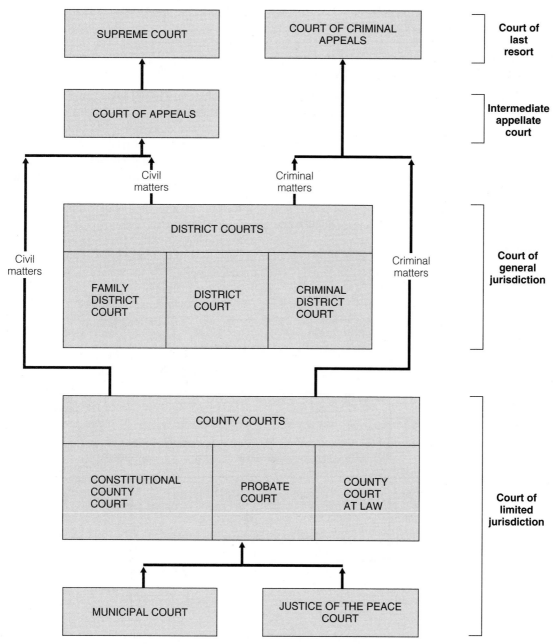

FIGURE 2.3 The Texas Court System. Source: U.S. Department of Justice/National Center for State Courts.

Contrasting Judicial Functions and Environments

As we noted in Chapter 1, trial courts primarily make factual determinations, often assisted by juries; apply settled law to established facts; and impose sanctions. Appellate courts, on the other hand, interpret the federal and state constitutions and statutes, correct errors in law made by trial courts, and develop the law by "filling in the gaps" that often become apparent in the application of statutory laws.

The difference in the roles of trial and appellate courts is also evident in the environment where trial and appellate judges perform their functions. A trial court usually sits in a county courthouse or other county judicial building. Trial judges preside over courtrooms where there is considerable daily activity with the impaneling of juries, testimony of witnesses, and attorneys making objections and pleas for their clients. At other times the judges are busy hearing arguments in their chambers. In short, the trial scene is one of high visibility and is often attended by numerous spectators and, where a high-profile case is being tried, by members of the print and television media. In short, the trial court setting is a venue of daily interaction between court personnel and the citizens of the community.

In contrast, appellate courts are often described as "invisible courts" because their public proceedings are generally limited to hearing legal arguments by attorneys on prescribed oral argument days. Few clients and even fewer spectators are generally in attendance. Media representatives usually attend only when some high-profile appeal is being argued. Many of the documents are delivered by mail to a staff of clerks. Proceedings are resolved primarily by review of records from the lower court or administrative agency, by study of the law briefs submitted by counsel, and by discussion among the panel of judges assigned a particular case, often supplemented by independent research by judges and their staff attorneys.

Unlike a trial court, which is normally surrounded by a busy atmosphere, an appellate court often sits in the state capitol building or in its own facility, usually with a complete law library. The décor in the buildings that house appellate courts is usually quite formal, and often features portraits of former judges regarded as oracles of the law. When a panel of judges sits to hear oral arguments, they normally emerge from behind a velvet curtain on a precise schedule and to the cry of the court's marshal. When not hearing oral arguments, appellate judges usually occupy a suite of offices with their secretaries and law clerks. It is in these individual chambers that appellate judges study and write their opinions on cases assigned to them.

The United States Supreme Court occupies a majestic building in Washington, D.C., with spacious office suites and impressive corridors and library facilities. With enhancements and attributes similar to those of appellate courts, the elegance and dignity of the facilities comport with the significant role of the Court as final arbiter in the nation's judicial system. There is a sparse crowd at most state and intermediate federal appellate courts; at the Supreme Court, by contrast, parties interested in the decisions that will result from arguments, a coterie of media persons, and many spectators fill the courtroom to hear arguments in cases that often significantly affect the economic, social, and political life of the nation. Photography is not allowed, and the arguments and dialogue between the counsel and the justices are observed silently and respectfully by those who attend. There is sometimes a contrasting scene outside the Supreme Court building, where demonstrators gather to give visibility to the causes they represent.

The Juvenile Justice System

juvenile delinquency
Actions of a juvenile in violation of the criminal law.

The juvenile justice system includes specialized courts, law enforcement agencies, social services agencies, and corrections facilities designed to address problems of **juvenile delinquency** as well as child neglect and abuse. "Delinquency" refers to conduct that would be criminal if committed by an adult. In addition to being charged with delinquency, young people may be subjected to the jurisdiction of a juvenile court for engaging in conduct that is prohibited only for minors. Such

status offenses Noncriminal conduct on the part of juveniles that may subject them to the authority of a juvenile court.

behaviors, which include truancy (chronic absence from school) and incorrigibility, are often called **status offenses**, because they are peculiar to the status of children.

Historical Basis

The common law treated all persons above the age of fourteen as adults for purposes of criminal responsibility. Because the American legal system was based on English common law, American courts followed the common-law rules for the treatment of juveniles. Young teenagers were treated essentially as adults for the purposes of criminal justice. During the colonial period of American history, it was not uncommon for teenagers to be hanged, flogged, or placed in the public pillory as punishment for their crimes. Later, as state penitentiaries were established, it was not unusual for 20 percent of prison populations to be juveniles.

In the late nineteenth century, public outcry against treating juveniles like adults led to the establishment of a separate juvenile justice system in the United States. Reformers were convinced that the existing system of criminal justice was inappropriate for young offenders who were more in need of guidance than punishment. Reformers proposed specialized courts to deal with young offenders not as hardened criminals, but as misguided youth in need of special care. This special treatment was justified legally by the concept of ***parens patriae***, the power of the state to act to protect the interests of those who cannot protect themselves.

parens patriae "The parent of the country." Refers to the role of the state as the guardian of minors, mentally ill individuals, and other legally disabled persons.

The first state to act in this area was Illinois in 1899. By the 1920s, many states had followed suit, and by 1945, juvenile court legislation had been enacted by Congress and all state legislatures. The newly created juvenile courts were usually separate from the regular tribunals. Often, the judges or referees presiding over these courts did not have formal legal training. The proceedings were generally nonadversarial, and there was little in the way of procedural regularity or even the opportunity for the juvenile offender to confront his or her accusers. In fact, juvenile delinquency proceedings were conceived as civil, as opposed to criminal, proceedings. Dispositions of cases were usually nonpunitive in character; therefore, accused juvenile offenders were not afforded most of the rights of criminal defendants.

Because the juvenile justice system emphasized rehabilitation (rather than retribution, incapacitation, or deterrence), juveniles who were found delinquent were often placed in reformatories for indeterminate periods, sometimes until they reached the age of majority. Juvenile courts often suffered from lack of trained staff and adequate facilities, and by the 1960s, a system that was conceived by reformers was itself under attack by a new generation of reformers.

The Constitutional Reform of Juvenile Justice

The abuses that came to be associated with juvenile courts were addressed by the Supreme Court in the landmark case of *In re Gault,* 387 U.S. 1, 87 S.Ct. 1428, 18 L.Ed.2d 527 (1967). In *Gault,* the Court essentially required that juvenile courts adhere to standards of due process, applying most of the basic procedural safeguards enjoyed by adults who are accused of crimes. Moreover, *Gault* held that juvenile courts must respect the right to counsel, the freedom from compulsory self-incrimination, and the right to confront (cross-examine) hostile witnesses. Writing for a nearly unanimous bench, Justice Fortas observed that "under our Constitution, the condition of being a boy does not justify a kangaroo court." 387 U.S. at 28, 87 S.Ct. at 1444, 18 L.Ed.2d at 546.

In re Gault, 387 U.S. 1, 87 S.Ct. 1428, 18 L.Ed.2d 527 (1967)

After a neighbor complained of receiving an obscene phone call, fifteen-year-old Gerald Gault was taken into custody and brought before a juvenile court in Gila County, Arizona. As was normal at that time, the case against Gault proceeded without many of the constitutional protections afforded to adult defendants in criminal courts. In particular, Gault was denied the right to an attorney, was not formally notified of the charges against him, was not informed of his protection against self-incrimination, and was not given an opportunity to confront his accuser. After a brief hearing, Gault was judged to be delinquent and was ordered to serve six years in juvenile detention. Two years later, the U.S. Supreme Court held that the process leading to Gault's detention was constitutionally defective: juvenile proceedings must observe the rudiments of due process of law. Justice Abe Fortas, writing for the Court in *Gault,* observed, "Under our Constitution, the condition of being a boy does not justify a kangaroo court."

Four years later in *McKeiver v. Pennsylvania,* 403 U.S. 528, 91 S.Ct. 1976, 29 L.Ed.2d 647 (1971), the Court refused to extend the right to trial by jury to juvenile proceedings. In *Schall v. Martin,* 467 U.S. 253, 104 S.Ct. 2403, 81 L.Ed.2d 207 (1984), the Court upheld a pretrial detention program for juveniles that might well have been found violative of due process had it applied to adults. Writing for the Court, Justice Rehnquist stressed that "the Constitution does not mandate elimination of all differences in the treatment of juveniles." 467 U.S. at 263, 104 S.Ct. at 2409, 81 L.Ed.2d at 216.

In the wake of *Gault,* a number of states revised their juvenile codes to reflect the requirements of those decisions and to increase the qualifications of persons serving as juvenile judges and to transform juvenile courts into courts of record. Today it is common for the juvenile court to be simply a division of a court of general jurisdiction, such as a circuit or a superior court. Nevertheless, juvenile courts retain their distinctive character. For example, juvenile court proceedings are not subject to the constitutional "public trial" requirement. The Federal Juvenile Delinquency Act, 18 U.S.C.A. §§ 5031–5042, gives the court discretion on the issue of whether to close proceedings involving a child and whether to grant public access to the records of the proceedings. State laws vary, often allowing the presiding judge to exercise discretion in these matters. Despite reforms enacted after *Gault,* there remain significant differences in the adjudication of juvenile cases and adult criminal proceedings as well as the punishments imposed.

The Corrections System

corrections system The system of prisons, jails, and other penal and correctional institutions.

The **corrections system** is designed to fulfill the criminal justice system's objective of providing punishment and rehabilitation of offenders. As with the court system, corrections facilities are operated at the federal and state levels. The system includes prisons and jails as well as a variety of programs such as probation, parole, and supervised community service.

Historical Background

Punishments inflicted under the English common law were quite severe—the death penalty was prescribed for most felonies, and those convicted of misdemeanors were generally subjected to such corporal punishment as flogging in the public square. The new American colonies generally followed common-law practice; by the time of the American Revolution, the death penalty was in wide use for a variety of felonies, and corporal punishment, primarily flogging, was widely used for a variety of crimes.

The Eighth Amendment to the U.S. Constitution prohibited the imposition of "**cruel and unusual punishments**." The framers sought to prevent the use of torture, which had been common in Europe as late as the eighteenth century; however, they did not intend to outlaw the death penalty or abolish all forms of corporal punishment.

During the nineteenth century, reformers introduced the concept of the **penitentiary**—literally, "a place to do penance." The idea was that criminals could be reformed through isolation, Bible study, and hard labor. This gave rise to the notion of *rehabilitation*—the idea that the criminal justice system could reform criminals and reintegrate them into society. Many of the educational, occupational training, and psychological programs found in modern prisons are based on this theory.

Contemporary Developments in Criminal Punishment

By the twentieth century, incarceration had largely replaced corporal punishment as the states, as well as the federal government, constructed prisons to house persons convicted of felonies. Even cities and counties constructed jails for the confinement of persons convicted of misdemeanors. The **death penalty**, an intensely controversial penalty, remains in effect today for certain federal offenses and in more than half the states for the most aggravated cases of murder. Today, the focus of criminal punishment is on the goal of incapacitation to prevent commission of further crimes.

There are procedural as well as substantive issues in the area of sentencing and punishment. Sharp disagreements exist regarding the roles that legislatures, judges, and corrections officials should play in determining punishments. Specifically, criminal punishment is limited by the Eighth Amendment prohibition of cruel and unusual punishments, the Due Process Clauses of the Fifth and Fourteenth Amendments, and by similar provisions in all fifty state constitutions. Today, the criminal law provides for a variety of criminal punishments, including **monetary fines**, **incarceration**, **probation**, **community service**, and, of course, the death penalty.

As with courts, there is a federal corrections system and fifty separate state corrections systems. Each of these systems is responsible for supervising those persons sentenced to prison by courts of law. As noted previously, prisons were conceived as places for criminals to reflect on their misdeeds and repent. In the twentieth century, the emphasis shifted to rehabilitation through psychological and sociopsychological methods. Unfortunately, these efforts were less than successful. Ironically, prisons appear to "criminalize" individuals more than they rehabilitate them. Inmates are exposed to an insular society with norms of conduct antithetical to those of civil society. As essentially totalitarian institutions, prisons do not encourage individuals to behave responsibly; furthermore, prisons provide an excellent venue for the spreading of criminal techniques. It is probably unrealistic to expect rehabilitation programs to succeed in such an environment. Today, prisons are generally regarded as little more than a way to punish and isolate those persons deemed unfit to live in civil society.

America's Massive Prison Population

At the end of 2011, there were slightly more than 2.2 million prison inmates in the United States. About 1.5 million prisoners were incarcerated in federal or state

cruel and unusual punishments Criminal penalties that shock the moral conscience of the community—for example, torture and other extreme forms of corporal punishment. Prohibited by the Eighth Amendment to the U.S. Constitution.

penitentiary A synonym for prison. Literally, a place for doing penance.

death penalty Capital punishment; a sentence to death for the commission of a crime.

monetary fines Sums of money that offenders are required to pay as punishment for the commission of crimes.

incarceration Imprisonment.

probation Conditional release of a convicted criminal in lieu of incarceration.

parole Conditional release from jail or prison of a person who has served part of his or her sentence.

community service A sentence or condition of probation requiring that the criminal perform some specific service to the community for some specified period of time.

prisons; the remainder were being held in local jails or other correctional facilities. In 2011, 6.98 million people were in jail or prison or on probation or parole, which is 2.9 percent of all adult residents in the United States (or one in every 34 adults). (U.S. Department of Justice, Office of Justice Programs, Bureau of Justice Statistics, "Correctional Population in the United States, 2011,"November 2012, NCJ 239972).

After decades of very rapid growth, the last several years have seen slower growth rates in state and federal prison populations. Nevertheless, most prisons are operating beyond design capacity, and some state prisons are seriously overcrowded. Responding to lawsuits based on the Eighth Amendment's Cruel and Unusual Punishments Clause, federal courts have imposed limits on some prison populations. In 2005, about one in eight state prisons were under federal court orders to reduce prison populations (U.S. Department of Justice, Office of Justice Programs, Bureau of Justice Statistics Bulletin, "Census of State and Federal Correctional Facilities, 2005," October 2008, NCJ 222182).

The Future Outlook

The public continues to demand harsh sentences for convicted felons, but legislators (and taxpayers) are often unwilling to pay the price of constructing more prisons. Moreover, local residents often object to prisons being built in their "backyards." Even those states that have been aggressive in prison construction have found that demand for cell space continues to exceed supply. In many instances, federal courts have ordered prison officials to reduce overcrowding to comply with the U.S. Constitution's prohibition against "cruel and unusual punishments."

In many state prisons, cells originally designed for one or two inmates now house three or four prisoners. Increasingly, state prison systems must rely on local jails to house inmates, a situation that presents its own set of problems relating both to security and to conditions of confinement. Aside from the threat of federal judicial intervention, overcrowded prisons are more likely to produce inmate violence and even riots.

In addition to prisons, corrections systems include agencies that supervise probation, parole, community service, and other forms of alternative sentences. With burgeoning prison populations, these alternatives to incarceration are assuming more importance and consuming more resources, especially at the state level.

Conclusion

The American system of criminal justice is extremely complicated. The primary reason for this complexity is the principle of federalism, which refers to the division of political and legal authority in this country between one national government and fifty state governments. The United States Congress on behalf of the national government and each state legislature on behalf of its respective state enact their own criminal laws. The national government and all fifty state governments have their own law enforcement agencies, prosecutors, courts, and prison systems. No two systems are exactly alike. Indeed, there is tremendous variation from one jurisdiction to the next, both in the substantive criminal law and in the practices and procedures used by the various components of the criminal process. Yet, despite their substantive and procedural differences, all jurisdictions share two basic goals: to protect society from crime and, at the same time, to protect the rights of the individuals suspected of having committed offenses. Much of the conflict and inefficiency inherent in our criminal justice system stems from the need to balance these two competing objectives.

Chapter Summary

- LO1

  - Under our system of federalism, the national government and each of the fifty states operates its own system of criminal justice. Each has its own legislature, law enforcement and corrections agencies, and courts of law.

  - Because the federal government and the government of each state enact its own criminal laws and have its own system of courts to interpret those laws, there are significant variations across the states and between the state and federal systems.

- LO2

  - The U.S. Congress enacts laws defining federal crimes and setting punishments for those crimes. State legislatures define offenses and set punishments for their states and authorize local governing bodies to enact ordinances defining minor offenses and setting penalties.

  - Federal courts interpret and apply acts of Congress; state courts do likewise with regard to their respective states' laws.

  - Federal law enforcement agencies enforce federal laws; state and local agencies enforce state criminal prohibitions.

- LO3

  - State legislatures have inherently broad powers to enact laws to further the public safety, order, health, and welfare.

  - Congress's legislative powers are restricted to constitutionally enumerated and implied powers, although in the modern era these powers have been exercised and interpreted quite broadly.

  - Criminal laws are written in general terms, and sometimes the meaning of criminal prohibitions is unclear. Courts must interpret statutes to determine their meaning as applied to particular cases.

  - American courts basically adhere to the doctrine of following precedent (*stare decisis*). This provides predictability and stability in the law.

  - Where legislative bodies use certain terms that are not defined, judges look to the common law for definitions and follow certain canons of construction for interpreting statutes that are unclear.

- LO4

  - Numerous federal and state agencies are responsible for enforcement of the criminal law. They investigate suspected criminal activity, arrest suspected criminals, and detain arrested persons until their cases come before the appropriate courts.

  - Unlike their medieval forebears, modern law enforcement agencies are highly constrained by law and emphasize professionalism.

- LO5

  - The U.S. Attorney General heads the Department of Justice. The U.S. Attorneys and their assistants prosecute federal offenses. At the state level, a state or district attorney is the prosecutor.

- The prosecutor serves a vital function in the criminal justice system and is vested with broad discretion in determining whether to bring charges and, if so, the level of those charges.

- Defense counsel are guardians of the defendant's constitutional rights and the legality of the system. Defense attorneys serve as counselors to assist defendants in determining their best course of action and represent a defendant at trial when he or she elects to plead not guilty.

- In all but criminal prosecutions except for petty offenses, indigent defendants are entitled to government-furnished counsel, usually a public defender.

- LO6

  - At the federal level and in many states, grand juries review evidence of criminal activity and determine whether to hand down an indictment or presentment.

  - Grand juries are not trial juries; they do not determine guilt or innocence, but only whether a criminal charge is warranted.

  - An alternative mechanism for charging defendants is an "information" filed by a prosecutor followed by a preliminary hearing.

- LO7

  - The judicial branch operates through trial and appellate courts at both the national and state levels.

  - At the national level the U.S. District Courts are staffed by judges and the U.S. Attorneys who prosecute federal offenses. The U.S. Courts of Appeal hear appeals from decisions of these courts.

  - At the state level, where most criminal trials occur, trial courts conduct trials, sentence defendants found guilty, and deal with posttrial functions. Appellate courts correct errors made at the trial level and, where it becomes necessary, fill in the gaps of the statutory law by exercising a lawmaking function.

  - At the apex of the system is the U.S. Supreme Court, where nine justices who serve for life become the final arbiters of whether federal and state laws pass constitutional muster.

  - The Supreme Court has jurisdiction to review, either on appeal or by writ of certiorari (discretionary review), all the decisions of the lower federal courts and many decisions of the highest state courts.

- LO8

  - Military tribunals are empowered to try any offense by military personnel under the Uniform Code of Military Justice. A military commander convenes a court-martial composed of military officers and, in some instances, enlisted personnel. A trial counsel serves as prosecutor, and defendants are furnished military lawyers unless they choose to employ civilian attorneys. Jurisdiction and the level of authorized punishment depend on whether the court-martial is summary, special, or general.

  - A military judge presides at special and general courts-martial. Military courts basically follow federal court procedures and rules of evidence. The military has an appellate system consisting of courts of review and the U.S. Court of Appeals for the Armed Forces.

- LO9

  ○ Every state has its own system for administering justice to juveniles. The system has evolved from an informal system that focused on rehabilitation to an adversarial system that emphasizes due process.

  ○ Today, the juvenile justice system includes specialized courts, law enforcement agencies, social services agencies, and corrections facilities that address juvenile delinquency and child neglect and abuse.

  ○ In addition to statutory offenses, juveniles are subject to punishment for certain status offenses. Juveniles are entitled to most constitutional rights afforded adults, but they are not entitled to jury trials.

- LO10

  ○ Federal and state corrections facilities include prisons and jails as well as probation, parole, and supervised community service.

  ○ The correctional system administers the death penalty for certain federal offenses and for murder under the laws of many states.

  ○ Additional corrective procedures include incarceration, monetary fines, probation, and parole.

  ○ Today, the focus of criminal punishment is on the goal of incapacitation to prevent commission of further crimes rather than the rehabilitation of offenders.

  ○ Increasingly, the public demands that those who commit the most serious felonies be sentenced to lengthy prison terms. As a result, prisons are overflowing, and in many instances federal courts have ordered prison officials to reduce overcrowding to comply with the U.S. Constitution's prohibition against "cruel and unusual punishments."

Key Terms

appellate courts	*en banc* hearing
Attorney General	enumerated powers
canons of construction	Federal Bureau of Investigation (FBI)
community policing	federalism
community service	grand jury
corrections system	implied exception
Court of Appeals for the Armed Forces	implied powers
court-martial	incarceration
courts of general jurisdiction	independent counsel
courts of limited jurisdiction	indictment
cruel and unusual punishments	indigent defendants
cybersecurity	information
death penalty	intermediate appellate courts
defense attorney	jurisdiction
Department of Justice (DOJ)	jury

juvenile court

juvenile delinquency

legislative intent

legislature

mala prohibita

monetary fines

no bill

nolle prosequi

order maintenance

parens patriae

parole

penitentiary

petit (trial) jury

plain meaning rule

police departments

probation

prosecutor

public defender

rules of procedure

rules of statutory interpretation

session laws

sheriff

special agents

speedy and public trial

state supreme court

state's attorneys

status offenses

statute

sworn officers

trial courts

true bill

U.S. Code

Uniform Code of Military Justice (UCMJ)

United States Attorneys

United States Code Annotated (U.S.C.A.)

United States Congress

United States Courts of Appeals

United States District Courts

United States Marshals Service

United States Supreme Court

void for vagueness

writ of certiorari

Key Court Decisions

Gideon v. Wainwright (1963): Due process requires states to appoint counsel to represent indigent defendants charged with felonies.

Hurtado v. California (1884): States do not have to use grand juries to charge people with felonies as long as they have an alternative procedure that provides due process of law.

Williams v. Florida (1970): The Sixth Amendment does not require states to use twelve-person juries; six person juries are acceptable.

Solorio v. United States (1987): Military court jurisdiction depends solely on whether an accused is a military member; thus, courts-martial may try all offenses committed by servicepersons in violation of the Uniform Code of Military Justice.

Hamdan v. Rumsfeld (2006). Military commissions set up by the Bush administration to try detainees at Guantanamo Bay were held invalid as they were not based on congressional authorization.

In re Gault (1967). Juvenile courts must follow the rudiments of due process of law.

Questions for Thought and Discussion

1. How does the concept of federalism complicate the administration of criminal justice in the United States?
2. Describe the functions of federal and state law enforcement agencies.

3. Compare and contrast the functions of trial and appellate courts. How are they similar? How are they different?

4. What function does a grand jury serve? Does replacement of the indictment function of grand juries at the state level with prosecutors authorized to charge crimes by filing a sworn information impair the rights of citizens charged with crimes?

5. Is there a justification for the broad discretion vested in a prosecutor?

6. To what extent does the United States Constitution protect the right to trial by jury in a criminal case?

7. What are the arguments for and against allowing trial judges broad discretion in criminal sentencing?

8. What factors do you think a prosecutor should take into consideration in determining whether to prosecute an individual the police have arrested for possession of illegal drugs?

9. What chief characteristics distinguish the military justice system under the Uniform Code of Military Justice from civilian criminal prosecutions?

10. What factors should a judge consider in determining whether to sentence a convicted felon to prison?

PART TWO

Law Enforcement and Criminal Procedure

CHAPTER **3**

Search and Seizure

CHAPTER OUTLINE

Introduction

Historical Background

When, Where, and to Whom the Fourth Amendment Applies

The Scope of Privacy Protected by the Fourth Amendment

The Warrant Requirement

Exceptions to the Warrant Requirement

Exceptions to the Probable Cause Requirement

Electronic Surveillance

The Exclusionary Rule

Conclusion

Chapter Summary

Key Terms

Questions for Thought and Discussion

Problems for Discussion and Solution

JURISPRUDENCE FEATURE BOXES

Katz v. United States (1967)

California v. Greenwood (1988)

United States v. Ross (1982)

Terry v. Ohio (1968)

United States v. Jones (2012)

Mapp v. Ohio (1961)

United States v. Leon (1984)

Herring v. United States (2009)

LEARNING OBJECTIVES

After reading this chapter, you should be able to explain

1. when, where, and to whom the Fourth Amendment applies

2. the scope of privacy protected by the Fourth Amendment

3. why searches based on consent are problematic

4. the meaning and importance of probable cause

5. the rules governing the issuance and execution of search warrants

6. the recognized exceptions to the warrant requirement

7. the circumstances under which police or other officials are permitted to conduct searches based on reasonable suspicion

8. how interpretation of the Fourth Amendment has evolved in response to electronic surveillance

9. how federal statutes, including the USA PATRIOT Act, affect electronic surveillance

10. the exclusionary rule and the good faith exception to the rule

CHAPTER OPENING VIGNETTE

Federal agents suspected that Danny Kyllo was growing marijuana inside his home in Florence, Oregon. But mere suspicion is not enough to justify the issuance of a search warrant. So the agents, sitting in a parked car across the street, used a thermal imaging device to scan the home.

The scan revealed that the roof over the garage and a side wall of Kyllo's home were significantly hotter than the rest of the house and much warmer than neighboring homes. Based on these results, as well as utility bills showing inordinate use of electricity, the agents concluded that Kyllo was using high-intensity lamps to grow marijuana inside his home. A federal magistrate determined that there was probable cause and issued a search warrant. After executing the warrant, agents found what they had suspected: an indoor growing operation with more than a hundred cannabis plants. Kyllo was arrested and later indicted by a federal grand jury for growing marijuana. Kyllo's attorney moved to have the evidence suppressed, claiming that the use of the thermal imager constituted an unconstitutional search of his home. When the motion was denied, Kyllo agreed to a guilty plea but reserved the right to appeal the ruling on the pretrial motion. In 2001, nine years after Kyllo was arrested, the case was decided by the U.S. Supreme Court.

The Fourth Amendment prohibits unreasonable searches and seizures, and the courts have long held that warrantless searches of the home are unreasonable in the absence of extraordinary circumstances. But was the thermal scan of Kyllo's home a "search"? At the time this case was being litigated, thermal imagers were being widely used by law enforcement agencies around the country as part of the national war on drugs. Police and prosecutors typically took the view that the thermal scan was not a search within the meaning of the Fourth Amendment, since it merely collected data on heat that was being released into the public space. In a 5–4 decision, the Supreme Court disagreed with this point of view. *Kyllo v. United States*, 533 U.S. 27, 121 S.Ct. 2038, 150 L.Ed.2d 94 (2001). Writing for the Court, Justice Antonin Scalia observed that "[w]here, as here, the Government uses a device that is not in general public use, to explore details of the home that would previously have been unknowable without physical intrusion, the surveillance is a search and is presumptively unreasonable without a warrant." 533 U.S. at 40, 121 S.Ct. at 2046, 150 L.Ed.2d at 106. As a result of the Supreme Court's decision, the evidence the government had obtained against Kyllo was thrown out. The case collapsed, and the government dropped the charges. The *Kyllo* case is interesting because it shows how changing technology creates new and difficult Fourth Amendment problems. As technology advances, courts will continue to confront such issues.

Introduction

search Inspection; attempt to locate a particular person or object.

seizure Action of police in taking possession or control of property or persons.

Search and seizure have always been essential tools of law enforcement. A **search** occurs when government agents look for evidence in a manner that intrudes into a person's legally protected zone of privacy. A **seizure** takes place when agents take possession or control of property or persons.

Today, as the United States simultaneously prosecutes a "war on drugs" and a "war on terrorism," search and seizure are crucial issues for law enforcement agencies, courts, and citizens. Without the powers to conduct searches and seize evidence, law enforcement agencies would be unable to perform their historic missions, let alone combat drug trafficking, organized crime, and international terrorism. On the other hand, unrestricted powers of search and seizure are antithetical to the American traditions of individual liberty, personal privacy, and limited government.

Because search and seizure often entails serious invasions of privacy, the power of law enforcement agencies to conduct searches and seizures is limited by the federal and state constitutions and by a number of federal and state statutes. Most important among these legal limitations is the Fourth Amendment to the U.S. Constitution, which provides:

> The right of the people to be secure in their persons, houses, papers and effects, against unreasonable searches and seizures, shall not be violated, and no Warrants shall issue but upon probable cause, supported by Oath or affirmation, and particularly describing the place to be searched and the persons or things to be seized.

warrant A judicial writ or order directed to a law enforcement officer authorizing the doing of a specified act, such as an arrest or a search.

probable cause A reasonable ground for belief in certain alleged facts.

reasonable suspicion A police officer's belief based on all relevant circumstances that criminal activity is afoot.

As a general rule, the Fourth Amendment requires law enforcement officers to obtain a **warrant** before conducting searches and seizures. Although some warrantless searches and seizures are permissible, they all must conform to a standard of reasonableness. Law enforcement officers are not permitted to conduct searches and seizures arbitrarily or even based on their hunches about criminal activity. For a search to be reasonable under the Fourth Amendment, police generally must have **probable cause** to believe that a search will produce evidence of crime. In certain instances, police may conduct limited searches based on the lesser standard of **reasonable suspicion**. Subject to certain exceptions, evidence obtained through unreasonable searches and seizures is not admissible in criminal prosecutions.

Historical Background

Before the late seventeenth century, there was very little protection at common law against invasions of privacy by unreasonable searches and seizures. Although a system of warrants had long been in place to provide legal authority for arrests, searches, and seizures, executive as well as judicial authorities could issue warrants. Moreover, there was no requirement that a search warrant specify the location to be searched or the items to be seized. For hundreds of years, English subjects (and, later, American colonists) were subjected to the abuse of the **general warrant**—that is, a warrant authorizing searches of unspecified persons and places.

general warrant A search or arrest warrant that is not particular as to the person to be arrested, place to be searched, or property to be seized.

The Glorious Revolution of 1688 was the real beginning of democracy in England. It was then that Parliament achieved supremacy over the monarchy. In the wake of the Glorious Revolution, English courts began to place more stringent and effective limitations on the Crown's power. The power of search and seizure was one area in which courts moved to limit royal authority.

By far, the most significant English case in the area of search and seizure before the American Revolution was *Entick v. Carrington*, 95 Eng. Rep. 807 (1765). John Entick, who edited a newspaper highly critical of the government, was arrested on a charge of seditious libel. A warrant was issued calling for the seizure of all his books, letters, and papers. Entick successfully sued for trespass. On appeal, the judgment was upheld, and the practice of general warrants was declared illegal. The opinion in *Entick v. Carrington* proved to be very influential. The next year, Parliament declared the notorious general warrant invalid. Addressing the House of Commons, William Pitt (the elder) declared that

> [t]he poorest man may, in his cottage, bid defiance to all the forces of the Crown. It may be frail; its roof may shake; the wind may blow through it; the storm may enter; but the King of England may not enter; all his force dares not cross the threshold of the ruined tenement.

Adoption of the Fourth Amendment

Although the common law provided some protection against general warrants, the framers of the American Bill of Rights adopted a more explicit, and more thorough, proscription of unreasonable searches and seizures. To a great extent, they were motivated by a distaste for the Writs of Assistance, which gave customs officials in the American colonies unlimited power to search for smuggled goods. In a famous debate in 1761, James Otis called the Writs of Assistance "the worst instrument of arbitrary power, the most destructive of English liberty and the fundamental principles of law, that ever was found in an English lawbook." Quoted in *Boyd v. United States*, 116 U.S. 616, 625, 6 S.Ct. 524, 529, 29 L.Ed. 746, 749 (1886). The Fourth Amendment was adopted to ensure that officials of the U.S. government would never be able to exercise such unlimited powers of search and seizure.

Their distaste for general warrants led the framers of the Bill of Rights to write a particularity requirement into the Warrant Clause of the Fourth Amendment. The Supreme Court has recognized that "limiting the authorization to search to the specific areas and things for which there is probable cause to search ... ensures that the search will be carefully tailored to its justifications, and will not take on the character of the wide-ranging exploratory searches the Framers intended to prohibit." *Maryland v. Garrison*, 480 U.S. 79, 84, 107 S.Ct. 1013, 1016, 94 L.Ed.2d 72, 80 (1987).

Extension of the Fourth Amendment to Apply to Searches by State and Local Authorities

The Fourth Amendment, like all the protections of the Bill of Rights, was originally conceived as a limitation on the powers of the newly created national government. Under the original conception of the Bill of Rights, citizens seeking legal protection against actions of state and local governments had to look to their state constitutions and state courts for relief. *Barron v. Baltimore*, 32 U.S. (7 Pet.) 243, 8 L.Ed. 672 (1833). However, the protection of the Fourth Amendment, along with most of the protections contained in the Bill of Rights, has been extended to defendants in state criminal prosecutions on the basis of the Fourteenth Amendment's limitations on state action. In 1949 the Supreme Court held that the freedom from unreasonable searches and seizures is "implicit in 'the concept of ordered liberty' and as such enforceable against the States through the Due Process Clause [of the Fourteenth Amendment]." *Wolf v. Colorado*, 338 U.S. 25, 27–28, 69 S.Ct. 1359, 1361, 93 L.Ed. 1782, 1785 (1949).

The judicial extension of the Fourth Amendment and other protections of the Bill of Rights to limit the actions of the state and local governments are referred to as the **doctrine of incorporation**. Under this doctrine, provisions of the Bill of Rights deemed to be essential to a scheme of ordered liberty are incorporated into the Fourteenth Amendment's broad limitations on state and local authority. *Palko v. Connecticut*, 302 U.S. 319, 58 S.Ct. 149, 82 L.Ed. 288 (1937).

doctrine of incorporation
The doctrine under which provisions of the Bill of Rights are held to be incorporated within the Due Process Clause of the Fourteenth Amendment and are thereby made applicable to actions of the state and local governments.

Judicial Federalism and the Fourth Amendment

As a result of *Wolf v. Colorado*, supra, the Fourth Amendment limits search and seizure activities by law enforcement agencies at all levels of government, whether federal, state, or local. The application of the Fourth Amendment to state prosecutions ensures a minimal national standard governing search and seizure. Under our system of federalism, state courts are free to provide higher levels of protection for individuals under applicable provisions of their state constitutions than are provided by the Fourth Amendment. But they cannot provide less protection to the individual without running afoul of the Fourteenth Amendment. Indeed, this is true of all constitutional protections. As long as state courts make clear that decisions that favor the rights of suspects, defendants, and prisoners rest on independent state constitutional grounds, those decisions are not subject to review by the federal courts. *Michigan v. Long*, 463 U.S. 1032, 103 S.Ct. 3469, 77 L.Ed.2d 1201 (1983).

State constitutional law in the search and seizure area has become extremely complex, as there are numerous issues on which certain state courts have refused to follow federal decisions restricting Fourth Amendment protections. We will mention a few examples on the pages that follow. In an attempt to reduce confusion and unnecessary complexity owing to different federal and state standards of search and seizure, Florida amended its constitution in 1982 to render its prohibition of unreasonable searches and seizures coextensive with that of the Fourth Amendment. West's Fla. Const. Art. 1, § 12 (as amended 1982). Interpreting this novel amendment, the Florida Supreme Court has held that, in effect, the Florida Constitution incorporates all decisions of the U.S. Supreme Court interpreting the Fourth Amendment, regardless of when they were rendered. *Bernie v. State*, 524 So.2d 988 (Fla. 1988).

When, Where, and to Whom the Fourth Amendment Applies

Because the Constitution limits government action, the Fourth Amendment protects a person's rights against the police and other government agents but not against searches and seizures conducted by private individuals. The Supreme Court has said that the Fourth Amendment "is wholly inapplicable to a search or seizure, even an unreasonable one, effected by a private individual not acting as an agent of the Government or with the participation or knowledge of any government official." *United States v. Jacobsen*, 466 U.S. 109, 113, 104 S.Ct. 1652, 1656, 80 L.Ed.2d 85, 94 (1984). In determining whether a private citizen has acted as an agent of the government, the court must consider (1) whether the government knew of and acquiesced in the activity and (2) whether the citizen was motivated on the basis of assisting the government. *United States v. Feffer*, 831 F.2d 734, 739 (7th Cir. 1987). Thus, a search by a privately employed security guard is ordinarily considered a search by a private citizen. Likewise, a search of a package by an employee of a common carrier is not considered a violation of the Fourth Amendment unless the search was instigated by government action. *United States v. Monroe*, 943 F.2d 884 (8th Cir. 1991).

On the other hand, states can interpret their own constitutional limitations more broadly to apply to searches by certain nongovernmental actors. Alternatively, they can enact statutes to that effect. For example, the Texas Code of Criminal Procedure provides, "No evidence obtained by an officer *or other person* [emphasis added] in violation of any provisions of the Constitution or laws of the State of Texas, or of the Constitution or laws of the United States of America, shall be admitted in evidence against the accused on the trial of any criminal case." Tex. Code Crim. Proc. Art. 38.23(a).

Border Searches and Searches Outside the United States

border searches Searches of persons entering the borders of the United States.

Travelers crossing the borders of the United States are routinely subjected to searches even when they are not the targets of suspicion. Suspicionless **border searches** are justified by the view that persons crossing the national border are not entitled to the protections of the Fourth Amendment. *United States v. Ramsey*, 431 U.S. 606, 97 S.Ct. 1972, 52 L.Ed.2d 617 (1977). This is not to say that agents conducting border searches are beyond the law. Regardless of the applicability of the Fourth Amendment, methods of search and seizure may not be so severe or extreme as to "shock the conscience." *Rochin v. California*, 342 U.S. 165, 72 S.Ct. 205, 96 L.Ed. 183 (1952).

The border search exception to the Fourth Amendment extends to searches conducted at established stations near the border or other functional equivalents of a border search. An example would be the search of a ship when it first docks after entering the territorial waters of the United States. *United States v. Prince*, 491 F.2d 655 (5th Cir. 1974). On the other hand, in *Almeida-Sanchez v. United States*, 413 U.S. 266, 93 S.Ct. 2535, 37 L.Ed.2d 596 (1973), the Supreme Court invalidated a search by a roving patrol some twenty-five miles within the border because agents lacked probable cause.

The Fourth Amendment does not apply to searches and seizures conducted by U.S. agents outside the territory of the United States. The purpose of the amendment is to restrict only those searches and seizures conducted domestically. *United States v. Verdugo-Urquidez*, 494 U.S. 259, 110 S.Ct. 1056, 108 L.Ed.2d 222 (1990).

The Home, Its Curtilage, and the Open Fields Doctrine

The English common law held that "a man's home is his castle," and it sought to protect persons in their homes by, among other things, creating the crime of burglary. The Fourth Amendment specifically mentions the right of the people to be secure in their houses. Of course, it also mentions their persons, papers, and effects. But it is fair to say that when a person is in his or her home, the protection afforded by the Fourth Amendment is at its maximum.

curtilage The enclosed space of ground surrounding a dwelling.

At common law, the concept of **curtilage** was developed to afford the area immediately surrounding a house the same protection under the law of burglary as the house itself. The term refers to the enclosed space of ground surrounding a dwelling. The Supreme Court has held that the Fourth Amendment provides the same protection to the curtilage as to the house itself. On the other hand, the open fields surrounding the house and curtilage are not entitled to Fourth Amendment protection. *Hester v. United States*, 265 U.S. 57, 44 S.Ct. 445, 68 L.Ed. 898 (1924). Writing for the Supreme Court in *Hester*, Justice Oliver Wendell Holmes noted that

> the special protection accorded by the Fourth Amendment to the people in their "persons, houses, papers and effects," is not extended to the open fields. The distinction between the latter and the house is as old as the common law. 265 U.S. at 59, 44 S.Ct. at 446, 68 L.Ed. at 900.

open fields doctrine The doctrine that the Fourth Amendment does not apply to the open fields around a home, even if these open fields are private property.

The **open fields doctrine** was reaffirmed by the Supreme Court in *Oliver v. United States*, 466 U.S. 170, 104 S.Ct. 1735, 80 L.Ed.2d 214 (1984). In *Oliver*, narcotics officers entered the defendant's land by going around a locked gate and ignoring NO TRESPASSING signs. When they observed a field of marijuana, they arrested the owner of the property for manufacturing contraband. The Court upheld the search because it concluded that the Fourth Amendment did not apply to the open fields around the owner's home, despite his attempt to protect it by posting signs. State courts are divided on whether to provide greater protection under their state constitutions. But in *United States v. Cuevas-Sanchez*, 821 F.2d 248 (5th Cir. 1987), the Fifth Circuit Court of Appeals held that the use of a video camera mounted on a utility pole to conduct surveillance of a defendant's fenced-in backyard was a search entitled to Fourth Amendment protection.

In *People v. Scott*, 593 N.E.2d 1328 (N.Y. 1992), New York's highest court ruled that where property owners fence or post NO TRESPASSING signs on their private property or, by some other means, indicate that entry is not permitted, they have a reasonable expectation of privacy that must be respected. The New York decision illustrates that a state is free to provide greater protection under its state constitution than the U.S. Supreme Court determines is required under the federal constitution. A New Jersey appellate court was unwilling to grant greater protection than afforded by the federal constitution when it excused a warrantless entry onto private lands by conservation officers investigating a suspected violation of fish and game law. *State v. Gates*, 703 A.2d 696 (N.J. Super. 1997).

Searches of Abandoned Property

abandoned property Property over which the former owner has relinquished any claim of ownership.

Police may search abandoned premises and seize **abandoned property** without the necessity of legally justifying their actions. *Abel v. United States*, 362 U.S. 217, 80 S.Ct. 683, 4 L.Ed.2d 668 (1960). The key question in such cases is whether the property was abandoned at the time of the search. In a 1960 decision, the Supreme Court observed that a "passenger who lets a package drop to the floor of the taxicab in which he is riding can hardly be said to have 'abandoned' it. An occupied taxicab is not to be compared to an open field … or a vacated hotel room." *Rios v. United States*, 364 U.S. 253, 262, n. 6, 80 S.Ct. 1431, 1437, 4 L.Ed.2d 1688, 1694 (1960). Similarly, in 1990 the Supreme Court held that "a citizen who attempts to protect his private property from inspection, after throwing it on a car to respond to a police officer's inquiry, clearly has not abandoned that property." *Smith v. Ohio*, 494 U.S. 541, 543–544, 110 S.Ct. 1288, 1290, 108 L.Ed.2d 464, 468 (1990).

Automobile Inventory Searches

inventory search An exception to the warrant requirement that allows police who legally impound a vehicle to conduct a routine inventory of the contents of the vehicle.

Most law enforcement agencies that impound automobiles for parking violations or abandonment, or pursuant to the arrest of a motorist, routinely conduct an inventory of the contents and remove any valuables for safekeeping. When conducted according to standard police procedures, an **inventory search** is generally regarded as an administrative search not subject to ordinary Fourth Amendment requirements. Inventory searches are justified by the need for protection of the owner's property while the vehicle remains in police custody, protection of the police from claims of lost property, and protection of the police from potential dangers that might be lurking inside closed automobiles. Of course, if a routine inventory search yields evidence of crime, it may be seized and admitted into evidence without violating the Fourth Amendment. *South Dakota v. Opperman*, 428 U.S. 364, 96 S.Ct. 3092, 49 L.Ed.2d 1000 (1976).

It should be recognized that police are not permitted to use an inventory search as a pretext for a criminal investigation. *Colorado v. Bertine*, 479 U.S. 367, 107 S.Ct. 738, 93 L.Ed.2d 739 (1987). Nevertheless, once the police have legitimately taken a vehicle into custody, they are not required to overlook contraband articles discovered during a valid inventory search, and such items may be used as evidence. Lower federal and state courts have emphasized that an inventory search must be in accordance with established inventory procedures. See, e.g., *United States v. Velarde*, 903 F.2d 1163 (7th Cir. 1990). In 1998, the Arkansas Supreme Court held that the fact that the defendant lacked a valid driver's license constituted good cause to justify a police officer's impounding his vehicle and completing a warrantless inventory of its contents pursuant to the police department's standards. *Thompson v. State*, 966 S.W.2d 901 (Ark. 1998).

Searches Based on Consent

consent to a search The act of a person voluntarily permitting police to conduct a search of person or property.

Constitutional rights may be waived, and Fourth Amendment rights are no exception. Voluntary cooperation with police officers often results in fruitful searches and seizures. The Supreme Court has refused to require law officers to inform suspects of their right to refuse to **consent to a search**. *Schneckloth v. Bustamonte*, 412 U.S. 218, 93 S.Ct. 2041, 36 L.Ed.2d 854 (1973). More recently, the Court held that police are not required to inform motorists who are stopped for other reasons that they are "free to go" before asking them to consent to a search of their automobile. *Ohio v. Robinette*, 519 U.S. 33, 117 S.Ct. 417, 136 L.Ed.2d 347 (1996).

To be valid, consent must be truly voluntary. If a person actually assists the police in conducting a search, or consents after having been advised that consent is not required, courts have little difficulty in finding that consent was voluntary. Yet, consent has to involve more than mere acquiescence to the authority of the police. Thus, in *Bumper v. North Carolina*, 391 U.S. 543, 88 S.Ct. 1788, 20 L.Ed.2d 797 (1968), the Court held that a claim of police authority based on a nonexistent warrant was so coercive as to invalidate the defendant's consent. Similarly, a Georgia appellate court invalidated an automobile search where the defendant and a companion were surprised by six heavily armed law officers, were searched at gunpoint, and were then asked to consent to a search of their automobile. *Love v. State*, 242 S.E.2d 278 (Ga. App. 1978).

When a person summons the police to the home to investigate a crime that has allegedly taken place there, there is an **implied consent** to a search of the premises related to the routine investigation of the offense. Of course, once police are lawfully on the premises, any evidence of crime that is in their plain view may be seized, even if the person who initially summoned the police may be ultimately prosecuted as a result of such evidence.

A perennial problem in the area of consent searches is that of **third-party consent**. The problem is especially acute in situations where several persons share a single dwelling, as is common among college students. For example, may an apartment dweller consent to the search of his or her roommate's bedroom? The Supreme Court has said that the consent of a third party is valid only when there is mutual use of the property by persons generally having joint access or control. Thus, any of the co-occupants has the right to permit the inspection. The others have assumed the risk that one of their number might permit the common area to be searched. *United States v. Matlock*, 415 U.S. 164, 94 S.Ct. 988, 39 L.Ed.2d 242 (1974). *Matlock* stands for the principle that the validity of third-party consent is tested by the degree of dominion and control exercised by the third party over the searched premises and that a joint occupant may provide valid consent only if the other party is not present.

In *Illinois v. Rodriguez*, 497 U.S. 177, 110 S.Ct. 2793, 111 L.Ed.2d 148 (1990), the Supreme Court shifted the focus from the dominion and control of the third party to the police officer's subjective belief that the third party has the authority to grant consent to a search of the premises. Writing for the Court, Justice Antonin Scalia opined that a warrantless entry is valid when based on the consent of a third party that the police reasonably believe to possess common authority over the premises, even if the third party does not in fact have such authority.

There are a number of well-established situations in which third-party consent is not valid. Tenancy arrangements are a good example. A landlord does not have the implied authority to consent to the search of a tenant's premises. *Chapman v. United States*, 365 U.S. 610, 81 S.Ct. 776, 5 L.Ed.2d 828 (1961). Likewise, a hotel manager or clerk does not have the right to consent to the search of a guest's room during the time the guest has a legal right to occupy the room. *Stoner v. California*, 376 U.S. 483, 84 S.Ct. 889, 11 L.Ed.2d 856 (1964).

Courts have taken different approaches to searches of college dormitory rooms, often depending on the regulations the student agrees to when occupying the dormitory room. A search routinely performed by college officials for reasons of health or safety that reveals incriminating evidence in plain view would probably not be in violation of the Fourth Amendment. On the other hand, a search of a dormitory room by police would ordinarily require a search warrant issued on the basis of probable cause. In *Commonwealth v. McCloskey*, 272 A.2d 271 (Pa. Super. 1970), the court held that absent **exigent circumstances**, police entry into a college dormitory room by means of a pass key possessed by the head resident was improper. Even though the university had reserved the right to check the room for damage and use of unauthorized appliances, the court found that in the absence of exigent circumstances the university did not have authority to consent to a governmental search of the student's room.

implied consent An agreement or acquiescence manifested by a person's actions or inaction.

third-party consent Consent, usually to a search, given by a person on behalf of another—for example, a college roommate who allows the police to search a roommate's effects.

exigent circumstances Unforeseen situations that demand unusual or immediate action.

Some current problems in the area of third-party consent involve parental consent to searches of premises occupied by their adult children and spousal consent to searches of the other spouse's property, such as an automobile. But again, the Supreme Court has shifted the focus to the police officer's subjective belief regarding the authority of third parties. In general, state courts have followed the *Matlock* approach. The Louisiana Supreme Court did that in 1999 by holding that a warrantless search may be valid even if consent was given by one without authority if the facts available to officers at the time of entry justified the officers' reasonable, albeit erroneous, belief that the one consenting to the search had authority over the premises. *State v. Edwards*, 750 So.2d 893 (La. 1999). But not all state courts have been willing to follow *Matlock*; some provide more protection to their citizens. For example, Oregon courts have ruled that the state constitution requires that consent by a third party must be based on actual authority. See *State v. Will*, 885 P.2d 715 (Or. App. 1994).

The Scope of Privacy Protected by the Fourth Amendment

wiretapping The use of electronic devices to intercept telephonic communications.

electronic eavesdropping Covert listening to or recording of a person's conversations or messages by electronic means.

The term "seizure" refers to the taking into custody of physical evidence, property, or even a person. What constitutes a "search"? The answer is not so clear. Originally, the protection of the Fourth Amendment was limited to physical intrusions on one's person or property. *Olmstead v. United States*, 277 U.S. 438, 48 S.Ct. 564, 72 L.Ed. 944 (1928). Historically, courts looked at whether a trespass had taken place in deciding whether the Fourth Amendment was implicated. Thus, surveillance without physical contact with the suspect or the suspect's property was deemed to fall outside the protections of the Fourth Amendment. Accordingly, the Fourth Amendment was not deemed applicable to **wiretapping** or **electronic eavesdropping**.

In *Katz v. United States*, 389 U.S. 347, 88 S.Ct. 507, 19 L.Ed.2d 576 (1967), the Supreme Court overruled *Olmstead* and abandoned the trespass doctrine, saying "the Fourth Amendment protects people, not places." 389 U.S. at 361, 88 S.Ct. at 516, 19 L.Ed.2d at 582. The contemporary approach to determining the scope of protected privacy under the Fourth Amendment is nicely stated in Justice John M. Harlan's concurring opinion in *Katz*:

> My understanding of the rule as it has emerged from prior decisions is that there is a twofold requirement, first, that a person has exhibited an actual (subjective) expectation of privacy and, second, that the expectation be one that society is prepared to recognize as "reasonable." 389 U.S. at 361, 88 S.Ct. at 516, 19 L.Ed.2d at 587.

Reasonable Expectations of Privacy

reasonable expectation of privacy Doctrine holding that the Fourth Amendment protects persons from official intrusions as long as they have a subjective expectation of privacy that society is prepared to accept.

Potentially, the term "search" applies to any official invasion of a person's reasonable expectation of privacy as to one's person, house, papers, or effects. In *Katz*, the Court held that a suspected bookie who was using a public telephone, allegedly to conduct a gambling business, enjoyed a **reasonable expectation of privacy** and that a police wiretap of the phone booth was a search within the meaning of the Fourth Amendment. This decision brought wiretapping and other forms of electronic eavesdropping within the limitations of the Fourth Amendment. Currently, any means of invading a person's reasonable expectation of privacy is considered a search for Fourth Amendment purposes. The critical question that courts must address in reviewing cases

Katz v. United States, 389 U.S. 347, 88 S.Ct. 507, 19 L.Ed.2d 576 (1967)

Government agents, acting without a warrant, attached a "bug," or listening device, to the outside of a public telephone booth from which Charles Katz, a suspected bookie, often placed calls. Agents recorded Katz's conversations and obtained evidence that led to an eight-count indictment charging him with transmitting wagering information by telephone. Katz was convicted despite his claim that the government's key evidence had been obtained in violation of the Fourth Amendment. In affirming his conviction, the Court of Appeals, relying on *Olmstead v. United States* (1928), found no constitutional violation because "[t]here was no physical entrance into the area occupied by [Katz]." In a landmark ruling, the Supreme Court reversed and overturned the conviction. The Court observed that "the underpinnings of [*Olmstead v. United States*] have been so eroded by our subsequent decisions that the 'trespass' doctrine there enunciated can no longer be regarded as controlling." Justice Potter Stewart's opinion for the Court concluded that "electronically listening to and recording the petitioner's words violated the privacy upon which he justifiably relied while using the telephone booth and thus constituted a "search and seizure" within the meaning of the Fourth Amendment." According to Justice Harlan's concurrence, which has come to be regarded as the most important opinion in *Katz*, the Fourth Amendment extends to any place or thing in which an individual has a "reasonable expectation of privacy."

where police conduct surveillance or eavesdropping without probable cause or prior judicial authorization is whether such surveillance intruded on a person's reasonable expectation of privacy.

The question of what constitutes a reasonable expectation of privacy has been litigated in hundreds of cases in federal and state courts. The uniqueness of individual situations has resulted in disparate views, with police frequently complaining that judicial decisions fail to furnish any "bright-line" rules. In a number of well-defined situations, however, courts have upheld minimally intrusive, suspicionless searches on the assumption that people's privacy expectations are reduced in such situations.

Police techniques such as canine sniffs are considered among the least intrusive means of government investigation. Thus, police were allowed to conduct a "sniff test" of a passenger's luggage at an airport without reasonable suspicion because it did not violate a person's reasonable expectation of privacy. *United States v. Place*, 462 U.S. 696, 106 S.Ct. 2637, 77 L.Ed.2d 110 (1983). More recently, however, the Supreme Court ruled that bringing a drug-sniffing dog to the front porch of a home was a search within the meaning of the Fourth Amendment. And because this was a search of a home, the police needed prior judicial authorization, which they did not obtain in this case. In his opinion for the Court, Justice Scalia, who has not been sympathetic to the "reasonable expectation of privacy" formulation, characterized the search as a physical intrusion into a person's property. *Florida v. Jardines*, 569 U.S. ___, 133 S.Ct. 1409, 185 L.Ed.2d 495 (2013).

Airport Security Procedures

With increased concern over airplane hijacking and terrorism has come increased security at the nation's airports. Passengers attempting to board aircraft routinely pass through metal detectors and other sorts of scanners; their carry-on baggage and checked luggage are routinely subjected to X-ray scans. Should these procedures suggest the presence of suspicious objects, physical searches are conducted to determine what the objects are. There is little question that such searches are reasonable given their minimal intrusiveness, the gravity of the safety interests involved, and the reduced privacy expectations associated with airline travel. Indeed, travelers are often notified through airport public address systems and signs that "all bags are subject to search." Such announcements place passengers on notice that ordinary Fourth Amendment protections do not apply.

In 2010, a controversy erupted over enhanced screening procedures adopted by the Transportation Security Administration in response to recent attempts by terrorists to carry nonmetallic explosives onto aircraft. These procedures involved the use of full-body scans that revealed considerable anatomical detail and, for passengers who opted out of the scans, fairly extensive pat-down searches. Clearly, the enhanced procedures were more intrusive and subjected passengers to considerable inconvenience and, in some cases, embarrassment. But most legal commentators agreed that, given the magnitude of the safety interests involved, the enhanced procedures were reasonable.

Sobriety Checkpoints

sobriety checkpoints
Roadblocks set up for the purpose of administering field sobriety tests to motorists who appear to be intoxicated.

In the last twenty-five years, society has become incensed about drunk driving and the resulting carnage on the nation's highways. One method increasingly used by law enforcement to combat this problem is the use of **sobriety checkpoints**, in which all drivers passing a certain point are stopped briefly and observed for signs of intoxication. To the extent that police officers at these checkpoints visually inspect the passenger compartments of stopped automobiles, these brief encounters involve searches, although in most instances these procedures entail only minor intrusion and inconvenience. Critics of sobriety checkpoints object to the fact that police temporarily detain and visually search cars without any particular suspicion. Yet, the courts have generally approved such measures. See, e.g., *Michigan Dept. of State Police v. Sitz*, 496 U.S. 444, 110 S.Ct. 2481, 110 L.Ed.2d 412 (1990). It is noteworthy, however, that in 2000, the U.S. Supreme Court disallowed a checkpoint that was established primarily for the purpose of detecting illegal drugs. *City of Indianapolis v. Edmond*, 531 U.S. 32, 121 S.Ct 447, 148 L.Ed.2d 333 (2000). (This topic is explored further in the next chapter.)

Jail and Prison Searches and Strip Searches

strip searches Searches of suspects' or prisoners' private parts.

Obviously, anyone lawfully incarcerated in a prison or jail has no reasonable expectation of privacy. Jail and prison cells are routinely "swept" for weapons and other contraband, and inmates are routinely subjected to searches of their persons. The Supreme Court in *Bell v. Wolfish*, 441 U.S. 520, 99 S.Ct. 1861, 60 L.Ed.2d 447 (1979), upheld **strip searches** of prison inmates because of the demands for institutional security. But the Court did not give prison officials carte blanche. Rather, the Court held that the Fourth Amendment requires balancing the need for the particular search against the invasion of personal rights. Thus, courts must consider the justification and scope of the intrusion and the manner and place in which it is conducted.

Absent cause for suspicion, visitors to a prison may be subjected to reasonable searches—for example, a pat-down search or a metal detector sweep. However, before conducting a strip search of a visitor, prison authorities must have at least a reasonable suspicion that the visitor is bearing contraband. *Spear v. Sowders*, 71 F.3d 626 (6th Cir. 1995).

Courts have generally disapproved of blanket policies that allow strip searches of all persons who have been arrested, particularly where traffic violators are concerned.

JURISPRUDENCE

California v. Greenwood, 486 U.S. 35, 108 S.Ct. 1625, 100 L.Ed.2d 30 (1988)

A police officer asked a trash collector to turn over bags of garbage collected from the Greenwoods' home in Laguna Beach, California. The officer searched the garbage bags and found evidence indicating illicit drug use. She used this evidence as a basis for obtaining a warrant to search the Greenwood home. During the search, the police discovered cocaine and hashish. As a result, the police charged the defendants with possession of illicit drugs. The trial court dismissed the charges on the ground that the warrantless trash search violated the Fourth Amendment, and the California appellate court affirmed. The U.S. Supreme Court granted review and reversed on the ground that the defendants, by placing their garbage outside the curtilage, had exposed their garbage to the public, and regardless of whether they may have had an expectation of privacy in their garbage, it was not an expectation that society is prepared to accept as being objectively reasonable.

Some courts hold that strip searches are violative of Fourth Amendment rights unless there is probable cause to believe the arrestee is concealing weapons or contraband. See, e.g., *Mary Beth G. v. Chicago*, 723 F.2d 1263 (7th Cir. 1983). Other courts have permitted such searches where there is a reasonable suspicion that the arrestee is concealing weapons or contraband. See, e.g., *Weber v. Dell*, 804 F.2d 796 (2d Cir. 1986).

Strip searches can also have civil consequences. For example, in *Jones v. Edwards*, 770 F.2d 739 (8th Cir. 1985), Marlin E. Jones was arrested and taken into custody for failing to sign a summons and complaint on an animal leash law violation. He was subjected to a visual strip search of his anal and genital area. The court ruled that such a search, under these circumstances, subjected the police and jail personnel to liability for the violation of the arrestee's civil rights. The court emphasized that the police had no reason to suspect that Jones was harboring weapons or contraband on his person.

The Warrant Requirement

As pointed out, when searches are challenged as being unreasonable, courts must first determine if the Fourth Amendment is applicable. The Fourth Amendment does not apply to border searches or searches conducted outside the United States, nor does it apply to open fields or abandoned property. Indeed, the Fourth Amendment does not apply to any situation where a person lacks a reasonable expectation of privacy. Where it does apply, the Fourth Amendment expresses a decided preference for searches and seizures to be conducted pursuant to a warrant. The warrant requirement is designed to ensure that the impartial judgment of a judge or a magistrate is interposed between the citizen and the state. The right of privacy is "too precious to entrust to the discretion of those whose job is the detection of crime and the arrest of criminals." *McDonald v. United States*, 335 U.S. 451, 455–456, 69 S.Ct. 191, 195–96, 93 L.Ed. 153, 158 (1948).

Probable Cause

With the exception of warrants permitting administrative searches, search warrants must be based on probable cause. Like many legal terms, "probable cause" is not susceptible to precise definition. Probable cause exists when prudent and cautious police officers have trustworthy information leading them to believe that evidence of crime might be obtained through a particular search. See *Brinegar v. United States*,

338 U.S. 160, 69 S.Ct. 1302, 93 L.Ed. 1879 (1949); *Carroll v. United States,* 267 U.S. 132, 45 S.Ct. 280, 69 L.Ed. 543 (1925).

The Supreme Court has said that courts should view the determination of probable cause as a "commonsense, practical question" that must be decided in light of the **totality of circumstances** in a given case. *Illinois v. Gates,* 462 U.S. 213, 230, 103 S.Ct. 2317, 2328, 76 L.Ed.2d 527, 543 (1983). This approach has been amplified by lower federal courts, which have observed that even though an innocent explanation might be consistent with the facts alleged in an affidavit seeking a search warrant, this does not negate probable cause. See, e.g., *United States v. Fama,* 758 F.2d 834 (2d Cir. 1985).

Although state courts are free to impose a higher standard, most have followed this approach. For example, the Ohio Supreme Court ruled that an affidavit by a police agent saying that he observed a tall marijuana plant growing in an enclosed backyard furnished probable cause for a magistrate to conclude there was marijuana or related paraphernalia in the residence. *State v. George,* 544 N.E.2d 640 (Ohio 1989). Some state courts have declined to follow the *Gates* approach and have opted to provide their citizens more protection than allowed by the federal view. In some instances, these state views result from linguistic variations in state constitutional counterparts to the Fourth Amendment. For example, in *Commonwealth v. Upton,* 476 N.E.2d 548 (Mass. 1985), the court noted the Massachusetts constitution provides more substantive protection to criminal defendants than does the Fourth Amendment to the U.S. Constitution in the determination of probable cause. Thus, the court held that an affidavit based on a telephone tip from an anonymous informer whose veracity was not shown did not establish probable cause for issuance of a warrant to search a mobile home.

Issuance of the Search Warrant

Under normal circumstances, a police officer with probable cause to believe that evidence of a crime is located in a specific place must submit under oath an application for a search warrant to the appropriate judge or magistrate. Rule 41 of the Federal Rules of Criminal Procedure allows a federal agent to obtain a search warrant from a federal magistrate or a judge of a state court of record within the district wherein the property or person sought is located. Either by statute or judicial rules, states usually provide similar authorization.

In *Coolidge v. New Hampshire,* 403 U.S. 443, 91 S.Ct. 2022, 29 L.Ed.2d 564 (1971), the Supreme Court invalidated a warrant issued by the state attorney general. The Court said that a warrant must be issued by a neutral and detached magistrate and certainly not by an official responsible for criminal prosecutions. Similarly, in *United States v. United States District Court,* 407 U.S. 297, 92 S.Ct. 2125, 32 L.Ed.2d 752 (1972), the Court invalidated a statute that permitted electronic eavesdropping to be authorized solely by the U.S. Attorney General in cases involving national security. Writing for the Court, Justice Lewis Powell observed that "unreviewed executive discretion may yield too readily to pressures to obtain incriminating evidence and overlook potential invasions of privacy. ... " 407 U.S. at 317, 92 S.Ct. at 2136, 32 L.Ed.2d at 766.

The Supporting Affidavit

An **affidavit** is a signed document attesting under oath to certain facts of which the **affiant** (the person submitting the affidavit) has knowledge (see Figure 3.1). Generally, an affidavit by a law enforcement officer requesting issuance of a search warrant is presented to a judge or magistrate. The manner in which the affidavit is recorded

totality of circumstances Circumstances considered in the aggregate as opposed to individually.

affidavit A written document attesting to specific facts of which the affiant has knowledge, and sworn to or affirmed by the affiant.

affiant A person who makes an affidavit.

ACODC NO. 29

Commonwealth of Massachusetts

Middlesex , ss.   Concord District Court
                                                                                    Court

AFFIDAVIT IN SUPPORT OF APPLICATION FOR SEARCH WARRANT*
G.L. c. 276, ss. 1 to 7; St. 1964, c. 557 As Amended

I, Sam Buckley _____ , being duly sworn, depose and say: 21   June   , 19 80
    Name of applicant

1. I am ___ Police Chief of Concord, Massachusetts ___
        (Describe position, assignment, office, etc.)

2. I have information based upon (describe sources, facts indicating reliability of source and nature of information; if based on personal knowledge and belief, so state) (If space is insufficient, attach affidavit or affidavits hereto)

    Based on information from a Federal Drug Enforcement Officer, the above has reason to belive at 123 Smith Street, one-story red brick house, with garage, 2 bedrooms, kitchen, living room, and bathroom, there is a small brown suitcase containing a controlled substance believed to be heroin.

*3. Based upon the foregoing reliable information - and upon my personal knowledge and belief - and ~~searched affidavits~~ - there is probable cause to believe that the property hereinafter described - has been stolen - or is being concealed, etc.
    and may be found in the possession of __ Miss Francine Taggart ___
                                                                    Name or person or persons

    at premises ___ 123 Smith Street, Concord ___
                    (Identify number, street, place, etc.)

4. The property for which I seek the issuance of a search warrant is the following (here describe the property as particularly as possible).

    One small brown suitcase taken from a station locker by Francine Taggart on June 19, 1980, containing heroin.

WHEREFORE, I respectfully request that the court issue a warrant and order of seizure, authorizing the search of (identify premises and the person or persons to be searched)

and directing that if such property or evidence or any part thereof be found that it be seized and brought before the court; together with such other and further relief that the court may deem proper.

                                                    Police Chief Sam Buckley
                                                        Signature of applicant

Then personally appeared the above named _Chief Buckley_
and made oath that the foregoing affidavit by him subscribed is true.

                    Before me this ___ 21 ___ day of __ June __ 19 80
                                    J. P. Jones - Special Justice
                                    Justice of Special Justice
                                    Clerk or Assistant Clerk of the Municipal Court.
                                                                    District

* Strike inapplicable clauses

                    REVISED JULY 1965   APPROVED BY THE CHIEF JUSTICE OF THE DISTRICT COURTS

FIGURE 3.1 Application for a Search Warrant.

and transmitted may vary. For example, the Idaho Supreme Court, finding that electronically recorded testimony is no less reliable than a sworn, written statement, held that the word "affidavit" under the Idaho constitution was sufficiently broad to include a tape recording of oral testimony. *State v. Yoder*, 534 P.2d 771 (Idaho 1975).

Rule 41(d)(3)(A) of the Federal Rules of Criminal Procedure provides that a federal magistrate judge may issue a warrant based upon sworn oral testimony communicated by phone or other appropriate means, including facsimile transmission. Some states follow this approach—for example, California law permits police officers to complete affidavits using the telephone to expedite the issuance of a warrant. West's Ann. Cal. Pen. Code. § 1526(b).

The officer's affidavit in support of a search warrant must always contain a rather precise description of the place(s) or person(s) to be searched and the things to be seized. Moreover, the affidavit must attest to specific facts (merely on the affiant's suspicion) that establish probable cause to justify a search. The information on which an affidavit is based must be sufficiently fresh to ensure that the items to be seized are probably located on the premises to be searched. The issue of when a search warrant becomes invalid because the information the affidavit is based on is stale has been litigated in many cases, with varying results. No set rule can be formulated. For example, a Delaware appellate court invalidated a search warrant where there was a delay of twenty-three days between the last alleged fact and the issuance of the warrant. In *State v. Pulgini*, 374 A.2d 822 (Del. 1977), the Delaware Supreme Court reversed the decision, noting the affidavit for the warrant recited facts indicating activity of a protracted and continuous nature during the period of delay. The court said that under such circumstances the passage of time becomes less significant. In *United States v. Rosenbarger*, 536 F.2d 715 (6th Cir. 1976), a twenty-one-day time lapse between observation of the receipt of stolen property and issuance of the warrant did not invalidate the warrant because the magistrate could determine there was a reasonable probability that the stolen goods were still in the defendant's home.

In *State v. Carlson*, 4 P.3d 1122 (Idaho App. 2000), an Idaho appellate court held that a warrant to search a defendant's residence was not based upon stale information even though there was a lapse of twenty-four days between the informant's initial observations and the issuance of the search warrant. The court considered the fact that the information was supplemented by a second report regarding observation of a marijuana plant three days prior to the issuance of the warrant and the implication that a marijuana operation continued in the interim period.

In *Hemler v. Superior Court*, 118 Cal. Rptr. 564 (Cal. App. 1975), the court acknowledged that the question of "stale" information depends upon the facts of each case. The court stated that an affidavit clearly furnished probable cause for the issuance of a search warrant either immediately or within a short time after observation of the sale of narcotics in an apartment. Nevertheless, the court held that the affidavit did not furnish probable cause for the issuance of a search warrant thirty-four days later.

Most appellate courts have not set specific time limits as to when information supporting the issuance of a search warrant becomes stale. While a magistrate must consider time as an element of probable cause when issuing a warrant, in *Copeland v. State*, 616 S.E.2d 189, 192 (Ga. App. 2005), the court pointed out that "[t]he mere passage of time does not equate with staleness."

Tips from Police Informants

A magistrate's finding of probable cause may be based on hearsay evidence. See, e.g., Fed. R. Crim. P. 41(c)(1), which permits police to obtain search warrants based on tips from anonymous or **confidential informants**. Confidential informants, or CIs, are often persons who have been involved with the police and are seeking favorable consideration in respect to their own offenses. Because their motivation may

confidential informants
An informant known to the police but whose identity is held in confidence.

be suspect, their reliability is checked carefully. For many years the Supreme Court required magistrates to apply a rigorous two-pronged test to determine probable cause. See *Aguilar v. Texas*, 378 U.S. 108, 84 S.Ct. 1509, 12 L.Ed.2d 723 (1964); *Spinelli v. United States*, 393 U.S. 410, 89 S.Ct. 584, 21 L.Ed.2d 637 (1969). The *Aguilar–Spinelli* test required that the officer's affidavit satisfy two criteria: (1) it had to demonstrate that the informant was both credible and reliable, and (2) it had to reveal the informant's basis of knowledge.

The *Aguilar–Spinelli* test made it very difficult for police to use anonymous tips. In 1983, the Supreme Court relaxed the test and permitted magistrates to consider the totality of circumstances when evaluating applications based on hearsay evidence. *Illinois v. Gates*, supra. The following year, the Court held that the standard for determining probable cause announced in the *Gates* decision was to be given a broad interpretation by lower courts. *Massachusetts v. Upton*, 466 U.S. 727, 104 S.Ct. 2085, 80 L.Ed.2d 721 (1984).

Despite the Supreme Court's relaxed standard for determining probable cause based on tips from informants, several states have chosen to follow the stricter standards formerly imposed by the *Aguilar* and *Spinelli* decisions. This, of course, is the prerogative of the states. In a comprehensive opinion in *State v. Cordova*, 784 P.2d 30 (N.M. 1989), the New Mexico Supreme Court reviewed an affidavit for a search warrant that recited that Cordova had brought heroin into town and was selling it at the house in question. However, the affidavit was devoid of explanation about how the informant gathered this information. Further, although the affidavit stated that the informant had personal knowledge that "heroin users" had been at the residence in question, there was nothing to indicate the source of the informant's knowledge and no explanation of how the informant knew that the persons in question were heroin users. Because the affidavit did not establish that the informant was both credible and reliable, the court found it did not provide a substantial basis for believing the informant and for concluding that the informant had gathered the information in a reliable manner. Further, the affidavit did not adequately state the informant's basis of knowledge that the defendant was selling heroin. In rejecting the state's appeal, the New Mexico Supreme Court declined to follow the *Gates* totality-of-circumstances rule and found the affidavit did not meet the requirements of the New Mexico Constitution and its rules of criminal procedure.

In 1985, the Connecticut Supreme Court criticized the totality-of-circumstances test as being "too amorphous" and an inadequate safeguard against unjustified police intrusions. Nevertheless, that court has recently held that if the information supplied by a CI fails the *Aguilar–Spinelli* test, probable cause may still be found if the affidavit sets forth other circumstances that bolster any deficiencies. *State v. Barton*, 594 A.2d 917 (Conn. 1991). Four years later, the Tennessee Supreme Court held that the two-pronged standard for probable cause inquiries incident to the issuance of a search warrant announced in the *Aguilar* and *Spinelli* cases, if not measured hypertechnically, is the standard to measure whether there is probable cause to issue a warrant. *State v. Jacumin*, 778 S.W.2d 430 (Tenn. 1989).

When a defendant demands to know the identity of the informant who provided the police with information on which they based their affidavit for a search warrant, courts face a delicate problem. There is a limited privilege to withhold the identity of the confidential informant. In determining whether to require disclosure, the court balances the interest of the public in preserving the anonymity of the informant against the defendant's need to have this information to prepare a defense, and where the questioned identity "is relevant and helpful to the defense of an accused, or is essential to a fair determination of a cause, the privilege must give way." *Roviaro v. United States*, 353 U.S. 53, 77 S.Ct. 623, 1 L.Ed.2d 639 (1957).

In *State v. Litzau*, 650 N.W.2d 177 (Minn. 2002), the Minnesota Supreme Court, citing *Roviaro*, pointed out that where an informant is merely a transmitter of information rather than an active participant in or a material witness to the crime, that disclosure is generally not required. But the court said, "Where an informant is an eyewitness to the crime, an *in camera* hearing is appropriate to determine whether there is a reasonable probability that the informer's testimony is necessary to a fair determination of guilt or innocence." *Id.* at 184. In considering a request for disclosure of the identity of an informant, the Minnesota court stated that the trial court considers (1) whether the informant is a material witness, (2) whether the informant's testimony will be material to the issue of guilt, (3) whether the state's evidence is suspect, and (4) whether the informant's testimony might disclose entrapment. *Id.* at 184.

Required Specificity of a Search Warrant

The Fourth Amendment mandates that "no warrants shall issue" except those "particularly describing the place to be searched and the persons or things to be seized." Thus, the scope of a search and seizure is bound by the terms of the warrant (see Figure 3.2). Consequently, a warrant that described property to be seized as "various long play phonographic albums, and miscellaneous vases and glassware" was held insufficient. Nevertheless, in 1999, the Maine Supreme Judicial Court upheld a search warrant that authorized the seizure of all computer-related equipment in the defendant's house. The police knew only that images of minors who were allegedly sexually exploited were taken by digital camera and downloaded on a computer. *State v. Lehman*, 736 A.2d 256 (Me. 1999).

Courts tend to be less strict when it comes to the description of contraband (such as heroin), because it is illegal per se, but stricter in cases involving First Amendment rights. For example, a federal appeals court invalidated a warrant authorizing the seizure of "a quantity of obscene materials, including books, pamphlets, magazines, newspapers, films and prints." *United States v. Guarino*, 729 F.2d 864, 865 (1st Cir. 1984). In *United States v. Hall*, 142 F.3d 988 (7th Cir. 1998), the court held that search warrants were written with sufficient particularity "because the items listed on the warrants were qualified by ... such phrases as 'child pornography,' 'minors engaged in sexually explicit conduct,' and 'sexual conduct between adults ... and minors.' *Id.* at 996–997.

CASE-IN-POINT

Required Specificity of a Search Warrant

A police officer was executing a search warrant that specified a particular copyrighted software program, gave its serial number, and added "all other computer related software." The officer was unable to find a floppy disk containing the program but did locate the program on the hard drive of the defendant's computer.

After making a diskette copy of the program, the officer seized the manuals for the program, the computer keyboard and terminal, and numerous related documents. In affirming the defendant's conviction for an offense involving intellectual property, the court held that these materials were properly seized even though not specifically listed in the warrant.

State v. Tanner, 534 So.2d 535 (La. App. 1988).

ACODC NO. 30

Commonwealth of Massachusetts

Middlesex, ss. Concord District Court

(Search Warrant)

TO THE SHERIFFS OF OUR SEVERAL COUNTIES, OR THEIR DEPUTIES, ANY STATE POLICE OFFICER, OR ANY CONSTABLE OR POLICE OFFICER OF ANY CITY OR TOWN, WITHIN OUR SAID COMMONWEALTH:

Proof by affidavit having been made this day before Special Justic J.Q. Jones
(Name of person issuing warrant)

by Police Chief Sam Buckley
(Name of person or persons signing affidavit)

*that there is probable cause for believing that certain property has been stolen, embezzled, or obtained by false pretences — certain property is intended for use or has been used as the means of committing a crime — certain property has been concealed to prevent a crime from being discovered — certain property is unlawfully possessed or kept or concealed for an unlawful purpose.

WE THEREFORE COMMAND YOU in the daytime (or at any time of the day or night) to make an immediate search of 123 Smith Street, Concord
(Identify premises)

(occupied by Francine Taggart) and of the person of
(Name of occupant)

__________, and of any person present who may
(Name of person)

be found to have such property in his possession or under his control or to whom such property may have been delivered, for the following property:

(Description of property)

One small brown suitcase believed to contain heroin.

and if you find any such property or any part therof to bring it and the persons in who possession it is found before the Concord District Court
(Name of Court)

at Concord, Massachusetts
(Court location)

in said County and Commonwealth, as soon as it has been served and in any event not later than seven days of issuance thereof. (Officer to make return on reverse side)

Witness J.Q. Jones, Esquire, Justice, at Concord Dist Court

aforesaid, this 21 day of June

in the year of our Lord one thousand nine hundred and 80

PL Norman

* Strike inapplicable clauses

Justice
Clerk
Assistant Clerk

G.L. c. 276, ss. 1 to 7; St. 1964, c. 557

APPROVED BY THE CHIEF JUSTICE OF THE DISTRICT COURTS

FIGURE 3.2 A Typical Search Warrant.

anticipatory search warrant A search warrant issued based on an affidavit that at a future time evidence of a crime will be at a specific place.

Anticipatory Search Warrants

The dramatic increase in drug trafficking over the last few decades has given rise to a countermeasure known as the **anticipatory search warrant**. Traditionally, police wait until a suspect receives contraband and then prepare an affidavit to obtain a search warrant. If the magistrate finds that probable cause exists at that time, a search warrant is issued. In the case of an anticipatory warrant, probable cause does not have to exist until the warrant is executed and the search conducted.

During the 1980s, several state appellate courts approved anticipatory search warrants. See, e.g., *State v. Coker*, 746 S.W.2d 167 (Tenn. 1987). In one of these cases, *Bernie v. State*, supra, a freight delivery service notified police that a package that broke in transit revealed a suspicious substance that later proved to be cocaine. An anticipatory warrant was issued to search the residence to which the package was addressed. Police were on the scene when the freight company delivered the package. The warrant was served, the cocaine seized, and the defendant taken into custody. On appeal, the search was upheld by the state supreme court, which observed that neither the federal nor the state constitution prohibited issuance of a search warrant to be served at a future date in anticipation of the delivery of contraband.

The Alaska Supreme Court has cautioned that a magistrate issuing an anticipatory warrant should make its execution contingent on the occurrence of an event that evidences probable cause that the items to be seized are in the place to be searched rather than directing that the warrant be executed forthwith. *Johnson v. State*, 617 P.2d 1117 (Alaska 1980).

In January 2000, a Michigan appellate court first addressed the issue; following the trend of appellate courts, it concluded that an anticipatory search warrant does not violate the federal and state constitutional prohibitions against unreasonable searches and seizures. *People v. Kaslowski*, 608 N.W.2d 539 (Mich. App. 2000).

While there has been a split of authority, the majority of federal appellate courts have upheld the basic concept that contraband does not have to be currently located at the place described in a search warrant if there is probable cause to believe it will be there when the warrant is executed.

In 1986, the Ninth Circuit Court of Appeals held that an anticipatory search warrant is permissible "where the contraband to be seized is on a sure course to its destination." *United States v. Hale*, 784 F.2d 1465, 1468 (9th Cir. 1986). Two years later, the U.S. Court of Appeals for the Fourth Circuit upheld an anticipatory search warrant permitting an inspector to search an apartment for child pornography where the issuing magistrate conditioned the validity of the warrant on the contraband being placed in the mail. Thus, when the mailing was accomplished, the contraband was on a certain course to its destination. *United States v. Dornhofer*, 859 F.2d 1195 (4th Cir. 1988).

In *United States v. Grubbs*, 547 U.S. 90, 126 S.Ct. 1494, 164 L.Ed.2d 195 (2006), the Supreme Court held that anticipatory search warrants do not contravene the Fourth Amendment. In an opinion by Justice Scalia, the Court said:

> Anticipatory warrants are ... no different in principle from ordinary warrants. They require the magistrate to determine (1) that it is now probable that (2) contraband, evidence of a crime, or a fugitive will be on the described premises (3) when the warrant is executed. It should be noted, however, that where the anticipatory warrant places a condition (other than the mere passage of time) upon its execution, the first of these determinations goes not merely to what will probably be found if the condition is met. ... Rather, the probability determination for a conditioned anticipatory warrant looks also to the likelihood that the condition will occur, and thus that a proper object of seizure will be on the described premises. In other words, for a conditioned anticipatory warrant to comply with the Fourth Amendment's requirement of probable cause, two prerequisites of probability must be satisfied. It must be true not only that if the triggering condition occurs "there is a fair probability that

contraband or evidence of a crime will be found in a particular place," ... but also that there is probable cause to believe the triggering condition will occur. The supporting affidavit must provide the magistrate with sufficient information to evaluate both aspects of the probable-cause determination. 547 U.S. at 96, 126 S.Ct. at 1500, 164 L.Ed.2d at 203.

By 2009, a majority of state courts approved issuance of anticipatory search warrants, but courts in at least eight states have held that statutory or constitutional provisions render such warrants invalid.

Execution of a Search Warrant

Applicable federal and state laws and rules of criminal procedure govern the manner and time in which warrants are executed. Rule 41(e) of the Federal Rules of Criminal Procedure provides that the warrant

> shall command the officer to search, within a specified period of time not to exceed 10 days, the person or place named or the property or person specified. The warrant shall be served in the daytime, unless the issuing authority ... authorizes its execution at times other than daytime.

Rule 41(a)(2)(B) defines "daytime" as the period between 6:00 A.M. and 10:00 P.M. according to local time. States have varying provisions governing the period of time within which a search warrant may be executed. Texas allows three days, excluding the date of issuance and the date of execution, Vernon's Ann. Texas C.C.P. Art. 18.07, whereas California allows ten, West's Ann. Cal. Penal Code § 1534. Likewise, state laws vary on the hours during which a search warrant may be executed. California law provides that upon a showing of good cause, the magistrate may, in his or her discretion, insert a direction in a search warrant that it may be served at any time of the day or night. In the absence of such a direction, the warrant shall be served only between the hours of 7:00 A.M. and 10:00 P.M. West's Ann. Cal. Penal Code § 1533. Some states, including Texas, do not impose restrictions on the hours when a warrant may be executed; others allow nighttime searches under special circumstances.

The Knock-and-Announce Rule

At the time the Constitution was adopted, there was a principle of the English common law that law enforcement officers should ordinarily announce their presence and authority before entering a residence to conduct a search or make an arrest pursuant to a warrant. Under federal law an officer is required to **knock and announce** on arrival at the place to be searched. 18 U.S.C.A. § 3109. That section stipulates:

knock and announce The provision under federal and most state laws that requires a law enforcement officer to first knock and announce his or her presence and purpose before entering a person's home to serve a search or arrest warrant.

> The officer may break open any outer or inner door or window of a house, or any part of a house, or anything therein, to execute a search warrant, if, after notice of his authority and purpose, he is refused admittance or when necessary to liberate himself or a person aiding him in the execution of the warrant.

Most states have similar "knock-and-announce" requirements, but courts have created some exceptions to protect officers and to prevent the destruction of evidence. In *Wilson v. Arkansas*, 514 U.S. 927, 115 S.Ct. 1914, 131 L.Ed.2d 976 (1995), the U.S. Supreme Court elevated the knock-and-announce rule to constitutional status under the Fourth Amendment. However, the Court did recognize that exigent circumstances may render the knock-and-announce requirement unnecessary.

The purpose of the knock-and-announce requirement is to reduce the potential for violence and to protect the right of privacy of the occupants. Courts have generally ruled that there are no rigid limits as to the time that must elapse between the announcement and the officers' entry. A few seconds may even suffice. Moreover, courts frequently excuse compliance when to require it would endanger the lives of the officers or simply provide an occasion for occupants to dispose of evidence. The most common example of disposing of evidence after police have announced their presence is the flushing of contraband down a toilet. For example, in *State v. Stalbert*, 783 P.2d 1005 (Or. App. 1989), the court found no violation of the knock-and-announce rule where police officers arrived at the defendant's residence to execute a search warrant, yelled, "Police officers, search warrant," and paused no more than two seconds between knocking and breaking through the door.

In *Wilson v. Arkansas*, supra, the Supreme Court noted that officers facing exigent circumstances such as the need to preserve evanescent evidence could dispense with the knock-and-announce requirement. But in *Richards v. Wisconsin*, 520 U.S. 385, 117 S.Ct. 1416, 137 L.Ed.2d 615 (1997), the Court ruled that states may not create a blanket "drug exception" to the requirement that police officers knock and announce prior to executing a search warrant. Writing for a unanimous bench, Justice John Paul Stevens observed that

> the fact that felony drug investigations may frequently present circumstances warranting a no knock entry cannot remove from the neutral scrutiny of a reviewing court the reasonableness of the police decision not to knock and announce in a particular case. Instead, in each case, it is the duty of a court confronted with the question to determine whether the facts and circumstances of the particular entry justified dispensing with the knock and announce requirement. 520 U.S. at 394, 117 S.Ct. at 1421, 137 L.Ed.2d at 624.

In *Hudson v. Michigan*, 547 U.S. 586, 126 S.Ct. 2159, 165 L.Ed.2d 56 (2006), the Supreme Court retreated from the position taken in *Wilson v. Arkansas*, holding that violations of the knock-and-announce requirement do not require the suppression of all evidence seized as the result of such violations. Speaking for a sharply divided Court, Justice Antonin Scalia concluded that when it comes to knock-and-announce violations, "Resort to the massive remedy of suppressing evidence of guilt is unjustified." 547 U.S. at 599, 126 S.Ct. at 2168, 165 L.Ed.2d at 69. Scalia also noted, "In addition to the grave adverse consequence that excluding relevant incriminating evidence always entails (viz. the risk of releasing dangerous criminals), imposing such a massive remedy would generate a constant flood of alleged failures to observe the rule. ..." 547 U.S. at 595, 126 S.Ct. at 2165, 165 L.Ed.2d at 66. Writing for four dissenters, Justice Stephen Breyer observed that the decision "destroys the strongest legal incentive to comply with the Constitution's knock-and-announce requirement." 547 U.S. at 605, 126 S.Ct. at 2171, 165 L.Ed.2d at 73.

Testing the Sufficiency of the Basis for Issuing a Search Warrant

In *Franks v. Delaware*, 438 U.S. 154, 98 S.Ct. 2674, 57 L.Ed.2d 667 (1978), the Supreme Court was faced with the issue of whether a defendant can challenge the affidavit for a search warrant in a pretrial proceeding. The Delaware Supreme Court had ruled that a defendant could not challenge the veracity of the statements made by the police to obtain their search warrant. The U.S. Supreme Court reversed and

Franks **hearing** A pretrial proceeding that allows a defendant to challenge the veracity of an affiant's statements in the affidavit that supports the issuance of a search warrant.

held that the Fourth Amendment requires an evidentiary hearing (called a ***Franks*** **hearing**) into the truthfulness of allegations in an affidavit in support of an application for a search warrant "where the defendant makes a substantial preliminary showing that a false statement knowingly and intentionally, or with reckless disregard for the truth, was included by the affiant in the warrant affidavit, and if the allegedly false statement is necessary to the finding of probable cause." 439 U.S. 154, 155–156, 98 S.Ct. 2674, 2676, 57 L.Ed.2d 667 (1978).

Return of Seized Property

Illegally seized property must be returned to the owner; however, the government may retain property lawfully seized as long as the government has a legitimate interest in its retention. Whether seized legally or illegally, contraband or property subject to forfeiture is not subject to being returned. See *United States v. Carter*, 859 F. Supp. 202 (E.D. Va. 1994). The return of other seized property is generally handled expeditiously based on a motion of the party seeking return. See, e.g., Fed. R. Crim. P. 41(g).

Exceptions to the Warrant Requirement

warrantless searches Searches made by police who do not possess search warrants.

Courts have recognized that an absolute warrant requirement would be impractical. Consequently, they have upheld the reasonableness of **warrantless searches** under so-called exigent circumstances. Yet, despite a number of exceptions, the warrant requirement remains a central feature of Fourth Amendment law. Whenever possible, police officers should obtain warrants, because their failure to do so can jeopardize the fruits of a successful search. The following are well-defined exceptions to the warrant requirement. However, it is important to understand that all these exceptions assume that police officers have probable cause to believe that a given search is likely to produce evidence of crime.

Evidence in Plain View

The Supreme Court has said that evidence in plain view of a police officer is not subject to the warrant requirement. *Harris v. United States*, 390 U.S. 234, 88 S.Ct. 992, 19 L.Ed.2d 1067 (1968). Police officers are not required to close their eyes or wear blinders in the face of evidence of a crime. Police officers have long been permitted to seize evidence that comes to their attention inadvertently, provided that (1) the officer has a legal justification to be in a constitutionally protected area when the seizure occurs, (2) the evidence seized is in the plain view of the officer who comes across it, and (3) it is apparent that the object constitutes evidence of a crime. *Coolidge v. New Hampshire*, supra. An officer may not seize anything and everything in plain view—the officer must have probable cause.

The "inadvertent discovery" requirement announced in *Coolidge v. New Hampshire* remained in effect for more than a decade. However, in *Horton v. California*, 496 U.S. 128, 110 S.Ct. 2301, 110 L.Ed.2d 112 (1990), the Supreme Court noted that the inadvertence requirement was not an essential part of the plurality opinion in *Coolidge v. New Hampshire*. As the Court observed in 1983, "There is no reason [the police officer] should be precluded from observing as an officer what would be entirely visible to him as a private citizen." *Texas v. Brown*, 460 U.S. 730, 740, 103 S.Ct. 1535, 1542, 75 L.Ed.2d 502 (1983). Notwithstanding, some state courts have continued to insist that the inadvertence requirement is a limitation on the plain view exception to the warrant requirement. See, e.g., *State v. Davis*, 828 A.2d 293 (N.H. 2003) (inadvertence requirement is satisfied if, immediately prior to the discovery, the police lacked sufficient information to establish probable cause to obtain a warrant to search for the object).

plain-view doctrine The Fourth Amendment doctrine under which a police officer may seize evidence of a crime that is readily visible to the officer's naked eye as long as the officer is legally in the place where the evidence becomes visible.

The **plain-view doctrine** may apply both where the item seized is in plain view before the commencement of a search and where it comes into the plain view of an officer conducting an otherwise valid search or entry. For example, in *United States v. Pacelli*, 470 F.2d 67 (2d Cir. 1972), the court invoked the plain view doctrine to uphold the seizure of illegal chemicals found during a search based on a warrant to search for heroin. The search warrant gave police officers the right to enter and search the premises; other items of contraband found in plain view during the search were deemed properly seized.

In contrast with *Pacelli*, consider the case of *Arizona v. Hicks*, 480 U.S. 321, 107 S.Ct. 1149, 94 L.Ed.2d 347 (1987). There, police who had lawfully entered an apartment to search for weapons noticed stereo equipment that seemed out of place, given the squalid condition of the apartment. His suspicion aroused, an officer moved the stereo equipment to locate the serial numbers. A check of the numbers indicated that the equipment was stolen. The Supreme Court disallowed the "search" of the serial numbers because they were not in plain view when the police entered the apartment.

Emergency Searches

emergency searches Searches by law enforcement officers in response to an emergency. In such an instance, police can seize evidence in plain view despite not having a search warrant.

Police frequently must respond to emergencies involving reports of crime or injuries. In other instances, they accompany firefighters to the scene of a fire. Increasingly, law enforcement authorities are called to investigate bomb threats where explosive devices are possibly sequestered inside buildings. Although these are among the most dramatic emergencies, in many other situations police are called to conduct **emergency searches**. The law recognizes that police do not have the time to obtain search warrants in such instances. Of course, police must possess probable cause to make warrantless emergency searches of dwellings. While they are on premises in response to an emergency, police may seize evidence in plain view during the course of their legitimate emergency activities. *Michigan v. Tyler*, 436 U.S. 499, 98 S.Ct. 1942, 56 L.Ed.2d 486 (1978).

Even when investigating a crime scene, police are not permitted to search anything and everything found. In *Flippo v. West Virginia*, 528 U.S. 11, 120 S.Ct. 7, 145 L.Ed.2d 16 (1999), the police responded to a 911 call reporting that a man and his wife had been attacked in a cabin at a state park. When they arrived, the police found the woman fatally wounded. While investigating the crime scene, they discovered a briefcase. They opened it and an envelope within it and found photographs that tended to incriminate the husband. The prosecutor attempted to justify the seizure based on a "crime scene" exception to the warrant requirement. While recognizing that police may make warrantless searches for perpetrators and victims at a crime scene, the Supreme Court rejected the contention that there is a "crime scene exception" to the Warrant Clause of the Fourth Amendment. In remanding the case to the lower court, the Court allowed that the police might have secured the evidence by consent, under the plain view doctrine, or under the inventory exception to the warrant requirement, but not on the basis of a claimed crime scene exception.

Police do not violate the Fourth Amendment if they stop a vehicle when they have adequate grounds to believe the driver is ill or falling asleep. *State v. Pinkham*, 565 A.2d 318 (Me. 1989). Likewise, police who make warrantless entries and searches when they reasonably believe that a person within is in need of immediate aid do not violate the protections against unreasonable search and seizure. Once inside, the police may justifiably seize evidence in plain view. See *Mincey v. Arizona*, 437 U.S. 385, 392, 98 S.Ct. 2408, 2413, 57 L.Ed.2d 290, 300 (1978). An officer's belief that an emergency exists must be reasonable, however. Judge Warren Burger (the future Chief Justice), in *Wayne v. United States*, 318 F.2d 205, 212 (D.C. Cir. 1963), opined that "the need to protect or preserve life or avoid serious injury is justification for what would be otherwise illegal absent an exigency or emergency." In *United States v. Al-Azzawy*, 784 F.2d 890 (9th Cir. 1985), the court upheld a warrantless search where a suspect was believed to be in possession of explosives and in such an agitated state as to create a risk of endangering the lives of others.

Preservation of Evidence

evanescent evidence
Evidence that tends to disappear or be destroyed. Often, police seek to justify a warrantless search on the ground that destruction of the evidence is imminent.

A frequently invoked justification for a warrantless search and seizure is the preservation of **evanescent evidence**—evidence that might be lost or destroyed. Where there is a reasonable belief that loss or destruction of evidence is imminent, a warrantless entry of premises may be justified, *United States v. Gonzalez*, 967 F.2d 1032 (4th Cir. 1992), but a mere possibility of such is insufficient, *United States v. Hayes*, 518 F.2d 675, 678 (6th Cir. 1975). The leading case in this area is *Schmerber v. California*, 384 U.S. 757, 86 S.Ct. 1826, 16 L.Ed.2d 908 (1966), where the Supreme Court upheld a warrantless blood-alcohol test of a person who appeared to be intoxicated. The Court characterized the forcible blood test as a "minor intrusion" and noted that the test was performed by qualified medical personnel. However, the most significant fact of the case was that the suspect's blood-alcohol level was rapidly diminishing, and the time required for police to obtain a search warrant could well have changed the results of the test.

In 1984, the Supreme Court narrowed the doctrine, saying that destruction of evidence does not constitute exigent circumstances if the underlying offense is relatively minor. *Welsh v. Wisconsin*, 466 U.S. 740, 104 S.Ct. 2091, 80 L.Ed.2d 732 (1984). In particular, drug offenses, many of which may be either felonies or misdemeanors depending on the quantity of contraband involved, have proven vexing to police and courts trying to apply the "relatively minor" standard. In 1993, the Idaho Supreme Court said that a minor offense is one that is nonviolent; thus, drug possession offenses, even if felonies, are "minor offenses." The court announced its decision in a case where police, acting with probable cause but without a warrant, entered a home and seized marijuana they believed was about to be destroyed. *State v. Curl*, 869 P.2d 224 (Idaho 1993). Following the Idaho Supreme Court's decision, other courts have applied the "relatively minor" standard to such offenses as disorderly conduct, indecent exposure, and underage drinking.

Search Incident to a Lawful Arrest

search incident to a lawful arrest Search of a person placed under arrest and the area within the arrestee's grasp and control.

A **search incident to a lawful arrest** is an exception to the warrant requirement in order that the police may disarm an arrestee and preserve evidence. It has long been recognized that such a search is permissible. *Weeks v. United States*, 232 U.S. 383, 34 S.Ct. 341, 58 L.Ed. 652 (1914). For many years, this rule was interpreted quite broadly.

For example, in *United States v. Rabinowitz*, 339 U.S. 56, 70 S.Ct. 430, 94 L.Ed. 653 (1950), the Supreme Court upheld a warrantless search of an entire home incident to a lawful arrest that occurred there. In 1969, the Supreme Court narrowed the permissible scope of searches incident to lawful arrests. *Chimel v. California*, 395 U.S. 752, 89 S.Ct. 2034, 23 L.Ed.2d 685 (1969). Under *Chimel*, police may search the body of an arrestee and the area within that person's immediate control. The area of immediate control is often defined as the area within the "grasp" or "lunge" of the arrestee. To conduct a more extensive search, police must generally obtain a search warrant.

Even if a formal arrest is not made until after a search, the search will be upheld as one incident to arrest if there was probable cause for the arrest before the search was begun. *Bailey v. United States*, 389 F.2d 305 (D.C. Cir. 1967). On the other hand, courts will not uphold a search where it is shown that the arrest was a mere pretext to conduct a warrantless search. See, e.g., *United States v. Jones*, 452 F.2d 884 (8th Cir. 1971).

There are definite limitations on police conducting a search incident to arrest. Despite the existence of probable cause, absent extraordinary circumstances, the police have no right to search a dwelling when an arrest occurs outside it. As the Supreme Court observed in *Payton v. New York*, 445 U.S. 573, 591, 100 S.Ct. 1371, 1382, 63 L.Ed.2d 639, 653 (1980), "The Fourth Amendment has drawn a firm line at the entrance to the house. Absent exigent circumstances, that threshold may not reasonably be crossed without a warrant." Exigent circumstances would most likely include a situation where, after an arrest, the officers have a reasonable basis to suspect there may be others on the premises who pose a danger to the police or who may destroy evidence. See *Vale v. Louisiana*, 399 U.S. 30, 90 S.Ct. 1969, 26 L.Ed.2d 409 (1970). Thus, police who made an arrest outside a residence and had knowledge regarding cocaine trafficking taking place inside were not barred from entering the house to conduct a "protective sweep" for other persons who might pose a threat to their safety. *United States v. Hoyos*, 892 F.2d 1387 (9th Cir. 1989). Nevertheless, once a person is arrested and in custody, searching that person's car at another location is not a search incident to arrest. *Preston v. United States*, 376 U.S. 364, 84 S.Ct. 881, 11 L.Ed.2d 777 (1964).

Hot Pursuit

hot pursuit (1) The right of police to cross jurisdictional lines to apprehend a suspect or criminal; (2) The Fourth Amendment doctrine allowing warrantless searches and arrests where police pursue a fleeing suspect into a protected area.

Officers in **hot pursuit** of a fleeing suspect already have probable cause to make an arrest. The Supreme Court has long recognized that police may pursue the suspect into a protected place, such as a home, without having to abandon their pursuit until a warrant can be obtained. *Warden v. Hayden*, 387 U.S. 294, 87 S.Ct. 1642, 18 L.Ed.2d 782 (1967). As the police enter a building and look for a suspect therein, they are by definition engaged in a search. If they find the suspect and make an arrest, they have in effect made a seizure. Once the suspect is in custody, police may engage in a warrantless search of the immediate area, which might produce evidence such as discarded weapons or contraband.

Automobile Stops and Roadside Searches of Motor Vehicles

Police may stop an automobile without a warrant and temporarily detain the driver as long as they have probable cause to believe that criminal activity is taking place or that traffic laws or automobile regulations are being violated. *Whren v. United States*, 517 U.S. 806, 116 S.Ct. 1769, 135 L.Ed.2d 89 (1996). Sometimes, police use a minor traffic or equipment violation as a pretext for stopping an automobile that they wish to investigate. When police make such stops, evidence of drug or alcohol use or some other criminal violation may become readily apparent, which allows police to make a warrantless arrest and a warrantless search incident to that arrest.

Quite often, automobile stops involve fairly extensive roadside searches and seizures. The Supreme Court has long recognized the validity of the so-called **automobile exception** to the warrant requirement, as long as police have probable cause to believe the vehicle contains contraband or evidence of crime, on the premise that the mobile character of a motor vehicle creates a practical necessity for an immediate search. *Carroll v. United States,* supra. The Court has held that once begun under exigent circumstances, a warrantless search of an automobile may continue after the vehicle has been taken to the police station. *Chambers v. Maroney,* 399 U.S. 42, 90 S.Ct. 1975, 26 L.Ed.2d 419 (1970).

Several state supreme courts have refused to go along with *Chambers v. Maroney.* For example, in August 1993, the Connecticut Supreme Court refused to adopt *Chambers v. Maroney* as a matter of state constitutional law. In *State v. Miller,* 630 A.2d 1315 (Conn. 1993), the court noted that any exigent circumstances that might justify a roadside automobile search disappear once the vehicle has been impounded. Writing for the court was Chief Justice Ellen A. Peters:

> We tolerate the warrantless on-the-scene automobile search only because obtaining a warrant would be impracticable in light of the inherent mobility of automobiles and the latent exigency that that mobility creates. The balance between law enforcement interests and individuals' privacy interests thus tips in favor of law enforcement in the context of an on-the-scene automobile search. If the impracticability of obtaining a warrant no longer exists, however, our state constitutional preference for warrants regains its dominant place in that balance, and a warrant is required. 630 A.2d at 1325.

The Scope of Warrantless Roadside Automobile Searches

One perennial problem associated with warrantless automobile searches is how closed containers, such as suitcases, that are found inside automobiles should be treated. In 1982, the U.S. Supreme Court held that a police officer who has probable cause to believe that evidence of a crime is concealed within an automobile may conduct a search as broad as one that could be authorized by a magistrate issuing a warrant. *United States v. Ross,* 456 U.S. 798, 102 S.Ct. 2157, 72 L.Ed.2d 572 (1982). This ruling effectively allowed police officers to search closed containers found during the course of an automobile search without first having to obtain a warrant.

In *United States v. Johns,* 469 U.S. 478, 105 S.Ct. 881, 83 L.Ed.2d 890 (1985), the Court upheld the warrantless search of plastic containers seized during an automobile search even though the police had waited several days before opening the containers. The Court reasoned that since police legitimately seized the containers during the original search of the automobile, no reasonable expectation of privacy could be maintained once the containers came under police control. The search of the containers, which produced a substantial quantity of marijuana, was therefore not unreasonable simply because it was delayed.

In 1998, a highway patrol officer in Wyoming stopped a speeding car. While speaking to the driver, the officer noticed a syringe in the driver's pocket. The driver admitted using the syringe to inject drugs. Having probable cause to search the car,

automobile exception
Exception to the Fourth Amendment warrant requirement. The exception allows the warrantless search of a vehicle by police who have probable cause to search but because of exigent circumstances are unable to secure a warrant.

JURISPRUDENCE

United States v. Ross, 456 U.S. 798, 102 S.Ct. 2157, 72 L.Ed.2d 572 (1982)

District of Columbia Police received a tip from a reliable confidential informant that Albert Ross was selling narcotics from his car. The informant provided the location of the vehicle, and the police immediately drove to where Ross's vehicle was allegedly located. When Ross entered the vehicle and began to drive away, the police stopped the vehicle and ordered Ross out of the car. Spotting a bullet on the front seat, one of the officers opened the glove compartment and found a pistol. Ross was then handcuffed and placed under arrest. Police then opened the "trunk, found a closed brown paper bag, and after opening the bag, discovered glassine bags containing white powder," which later tested positive for heroin. The vehicle was driven to police headquarters where a second warrantless search was performed, which "revealed a zippered leather pouch containing cash." As a result of the two searches, Ross was tried and convicted of possession of heroin with intent to distribute, his objection to the admission of the seized evidence notwithstanding. The Supreme Court held where police officers have "legitimately stopped an automobile and have probable cause to believe that contraband is concealed somewhere within it may conduct a warrantless search of the vehicle that is as thorough as a magistrate could authorize by warrant." The Court applied the "automobile exception" articulated in *Carroll v. United States* (1925) to searches "of vehicles that are supported by probable cause to believe that the vehicle contains contraband." As a result, the search was not unreasonable as it was based on "objective facts that would justify the issuance of a warrant," even though a warrant was not actually obtained.

the officer then opened a passenger's purse on the back seat and found contraband. The Wyoming Supreme Court ruled that the search that yielded the contraband was not within the permissible scope of search of the vehicle and thus violated the Fourth Amendment. *Houghton v. State*, 956 P.2d 363 (1998). On review, the U.S. Supreme Court held that police officers who have probable cause to search a vehicle may search the belongings of passengers who are capable of concealing objects of the search. *Wyoming v. Houghton*, 526 U.S. 295, 119 S.Ct. 1297, 140 L.Ed.2d 408 (1999).

Warrantless Automobile Searches Incident to the Arrest of an Occupant

In *New York v. Belton*, 453 U.S. 454, 101 S.Ct. 2860, 69 L.Ed.2d 768 (1981), the Supreme Court held that the police may search the passenger compartment of a vehicle and any containers therein, even absent probable cause, as a contemporaneous incident of an occupant's lawful arrest. *Belton*, provided police with a "bright-line" rule; however, it did not answer the question of whether officers may conduct such a search once the scene has been secured. *Belton* was criticized as moving beyond the rationale of *Chimel*. Most state courts have followed the *Belton* approach, but several have not. In *State v. Brown*, 588 N.E.2d 113 (Ohio 1992), the Ohio Supreme Court rejected *Belton*, which it characterized as allowing police "to search every nook and cranny of an automobile just because the driver is arrested for a traffic violation." 588 N.E.2d at 115.

Until 1998, Iowa law allowed an officer to conduct a full-blown search of an automobile and its driver when the officer stopped a motorist for speeding and issued a traffic citation. Pursuant to that rule, the officer searched the vehicle without consent or probable cause, and the search revealed a bag of marijuana and a "pot pipe." The search was upheld by the Iowa Supreme Court. *State v. Knowles*, 569 N.W.2d 601

(Iowa 1997). But, the U.S. Supreme Court granted review and the following year held that a search under these circumstances (where a traffic citation was issued and no custodial arrest was involved) violates the Fourth Amendment. *Knowles v. Iowa*, 525 U.S. 113, 119 S.Ct. 484, 142 L.Ed.2d 492 (1998).

Some twenty-eight years after its decision in *Belton*, the Supreme Court in *Arizona v. Gant*, 556 U.S. 332, 129 S.Ct. 1710, 173 L.Ed.2d 485 (2009), substantially distinguished the rule that it had arrived at in the factual context of *Belton*. In doing so the Court placed limits on a search incident to arrest of an occupant of a vehicle. Writing for a 5–4 majority, Justice John Paul Stevens announced the new standard by saying:

> Police may search a vehicle incident to a recent occupant's arrest only if the arrestee is within reaching distance of the passenger compartment at the time of the search or it is reasonable to believe the vehicle contains evidence of the offense of arrest. When these justifications are absent, a search of an arrestee's vehicle will be unreasonable unless police obtain a warrant or show that another exception to the warrant requirement applies. 556 U.S. at 351, 129 S.Ct. at 1723–24, 173 L.Ed.2d at 501.

Dissenting, Justice Samuel Alito pointed out that the doctrine of *stare decisis* commands the "bright-line" rule adopted in *Belton* should not be discarded.

Exceptions to the Probable Cause Requirement

Warrantless searches are now well established in the law, and although reasonable people might disagree about specific cases, there is consensus that warrantless searches are often necessary and proper. The same cannot be said for the next category of searches—those based on something less than probable cause. In these special situations, courts permit limited searches based on the lesser standard of reasonable suspicion. Reasonable suspicion is the belief, based on articulable circumstances, that criminal activity might be afoot. The classic application of the reasonable suspicion standard is to the so-called "stop-and-frisk."

Stop-and-Frisk

stop-and-frisk An encounter between a police officer and a suspect during which the latter is temporarily detained and subjected to a pat-down search for weapons.

The **stop-and-frisk** is a routine law enforcement technique whereby police officers stop, question, and sometimes search suspicious persons. In *Terry v. Ohio*, 392 U.S. 1, 88 S.Ct. 1868, 20 L.Ed.2d 889 (1968), the Supreme Court upheld the authority of police officers to detain and conduct a limited "pat-down" search of several men who were acting suspiciously. Given the limited intrusiveness of the pat-down and the compelling need to protect officers in the field, the Court allowed the warrantless search for weapons on a reasonable suspicion standard instead of imposing the traditional probable cause requirement. Subsequently, the Court stressed the narrow scope of the stop-and-frisk exception by saying that "nothing in *Terry* can be understood to allow ... any search whatever for anything but weapons." *Ybarra v. Illinois*, 444 U.S. 85, 93–94, 100 S.Ct. 338, 343, 62 L.Ed.2d 238, 247 (1979).

In *Michigan v. Long*, 463 U.S. 1032, 103 S.Ct. 3469, 77 L.Ed.2d 1201 (1983), the Supreme Court held that seizure of contraband other than weapons during a lawfully conducted *Terry* search was justified under the plain view doctrine. Going a step further in *Minnesota v. Dickerson*, 508 U.S. 366, 113 S.Ct. 2130, 124 L.Ed.2d 334 (1993), the Court said that police may seize nonthreatening contraband detected

JURISPRUDENCE

Terry v. Ohio, 392 U.S. 1, 88 S.Ct. 1868, 20 L.Ed.2d 889 (1968)

An experienced police officer on routine patrol in downtown Cleveland observed two men repeatedly walking up and down a street while stopping to stare into a store window. Each time one of the men walked up the street and stopped to look into the store window and returned, a conference was held between the two men and a third individual. The officer believed the men were "casing a job, a stick up." The officer approached the men, "identified himself as a policeman, and asked their names," but the men were less than forthcoming and mumbled something under their breaths. The officer "spun [Terry] around, patted down his outside clothing, and found in his overcoat pocket … a pistol." The officer then removed the overcoat from Terry, removed the pistol, and ordered the men "to face the wall with their hands raised." The officer repeated the same procedure with the other two men, finding a pistol during the pat-down on one, but nothing on the other. Terry and the second man with a pistol were charged with carrying a concealed weapon. The trial court denied defense's motion to suppress the evidence "on the ground that the officer had cause to believe the men were acting suspiciously, their interrogation was warranted, and the officer, for his own protection, had the right to pat down their outer clothing having reasonable cause to believe that they might be armed." The Supreme Court determined that the officer's actions to detain did constitute a search and seizure under the Fourth Amendment, but that the search and seizure were not unreasonable. The Court expressly held that "where a reasonably prudent officer is warranted in the circumstances of a given case in believing that his safety or that of others is endangered, he may make a reasonable search for weapons of the person believed by him to be armed and dangerous."

through their sense of touch during a protective pat-down search as long as that search stays within the bounds of a *Terry* search. This extension of *Terry* is sometimes referred to as a "plain feel" exception to the warrant requirement of the Fourth Amendment. Nevertheless, in *Dickerson* the Court found the search and seizure of contraband invalid because the officer conducting the search determined that the item he seized was contraband only after searching beyond the scope authorized in *Terry*. (More attention is given to the so-called *Terry* stop in Chapter 4.)

Is a Stop-and-Frisk Permissible Based Solely on an Anonymous Tip?

In *Alabama v. White*, 496 U.S. 325, 110 S.Ct. 2412, 110 L.Ed.2d 301 (1990), police received an anonymous tip that a certain female was carrying cocaine and that she would leave a certain apartment at a specified time, get into a car matching a particular description, and drive to a particular motel. The police conducted surveillance of the woman, which verified elements of the tip. Only then did they move in to stop her car, detain her, and seize the cocaine.

Characterizing the case as a "close" one, the Supreme Court upheld the police procedure but said that the tip alone would not have justified the stop-and-frisk. It was on that basis that the Court invalidated a seizure of a firearm in *Florida v. J.L.*, 529 U.S. 266, 120 S.Ct. 1375, 146 L.Ed.2d 254 (2000). In the latter case, the Court observed that "an anonymous tip lacking indicia of reliability … does not justify a stop and frisk whenever and however it alleges the illegal possession of a firearm." 529 U.S. at 274, 120 S.Ct. at 1380, 146 L.Ed.2d at 262.

Drug Courier Profiles

In attempting to identify and to apprehend drug smugglers, law enforcement agencies have developed **drug courier profiles**. These profiles are sets of characteristics that typify drug couriers, such as paying for airline tickets in cash, appearing nervous, carrying certain types of luggage, and so forth. In *Reid v. Georgia*, 448 U.S. 438, 100 S.Ct. 2752, 65 L.Ed.2d 890 (1980), the Supreme Court suggested that fitting a drug courier profile was not in itself sufficient to give rise to the reasonable suspicion necessary to allow police to detain an airline passenger. Therefore, the stopping of an airline passenger on that basis violated the Fourth Amendment. However, in *United States v. Sokolow*, 490 U.S. 1, 109 S.Ct. 1581, 104 L.Ed.2d 1 (1989), the Court upheld a similar investigatory detention in which a drug courier profile was employed. It is instructive to examine these decisions side by side to determine how and why the Court distinguished the two situations.

School Searches

In the First Amendment context, the Supreme Court has said that students in public schools do not "shed their constitutional rights ... at the schoolhouse gate." *Tinker v. Des Moines Independent Community School District*, 393 U.S. 503, 506, 89 S.Ct. 733, 736, 21 L.Ed.2d 731, 737 (1969). Following this premise, the Court has held that the Fourth Amendment protects children in the public schools from unreasonable searches and seizures. However, the Court has said that such searches are to be judged by a reasonableness standard and are not subject to the requirement of probable cause. Moreover, the Court has said that the warrant requirement is particularly unsuited to the unique circumstances of the school environment. *New Jersey v. T.L.O.*, 469 U.S. 325,105 S.Ct. 733, 83 L.Ed.2d 720 (1985). The pervasive problem of illicit drug use in the schools, as well as the notorious incidents of school violence in recent years, have added pressure to relax Fourth Amendment standards in the public school context.

Although there are certainly exceptions, most search and seizure policies implemented by public schools have been upheld by the courts. These include "sweeps" for drugs and guns, using such devices as drug-sniffing dogs and metal detectors, as well as routine searches of backpacks, lockers, and even automobiles coming onto school grounds. Courts have generally upheld searches of students in the public schools where the search is reasonably related to its objectives and is not excessively intrusive in light of the age and sex of the student and the nature of the infraction. See *Brannum v. Overton County School Bd.*, 516 F.3d 489 (6th Cir. 2005). But until recently the law has been unclear when it involves school officials going to the extent of strip searches. In 2003, Safford, Arizona, school officials searching for ibuprofen ordered a search of a thirteen-year-old female student's backpack and pockets. Finding none, they conducted a strip search. In 2008, the Ninth Circuit Court of Appeals in a 6–5 decision held that the search was a violation of the student's Fourth Amendment right to privacy. *Redding v. Safford Unified School Dist. No. 1*, 531 F.3d 1071 (9th Cir. 2008). On review, the Supreme Court affirmed this decision, holding that the strip search was unjustified. *Safford Unified School Dist. No. 1 v. Redding*, 557 U.S. 364, 129 S. Ct. 2633; 174 L. Ed. 2d 354 (2009). This decision shows that school officials do not have unbridled authority to subject students to strip searches.

In *Commonwealth v. Cass*, 709 A.2d 350 (Pa. 1998), a leading case decided by the Pennsylvania Supreme Court, a public high school principal brought in police and drug-sniffing dogs to detect drugs sequestered in student lockers. When a dog "alerted" to a particular locker, school officials would open it and search the contents. Eighteen lockers were searched, and one of them was found to contain a small amount of marijuana and some related paraphernalia. The student to whom that locker was assigned was suspended from school for ten days, required to attend drug counseling, and charged criminally with possession of marijuana and possession of drug paraphernalia. In rejecting a challenge to the constitutionality of the search that led to the discovery of the contraband, the Pennsylvania Supreme court observed:

> Common sense dictates that when a student is given permission to store his or her belongings in a locker designated for his or her personal and exclusive use, that student can reasonably expect a measure of privacy within that locker. Common sense further dictates that when the student's use of the locker is expressly conditioned upon the acknowledgment that the locker belongs to the school, that measure of privacy is necessarily limited. *Id.* at 359.

Drug Testing

Because of the paramount interest in ensuring the public safety, courts have upheld the constitutionality of regulations permitting supervisory personnel to order urinalysis testing of public safety officers based on reasonable suspicion of drug abuse. See, e.g., *Turner v. Fraternal Order of Police*, 500 A.2d 1005 (D.C. App. 1985). In 1989, the U.S. Supreme Court upheld federal regulations requiring drug and alcohol testing of railroad employees involved in train accidents. *Skinner v. Railway Labor Executives' Association*, 489 U.S. 602, 109 S.Ct. 1402, 1411, 103 L.Ed.2d 639 (1989). The Court has also sustained a U.S. Customs Service policy requiring drug tests for persons seeking positions as customs inspectors. *Treasury Employees Union v. Von Raab*, 489 U.S. 656, 109 S.Ct. 1384, 103 L.Ed.2d 685 (1989). As yet, the Supreme Court has not addressed the issue of general, random **drug testing** of public employees. However, it has invalidated a policy under which all political candidates were required to submit to drug testing as a condition of qualifying for the ballot. *Chandler v. Miller*, 520 U.S. 305, 117 S.Ct. 1295, 137 L.Ed.2d 513 (1997).

drug testing Procedures, usually involving urinalysis, designed to test for the presence of illegal drugs in the body.

In 1995, the U.S. Supreme Court stated that a public school district's student athlete drug policy, which authorized random urinalysis drug testing of students who participated in athletic programs, did not violate a student's right to be free from unreasonable searches. While mandatory drug testing is a search, Justice Antonin Scalia, writing for a 6–3 majority of the Court, pointed out that, given the decreased expectation of privacy of a public school student, the relative unobtrusiveness of the search, and the severity of the need, such a search was not unreasonable. *Vernonia School District v. Acton*, 515 U.S. 646, 115 S.Ct. 2386, 132 L.Ed.2d 564 (1995).

State courts have addressed random drug testing of municipal employees under both state and federal constitutional standards. In 2001, the Alaska Supreme Court held that where there was no documented history of substance abuse problems by firefighters and police employees, the random testing program violated the Alaska Constitution. *Anchorage Police Department Employees Ass'n v. Municipality of Anchorage*, 24 P.3d 547 (Alaska 2001). Three years later the Arizona Supreme Court found that the city of Mesa's random drug testing of firefighters was not justified by a generalized and unsubstantiated interest in deterring and detecting alcohol and drug use. Thus, it concluded that such random testing violated Fourth Amendment privacy interests of the firefighters. *Petersen v. City of Mesa*, 83 P.3d 35 (Ariz. 2004). The U.S. Supreme Court denied review.

When administrative personnel turn over results of drug tests to law enforcement agencies for criminal prosecution, courts tend to exercise a higher level of scrutiny. The leading case in this regard is *Ferguson v. City of Charleston*, 532 U.S. 67, 121 S.Ct. 1281, 149 L.Ed.2d 205 (2001). There, the U.S. Supreme Court invalidated a policy under which a public hospital turned over to police urine samples of pregnant women who had tested positive for cocaine. The Court noted that

> The fact that positive test results were turned over to the police does not merely provide a basis for distinguishing our prior cases applying the "special needs" balancing approach to the determination of drug use. It also provides an affirmative reason for enforcing the strictures of the Fourth Amendment. 532 U.S. at 84, 121 S.Ct. at 1292, 149 L.Ed.2d at 220.

Electronic Surveillance

The drafters of the Fourth Amendment obviously did not contemplate present-day technology. Yet, in framing the Bill of Rights, they used simple, straightforward language that has endured through the centuries—language capable of being adapted to the needs of the people. Today's technology makes possible silent and invisible intrusions on the privacy of the individual, and the courts are responding to these new, innovative means of surveillance, always cognizant that the touchstone of the Fourth Amendment is its prohibition of "unreasonable" searches and seizures. Of course, the interpretation of what is "reasonable" is apt to be affected by pressing public needs. The attacks on American cities on September 11, 2001, and the subsequent "war on terrorism" have had an enormous impact in the area of electronic surveillance, both in terms of what law enforcement agencies are now doing and what legislation and judicial opinions authorize.

Expectations of Privacy with Respect to Electronic Surveillance

Generally speaking, the use of wiretaps, microphones, video recorders, and other devices that permit agencies to intercept the content of what would otherwise be private communications implicates the Fourth Amendment. *Katz v. United States*, supra. However, merely using technology to augment the senses does not necessarily trigger Fourth Amendment protections. For example, the Supreme Court has approved the use of searchlights, field glasses, aerial photography, and various other means of enhancing the police's powers of observation, even in the absence of a warrant or probable cause. *United States v. Lee*, 274 U.S. 559, 47 S.Ct. 746, 71 L.Ed. 1202 (1927); *Texas v. Brown*, 460 U.S. 730, 103 S.Ct. 1535, 75 L.Ed.2d 502 (1983). Lower federal courts have even approved miniaturized television camera surveillance. *United States v. Torres*, 751 F.2d 875 (7th Cir. 1984). The question is whether the police use methods that infringe on a person's reasonable expectations of privacy. If so, they need a warrant or some other form of judicial authorization before deploying these technologies.

Cordless and Cellular Telephones

Changes in technology often create new legal questions. An excellent example is the proliferation of cordless telephones in the 1980s. When one uses a cordless phone, one is essentially broadcasting a low-power radio signal to a nearby receiver (the base unit) that is connected to a phone line. But any nearby receiver tuned to the correct frequency can intercept a conversation being conducted on a cordless phone. Analog cellular telephones operate in much the same way, although their signals are more powerful so that they can communicate with towers located within "cells." The new digital cell phones are more difficult to eavesdrop upon because their signals are encrypted. Realizing the potential for monitoring conversations on cordless telephones and analog cellular phones, police sometimes employ receivers or scanners mounted in vehicles to eavesdrop on conversations. When they do this without a warrant or even probable cause, are police in violation of the Fourth Amendment?

In *Tyler v. Berodt*, 877 F.2d 705 (8th Cir. 1989) and *United States v. Smith*, 978 F.2d 171, 177 (5th Cir. 1992), two federal courts ruled that users of cordless phones had no reasonable expectation of privacy; therefore, the interception of their calls was not a "search" within the meaning of the Fourth Amendment. However, in *State v. Mozo*, 655 So.2d 1115 (Fla. 1995), the Florida Supreme Court held that nonconsensual interception of cordless phone calls without prior judicial approval violates a state statute protecting the privacy of communications. That court declined to reach the constitutional issues in the case, preferring to base its decision on statutory grounds. In 1986 Congress enacted a statute to provide nationwide protection against eavesdropping on cellular phone conversations, and in 1994 the statute was amended to provide protection for cordless phones as well. Thus, through legislation Congress provided protection to individual privacy that federal courts were unable or unwilling to provide via the Fourth Amendment.

The Supreme Court's Major Decisions in the Area of Electronic Surveillance

pen register Device that enables law enforcement to obtain the numbers that have been dialed by use of a specific telephone instrument.

The U.S. Supreme Court has rendered only a few decisions affecting the legality of electronic surveillance by police, but these decisions have had a major impact on law enforcement practices. In *Smith v. Maryland*, 442 U.S. 735, 99 S.Ct. 2577, 61 L.Ed.2d 220 (1979), the Court determined that the employment of a **pen register** is not a search within the meaning of the Fourth Amendment. A pen register is a device that records the phone numbers that are dialed from a particular phone number. Writing for the Court, Justice Harry Blackmun observed that merely by using the phone, the defendant "voluntarily conveyed numerical information to the telephone company and 'exposed' that information to its equipment in the ordinary course of business." 442 U.S. at 744, 99 S.Ct. at 2582, 61 L.Ed.2d at 229. Blackmun concluded that in so doing, the defendant "assumed the risk that the company would reveal to police the numbers he dialed." *Ibid*. In a vigorous dissenting opinion, Justice Potter Stewart asserted, "It is simply not enough to say, after *Katz*, that there is no legitimate expectation of privacy in the numbers dialed because the caller assumes the risk that the telephone company will disclose them to the police." 442 U.S. at 747, 99 S.Ct. at 2583, 61 L.Ed.2d at 231. In another dissenting opinion, Justice Thurgood Marshall observed that "[p]rivacy in placing calls is of value not only to those engaged in criminal activity" and predicted that "[t]he prospect of unregulated governmental monitoring will undoubtedly prove disturbing even to those with nothing illicit to hide." 442 U.S. at 751, 99 S.Ct. at 2586, 61 L.Ed.2d at 234.

In *Dow Chemical Co. v. United States*, 476 U.S. 227, 106 S.Ct. 1819, 90 L.Ed.2d 226 (1986), the Supreme Court held that high-altitude photography of a chemical plant was not a search within the meaning of the Fourth Amendment. The Court concluded that the means of surveillance was incapable of revealing intimate activities that would give rise to constitutional concerns. That same year, in *California v. Ciraolo*, 476 U.S. 207, 106 S.Ct. 1809, 90 L.Ed.2d 210 (1986), the Court upheld a conviction where police, acting on a tip, conducted a low-altitude flight and photographed marijuana plants growing in the defendant's backyard. The police then used the photos to obtain a warrant and seize the contraband. In upholding the search, the Court said, "[W]e readily conclude that [the defendant's] expectation that his garden was protected from [aerial] observation is unreasonable and is not an expectation that society is prepared to honor." 476 U.S. at 214, 106 S.Ct. at 1813, 90 L.Ed.2d at 217. Dissenting, Justice Lewis Powell suggested that the Court's decision was inconsistent with the broad interpretation of the Fourth Amendment suggested by the Court's seminal decision in *Katz v. United States*:

> Rapidly advancing technology now permits police to conduct surveillance in the home itself, an area where privacy interests are most cherished in our society, without any physical trespass. While the rule in *Katz* was designed to prevent silent and unseen invasions of Fourth Amendment privacy rights in a variety of settings, we have consistently afforded heightened protection to a person's right to be left alone in the privacy of his house. The Court fails to enforce that right or to give any weight to the longstanding presumption that warrantless intrusions into the home are unreasonable. 476 U.S. at 226, 106 S.Ct. at 1819, 90 L.Ed.2d at 225.

In the 1980s, police looking for marijuana being grown indoors under artificial light began to use infrared thermal imagers, which detect heat waves. These devices can provide a strong indication of whether marijuana is being grown inside a closed structure. Prior to 2001, most courts that considered this issue ruled that using thermal imaging devices was not a search within the meaning of the Fourth Amendment. See, e.g., *United States v. Pinson*, 24 F.3d 1056 (8th Cir. 1994); *United States v. Ford*, 34 F.3d 992 (11th Cir. 1994); and *United States v. Penny-Feeney*, 773 F. Supp. 220 (D.C. Hawaii 1991). A notable exception was *State v. Young*, 867 P.2d 593 (Wash. 1994), where the Washington Supreme Court held that the use of a thermal imaging device was a search within the meaning of the Washington state constitution. In *Kyllo v. United States*, 533 U.S. 27, 121 S.Ct. 2038, 150 L.Ed.2d 94 (2001), the U.S. Supreme Court adopted the view taken by the Washington Supreme Court. Writing for the Court, Justice Antonin Scalia concluded that when "the Government uses a device that is not in general public use, to explore details of the home that would previously have been unknowable without physical intrusion, the surveillance is a 'search' and is presumptively unreasonable without a warrant." 533 U.S. at 40, 121 S.Ct. at 2046, 150 L.Ed.2d at 106.

In *United States v. Jones*, 565 U.S. ___, 132 S.Ct. 945, 181 L.Ed.2d 911 (2012), the Supreme Court invalidated the use of GPS tracking devices without prior judicial authorization. Although the decision was a unanimous one, the justices split on the underlying rationale for the ruling, with five justices focusing on the physical intrusion of placing the GPS locator on the car and four justices focusing on the overall violation of a "reasonable expectation of privacy" entailed by lengthy electronic surveillance.

Federal Legislation Governing Interception of Electronic Communications

As noted above, Congress has enacted legislation governing the interception of electronic communications. The cornerstone of this statutory edifice is Title III of the Omnibus Crime Control and Safe Streets Act of 1968, codified at 18 U.S.C.A.

> ## JURISPRUDENCE
>
> *United States v. Jones*, 565 U.S. ___, 132 S.Ct. 945, 181 L.Ed.2d 911 (2012)
>
> Antoine Jones, a nightclub owner in the District of Columbia, was suspected by federal agents of trafficking in cocaine. Agents obtained a warrant authorizing them to install a GPS tracking device on Jones' car in D.C. within ten days. A day after the warrant expired, agents placed the tracking device on the Jones vehicle while it was parked in Maryland. They then used the device to follow Jones for twenty-eight days. The investigation led to a multiple-count indictment charging Jones with conspiracy to distribute cocaine and other offenses. A jury found Jones not guilty on all charges except for conspiracy, where they were not able to reach a verdict. Prosecutors then re-filed a single charge of conspiracy against Jones, who was convicted and sentenced to life in prison. The U.S. Court of Appeals for the D.C. Circuit reversed, holding that the warrantless use of the GPS device violated the Fourth Amendment. The U.S. Supreme Court affirmed the circuit court decision, holding that the Government's physical intrusion into Jones' property for the purpose of obtaining information constituted a "search." In an opinion concurring only in the judgment, four justices focused on what they believed to be a violation of Jones's reasonable expectations of privacy.

§§ 2510–20. The act prohibits interception of electronic communications without a court order unless one party to the conversation consents. Interception is defined as "aural or other acquisition of the contents of any wire, electronic or oral communication through the use of any electronic, mechanical, or other device." 18 U.S.C.A. § 2510(4). In 1986, Congress expanded the meaning of "wire communications" to include conversations through "switching stations." 18 U.S.C.A. § 2510(1). Therefore, the statute now covers cellular telephones.

wiretap orders Court orders permitting electronic surveillance for a limited period.

Title III permits issuance of **wiretap orders** by federal and state courts on sworn applications authorized by the U.S. Attorney General, a specially designated assistant, or a state official at a similar level. The act expressly preempts state law. Therefore, to permit the use of electronic surveillance, a state must adopt legislation along the lines of the federal act, and many states have done so. See, e.g., the New Jersey Wiretapping and Electronic Surveillance Control Act of 1968, N.J. Stat. Ann. § 2A: 156A-(1), *et seq.*

An application for a wiretap order must contain considerable detailed information along with an explanation of why less intrusive means of investigation will not suffice. 18 U.S.C.A. § 2518(1)(c). The statute requires that normal investigative procedures be employed first. But it does not require an officer to exhaust all possible investigative methods before applying for a wiretap order. Before a court may issue a wiretap order, it must find probable cause that the subject of the wiretap has committed or is committing one of a series of enumerated crimes for which wiretapping is authorized and that conventional modes of investigation will not suffice. 18 U.S.C.A. § 2518(3). Originally these offenses included narcotics, organized crime, and national security violations. In 1986, the act was amended to include numerous other serious crimes, including interstate transportation of stolen vehicles; bribery in sports contests; weapons of mass destruction threats; sex trafficking of children by force, fraud, or coercion; mail fraud; and money laundering. 18 U.S.C.A. § 2516(1)(c).

Court orders permit surveillance for no longer than a thirty-day period. 18 U.S.C.A. § 2518(5). At the period's expiration, the recordings made of intercepted communications must be delivered to the judge who issued the order. They are then sealed under the judge's direction. 18 U.S.C.A. § 2518(8)(a).

The Electronic Communications Privacy Act of 1986 (ECPA), 18 U.S.C.A. § 2701 *et seq.*, established federal standards for access to e-mail and other electronic

trap-and-trace devices
Devices that capture incoming electronic impulses that identify the originating number of a device from which an electronic communication was transmitted.

communications and to "transactional records," including subscriber identifying information, call logs, phone bills, and so forth. The law established a high standard for access to the contents of electronic communications but allowed agencies to easily gain access to transactional records. One part of the act, 18 U.S.C.A. § 3121 *et seq.*, governs the use of pen registers and **trap-and-trace devices**. It requires judges to issue orders to allow the use of such devices when properly requested by prosecutors. There is no standard of proof that prosecutors have to meet in order to obtain such orders. The courts have generally taken the position that users of telephones have no reasonable expectations of privacy with regard to numbers associated with incoming or outgoing phone calls. Congress has chosen not to provide significant statutory protection in this area, much to the chagrin of civil libertarians.

In 2007, the Ninth Circuit Court of Appeals reviewed a case of first impression involving the use of computer surveillance. During its investigation of Defendants Forrester and Alba's Ecstasy manufacturing operation, the government used computer surveillance techniques to monitor Alba's e-mail and Internet activity. Alba argued that these techniques violated the Fourth Amendment. The court disagreed and pointed out that the messages are sent and the Internet protocol (IP) addresses are accessed through the equipment of their Internet service provider and other third parties. Therefore, e-mail and Internet users have no reasonable expectation of privacy in the to/from addresses of their messages or the IP addresses of the websites they visit. The court reasoned that because these computer surveillance techniques are constitutionally indistinguishable from the use of a pen register they do not violate the Fourth Amendment. *United States v. Forrester*, 495 F.3d 1041 (9th Cir. 2007).

The Foreign Intelligence Surveillance Act

In 1978, Congress enacted the Foreign Surveillance Intelligence Act (FISA), 50 U.S.C.A. § 1861 *et seq.*, to create a separate legal regime with respect to surveillance conducted by federal agents as part of the gathering of foreign intelligence. Originally applicable only to surveillance of foreign nationals operating inside the United States, the Act was amended in 2008 to cover surveillance of foreign nationals and the U.S. nationals outside the country as well. See 50 U.S.C.A. § 1802; 50 U.S.C.A. § 1881b.

FISA created a specialized court, the Foreign Intelligence Surveillance Court (FISC), to review requests for wiretaps, trap and trace devices, pen registers, and so forth pursuant to a foreign intelligence gathering operation aimed at foreign nationals located within the United States. Under the FISA Amendments Act of 2008, the FISC acquired jurisdiction over surveillance requests targeting the U.S. nationals outside the country. 50 U.S.C.A. § 1881b. These amendments also authorized FISC to approve annual certifications made by the Attorney General to allow ongoing surveillance of foreign nationals outside the United States. 50 U.S.C.A. § 1881a. And, under specified circumstances, the Attorney General may authorize surveillance of foreign nationals located outside the United States without obtaining an order from the FISC. 50 U.S.C.A. § 1802.

Although FISA was enacted to provide a legal framework for the gathering of foreign intelligence (an activity that was theretofore largely unregulated), it has implications for criminal justice as well, especially in an age of terrorism. Information gleaned through foreign intelligence gathering can be handed over to the FBI and used to further criminal investigations. And, assuming proper legal procedures were followed in the gathering of that information, it can be admissible in a criminal trial as well.

FISA is extremely controversial. Much of the controversy involves the FISC, which operates to a considerable degree in secret. The judges of the court are appointed by the Chief Justice of the Supreme Court without any need for congressional approval. The court tends to approve nearly all surveillance requests it receives, leading critics to regard it as little more than a rubber stamp. There is also concern about the breadth of FISA's provisions, especially provisions added by the FISA Amendments Act of 2008. On the other hand, federal authorities tend to regard FISA as an essential tool in the ongoing war on terrorism. On December 30, 2012, President Obama signed HR 5949, the FISA Amendments Act Reauthorization Act of 2012, which extended the provisions of the FISA Amendments Act of 2008 through the end of 2017.

The USA PATRIOT Act

Shortly after the terrorist attacks of September 11, 2001, President George W. Bush signed the Uniting and Strengthening America by Providing Appropriate Tools to Intercept and Obstruct Terrorism (USA PATRIOT) Act. This controversial statute was designed to deter and punish terrorist acts in the United States and around the world and to enhance the federal government's law-enforcement investigatory tools. The USA PATRIOT Act was reauthorized in 2006 under President Bush and again in 2011 under President Obama.

USA PATRIOT Act
Controversial act of Congress enacted in 2001 to strengthen the federal government's efforts to combat terrorism.

Many of the measures enacted into law by the **USA PATRIOT Act** are outside the scope of this chapter; however, Title II, "Enhanced Surveillance Procedures," includes provisions of particular relevance to our discussion of search and seizure. Title II enables law enforcement agencies to access Internet communications and expands their authority to use pen registers and trap-and-trace surveillance. Listed below are several significant changes, most of which focus on expanding the government's power to conduct electronic surveillance:

- § 202. Computer fraud and abuse are added to the predicate crimes listed in 18 U.S.C.A. § 2516(1)(c) for seeking authorization for interception of wire, oral, or electronic communications.
- § 203. Rule 6(e)(3)(C), Federal Rules of Criminal Procedure and 18 U.S.C.A. § 2517 are amended to allow intelligence obtained in grand jury proceedings and from wiretaps to be shared with federal law enforcement and national security personnel for use in connection with their official duties.
- § 204. The act amends 18 U.S.C.A. § 2511(2)(f) in regard to interception and disclosure of electronic communications by inserting "wire, oral and electronic" in place of "wire and oral," thereby broadening the right of government to intercept electronic communications in foreign intelligence matters.
- § 206. The act also amends 18 U.S.C.A. § 1805(c)(2)(B) to authorize federal courts to issue "roving" surveillance orders in connection with foreign intelligence matters, enabling investigators to intercept e-mail and cell phone communications in circumstances where suspects frequently change their account numbers.
- § 209. The act amends 18 U.S.C.A. § 2510 to authorize law enforcement officers to seize voicemail messages pursuant to a search warrant instead of a wiretap order.
- § 210. The act amends 18 U.S.C.A. § 2703(c) to allow law enforcement officers to obtain by subpoena subscriber records of local and long-distance telephone connection records, "records of session times and durations," and means of payment including credit card numbers from Internet service providers (ISPs).
- § 212. ISPs are allowed to reveal data concerning their customers without first notifying them if the ISP reasonably believes that "death or serious physical injury to any person" requires such disclosure without delay.

- § 214. The government only has to certify that the information that it obtains would be relevant to an "ongoing investigation" to secure a pen register or trap-and-trace order. Formerly, under 50 U.S.C.A. § 1842(c)(3), the government had to certify that it had reason to believe that surveillance was being conducted on a line or device that is or was used in "communications with" someone involved in international terrorism or intelligence activities that may violate the U.S. criminal law, or a foreign power or its agent whose communication is believed to concern terrorism or intelligence activities that violate the U.S. law.

- § 215. Among the very controversial provisions of the act is an amendment to the Foreign Intelligence Security Act (FISA), 50 U.S.C.A. § 1861 *et seq.*, which removes the limitations on the FBI's ability to obtain business records pursuant to an *ex parte* court order and grants the FBI the power in terrorism investigations to obtain records and other "tangible things" from entities that include libraries and Internet providers. The act forbids those who are served such orders from disclosing such fact to other than official sources. Section 215 became the focus of the first direct constitutional assault on the act, in a suit filed by the American Civil Liberties Union and other organizations in July of 2003. In *Muslim Community Association of Ann Arbor v. Ashcroft*, 459 F. Supp. 2d 592 (E.D. Mich.), a federal district judge denied the government's motion to dismiss the complaint, but after the statute was amended in 2006, the ACLU dropped the case. (See amendments to the act in the topic that follows on the 2006 Reauthorization Act.)

- § 216. Sections of the Electronic Communications Privacy Act (ECPA), 18 U.S.C.A. §§ 3121, 3123 (previously discussed), are amended to add the terms "routing" and "addressing" to the phrase "dialing and signaling information," thus expanding the federal government's authority to monitor Internet activities, as well as telephone conversations, by using systems similar to pen registers and trap-and-trace devices. This enables a U.S. Attorney, acting at the behest of the FBI, to obtain a court order allowing use of technology that records e-mail addresses and URLs of websites being accessed from a particular computer.

- § 216. The act also amends 18 U.S.C.A. § 3123(a) to provide that the court shall enter an *ex parte* order authorizing the installation and use of a pen register or trap-and-trace device anywhere within the United States if the court finds that the attorney for the government has certified to the court that the information likely to be obtained by such installation and use is relevant to an ongoing criminal investigation. (Recall our previous discussion that a pen register or trap-and-trace device ordinarily reveals only such telephone transactions as numbers called from particular telephones.)

- § 219. The act also permits federal magistrate judges in any district in which terrorism-related activities may have occurred to issue search warrants for searches within or outside the district. This greatly facilitates the issuance of nationwide warrants for investigations involving terrorism.

Soon after the adoption of the USA PATRIOT Act in October 2001, controversy erupted about the necessity and constitutionality of several provisions of the act. Some of the most significant complaints were lodged by libraries that could be directed to turn over records to the FBI and that, if served with § 215 orders, would be prohibited from disclosing that fact to anyone.

Congress enacted—and on March 9, 2006, President George W. Bush signed—the Reauthorizing Amendments Act of 2006. The 2006 law contained a number of technical revisions of the original USA PATRIOT Act. Many were designed to clarify that individuals who receive Foreign Intelligence Service Act (FISA) orders can challenge nondisclosure requirements. Specifically, recipients of a § 215 order (often libraries) are granted the right to petition a judge of the special FISA court to modify or quash the nondisclosure requirement of such an order. The 2006 act removed the requirement that recipients of § 215 orders or National Security Letters (NSLs) provide the FBI with the name of the attorney they consulted. Finally, it clarified that libraries, whose services include offering patrons access to the Internet, are not subject to NSLs unless they are functioning as electronic communication service providers.

On September 6, 2007, the U.S. District Court for the Southern District of New York struck down the National Security Letter provisions of the USA PATRIOT Act on grounds that subsection 18 U.S.C.A. § 2709(c) (which incorporates the nondisclosure requirements referred to above) violates the First Amendment freedom of speech and the principle of separation of powers. *Doe v. Gonzales*, 500 F.Supp. 379 (S.D.N.Y. 2007). On appeal, the Second Circuit agreed that National Security Letter provisions violate the First Amendment. But the court said:

> We will adjudicate the constitutionality of the nondisclosure requirement in subsection 2709(c) by construing this requirement to apply only when senior FBI officials certify that disclosure may result in an enumerated harm that is related to "an authorized investigation to protect against international terrorism or clandestine intelligence activities." *Doe, Inc. v. Mukasey*, 549 F.3d 861, 875 (2d Cir. 2008).

The USA PATRIOT Act continues to spark controversy, as does FISA. In 2013, the controversy was intensified when it was revealed that the National Security Agency was collecting metadata on Americans' phone calls and e-mails in order to identify terrorists. Although the scope of the program was not made clear, many suspected that the government had exceeded its authority under the aforementioned statutes and had invaded the realm of constitutionally protected privacy. As litigation is already underway, one can expect the Supreme Court to address these concerns in the coming years.

As Americans have come to rely more extensively on computers, e-mail, and the Internet, many see these new measures of exposing their electronic communications as a necessary evil in pursuit of a greater good, namely, prevention of terrorism. Others worry that their constitutional rights are being substantially diminished. While acknowledging that effective legislation is essential to protect the national security of the United States, they believe that greatly expanding the government's right to collect telephone metadata and eavesdrop on e-mail, text messaging and other Internet communications increases the potential for official mischief and diminishes individual liberty and privacy. Although recognizing the imperatives of national security, many Americans would ask courts, legislatures, and their fellow citizens to heed the words of Justice Louis Brandeis written in a dissenting opinion more than seventy-five years ago:

> The makers of our Constitution undertook to secure conditions favorable to the pursuit of happiness. They recognized the significance of man's spiritual nature, of his feelings and of his intellect. They knew that only a part of the pain, pleasure and satisfactions of life are to be found in material things. They sought to protect Americans in their beliefs, their thoughts, their emotions and their sensations. They conferred, as against the government, the right to be let alone—the most comprehensive of rights and the right most valued by civilized men. To protect that right, every unjustifiable intrusion by the government upon the privacy of the individual, whatever the means employed, must be deemed a violation of the 4th Amendment. ... *Olmstead v. United States*, 277 U.S. 438, 478, 48 S.Ct. 564, 572, 72 L.Ed. 944, 956 (1928).

The Exclusionary Rule

exclusionary rule Judicial doctrine forbidding the use of evidence in a criminal trial where the evidence was obtained in violation of the defendant's constitutional rights.

The **exclusionary rule** is a judicially created rule that prohibits the use of illegally obtained evidence in a criminal prosecution of the person whose rights were violated by the police in obtaining that evidence. In 1914, the U.S. Supreme Court first held that evidence obtained through an unlawful search and seizure could not be used to convict a person of a federal crime. *Weeks v. United States*, supra. The rationale for the rule is to deter illegal searches and seizures by police and thereby enforce the constitutional requirements. In 1949, in *Wolf v. Colorado*, supra, the Supreme Court refused to require the states to follow the exclusionary rule, saying that it was not an essential element of Fourth Amendment protection. But in *Mapp v. Ohio*, 367 U.S. 643, 81 S.Ct. 1684, 6 L.Ed.2d 1081 (1961), the Court held that there was no other effective means of enforcing the protections of the Fourth Amendment. The Court reasoned that if the Fourth Amendment was applicable to the states under the Fourteenth Amendment, then the exclusionary rule was also because it was the only effective means of enforcing the Fourth Amendment against overzealous police officers. The *Mapp* decision had an immediate impact. In New York City, for example, in the year preceding *Mapp*, police officers had not bothered to obtain a single search warrant. In the year following *Mapp*, they obtained more than 800.

The Fruit of the Poisonous Tree Doctrine

fruit of the poisonous tree doctrine A doctrine based on the judicial interpretation of the Fourth Amendment that holds that evidence derived from other, illegally seized evidence cannot be used by the prosecution.

The **fruit of the poisonous tree doctrine** holds that evidence derived from other evidence that is obtained through an illegal search or seizure is itself inadmissible. *Wong Sun v. United States*, 371 U.S. 471, 83 S.Ct. 407, 9 L.Ed.2d 441 (1963). The general rule is that where there has been an illegal seizure of property, such property cannot be introduced into evidence and no testimony may be given relative to any facts surrounding the seizure. However, the Fourth Amendment does not require evidence to be excluded, even if it was initially discovered during an illegal search

JURISPRUDENCE

Mapp v. Ohio, 367 U.S. 643, 81 S.Ct. 1684, 6 L.Ed.2d 1081 (1961)

Cleveland, Ohio police arrived at Dollree Mapp's home pursuant to information that a bombing suspect was hiding there. They demanded access, but failing to produce a search warrant, were denied. Police returned some four hours later and forced their way into the home. Mapp, who protested the entry, was forcibly detained while officers searched the home. Although police failed to locate the bombing suspect, they did find in a trunk in the basement some sexually explicit materials. Mapp was arrested, tried, and convicted under the Ohio statute proscribing possession of obscene materials. The Ohio appellate courts upheld the conviction. Dividing 7–2, the U.S. Supreme Court reversed, holding that the evidence had been improperly admitted against her since it had been obtained in violation of the Fourth Amendment warrant requirement. In this landmark decision, the Court overturned precedent and applied the exclusionary rule to the state courts via the Fourteenth Amendment. Dissenting, Justice Harlan asserted that the Court had "forgotten the sense of judicial restraint which, with due regard for *stare decisis*, is one element that should enter into deciding whether a past decision of this Court should be overruled." The majority, however, concluded that its decision "gives to the individual no more than that which the Constitution guarantees him, to the police officer no less than that to which honest law enforcement is entitled, and, to the courts, that judicial integrity so necessary in the true administration of justice."

of private property, if that evidence is later discovered during a valid search that is wholly independent of the initial illegal activity. *Murray v. United States*, 487 U.S. 533, 108 S.Ct. 2529, 101 L.Ed.2d 472 (1988). The Supreme Court has also held that evidence obtained through a search guided by information obtained from an inadmissible confession is likewise inadmissible unless the search would inevitably have recovered the evidence in the absence of the tainted information. *Nix v. Williams*, 467 U.S. 431, 444, 104 S.Ct. 2501, 2509, 81 L.Ed.2d 377 (1984).

Erosion of the Exclusionary Rule

The exclusionary rule is justified by the need to deter police misconduct, but it exacts a high price to society in that "the criminal is to go free because the constable has blundered." As crime rates rose dramatically during the 1960s and 1970s, the exclusionary rule came under attack from critics who argued that the social cost of allowing guilty persons to avoid prosecution outweighed the benefit of deterring police from violating the Fourth Amendment. During the 1970s, the Supreme Court used this sort of cost–benefit analysis in curtailing the scope of the exclusionary rule in a series of controversial decisions. In *United States v. Calandra*, 414 U.S. 338, 94 S.Ct. 613, 38 L.Ed.2d 561 (1974), the Court held that illegally obtained evidence could be used to obtain grand jury indictments. In *Michigan v. DeFillippo*, 443 U.S. 31, 99 S.Ct. 2627, 61 L.Ed.2d 343 (1979), the Court allowed the use of evidence obtained through a search incident to arrest pursuant to a law that was later ruled unconstitutional. But the most significant erosions of the rule came in the 1980s.

The Good-Faith Exception

In the most significant exclusionary rule cases decided in the 1980s, the Supreme Court held that evidence obtained on the basis of a search warrant that is later held to be invalid may be admitted as evidence at trial if the police officer who conducted the search relied on the warrant in "good faith." *United States v. Leon*, 468 U.S. 897,

JURISPRUDENCE

United States v. Leon, 468 U.S. 897, 104 S.Ct. 3405, 82 L.Ed.2d 677 (1984)

Police officers obtained a search warrant based on a tip from a confidential informant of unproven reliability. A subsequent search of a residence turned up a substantial amount of illegal drugs. At an evidentiary hearing prior to trial, a judge ruled that the warrant had been wrongly issued; that there was insufficient information to constitute probable cause. The Supreme Court ultimately held that the evidence could nevertheless be admitted against the defendants, because to exclude such evidence would have no deterrent effect on police misconduct. The error was made by the magistrate who issued the warrant, not by the police who

were deemed to be acting in good faith. Writing for the Court, Justice Byron White concluded that "that the marginal or nonexistent benefits produced by suppressing evidence obtained in objectively reasonable reliance on a subsequently invalidated search warrant cannot justify the substantial costs of exclusion." Dissenting, Justice William Brennan asserted that "it is clear that we have not been treated to an honest assessment of the merits of the exclusionary rule but have instead been drawn into a curious world where the 'costs' of excluding illegally obtained evidence loom to exaggerated heights and where the 'benefits' of such exclusion are made to disappear with a mere wave of the hand."

good-faith exception An exception to the exclusionary rule (which bars the use of evidence obtained by a search warrant found to be invalid). The exception allows use of the evidence if the police relied in good faith on the search warrant, even though the warrant is subsequently held to be invalid.

104 S.Ct. 3405, 82 L.Ed.2d 677 (1984); *Massachusetts v. Sheppard*, 468 U.S. 981, 104 S.Ct. 3424, 82 L.Ed.2d 737 (1984). In *Illinois v. Krull*, 480 U.S. 340, 107 S.Ct. 1160, 94 L.Ed.2d 364 (1987), the Court held that the **good-faith exception** to the exclusionary rule permits the introduction of evidence obtained by an officer in reliance upon a statute authorizing warrantless administrative searches where the statute is later determined to be unconstitutional. It must be noted that the good-faith exception to the exclusionary rule, as it has been developed thus far by the Supreme Court, applies only to cases where police officers rely on warrants that are later held to be invalid; it does not apply to warrantless searches.

In *United States v. Leon*, supra, the Supreme Court identified four situations involving police reliance on a warrant where the good-faith exception to the exclusionary rule does not apply:

1. if the magistrate was misled by an affidavit that the affiant knew was false or would have known was false except for reckless disregard for the truth
2. if the magistrate wholly abandons his or her judicial role
3. if the affidavit is so lacking in indicia of probable cause as to render belief in its existence unreasonable
4. if the warrant is so facially deficient that the executing officer cannot reasonably presume its validity

The Good-Faith Exception under State Constitutional Law

As previously noted, the Fourth Amendment sets a minimum national standard. Most states have adopted the good-faith exception. State courts are free to provide

---

JURISPRUDENCE

Herring v. United States, 555 U.S. 135, 129 S.Ct. 695, 172 L.Ed.2d 496 (2009)

On July 7, 2004, Investigator Mark Anderson of the Coffee County, Alabama, Sheriff's Department, learned that Bennie Dean Herring had driven in to retrieve something from his impounded truck. Anderson requested the county's warrant clerk, Sandy Pope, to check for any outstanding warrants for Herring's arrest. She found none. He then requested her to check with Sharon Morgan, her counterpart in the neighboring county. Morgan replied that there was an active arrest warrant for Herring's failure to appear on a felony charge. Pope then relayed the information to Anderson, and he and a deputy followed Herring and arrested him. A search incident to arrest yielded methamphetamine in Herring's pocket and a pistol in his vehicle. There had, however, been a mistake about the warrant. When Morgan sought to retrieve the actual warrant to fax it to Pope, she learned it had been recalled five months earlier. Morgan immediately called Pope to alert her to the mix-up, and Pope in turn contacted Anderson by radio, but by this time, Anderson had already arrested Herring and seized a gun and drugs incident to arrest. Herring was convicted in federal district court and the Eleventh Circuit Court of Appeal affirmed. The Supreme Court granted review.

Chief Justice John Roberts delivered the Court's 5–4 decision. Assuming the arrest was unlawful, the Court held that because the mistake was merely negligence, the evidence need not be suppressed. Pointing out that the exclusionary rule serves "to deter deliberate, reckless, or grossly negligent conduct," Roberts observed: "When a probable-cause determination was based on reasonable but mistaken assumptions, the person subjected to a search or seizure has not necessarily been the victim of a constitutional violation." In dissent, Justice Ruth Bader Ginsburg argued that negligent recordkeeping errors by law enforcement are susceptible to deterrence by the exclusionary rule and cannot effectively be remedied through other means.

greater levels of protection under the search and seizure sections of state constitutions. This latter approach was followed by the New Jersey Supreme Court in *State v. Novembrino*, 519 A.2d 820 (N.J. 1987), where it refused to follow the good-faith exception to the exclusionary rule as a matter of state law. The court observed that the exclusionary rule was firmly embedded in its own jurisprudence and that a good-faith exception would "ultimately reduce respect for and compliance with the probable cause standard." 519 A.2d 854.

Standing to Invoke the Exclusionary Rule

standing The right to initiate a legal action or challenge based on the fact that one has suffered or is likely to suffer a real and substantial injury.

A person who seeks the benefits of the exclusionary rule must have **standing** to invoke the rule. The concept of standing limits the class of defendants who may challenge an allegedly illegal search and seizure. In *Jones v. United States*, 362 U.S. 257, 80 S.Ct. 725, 4 L.Ed.2d 697 (1960), the Supreme Court granted automatic standing to anyone who was legitimately on the premises that were searched. In *Rakas v. Illinois*, 439 U.S. 128, 99 S.Ct. 421, 58 L.Ed.2d 387 (1978), however, the Court restricted the *Jones* doctrine by refusing to allow passengers of an automobile to challenge the search of the vehicle in which they were riding.

When police stop an automobile, the driver of the car is "seized" within the meaning of the Fourth Amendment. Therefore the driver has standing to challenge the constitutionality of the stop and everything that transpires during the stop. In *Brendlin v. California*, 551 U.S. 249, 127 S.Ct. 2400, 168 L.Ed.2d 132 (2007), the Supreme Court held that a passenger is seized as well and so has standing to challenge the constitutionality of the stop. However, under *Rakas v. Illinois*, supra, passengers have standing to challenge only searches and seizures of things in which they have a property interest. Therefore, while the passenger can challenge the validity of the automobile stop, under *Rakas v. Illinois* the passenger may not challenge the constitutionality of the stop of the automobile.

In *United States v. Salvucci*, 448 U.S. 83, 100 S.Ct. 2547, 65 L.Ed.2d 619 (1980), the Court took the final step in overruling the automatic-standing rule of *Jones v. United States*. Salvucci was charged with possession of stolen mail. The evidence was recovered by police in a search of an apartment that belonged to

CASE-IN-POINT

The Good-Faith Exception under State Constitutional Law

Acting on the basis of an informant's tip, police obtained a warrant to search a building owned by the defendant. Inside the building they discovered seventeen growing marijuana plants, as well as cultivating equipment. After a suppression hearing, the trial judge determined that the warrant upon which the search was based was defective in that it had not been adequately supported by probable cause. Nevertheless, the judge refused to suppress the evidence, citing the good-faith exception

to the exclusionary rule created by the U.S. Supreme Court's decision in *United States v. Leon*. On appeal, the Pennsylvania Supreme Court interpreted its state constitution as affording more protection to a defendant against unreasonable searches and seizures than the federal constitution, as interpreted in *Leon*. Thus, the court concluded that the Pennsylvania constitution does not permit a *Leon*-style good-faith exception to the exclusionary rule.

Commonwealth v. Edmunds, 586 A.2d 887 (Pa. 1991).

the mother of Salvucci's accomplice. The federal district court granted Salvucci's motion to suppress the evidence, relying on the automatic-standing doctrine. The Supreme Court reversed, holding that Salvucci was not automatically entitled to challenge the search of another person's apartment. Justice William H. Rehnquist explained the Court's more conservative stance on the issue of standing:

> We are convinced that the automatic standing rule ... has outlived its usefulness in this Court's Fourth Amendment jurisprudence. The doctrine now serves only to afford a windfall to defendants whose Fourth Amendment rights have not been violated. 448 U.S. at 95, 100 S.Ct. at 2554, 65 L.Ed.2d at 630.

Thus, a casual visitor to an apartment has no legitimate expectation of privacy in an apartment hallway that would grant the visitor standing to contest a search of those premises. *United States v. Burnett*, 890 F.2d 1233 (D.C. Cir. 1989). To successfully invoke the exclusionary rule now, a defendant must show that a legitimate expectation of privacy was violated.

In *United States v. Edwards*, 242 F.3d 928 (10th Cir. 2001), the court held the defendant lacked standing to challenge the search of a rented car because it was rented in another person's name and the defendant was not an authorized driver of the vehicle, whereas in *United States v. Walker*, 237 F.3d 845 (7th Cir. 2001), the defendant had standing to challenge the search of a rental car because he was listed on the rental agreement as an authorized driver.

In 1983, the Pennsylvania Supreme Court determined that under its state constitution a defendant accused of a possessory crime who seeks to challenge a search and seizure must be accorded automatic standing notwithstanding the more restrictive view announced by the U.S. Supreme Court. *Commonwealth v. Sell*, 470 A.2d 457 (Pa. 1983). Of course, states may still grant automatic standing to challenge evidence that has been seized. For example, "under Louisiana jurisprudence, any defendant against whom evidence is acquired as a result of an allegedly unreasonable search and seizure, whether or not it was obtained in violation of his rights, has standing to challenge the constitutionality of the search or seizure." *State v. Dakin*, 495 So.2d 344, 346 (La. 1986). Likewise, in *Commonwealth v. Amendola*, 550 N.E.2d 121, 126 (Mass. 1990), the court refused to abandon the automatic-standing rule: "When a defendant is charged with a crime in which possession of the seized evidence at the time of the contested search is an essential element of guilt, the defendant shall be deemed to have standing to contest the legality of the search and the seizure of that evidence." Courts in Michigan, New Hampshire, New Jersey, and Vermont have reached similar conclusions.

Conclusion

The constitutional protection against unreasonable searches and seizures is a fundamental right, yet determining the precise scope and meaning of the right is not easy. The constitutional law governing search and seizure is extremely complex. Moreover, it is highly dynamic, as courts decide countless cases in this area each year. Figure 3.3 provides an overview of search and seizure law—actually, a decision tree that highlights the important questions that courts must answer in determining whether a particular search or seizure was lawful.

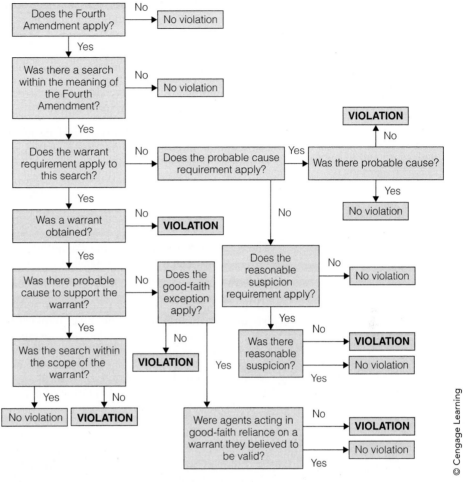

FIGURE 3.3 Fourth Amendment Decision Tree. The Decision Tree Depicted Here is Based on General Principles of Federal Law and may not Correctly Portray Applicable Laws in all States.

Chapter Summary

- LO1

  o The Fourth Amendment was conceived as a limitation on the powers of the national government but in 1949 the Supreme Court held that freedom from unreasonable searches and seizures is "implicit in the concept of ordered liberty" and ruled that the Fourth Amendment is enforceable against the States through the Due Process Clause of the Fourteenth Amendment.

  o State courts are free to provide higher levels of protection under their state constitutions but cannot provide less without running afoul of the Fourteenth Amendment.

o The Fourth Amendment protects a person's rights against the police and other government agents from unreasonable searches and seizures but does not protect against searches and seizures by private individuals.

o Persons crossing the national border or other functional equivalents, and searches and seizures conducted by the U.S. agents outside the territory of the United States, are not protected by the Fourth Amendment. Nor does it apply to open fields or to abandoned property.

o Fourth Amendment protection is at its maximum for persons in their home and its curtilage (the area immediately surrounding the house). Protections extend to stores, offices, and places of business, but not to those areas of commercial properties that carry an implied invitation for the public to enter.

- LO2

  o The term "seizure" refers to the taking into custody of physical evidence, property, or even a person. But what constitutes a "search" can be more difficult.

  o Historically, courts looked at whether a trespass had taken place in deciding whether the Fourth Amendment was implicated. But in 1967 the Supreme Court abandoned the trespass doctrine, saying "the Fourth Amendment protects people, not places."

  o Today courts employ a twofold requirement: first whether a person has exhibited an actual (subjective) expectation of privacy and, second, whether the expectation is one that society recognizes as "reasonable."

  o Obviously, anyone lawfully incarcerated in a prison or jail has no reasonable expectation of privacy. Inmates are routinely subjected to searches of their persons, although some courts hold that strip searches violate Fourth Amendment rights unless there is probable cause to believe the arrestee is concealing weapons or contraband. Other courts permit such searches where there is a reasonable suspicion that the arrestee is concealing weapons or contraband.

  o When conducted according to standard police procedures, an inventory search of a vehicle is regarded as an administrative search not subject to ordinary Fourth Amendment requirements. Inventory searches are justified by the need to protect the owner's property and to protect the police from claims of lost property and potential dangers lurking inside closed automobiles.

  o Courts have approved properly established and conducted sobriety checkpoints where all drivers passing a certain point are stopped briefly for license checks and signs of intoxication.

- LO3

  o Consent to a search must be truly voluntary and involve more than mere acquiescence to the authority of the police.

  o Courts have said that police may not search a home when one resident invites them in but another refuses to grant access.

o In 1990, the Supreme Court shifted the focus from the dominion and control of the third party to the police officer's subjective belief that the third party has the authority to grant consent to a search of the premises.

o The problem of consent is especially acute in situations where several persons share a single dwelling, as is common among college students.

- LO4

  o The Fourth Amendment expresses a preference for searches and seizures to be conducted pursuant to a warrant, which in turn must be supported by probable cause. Probable cause exists when prudent and cautious police officers have trustworthy information leading them to believe that evidence of crime might be obtained through a particular search.

  o Courts say officers are to determine probable cause as a "commonsense, practical question" in light of the totality of circumstances in a given case.

- LO5

  o To obtain a search warrant, agents submit an affidavit to a judge or magistrate who must then determine whether the stated facts support a finding of probable cause. The officer's affidavit must always contain a rather precise description of the place(s) or person(s) to be searched and the things to be seized. The information on which an affidavit is based must be sufficiently fresh to ensure that the items to be seized are probably located on the premises to be searched.

  o A magistrate's finding of probable cause may be based on hearsay evidence, but because hearsay evidence is often provided by confidential informants (CIs), whose motivations may be suspect, their reliability and basis of knowledge must be carefully checked. The Supreme Court formerly required that the officer's affidavit show that a CI was both credible and reliable, and give the basis of the CI's knowledge. In 1983, the Court relaxed the standards and permitted magistrates to consider the totality of circumstances when evaluating applications for search warrants based on hearsay evidence. Most states follow the relaxed standard, but many have opted adhere to the more strict requirements.

  o The scope of a search and seizure is bound by the terms of the warrant. Courts tend to be less strict when it comes to the description of contraband because it is illegal per se, but stricter in cases involving First Amendment rights. Traditionally, police wait until a suspect receives contraband before obtaining a search warrant.

  o Dramatic increases in drug trafficking over the last few decades gave rise to a number of state courts approving anticipatory search warrants where probable cause does not have to exist until the warrant is executed. In 2006, the Supreme Court approved anticipatory search warrants, noting that the magistrate must determine that it is probable that contraband will be on the described premises when the warrant is executed.

  o The Federal Rules of Criminal Procedure provide that a warrant "shall command the officer to search, within a specified period of time not to exceed 10 days, the person or place named or the property or person specified. The warrant shall be served in the daytime, unless the issuing authority . . . authorizes its execution at times other than daytime."

- States have varying requirements that govern the period of time and hours for execution of a search warrant. An officer may break open door or window of a house to execute a search warrant, if, after notice of his or her authority and purpose, the officer is refused admittance. Giving notice is known as the "knock-and-announce requirement." Officers facing exigent circumstances such as the need to preserve evanescent evidence can dispense with the knock and announce requirement. But in 1997, the Court ruled that states may not create a blanket "drug exception" to the knock-and-announce requirement. In 2006 a divided Supreme Court held that violations of the knock-and-announce requirement do not require the suppression of all evidence seized as the result of such violations.

- LO6

  - Because an absolute warrant requirement would be impractical, courts uphold warrantless searches under "exigent circumstances." All exceptions assume that police officers have probable cause to believe that a given search is likely to produce evidence of crime.

  - Police may seize evidence that comes to their attention when they are lawfully in an area and the evidence is in plain view and apparently constitutes evidence of a crime.

  - Police in "hot pursuit" may continue to pursue a suspect into a protected place, such as a home, without having to wait until a warrant can be obtained. When police reasonably believe that a person is in need of immediate aid, they may make a warrantless entry of a dwelling. Once inside, they may justifiably seize evidence in plain view.

  - Where police have a reasonable belief that loss or destruction of evidence is imminent, a warrantless entry of premises may be justified. In 1984, the Supreme Court narrowed the doctrine, saying that destruction of evidence does not constitute exigent circumstances if the underlying offense is relatively minor.

  - In 1969, the Supreme Court limited the historic doctrine of search incident to arrest to allow police to search only the body of an arrestee and the arrestee's immediate "grasp" or "lunge" area. Police may not search a dwelling when an arrest occurs outside it.

  - Police may stop an automobile without a warrant and temporarily detain the driver as long as they have probable cause to believe that criminal activity is taking place or that traffic laws or automobile regulations are being violated.

  - In 1996, the Supreme Court held that police may use a minor traffic or equipment violation as a pretext for stopping an automobile that they wish to investigate. When evidence of drug or alcohol use or other criminal violation becomes apparent, police may make a warrantless arrest and search incident to that arrest.

  - Once begun under exigent circumstances, a warrantless search of an automobile may continue after the vehicle has been taken to the police station.

  - In 2009, the Supreme Court substantially revised the rule on a search incident to arrest of an occupant of a vehicle to provide: that police may search a vehicle incident to a recent occupant's arrest only if the arrestee is within reaching distance of the passenger compartment at the time of the search or it is reasonable to believe the vehicle contains evidence of the offense of arrest.

- LO7

  o The courts have also recognized that certain types of searches may be reasonable in the absence of probable cause.

  o To protect law enforcement personnel, in 1968 the Supreme Court upheld the authority of police officers to stop and frisk an individual and conduct a limited "pat-down" search for weapons based on reasonable suspicion.

  o Stop-and-frisk laws generally also allow police to stop a motor vehicle on reasonable suspicion that crime is afoot and make a limited search for weapons. In attempting to identify and to apprehend drug smugglers, law enforcement agencies developed sets of characteristics that typify drug couriers.

  o In 1980, the Supreme Court suggested that fitting a drug courier profile was not in itself sufficient to constitute the reasonable suspicion necessary to allow police to detain an airline passenger.

  o The Supreme Court has also said searches of public school students can be based on a reasonableness standard rather than on probable cause.

  o To insure public safety, courts have upheld the constitutionality of regulations permitting supervisory personnel to order urinalysis testing of public safety officers based on reasonable suspicion of drug abuse.

- LO8

  o The use of technology searchlights, field glasses, aerial photography, and other means of enhancing observation does not necessarily trigger Fourth Amendment protections.

  o In 1979, the Supreme Court determined that use of a pen register to record phone numbers dialed from a particular phone number is not a search within the meaning of the Fourth Amendment.

  o In 1986, the Court held that neither the high-altitude photography of a chemical plant nor use in evidence of photos, taken in a low-altitude flight, of marijuana plants growing in a defendant's backyard constituted searches under the Fourth Amendment.

  o In 2001, the Court said, "when the Government uses a device that is not in general public use, to explore details of the home that would previously have been unknowable without physical intrusion, the surveillance is a 'search' and is presumptively unreasonable without a warrant."

- LO9

  o The Omnibus Crime Control and Safe Streets Act of 1968 prohibits interception of electronic communications without a court order unless one party to the conversation consents. Interception is defined as "aural or other acquisition of the contents of any wire, electronic or oral communication through the use of any electronic, mechanical, or other device."

- o In 1986, Congress expanded the meaning of "wire communications" to include conversations through "switching stations," which covers cellular telephones. An application for a wiretap order must contain detailed information along with an explanation of why less intrusive means of investigation will not suffice.

- o The Electronic Communications Privacy Act of 1986 established federal standards for access to e-mail and other electronic communications and to "transactional records," including subscriber identifying information, call logs, phone bills, and so forth. The act requires judges to issue orders to allow using pen registers and trap-and-trace devices on request of prosecutors. Courts generally hold that users of telephones have no reasonable expectations of privacy with regard to numbers associated with incoming or outgoing phone calls.

- o In 2007, a federal appeals court reasoned that because computer surveillance techniques are constitutionally indistinguishable from the use of a pen register they do not violate the Fourth Amendment.

- o The USA PATRIOT Act enables law enforcement to access Internet communications, expands the authority for use of pen registers and trap-and-trace surveillance, and allows federal courts to issue "roving" surveillance orders in connection with foreign intelligence matters. Law enforcement officers are authorized to seize voicemail messages pursuant to a search warrant and to subpoena subscriber records of local and long-distance telephone connection records and means of payment. The act also permits federal magistrate judges in any district in which terrorism-related activities may have occurred to issue search warrants for searches within or outside the district.

- o A section of the USA PATRIOT Act became controversial because it prohibited libraries that were directed to turn over records to the FBI from disclosing that fact to anyone. Amendments in 2006 made a number of technical revisions to the original USA PATRIOT Act, and libraries now have the right to petition to modify or quash the nondisclosure requirement of such an order. In 2008, the Second Circuit said it would construe the nondisclosure requirement to apply only when senior FBI officials certify that disclosure may result in an enumerated harm related to "an authorized investigation to protect against international terrorism or clandestine intelligence activities."

- LO10

  - o The exclusionary rule was judicially created to prohibit the use of illegally obtained evidence in a criminal prosecution of a person whose rights were violated by the police in obtaining that evidence.

  - o The "fruit of the poisonous tree doctrine" holds that evidence derived from other evidence that is obtained through an illegal search or seizure is itself inadmissible. Also, evidence obtained through a search guided by information obtained from an inadmissible confession is inadmissible unless the search would inevitably have recovered the evidence in the absence of the taint.

  - o Evidence does not have to be excluded, even if it was initially discovered during an illegal search of private property, if that evidence is later discovered during a valid search wholly independent of the initial illegal activity.

○ In 1984, the Supreme Court instituted a "good-faith exception" to the exclusionary rule where the police officer who conducted the search relied in "good faith" on the validity of a search warrant. But the good-faith exception to the exclusionary rule does not apply if (1) the magistrate was misled by an affidavit that the affiant knew was false, or would have known was false except for reckless disregard for the truth; (2) the magistrate wholly abandons his or her judicial role; (3) the affidavit is so lacking in indicia of probable cause as to render belief in its existence unreasonable; or (4) the warrant is so facially deficient that the executing officer cannot reasonably presume its validity.

Key Terms

abandoned property

affiant

affidavit

anticipatory search warrant

automobile exception

border searches

confidential informants

consent to a search

curtilage

doctrine of incorporation

drug courier profiles

drug testing

electronic eavesdropping

emergency searches

evanescent evidence

exclusionary rule

exigent circumstances

Franks hearing

fruit of the poisonous tree doctrine

general warrant

good-faith exception

hot pursuit

implied consent

inventory search

knock and announce

open fields doctrine

pen register

plain-view doctrine

probable cause

reasonable expectation of privacy

reasonable suspicion

search

search incident to a lawful arrest

seizure

sobriety checkpoints

standing

stop-and-frisk

strip searches

third-party consent

totality of circumstances

trap-and-trace devices

USA PATRIOT Act

warrant

warrantless searches

wiretap orders

wiretapping

Key Court Decisions

Katz v. United States (1967): Wiretapping implicates the Fourth Amendment even without a physical intrusion onto a suspect's property, because "the Fourth Amendment protects people, not places."

California v. Greenwood (1988): There is no "reasonable expectation of privacy" with respect to garbage that one places by the curb.

United States v. Ross (1982): A police officer who has probable cause to believe that evidence of a crime is concealed within an automobile may conduct a search as broad as one that could be authorized by a magistrate issuing a warrant.

Terry v. Ohio (1968): Police officers may stop and frisk persons based on reasonable suspicion that criminal activity is afoot.

United States v. Jones (2012): Police may not place a GPS tracking device on a suspect's car without first obtaining a search warrant.

Mapp v. Ohio (1961): Evidence obtained in violation of the Fourth Amendment is inadmissible in a state criminal prosecution.

United States v. Leon (1984): Evidence obtained on the basis of a search warrant that is later held to be invalid may be admitted as evidence at trial if the police officer who conducted the search relied on the warrant in good faith.

Herring v. United States (2009): When a police officer seizes evidence during a search incident to an arrest based on reasonable but mistaken assumptions, the evidence need not be suppressed.

Questions for Thought and Discussion

1. Today, many security personnel are "private police," yet Fourth Amendment protection has been extended only to those searches conducted by government officials. What arguments can be made for and against expanding the prohibitions of the Fourth Amendment to include security personnel?

2. What rationale supports the "search incident to arrest" exception to the warrant requirement? What limitations do the courts impose on such searches?

3. Should one have a reasonable expectation of privacy from infrared detectors and other high-tech devices that enable law enforcement officers to "see" heat emanating from a person's home? Why or why not?

4. Does a person using a public restroom in a government office building have a reasonable expectation of privacy from television security surveillance?

5. In *New Jersey v. T.L.O.* (1985), the Supreme Court adopted a reasonableness standard for public school searches. Should this standard be applied to searches of students in public colleges and universities? What about private colleges? Does it make a difference if the search is conducted in a public setting or in the student's dormitory room?

6. What is the rationale for excluding from trial evidence obtained in violation of the Fourth Amendment? Is this a compelling justification for the exclusion of criminal evidence from the trial of a defendant accused of a serious felony such as aggravated battery?

7. What alternatives to the exclusionary rule might be adopted to enforce the protections of the Fourth Amendment? How effective are such alternatives likely to be?

8. The Supreme Court has created a "good-faith" exception to the exclusionary rule where police rely on a search warrant that is later held to be invalid because the magistrate erred in finding probable cause for a search. Should the good-faith exception be extended to cases where police who were acting in good faith conduct *warrantless* searches that are later held to be unlawful?

9. What is meant by the "fruit of the poisonous tree doctrine" in relation to searches and seizures?

10. What is the "standing" requirement in the law of search and seizure? What is its purpose?

11. In 2006, in *Hudson v. Michigan*, Justice Antonin Scalia, writing for a sharply divided Supreme Court, concluded that when it comes to knock-and-announce violations, "[r]esort to the massive remedy of suppressing evidence of guilt is unjustified." Writing for the four dissenters, Justice Stephen Breyer contended that the decision "destroys the strongest legal incentive to comply with the Constitution's knock-and-announce requirement." Evaluate these opposing views.

12. In *United States v. Salvucci* (1980), the U.S. Supreme Court concluded that "the automatic standing rule ... has outlived its usefulness in this Court's Fourth Amendment jurisprudence." Yet, several state courts have held that under their state constitutions a defendant accused of a possessory crime who challenges a search and seizure must be accorded automatic standing. What are the merits of states', based on their own constitutions, affording defendants more protection in this area than is required by the Supreme Court?

13. In 2013, it was revealed that the National Security Agency was collecting metadata from the phone calls of millions of Americans without particularized suspicion. Apparently the NSA was relying on broad orders from the Foreign Intelligence Surveillance Court, which, in turn, was relying on broad interpretations of the Foreign Intelligence Surveillance Act Amendments of 2008 and the USA PATRIOT Act. In your view, does the collection of such metadata implicate the Fourth Amendment?

Problems for Discussion and Solution

1. Police observed an automobile traveling at a high rate of speed and swerving on the road. They gave pursuit and stopped the vehicle after a five-minute chase. The driver, later identified as Jerome Johnson, emerged from the car and began to verbally abuse and threaten the officers. Johnson appeared intoxicated but refused to take any of the standard field sobriety tests. Under state law, refusal to perform a sobriety test results in the loss of a driver's license for a period of one year. The law does not authorize police to force suspects to perform any sobriety tests against their will. Johnson was arrested and transported to a local hospital, where he was forcibly restrained and asked to submit to a blood-alcohol test. Johnson refused, saying "I'd rather lose my license than let you stick me with that needle." The test was administered over Johnson's objection, and the results indicated that Johnson's blood-alcohol level was substantially above the legal limit. Johnson was charged with driving under the influence of alcohol. Before trial, Johnson's attorney moved to suppress the results of the blood-alcohol test, arguing that it was taken without Johnson's consent, without probable cause, and in violation of the state's implied consent law. If you were the judge in this case, how would you be inclined to rule on the admissibility of this evidence? What additional information would you need to render your decision?

2. Acting without a search warrant, police arrive at a home after receiving an anonymous tip that a man has been making illegal explosives in his workshop. The officers find that the man is not at home. Can the man's wife consent to a warrantless search of her husband's workshop, or must police wait until the husband returns to obtain his consent? What would be the result if the man and his wife were both at home and the wife consented to the search but the man did not?

3. The sheriff's department in a rural north Georgia county receives an anonymous letter stating that there is a "meth lab" being operated in a trailer home belonging to Danny Dawgmire, and that children living in the trailer are being exposed to methamphetamine and other toxic chemicals. Without obtaining a

warrant, deputies drive to the trailer home, where they detect strong chemical odors associated with the production of methamphetamines. The deputies knock and announce their presence, but no one answers. They then forcibly enter the trailer, where they discover large quantities of methamphetamines and associated equipment, paraphernalia, and supplies. No children are found in the trailer. The deputies call a hazardous materials disposal unit to the scene. Two hours later, as the meth lab is being cleaned up and evidence secured, Dawgmire arrives at the scene in his pickup truck and is promptly arrested and charged with manufacture of and possession with intent to distribute a controlled substance. In a pretrial motion, Dawgmire's attorney moves to suppress the evidence on the ground that no warrant had been obtained to authorize the search. The attorney claims that Dawgmire, who is unmarried, lives in the trailer alone and that at no time have any children been inside the trailer. How would the state likely counter the motion? How would the judge likely rule on the motion to suppress?

4. Police receive a call from Johann Besch, who lives at 123 Pauline Place. Besch tells the police that he is convinced that his next-door neighbor is running a drug dealing operation. Police go to Besch's residence. There they meet with Besch, who tells them of the many different cars that come and go at all hours of the day. Besch also says that he doesn't think his neighbor has a "real job" because he never sees him leaving the house. Based on Besch's statements, police drive by the neighbor's house several times over the next three days. Each time they drive by they observe different cars parked in the driveway. They check departmental records and discover that a search warrant had been executed at that home two years before and that the search had resulted in seizure of illegal drugs. At this point they go to a magistrate to obtain a search warrant. If you were the magistrate, would you issue the warrant based on the information police have obtained thus far? Why or why not?

CHAPTER 4

Arrest, Interrogation, and Identification Procedures

JURISPRUDENCE FEATURE BOXES

Dunaway v. New York (1979)

Tennessee v. Garner (1985)

Minnesota v. Dickerson (1993)

Illinois v. Wardlow (2000)

Whren v. United States (1996)

United States v. Sokolow (1989)

City of Indianapolis v. Edmond (2000)

Hiibel v. Sixth Judicial Dist. Court of Nevada (2004)

Miranda v. Arizona (1966)

Nix v. Williams (1984)

New York v. Quarles (1984)

Arizona v. Fulminante (1991)

United States v. Wade (1967)

LEARNING OBJECTIVES

After reading this chapter, you should be able to explain

1. why an arrest triggers the Fourth Amendment warrant requirement and when a warrantless arrest is permissible

2. the extent to which officers may use force to make an arrest

3. how an investigatory detention differs from an arrest and the applicable constitutional standards

4. the controversy over racial profiling as a basis for investigatory detentions

5. the legal issues surrounding the use of roadblocks and sobriety checkpoints

6. the circumstances under which police may require a person to produce identification

7. why police interrogation implicates constitutional rights and why the courts have required police to warn suspects in custody of their constitutional rights before questioning them

8. whether police can use deception to induce suspects to confess

9. why inadmissible confessions can result in the suppression of physical evidence as well

10. the various methods police employ to identify suspects, and the constitutional standards that apply to identification procedures

CHAPTER OPENING VIGNETTE

The name "Miranda" is well known. Countless movies and television programs have shown police officers advising suspects who have just been arrested of their right to remain silent and their right to have counsel present during questioning, as dictated by the Supreme Court's landmark decision in *Miranda v. Arizona*, 384 U.S. 436, 86 S.Ct. 1602, 16 L.Ed.2d 694 (1966). Indeed, a new verb, "Mirandize," has been coined to refer to the process of advising suspects of their rights. Ernesto Miranda, a suspect in a rape case, was interrogated for two hours without being advised of the aforementioned rights. The Supreme Court invalidated his confession, saying that unless police advise suspects of their rights, incriminating statements made by suspects in custody cannot be used as evidence against them. Probably more than any other decision, *Miranda* has come to represent the importance of the rule of law in criminal justice—the idea that everyone taken into custody and charged with a crime by the police has constitutional rights that must be respected. In this chapter, we examine those constitutional rights in depth.

Introduction

arrest To take someone into custody or otherwise deprive that person of freedom of movement.

In its most general sense, the term **arrest** refers to the deprivation of a person's liberty by someone with legal authority. In the contemporary criminal justice system, an arrest usually occurs when police take an individual into custody and charge that person with the commission of a crime. Generally, an arrest is made by a police officer, although there are some circumstances in which an arrest can be effected by a private individual.

As a form of "seizure," an arrest is governed by requirements of the Fourth Amendment. However, the formal arrest is not the only type of encounter between police and citizens that implicates the Fourth Amendment. A seizure, for Fourth Amendment purposes, occurs when a police officer, "by means of physical force or show of authority, has in some way restrained the liberty of a citizen." *Terry v. Ohio*, 392 U.S. 1, 19 n. 16, 88 S.Ct. 1868, 1879 n. 16, 20 L.Ed.2d 889, 905 n. 16 (1968). The traditional full-blown arrest clearly constitutes a seizure. So, too, does a police officer's fatal shooting of a fleeing suspect. *Tennessee v. Garner*, 471 U.S. 1, 105 S.Ct. 1694, 85 L.Ed.2d 1 (1985). Other instances may not be so clear, however. In 1988, the Supreme Court declined to formulate a "bright-line" rule delineating what constitutes a seizure; rather, the Court asserted that the test requires an assessment of whether, in view of all the circumstances surrounding an incident, "a reasonable person would have believed that he was not free to leave." *Michigan v. Chesternut*, 486 U.S. 567, 108 S.Ct. 1975, 100 L.Ed.2d 565 (1988). The following year, the Court ruled that stopping a motorist at a police roadblock is a seizure for Fourth Amendment purposes. *Brower v. County of Inyo*, 489 U.S. 593,109 S.Ct. 1378, 103 L.Ed.2d 628 (1989).

Encounters between citizens and police range from formal arrests to situations in which police approach an individual and ask questions. Police–citizen encounters can be placed in four categories:

1. Arrest
2. Investigatory detention (also referred to as stop-and-frisk, as introduced in Chapter 3)
3. The use of roadblocks and sobriety checkpoints
4. The request for information or identification

Each type of encounter is unique from the standpoint of the Fourth Amendment. Accordingly, we examine each of these separately in this chapter.

interrogation Questioning of a suspect by police or questioning of a witness by counsel.

Interrogation refers to the questioning of a suspect by law enforcement officers to elicit a confession, an admission, or information that otherwise assists them in solving a crime. Typically, interrogation takes place behind closed doors in a law enforcement facility, although today a suspect being questioned is often accompanied by an attorney. Because interrogation of a suspect carries with it a risk of coercion, confessions obtained by police are subject to constitutional attack under the Self-Incrimination Clause of the Fifth Amendment.

identification procedures Scientific and nonscientific procedures employed by police to assist in the identification of suspects.

Identification procedures are techniques employed by law enforcement agencies to identify suspects. These fall into two basic categories: scientific means to match physical evidence taken from a suspect with that found at a crime scene, and procedures to determine whether victims or witnesses can identify perpetrators. Both types of identification procedure are extremely important in building cases against defendants, and both present unique legal problems.

Arrest

Because arrest is the most serious type of police–citizen encounter, it is subject to the most stringent constitutional requirements. Specifically, arrest is subject to the probable cause and warrant requirements of the Fourth Amendment, although there are exceptions to the latter. The Supreme Court has said that the legality of arrests by state and local officers is to be judged by the same constitutional standards applicable to federal agents. *Ker v. California*, 374 U.S. 23, 83 S.Ct. 1623, 10 L.Ed.2d 726 (1963).

The Probable Cause Requirement

For any arrest or significant deprivation of liberty to occur, police officers must have probable cause. Although it is not easy to define, probable cause in the context of arrest means the same thing as in the context of search and seizure (see Chapter 3). The Supreme Court has said that probable cause exists where "the facts and circumstances within [the officers'] knowledge and of which they had reasonably trustworthy information [are] sufficient in themselves to warrant a man of reasonable caution in the belief" that a particular crime had been or was being committed. *Carroll v. United States*, 267 U.S. 132, 162, 45 S.Ct. 280, 288, 69 L.Ed. 543, 555 (1925).

Police can establish probable cause without personally observing the commission of a crime as long as they have sufficient information to conclude that the suspect probably committed it. Officers often obtain their information from crime victims, eyewitnesses, official reports, and confidential or even anonymous informants.

The Warrant Requirement

arrest warrant A document issued by a magistrate or judge directing that a named person be taken into custody for allegedly having committed an offense.

capias "You are to take." A general term for various court orders requiring that some named person be taken into custody.

An **arrest warrant** (see Figure 4.1) is routine in cases where an arrest is to be made based on an indictment by a grand jury. When a prosecutor files an accusatorial document known as an information, the court issues a *capias*, a document directing the arrest of the defendant. In such cases, suspects are often not aware that they are under investigation, and police officers have ample time to obtain an arrest warrant without fear that suspects will flee. However, most arrests are not made pursuant to secret investigations but instead are made by police officers who observe a criminal act, respond to a complaint filed by a crime victim, or have probable cause to arrest after completing an investigation. In such cases, it is often unnecessary for police to obtain an arrest warrant, but it is always essential that they have probable cause to make the arrest.

Warrantless Arrests

warrantless arrest An arrest made by police who do not possess an arrest warrant.

plain view Readily visible to the naked eye.

At common law, police officers had the right to make a **warrantless arrest** if they observed someone in the commission of a felony or had probable cause to believe that a person had committed or was committing a felony. To make a warrantless arrest for a misdemeanor, an officer had to observe someone in the commission of the act. Otherwise, to make an arrest, a warrant was required. Many states adopted common-law rules of arrest in statutes allowing police officers broad discretion to make warrantless arrests. As with warrantless searches and seizures, the Supreme Court has approved warrantless arrests (1) where crimes are committed in **plain view** of police officers or (2) where officers possess probable cause to make an arrest but exigent circumstances prohibit

---

WARRANT OF ARREST

County of _____. State of _____.

To any peace officer of said state:

Complaint on oath having this day been laid before me that the crime of _____ (designating it generally) has been committed and accusing _____ (naming defendant) thereof, you are therefore commanded forthwith to arrest the above named defendant and bring him/her before me at _____ (naming the place), or in case of my absence or inability to act, before the nearest or most accessible magistrate in this county. Dated at _____ (place) this _____ day of _____, 20 ___.

_____
(signature and full official title of magistrate)

© Cengage Learning

FIGURE 4.1 Typical Form of an Arrest Warrant.

JURISPRUDENCE

Dunaway v. New York, 442 U.S. 200, 99 S.Ct. 2248, 60 L.Ed.2d 824 (1979)

On March 26, 1971, the owner of a pizza parlor in Rochester, New York, was killed during an attempted armed robbery. Acting without a warrant, police took Irving Dunaway into custody and interrogated him in connection with the attempted robbery and murder. Dunaway was not told that he was under arrest, but he was interrogated, he confessed, and he was ultimately convicted. On appeal, Dunaway contended the police officers violated his rights under the Fourth and Fourteenth Amendments when, without probable cause, they seized him and transported him to the police station for interrogation. The state argued that although the police did not have probable cause to make an arrest, the "station-house detention" and interrogation of the suspect could be allowed on the lesser standard of reasonable suspicion. The Supreme Court, however, reversed the conviction, saying that probable cause is necessary to justify a station-house detention and interrogation, irrespective of whether it is termed an "arrest."

them from obtaining a warrant. Absent plain view or compelling exigencies, the need to obtain an arrest warrant is unclear. As a matter of policy, it makes sense for police officers to obtain arrest warrants when possible. However, given the time that it takes to obtain an arrest warrant and the fact that magistrates are not always available around the clock, it is not always feasible for police to obtain warrants before making arrests.

The Supreme Court has upheld the authority of police officers to make warrantless arrests in public, assuming they have probable cause to do so. *United States v. Watson*, 423 U.S. 411, 96 S.Ct. 820, 46 L.Ed.2d 598 (1976). More problematic are warrantless arrests involving the forcible entry of a dwelling. Here, we encounter the classic Fourth Amendment concern for the sanctity of the home. For example, in *Payton v. New York*, 445 U.S. 573, 100 S.Ct. 1371, 63 L.Ed.2d 639 (1980), the Supreme Court held that, absent exigent circumstances, a warrantless, nonconsensual entry into a suspect's home to make a routine felony arrest violates the Fourth Amendment. In a footnote, the Court pointed out that at that time, twenty-three states had laws permitting a warrant-less entry into the home for the purpose of making an arrest, even in the absence of exigent circumstances. 445 U.S. at 598, n. 46, 100 S.Ct. at 1386, n. 46, 63 L.Ed.2d at 658, n. 46. Courts are generally inclined to uphold warrantless entries into homes for the purpose of making an arrest when all of the following conditions are met:

1. There is probable cause to arrest the suspect.
2. The police have good reason to believe the suspect is on the premises.
3. There is good reason to believe the suspect is armed and dangerous.
4. There is a strong probability that the suspect will escape or evidence will be destroyed if the suspect is not soon apprehended.
5. The entry can be effected peaceably.
6. The offense under investigation is a serious felony.

The Right of an Arrestee to a Prompt Appearance before a Magistrate

Although the Supreme Court has recognized the practical necessity of permitting police to make warrantless arrests, it has stressed the need for immediate *ex post facto* judicial review of the detention of a suspect. Writing for the Supreme Court in *Gerstein v. Pugh*, 420 U.S. 103, 95 S.Ct. 854, 43 L.Ed.2d 54 (1975), Justice Potter Stewart observed that "once the suspect is in custody . . . the reasons that justify dispensing with the magistrate's neutral judgment evaporate." 420 U.S. at 114, 95 S.Ct. at 863, 43 L.Ed.2d at 65. When a suspect is in custody pursuant to a warrantless arrest, "the detached judgment of a neutral magistrate is essential if the Fourth Amendment is to furnish meaningful protection from unfounded interference with liberty." 420 U.S. at 114, 95 S.Ct. at 863, 43 L.Ed.2d at 65. In *County of Riverside v. McLaughlin*, 500 U.S. 44, 111 S.Ct. 1661, 114 L.Ed.2d 49 (1991), the Supreme Court ruled that if an arrested person is brought before a magistrate within forty-eight hours, the requirements of the Fourth Amendment are satisfied.

Actually, any person who is arrested, regardless of whether the arrest was based on a warrant, must be brought promptly before a court of law. Although this is not a federal constitutional right in instances where arrests are made pursuant to warrants, all states now have rules that require the police to promptly bring an arrestee before a magistrate. Similarly, as Fed. R. Crim. P. 5(a) states, "A person making an arrest within the United States must take the defendant without unnecessary delay before a magistrate judge, or before a state or local judicial officer as Rule 5(c) provides, unless a statute provides otherwise."

Use of Force by Police Making Arrests

Because suspects frequently resist attempts to take them into custody, police officers often must use force in making arrests. An officer is entitled to use whatever reasonable force is necessary to effect an arrest. Sometimes, the use of force by police is challenged in civil suits seeking damages. Typically, in such cases, the courts have said that in making a lawful arrest, police officers may use such force as necessary to effect the arrest and prevent the escape of the suspect. See, e.g., *Martyn v. Donlin*, 198 A.2d 700 (Conn. 1964). Generally, a police officer has less discretion to use force in apprehending suspected misdemeanants than suspected felons. See, e.g., *City of Mason v. Banks*, 581 S.W.2d 621 (Tenn. 1979). Most states have statutes providing that police officers have the right to require bystanders to assist them in making arrests. See, e.g., West's Ann. Cal. Penal Code § 839. Nearly every state has a law governing the use of force by police attempting to make arrests. The Illinois statute is typical:

(a) A peace officer, or any person he has summoned or directed to assist him, need not retreat or desist from efforts to make a lawful arrest because of resistance or threatened resistance to the arrest. He is justified in the use of any force which he reasonably believes to be necessary to effect the arrest and of any force which he reasonably believes to be necessary to defend himself or another from bodily harm while making the arrest. However, he is justified in using force likely to cause death or great bodily harm only when he reasonably believes that such force is necessary to prevent death or great bodily harm to himself or other such person, or when he reasonably believes both that

1. Such force is necessary to prevent the arrest from being defeated by resistance or escape; and

2. The person to be arrested has committed or attempted a forcible felony which involves the infliction or threatened infliction of great bodily harm or is attempting to escape by use of a deadly weapon, or otherwise indicates that he will endanger human life or inflict great bodily harm unless arrested without delay.

(b) A peace officer making an arrest pursuant to an invalid warrant is justified in the use of any force which he would be justified in using if the warrant were valid, unless he knows that the warrant is invalid. 720 Ill. Comp. Stat. Ann. § 5/7-5(a).

JURISPRUDENCE

Tennessee v. Garner, 471 U.S. 1, 105 S.Ct. 1694, 85 L.Ed.2d 1 (1985)

At the time this case reached the Supreme Court, a Tennessee Statute provided that "if, after a police officer has given notice of an intent to arrest a criminal suspect, and the suspect flees or forcibly resists, 'the officer may use all the necessary means to effect the arrest.'" A Memphis police officer, acting under this statute, shot and killed Garner's teenage son. The teenager was told to halt by the officer, but instead he "fled over a fence at night in the backyard of a house he was suspected of burglarizing." The officer "used deadly force despite being 'reasonably sure' the suspect was unarmed, 17 or 18 years old, and of slight build." As a result, the father filed a lawsuit under 42 U.S.C. § 1983 for violating his son's constitutional rights. The district court held that the statute and the officer's actions were constitutional; however, the Court of Appeals reversed. The Supreme Court, speaking through Justice Byron White, held the Tennessee statute unconstitutional "insofar as it authorizes the use of deadly force against . . . an apparently unarmed, nondangerous fleeing suspect." Under these circumstances, "force may not be used unless necessary to prevent the escape and the officer has probable cause to believe that the suspect poses a significant threat of death or serious physical injury to the officer or others."

In *Tennessee v. Garner*, supra, the Supreme Court struck down a state statute that permitted police to use deadly force against fleeing suspects even when there was no threat to the safety of the officer or the public. This ruling effectively narrowed the discretion of police officers to use force to make arrests and broadened the possibility for civil actions against police for using excessive force.

The Rodney King Episode

Concern over police brutality took center stage in 1991, when the nation viewed on television a videotape of what appeared to be the unnecessarily brutal beating of a motorist, Rodney King, by Los Angeles police officers. In response to public outrage, four police officers involved in the incident were prosecuted by state authorities for assault and battery and related crimes. On the motion of the defense, the trial was moved from Los Angeles to a suburban community. A riot ensued in Los Angeles in April 1992 after the jury returned its verdict of not guilty. In response to the widespread perception that a miscarriage of justice had occurred, the U.S. Justice Department launched its own investigation of the case. In the summer of 1992, a federal grand jury indicted the four officers for violating Rodney King's Fourth Amendment rights. In April 1993, a trial jury returned verdicts of guilty against two of the officers; the other two were acquitted. See, e.g., *Koon v. United States*, 518 U.S. 81, 116 S.Ct. 2035, 135 L.Ed.2d 392 (1996). In 1997, Rodney King was awarded $3.8 million in a civil suit he brought against the City of Los Angeles.

The Amadou Diallo Case

In February 1999, four New York City police officers looking for a serial rapist shot and killed Amadou Diallo, a recent immigrant from the African nation of Guinea. The officers cornered Diallo in the vestibule of his apartment building in the Bronx. It remains unclear as to whether the officers considered Diallo to be a suspect in the rapes. The officers later claimed that they had ordered Diallo to put his hands in the air and that he had not complied but instead turned around and reached into his pocket. The officers claimed that they believed that Diallo was armed and was going for a gun. Reacting immediately, the officers fired forty-one bullets, nine of which struck Diallo. It turned out that Diallo was unarmed. Some speculated that he might have been reaching into his pocket for his identification card. The shooting spawned a wave of protest and demands that the officers be held criminally responsible for Diallo's death. The state of New York charged the four police officers with second-degree murder and reckless endangerment. On the motion of the defense, the trial was moved upstate from the Bronx to Albany. In February 2000, after deliberating for roughly twenty hours, a jury composed of seven white males, one white female, and four African-American females acquitted the police officers on all counts. The verdict prompted protests around the country and rekindled a debate over police treatment of minorities. Although the Diallo case was national news, there have been many such cases around the country. In many such cases, what initially appears to be reckless or wanton use of force by the police appears more understandable when all of the evidence comes to light in court.

Use of Police Dogs to Apprehend Suspects

In addition to using trained dogs to sniff for drugs and other contraband, police often use dogs to assist them in apprehending uncooperative or fleeing suspects. Sometimes the use of a dog to take down a suspect results in serious injury to that person. Police dogs are trained to bite and hold a suspect on the arm. The bite of a German shepherd has a force in the range of 1,200 to 1,600 pounds per square inch. If the bite lasts more than a few seconds, it can result in a severe wound, a fracture, or possibly even the severing of the arm. Of course, police are trained that once the dog has subdued the suspect, the dog is to be called off. The dogs tend to be very well trained and almost always obey immediately when given the command to release the suspect. In an interesting case decided by the U.S. Court of Appeals for the Ninth Circuit in August of 2003, a deputy sheriff sent a police dog into a wooded area to apprehend a suspect who had fled on foot into the woods. Before the deputy dispatched the dog, he yelled into the woods, "This is the Sheriff's Office. You have five seconds to make yourself known, or a police dog will be sent to find you." When the suspect did not respond after five seconds, the deputy sent the dog into the woods. About a minute later loud screaming could be heard from the woods. The deputy moved toward the sound and within about forty-five seconds located the police dog with a firm bite on the suspect's arm. The deputy called off the dog and arrested the suspect, whose badly injured arm required immediate surgery. The suspect eventually brought suit under 42 U.S.C.A. § 1983 against the deputy and the county, claiming that the use of the police dog constituted excessive force in violation of the Fourth Amendment. The federal district judge who tried the case entered judgment in favor of the defendants, holding that the use of the dog was not unreasonable under the circumstances. In a unanimous opinion, the Ninth Circuit agreed. The court noted that the suspect was being sought for a felony, that the deputy had reason to believe the suspect was armed with a knife and therefore posed a danger, and that because it was nighttime the deputy would have had great difficulty in locating the suspect promptly without the assistance of the dog. Given the totality of the circumstances, the court determined that the deputy's use of the police dog was reasonable. *Miller v. Clark County*, 340 F.3d 959 (9th Cir. 2003).

Use of Tasers to Subdue Persons Who Resist Arrest

Taser is the trade name of a stun gun that shoots metal barbs attached to wires. The barbs stick into a person's skin or clothing, whereupon 50,000 volts of electricity are transmitted from the gun via the wires. Tasers are now in wide use among police departments and are certainly effective in incapacitating most suspects who resist arrest. Typically, persons subjected to Taser shocks experience tremendous pain for about five seconds, but in most cases there is no permanent injury. However, a number of persons subjected to Taser shocks have been hospitalized and, according to a February 2003 report by Amnesty International, at least three persons died in the United States in 2002 as the result of being struck by Tasers. Generally, the courts have upheld the use of Tasers as an alternative to more injurious force. For example, in *Ewolski v. City of Brunswick*, 287 F.3d 492 (6th Cir. 2003), a federal appeals court held that use of a Taser to subdue a potentially homicidal individual did not constitute excessive force. Of course, courts will not permit police to use Tasers against resisting suspects when equally effective but less risky measures are readily available.

Arrest of Persons with Disabilities

There are special concerns stemming from police encounters with persons with disabilities. Persons who are deaf or mentally retarded may appear to be uncooperative. Persons experiencing epileptic seizures are likely to be perceived as "drunk and disorderly." Similarly, someone experiencing the effects of hypoglycemia, which is common among diabetics, may appear to be intoxicated. A disabled motorist who reaches behind the seat when stopped by the police may be trying to retrieve a walking assistance device, but this act might be perceived by police as an attempt to retrieve a weapon. Arresting and booking someone confined to a wheelchair poses obvious problems. According to the U.S. Department of Justice, the Americans with Disabilities Act requires public agencies "to make reasonable modifications in their policies, practices, and procedures that are necessary to ensure accessibility for individuals with disabilities, unless making such modifications would fundamentally alter the program or service involved." The U.S. Department of Justice, Civil Rights Division, Disability Rights Section, "Commonly Asked Questions about the Americans with Disabilities Act and Law Enforcement," last revised April 4, 2006. The document recommends modifying the "regular practice of handcuffing arrestees behind their backs, and instead handcuff[ing] deaf individuals in front in order for the person to sign or write notes." The document also suggests that "[s]afe transport of other individuals who use manual or power wheelchairs might require departments to make minor modifications to existing cars or vans, or to use lift-equipped vans or buses."

Citizen's Arrest

citizen's arrest An arrest made by a person who is not a law enforcement officer.

At common law, a private individual could make a **citizen's arrest** without a warrant for a felony or breach of the peace committed in the presence of that individual. The common-law rule prevails in some states; in others, it has been revised by statute. A California law enacted in 1872 broadened the common law in that it permits a private person to make a warrantless arrest in any of three situations:

A private person may arrest another:

1. For a public offense committed or attempted in his presence.
2. When the person arrested has committed a felony, although not in his presence.
3. When a felony has been in fact committed, and he has reasonable cause for believing the person arrested to have committed it. West's Ann. Cal. Penal Code § 837.

Arrests for Minor Traffic Offenses

In most states, a police officer is vested with discretion to make an arrest of or issue a citation to a person who commits a minor traffic violation. Generally, police exercise their discretion by giving the motorist a ticket, yet there is little judicial guidance for the proper action to be taken in such situations. That this area of broad police discretion is subject to abuse was recognized in *State v. Hehman*, 578 P.2d 527 (Wash. 1978), where the Washington Supreme Court ruled that arrests for minor traffic offenses are unjustified if the defendant signs a promise to appear in court as provided by statute. By contrast, an Illinois appellate court upheld the arrest and jailing of a motorist for lacking a front license plate and being unable to produce a driver's license. *People v. Pendleton*, 433 N.E.2d 1076 (Ill. App. 1982).

In *Atwater v. City of Lago Vista*, 532 U.S. 318, 121 S.Ct. 1536, 149 L.Ed.2d 549 (2001), the U.S. Supreme Court ruled that the Fourth Amendment does not forbid a warrantless arrest for a minor traffic offense, specifically a seat belt violation. Writing for the Court, Justice David Souter concluded that

> Atwater's arrest was surely "humiliating," . . . but it was no more "harmful to . . . privacy or . . . physical interests" than the normal custodial arrest. She was handcuffed, placed in a squad car, and taken to the local police station, where officers asked her to remove her shoes, jewelry, and glasses, and to empty her pockets. They then took her photograph and placed her in a cell, alone, for about an hour, after which she was taken before a magistrate, and released on $310 bond. The arrest and booking were inconvenient and embarrassing to Atwater, but not so extraordinary as to violate the Fourth Amendment. 532 U.S. at 354, 121 S.Ct. at 1558, 149 L.Ed.2d at 577.

Four justices dissented, characterizing Atwater's arrest for not wearing a seat belt as a "pointless indignity." Writing for the dissenters, Justice Sandra Day O'Connor opined:

> The majority takes comfort in the lack of evidence of "an epidemic of unnecessary minor-offense arrests." . . . But the relatively small number of published cases dealing with such arrests proves little and should provide little solace. Indeed, as the recent debate over racial profiling demonstrates all too clearly, a relatively minor traffic infraction may often serve as an excuse for stopping and harassing an individual. After today, the arsenal available to any officer extends to a full arrest and the searches permissible concomitant to that arrest. An officer's subjective motivations for making a traffic stop are not relevant considerations in determining the reasonableness of the stop. . . . But it is precisely because these motivations are beyond our purview that we must vigilantly ensure that officers' poststop actions—which are properly within our reach—comport with the Fourth Amendment's guarantee of reasonableness. 532 U.S. at 372, 121 S.Ct. at 1567, 149 L.Ed.2d at 587.

State courts can interpret their state constitutions to provide more protection than does the federal constitution as interpreted in the *Atwater* decision. Perhaps a more feasible solution is for state legislatures to provide that misdemeanor offenses are subject to "ticketing" under a "cite and release" statute. For example, Tennessee law provides that "[a] peace officer who has arrested a person for the commission of a misdemeanor committed in such peace officer's presence . . . shall issue a citation to such arrested person to appear in court in lieu of the continued custody and taking of the arrested person before a magistrate." Tenn. Code Ann. § 40-7-118 (1997). In 1999 the legislature added, "No citation shall be issued under the provisions of this section if . . . [t]he person arrested cannot or will not offer satisfactory evidence of identification, including the providing of a field-administered fingerprint or thumb-print which a peace officer may require to be affixed to any citation. . . ." Tenn. Code Ann. § 40-7-118(c)(3) (Supp. 1999). The state's "cite and release" statute creates a presumptive right to be cited and released for the commission of a misdemeanor. *State v. Walker*, 12 S.W.3d 460 (Tenn. 2000).

Search Incident to Arrest

When making an arrest, police usually conduct a limited search. As we noted in Chapter 3, the Supreme Court has said that such a search incident to arrest must be limited to the body of an arrestee and to the area within that person's immediate control. *Chimel v. California*, 395 U.S. 752, 89 S.Ct. 2034, 23 L.Ed.2d 685 (1969).

Normally, a search incident to arrest takes place after the arrest has been effected. In *Rawlings v. Kentucky*, 448 U.S. 98, 100 S.Ct. 2556, 65 L.Ed.2d 633 (1980); how-ever, the Supreme Court upheld a search incident to arrest even though the search briefly preceded the arrest. The key point is that probable cause to make the arrest must precede the search; police may not use the search as a means to justify the arrest.

The Supreme Court has limited the ability of police to conduct an automobile search incident to arrest when issuing a traffic citation. See, e.g., *Knowles v. Iowa*, 525 U.S. 113, 119 S.Ct. 484, 142 L.Ed.2d 492 (1998). In some instances, police may opt to make an arrest rather than issue a citation so that they can conduct a search of the automobile. See, e.g., *Gustafson v. Florida*, 414 U.S. 260, 94 S.Ct. 488, 38 L.Ed.2d 456 (1973). If a driver is arrested and there is no one else who is authorized to take possession of the vehicle, police will impound the vehicle and thoroughly search its contents. This will often lead to the discovery of incriminating evidence that has been sequestered in the vehicle. There is no Fourth Amendment barrier to using such evidence in a criminal prosecution. *South Dakota v. Opperman*, 428 U.S. 364, 96 S.Ct. 3092, 49 L.Ed.2d 1000 (1976). (For more information on inventory searches of impounded automobiles, see Chapter 3.)

Investigatory Detention

investigatory detention
Brief detention of a sus-pect by a police officer who has reasonable suspicion that criminal activity is afoot.

The second major category of police-citizen encounters involves the so-called stop-and-frisk, discussed in Chapter 3. A more descriptive term for this type of encounter is **investigatory detention**. Police are permitted to detain persons temporarily for questioning as long as they have reasonable suspicion that criminal activity is afoot. If they have reasonable suspicion that the detained person is armed, police may perform a **pat-down search** of the suspect's outer clothing to locate weapons. *Terry v. Ohio*, supra. In conducting the "frisk," police may seize items that plainly feel like contra-band. *Minnesota v. Dickerson*, 508 U.S. 366, 113 S.Ct. 2130, 124 L.Ed.2d 334 (1993).

pat-down search
A manual search by a police officer of the exterior of a suspect's outer garments.

What Constitutes Reasonable Suspicion?

After the U.S. Supreme Court's 1968 decision in *Terry v. Ohio*, supra, the concept of what constitutes "reasonable suspicion" became extremely important both in law enforcement and in criminal procedure in the courts. The concept does not lend itself to a precise definition. In *United States v. Cortez*, 449 U.S. 411, 101 S.Ct. 690, 66 L.Ed.2d 621 (1981), Chief Justice Warren E. Burger said that a trained officer develops a reasonable suspicion that a person is, or is about to be, engaged in criminal activity from the officer's objective observations and from inference and deductions.

Minnesota v. Dickerson, 508 U.S. 366, 113 S.Ct. 2130, 124 L.Ed.2d 334 (1993)

Police officers observed Timothy Dickerson leaving a building known for selling and trafficking cocaine. When the officers approached Dickerson, he seemed to make "evasive actions." Therefore, the police decided to investigate further and told Dickerson to submit to a "pat-down" *Terry* search. The search resulting in finding no weapons, but the officer "felt a small lump" in Dickerson's pocket, "believed it to be a lump of crack cocaine upon examining it with his fingers." The officer "then reached into the pocket and retrieved a small bag of cocaine." Dickerson moved to suppress the evidence at his trial for possession of a controlled substance, but the trial court denied the motion. The Supreme Court reversed the trial court stating that the "police may seize nonthreatening contraband detected through the sense of touch during a protective pat-down search of the sort permitted by *Terry*, so long as the search stays within the bounds marked by *Terry*." The Court refused to accept a "plain feel exception" to *Terry*. According to the Supreme Court, *Terry* "permits a brief stop of a person whose suspicious conduct leads an officer to conclude in light of his experience that criminal activity may be afoot, and a pat-down search of the person for weapons when the officer is justified in believing that the person may be armed and presently dangerous." This is a "protective search" that is "not meant to discover evidence of crime, [and] must be strictly limited to that which is necessary for the discovery of weapons which might be used to harm the officer or others." The Supreme Court explicitly held that if "the protective search goes beyond what is necessary to determine if the suspect is armed, it is no longer valid under *Terry* and its fruits will be suppressed."

In other words, an officer must be able to articulate some legitimate, objective basis for forming suspicion about a person; it cannot be based on whim, caprice, prejudice or even a "hunch."

Thousands of federal and state judicial decisions have applied the standard of reasonable suspicion, often with degrees of variation. However, courts generally agree that the totality of the circumstances of any given scenario must be examined to determine whether a law officer had a reasonable suspicion as a basis for making an investigatory stop. In *United States v. Arvizu*, 534 U.S. 266, 122 S.Ct. 744, 151 L.Ed.2d 740 (2002), the Supreme Court said that courts are not to view in isolation the factors upon which police officers develop reasonable suspicion. Instead, courts should consider all of an officer's observations, giving appropriate weight to any inferences drawn by an officer based on his or her training or experience.

The Length of an Investigatory Detention

The Supreme Court has said that investigatory detentions must be brief (unless, that is, they confirm police suspicions of criminal conduct). *Dunaway v. New York*, 442 U.S. 200, 99 S.Ct. 2248, 60 L.Ed.2d 824 (1979). Nevertheless, the Supreme Court has been disinclined to place an arbitrary time limit on detention. Instead, the Court has considered the purpose of the stop and the reasonableness of the time required for the police to obtain any additional required information. This approach looks at the totality of the circumstances to determine whether there has been an infringement of the suspect's Fourth Amendment rights. In *Florida v. Royer*, 460 U.S. 491, 103 S.Ct. 1319, 75 L.Ed.2d 229 (1983), the Court held that a fifteen-minute detention of a suspect in a police room was unreasonable when the police detained the suspect while they brought his luggage to him. Yet, a twenty-minute detention of a truck driver stopped on suspicion of transporting marijuana was found to be reasonable because the time

---

JURISPRUDENCE

Illinois v. Wardlow, 528 U.S. 119, 120 S.Ct. 673, 145 L.Ed.2d 570 (2000)

Around noon on September 9, 1995, William Wardlow was standing in front of a building in a high crime area in Chicago known for narcotics trafficking. When he saw a caravan of four police cars pass by, he ran through an alley. Officers in one of the patrol cars pursued and eventually stopped him, patted him down in a protective search for weapons, and searched an opaque bag he was holding. They found him in possession of a handgun and arrested him. Wardlow sought to suppress the weapon on the ground that the officers had no reasonable suspicion to stop and frisk him. Therefore, he argued the seizure of the handgun was in violation of the Fourth Amendment. His motion was denied, and he was convicted. The Illinois Supreme Court reversed, holding the stop illegal. On review, the U.S. Supreme Court, in a 5–4 decision, reversed the Illinois Supreme Court. The justices agreed that the "totality of the circumstances" governs in determining if there is reasonable suspicion for the stop, but they disagreed on the application of that test to the factual situation here. Writing for the majority, Chief Justice William Rehnquist found that the officers had a reasonable suspicion based on Wardlow's presence in a high crime area coupled with his headlong, unprovoked flight from the police. Four justices, in an opinion written by Justice John Paul Stevens, disagreed with the majority's conclusion that the Chicago police were justified in stopping Wardlow.

---

was used by police in pursuing a second, related vehicle necessary to the investigation, and the suspect's actions contributed to the delay. *United States v. Sharpe*, 470 U.S. 675, 105 S.Ct. 1568, 84 L.Ed.2d 605 (1985). Consequently, although detention must be brief in stop-and-frisk situations, the time span must be evaluated in light of the totality of circumstances. In *State v. Merklein*, 388 So.2d 218 (Fla. App. 1980), a Florida appellate court said it was reasonable for officers to detain suspects for twenty to forty minutes pending arrival of another officer, witnesses, and the victim of a robbery. The key is whether the police are diligently investigating to confirm or dispel the suspicions that led to the stop. *State v. Werner*, 848 P.2d 11 (N.M. App. 1992).

In *United States v. Mayo*, 394 F.3d 1271 (9th Cir. 2005), the court held that although the duration of detention bears on whether a *Terry* stop is justified, there is no strict time requirement. In *Mayo* the court found that a detention of forty minutes was not unreasonable where after the initial investigation new grounds for suspicion of criminal activity continued to unfold.

When May Police Conduct a Frisk?

Terry stop An encounter between a police officer and a suspect during which the latter is temporarily detained and subjected to a pat-down search for weapons.

A valid **Terry stop** (a synonym for investigatory detention) does not necessarily permit an officer to conduct a frisk. Rather, the need for protecting the police justifies a frisk. Therefore, an officer who undertakes to frisk a suspect must be able to point to specific facts and reasonable inferences to believe that the individual is armed. Initially, a frisk is limited to a pat-down search of an individual's outer garments. If during the pat-down search the officer feels an object that may be a weapon, the officer may seize it. If it turns out that the object is something other than a weapon, it may still be seized if it is contraband. As we have noted, a stop-and-frisk may be based on reasonable suspicion, but absent probable cause, an officer is not justified in simply searching a suspect for contraband when a pat-down does not reveal any weapon-like objects. *Terry v. Ohio*, supra.

In *Ybarra v. Illinois*, 444 U.S. 85, 100 S.Ct. 338, 62 L.Ed.2d 238 (1979), the Supreme Court ruled that because police could not point to any specific facts to support their belief that the suspect was armed and dangerous, they had no grounds for frisking him. The Court has made it amply clear that a frisk must be based on an officer's reasonable suspicion that the suspect is armed rather than on a desire to locate incriminating evidence. *Sibron v. New York*, 392 U.S. 40, 88 S.Ct. 1889, 20 L.Ed.2d 917 (1968). Under the doctrine of plain view (discussed in Chapter 3), however, contraband that is discovered during a legitimate pat-down for weapons may be admissible in evidence. For example, if during the course of a lawful frisk a police officer feels what the officer suspects is a knife concealed in the suspect's pocket, the officer may retrieve the object. If the object turns out to be a metal smoking pipe wrapped inside a plastic bag containing crack cocaine, the crack would most likely be admissible as evidence of crime under the plain-view doctrine.

Investigatory Automobile Stops

Lower federal and state courts have routinely applied the stop-and-frisk doctrine to stops of vehicles as well as individuals. In many instances, this was stipulated in state statutes codifying the *Terry* standard; otherwise, it was based on the *Terry* rationale. A traffic stop involves a seizure of the driver under the Fourth Amendment "even though the purpose of the stop is limited and the resulting detention quite brief." Therefore, the police must have reasonable suspicion that criminal activity is afoot before stopping a motor vehicle. *Delaware v. Prouse*, 440 U.S. 648, 653, 99 S.Ct. 1391, 59 L.Ed.2d 660 (1979).

Normal police practice is for the officer who makes an automobile stop to examine the suspect's driver's license, vehicle registration, and license plate. A rapid computer check can reveal whether there are any outstanding warrants on the driver, whether the license has been suspended or revoked, and whether the automobile has been reported stolen. During the stop, the officer also visually scans the driver, any passengers, and any objects in plain view. Such visual scans sometimes provide probable cause to make an arrest or conduct a warrantless automobile search.

In *Michigan v. Long*, 463 U.S. 1032, 103 S.Ct. 3469, 77 L.Ed.2d 1201 (1983), the Supreme Court held that "the search of the passenger compartment of an automobile, limited to those areas in which a weapon may be placed or hidden, is permissible if the police officer possesses a reasonable belief based on 'specific and articulable facts which, taken together with the rational inferences from those facts, reasonably warrant' the officers in believing that the suspect is dangerous and the suspect may gain immediate control of weapons." Among these are the knowledge, expertise, and experience of the officer; the physical appearance of a person or vehicle as fitting the description of a person or vehicle wanted for a crime; the item and place where the suspect or vehicle is seen; and their nearness to the scene of a crime. In addition, the suspect's demeanor and any furtive gestures or attempts to flee are relevant considerations. In *Arizona v. Gant*, 556 U.S. 332, 129 S.Ct. 1710, 173 L.Ed.2d 485 (2009), the Supreme Court held that

> Police may search a vehicle incident to a recent occupant's arrest only if the arrestee is within reaching distance of the passenger compartment at the time of the search or it is reasonable to believe the vehicle contains evidence of the offense of arrest. When these justifications are absent, a search of an arrestee's vehicle will be unreasonable unless police obtain a warrant or show that another exception to the warrant requirement applies.

Automobile Stops Based on Anonymous Tips

anonymous tip Information given to the police by an unknown individual.

An issue that often comes before appellate courts is whether reasonable suspicion can be developed on the basis of an **anonymous tip**. In *Alabama v. White*, 496 U.S. 325, 110 S.Ct. 2412, 110 L.Ed.2d 621 (1990), the U.S. Supreme Court reviewed a case where the police stopped a vehicle based on an anonymous phone tip. The Court held that an anonymous tip corroborated by independent police work was sufficient to establish a reasonable suspicion to make an investigatory stop of the vehicle described by the one who gave police the tip.

Since the Supreme Court's decision in *Alabama v. White*, state courts have been addressing cases where police have made an investigatory stop based on an anonymous tip. State courts have been disinclined to approve an investigatory stop where the anonymous tip lacks indicia of credibility and is not sufficiently verified by independent evidence. See, e.g., *State v. Hjelmstad*, 535 N.W.2d 663 (Minn. App. 1995). Nevertheless, many state courts now agree that information supplied by an anonymous source can warrant an investigatory stop if verified by sufficient independent evidence of criminal activity. See, e.g., *People v. George*, 914 P.2d 367 (Colo. 1996). In 2000, the Supreme Court of Pennsylvania held that an uncorroborated anonymous tip alleging a defendant was selling marijuana did not create a reasonable suspicion that would justify an investigatory stop of the defendant's car. *Commonwealth v. Goodwin*, 750 A.2d 795 (Pa. 2000).

Pretextual Automobile Stops

pretextual stops An incident in which police stop a suspicious vehicle on the pretext of a motor vehicle infraction.

Police have been known to use a minor or technical motor vehicle infraction as a pretext for stopping a vehicle and conducting an investigatory detention. In the past, most federal courts ruled that the police may not use minor traffic violations to justify **pretextual stops**. For example, in *United States v. Smith*, 799 F.2d 704

CASE-IN-POINT

An Anonymous Tip as the Basis of Reasonable Suspicion

Police in Memphis, Tennessee, received an anonymous telephone tip through a "drug hotline" that a number of African-American men were dealing drugs at a particular street corner known to police as a "hot spot" for drug sales. When an officer and his partner approached the area, they saw a group of around eight African-American males standing by the curb. When the officers approached the group, the men began to walk away. One of the men made a throwing motion toward the bushes. At this point the officers instructed the men to stop, take their hands out of their pockets, and place them on a nearby vehicle. A pat-down search of one of the men revealed a .40 caliber revolver tucked into his waistband. The man, who had been previously convicted of a felony, was

subsequently convicted in federal court of violating 18 U.S.C. § 922(g), which prohibits the possession of a firearm by a convicted felon. In reversing the defendant's conviction, the U.S. Court of Appeals for the Sixth Circuit held that the anonymous tip the police received failed to provide sufficient specific information in support of reasonable suspicion and that, in the absence of the tip, the defendant's behavior was insufficient to support reasonable suspicion. One judge dissented, arguing that the court's approach departed from that required by the Supreme Court's 2002 decision in *United States v. Arvizu*, supra, which instructs lower courts not to consider in isolation the factors that support determinations of reasonable suspicion.

United States v. Patterson, 340 F.3d 368 (6th Cir. 2003).

(11th Cir. 1986), the court said the appropriate analysis was whether a reasonable officer would have stopped the car absent an additional invalid purpose. Many state courts followed this approach.

In *Whren v. United States*, 517 U.S. 806, 116 S.Ct. 1769, 135 L.Ed.2d 89 (1996), the U.S. Supreme Court ruled that the motives of an officer in stopping a vehicle are irrelevant as long as there is an objective basis for the stop. Thus, the Court held there is no violation of the Fourth Amendment as long as there is probable cause to believe that even a minor violation has taken place. It remains to be seen whether the states, which may apply a stricter standard under their constitutions, will follow the federal standard.

Can Police Require Drivers and Passengers to Exit Their Vehicles?

During automobile stops, police routinely request that drivers exit their cars. Sometimes they also request that passengers exit. These practices are justified by the need to protect police officers from weapons that might be concealed inside the passenger compartment of a stopped vehicle. In upholding these practices, the U.S. Supreme Court noted that in 1994 eleven police officers were killed and more than five thousand officers assaulted during traffic stops. *Maryland v. Wilson*, 519 U.S. 408, 117 S.Ct. 882, 137 L.Ed.2d 41 (1997). Of course, when drivers and passengers are required to exit their automobiles, police often discover contraband or observe behavior that indicates intoxication. Such was the case in *Maryland v. Wilson*, where a passenger who had been ordered to exit a vehicle dropped a quantity of crack cocaine onto the ground. This evidence was used to secure a conviction for possession with intent to distribute; ultimately, the conviction was sustained by the Supreme Court. For the duration of a traffic stop, a police officer effectively seizes everyone in the vehicle. *Brendlin v. California*, 551 U.S. 249, 127 S.Ct. 2400, 168 L.Ed.2d 132 (2007). It followed therefore that in *Arizona v. Johnson*, 555 U.S. 323, 129 S.Ct. 781, 172 L.Ed.2d 694 (2009), the Supreme Court confirmed that during

---

JURISPRUDENCE

Whren v. United States, 517 U.S. 806, 116 S.Ct. 1769, 135 L.Ed.2d 89 (1996)

Police were traveling in an unmarked police vehicle through a "high drug area" when they observed a truck waiting at a stop sign for an unusually long time. After some time, "the truck turned without signaling and sped off at an 'unreasonable' speed." The officers stopped the truck with the intention of giving the driver a warning; however, when they approached the truck, they saw "plastic bags of crack cocaine in Whren's hands and arrested him. Whren moved to suppress the drugs on the grounds that the officers did not have "reasonable suspicion or probable cause to believe" that Whren was "engaged in illegal drug-dealing activity, and that the officers' traffic-violation

ground for stopping the truck was pretextual." The trial court denied the motion to suppress. The Supreme Court held that the "temporary detention of a motorist upon probable cause to believe that he has violated the traffic laws does not violate the Fourth Amendment's prohibition against unreasonable seizures, even if a reasonable officer would not have stopped the motorist absent some additional law enforcement objective." As long as the officer has probable cause to believe a traffic law has been violated, the detention of the motorist is reasonable. Furthermore, the Court held that "ulterior motives" will not invalidate police conduct on their own because "subjective intentions play no role in ordinary, probable-cause Fourth Amendment analysis."

a traffic stop both the driver and passengers are lawfully detained. Accordingly, an officer may, without violating the Fourth Amendment, ask the driver and all passengers to exit the vehicle and submit to a frisk on reasonable grounds that they may be armed and dangerous.

Drug Courier Profiles

drug courier profiles Sets of characteristics that are believed to typify drug couriers.

In recent years, police have developed **drug courier profiles** based on typical characteristics and behaviors of drug smugglers. The profiles include such factors as paying cash for airline tickets, taking short trips to drug-source cities, not checking luggage, and appearing nervous. Police often use these profiles to identify and detain suspected drug couriers, a controversial practice that has resulted in disparate court decisions. As we pointed out in Chapter 3, the Supreme Court has held that fitting a drug courier profile is not by itself sufficient to constitute the reasonable suspicion necessary to allow police to detain an airline passenger. *Reid v. Georgia*, 448 U.S. 438, 100 S.Ct. 2752, 65 L.Ed.2d 890 (1980). The critical question is whether the behavior of the suspect is inherently suspicious. In 1989, the Supreme Court upheld an investigative stop of an air passenger for which a number of circumstances, including the use of the profile, furnished the police a reasonable suspicion of criminal activity. Although the Court found that any one of the several factors relied on by the police may have been consistent with innocent travel, it observed that the evaluation of the stop requires a consideration of the "totality of the circumstances." *United States v. Sokolow*, 490 U.S. 1, 109 S.Ct. 1581, 104 L.Ed.2d 1 (1989).

Although the Supreme Court has upheld the use of profiles in locating suspicious persons, courts must remain on guard against abuse of the practice. In 1990, a Minnesota appellate court reversed a conviction in which the defendant, who was in an automobile, had been stopped not on the basis of a particular suspicion but because the driver's behavior loosely fit the police profile of a person looking for prostitutes. In rejecting the use of the profile, the court distinguished the case from *Sokolow*, supra, saying that "the observable facts taken together do not approach the composite bundle available to the DEA in *Sokolow*." *City of St. Paul v. Uber*, 450

◻ JURISPRUDENCE

United States v. Sokolow, 490 U.S. 1, 109 S.Ct. 1581, 104 L.Ed.2d 1 (1989)

When Drug Enforcement Agents stopped Andrew Sokolow at the Honolulu International Airport, agents found 1,063 grams of cocaine in his carry-on luggage. Prior to apprehending Sokolow, agents discovered during the course of an investigation that he paid cash for two round-trip plane tickets, traveled under a name that did not match the name under which his telephone number was listed, travelled to Miami, a city known for illicit drugs, stayed in Miami for only forty-eight hours when a trip from Hawaii takes twenty hours, appeared nervous during the flight, and failed to check any luggage. Sokolow was subsequently indicted for possession with intent to distribute cocaine. Sokolow moved to suppress the evidence; however, the trial court denied the motion on the grounds that the stop was justified by a reasonable suspicion that he was engaged in criminal activity, as required by the Fourth Amendment. The Supreme Court agreed that there was sufficient reasonable suspicion to believe Sokolow was transporting illegal drugs when they detained him; thus, the stop was justified under the premise of *Terry v. Ohio*. The Court said that the reasonableness of the stop does not turn on whether the police used the least restrictive means, but rather whether the stop was reasonable under the circumstances.

N.W.2d 623, 626 (Minn. App. 1990). The court concluded that "we cannot sustain what was, in effect, a random stop." 450 N.W.2d at 629.

Racial Profiling

racial profiling Practice of singling out members of minority groups by law-enforcement officers for purposes of investigation.

Recent years have seen a continuing controversy over **racial profiling**, a term that is loosely applied to a variety of police practices that are alleged to be racially biased. The Department of Justice defines racial profiling as "any police-initiated action that relies on the race, ethnicity or national origin rather than the behavior of an individual or information that leads the police to a particular individual who has been identified as being, or having been, engaged in criminal activity." Deborah Ramirez, Jack McDevitt, and Amy Farrell, *A Resource Guide on Racial Profiling Data Collection Systems: Promising Practices and Lessons Learned*, Washington, D.C.: U.S. Department of Justice, 2000, p. 3.

Most of the debate over racial profiling has focused on motor vehicle stops. The sarcastic phrase "driving while black" has been used to denote what critics allege to be a widespread police practice of stopping African-American motorists solely or primarily based on their race. The movement to halt racial profiling has taken both legislative and judicial directions. Several state legislatures have passed laws to require data collection for police stops, while defendants who contend they were stopped on the basis of race have sought to dismiss charges arising out of police stops, arguing they were denied due process and equal protection of the laws. Others have sought and won relief through civil litigation under 42 U.S.C.A. § 1983. See, e.g., *National Congress of Puerto Rican Rights v. City of New York*, 191 F.R.D. 52 (S.D.N.Y. 1999).

In the spring of 2010 controversy erupted over a proposed Arizona law (S.B. 1070) that provided, among other things, "[f]or any lawful contact made by a law enforcement official or a law enforcement agency . . . where reasonable suspicion exists that the person is an alien who is unlawfully present in the United States, a reasonable attempt shall be made, when practicable, to determine the immigration status of the person. . . ." Critics claimed that the new law would encourage racial profiling in that police would target persons who appeared to be Hispanic. On May 19, 2010, President Obama attacked the bill, saying, "In the United States of America, no law-abiding person—be they an American citizen, a legal immigrant, or a visitor or tourist from Mexico—should be subject to suspicion simply because of what they look like." Despite the President's protestations, the Arizona legislature enacted the law anyway. On July 6, the U.S. Department of Justice filed suit in federal court against the state of Arizona and Arizona's governor, claiming that S.B. 1070 was a usurpation of the federal government's authority to regulate immigration. In 2012, the Supreme Court upheld the controversial provision pending a full hearing in the federal district court regarding its compatibility with federal law. *Arizona v. United States*, 567 U.S. ___, 132 S.Ct. 2492, 183 L.Ed.2d 351 (2012). As this book was being completed, the fate of S.B. 1070 was still very much in doubt.

In the summer of 2013, a federal judge struck down New York City's stop-and-frisk policy, a major element of Mayor Michael Bloomberg's crime-fighting program. Judge Shira A. Scheindlin found that NYPD had a policy of indirect racial profiling under which officers routinely stopped African-Americans and Hispanics without reasonable suspicion. *Floyd v. City of New York*, ___ F.Supp. ___ (SDNY 2013). The City had argued that by removing thousands of illegal guns from the streets, the stop-and-frisk policy had saved the lives of numerous African-American and Hispanic men who might otherwise have been victims of gun violence. In a lengthy opinion, Judge

Scheindlin noted that the number of stops increased dramatically in recent years, even as crime rates declined. She ordered NYPD to require officers walking the beat in certain precincts to wear cameras to record their encounters with citizens. For its part, the City vowed to appeal. Interestingly, officials in other cities plagued by gang violence had been considering emulating New York City's program, which despite its legal shortcomings, appeared to be effective in reducing murder, armed robbery and other violent crime in the Big Apple.

Roadblocks, Sobriety Checkpoints, and Drug Checkpoints

roadblocks Barriers set up by police to stop motorists.

The third major category of police–citizen encounters includes **roadblocks** and sobriety checkpoints. Police often set up roadblocks for apprehending fleeing suspects, conducting field sobriety tests, or even for merely performing safety checks on automobiles. In addition to locating drunk drivers, roadblocks often lead to the discovery of illegal weapons, drugs, and other contraband. Because roadblocks do constitute a restraint on the liberty of the motorist, courts have held that they are susceptible to challenge under the Fourth Amendment. Therefore, police agencies must take care that roadblocks are established and operated according to guidelines that minimize the inconvenience to motorists and constrain the exercise of discretion by police officers.

In *Michigan Dept. of State Police v. Sitz*, 496 U.S. 444, 110 S.Ct. 2481, 110 L.Ed.2d 412 (1990), the Supreme Court recognized that a Fourth Amendment "seizure" occurs when a vehicle is stopped at a checkpoint but upheld the use of roadblocks for conducting field sobriety tests. In *Sitz*, the Michigan State Police operated a pilot roadblock program under guidelines drafted by an advisory committee. The guidelines set forth procedures governing checkpoint operations, site selection, and publicity. The sobriety checkpoints operated essentially as follows: Police set up roadblocks at predetermined points along state highways. All vehicles passing through the checkpoints were stopped, and drivers were briefly observed for signs of intoxication. The average length of the stop was less than thirty seconds, except where drivers appeared to be intoxicated. These drivers were instructed to pull their vehicles over to the side of the road for a license and registration check and, if indicated, a field sobriety test. Drivers who failed the test were placed under arrest. At one checkpoint, which was in operation for seventy-five minutes, 126 vehicles were stopped. Two drivers were given field sobriety tests, and one was arrested for driving under the influence of alcohol. One vehicle failed to stop at the roadblock but was apprehended and its driver arrested for driving under the influence.

Drug Checkpoints

After the Supreme Court's 1990 decision upholding sobriety checkpoints, some police departments began running drug checkpoints that operated in much the same way but often involved the use of drug-sniffing dogs. In 2000, the U.S. Supreme Court invalidated an Indianapolis police practice of establishing checkpoints primarily for the purpose of detecting illegal drugs. Writing for the Court, Justice Sandra Day O'Connor distinguished between sobriety checkpoints, which are geared toward elimination of an imminent public safety threat, and drug checkpoints designed

---

JURISPRUDENCE

City of Indianapolis v. Edmond, 531 U.S. 32, 121 S.Ct 447, 148 L.Ed.2d 333 (2000)

In August 1998, the City of Indianapolis began to operate vehicle checkpoints in an effort to interdict unlawful drugs. The overall "hit rate" of the program was approximately 9 percent. The checkpoint locations were predetermined weeks in advance based on area crime statistics and traffic flow. The checkpoints were conducted during daylight hours and were identified with lighted signs reading, NARCOTICS CHECKPOINT ___ MILE AHEAD, NARCOTICS K-9 IN USE, BE PREPARED TO STOP. Respondent James

Edmonds was stopped at a checkpoint and later filed a motion for injunctive relief claiming that the roadblocks violated the Fourth Amendment of the Constitution. The federal district court denied the motion for injunctive relief; however, the Court of Appeals for the Seventh Circuit reversed, holding that the checkpoints contravened the Fourth Amendment. The Supreme Court affirmed holding the checkpoints in violation of the Fourth Amendment because their primary purpose was indistinguishable from general interest crime control. The Court refused to validate suspicionless stops.

---

primarily to snare traffickers in contraband. *City of Indianapolis v. Edmond*, 531 U.S. 32, 121 S.Ct 447, 148 L.Ed.2d 333 (2000).

An interesting (and often productive) variation of the drug checkpoint procedure is for the police to place a sign on an interstate highway indicating NOTICE: DRUG CHECKPOINT AHEAD. The sign is placed just before an exit, tempting drivers who wish to avoid the checkpoint to take the exit. Of course, there really is no drug checkpoint on the interstate highway. Rather, police are waiting at the bottom of the exit ramp to see who takes the exit. Typically, the exit chosen is one where there is little or no commercial activity and no connection to a major road. When a van with out-of-state plates takes the exit, is this inherently suspicious? Can police assume that the only reason the driver took the exit was to avoid the spurious drug checkpoint? Can police stop this vehicle, order the driver and passengers to exit the vehicle, and bring out a drug-sniffing canine? Federal courts have reached different conclusions on this issue. For example, in *United States v. Huguenin*, 154 F.3d 547 (6th Cir. 1998), the Sixth Circuit held that it was a pretextual seizure for police to selectively detain motorists without a traffic violation or reasonable suspicion of drug trafficking. But in *United States v. Brugal*, 209 F.3d 353 (4th Cir. 2000), the Fourth Circuit held that the totality of factors used by police in screening motorists eliminated a substantial portion of innocent travelers and that the conduct of the particular motorist involved gave officers reasonable suspicion that justified instructing him to pull his vehicle over.

After the Supreme Court's decision in the Indianapolis case, some law enforcement agencies expressed their intention to continue running drug checkpoints featuring the deceptive tactic described above. In their view, a drug checkpoint of this type is distinguishable from that which was invalidated in the Indianapolis case. It will be interesting to see if the Supreme Court examines this practice and whether it recognizes a distinction that can salvage the constitutionality of the deceptive drug checkpoint.

In *Illinois v. Lidster*, 540 U.S. 419, 124 S.Ct. 885, 157 L.Ed.2d 843 (2004), the Supreme Court reversed a state supreme court decision striking down a police checkpoint based on *Indianapolis v. Edmond*, supra. Police in Lombard, Illinois, set up a checkpoint along a highway, stopping motorists to ask them if they knew anything about a recent hit-and-run accident. Approaching the checkpoint in his minivan, Lidster swerved and nearly hit a police officer. Detecting the odor of alcohol,

The Use of Roadblocks

CASE-IN-POINT

On August 8, 1992, Deputy Sheriff Robert Starnes stopped Sarah Hutton Downey at a highway roadblock on Hixson Pike in Hamilton County, Tennessee. The roadblock had been set up without advance publicity by Lt. Ronnie Hill of the Tennessee Highway Patrol, who was assisted by members of the Chattanooga Police Department DUI task force, the Hamilton County DUI task force, and auxiliary sheriff's officers. Hill did not obtain the approval of a superior officer regarding the establishment, time, or location of the roadblock. When Deputy Starnes checked Downey's driver's license, he smelled an odor of alcohol. After field sobriety testing, he arrested her for driving under the influence.

At trial, evidence revealed the defendant did nothing to arouse the deputy's suspicion as she approached the roadblock; rather, she was stopped for the same purpose and in the same manner as other motorists. The defendant moved to suppress the evidence on grounds there was no suspicion that a crime had been committed before the stop, and therefore her detention violated the section of the state constitution that parallels the Fourth Amendment to the U.S. Constitution. The trial court denied her motion. The Court of Criminal Appeals ruled that use of the roadblock was not a per se violation of the state constitution, but in this case no General Order was in effect granting authority to set up highway roadblocks. Thus, the court ruled that the defendant's arrest constituted an unreasonable seizure. The Tennessee Supreme Court granted review to determine the constitutionality of highway roadblocks.

Referring to the U.S. Supreme Court's 1990 decision in *Michigan Dept. of State Police v. Sitz*, the court agreed that highway roadblocks established and operated in accordance with predetermined guidelines do not violate the Tennessee Constitution. But here, the court observed, "[T]he decision to set up a roadblock was made by an officer in the field . . . the site selected for the roadblock and the procedure to be used in operating the roadblock were matters left to the discretion of an officer in the field. No supervisory authority was sought or obtained, and no administrative decisions were made with regard to these critical factors." Because the roadblock was not conducted in accordance with proper, predetermined operational guidelines and supervisory authority, the court found it constituted an unreasonable seizure under the Tennessee Constitution and affirmed the Court of Criminal Appeals.

State v. Downey, 945 S.W.2d 102 (Tenn. 1997).

police performed a field sobriety test, determined that Lidster was impaired, and placed him under arrest. Lidster challenged his DUI conviction on the ground that the government had obtained evidence through use of a checkpoint stop that violated the Fourth Amendment. The Illinois appellate courts agreed that, based on *Indianapolis v. Edmond*, the automobile stop was unconstitutional. The U.S. Supreme Court reversed, making clear in an opinion by Justice Stephen Breyer that *Indianapolis v. Edmond* was not intended to prevent the police from using checkpoints to obtain the motoring public's assistance in locating the perpetrator of a crime involving a traffic accident.

Requests for Information or Identification

The lowest level of police–citizen encounter takes place when a police officer approaches an individual in public and asks questions or requests identification. Is there a legal duty to cooperate with the police in such instances? In a concurring opinion in *Terry v. Ohio*, supra, Justice Byron White observed:

There is nothing in the Constitution which prevents a policeman from addressing questions to anyone on the streets. Absent special circumstances, the person approached may not be detained or frisked but may refuse to cooperate and go on his way. However, given the proper circumstances . . . the person may be briefly detained against his will while pertinent questions are directed to him. Of course, the person stopped is not obliged to answer, answers may not be compelled, and refusal to answer furnishes no basis for an arrest, although it may alert the officer to the need for continued observation. 392 U.S. at 34, 88 S.Ct. at 1886, 20 L.Ed.2d at 913.

Historically, many states had laws making it a misdemeanor for persons to refuse to identify themselves when asked to do so by police. In *Brown v. Texas*, 443 U.S. 47, 99 S.Ct. 2637, 61 L.Ed.2d 357 (1979), the Supreme Court reviewed the constitutionality of this provision of a Texas statute: "A person commits an offense if he intentionally refuses to report or gives a false report of his name and residence address to a peace officer who has lawfully stopped him and requested the information." The Court held that the statute could not be constitutionally applied in the absence of reasonable suspicion that the individual who was asked for identification was engaged in or had engaged in criminal conduct.

In *Kolender v. Lawson*, 461 U.S. 352, 103 S.Ct. 1855, 75 L.Ed.2d 903 (1983), the Supreme Court reviewed a California statute that required persons who were loitering or wandering on the streets to provide a "credible and reliable" identification and to account for their presence when requested to do so by a police officer. The Court found that the statute was "unconstitutionally vague on its face because it encourages arbitrary enforcement by failing to describe with sufficient particularity what a suspect must do in order to satisfy the statute." 461 U.S. at 361, 103 S.Ct. at 1860, 75 L.Ed.2d at 911.

Over the last two decades, a number of states have enacted "stop-and-identify" statutes. These laws make it a misdemeanor for suspect to refuse to identify himself or herself during a valid police stop or detention. One such law, Nevada Revised Statute § 171.123(3), was upheld by the U.S. Supreme Court in *Hiibel v. Sixth Judicial District Court of Nevada*, 542 U.S. 177, 124 S.Ct. 2451, 159 L.Ed.2d 292 (2004). The decision was close, however, with four justices voting to strike down the law. For the majority, the determining factor appeared to be that the law only required suspects to identify themselves during a valid *Terry*-stop.

CASE-IN-POINT

Validity of an Ordinance Requiring Self-Identification

Section 17-13 of the Arlington, Virginia, County Code provides that "[i]t shall be unlawful for any person at a public place . . . to refuse to identify himself by name and address at the request of a uniformed police officer . . . if the surrounding circumstances are such as to indicate to a reasonable man that the public safety requires such identification." The defendant was convicted of failing to identify himself at the request of a police officer and appealed. The Virginia Supreme Court held that the police validly stopped the defendant under a *Terry v. Ohio* standard and that the "stop and identify" provision in the county code did not violate the Fourth Amendment. The court distinguished the case from the statute the U.S. Supreme Court struck down in *Kolender v. Lawson*, saying that the California statute at issue there required an individual to provide a credible and reliable identification and required a person to account for his or her presence.

Jones v. Commonwealth of Virginia, 334 S.E.2d 536 (Va. 1985).

Hiibel v. Sixth Judicial Dist. Court of Nevada, 542 U.S. 177, 124 S.Ct. 2451, 159 L.Ed.2d 292 (2004)

Larry D. Hiibel was arrested after telling a deputy sheriff that he did not have to reveal his name or show any identification during his encounter with law enforcement officers. Hiibel was convicted under Nevada Revised Statute § 171.123(3), which authorizes *Terry* stops and provides, "Any person so detained shall identify himself, but may not be compelled to answer any other inquiry of any peace officer." After the Nevada Supreme Court upheld his conviction in 2002, the U.S. Supreme Court granted review. In a 5–4 decision in the Court upheld the statute and affirmed Hiibel's conviction. Justice Anthony Kennedy, writing for the Court, pointed out that there was no issue here as to the validity of the *Terry* stop. Justice Kennedy then explained that unlike the Court's 1983 decision in *Kolender v. Lawson*, supra, where the law required a suspect to give an officer "credible and reliable" identification when asked to identify himself, the Nevada statute only required

that a suspect disclose his or her name. Here, the officer's request for identification was reasonably related to circumstances justifying the *Terry* stop. Thus, the officer's request was a commonsense inquiry, and Hiibel's arrest for failure to comply with the "stop and identify" law did not violate Fourth Amendment prohibition against unreasonable searches and seizures. Further, the Court held that the Nevada law did not violate Hiibel's Fifth Amendment rights against self-incrimination as there was no showing that disclosure of his name presented any reasonable danger of incrimination. Justice John Paul Stevens dissented on the grounds that the statute violates the Fifth Amendment privilege against self-incrimination. Also dissenting, Justices Stephen Breyer, David Souter, and Ruth Bader Ginsburg argued that while an officer is permitted to stop a suspect and ask a moderate number of questions in a *Terry* stop without having "probable cause" that the Court's Fourth Amendment precedents invalidate laws that compel responses to police questioning.

Interrogation and Confessions

Although the courts have long recognized the need for police interrogation of suspects, they have also recognized the potential for abuse that is inherent in the practice of incommunicado interrogation. At early common law, any confession was admissible even if extracted from the accused by torture. As the common law progressed, judges came to insist on proof that a confession was made voluntarily before it could be admitted in evidence.

In 1897, the Supreme Court held that to force a suspect to confess violates the Self-Incrimination Clause of the Fifth Amendment. *Bram v. United States*, 168 U.S. 532, 18 S.Ct. 183, 42 L.Ed. 568. In 1936, the Court held that a **coerced confession** deprived a defendant in a state criminal case of due process of law as guaranteed by the Fourteenth Amendment. *Brown v. Mississippi*, 297 U.S. 278, 56 S.Ct. 461, 80 L.Ed. 682 (1936). In 1964, the Self-Incrimination Clause was made applicable to state criminal prosecutions. *Malloy v. Hogan*, 378 U.S. 1, 84 S.Ct. 1489, 12 L.Ed.2d 653 (1964). As a result, federal and state police are held to the same standards in evaluating the voluntariness of confessions of guilt. In *Malloy*, the Court said that the Fifth Amendment prohibits the extraction of a confession by "exertion of any improper influence." 378 U.S. at 7, 84 S.Ct. at 1493, 12 L.Ed.2d at 659. A confession is voluntary when it is made with knowledge of its nature and consequences and without duress or inducement. *United States v. Carignan*, 342 U.S. 36, 72 S.Ct. 97, 96 L.Ed. 48 (1951).

coerced confession
A confession or other incriminating statements obtained from a suspect by police through force, violence, threats, intimidation, or undue psychological pressure.

Coerced Confessions

As an example of psychological coercion, a confession was ruled involuntary where a defendant was incarcerated and subjected to questioning over a four-day period. The defendant's relatives were denied permission to see him, and he was unable to communicate with anyone outside the jail. At one point during the interrogation, the defendant was forced to hold for twenty-five minutes a gory picture of the deceased lying in a pool of blood.

Davis v. State, 308 S.W.2d 880, 882 (Tex. Crim. App. 1957).

In *Escobedo v. Illinois*, 378 U.S. 478, 84 S.Ct. 1758, 12 L.Ed.2d 977 (1964), the Supreme Court recognized the right of suspects to have counsel present during interrogation. Anticipating the criticism that the Court's decision would hamper law enforcement, Justice Arthur Goldberg observed the following: "If the exercise of constitutional rights will thwart the effectiveness of a system of law enforcement, then there is something very wrong with that system." However, the Court's work in this area was not finished. Two years later, in its landmark decision in *Miranda v. Arizona*, 384 U.S. 436, 86 S.Ct. 1602, 16 L.Ed.2d 694 (1966), the Supreme Court held that before interrogating suspects who are in custody, police must warn them of their right to remain silent and their right to have counsel present during questioning. The typical form of the ***Miranda* warnings** used by law enforcement is as follows:

> You are under arrest. You have the right to remain silent. Anything you say can and will be used against you in a court of law. You are entitled to have an attorney present during questioning. If you cannot afford an attorney, one will be appointed to represent you.

Unless these warnings have been given, no statement by the suspect may be used in evidence, subject to certain narrow exceptions.

The *Miranda* decision was severely criticized by law enforcement interests when it was handed down in 1966. But now it is accepted, even supported, by most law enforcement agencies and has been integrated into routine police procedure. It is also firmly established in the Supreme Court's jurisprudence, as evidenced by the Court's recent decision in *United States v. Dickerson* (2000).

Miranda **warnings** Based on the Supreme Court's decision in *Miranda v. Arizona* (1966), these warnings are given by police to individuals who are taken into custody before they are interrogated. The warnings inform persons in custody that they have the right to remain silent and to have a lawyer present during questioning and that anything they say can and will be used against them in a court of law.

The Fruit of the Poisonous Tree Doctrine

The *Miranda* decision essentially established an exclusionary rule applicable to statements made by suspects during custodial interrogation. But the loss of a confession or statement may have consequences for other evidence gathered by the police. Under the doctrine of the fruit of the poisonous tree, evidence that is derived from inadmissible evidence is likewise inadmissible. *Wong Sun v. United States*, 371 U.S. 471, 83 S.Ct. 407, 9 L.Ed.2d 441 (1963). For example, if police learn of the location of a weapon used in the commission of a crime by interrogating a suspect who is in custody, that weapon is considered **derivative evidence**. If the police failed to provide the *Miranda* warnings, not only the suspect's responses to their questions but also the weapon discovered as the fruit of the interrogation are tainted. On the other hand, if the physical evidence was located on the basis of independently and lawfully obtained information, it may be admissible under the **independent source doctrine**.

derivative evidence Evidence that is derived from or obtained only as a result of other evidence.

independent source doctrine The doctrine that permits evidence to be admitted at trial as long as it was obtained independently from illegally obtained evidence.

JURISPRUDENCE

Miranda v. Arizona, 384 U.S. 436, 86 S.Ct. 1602, 16 L.Ed.2d 694 (1966)

Police arrested Ernesto Miranda, a twenty-three-year-old indigent with a ninth grade education, and charged him with raping an eighteen-year-old girl. At the police station, the victim picked Miranda out of a lineup. Two officers then took Miranda to a room where they interrogated him. After first denying his guilt, Miranda eventually confessed to the crime. Following his conviction, Miranda appealed on the ground that his confession had been coerced. The Supreme Court granted review, consolidating Miranda's appeal with three other cases involving the admissibility of confessions. The Court reversed Miranda's conviction, holding that his confession had been improperly admitted into evidence. Per Chief Justice Earl Warren, the Court held that, henceforth, police must advise suspects of their right to remain silent and their right to have counsel present during interrogation. Failure to provide these warnings will result in the suppression of a confession, even if it is deemed reliable. These new requirements were based on the Court's conclusion that "without proper safeguards the process of in-custody interrogation ... contains inherently compelling pressures which work to undermine the individual's will to resist and to compel him to speak where he would not otherwise do so freely." In a bitter dissent, Justice White complained that "[i]n some unknown number of cases the Court's rule will return a killer, a rapist or other criminal to the streets . . . to repeat his crime whenever it pleases him."

---

inevitable discovery doctrine The doctrine that holds that evidence derived from inadmissible evidence is admissible if it inevitably would have been discovered independently by lawful means.

public safety exception Exception to the requirement that police officers promptly inform suspects taken into custody of their rights to remain silent and have an attorney present during questioning. Under the public safety exception, police may ask suspects questions motivated by a desire to protect public safety without jeopardizing the admissibility of suspects' answers to those questions or subsequent statements.

Segurra v. United States, 468 U.S. 796, 104 S.Ct. 3380, 82 L.Ed.2d 599 (1984). Thus, in our hypothetical case, if police learned of the location of the weapon from an informant, the weapon might well be admissible in court, even though the suspect's admissions are still inadmissible.

A variation on the independent source doctrine is the **inevitable discovery doctrine**. A grisly case that illustrates this doctrine is *Nix v. Williams*, 467 U.S. 431, 104 S.Ct. 2501, 81 L.Ed.2d 377 (1984). In this case, a jury in a murder defendant's retrial was not permitted to learn of the defendant's incriminating statements because the police had violated *Miranda*. He was convicted nevertheless, largely on evidence derived from the girl's corpse. The body was discovered when Williams, before meeting with his attorney, led police to the place where he had dumped it. On appeal, Williams argued that evidence of the body was improperly admitted at trial because its discovery was based on inadmissible statements and thus constituted the fruit of the poisonous tree. In reviewing the case, the U.S. Supreme Court held that the evidence of the body was properly admissible at trial because a search party operating in the area where the body was discovered would eventually have located the body, even without assistance from the defendant.

The Public Safety Exception to *Miranda*

Police generally provide the *Miranda* warnings immediately on arrest or as soon as is practicable to preserve as evidence any statements that the suspect might make, as well as any other evidence that might be derived from these statements. In some situations, however, the *Miranda* warnings are delayed because police are preoccupied with apprehending other individuals or taking actions to protect themselves or others on the scene. In *New York v. Quarles*, 467 U.S. 649, 104 S.Ct. 2626, 81 L.Ed.2d 550 (1984), the Supreme Court recognized a **public safety exception** to the *Miranda* exclusionary rule. Under *Quarles*, before providing the *Miranda* warnings police may ask suspects questions that are designed to locate weapons that might be used to harm the police or other persons. If this

---

JURISPRUDENCE

Nix v. Williams, 467 U.S. 431, 104 S.Ct. 2501, 81 L.Ed.2d 377 (1984)

Robert Anthony Williams was arrested in Davenport, Iowa, for the kidnapping of a ten-year-old girl in Des Moines. He was given the *Miranda* warnings and indicated his desire to have counsel present during questioning. Des Moines police informed counsel that they would pick Williams up in Davenport and return him to Des Moines without questioning the suspect. During the car ride back to Des Moines, one of the police officers made a speech emphasizing the need for a "Christian burial" for the victim. In the ensuing conversation, Williams made incriminating statements and ultimately led police to where he had disposed of the victim's body. Prior to the beginning of this "conversation" a systematic search of the area was being conducted with the aid of two hundred volunteers. The

search was terminated when Williams guided police to the body. At trial, Williams' counsel moved unsuccessfully for his client's incriminating statements to be suppressed along with evidence of the condition of the victim's body as it was found, articles and photographs of her clothing, and the results of tests on the body. Williams was convicted of first-degree murder. Then began an appellate odyssey lasting fifteen years and involving two decisions by the U.S. Supreme Court. In the latter of these decisions, the Court upheld the admissibility of the victim's body and related evidence. Speaking through Chief Justice Warren E. Burger, the Court reasoned that the body was not the fruit of the poisonous tree because the search that had been underway in the area would eventually have located the body anyway. Hence, the Court created the inevitable discovery exception to the fruit of the poisonous tree doctrine.

---

interaction produces incriminating statements or physical evidence, the evidence need not be suppressed.

What Constitutes an Interrogation?

Although interrogation normally occurs at the station house after arrest, it may occur anywhere. For the purpose of determining when the *Miranda* warnings must be given, the Supreme Court has defined interrogation as "express questioning or its functional equivalent," including "any words or actions on the part of the police that the police should know are reasonably likely to elicit an incriminating response

---

JURISPRUDENCE

New York v. Quarles, 467 U.S. 649, 104 S.Ct. 2626, 81 L.Ed.2d 550 (1984)

Two New York City police officers were approached by a woman who claimed she had just been raped and reported that her assailant had gone into a nearby grocery store. The police were informed that the assailant was carrying a gun. The officers proceeded to the store and immediately spotted Benjamin Quarles, who matched the description given by the victim. Upon seeing the police, Quarles turned and ran. One of the police officers drew his service revolver and ordered Quarles to "freeze." Quarles complied with the officer's request. The officer frisked Quarles and discovered an empty shoulder holster. Before reading Quarles the

Miranda warnings, the officer asked where the gun was. Quarles nodded in the direction of some empty boxes and said, "The gun is over there." He was then placed under arrest and "Mirandized." Later Quarles moved to have his statement suppressed from evidence since it was made prior to the *Miranda* warnings. He also moved for suppression of the gun under the fruit of the poisonous tree doctrine. The Supreme Court allowed both pieces of evidence to be used against Quarles, notwithstanding the delay in the *Miranda* warnings. Obviously, the Court felt that the officers were justified in locating a discarded weapon prior to Mirandizing Quarles. In so holding, the Court created the public safety exception to *Miranda*.

from the suspect." *Rhode Island v. Innis*, 446 U.S. 291, 301, 100 S.Ct. 1682, 1693, 64 L.Ed.2d 297, 308 (1980). Before police may engage in such interaction, they must provide the *Miranda* warnings or risk the likelihood that useful **incriminating statements** will be suppressed as illegally obtained evidence.

incriminating statements
Statements, typically made to police, that increase the likelihood that one will be found guilty of a crime.

Waiver of *Miranda* Rights

It is axiomatic that all constitutional rights may be waived. A suspect may elect to waive the right to remain silent or the right to have counsel present during questioning as long as he or she does so knowingly and voluntarily. Courts are apt to strictly scrutinize a **waiver of *Miranda* rights** to make sure it is not the product of some coercion or deception by police. In *United States v. Carra*, 604 F.2d 1271 (10th Cir. 1979), the court observed: "Voluntary waiver of the right to remain silent is not mechanically to be determined but is to be determined from the totality of circumstances as a matter of fact." For example, in *United States v. Blocker*, 354 F. Supp. 1195 (D.D.C. 1973), a federal district court, citing decisions from the U.S. Court of Appeals for the Fifth Circuit, observed that a written waiver signed by the accused is not in itself conclusive evidence: "The court must still decide whether, in view of all the circumstances, defendant's subsequent decision to speak was a product of his free will." 354 F. Supp. at 1198 n. 11.

waiver of *Miranda* rights A known relinquishment of the right to remain silent and/or have counsel present during police interrogation.

Although they must honor a suspect's refusal to cooperate, police are under no duty to inform a suspect who is considering whether to cooperate that arrangements have been made to provide counsel. In *Moran v. Burbine*, 475 U.S. 412, 106 S.Ct. 1135, 89 L.Ed.2d 410 (1986), police arrested a man on a burglary charge and subsequently linked him to an unsolved murder. The suspect's sister, not aware that a murder charge was about to be filed against her brother, arranged for a lawyer to represent her brother on the burglary charge. The attorney contacted the police to arrange a meeting with her client. The police did not mention the possible murder charge and told the attorney that her client was not going to be questioned until the next day. The police then began to interrogate Burbine, failing to tell him that a lawyer had been arranged for him and had attempted to contact him. Burbine waived his rights and eventually confessed to the murder. The Supreme Court upheld the use of the confession in evidence.

Miranda Turned Upside Down?

Police "Mirandized" and then interrogated the suspect in a fatal shooting that occurred on January 10, 2000. At no point did the suspect, Van Chester Thompkins, indicate that that he wished to remain silent or have a lawyer present during the interrogation. Three hours into the questioning, Thompkins answered "Yes" when asked if he prayed to God to forgive him for his role in the shooting. After being charged with first-degree murder, Thompkins filed a pretrial motion to suppress that statement, claiming that it was obtained in violation of *Miranda*. The trial court denied the motion; in June 2010 the Supreme Court agreed. *Berghuis v. Thompkins*, 560 U.S. ___, 130 S.Ct. 2250, 176 L.Ed.2d 1098 (2010). Speaking through Justice Anthony Kennedy, a sharply divided Court held that a suspect's *Miranda* right to counsel must be invoked "unambiguously," which Thompkins failed to do. Moreover, Thompkins' answer to the question about prayer, albeit three hours into the interrogation, constituted a waiver of the right to remain silent. The fact that the waiver came three hours after interrogation began did not invalidate the interrogation.

In dissent, Justice Sonia Sotomayor claimed that the Court's decision had turned *Miranda* "upside down."

> Criminal suspects must now unambiguously invoke their right to remain silent—which, counterintuitively, requires them to speak. At the same time, suspects will be legally presumed to have waived their rights even if they have given no clear expression of their intent to do so. Those results, in my view, find no basis in *Miranda* or our subsequent cases and are inconsistent with the fair-trial principles on which those precedents are grounded. 560 U.S. at ___, 130 S.Ct. at 2278, 176 L.Ed.2d at 1130.

In 2013, the Supreme Court rendered a similar decision. Genovevo Salinas, who had not been placed in custody or received the *Miranda* warnings, voluntarily answered a police officer's questions about a murder. But when Salinas was asked whether ballistics testing would match his shotgun to shell casings found at the scene of the crime, he fell silent. At Salinas' trial, the state characterized his failure to answer the officer's questions as evidence of guilt. Salinas was convicted and sentenced to twenty years in prison. The U.S. Supreme Court affirmed the conviction, but was unable to produce a majority opinion, which gives the *Salinas* decision limited precedential value. *Salinas v. Texas*, 570 U.S. ___, 133 S.Ct. 2174, 186 L.Ed.2d 376 (2013).

Coerced Confessions

Even where police officers provide the *Miranda* warnings and the suspect agrees to talk to police without having counsel present, a confession elicited from the suspect is inadmissible if it is obtained through coercion, whether in the form of physical intimidation or psychological pressure. *United States v. Tingle*, 658 F.2d 1332 (9th Cir. 1981). A classic example of psychological coercion is the so-called Mutt and Jeff strategy. Under this tactic, one police officer, the "bad guy," is harsh, rude, and aggressive, while another police officer, the "good guy," is friendly and sympathetic to the suspect. Obviously the objective of the strategy is to get the accused to confess to the "good guy," and many believe that it is an effective technique. There is controversy about whether the Mutt and Jeff tactic is a constitutional means of eliciting a confession from a suspect who has waived his or her *Miranda* rights and agreed to talk to police without the presence of counsel. In *Miranda*, the Supreme Court alluded to the Mutt and Jeff routine as a possible example of impermissible psychological coercion. 384 U.S. at 452, 86 S.Ct. at 1614, 16 L.Ed.2d at 711. Yet, absent other indications of coercion, courts have generally acquiesced in the practice.

Police Deception

voluntariness of a confession The quality of a confession having been freely given.

The use of tricks or factual misstatements by police in an effort to induce a defendant to confess does not automatically invalidate a confession. A misstatement by police may affect the **voluntariness of a confession**, but the effect of any misstatements must be considered in light of the totality of surrounding circumstances. In *Frazier v. Cupp*, 394 U.S. 731, 89 S.Ct. 1420, 22 L.Ed.2d 684 (1969), the Supreme Court reversed a conviction where the police had falsely informed a suspect that his codefendant had confessed. Although the Supreme Court found the misstatement relevant to the issue of whether the confession had been given voluntarily, it did not find that the misstatement per se made the confession inadmissible. The Nebraska

Supreme Court has held that even deceptive statements referring to nonexistent autopsies of victims will not automatically render a confession involuntary. *State v. Norfolk*, 381 N.W.2d 120 (Neb. 1986).

How far may police go in their use of deception? In 1989, a Florida appellate court affirmed a trial judge's order holding a confession involuntary where police had presented fabricated laboratory reports to the defendant to secure a confession. The "reports," which were on the stationery of a law enforcement agency and a DNA testing firm, indicated that traces of the defendant's semen had been found on the victim's underwear. Among the factors cited by the appellate court in support of the exclusion of the confession were the indefinite life span of manufactured documents, their self-authenticating character, and their ease of duplication. The court expressed concern that false documents could find their way into police files or the courtroom and be accepted as genuine. *State v. Cayward*, 552 So.2d 971 (Fla. App. 1989).

In *State v. Patton*, 826 A.2d 783 (N.J. Sup. 2003), a police officer, posing as an eyewitness, was "interviewed" on an audiotape and fabricated an account of the victim's murder. The tape was later played to the defendant. Despite his earlier denials of involvement, upon hearing the audiotape, the defendant confessed to the murder. The fabricated audiotape, identified as such, was later introduced into evidence at trial, and the defendant was found guilty. Relying heavily on the Florida court's opinion in *State v. Cayward*, supra, the New Jersey appellate court held this fabrication of evidence violated due process. The court found the defendant's resulting confession to be inadmissible and reversed the defendant's conviction.

police deception Intentional deception by police in order to elicit incriminating statements from a suspect.

Police deception must be distinguished from cases where the police use or threaten force or promise leniency to elicit a confession. In instances where force is used or leniency is promised, courts will suppress confessions obtained. See, e.g., *Spano v. New York*, 360 U.S. 315, 79 S.Ct. 1202, 3 L.Ed.2d 1265 (1959). Moreover, when the police furnish a suspect with an incorrect or incomplete advisory statement of the penalties provided by law for a particular crime, courts will generally suppress the suspect's confession. See, e.g., *People v. Lytle*, 704 P.2d 331 (Colo. App. 1985).

Factors Considered by Judges in Evaluating Confessions

Judges consider several variables when determining whether a challenged confession was voluntary. These include the duration and methods of the interrogation, the length of the delay between arrest and appearance before a magistrate, the conditions of detention, the attitudes of the police toward the defendant, the defendant's physical and psychological state, and anything else that might bear on the defendant's resistance. *Commonwealth v. Kichline*, 361 A.2d 282, 290 (Pa. 1976). Courts are particularly cautious when receiving confessions by juveniles. See, e.g., *Haley v. Ohio*, 332 U.S. 596, 68 S.Ct. 302, 92 L.Ed. 224 (1948).

In a landmark ruling, *Arizona v. Fulminante*, 499 U.S. 279, 111 S.Ct. 1246, 113 L.Ed.2d 302 (1991), the Supreme Court said that the use of a confession that should have been suppressed does not automatically require reversal of a defendant's conviction. Rather, the appellate court must determine whether the defendant would have been convicted in the absence of the confession. If so, the admission of the confession is deemed to be a harmless error that does not require reversal. See, e.g., *State v. Tart*, 672 So.2d 116 (La. 1996).

JURISPRUDENCE

Arizona v. Fulminante, 499 U.S. 279, 111 S.Ct. 1246, 113 L.Ed.2d 302 (1991)

Oreste Fulminante's eleven-year-old daughter was murdered in Arizona. After the murder, Fulminante left Arizona for New York, where he was convicted of an unrelated crime and sentenced to prison. While in prison, Fulminate became friends with a fellow inmate named Anthony Sarivola, who was a paid informant for the Federal Bureau of Investigation. In the course of conversation, Sarivola told Fulminante that the reason for his harsh treatment by other inmates was a rumor circulating that he had murdered a child. Sarivola told him that he would provide protection in exchange for the truth. Fulminante disclosed that he had killed his daughter in Arizona and gave details about the crime. After being released from prison in New York, Fulminante was indicted for first-degree murder in Arizona. The confession to Sarivola was the key piece of evidence, and

Fulminate sought to have it suppressed. The trial court rejected the notion that the confession was coerced and barred by the Fifth and Fourteenth Amendments. The Arizona Supreme Court reversed holding that "the confession was coerced" and ordered a new trial without the use of the confession. The Supreme Court agreed that the confession was coerced because Fulminante's primary motivation to confess was to prevent physical violence. Thus, the confession could not be used against him under the Fifth and Fourteenth Amendments. However, the Court also ruled that the use in evidence of a confession that should have been suppressed does not automatically require reversal of a defendant's conviction. But the Court concluded that admitting Fulminante's confession was not harmless beyond a reasonable doubt, thus affirming the Arizona Supreme Court's conclusion that Fulminante was entitled to a new trial in which the confession was not be used in evidence.

Identification Procedures

lineups Police identification procedure where suspects are included in a group with other persons and the group is exhibited to victims.

Police identification procedures include those in which victims and witnesses are asked to identify perpetrators, such as **lineups**, **showups**, and **photo packs**. They also encompass scientific techniques comparing **forensic evidence** taken from a suspect with that found at a crime scene. All of these procedures are extremely important in police work, but each poses unique legal problems.

showups Events in which victims are taken to see suspects to make an identification.

Forensic Methods

photo packs Collections of "mug shots" exhibited to a victim or witness in an attempt to identify the perpetrator of a crime.

Forensic methods involve the application of scientific principles to legal issues. In the context of police work, forensic methods commonly include fingerprint identification, comparison of blood samples, matching of clothing fibers, head and body hair comparisons, identification of semen, and, more recently, DNA tests. When these methods are conducted by qualified persons, the results are usually admissible evidence. Indeed, the courts have ruled that obtaining such physical evidence from suspects does not violate the constitutional prohibition of compulsory self-incrimination. *Schmerber v. California,* 384 U.S. 757, 86 S.Ct. 1826, 16 L.Ed.2d 908 (1966).

forensic evidence Evidence obtained through scientific techniques of analyzing physical evidence.

In *Gilbert v. California,* 388 U.S. 263, 87 S.Ct. 1951, 18 L.Ed.2d 1178 (1967), the U.S. Supreme Court held that a suspect could be compelled to provide a **handwriting exemplar**, explaining that it is not testimony but an identifying physical characteristic. Similarly, in *United States v. Dionisio,* 410 U.S. 1, 93 S.Ct. 764, 35 L. Ed.2d 67 (1973), the Court held that a suspect could be compelled to provide a **voice exemplar** on the ground that the recording is being used only to measure the physical properties of the suspect's voice, as distinct from the content of what the suspect has said. And in *Maryland v. King,* 570 U.S. ___, 133 S.Ct. 1958, 186 L.Ed.2d 1 (2013), the Court held that police collection of DNA by swabbing the mouth of

handwriting exemplar A sample of a suspect's handwriting.

voice exemplar A sample of a person's voice, usually taken by police for the purpose of identifying a suspect.

an arrested person is a legitimate booking procedure, that is essentially no different from fingerprinting and taking mug shots.

Of course, police may not use methods that "shock the conscience" in obtaining physical evidence from suspects. *Rochin v. California*, 342 U.S. 165, 72 S.Ct. 205, 96 L.Ed. 183 (1952). Courts will scrutinize closely procedures that subject the suspect to major bodily intrusions. For example, in *Winston v. Lee*, 470 U.S. 753, 105 S.Ct. 1611, 84 L.Ed.2d 662 (1985), the prosecution sought a court order requiring a suspect to have surgery to remove a bullet lodged in his chest. The prosecution believed that ballistics tests on the bullet would show that the suspect had been wounded during the course of a robbery. The Supreme Court, weighing the risks to the suspect against the government's need for evidence and noting that the prosecution had other evidence against the suspect, disallowed the procedure. The Court declined to formulate a broad rule to govern such cases. Therefore, courts must consider such matters on a case-by-case basis, carefully weighing the interests on both sides.

As the 1995 O.J. Simpson murder trial demonstrated, defense lawyers can attack the methodology of forensic procedures as well as the qualifications of those administering them. If the evidence is inherently unreliable, it is inadmissible regardless of whether there were violations of the suspect's constitutional rights. In 1996, the FBI crime laboratory was criticized for allegedly sloppy procedures in the conduct of DNA and other forensic tests. This encouraged defense lawyers to challenge the reliability of the evidence in several cases where prosecutors were using evidence analyzed by the FBI crime lab.

With the rapid progress of science and technology, forensic procedures are constantly evolving, and new procedures are becoming available to the police. Evidence obtained through scientific and technological innovations can be both relevant and probative in a criminal case. Yet, care must be taken to ensure that a new method is clearly supported by research.

Until recently, federal and state courts followed the test articulated in *Frye v. United States*, 293 F. 1013 (D.C. Cir. 1923), and admitted scientific evidence only if it was based on principles or theories generally accepted in the scientific community. In *Daubert v. Merrell Dow Pharmaceuticals, Inc.*, 509 U.S. 579, 113 S.Ct. 2786, 125 L.Ed.2d 469 (1993), the Supreme Court held that the Federal Rules of Evidence supersede *Frye* and govern the admissibility of scientific evidence in the federal courts. This approach causes admissibility of scientific evidence to hinge on such factors as whether the evidence can be tested and whether it has been subjected to peer review. State courts are now divided on whether to accept the newer *Daubert* standard or remain with the classic standard announced in 1923 in *Frye*. (This topic is discussed further in Chapter 6.)

Lineups

Eyewitness identification may be more persuasive to juries than forensic evidence, but it can also present problems. One of the most common nonscientific methods of identification is the lineup. In a lineup, a group of individuals, one of whom is the suspect in custody, appears before a victim or witness, who is usually shielded from the suspect's view. Often, the individuals in the lineup are asked to walk, turn sideways, wear certain items of clothing, or speak to assist the victim or eyewitness in making a positive identification. The Supreme Court has held that there is no Fifth Amendment immunity against being placed in a lineup as an identification procedure. *United States v. Wade*, 388 U.S. 218, 87 S.Ct. 1926, 18 L.Ed.2d 1149 (1967). However, courts must guard against the possibility that identification procedures,

JURISPRUDENCE

United States v. Wade, 388 U.S. 218, 87 S.Ct. 1926, 18 L.Ed.2d 1149 (1967)

Billy Joe Wade was indicted for conspiracy and bank robbery. Several weeks afterwards, police placed Wade in a "lineup in which each person wore strips of tape on his face, as the robber allegedly had done, and, on direction, repeated words like those the robber allegedly had used." This was done without notice to Wade's appointed counsel. During the lineup, two bank employees identified Wade as the robber. At Wade's trial, the employees identified Wade as the robber when asked whether the guilty person was in the courtroom. However, Wade's attorney argued that the lineup "violated [Wade's] Fifth Amendment privilege against self-incrimination and his Sixth Amendment right to counsel, and filed a motion for judgment of acquittal or, alternatively, to strike the courtroom identifications." The trial court denied the motions, and Wade was convicted. In reviewing the case, the Supreme Court held "neither the lineup itself nor anything required therein violated [Wade's] Fifth Amendment privilege against

self-incrimination, since merely exhibiting his person for observation by witnesses and using his voice as an identifying physical characteristic involved no compulsion of the accused to give evidence of a testimonial nature against himself which is prohibited by that Amendment." However, the Court held the postindictment lineup without the presence of his attorney violated Wade's Sixth Amendment right to counsel because such a right "guarantees an accused the right to counsel not only at his trial but at any critical confrontation by the prosecution at pretrial proceedings where the results might determine his fate and where the absence of counsel might derogate from his right to a fair trial." The postindictment lineup was held to be a "critical prosecutive stage," and therefore Wade was entitled to have counsel present. Yet the Court held that this violation did not necessitate reversal of Wade's conviction and said that his conviction could be upheld if the prosecution could show that the witnesses' in-court identification of Wade as the perpetrator was based on their observations of him during the crime.

especially lineups, are unfair when a victim or witness is prompted to identify a particular suspect as the perpetrator. See, e.g., *Foster v. California*, 394 U.S. 440, 89 S.Ct. 1127, 22 L.Ed.2d 402 (1969). Obviously, if the perpetrator is known to be black, it is impermissibly suggestive for police to place one African-American suspect in a lineup with five white individuals. In practice, however, the more subtle suggestiveness of lineups causes problems for the courts. To avoid such problems, police should place several persons with similar physical characteristics in a lineup.

To further protect the rights of the accused, the Supreme Court has said that after formal charges have been made against a defendant, the defendant has the right to have counsel present at a lineup. *Kirby v. Illinois*, 406 U.S. 682, 92 S.Ct. 1877, 32 L.Ed.2d 411 (1972). To ensure that police and prosecutors honor that right, the Supreme Court has said that a pretrial identification obtained in violation of the right to counsel is per se inadmissible at trial. *Gilbert v. California*, supra. A per se exclusionary rule was deemed necessary to ensure that the police and the prosecution would respect the defendant's right to have counsel present at a lineup. On the other hand, a pretrial identification obtained through impermissibly suggestive identification procedures is not per se inadmissible. Instead, such an identification may be introduced into evidence if the trial judge first finds that the witness's in-court identification is reliable and based on independent recall. In making this determination, the trial judge must consider (1) the opportunity of the witness to view the accused at the time of the crime, (2) the witness's degree of attention, (3) the accuracy of the witness's prior description of the accused, (4) the level of certainty demonstrated at the confrontation, and (5) the time that elapsed between the crime and the confrontation. *Neil v. Biggers*, 409 U.S. 188, 93 S.Ct. 375, 34 L.Ed.2d 401 (1972); see also *Wethington v. State*, 560 N.E.2d 496 (Ind. 1990).

Showups

The showup is a frequently used method of identification of a suspect. In a showup, the police usually take the victim to the suspect to determine whether the victim can make an identification, and at least one state supreme court has held the that police may transport a person stopped for an investigatory stop a short distance for purposes of a showup. *People v. Lippert*, 432 N.E.2d 605 (Ill. 1982).

In 1967, the U.S. Court of Appeals for the District of Columbia Circuit approved the use of showups, commenting, "[W]e do not consider a prompt identification of a suspect close to the time and place of an offense to diverge from the rudiments of fair play that govern the due balance of pertinent interests that suspects be treated fairly while the state pursues its responsibility of apprehending criminals." *Wise v. United States*, 383 F.2d 206, 210 (D.C. Cir. 1967).

In *Stovall v. Denno*, 308 U.S. 293, 87 S.Ct. 198, 18 L.Ed.2d 1199 (1967), the Supreme Court recognized a defendant's due process right to exclude identification testimony that results from unnecessarily suggestive procedures that may lead to an irreparably mistaken identification. This form of "on-the-scene" confrontation between an eyewitness and a suspect is inherently suggestive because it is apparent that when law enforcement takes a victim for a showup of a suspect, they usually believe they have caught the offender. Therefore, courts review identification testimony carefully to make sure a witness's identification testimony is not based on impermissibly suggestive identification procedures. In making such a determination, courts often look to the length of time between the crime and the confrontation and the level of certainty demonstrated by the witness at the confrontation.

Although critics complain of the use of showups, such a confrontation may be justified by the necessity to preserve a witness's memory of a suspect before the suspect has had an opportunity to alter his or her clothing and appearance. Appellate courts consistently admonish caution in the use of showups; however, they generally approve of their use when the identification occurs shortly after the crime has been committed and the showup is conducted near the scene of the crime under circumstances that are not unduly suggestive. In approving showups, some courts have pointed out that a victim's or eyewitness's on-the-scene identification is likely to be more reliable than a later identification because the memory is fresher. See, e.g., *Jones v. State*, 600 P.2d 247, 250 (Nev. 1979). Courts base their judgments of the reliability of showups on many factors and circumstances. For example, in *United States v. Bautista*, 23 F.3d 726 (2d Cir. 1994), in its review of a challenge to an on-the-scene identification immediately following a nighttime narcotics raid, the court observed, "The fact that the suspects were handcuffed, in the custody of law enforcement officers, and illuminated by flashlights . . . did not render the pretrial identification procedure unnecessarily suggestive." *Id*. at 731. The court went on to explain that because the on-the-scene identification was necessary to allow the officers to release the innocent, the incidents of that identification were also necessary.

Photo Packs

A photo pack is simply a set of "mug shots" that are shown individually to the victim or eyewitness in the hope that he or she will be able to identify the perpetrator. To produce a reliable, hence admissible, identification, the presentation of the photo pack should not emphasize one photo over the others. For example, in *Commonwealth v. Thornley*, 546 N.E.2d 350 (Mass. 1989), the Supreme Judicial Court of Massachusetts found that the photographic array was impermissibly suggestive because the witnesses admitted they made their selection of the defendant's photograph because the man in the photo was wearing glasses. The defendant was the only one of thirteen men in the photo array who was wearing glasses.

The words and actions of the officers making the presentation must manifest an attitude of disinterest. *State v. Thamer*, 777 P.2d 432 (Utah 1989). In analyzing a defendant's claim of being the victim of an impermissibly suggestive photo pack identification, courts generally apply a two-part test. First, did the photo array present the defendant in an impermissibly suggestive posture? Second, if so, under the totality of circumstances, did the procedure give rise to a substantial likelihood of misidentification? *State v. Bedwell*, 417 N.W.2d 66 (Iowa 1987).

Conclusion

Police are permitted broad discretion in their interactions with the public. There are no legal prerequisites to the many consensual encounters through which police routinely perform their investigative and preventive duties. But the whole array of nonconsensual encounters with the public, including arrest, investigatory detention, interrogation, roadblocks, and identification procedures, are subject to strict constitutional requirements.

Chapter Summary

- LO1

  o Because an arrest is a form of "seizure," it must conform to the requirements of the Fourth Amendment. Thus, an arrest must be based on probable cause and, with certain exceptions, is subject to the warrant requirement of the Fourth Amendment.

  o At common law, and under contemporary American law, police who have probable cause to believe that a person has committed or is committing a felony or who observes someone committing a misdemeanor can make a warrantless arrest. Otherwise, an arrest requires a warrant.

  o An arrest warrant issues based on a grand jury indictment; a *capias* directs the defendant's arrest following a prosecutor's information.

  o The Supreme Court has approved warrantless arrests where crimes are committed in plain view of police officers or where officers possess probable cause but exigent circumstances prohibit obtaining a warrant.

  o The Fourth Amendment is very protective of homes. Nevertheless, courts generally uphold a peaceful warrantless entry into a home where there is probable cause to arrest an armed suspect for a serious felony and the suspect will likely escape or evidence will be destroyed.

  o By statute or court rules, federal and state officers are required to promptly take persons arrested before a magistrate, regardless of whether the arrest was based on a warrant.

  o At common law, a private individual could make a citizen's arrest without a warrant for a felony or breach of the peace committed in that person's presence. The rule prevails in some states; in others, it has been revised by statute.

- o In most states, a police officer has discretion to either make an arrest or issue a citation to a person who commits a minor traffic violation. In 2001, the Supreme Court ruled that the Fourth Amendment does not forbid a warrantless arrest, even for a minor traffic offense. Some states have "cite and release" statutes that create a presumptive right to be cited and released for the commission of a misdemeanor.

- • LO2

  - o Laws typically allow police officers to use force reasonably necessary to make an arrest. This includes use of stun guns (Tasers) to incapacitate suspects who resist arrest and trained dogs to apprehend fleeing suspects.

  - o In 2003, a federal appeals court held that use of a Taser to subdue a potentially homicidal individual did not constitute excessive force.

  - o In 1985, the Supreme Court struck down a state statute that permitted police to use deadly force against fleeing suspects when there was no threat to the safety of the officer or the public.

- • LO3

  - o Police who have "reasonable suspicion" that criminal activity is afoot may temporarily detain a person for questioning and, based on a reasonable suspicion that the detainee is armed, may perform a pat-down search of the suspect's outer clothing to locate weapons. An officer who feels an object that may be a weapon may seize it, and if it turns out to be something other than a weapon, it may be seized if it is contraband. Stops as long as forty minutes have been held to be reasonable.

  - o Courts have applied this rationale to stops of vehicles. An anonymous tip corroborated by independent police work is generally held to be sufficient to establish a reasonable suspicion to make an investigatory stop of a vehicle.

  - o In 1983, the Supreme Court held that when police stop an automobile based on reasonable suspicion, they may search the passenger compartment for weapons, assuming they have reason to believe that a suspect is dangerous. The search must be limited to areas in which a weapon may be placed or hidden. Passengers and the driver may be frisked if there is a reasonable suspicion they may be armed and dangerous. This often results in discovery of contraband or evidence of intoxication that police can use in a criminal prosecution.

  - o In 1996, the Court ruled that the motives of an officer in stopping a vehicle for a traffic violation are irrelevant if there is an objective basis for the stop.

  - o In 1989, the Supreme Court upheld an investigative stop of an air passenger for which a number of circumstances, including the use of a drug courier profile, gave the police reasonable suspicion of criminal activity.

- • LO4

  - o Racial profiling involves "police-initiated action that relies on the race, ethnicity or national origin rather than the behavior of an individual or information that leads the police to a particular individual who has been identified as being, or having been, engaged in criminal activity."

- ○ Some defendants who claim to have been stopped on the basis of race have sought to dismiss charges, arguing they were denied due process and equal protection of the laws. The racial profiling debate was recharged in 2010 when Arizona enacted a law allowing officers to determine the immigration status of those persons reasonably suspected to be in this country illegally.

- **LO5**

  - ○ Police are permitted to stop motorists at roadblocks to perform safety checks on automobiles or apprehend fleeing suspects. They also may establish sobriety checkpoints designed to locate drunk drivers, as long as procedures are in place to ensure reasonableness. Roadblocks often reveal illegal weapons, drugs, and other contraband.

  - ○ In 1990, the Supreme Court recognized that a "seizure" occurs when a vehicle is stopped at a checkpoint but upheld the use of roadblocks for conducting field sobriety tests, provided they are established and operated according to guidelines that minimize the inconvenience to motorists and constrain the exercise of discretion by police officers.

  - ○ In 2000, the Court invalidated an ordinance establishing checkpoints primarily for snaring drug traffickers, but in 2004 the Court noted that its decision was not intended to prevent the police from using checkpoints to obtain assistance in locating perpetrators of a crime involving a traffic accident.

- **LO6**

  - ○ In 1979, the Supreme Court said that a law making it an offense to refuse to report or to give a false name and residence address to a peace officer could not be constitutionally applied in absence of reasonable suspicion that the individual asked for identification was engaged in or had engaged in criminal activity.

  - ○ In 1983, the Court found unconstitutional a statute that required persons loitering or wandering on the streets to provide a "credible and reliable" identification and to account for their presence when requested to do so by a police officer.

  - ○ In 2004, in a 5–4 decision, the Court affirmed a conviction of a defendant who violated an ordinance that provided, "Any person so detained shall identify himself, but may not be compelled to answer any other inquiry of any peace officer."

- **LO7**

  - ○ In 1897, the Supreme Court held that to force a suspect to confess violates the Self-Incrimination Clause of the Fifth Amendment; in 1936, it held that a coerced confession deprived a defendant in a state criminal case of due process of law.

  - ○ Through a series of decisions in 1960s the Supreme Court reformed the law on confessions. In 1964, it made the Self-Incrimination Clause applicable to state criminal prosecutions and recognized the right of suspects to have counsel present during interrogation.

  - ○ In its seminal *Miranda* decision in 1966, the Court required police to advise suspects in custody of their rights to remain silent and to have counsel present during questioning. Before police engage in questioning, they must provide the *Miranda* warnings or risk the likelihood that incriminating statements will be suppressed as illegally obtained evidence.

o A public safety exception allows police to ask suspects questions about the location of weapons before providing *Miranda* warnings.

o A waiver of *Miranda* rights by a suspect must be knowing and voluntary. Courts scrutinize waivers closely, especially waivers by juveniles.

o In 1986, the Court held that police are under no duty to inform a suspect considering whether to cooperate that arrangements have been made to provide counsel.

o In 1991, the Court said that the use of a confession that should have been suppressed does not automatically require reversal of a defendant's conviction if an appellate court determines the defendant would have been convicted in the absence of the confession.

- LO8

o The use of tricks or factual misstatements by police in an effort to induce a defendant to confess does not automatically invalidate a confession. This is distinguishable from instances where police furnish a suspect with an incorrect or incomplete advisory statement of the penalties the law provides for a particular crime or where they use threats to use force or promises of leniency to elicit a confession. In such instances courts will suppress confessions.

- LO9

o The Supreme Court held in 1963 that under the "fruit of the poisonous tree" doctrine, evidence derived from inadmissible evidence is likewise inadmissible to prove guilt.

o Evidence obtained in violation of the *Miranda* rules is inadmissible in criminal prosecutions to prove guilt unless it was located on the basis of independently and lawfully obtained information (the independent source doctrine) or would have been discovered inevitably by an independent search (the inevitable discovery rule).

- LO10

o Law enforcement agencies use forensic means (such as fingerprints, blood samples, matching of clothing fibers, hair comparisons, identification of semen, and DNA tests) as well as witness identification of suspects.

o The Supreme Court has held that neither obtaining such physical evidence nor compelling suspects to provide handwriting and voice exemplars violates the constitutional prohibition of compulsory self-incrimination.

o Police use lineups in which a group of individuals, one of whom is the suspect in custody, appears before a victim or witness, who is usually shielded from the suspect's view.

o The Supreme Court held that there is no Fifth Amendment immunity against being placed in a lineup as a means of identification, but has recognized a defendant's due process right to exclude identification testimony that results from unnecessarily suggestive procedures that may lead to an irreparably mistaken identification.

○ After formal charges have been made against a defendant, the defendant has the right to have counsel present at a lineup, and a pretrial identification obtained in violation of the right to counsel is per se inadmissible at trial.

○ In a showup police take the victim to the suspect to make an identification. This form of "on-the-scene" confrontation between an eyewitness and a suspect is inherently suggestive because when the police take a victim for a showup, they usually believe they have caught the offender.

○ A photo pack is simply a set of "mug shots" that are shown individually to the victim or eyewitness in the hope that he or she will be able to identify the perpetrator. In analyzing a defendant's claim of being the victim of an impermissibly suggestive photo pack identification, courts generally apply a two-part test. First, did the photo array present the defendant in an impermissibly suggestive posture? Second, if so, under the totality of circumstances, did the procedure give rise to a substantial likelihood of misidentification?

Key Terms

anonymous tips	lineups
arrest	*Miranda* warnings
arrest warrant	pat-down search
capias	photo packs
citizen's arrest	plain view
coerced confession	police deception
derivative evidence	pretextual stops
drug courier profiles	public safety exception
forensic evidence	racial profiling
handwriting exemplar	roadblocks
identification procedures	showups
incriminating statements	*Terry* stop
independent source doctrine	voice exemplar
inevitable discovery doctrine	voluntariness of a confession
interrogation	waiver of *Miranda* rights
investigatory detention	warrantless arrest

Key Court Decisions

Dunaway v. New York (1979): Probable cause is necessary to justify a station-house detention and interrogation, irrespective of whether it is termed an "arrest."

Tennessee v. Garner (1985): Police may not use deadly force to prevent the escape of a fleeing felony suspect unless they have probable cause to believe that the suspect poses a significant threat of death or serious physical injury to them or other persons.

Minnesota v. Dickerson (1993): In conducting pat-down search after detaining a suspect based on reasonable suspicion, police may seize items that plainly feel like contraband.

Illinois v. Wardlow (2000): In determining whether there was reasonable suspicion to justify an investigatory detention, courts must consider the totality of circumstances.

Whren v. United States (1996): The motives of an officer in stopping a motor vehicle are irrelevant as long as there is an objective basis for the stop.

United States v. Sokolow (1989): Police may use a drug courier profile to determine whether there is reasonable suspicion to conduct an investigatory detention of an airport traveler.

Indianapolis v. Edmond (2000): Checkpoints in which all drivers are stopped in an effort to detect illegal drugs, as distinct from sobriety checkpoints, are not permissible as they are not aimed at an imminent public safety threat.

Hiibel v. Sixth Judicial Dist. Court of Nevada (2004): When conducting an investigatory detention based on reasonable suspicion, officers may require suspects to identify themselves.

Miranda v. Arizona (1966): Before questioning a suspect in custody, police must advise the suspect of the right to remain silent and the right to have counsel present during questioning; otherwise incriminating statements made by the suspect are inadmissible in court.

Nix v. Williams (1984): Physical evidence subject to the fruit of the poisonous tree doctrine is admissible in court if it would inevitably have been discovered independently.

New York v. Quarles (1984): Police may engage in limited questioning of a suspect in custody prior to providing the *Miranda* warnings if necessary to prevent an imminent threat to public safety.

Arizona v. Fulminante (1991): Use of a confession that should have been suppressed does not automatically require reversal of a defendant's conviction. The appellate court must determine whether the defendant would have been convicted in the absence of the confession. If so, the admission of the confession is deemed to be a harmless error that does not require reversal.

United States v. Wade (1967): A suspect in custody has no Fifth Amendment immunity against being placed in a lineup as an identification procedure.

Questions for Thought and Discussion

1. Practically speaking, what is the difference between "probable cause" and "reasonable suspicion"? How long can police detain a suspect based on reasonable suspicion?

2. What are the practical arguments for and against allowing private citizens to make arrests when they observe criminal activity taking place? What is the law in your state governing "citizen's arrests"?

3. Does your state make any distinction between minor and serious traffic offenses in permitting arrests? Is the use of arrest procedures for relatively minor traffic offenses unnecessary? Is it better to give the individual police officer discretion in these matters or to adopt laws decriminalizing such infractions?

4. In the *Miranda* case, the Supreme Court released a convicted rapist when it imposed a requirement that police advise suspects of their constitutional rights before conducting interrogations. Was the Court's decision a wise one? What has been the impact of the *Miranda* decision on law enforcement?

5. What factors do courts consider in determining whether an individual is "in custody" when a police interrogation takes place?

6. What limitations do courts impose on police in the use of deception in interrogations of suspects?

7. How might police coerce a suspect into waiving the rights to counsel and to remain silent during interrogation? How can courts ensure that cooperation with police was voluntary?

8. What factors do courts consider in evaluating whether a confession has been coerced?

9. Are the courts correct in limiting the scope of the Fifth Amendment Self-Incrimination Clause to verbal statements so that there is no constitutional protection against compulsory police identification procedures? What would be the implications for law enforcement if the courts included physical evidence like fingerprints or handwriting samples within the scope of the Fifth Amendment privilege?

10. Describe the methods of nonscientific identification used by law enforcement in their attempts to identify suspects. Which do you think is the most reliable?

11. Would it be permissible for police to construct a lineup including four visibly overweight persons along with a slim one where the victim told police that her assailant was "very thin"?

12. Discuss racial profiling, which results in a disproportionate number of minorities being stopped for disobeying traffic laws. Should this problem be addressed by (a) courts' dismissing charges or suppressing evidence seized as a result of racial profiling based on denial of due process and equal protection of the law, (b) civil litigation seeking financial redress, (c) disciplinary action against law enforcement officers responsible for racial profiling, or (d) some other proposed remedy?

Problems for Discussion and Solution

1. Police obtained a warrant to search a single-family residence for "illegal amphetamines and equipment used in the manufacture of same." The warrant also authorized the search of the person of Harry Hampton, described in the warrant as a white male, thirty-two years of age, six feet two inches tall, and weighing 225 lbs. When police arrived at the scene, one officer began to search Hampton. When that search yielded contraband, another officer detained a second man sitting on the porch. (He was later identified as Jimmy Jaffers.) The officer subjected Jaffers to a pat-down search. No weapons were discovered on Jaffers's person, but the officer, having felt a "suspicious lump" in Jaffers's front pants pocket, retrieved a plastic bag of capsules that later proved to be illegal amphetamines. In a pretrial motion, Jaffers's counsel moves to suppress the contraband, arguing that his client was the victim of an unreasonable search. Is Jaffers likely to prevail in this contention? Why or why not?

2. A police officer on night patrol saw a car parked off a dirt road in an area known to be a "lovers' lane." As his cruiser approached the car, he observed a male and a female sitting inside. He noticed the male occupant make a movement that the officer interpreted as an attempt to hide something under the seat. The officer approached the vehicle and directed the occupants to get out. As they did, he observed a marijuana "roach" in the open ashtray. The officer then reached under the front seat and retrieved a small quantity of marijuana. The officer placed both individuals under arrest. In court, the officer admitted that he was not concerned for his safety but simply had a "hunch" that the couple could be "doing drugs." Did the officer make a legal arrest? Why or why not?

3. Deputy Dennis D. Mennis was conducting a routine patrol in his police cruiser at 4 A.M. in an area known to have high levels of gang, drug, and gun activity. He witnessed two young men standing near a parked car. He stopped to investigate. As he approached the two men, one of the men got into the car and attempted to drive away. Deputy Mennis ordered the man to stop and exit the vehicle, which he did. Deputy Mennis did not observe any criminal activity, but nevertheless ordered both men to place their hands on the hood of the car while he conducted a pat-down search of both of them. The pat-down search of one of the men resulted in the seizure of a small caliber handgun, which has been concealed in the man's jacket pocket. The man from whom the gun was seized was immediately arrested for possession of a concealed weapon. The other man, who turned out to be the owner of the vehicle, was permitted to leave the scene. Did Deputy Mennis act properly in conducting the pat-down searches, seizing the concealed firearm, and making the warrantless arrest? What standards would a judge employ in reviewing the deputy's actions?

4. Police were called to a residence by a homeowner who claimed she had just been the victim of a burglary and armed robbery. She gave the police a precise description of the perpetrator and informed police that the suspect had pointed a handgun at her during the crime. Thirty minutes later the same officers confronted a suspect who matched the homeowner's description walking down the road about a mile from the crime scene. When the police approached the suspect, he turned and ran toward nearby woods. The police gave chase while calling for the suspect to stop. Fearing that the suspect would avoid arrest, an officer drew his revolver and shot the suspect in the back, killing him. Was the officer's use of deadly force permissible in this instance? Why or why not?

5. Police got a phone call from someone who claimed he had just planted a bomb in a nearby high school and that it would go off in forty-five minutes. Police officers, including the bomb squad, rushed to the scene as the school was being evacuated. While surveying the area outside the school, an officer came upon a young man perched in a tree. The man appeared to be observing the scene with a pair of binoculars. The officer demanded that the man come down from the tree. As he was climbing down, a cell phone fell from his pocket. The officer picked up the phone and pushed the button to display the call history. The officer noticed that the last number called was the police station. The officer immediately placed the man in handcuffs and asked him, "Where's the bomb?" The man replied that there was no bomb and that the whole thing had been a prank. The man was arrested on a charge of making a false bomb threat. In a pretrial motion, his attorney moved to suppress the statements made by the suspect in response to the officer's questions. How would a judge likely rule on this motion? Why?

6. Police arrested Sam Shady for an alleged rape. Police required Shady, who was unusually tall and lean, to stand in a lineup with four other men, all of whom were of average height and weight. The victim did not hesitate to identify Shady as the perpetrator. Is this identification likely to withstand a challenge by the defense?

CHAPTER OUTLINE

JURISPRUDENCE FEATURE BOXES

Scott v. Illinois (1980)

Stack v. Boyle (1951)

United States v. Salerno (1987)

United States v. Armstrong (1996)

United States v. Calandra (1974)

Bruton v. United States (1968)

Bordenkircher v. Hayes (1978)

LEARNING OBJECTIVES

After reading this chapter, you should be able to explain

1. why constitutional rights, especially the right to counsel, are critically important during the pretrial process

2. why petty offenses are disposed of through summary trials and more serious charges entail more complex procedures

3. what factors determine whether a defendant will be granted pretrial release or be remanded to custody

4. the different mechanisms by which formal charges are brought

5. the role and function of the grand jury in the pretrial process

6. how extradition works and why it is necessary

Continued

Continued

7. the various pretrial motions employed by defense counsel and prosecutors

8. the defendant's options with respect to entry of a plea and why plea bargaining is both prevalent and controversial

9. what is meant by pretrial discovery and how that process works

10. the requirements for speedy trials in federal and state courts

CHAPTER OPENING VIGNETTE

On March 25, 1931, a sheriff's posse stopped a freight train in Paint Rock, Alabama, and arrested nine young African-American men. The sheriff had been alerted by several white teenagers who had jumped off the train earlier and claimed that they had been assaulted by the African Americans. Later that day, two young white women who also were on the train claimed that they had been raped by the African Americans now in custody. The next day an angry mob surrounded the jail in Scottsboro, Alabama, where the suspects were being held. Thus began one of the most infamous cases in American legal history. The nine "Scottsboro boys," as they were dubbed by the press, were indicted for rape on March 30, 1931. Less than a week later they were tried before an all-white jury. During the rushed investigation and trial, which was conducted in an atmosphere of extreme racial animosity, the defendants were not represented by counsel in any meaningful sense. Eight of the nine defendants were convicted of rape and sentenced to death—the jury could not agree on whether one defendant should receive the death penalty or life imprisonment. In *Powell v. Alabama*, 287 U.S. 45, 53 S.Ct. 55, 77 L.Ed. 158 (1932), the U.S. Court reversed the convictions, holding that that the defendants had been denied due process of law in violation of the Fourteenth Amendment. Saying that the Due Process Clause of the Fourteenth Amendment incorporates the "fundamental principles of liberty and justice which lie at the base of all our civil and political institutions," the Court foreshadowed modern judicial decisions protecting the rights of the accused. Unfortunately for the Scottsboro Boys, the High Court's decision did not end their legal troubles. The story of what happened in the years that followed is too long and complex to be recounted here. Suffice it to say that evidence later revealed that all of the defendants had been falsely accused. Ultimately, all were paroled or pardoned and the state of Alabama apologized for a horrific miscarriage of justice.

Introduction

The U.S. Constitution and the constitutions of all fifty states guarantee due process of law to all persons accused of criminal wrongdoing. Due process requires that persons accused of crimes be given fair notice of criminal charges and an adequate opportunity to contest them. As the Supreme Court has said,

> No principle of procedural due process is more clearly established than that of notice of the specific charge, and a chance to be heard in a trial of the issues raised by that charge, if desired, are among the constitutional rights of every accused in a criminal proceeding, in all courts, state or federal. *Cole v. Arkansas*, 333 U.S. 196, 201, 68 S.Ct. 514, 517, 92 L.Ed. 644, 647 (1948).

For **petty offenses** (minor misdemeanors), due process may require no more than the opportunity for the accused to contest the charge before a magistrate in a single, summary proceeding. For more serious offenses (treason, felonies, and major misdemeanors), the federal and state constitutions impose more elaborate procedural requirements.

As a practical matter, judicial decisions that interpret the generalities of the federal and state constitutions have greatly expanded the procedural rights that must be observed in criminal prosecutions. One result of this judicial activity is that the area of law known as criminal procedure has developed substantially over the past several decades.

Although many people equate the term **criminal procedure** with the criminal trial, the former term is actually much broader. Criminal procedure includes search and seizure, arrest, and interrogation (see Chapters 3 and 4), as well as a variety of other procedures that must occur before a trial can take place. The main components of the pretrial process are the **initial appearance** before a magistrate, the **preliminary hearing**, the **grand jury** proceeding, and the **arraignment** (see Figure 5.1). In addition, judges consider various motions made by the defense and prosecution at pretrial hearings. These pretrial procedures are designed to eliminate from the system those cases for which there is insufficient evidence of criminal wrongdoing and to set the stage for a fair and orderly resolution of cases for which the evidence is sufficiently strong to proceed to trial.

What happens during the pretrial process often determines the outcome of a criminal case. Indeed, the overwhelming majority of criminal cases never make it to trial. Some cases are dropped or dismissed for lack of sufficient evidence; many others result in convictions pursuant to guilty pleas. A substantial number of these guilty pleas result from negotiations between prosecutors and defense counsel. In such cases, trials are unnecessary. Where a defendant pleads guilty or no contest to an offense, there is a factual basis for the plea, and the court is satisfied that the plea

petty offenses Minor crimes for which fines or short jail terms are the only prescribed modes of punishment.

criminal procedure The rules of law governing the procedures by which crimes are investigated, prosecuted, adjudicated, and punished.

initial appearance After arrest, the first appearance of the accused before a judge or magistrate, at which the charges against a defendant are read and the defendant is advised of his or her constitutional rights. Sometimes referred to as the "first appearance."

preliminary hearing A hearing held to determine whether there is sufficient evidence to hold an accused for trial.

grand jury A group of citizens who are convened either to conduct an investigation or to determine whether there is sufficient evidence to warrant the prosecution of an accused.

arraignment An appearance before a court of law for the purpose of pleading to a criminal charge.

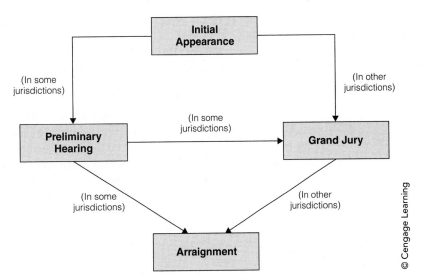

FIGURE 5.1 Major Components of Pretrial Process.

has been entered voluntarily, guilt is pronounced, and the process moves along to the sentencing stage. Given the relative infrequency of trials, pretrial procedures have great importance in the day-to-day operation of the criminal justice system.

The Right to Counsel

right to counsel (1) The right to retain an attorney to represent oneself in court. (2) The right of an indigent person to have an attorney provided at public expense.

Before undertaking a detailed examination of pretrial procedures, we must consider the contours of the **right to counsel**, which is essential to preserving the fundamental fairness of all criminal procedures. The defense attorney not only represents the accused in pretrial court proceedings, but also advises on strategy, and often serves as the negotiator between the defendant and the prosecutor. Thus, the attorney for the defense plays an essential role in the criminal process. Indeed, in our adversarial legal system, the right to counsel may be the single most important right possessed by persons accused of serious crimes. The Supreme Court has observed that "the right of one charged with crime to counsel may not be deemed fundamental and essential in some countries, but it is in ours." *Gideon v. Wainwright*, 372 U.S. 335, 344, 83 S.Ct. 792, 796, 9 L.Ed.2d 799, 805 (1963).

Common-Law Background of the Right to Counsel

Under the early English common law, there was no right to counsel for persons accused of treason or felonies. Somewhat ironically, by modern standards, the common law did recognize a right to counsel in misdemeanor cases. In 1698, Parliament enacted a law recognizing a right to counsel in cases of treason. By the late eighteenth century, the common law recognized a limited right to counsel in felony cases, and in 1836 Parliament passed legislation recognizing the right to counsel for all criminal defendants. Under the common law and the aforementioned acts of Parliament, the right to counsel meant the right to hire a barrister (a lawyer admitted to trial practice) at a person's own expense. It was not until 1903 that Parliament passed the Poor Prisoner's Defense Act, requiring that indigent defendants be provided counsel at public expense.

The Modern American Approach

In the United States, the right to counsel has likewise evolved through both judicial decisions and legislation. As the Sixth Amendment to the U.S. Constitution provides, "In all criminal prosecutions, the accused shall enjoy the right . . . to have the Assistance of Counsel for his defense."

The Sixth Amendment has been consistently interpreted to allow defendants to employ counsel in all federal prosecutions, including treason, felony, and misdemeanor cases. Similar provisions in the fifty state constitutions have been interpreted to allow defendants to retain counsel in state criminal prosecutions. Irrespective of state constitutional protection, the accused is protected by the federal constitution. In 1963, the Supreme Court held that the Sixth Amendment right to counsel applies to prosecutions in the state courts by way of the Due Process Clause of the Fourteenth Amendment. *Gideon v. Wainwright*, supra. Today, criminal defendants have the right to retain attorneys to represent them in all types of criminal prosecutions, whether in state court, in federal court, or before military tribunals.

Indigency and the Right to Counsel

Although criminal defendants have the right to employ attorneys to represent them, many defendants are too poor to afford private counsel. To what extent does the law mandate that they be provided counsel at public expense?

indigency Poverty: in context, the inability to afford an attorney.

In 1790, Congress first addressed the issue of **indigency** in the context of federal criminal prosecutions for capital crimes. The Federal Crimes Act of 1790, 1 Stat. 112, required federal judges to assign counsel to indigent defendants in capital cases, at least where defendants requested representation. Some states emulated the act of Congress by providing for appointed counsel in capital cases, but most did not.

The Scottsboro Case

In this highly publicized case in the early 1930s, the Supreme Court held that the Fourteenth Amendment required states to observe the requirement long since imposed on federal courts by Congress. *Powell v. Alabama*, 287 U.S. 45, 53 S.Ct. 55, 77 L.Ed. 158 (1932). In the "Scottsboro case," as it has become known, several black youths were charged with raping two white women. Within a week of being arrested, the defendants were tried, convicted, and sentenced to death, all without meaningful assistance of counsel. The Supreme Court reversed their convictions:

> In light of the . . . ignorance and illiteracy of the defendants, their youth, the circumstances of public hostility, the imprisonment and the close surveillance of the defendants by the military forces, the fact that their friends and families were all in other states and communication with them necessarily difficult, and above all that they stood in deadly peril of their lives . . . we think that . . . the failure of the trial court to make an effective appointment of counsel was . . . a denial of due process within the meaning of the Fourteenth Amendment. 287 U.S. at 71, 53 S.Ct. at 65, 77 L.Ed. at 171 (1932).

Relying heavily on its reasoning in *Powell v. Alabama*, the Supreme Court held four years later that the Sixth Amendment requires federal courts to appoint counsel for indigent defendants in all felony cases. *Johnson v. Zerbst*, 304 U.S. 458, 58 S.Ct. 1019, 82 L.Ed. 1461 (1938). Subsequently, Congress passed the Criminal Justice Act of 1964, 18 U.S.C.A. § 3006A, which provided that all indigent defendants in federal criminal cases are entitled to have appointed counsel.

In the wake of *Powell v. Alabama*, many states adopted laws creating a right to counsel at state expense, at least in capital cases. Some states went further by providing counsel for all indigent defendants in felony prosecutions. In states where appointed counsel was not a legal requirement, it was not uncommon for trial judges to appoint new members of the bar to represent indigent felony defendants *pro bono* (free of charge).

In *Betts v. Brady*, 316 U.S. 455, 62 S.Ct. 1252, 86 L.Ed. 1595 (1942), the Supreme Court held that state courts were under no federal constitutional obligation to provide counsel to indigent defendants. Writing for the Court, Justice Owen Roberts concluded that "while want of counsel in a particular case may result in a conviction lacking in such fundamental fairness, we cannot say that the Amendment embodies an inexorable command that no trial for any offense, or in any court, can be fairly conducted and justice accorded a defendant who is not represented by counsel." 316 U.S. at 473, 62 S.Ct. at 1262, 86 L.Ed. at 1607.

The *Gideon* Decision

In 1963, the Supreme Court under Chief Justice Earl Warren overturned *Betts v. Brady* and held that the Fourteenth Amendment requires states to provide counsel to indigent defendants in all felony cases. In his opinion for a unanimous bench in *Gideon v. Wainwright*, supra, Justice Hugo Black observed:

> From the very beginning, our state and national constitutions and laws have laid great emphasis on procedural and substantive safeguards designed to assure fair trials before impartial tribunals in which every defendant stands equal before the law. This noble ideal cannot be realized if the poor man charged with crime has to face his accusers without a lawyer to assist him. 372 U.S. at 344, 83 S.Ct. at 796–797, 9 L.Ed.2d at 805.

Because the *Gideon* decision was made retroactive, it allowed numerous persons serving time in state prisons to win their freedom by seeking a writ of *habeas corpus* in the state or federal courts. In Florida, where the *Gideon* case originated, the state was forced to release or retry hundreds of convicted criminals. Other states experienced similar challenges. Today, *Gideon v. Wainwright* has come to be widely accepted by state officials who recognize that representation by counsel is essential to the fair and effective functioning of the adversary system of justice.

Indigent Misdemeanor Defendants

In 1972, the Supreme Court extended the *Gideon* decision to encompass defendants who were sentenced to jail terms for misdemeanors. *Argersinger v. Hamlin*, 407 U.S. 25, 92 S.Ct. 2006, 32 L.Ed.2d 530 (1972). But the Court's decision did not resolve the question of whether counsel had to be provided to misdemeanor defendants who faced possible jail terms, as distinct from those who are actually sentenced to jail. In 1979, the Court opted for the **actual imprisonment standard**. *Scott v. Illinois*, 440 U.S. 367, 99 S.Ct. 1158, 59 L.Ed.2d 383 (1979). The actual imprisonment standard poses a problem for judges, for if an indigent defendant to a misdemeanor charge is denied counsel and is subsequently found guilty, the judge is barred from imposing a jail term. To do so would be a constitutional violation likely to result in a reversal of the defendant's conviction. This places the judge in the anomalous position of having to consider the sentence before determining the guilt or innocence of the accused. As a result, several states have gone beyond the federal constitutional requirement announced in *Scott v. Illinois* by providing counsel to indigent defendants in all misdemeanor cases where defendants face possible jail terms.

actual imprisonment standard The standard governing the applicability of the federal constitutional right of an indigent person to have counsel appointed in a misdemeanor case. For the right to be violated, the indigent defendant must actually be sentenced to jail or prison after having been tried without appointed counsel.

JURISPRUDENCE

Scott v. Illinois, 440 U.S. 367, 99 S.Ct. 1158, 59 L.Ed.2d 383 (1979)

Aubrey Scott was convicted of shoplifting and fined $50; however, Scott was unable to afford counsel to represent him. The statute under which Scot was prosecuted set the maximum penalty for shoplifting at a $500 fine and/or one year in jail. At his summary trial, Scott requested the appointment of counsel; however, the trial court denied his request. In a 5–4 decision, the Supreme Court held the Sixth and Fourteenth Amendments require "that no indigent criminal defendant be sentenced to a term of imprisonment unless the State has afforded him the right to assistance of appointed counsel in his defense." However, the Court also held that the Sixth and Fourteenth Amendments "do not

require a state trial court to appoint counsel for a criminal defendant, such as Scott, who is charged with a statutory offense for which imprisonment upon conviction is authorized but not imposed." Therefore, the Court explained that *Argersinger v. Hamlin* "limits the constitutional right to appointed counsel in state criminal proceedings to a case that actually leads to imprisonment." Dissenting, Justice William Brennan opined: "The Court, in an opinion that at best ignores the basic principles of prior decisions, affirms Scott's conviction without counsel because he was sentenced only to pay a fine. In my view, the plain wording of the Sixth Amendment and the Court's precedents compel the conclusion that Scott's uncounseled conviction violated the Sixth and Fourteenth Amendments and should be reversed."

Representation of Indigent Persons at Pretrial Proceedings

Most people think of the right to counsel in terms of a defendant being represented at trial. Although this may be the most important stage of the criminal process for a defendant who pleads not guilty, most criminal cases do not go to trial. For the defendant who elects to plead guilty, the pretrial procedures are critically important. The right of indigent persons to be provided counsel extends to many pretrial procedures. The U.S. Supreme Court has specifically identified a number of critical stages where counsel must be provided to indigent persons. Such **critical pretrial stages** include preliminary hearings, *White v. Maryland*, 373 U.S. 59, 83 S.Ct. 1050, 10 L.Ed.2d 193 (1963); lineups after charges have been filed against the accused, *United States v. Wade*, 388 U.S. 218, 87 S.Ct. 1926, 18 L.Ed.2d 1149 (1967); postindictment interrogations, *Massiah v. United States*, 377 U.S. 201, 84 S.Ct. 1199, 12 L.Ed.2d 246 (1964); and arraignments, *Hamilton v. Alabama*, 368 U.S. 52, 82 S.Ct. 157, 7 L.Ed.2d 114 (1961).

critical pretrial stages
Significant procedural steps that occur before a criminal trial. A defendant has the right to counsel at these critical stages.

Alternative Means of Providing Counsel to Indigent Persons

The representation that is provided to indigent defendants may take the form of a public defender or an attorney appointed ad hoc by the court. Many states have established successful public defender systems. In most states that use this system, the public defender is an elected official provided with funds to hire a staff of lawyers, much like the public prosecutor. In other states, indigent defendants still depend largely on ad hoc appointment of counsel. Very often the attorneys appointed to represent indigent defendants in noncapital cases are new members of the bar with limited trial experience. Remuneration for appointed counsel tends to be modest.

There remains considerable controversy over which method of providing counsel is more cost effective and which method more effectively meets a state's constitutional responsibilities. Proponents of the public defender system note that public defenders are full-time specialists in criminal law, whereas appointed counsel may be relatively inexperienced in the field. Critics of the public defender system express concern about the constant contact between public defenders and prosecutors.

They argue that this undermines the adversary system, resulting in a routinization of the criminal process in which the interests of the accused become subordinated to a bureaucratic effort to maximize efficiency in the processing of cases.

Sometimes the public defender's office has a conflict in which codefendants want to pursue inconsistent defenses. In such instances, an outside attorney should be appointed. If trial counsel representing multiple defendants brings a conflict of interest to the judge's attention, separate counsel must be appointed unless the judge determines that the risk of conflict is remote. *Holloway v. Arkansas*, 435 U.S. 475, 98 S.Ct. 1173, 55 L.Ed.2d 426 (1978). Most states have statutes that provide for the appointment of private counsel in instances where public defenders have conflicts, but even in the absence of such statutes, courts generally take the position that they have the inherent authority to make such appointments.

Determining Who Is Indigent

Federal law leaves the determination of indigency to the discretion of the courts. This is also the case in most states. See, e.g., Ala. Rule Crim. Proc. 6.3. Courts tend to be liberal in this regard, refusing to equate indigency with destitution, and are generally inclined to appoint counsel if the cost of hiring a lawyer would prevent the defendant from making bail.

After arrest, the accused is asked to complete a form to elicit information about employment, income, assets, and liabilities. Before the defendant's first appearance in court, judicial staff members will attempt to verify the accuracy of the defendant's statement. This information is then passed along to assist the magistrate in determining whether the defendant is entitled to appointed counsel. In most jurisdictions, more than 75 percent of felony defendants are classified as indigent. Some state statutes provide for an assessment of an attorney's fee against a defendant who is represented by the public defender's office. See, e.g., West's Ann. Cal. Penal Code § 987.8. An indigent defendant may be assessed the costs of appointed counsel, and these costs may be collected at some later time if the defendant becomes solvent. See, e.g., *Fuller v. Oregon*, 417 U.S. 40, 94 S.Ct. 2116, 40 L.Ed.2d 642 (1974).

Self-Representation

self-representation Also known as a *pro se* defense, representing oneself in a criminal case.

The Supreme Court has held that there is a constitutional right to represent oneself in a criminal prosecution. *Faretta v. California*, 422 U.S. 806, 95 S.Ct. 2525, 45 L.Ed.2d 562 (1975). In *Faretta*, the Court said that the defendant's legal knowledge or skill has no bearing on the right to **self-representation**. However, the Court stressed that the defendant who waives the right to counsel and proceeds *pro se* (Latin, meaning "for oneself") must do so "knowingly and intelligently." Critics of the *Faretta* decision believe that criminal law and procedure have become too complex and technical to permit the nonlawyer defendant to engage in effective self-representation. They argue that due process requires that defendants be represented by trained counsel, lest fundamental fairness be denied. As the Supreme Court recognized in *Powell v. Alabama*,

> Even the intelligent and educated layman has small and sometimes no skill in the science of the law. If charged with a crime, he is incapable, generally, of determining for himself whether the indictment is good or bad. He is unfamiliar with the rules of evidence. Left without the aid of counsel he may be put on trial without a proper charge, and convicted upon incompetent evidence, or evidence irrelevant

to the issue or otherwise inadmissible. He lacks both the skill and knowledge adequately to prepare his defense, even though he may have a perfect one. He requires the guiding hand of counsel at every step in the proceedings against him. Without it, though he be not guilty, he faces a danger of conviction because he does not know how to establish his innocence. 287 U.S. 45, 69, 53 S.Ct. 55, 64, 77 L.Ed. 158, 170 (1932).

Despite the potential dangers of the *pro se* defense, the Supreme Court held in *Faretta* that the Constitution places the defendant's "free choice" above the need for effective representation in a criminal trial. The constitutional issue aside, many lawyers have said that "the defendant who chooses to represent himself has a fool for a client."

In 1984, the Supreme Court ruled that "a defendant does not have a constitutional right to receive personal instruction from the trial judge on courtroom procedure. Nor does the Constitution require judges to take over chores for a *pro se* defendant that would normally be attended to by trained counsel as a matter of course." *McKaskle v. Wiggins*, 465 U.S. 168, 183–184, 104 S.Ct. 944, 954, 79 L.Ed.2d 122, 136–137 (1984). Numerous appellate decisions from state courts have emphasized that before approving self-representation by a criminal defendant, the trial court must conduct a thorough *Faretta* hearing to determine whether the defendant has competently and intelligently exercised the right to choose self-representation. Basic to the conduct of such a hearing is that the trial judge must make the defendant aware of the dangers and disadvantages of self-representation. The objective is to ensure that the defendant seeking to represent himself or herself makes such choice only after being fully informed of the disadvantages of self-representation. Failure to conduct a thorough *Faretta* hearing can result in reversal of a conviction. See, for example, *State v. Chavis*, 644 P.2d 1202 (Wash. App. 1982), in which the court held that the trial judge's questions to the defendant must reveal the defendant's understanding and not merely consist of questions that call for a simple "yes" or "no" response.

But once a defendant has made the choice "knowingly and intelligently," the trial court is not required to give the defendant instructions on the law. This is illustrated by a 1993 decision of the California Supreme Court, reversing lower state courts. In *People v. Barnum*, 64 P.3d 788 (Cal. 2003), the state supreme court ruled that a trial court is not required to advise self-represented defendants of the privilege against compelled self-incrimination. Moreover, the constitutional right to self-representation does not imply a right to obstruct the workings of the criminal process. A trial judge may terminate self-representation by a defendant who engages in obstructionist conduct. *Illinois v. Allen*, 397 U.S. 337, 90 S.Ct. 1057, 25 L.Ed.2d 353 (1970).

Judges sometimes appoint standby counsel to assist defendants who choose self-representation. There are two principal advantages: (1) standby counsel can be available to answer questions by a *pro se* defendant; and (2) if it is necessary to terminate the *pro se* defense because of misconduct, standby counsel is available to complete the case.

Although a defendant has the right to self-representation, he or she may not be represented by another person who is not a member of the bar. Nor may a defendant force an unwilling attorney to represent him or her. *Wheat v. United States*, 486 U.S. 153, 108 S.Ct. 1692, 100 L.Ed.2d 140 (1988). By the same token, a trial judge does have the discretion to deny an attorney's motion to withdraw from representation—after, of course, examining counsel's reasons for wanting to withdraw.

Disposition of Petty Offenses

Petty (or petit) offenses are minor misdemeanors for which fines or short jail terms are the only prescribed modes of punishment. Usually, police issue citations rather than arrest people for such offenses. Common traffic violations fall under the category of petty offenses, as do most violations of local ordinances. Many states have decriminalized routine traffic violations altogether. This means that an officer who stops a motorist for committing such an infraction has no authority to make an arrest (unless, of course, there is probable cause to believe the motorist has committed another offense for which he or she may be arrested). Rather, the officer simply issues the motorist a **citation**. In other jurisdictions in which minor traffic violations are still considered criminal offenses, legislatures have passed **cite and release statutes** that instruct officers to issue citations rather than arrest motorists who are stopped only for minor traffic offenses.

citation A summons to appear in court, often used in traffic violations and other minor offenses.

cite and release statutes Laws permitting or requiring police officers to issue citations instead of making arrests for traffic violations or other minor misdemeanors or infractions.

A person who is cited for an infraction or minor misdemeanor may simply elect to waive the right to appear in court to contest the charge, in which case he or she is required to pay a predetermined fine. If the individual appears in court to contest the charges, the entire matter is typically resolved in one proceeding. Under most statutes decriminalizing minor traffic violations, the court must find that there is a preponderance of evidence to support the citation. If the court so finds, the cited party is ordered to pay a fine (along with court costs), but there is no criminal record because the infraction is a civil one. In the case of the minor misdemeanor, the accused may plead guilty or no contest, in which case guilt is pronounced and the sentence is imposed immediately. If the plea is not guilty, the court conducts a **summary trial** and determines guilt or innocence according to the reasonable doubt standard.

summary trial A trial that is conducted by a trial court to determine guilt or innocence in minor misdemeanor cases where defendants plead not guilty.

Although defendants clearly have a right to hire attorneys to represent them in minor misdemeanor cases, few exercise this right. Most people would rather go it alone before the magistrate. If they lose, which is highly probable, they typically pay a fine, which tends to be substantially less expensive than hiring an attorney. As noted earlier, the Supreme Court has said that there is no constitutional right for indigent persons to have counsel appointed in such minor cases except where defendants are actually sentenced to jail terms. *Scott v. Illinois*, supra.

The Initial Court Appearance

In major misdemeanor and felony cases, the procedure is much more complex and protracted. Typically, individuals charged with felonies are placed under arrest before any appearance in court. However, all persons placed under arrest must promptly be taken before a court of law. The purpose of the initial appearance is to begin the formal charging process. Essentially, the magistrate must perform three important functions at the initial appearance: (1) the charges must be read so that the accused knows exactly what he or she is being charged with; (2) the accused must be informed of relevant constitutional rights, including the right to remain silent and the right to counsel; and (3) a determination must be made of whether the accused should be released pending trial or remanded to custody to await the disposition of the case. As we shall discuss, the court may order the defendant to post bond in order to ensure future court appearances. If so, the amount of bail is determined at this time.

All jurisdictions require the prompt appearance of an arrestee before a court of law, but what constitutes "prompt"? Many jurisdictions require a suspect to be brought before a magistrate for an initial appearance within twenty-four hours after arrest. See, e.g., Fla. R. Crim. P. Rule 3.130(a). However, the U.S. Supreme Court has ruled that suspects may be detained for as long as forty-eight hours before being taken before a magistrate. *County of Riverside v. McLaughlin*, 500 U.S. 44, 111 S.Ct. 1661, 114 L.Ed.2d 49 (1991).

Rule 5(a) of the Federal Rules of Criminal Procedure provides that a person arrested for a federal offense shall be taken before a magistrate "without unnecessary delay" for a first appearance. Under the so-called *McNabb–Mallory* rule (see *McNabb v. United States,* 318 U.S. 332, 63 S.Ct. 608, 87 L.Ed. 819 [1943], and *Mallory v. United States,* 354 U.S. 449, 77 S.Ct. 1356, 1 L.Ed.2d 1479 [1957]), confessions made during periods of detention that violate the prompt presentment requirement of Rule 5(a) are inadmissible at trial. Under 18 U.S.C.A. § 3501(c), however, Congress provided that a confession made within six hours after arrest is not rendered inadmissible solely because of a delay in bringing the accused before the magistrate.

In *Alvarez-Sanchez v. United States*, 975 F.2d 1396 (9th Cir. 1992), the U.S. Court of Appeals for the Ninth Circuit reversed a federal counterfeiting conviction because of a delay in the pretrial process. The defendant was originally arrested on a Friday by state authorities on state charges. A search of his home turned up evidence of counterfeit U.S. currency. On Monday, federal agents took the defendant into custody and obtained a confession. Because of congestion in court, the defendant was not taken before a federal magistrate until Tuesday. The Ninth Circuit held that the confession could not be used as evidence because of the delay in the first appearance. In reversing the Court of Appeals, the Supreme Court held that the promptness requirement is inapplicable where an accused person is first arrested on state charges and is later turned over to federal authorities on related charges. As Justice Clarence Thomas explained, "Until a person is arrested or detained for a federal crime, there is no duty, obligation, or reason to bring him before a judicial officer 'empowered to commit persons charged with offenses against the laws of the United States,' and therefore, no 'delay' under § 3501(c) can occur." *United States v. Alvarez-Sanchez*, 511 U.S. 350, 358, 114 S.Ct. 1599, 1604, 128 L.Ed.2d 319, 328 (1994).

Pretrial Release and Pretrial Detention

The immediate goal for anyone who has been arrested and confined to jail is to secure release as soon as possible. Beyond the obvious desirability of freedom, an accused who remains at liberty can be of considerable assistance to defense counsel in locating witnesses and being able to confer with counsel outside the jail setting. In addition, a person who remains at liberty can usually pursue gainful employment and discharge family responsibilities pending the disposition of the criminal charges.

pretrial release Release of a defendant on bail or personal recognizance pending adjudication of criminal charges.

Granting an accused **pretrial release** is commonly referred to as granting bail. Judicial authority to grant a defendant bail originated in English common law. Statutes or court rules commonly grant judges this authority today. In determining whether a defendant is entitled to pretrial release, the court usually considers the accused's prior convictions (if any), character, employment history, and ties to family and the community, as well as the nature and scope of the current charges. In making these determinations, judges rely on reports prepared by court personnel. In the federal system, these reports are prepared by an agency called Pretrial Services. Increasingly, courts are requiring that arrested persons be drug tested. Although not used as evidence, the results of the drug test help the judge decide whether to grant pretrial release and whether to impose conditions upon that release. As with probation and parole, pretrial release may be contingent on a defendant's willingness to abide by certain conditions, such as avoiding certain places or activities or remaining at home after dark.

Modes of Pretrial Release

release on personal recognizance Pretrial release of a defendant based solely on the defendant's promise to appear for future court dates.

Pretrial release can take several forms. The four most common are **release on personal recognizance**, release to the custody of another, posting an individual bond, and posting a **surety bond**.

- *Personal recognizance.* A recognizance is a person's promise to appear in court as required. The defendant signs a guarantee to appear at all required proceedings and, in some cases, acknowledges certain restrictions on his or her activities.

surety bond A sum of money or property that is posted or guaranteed by a party, usually an insurer, to ensure the future court appearance of another person.

- *Release to the custody of another.* The magistrate may release the defendant to the custody of some responsible person, often the defendant's attorney, who agrees to exercise custodial supervision and to assume responsibility for the defendant's required court appearances.
- *Posting an individual bond.* The defendant posts a bond agreeing to appear in court as required. The defendant may or may not be required to post an amount of cash or other security to guarantee the undertaking.

bail bond Sum of money posted to ensure a defendant's subsequent appearance in court.

- *Posting a surety bond.* Also known as a **bail bond**, this is the common method of securing pretrial release by paying a premium to a third party that agrees to post the bond for the accused. The magistrate sets the amount of a bond for the particular offense. Often, this is based on a schedule of bonds set by the judge of the court having jurisdiction over the offense. The defendant signs the bond, agreeing to appear as required. The bond is guaranteed by the defendant's surety, which means that should the defendant default, the surety, or bonding company, is bound to pay the court the amount of the bond (called the "penal sum"). A defendant usually pays a premium of about 10 percent of the amount of the bond and in most instances provides the surety with collateral to induce the surety to sign the bond. Sureties bonding a defendant are responsible for ensuring the defendant's appearance; therefore, they are commonly given the statutory authority to arrest an absconding defendant. To this end, sureties often employ **skip tracers**, who are, in effect, modern bounty hunters who seek out and return absconding defendants. When a surety promptly produces a defendant, it can usually recover any money forfeited to the court because of the defendant's failure to appear.

skip tracers People who track down alleged offenders who have fled to avoid prosecution. Also known as bounty hunters.

The Issue of Excessive Bail

excessive bail Where a court requires a defendant to post an unreasonably large amount or imposes unreasonable conditions as a prerequisite for a defendant to be released before trial. The Eighth Amendment to the U.S. Constitution prohibits courts from requiring "excessive bail."

Recognizing the common-law practice of allowing pretrial release on bail, the Eighth Amendment to the federal constitution states that "excessive bail shall not be required." The Supreme Court has made it clear that the purpose of bail is to ensure the appearance of the accused in court, not to inflict punishment: "Bail set at a figure higher than an amount reasonably calculated to fulfill this purpose is 'excessive' under the Eighth Amendment." *Stack v. Boyle*, 342 U.S. 1, 5, 72 S.Ct. 1, 3, 96 L.Ed. 3, 6 (1951). However, the Supreme Court has never held that the Excessive Bail Clause of the Eighth Amendment is enforceable against the states via the Fourteenth Amendment, leaving the matter of **excessive bail** in state criminal cases to the state constitutions, legislatures, and courts.

JURISPRUDENCE

Stack v. Boyle, 342 U.S. 1, 72 S.Ct. 1, 96 L.Ed. 3 (1951)

Loretta Starvus Stack and eleven other members of the Communist Party were arrested and charged with "subversive activities" in violation of the Alien Registration Act of 1940, better known as the Smith Act. Their bail was initially set at different amounts ranging from $2,500 to $100,000, but later was fixed "pending trial in the uniform amount of $50,000." Each defendant moved for a reduction in bail under the theory that the $50,000 was "excessive under the Eighth Amendment." The Government's only argument against lowering the bail was that four other individuals previously convicted under the Smith Act "had forfeited bail." While the Government presented no evidence relating specifically Stack and the other

defendants, the U.S. District Court denied the motion to reduce bond. The defendants, who could not make the $50,000 bail, sought unsuccessfully to challenge their pretrial detention via habeas corpus. In reviewing the denial of relief by the U.S. Court of Appeals, the Supreme Court held that the bail was not "fixed by proper methods." The Court stated that bail "set before trial at a figure higher than an amount reasonably calculated to fulfill the purpose of ensuring the presence of the defendant is 'excessive' under the Eighth Amendment." The Court went on to establish the standards for setting bail by stating that the amount of bail "must be based upon standards relevant to the purpose of assuring the presence of that defendant." The Court sent the case back to the District Court for new bail hearings.

The Illinois Code of Criminal Procedure provides that "the amount of bail shall be: (1) Sufficient to assure compliance with the conditions set forth in the bail bond; (2) Not oppressive; (3) Considerate of the financial ability of the accused." 725 Ill. Comp. Stat. Ann. § 5/110-5(b). Similarly, the Texas Code of Criminal Procedure states that "the power to require bail is not to be so used as to make it an instrument of oppression." Vernon's Tex. Code Crim. P. § 17.15(2).

Pretrial Detention

Federal Bail Reform Act of 1984 An act that provides that a defendant charged with a federal crime may be denied bail if the prosecution can show that the defendant poses a threat to public safety.

The Eighth Amendment prohibition of "excessive bail" is vague regarding the existence of a constitutional right to pretrial release. However, the Supreme Court has ruled that there is no right to bail under the Eighth Amendment. *United States v. Salerno*, 481 U.S. 739, 107 S.Ct. 2095, 95 L.Ed.2d 697 (1987). The **Federal Bail Reform Act of 1984**, 18 U.S.C.A. § 3141 *et seq.*, allows federal courts to detain arrestees without bail on the ground of the arrestee's danger to the community, as well as the need to ensure future court appearances. First, the court must determine whether the government has established "by a preponderance of the evidence that the defendant either has been charged with one of the crimes enumerated in Section 3142(f)(1) or that the defendant presents a risk of flight or obstruction of justice." *United States v. Friedman*, 837 F.2d 48, 49 (2d Cir. 1988). If the government satisfies that burden, the court must determine whether there are "conditions or a combination of conditions which reasonably will assure the presence of the defendant at trial." *United States v. Shakur*, 817 F.2d 189, 195 (2d Cir. 1987).

pretrial detention Holding a defendant in jail pending trial.

Congress has set forth various factors that a court must consider in weighing the appropriateness of **pretrial detention**. Among these are the nature of the offense, the weight of the evidence against the suspect, the history and character of the person charged, and the nature and seriousness of the risk to the community. 18 U.S.C.A. § 3142(g). The statute provides for an adversary hearing on the issue of detention. The government must show by clear and convincing evidence that pretrial release

JURISPRUDENCE

United States v. Salerno, 481 U.S. 739, 107 S.Ct. 2095, 95 L.Ed.2d 697 (1987)

Anthony Salerno and Vincent Cafaro, members of the Genovese crime family, were arrested after being charged with violating the Racketeer Influenced and Corrupt Organizations (RICO) Act as well as mail fraud, wire fraud, extortion, and various gambling offenses. On the government's motion, they were denied bail under the Bail Reform Act of 1984, which allows pretrial detention when the prosecution establishes by clear and convincing evidence that no conditions of release will ensure the safety of the community or any person. Concluding that the statute allows defendants to be punished for crimes they might commit in the future, the U.S. Court of Appeals found the Bail Reform Act to be facially unconstitutional.

The Supreme Court reversed, "given the Act's legitimate and compelling regulatory purpose and the procedural protections it offers" to the accused. The Court's examination of the legislative history revealed the Act was not intended as pretrial punishment, but rather "as a potential solution to the pressing societal problem of crimes committed by persons on release" and to prevent "danger to the community." In effect, the Court held that there is no constitutional right to bail under the Eighth Amendment. In a forceful dissenting opinion, Justice Thurgood Marshall noted that the case "brings before the Court for the first time a statute in which Congress declares that a person innocent of any crime may be jailed indefinitely, pending the trial of allegations which are legally presumed to be untrue...."

will not reasonably ensure the appearance of the accused or the safety of other persons and the community. *United States v. Orta*, 760 F.2d 887 (8th Cir. 1985).

The judge or magistrate who denies pretrial release must prepare a written statement justifying the decision to detain the accused and direct that the detainee be afforded a reasonable opportunity for private consultation with counsel. 18 U.S.C.A. § 3142(i). Finally, the law provides for a prompt appellate review of the detention decision. 18 U.S.C.A. § 3145(c). In upholding the Bail Reform Act of 1984 against an Eighth Amendment challenge, the Supreme Court in *United States v. Salerno* said that "when Congress has mandated detention on the basis of a compelling interest other than prevention of flight, as it has here, the Eighth Amendment does not require release on bail." 481 U.S. at 754–755, 107 S.Ct. at 2105, 95 L.Ed.2d at 713–714.

The *Salerno* decision, although technically limited to the constitutionality of federal pretrial detention, suggests the validity of state laws or court decisions that deny bail to persons accused of violent crimes, especially where arrestees already have a record of violent crime.

In many states, a defendant is ineligible for pretrial release if charged with a crime that is punishable by death or life imprisonment and if the "proof is evident or the presumption [of guilt] is great." See, e.g., *State v. Arthur*, 390 So.2d 717, 718 (Fla. 1980). In the majority of these states, before denying pretrial release, courts must determine whether the facts, viewed in light most favorable to the state, are legally sufficient to sustain a verdict of guilty. See, e.g., *Fontaine v. Mullen*, 366 A.2d 1138 (R.I. 1976).

The Formal Charging Process

subpoenas Judicial orders to appear at a certain place and time to give testimony.

Prosecutors occupy a uniquely important role in the criminal justice system. The prosecutor decides whether to proceed with a criminal case and whether to negotiate charges with the defense, and must, at various stages of the process, demonstrate the veracity of the government's case to the satisfaction of the court. The prosecutor causes the court to issue **subpoenas** to compel the attendance of witnesses to testify, to bring in documents, and to provide nontestimonial physical evidence such as handwriting specimens, *United States v. Mara*, 410 U.S. 19, 93 S.Ct. 774, 35 L.Ed.2d 99 (1973), and voice exemplars, *United States v. Dionisio*, 410 U.S. 1, 93 S.Ct. 764, 35 L.Ed.2d 67 (1973).

State and federal prosecutors have broad discretion in deciding whether to proceed with criminal charges initiated by a complainant or the police. The prosecutor may decide to drop a case for a variety of reasons, ranging from insufficient evidence to a judgment that the criminal sanction is inappropriate in a given situation. Alternatively, the prosecutor may decide to proceed on a lesser charge.

The American Bar Association's *Standards Relating to the Prosecution and Defense Function* offers prosecutors guidelines for the exercise of their discretion in making the decision to charge. The standards admonish prosecutors not to be influenced by personal or political motivations and not to bring more charges, in number or degree, than can reasonably be supported at trial.

prosecutorial discretion
The leeway afforded prosecutors in deciding whether or not to bring charges and to engage in plea bargaining.

Prosecutorial discretion facilitates the widespread yet controversial practice of plea bargaining, which we discuss later in the chapter. Although very broad, prosecutorial discretion is not unlimited. The Equal Protection Clause of the Fourteenth Amendment is offended by selective prosecution. Prosecutors may not single out defendants for prosecution on the basis of race, religion, or other impermissible classifications. *Oyler v. Boles*, 368 U.S. 448, 82 S.Ct. 501, 7 L.Ed.2d 446 (1962).

One of the long-standing controversies in the criminal justice field is whether police and prosecutors unfairly target people on the basis of race in the enforcement of certain types of criminal prohibitions. In 1996, the U.S. Supreme Court made it more difficult for criminal defendants to make prosecutors respond to claims that they are engaging in racially motivated selective prosecution. *United States v. Armstrong*, 517 U.S. 456, 116 S.Ct. 1480, 134 L.Ed.2d 687 (1996). A party making such a claim must show that similarly situated individuals of a different race were not prosecuted. Obviously, this is a difficult showing to make.

prosecutorial immunity
A prosecutor's legal shield against civil suits stemming from his or her official actions

Courts have not only cloaked prosecutors with broad discretion in determining whether to prosecute, but they have also long held prosecutors immune from civil actions for malicious prosecution, as long as they are acting within the scope of their offices. *Griffith v. Slinkard*, 44 N.E. 1001 (Ind. 1896). More recently, the U.S. Supreme Court has ruled that the same considerations that underlie **prosecutorial immunity** in tort actions require that prosecutors be immune from damages for deprivation of defendants' constitutional rights under 42 U.S.C.A. § 1983. See, e.g., *Imbler v. Pachtman,* 424 U.S. 409, 96 S.Ct. 984, 47 L.Ed.2d 128 (1976).

JURISPRUDENCE

United States v. Armstrong, 517 U.S. 456, 116 S.Ct. 1480, 134 L.Ed.2d 687 (1996)

Five African Americans charged with selling crack cocaine persuaded lower courts to dismiss the charges against them because prosecutors refused to explain how they chose which crack cocaine cases to pursue. Dividing 8–1, the Court held that defendants who make selective prosecution claims must show that people of other races were not prosecuted for the same crimes. "To establish a discriminatory effect in a race case, the claimant must show that similarly situated individuals of a different race were not prosecuted," Chief Justice William H. Rehnquist wrote for the court. Because the defendants did not make such a showing, the prosecutors were not required to respond to their allegation of discrimination. In his solo dissent, Justice Stevens stressed "the need for judicial vigilance over certain types of drug prosecutions," referring to the fact that the overwhelming majority of individuals charged with offenses involving crack cocaine are black.

Limitations on Prosecutorial Conduct

E. J. Reagan was charged with torturing a child and assault with intent to do great bodily harm. The prosecutor agreed to drop the charges if Reagan could pass a lie detector test. The defendant agreed and passed the test. Pursuant to the agreement, the prosecutor filed a *nolle prosequi* (Latin for "not wish to prosecute"), and the charges were dismissed. Subsequently, the prosecutor became convinced that the polygraph examination was flawed. He then filed a new complaint on the same charges. The defendant was tried and convicted. The Michigan Supreme Court reversed the conviction and discharged the defendant. The court said that "a pledge of public faith in this instance gave force to an unwise agreement."

People v. Reagan, 235 N.W.2d 581 (Mich. 1975).

Determining the Sufficiency of the Government's Case

Assuming that the prosecutor decides to proceed with criminal charges, an examination of the sufficiency of the evidence generally follows. The purpose of this procedure is to ensure that there is probable cause for trial. This determination is made by a magistrate, a grand jury, or both. In some jurisdictions, the prosecutor files a document called an **information** in the appropriate court of law. An information is a formal accusatorial document detailing the specific charges against a defendant. After the filing of the information, a preliminary hearing may be requested to determine the sufficiency of the evidence in support of the information. In Florida, a defendant who is not charged in an information or indictment within twenty-one days from the date of arrest or service of the capias shall have a right to an adversary preliminary hearing on any felony charge. Fla. R. Crim. P. 3.133(b)(1). In other jurisdictions, the prosecutor must obtain an indictment from a grand jury. Some jurisdictions employ a combination of both mechanisms. In Tennessee, for example, a person accused of a felony must be indicted by a grand jury; a preliminary examination before the grand jury proceeding is available at the option of the accused. Tenn. R. Crim. P., Rule 5.

information A document filed by a prosecutor under oath charging one or more persons with commission of a crime.

The Preliminary Hearing

In a preliminary hearing (not to be confused with the initial appearance), a judge or magistrate examines the state's case to determine whether there is probable cause to bind the accused over to the grand jury or (in the absence of a grand jury requirement) hold the accused for trial. The Supreme Court has said that when an arrest is made without a warrant, a preliminary hearing is constitutionally required in the absence of grand jury review to determine the sufficiency of an information. *Gerstein v. Pugh*, 420 U.S. 103, 95 S.Ct. 854, 43 L.Ed.2d 54 (1975). *Gerstein* does not require preliminary hearings to be full-blown adversarial proceedings. Nevertheless, most states do provide for open hearings with both parties represented. Typically, in a preliminary hearing the defense has the privilege of cross-examining witnesses for the prosecution and can learn the details and strengths of the state's case. The state can preserve testimony of witnesses who may balk at testifying at the trial. Thus, the preliminary hearing serves the interests of both the prosecution and the defense by providing an inquiry into probable cause for arrest and detention, a screening device for prosecutors, and an opportunity for the defense to discover the prosecutor's case.

The Grand Jury

In many jurisdictions, prosecutors must obtain an indictment or "true bill" from the grand jury in addition to, or instead of, the preliminary hearing. The Fifth Amendment to the U.S. Constitution states that "[n]o person shall be held to answer for a capital, or otherwise infamous crime, unless on a presentment or indictment of a grand jury."

The Supreme Court has held that states are not bound by the Fourteenth Amendment to abide by the grand jury requirement imposed on the federal courts by the Fifth Amendment. *Hurtado v. California*, 110 U.S. 516, 4 S.Ct. 111, 28 L.Ed. 232 (1884). Nevertheless, about half the states have constitutional provisions or statutes requiring the use of grand juries in certain types of criminal cases. Other states use grand juries primarily in an investigatory or supervisory capacity.

The grand jury is an institution deeply rooted in English common law. For a detailed discussion, see *Costello v. United States*, 350 U.S. 359, 362, 76 S.Ct. 406, 408, 100 L.Ed. 397, 401 (1956). At common law, the grand jury comprised twenty-three persons, at least twelve of whom had to agree to hand down an indictment. Today, federal grand juries comprise sixteen to twenty-three persons, Fed. R. Crim. P. 6(a), but the "twelve votes for indictment" rule applies in every case, Fed. R. Crim. P. 6(f). States vary in the size of grand juries, but in every state at least a majority of grand jurors must agree that there is probable cause in order to hand down an indictment against the accused. In Texas, for example, the grand jury consists of twelve jurors. Texas Const., Art. V, § 13. At least nine grand jurors must agree to hand down an indictment. Vernon's Tex. Code Crim. P. § 20.19.

Exclusion of Minorities from Grand Juries

As with trial jurors, the selection of grand jurors must not systematically exclude certain groups in the community. A defendant may be able to obtain a reversal of a conviction on this basis. For example, in *Castaneda v. Partida*, 430 U.S. 482, 97 S.Ct. 1272, 51 L.Ed.2d 498 (1977), the Supreme Court reversed a conviction after finding that Mexican Americans had been grossly underrepresented on a grand jury that indicted a Mexican American defendant. In his opinion for the Court, Justice Harry Blackmun outlined the necessary steps to make a case that such a violation has occurred:

> [I]n order to show that an equal protection violation has occurred in the context of grand jury selection, the defendant must show that the procedure employed resulted in substantial underrepresentation of his race or of the identifiable group to which he belongs. The first step is to establish that the group is one that is a recognizable, distinct class, singled out for different treatment under the laws, as written or as applied. . . . Next, the degree of underrepresentation must be proved, by comparing the proportion of the group in the total population to the proportion called to serve as grand jurors, over a significant period of time. . . . This method of proof, sometimes called the "rule of exclusion," has been held to be available as a method of proving discrimination in jury selection against a delineated class. . . . Finally, a selection procedure that is susceptible of abuse or is not racially neutral supports the presumption of discrimination raised by the statistical showing. . . . Once the defendant has shown substantial underrepresentation of his group, he has made out a *prima facie* case of discriminatory purpose, and the burden then shifts to the State to rebut that case. 430 U.S. at 494, 97 S.Ct. at 1280, 51 L.Ed.2d at 510–511 (1977).

Functions and Powers of the Grand Jury

Historically, the grand jury acted as a shield to prevent unfounded charges and arbitrary and overzealous prosecution. Today, grand juries seldom refuse to hand down indictments sought by prosecutors, causing some critics to question the institution's use as a safeguard for the rights of the accused. Perhaps this perception has led several states to adopt the information/preliminary hearing mechanism in lieu of the grand jury. In most midwestern and western states, the grand jury is seldom used to charge persons with crimes.

The grand jury, like the magistrate presiding over the preliminary hearing, examines testimony and other evidence the prosecution has collected against the accused. Unlike the preliminary hearing, the grand jury proceeding is normally closed: the defendant is generally not represented by counsel or even present at the proceeding. Although controversial, grand jury secrecy encourages uninhibited testimony by witnesses and prevents the circulation of derogatory statements about persons who are ultimately not indicted. *Pittsburgh Plate Glass Co. v. United States*, 360 U.S. 395, 79 S.Ct. 1237, 3 L.Ed.2d 1323 (1959). Grand jury secrecy also protects grand jurors from intimidation and possible reprisals. In a federal grand jury, except while it is deliberating or voting, all proceedings must be recorded by a court reporter or by a suitable recording device. Traditionally, proceedings before a grand jury remain secret; however, a trial judge has discretion to allow disclosure subject to conditions. Fed. R. Crim. P. 6(e). In the states, testimony before the grand jury is not always transcribed, and if it is, access to transcripts is either limited or nonexistent.

After the prosecutor has presented testimony and physical evidence, the members of the grand jury vote on whether to hand down an indictment. Rules that determine grand jury indictments vary among jurisdictions, but in no case can a grand jury return a true bill unless a majority of grand jurors vote to indict.

Grand juries possess the authority to compel the appearance of witnesses, to subpoena documents, to hold individuals in contempt, and to grant immunity from prosecution in exchange for testimony. Immunity is of two kinds. Transactional immunity bars any further prosecution of the witness for the specific transaction as to which the witness testified. Use immunity is more limited, barring only the use of the witness's testimony against the witness in a subsequent prosecution. Federal grand juries are authorized to grant use immunity. 18 U.S.C.A. § 6002. The basic purpose of granting immunity is to permit compulsion of testimony that otherwise would be privileged by the Fifth Amendment. *United States v. Weiss*, 599 F.2d 730 (5th Cir. 1979). Many states follow the federal statute; some states go further and permit grand juries to grant transactional immunity. The federal statutory bar against the use of immunized testimony applies equally to federal and state proceedings. *In re Grand Jury Proceedings*, 860 F.2d 11 (2d Cir. 1988).

Rights of Witnesses and Suspects

The Supreme Court has held that grand jury witnesses retain their Fifth Amendment privileges against compulsory self-incrimination. *Lefkowitz v. Turley*, 414 U.S. 70, 94 S.Ct. 316, 38 L.Ed.2d 274 (1973). Nevertheless, through a limited grant of immunity, a grand jury can override a witness's refusal to answer questions on Fifth Amendment grounds. The Supreme Court has also held that a grand jury's grant of immunity must be coextensive with the privilege against self-incrimination. Use immunity satisfies this requirement; transactional immunity is not required by the Constitution.

Kastigar v. United States, 406 U.S. 441, 92 S.Ct. 1653, 32 L.Ed.2d 212 (1972). Witnesses testifying before grand juries have no right to be represented by counsel, *In re Groban's Petition*, 352 U.S. 330, 77 S.Ct. 510, 1 L.Ed.2d 376 (1957), although some jurisdictions allow witnesses to consult with counsel outside the grand jury room. An attorney's appearance before a grand jury on behalf of a witness is generally thought to cause unnecessary delays and violate the secrecy of the proceeding.

In only a few states does the defendant have a right to appear before the grand jury to confront his or her accusers. Like witnesses, a suspect has no federal constitutional right to be represented by counsel inside the grand jury room. *United States v. Mandujano*, 425 U.S. 564, 96 S.Ct. 1768, 48 L.Ed.2d 212 (1976).

Evidence before the Grand Jury

Many rules of evidence that apply to the criminal trial do not apply to the grand jury. *Costello v. United States*, 350 U.S. 359, 76 S.Ct. 406, 100 L.Ed. 397 (1956). For example, hearsay evidence is generally admissible, whereas at trial it is not admitted over the defendant's objection. Moreover, evidence excluded from trial on Fourth or Fifth Amendment grounds is nevertheless admissible before a grand jury. *United States v. Calandra*, 414 U.S. 338, 94 S.Ct. 613, 38 L.Ed.2d 561 (1974). The theory is that the grand jury is an investigative body and that any infringement of the rights of the accused can be corrected in subsequent adversary court proceedings. Notwithstanding that a grand jury may consider evidence that is inadmissible at trial, it may not violate a valid evidentiary privilege (see Chapter 6) established under the Constitution, statutes, or the common law. *Branzburg v. Hayes*, 408 U.S. 665, 92 S.Ct. 2646, 33 L.Ed.2d 626 (1972).

JURISPRUDENCE

United States v. Calandra, 414 U.S. 338, 94 S.Ct. 613, 38 L.Ed.2d 561 (1974)

Federal agents searched John Calandra's place of business pursuant to a warrant authorizing seizure of bookmaking records and wagering paraphernalia. During the course of the search, an agent discovered and seized a document implicating Calandra in loansharking. As a result, a grand jury was convened to investigate loansharking, which subpoenaed Calandra to appear before it for the purposes of questioning him on the seized evidence. Calandra refused to testify on Fifth Amendment grounds against self-incrimination. Calandra then moved to suppress the loansharking evidence seized during the search of his office on the grounds that the affidavit supporting the warrant was insufficient and that the search exceeded the scope of the warrant. The trial court granted the motion and further ordered that Calandra did not have to answer any questions posed by the grand jury related to the loansharking evidence. However,

the Supreme Court held that "a witness summoned to appear and testify before a grand jury *may not* refuse to answer questions on the ground that they are based on evidence obtained from an unlawful search and seizure." The Court, speaking through Justice Powell, reinforced the notion that the exclusionary rule is a "judicially created remedy designed to safeguard Fourth Amendment rights generally through its deterrent effect on future unlawful police conduct, rather than a personal constitutional right of the party aggrieved." As a result of this purpose, the Court held that "allowing a grand jury witness to invoke the exclusionary rule would unduly interfere with the effective and expeditious discharge of the grand jury's duties, and extending the rule to grand jury proceedings would achieve only a speculative and minimal advance in deterring police misconduct at the expense of substantially impeding the grand jury's role." As a result, the exclusionary rule does not apply in grand jury proceedings.

Right to a Prompt Indictment

Under federal law an indictment must be filed within thirty days of arrest, 18 U.S.C.A. § 3161. Where delay in filing an indictment prejudices the presentation of a defense and is engaged in for an improper purpose, it violates the Due Process Clause. *United States v. Lovasco*, 431 U.S. 783, 97 S.Ct. 2044, 52 L.Ed.2d 752 (1977). Prejudice in this context means the sort of deprivation that impairs a defendant's right to a fair trial. See, e.g., *United States v. Elsbery*, 602 F.2d 1054 (2d Cir. 1979). In *United States v. Mmahat*, 106 F.3d 89 (5th Cir. 1997), the court said that the defendant must show actual prejudice and deliberate design by the government to gain tactical advantage to establish a claim of preindictment delay. Usually a defendant attempts to meet this standard by demonstrating that the prosecution's delay resulted in the loss of documentary evidence or the unavailability of a key witness.

State courts generally take a similar the approach. Illustrative is *State v. Smith*, 699 P.2d 711 (Utah 1985), where the court observed:

> A hard and fast rule that a prosecutor must file charges as soon as he has probable cause could result in the charging of innocent persons. Such a rule could also result in the acquittal of guilty persons by hampering the investigation of crimes. Therefore, a prosecutor is not required to file charges as soon as probable cause exists but before the prosecutor is reasonably satisfied that he will be able to establish the suspect's guilt beyond a reasonable doubt. For preaccusation delay to constitute reversible error, the delay must cause actual prejudice to the defendant's case and result in a tactical advantage for the prosecutor. *Id.* at 713.

Extradition

extradition The surrender of a person by one jurisdiction to another for the purpose of criminal prosecution.

Extradition is the surrender, on demand, of an individual accused or convicted of an offense committed within the territorial jurisdiction of the demanding government and outside the territory of the ceding government. See, e.g., *Terlinden v. Ames*, 184 U.S. 270, 22 S.Ct. 484, 46 L.Ed. 534 (1902). The objective is to prevent the escape of persons who stand accused or convicted of crimes and to secure their return to the jurisdiction from which they fled.

In a mobile society such as ours, it is not uncommon for persons accused of crimes to flee across state lines to avoid prosecution. Anticipating this problem, Article IV, Section 2 of the Constitution provides, "A Person charged in any State with Treason, Felony or any other crime, who shall flee from Justice, and be found in another state, shall on demand of the executive Authority of the State from which he fled, be delivered up, to be removed to the State having Jurisdiction of the crime."

To effectuate the constitutional provision, Congress has enacted statutes governing interstate extradition. 18 U.S.C.A. § 3182. Interstate extradition is a summary executive proceeding designed to enable each state to bring offenders to trial swiftly in the state where the alleged crime was committed. *Michigan v. Doran*, 439 U.S. 282, 99 S.Ct. 530, 58 L.Ed.2d 521 (1978). Every offense punishable by law in the jurisdiction where it was committed can subject the offender to extradition, but extradition is usually sought only in serious offenses. Frequently it is used to regain custody of parole violators, prison escapees, or persons who have "jumped bail."

Most states have adopted the Uniform Criminal Extradition Law, which sets out procedural rules for handling interstate extradition. The governor of the "demanding" state issues a requisition warrant seeking return of the fugitive. This is presented to the governor of the "asylum" state (that is, the state in which the fugitive is located). After investigation, the governor of the asylum state issues a warrant for the fugitive's arrest. An opportunity exists for the person sought as a fugitive to contest the extradition in a court of law in the asylum state. Often this challenge takes the form of a petition for a writ of habeas corpus challenging whether the petitioner is in fact the person charged or attacking the regularity of the proceedings. See, e.g., N.J. Stat. Ann. § 2A:160-18. Extradition proceedings seek the release of the prisoner who is to be extradited but do not focus on the issue of the prisoner's guilt or innocence.

Extradition of suspects or convicted criminals between nations is regulated by treaties, which usually provide that the crime involved must be a serious one in both nations and that the penalty for the person extradited will not be disproportionate to the crime. The United States does not have extradition treaties with all nations. Even where treaties are in force, some countries, including many European nations, will not extradite unless they are assured that the death penalty will not be imposed on a suspect. In addition, many nations will not extradite persons charged with offenses regarded as political offenses, such as treason, sedition, and espionage.

Jurisdiction and Venue

jurisdiction The authority of a court to hear and decide certain categories of legal disputes. Jurisdiction relates to the authority of a court over the person, subject matter, and geographical area.

venue The location of a trial or hearing.

Before it may hear and adjudicate a case, a court must possess **jurisdiction** over the subject matter and the parties to the case. State courts have jurisdiction only over persons who commit crimes in their particular states. Of course, it is necessary for a court to acquire jurisdiction over a person before that individual can be tried for an offense. When a person is arrested, a court with jurisdiction over the offense acquires jurisdiction over that person. In other instances, the court acquires jurisdiction when an arrest warrant is issued following an indictment or after a capias is issued once a prosecutor files an information.

The term **venue** is sometimes confused with the concept of jurisdiction, but it is a distinct concept. Venue refers to the place of the trial, and its importance is underscored by the fact that it is twice mentioned in the U.S. Constitution. Article III, Section 2 provides, in part, "Trial shall be held in the State where the said crimes shall have been committed; but when not committed within the State, the Trial shall be at such Place or Places as the Congress may by law have directed." And the Sixth Amendment provides, "In all criminal prosecutions, the accused shall enjoy the right to a . . . public trial, by an impartial jury of the State and district wherein the crime shall have been committed."

The Sixth Amendment applies to state criminal trials via the Fourteenth Amendment. *Duncan v. Louisiana*, 391 U.S. 145, 88 S.Ct. 1444, 20 L.Ed.2d 491 (1968). State constitutions, statutes, or court rules usually mirror the provisions of the Sixth Amendment.

Federal courts sit in all fifty states, as well as in federal territories. In some states, federal court jurisdiction is divided into two or more districts. A federal offense is normally tried in the particular federal district where the crime was committed. State courts are usually organized by districts of one or more counties. Likewise, a state criminal case is tried in the particular jurisdiction (district, county, circuit, and so forth) where the offense was committed.

Although venue lies in the district where the offense was committed, there are unique situations in which the nature of the crime makes it difficult to determine in which of two districts the crime occurred. For example, consider the situation where a person fires a rifle across a county or state line, killing a victim in the adjoining county or state. A more probable scenario is a kidnapping in which the perpetrator takes the victim across county or state lines. Courts must resolve these jurisdictional quandaries according to the relevant statutes and precedents.

Defendants commonly seek a **change of venue** if they believe it is impossible to obtain a fair trial in the venue in which the crime occurred. Rule 21(a) of the Federal Rules of Criminal Procedure stipulates,

change of venue The removal of a legal proceeding, usually a trial, to a new location.

> Upon the defendant's motion, the court must transfer the proceeding as to that defendant to another district . . . if the court is satisfied that there exists in the district where the prosecution is pending so great a prejudice against the defendant that the defendant cannot obtain a fair and impartial trial at any place fixed for holding court in that district.

State statutes and court rules generally contain similar provisions. Indeed, some states permit prosecutors, as well as defendants, to seek a change of venue. See, e.g., Fla. R. Crim. P. 3.240. In determining whether to grant a change of venue, courts consider a variety of factors, including (1) the nature of the pretrial publicity and the degree to which it has circulated in the community, (2) the connection of government officials with the release of the publicity, (3) the length of time elapsing between the dissemination of the publicity and the trial, (4) the severity and notoriety of the offense, (5) the area from which the jury is to be drawn, (6) other events occurring in the community that either affect or reflect the attitude of the community or individual jurors toward the defendants, and (7) any factor likely to affect the candor and veracity of the prospective jurors. See, e.g., *State v. Bell*, 315 So.2d 307 (La. 1975).

A defendant seeking a change of venue bears the burden of showing the necessity for the change. Changing venue can offend the community sense of justice in not having a trial take place within the community. In addition, it can create hardships and inefficiencies because of the need to transport witnesses and court personnel to sometimes-distant locations. Because a decision to change venue depends on many factors that can best be determined by the local judge, trial courts are accorded considerable discretion in determining whether to grant a motion to change venue in a criminal case.

Joinder and Severance

Very often, a defendant stands accused of several distinct offenses arising from one set of related facts. Conceivably, each offense could be prosecuted separately, but it would be more efficient, in most instances, to prosecute such offenses jointly. Most state rules of criminal procedure follow the federal rule on **joinder of offenses**:

joinder of offenses The uniting of different charges or counts alleged in an information or indictment into one case for trial.

> (a) Joinder of Offenses. The indictment or information may charge a defendant in separate counts with 2 or more offenses if the offenses charged—whether felonies or misdemeanors or both—are of the same or similar character, or are based on the same act or transaction, or are connected with or constitute parts of a common scheme or plan.

> Fed. R. Crim. P. 8(a).

In determining whether to proceed on multiple criminal charges jointly or separately, a prosecutor must consider the Double Jeopardy Clause of the Fifth Amendment. This clause bars successive prosecutions for the "same offense." A particular set of actions by the defendant may constitute distinct violations of criminal law and yet be considered part of the same offense under the Double Jeopardy Clause.

For example, in *Harris v. Oklahoma*, 433 U.S. 682, 97 S.Ct. 2912, 53 L.Ed.2d 1054 (1977), the Supreme Court held that a defendant could not be prosecuted for armed robbery after being convicted of felony murder for a homicide committed during the armed robbery "because proof of the underlying felony, i.e., armed robbery, was required to prove the intent necessary for the felony-murder conviction."

The basic test laid down by the Supreme Court for determining whether there are two separate offenses is "whether each provision [of the criminal law] requires proof of an additional fact that the other does not." *Blockburger v. United States*, 284 U.S. 299, 304, 52 S.Ct. 180, 182, 76 L.Ed. 306, 309 (1932). Separate statutory crimes need not be identical—either in constituent elements or in actual proof—to be the "same offense" within the meaning of the Double Jeopardy Clause of the Fifth Amendment. Thus, a defendant cannot be convicted of an offense and a lesser included offense. *Brown v. Ohio*, 432 U.S. 161, 97 S.Ct. 2221, 53 L.Ed.2d 187 (1977). State courts have held that a person cannot be convicted of two separate homicide charges where there is only one victim. See, e.g., *Wilcox v. Leapley*, 488 N.W.2d 654 (S.D. 1992).

Severance of Charges

severance of the charges
Conducting multiple trials for multiple charges, as distinct from joinder, which refers to trying all charged offenses at once. Where two or more related offenses are charged in a single indictment or information, the trial judge often grants a severance of the charges on the motion of either the defense or the prosecution.

Where two or more related offenses are charged in a single indictment or information, the trial judge ordinarily grants a **severance of the charges** on the motion of either the defense or prosecution if it is necessary to achieve a fair determination of the defendant's guilt or innocence on each offense. A defendant seeking severance bears the burden of showing that a joint trial would be so unfairly prejudicial that it would result in a miscarriage of justice. *United States v. Williams*, 10 F.3d 1070 (4th Cir. 1993).

Trial judges have considerable discretion in this area, but there are certain situations in which severance seems mandatory. For example, a defendant charged with two offenses may want to testify in one case but decline to testify in the other. Or a defendant might be charged in one case with possession of a firearm by a convicted felon and in another case with robbery. To sustain the charge in the firearm case, the prosecution would have to show the defendant's prior conviction of a felony. Such a showing would obviously be prejudicial to defense of the robbery charge being heard by the same jury.

Joinder and Severance of Parties

As with multiple offenses, prosecutors generally have broad discretion in deciding whether to prosecute multiple defendants separately or jointly. However, here too there are constitutional considerations. For example, it has been held that separate trials are required where the prosecution plans to use against one defendant evidence that has no relevance to the other defendants. *Kotteakos v. United States*, 328 U.S. 750, 66 S.Ct. 1239, 90 L.Ed. 1557 (1946).

Rule 8(b) of the Federal Rules of Criminal Procedure authorizes joinder of two or more defendants in the same indictment "if they are alleged to have participated in the same act or transaction or the same series of acts or transactions constituting an offense or offenses." However, rule 14(a) states that the court "may grant" a severance "if it appears that a defendant or the government is prejudiced by a joinder of offenses or of defendants." Thus, federal judges try to determine whether the failure to sever prevents the moving party from getting a fair trial. Denial of a motion for severance is generally held to be an abuse of discretion if the defendants present conflicting and irreconcilable defenses and if there is a danger that the jury will infer that such conflict demonstrates that both are guilty. *United States v. Tarantino*, 846 F.2d 1384 (D.C. Cir. 1988).

joinder and severance of parties The uniting or severing of two or more parties charged with a crime or crimes.

Rules governing **joinder and severance of parties** are usually spelled out in the rules of criminal procedure in each jurisdiction. The purpose of such rules is to ensure that when two or more persons are charged jointly, each will receive a fair determination of guilt or innocence. The Tennessee Rules of Criminal Procedure are fairly typical in this respect:

The Court, on motion of the State or on motion of the defendant . . . shall grant a severance of defendants if:

> I. before trial, it is deemed necessary to protect a defendant's right to a speedy trial or it is deemed appropriate to promote a fair determination of the guilt or innocence of one or more defendants; or
>
> II. during trial, with the consent of the defendant to be severed, it is deemed necessary to promote a fair determination of the guilt or innocence of one or more defendants.

Tenn. R. Crim. P., Rule 14(c)(2).

Severance of defendants is almost always granted when jointly charged defendants pursue inconsistent defenses, when their interests are otherwise antagonistic, or when one defendant chooses to testify and the other does not. Severance is required when a codefendant's confession implicates another, nontestifying codefendant. *Bruton v. United States*, 391 U.S. 123, 88 S.Ct. 1620, 20 L.Ed.2d 476 (1968).

The Florida courts developed the following procedural rule to cope with the *Bruton* problem. The rule gives the state three options when the trial court determines that a defendant's statement is not admissible against a codefendant.

If a defendant moves for a severance of defendants on the ground that an oral or written statement of a co-defendant makes reference to him but is not admissible against him, the court shall determine whether the State will offer evidence of the statement at the trial. If the State intends to offer the statement in evidence, the

---

JURISPRUDENCE

Bruton v. United States, 391 U.S. 123, 88 S.Ct. 1620, 20 L.Ed.2d 476 (1968)

Bruton and his codefendant, Evans, were tried jointly and convicted for armed postal robbery. While Evans did not testify, a postal inspector testified that Evans confessed that he and Bruton committed the robbery. As a result of the testimony, "the trial judge instructed the jury that, although Evans's confession was evidence against him it was inadmissible hearsay against [Burton] and had to be disregarded in determining [Bruton's] guilt or innocence." The Court of Appeals affirmed Bruton's conviction in view of the trial judge's jury instructions. The Supreme Court held that due to "the substantial risk that the jury, despite instructions to the contrary, looked to the incriminating statements in determining [Bruton's] guilt, the admission of Evans's confession in the joint trial violated his right of cross-examination secured by the Confrontation Clause of the Sixth Amendment." The Court reversed Bruton's conviction and remanded the case for a new trial.

court shall order the State to submit its evidence of such statement for consideration by the court and counsel for defendants and if the court determines that such statement is not admissible against the moving defendant, it shall require the State to elect one of the following courses: (i) a joint trial at which evidence of the statement will not be admitted; (ii) a joint trial at which evidence of the statement will be admitted after all references to the moving defendant have been deleted, provided the court determines that admission of such evidence with deletions will not prejudice the moving defendant; or (iii) severance of the moving defendant.

Fla. R. Crim. P. 3.152.

Redaction of Incriminating Statements Introduced in a Joint Trial

redaction Editing out portions of a transcript in order to maintain secrecy of someone's identity or other information.

One of the options allowed by the rule is **redaction** (editing) of a confession or incriminating statement made by one defendant so that it may be used at a joint trial without implicating any other defendant. In *Gray v. Maryland*, 523 U.S. 185, 118 S.Ct. 1151, 140 L.Ed.2d. 294 (1998), the Supreme Court addressed the redaction problem in a case that resulted in Kevin Gray's conviction for involuntary manslaughter. Gray's codefendant, Bell, had given a confession to the police in which he said that Bell, Gray, and Vanlandingham had participated in a beating that resulted in the victim's death. Vanlandingham later died, and Bell and Gray were tried jointly for murder. The trial judge, after denying Gray's motion for a separate trial, permitted a police detective to read Bell's redacted confession into evidence. The detective said the word "deleted" or "deletion" whenever Gray's name or Vanlandingham's name appeared. The state then introduced into evidence a written copy of Bell's confession with Gray's and Vanlandingham's names omitted, leaving in their place blank white spaces separated by commas. The Maryland Court of Appeals upheld Gray's conviction. A sharply divided Supreme Court vacated the decision and stated that "redactions that replace a proper name with an obvious blank, the word 'delete,' a symbol, or similarly notify the jury that a name has been deleted are similar enough to *Bruton's* unredacted confession as to warrant the same legal results." 523 U.S. at 195, 118 S.Ct. at 1156, 140 L.Ed.2d. at 302. Writing for the Court's four dissenters, Justice Antonin Scalia contended that allowing the confession to be admitted with limiting instructions "represents a reasonable practical accommodation of the interests of the state and the defendant in the criminal justice process." 523 U.S. at 200, 118 S.Ct. at 1159, 140 L.Ed.2d. at 306.

Severance in Cases Where Defendants Pursue Mutually Contradictory Defenses

Lower federal courts have generally taken the position that defendants are entitled to separate trials if their defenses are mutually contradictory. See, e.g., *United States v. Tarantino*, supra. In 1993, the U.S. Supreme Court addressed the issue. Writing for the Court, Justice Sandra Day O'Connor made it clear that severance of defendants is not required, as a matter of law, when defendants present mutually antagonistic defenses. Rather, severance is required only if the trial court finds a serious risk that a joint trial would compromise a specific trial right of a properly joined defendant or prevent the jury from making a reliable judgment about guilt or innocence.

Circumstances that may require a severance include a case in which joinder results in the admission of evidence that the jury could consider against one defendant but not another, or a case in which evidence exculpating one defendant would have to be excluded at a joint trial. But in federal courts, simply relying on antagonistic defenses without articulating any specific prejudice is not sufficient to require that a trial court sever the trial of a codefendant. *Zafiro v. United States*, 506 U.S. 534, 113 S.Ct. 933, 122 L.Ed.2d 317 (1993).

Pretrial Motions

pretrial motions Requests for rulings or orders before the commencement of a trial.

Pretrial motions are written requests to the court on behalf of the government or the defendant. They are the means by which defense counsel and prosecutors seek to attain certain objectives before trial. Typically, many motions are available to both the defense and the prosecution during the pretrial phase of a criminal case. One common set of motions deals with joinder and severance of offenses and defendants, as previously discussed. Other common pretrial motions include the following:

motion to dismiss A formal request to a trial court to dismiss the criminal charges against the defendant.

1. *Motion to dismiss.* Frequently the defense files a **motion to dismiss** the indictment or information, alleging (a) that the government's allegations, assuming the truth thereof, do not allege a crime, or that the accusatorial document is not correct in form; or (b) that the undisputed facts do not establish a case of *prima facie* guilt against the defendant. Often the court's determination on a motion to dismiss is not final, as the government may be given an opportunity to amend its documentation. In addition, a defendant may file a motion to dismiss on grounds of double jeopardy or having been granted immunity.

2. *Motion to determine the competency of the accused to stand trial.* In cases where the defendant is mentally disturbed, the defendant may be declared incompetent to stand trial on the motion of the defense. In federal cases the trial judge must determine whether the defendant has (1) a rational and factual understanding of the pending proceedings and (2) the ability to consult with his or her lawyer with a reasonable degree of rational understanding. *Dusky v. United States*, 362 U.S. 402, 80 S.Ct. 788, 4 L.Ed.2d 824 (1960). State courts use varying standards to determine whether an accused person is competent to stand trial. The differences are largely semantic. Some state courts apply the federal standard, with the additional requirement that the accused must understand the range of penalties that would attend conviction and be able to perceive the adversarial nature of the trial process. A person restored to competency may then be tried for the criminal offense originally charged. States generally require a defendant to prove incompetency by a preponderance of the evidence. In *Cooper v. Oklahoma*, 517 U.S. 348, 116 S.Ct. 1373, 134 L.Ed.2d 498 (1996), the Supreme Court held that a law that required defendants to prove incompetence to stand trial by clear and convincing evidence violated the Due Process Clause.

3. *Motion to suppress evidence obtained through unlawful search or seizure.* Evidence obtained in violation of a defendant's Fourth Amendment rights cannot be used against the defendant in a criminal trial. *Weeks v. United States*, 232 U.S. 383, 34 S.Ct. 341, 58 L.Ed. 652 (1914); *Mapp v. Ohio*, 367 U.S. 643, 81 S.Ct. 1684, 6 L.Ed.2d 1081 (1961). When the defense moves to suppress evidence on Fourth Amendment grounds, the court generally holds an evidentiary hearing. If the defense is successful in causing the **suppression of evidence**, it may undermine the government's case, leading to a favorable ruling on a subsequent defense motion to dismiss. When the state's case depends solely on the

suppression of evidence Judicial rule forbidding the use of evidence in a criminal trial where the evidence was obtained in violation of the defendant's constitutional rights. See **exclusionary rule**.

evidence sought to be suppressed, the defense's attempt is often referred to as a **dispositive motion**.

dispositive motion
A motion made to a court where the ruling on the motion will determine the outcome of the case.

4. *Motion to suppress confessions, admissions, or other statements made to the police.* A defendant is constitutionally entitled to a determination by the court of whether a confession is voluntary before the confession is made known to the jury. *Jackson v. Denno*, 378 U.S. 368, 84 S.Ct. 1774, 12 L.Ed.2d 908 (1964). The motion to suppress the confession is the means of bringing this issue before the court. The motion can initiate a number of related inquiries, such as whether the confession was obtained in violation of the *Miranda* rules. Generally, before ruling on a motion to suppress a confession, the court holds an evidentiary hearing. Again, the disposition of such a motion can have a significant impact on the prosecution of a criminal case. If the confession is crucial to the prosecution's case, a favorable ruling on the motion to suppress may lead to a dismissal of the charges.

5. *Motion to suppress a pretrial identification of the accused.* This motion by the defendant is designed to determine whether the pretrial identification procedures employed by the police in having an eyewitness identify the accused violated the due process standards outlined in *Neil v. Biggers*, 409 U.S. 188, 93 S.Ct. 375, 34 L.Ed.2d 401 (1972). The court's inquiry here focuses on whether the identification procedures were impermissibly suggestive to the witness (see Chapter 4).

6. *Motion to require the prosecution to disclose the identity of a confidential informant.* The prosecution is not ordinarily required to disclose the identity of a confidential informant who merely furnishes the probable cause on which an arrest or search is predicated. Nevertheless, if the informant was an "active participant" in the offense, the prosecution may be required to disclose the informant's identity. The test calls for balancing the public interest in protecting the free flow of information to the police against the individual's right to prepare a defense. See, e.g., *Roviaro v. United States*, 353 U.S. 53, 77 S.Ct. 623, 1 L.Ed.2d 639 (1957). Trial judges have considerable discretion in ruling on this motion.

7. *Motion for change of venue.* The defendant, and in some instances the government, may move for a change of venue (that is, place of trial) on the ground that a fair and impartial trial cannot be had where the case is pending. In recent years, heightened media coverage of crime and criminal prosecutions has generated tremendous concern over the ability of defendants to receive a fair trial. The concern usually focuses on the difficulty of selecting an impartial jury when potential jurors have been exposed to intensive newspaper, radio, and television coverage of a crime. The Supreme Court, in *Sheppard v. Maxwell*, 384 U.S. 333, 86 S.Ct. 1507, 16 L.Ed.2d 600 (1966), established some guidelines for dealing with the effects of pretrial publicity (see Chapter 6). Since then, an increasing number of defendants have filed motions seeking a change of venue.

continuance Delay of a judicial proceeding on the motion of one of the parties.

8. *Motion for a continuance.* Either the government or the defendant may seek a **continuance**, or postponement, of the trial. A variety of grounds may be asserted, including illness or emergency, that make it difficult or impossible for the defendant, prosecutor, defense counsel, or an important witness to be present as scheduled; the unavailability of a significant witness or piece of documentary evidence; or the lack of adequate time to prepare for trial. Appellate courts consistently hold that there is no abuse of discretion unless a party can show that specific prejudice has resulted to the defendant as a result of the denial of the requested continuance.

deposition The recorded sworn testimony of a witness; not given in open court.

9. *Other pretrial motions.* Other common pretrial motions include motions to take a **deposition** to preserve the testimony of an infirm witness or one who may

not be available for trial; to appoint an interpreter; to inspect the minutes of the grand jury proceeding; to compel the prosecutor to disclose evidence that may be favorable to the accused; and to disqualify the trial judge on grounds of bias, close relationship to parties, or that the judge will be a material witness.

Arraignment

plea of not guilty
A formal answer to a criminal charge in which the accused denies guilt and thus exercises the right to a trial.

plea of guilty A formal answer to a criminal charge in which the accused acknowledges guilt and waives the right to a trial.

Alford plea A plea of guilty with a protestation of innocence.

no-contest plea Also called nolo contendere, a defendant's plea to a criminal charge that, although it is not an admission of guilt, generally has the same effect as a plea of guilty. A no-contest plea is usually not admissible in evidence in a subsequent civil suit.

factual basis When a defendant pleads guilty to an offense, the court requires a recitation of facts (usually by counsel) to establish that proof is available to show the defendant's guilt of the elements of the offense.

The arraignment is the accused's first appearance before a court of law with the authority to conduct a criminal trial. At this stage of the process, the accused must enter a plea to the charges contained in the indictment or information. There are several options. The accused may choose to enter a **plea of not guilty**, in which case the plea is noted and a trial date is set. The accused may enter a **plea of guilty**, in which case no trial is necessary. Instead, guilt is simply pronounced and sentencing follows, either immediately or at some future court appearance, after a presentence investigation has been completed (see Chapter 7). A plea of guilty containing a protestation of innocence, sometimes called an ***Alford plea***, can be made when a defendant intelligently concludes that his or her interests require the entry of a guilty plea. *North Carolina v. Alford*, 400 U.S. 25, 91 S.Ct. 160, 27 L.Ed.2d 162 (1970). In some jurisdictions, the accused has the option of pleading *nolo contendere* (no contest). The **no-contest plea**, although functionally equivalent to a guilty plea has the advantage that it generally cannot be construed as an admission of guilt in a related civil suit. Although a judgment is entered on a no-contest plea, the defendant neither admits nor denies anything.

Because a plea of guilty or *nolo contendere* represents a waiver of constitutional rights, it is essential that the plea be made knowingly and voluntarily. The Federal Rules of Criminal Procedure preclude trial judges from accepting such a plea unless the court determines the plea is "voluntary and not the result of force or threats or of promises apart from a plea agreement." Fed. R. Crim. P. 11(b)(2). In addition to determining voluntariness, a judge must decide whether a **factual basis** exists for a plea of guilty or *nolo contendere*. A factual basis is necessary to ensure that the accused does not admit to an offense when his or her conduct does not fall within the bounds of the government's accusations. See, e.g., *United States v. Montoya-Camacho*, 644 F.2d 480 (5th Cir. 1981).

Most states have adopted similar rules of procedure to ensure that pleas are voluntary and comply with constitutional requirements. For example, rule 3.170(k) of the Florida Rules of Criminal Procedure specifies that "[n]o plea of guilty or *nolo contendere* shall be accepted by a court without first determining . . . that the circumstances surrounding the plea reflect . . . its voluntariness and that there is a factual basis for the plea."

Rules concerning voluntariness and factual basis generally do not specify any precise method to be followed by the court. Judges employ various methods to determine voluntariness. Often these methods include interrogation of the defendant by the judge, and sometimes by the prosecutor and/or defense counsel. The extent of questioning often depends on the defendant's educational level and maturity. Frequently, judges ask indigent defendants about their satisfaction with court-appointed counsel. The objective is to establish that no improper inducements have been made to secure a plea, that the defendant understands the basic constitutional rights incident to a trial, that these rights are being waived, and that he or she comprehends the consequences of the plea. *Boykin v. Alabama*, 395 U.S. 238, 89 S.Ct. 1709, 23 L.Ed.2d 274 (1969).

In determining that a factual basis exists for the defendant's plea, judges often have the prosecutor briefly outline available proof to establish a *prima facie* case of the defendant's guilt. A more extensive inquiry is usually necessary for specific-intent crimes. The thoroughness of the court's determination of voluntariness and factual basis becomes important if a defendant later moves to withdraw a plea and enter a plea of not guilty.

Federal Rule of Criminal Procedure 11(d) provides that after a court accepts a plea, but before it imposes sentence, a defendant may withdraw a plea of guilty or *nolo contendere* if the defendant can show a just reason for requesting the withdrawal. "The fact that a defendant has a change of heart prompted by his reevaluation of either the Government's case against him or the penalty that might be imposed is not a sufficient reason to permit withdrawal of a plea." *United States v. Gonzalez*, 970 F.2d 1095, 1100 (2d Cir. 1992). Subsection (e) stipulates that after sentencing a defendant may not withdraw a plea, and that the plea may be set aside only on direct appeal or collateral attack. The rules of procedure in state courts generally allow the court, in its discretion, to permit a defendant to withdraw a plea for good cause before sentencing. But once sentence has been imposed, a defendant must demonstrate that a manifest injustice requires correction in order to be permitted to withdraw a plea. See, e.g., *State v. Barney*, 570 N.W.2d 731 (1997).

Plea Bargaining

In most jurisdictions, more than 90 percent of felony suspects arraigned plead guilty or no contest. Very often the guilty plea is the result of a bargain struck between the defense and the prosecution. In a plea bargain, the accused agrees to plead guilty in exchange for a reduction in the number or severity of charges or a promise by the prosecutor not to seek the maximum penalty allowed by law. Often bargains are quite specific in terms of punishment to be imposed, conditions of probation, restitution to the victim, and so forth.

Plea negotiations are subject to the approval of the trial court. In most instances, the bargain is arranged by experienced and knowledgeable counsel on both sides and is readily approved by the court. If the court is unwilling to approve the plea bargain, the defendant must choose between withdrawing the guilty plea (and thus going to trial) and accepting the plea bargain with such modifications as the judge may approve. Once the court has accepted a guilty plea pursuant to a plea bargain, the court cannot unilaterally alter it without permitting the defendant the opportunity to withdraw the plea.

In some jurisdictions, judges participate directly in plea bargaining discussions. The justification for this practice is that a judge can guide the parties to an equitable and expeditious resolution of the case. On the other hand, some courts disfavor the participation of a trial judge in plea bargaining discussions on the basis that the power and position of the judge may improperly influence the defendant to enter a guilty plea. See, e.g., *Perkins v. Court of Appeals*, 738 S.W.2d 276, 282 (Tex. Crim. App. 1987).

Plea bargaining has been sharply criticized by observers with different perspectives on the criminal process. Some critics fault plea bargaining for reducing the severity of criminal penalties. Others view plea bargaining as an unconstitutional effort to deprive defendants of their right to a fair trial. Plea bargaining has never been popular, but few who oppose the practice stop to consider the tremendous costs

The Realities of Plea Bargaining

CASE-IN-POINT

Paul LaVallee was charged in a New Hampshire court with the crime of aggravated assault. He elected to plead not guilty, was convicted at trial, and was sentenced to ten to thirty years in prison. LaVallee brought a habeas corpus action challenging his sentence, arguing that it was disproportionate to the sentences given defendants who agreed to plead guilty. He claimed that it was impermissible for the courts to give harsher sentences to defendants who insist on their constitutional right to a trial. The state supreme court rejected LaVallee's challenge. The court said that the defendant's argument ignored "the realities of the plea bargaining process." Further, it noted that "[i]n this state, we have rejected the notion that it is impermissible to compensate one who pleads guilty by extending him a proper degree of leniency."

LaVallee v. Perrin, 466 A.2d 932 (N.H. 1983).

and delays that would result if the numerous cases currently resolved through plea bargaining were to go to trial.

Despite frequent criticism, the practice of plea bargaining is widespread among American jurisdictions today. In addition to permitting a substantial conservation of prosecutorial and judicial resources, plea bargaining provides a means by which, through mutual concession, the parties can obtain a prompt resolution of criminal proceedings with the benefits that flow from final disposition of a case. The plea bargain, or negotiated sentence, enables the parties to avoid the delay and uncertainties of trial and appeal, and it permits swift and certain punishment of law violators with a sentence tailored to the circumstances of the case at hand.

Despite constitutional attacks, the Supreme Court has upheld the practice of plea bargaining. In *Brady v. United States,* 397 U.S. 742, 753, 90 S.Ct. 1463, 1471, 25 L.Ed.2d 747, 759 (1970), the Court said that "we cannot hold that it is unconstitutional for the State to extend a benefit to a defendant who in turn extends a substantial benefit to the State." In a subsequent case, the Court was even more sanguine about plea bargaining:

> The disposition of criminal charges by agreement between the prosecutor and the accused, sometimes loosely called "plea bargaining," is an essential component of the administration of justice. Properly administered, it is to be encouraged. If every criminal charge were subjected to a full-scale trial, the States and the Federal Government would need to multiply by many times the number of judges and court facilities. *Santobello v. New York,* 404 U.S. 257, 260, 92 S.Ct. 495, 498, 30 L.Ed.2d 427, 432 (1971).

The plea bargain necessarily entails a waiver of the constitutional right to trial, so it must be examined by the trial court to determine whether the accused has knowingly waived his or her rights and agreed to plead guilty without coercion by the state. *Boykin v. Alabama,* supra. Despite such procedural protections, cases still arise challenging the fundamental fairness of certain plea bargaining tactics. See, e.g., *Bordenkircher v. Hayes,* 434 U.S. 357, 98 S.Ct. 663, 54 L.Ed.2d 604 (1978), where the Court found no due process violation when the prosecutor threatened during plea negotiations to reindict the defendant on a more serious charge if the defendant refused to plead guilty to the lesser crime originally charged.

JURISPRUDENCE

Bordenkircher v. Hayes, 434 U.S. 357, 98 S.Ct. 663, 54 L.Ed.2d 604 (1978)

Here the Supreme Court held that the Due Process Clause of the Fourteenth Amendment "is not violated when a state prosecutor carries out a threat made during plea negotiations to have the accused reindicted on more serious charges on which he is plainly subject to prosecution if he does not plead guilty to the offense with which he was originally charged." Paul Lewis Hayes was charged with uttering a forged instrument, which carried a prison term of two to ten years. The prosecutor offered to recommend a sentence of five years if Hayes would plead guilty. Hayes decided not to plead guilty and the prosecutor went back to the grand jury and obtained an indictment under Kentucky's habitual offender law. Hayes, who had two prior felony convictions, was found guilty and sentenced to life in prison as a habitual offender. Justice Potter Stewart, writing for the Supreme Court, stated that "though to punish a person because he has done what the law allows violates due process, there is no such element of punishment in the 'give-and-take' of plea bargaining as long as the accused is free to accept or reject the prosecutor's offer."

Availability of Compulsory Process

compulsory process The power to subpoena witnesses to appear in court.

The Sixth Amendment to the Constitution guarantees a defendant in a criminal case the right to "have the **compulsory process** of the law to obtain witnesses in his favor." The Compulsory Process clause was applied to the states in *Washington v. Texas*, 388 U.S. 14, 87 S.Ct. 1920, 18 L.Ed.2d 1019 (1967), although the right previously existed in state constitutions and laws. The method of securing this right is through use of a subpoena, which is a formal written demand available in all federal and state jurisdictions. Subpoenas are available to both the prosecution and defense.

Rule 17 of the Federal Rules of Criminal Procedure implements this right at the federal level by allowing a defendant to have the court issue a subpoena for witnesses, documents, and objects and providing for service of such subpoenas. Court clerks, and sometimes judges, issue subpoenas. They are usually served by a marshal in the federal system and by a sheriff or process server in the state system. There are costs associated with subpoenas, but the federal rule provides for issuance without cost when a defendant is financially unable to pay the costs, as long as the witness is "necessary to an adequate defense." States generally have statutes or court rules closely paralleling the federal rule.

In the pretrial stages, challenges may be made to the right to subpoena a witness, document, or object. Challenges are usually based on the contention that such witnesses or items are not material to issues in the case. Judges have considerable discretion in ruling on these challenges.

Pretrial Discovery

The courts have long recognized a prosecutorial duty to disclose to the defense exculpatory information (that is, information that tends to vindicate the accused). This duty is based on the fundamental concept of our system of justice—that individuals accused of crimes must be treated fairly. The Supreme Court has stated that "the suppression by the prosecution of evidence favorable to the accused upon request violates due process where the evidence is material either to guilt or punishment, irrespective of the good faith or bad faith of the prosecution." *Brady v. Maryland*, 373 U.S. 83, 87, 83 S.Ct. 1194, 1996, 10 L.Ed.2d 215, 218 (1963).

The Supreme Court has held that, in addition to substantive exculpatory evidence, evidence tending to impeach (i.e., challenge the credibility of) prosecution witnesses falls within *Brady's* definition of evidence favorable to an accused. Therefore, under *Brady* a defendant is entitled to disclosure of information that might be used to impeach government witnesses. See, e.g., *United States v. Bagley,* 473 U.S. 667, 105 S.Ct. 3375, 87 L.Ed.2d 481 (1985).

Generally, the defense must request the disclosure of the **exculpatory evidence**. If the defense is unaware of the existence of the evidence, however, such a request is impossible. The Supreme Court has held that failure to request disclosure is not necessarily fatal to a later challenge based on *Brady,* but it may significantly affect the standard for determining materiality. *United States v. Agurs,* 427 U.S. 97, 96 S.Ct. 2392, 49 L.Ed.2d 342 (1976).

In a similar vein, it has been held to be a denial of due process if a prosecutor knowingly allows perjured testimony to be used against the accused. *Mooney v. Holohan,* 294 U.S. 103, 55 S.Ct. 340, 79 L.Ed. 791 (1935); *Alcorta v. Texas,* 355 U.S. 28, 78 S.Ct. 103, 2 L.Ed.2d 9 (1957).

Evidence that impeaches the credibility of a prosecution witness is considered to be exculpatory. The Supreme Court of Virginia in 1993 held that before the prosecution is obliged to produce evidence, it must be established that the undisclosed evidence is exculpatory and material to the defendant's guilt or punishment. Accordingly, where the record did not establish that there was any exculpatory evidence in the defendant's accomplices' polygraph tests, the state supreme court said that the trial court did not err in denying the defendant's motion seeking to discover the results of the tests. *Ramdass v. Commonwealth,* 437 S.E.2d 566 (Va. 1993).

Most states have now adopted liberal rules pertaining to **pretrial discovery**, rules designed to avoid unfairness to the defense resulting from abdications of prosecutorial duty. Using appropriate pretrial motions, the defense and prosecution can gain access to the evidence possessed by the opposing party. Thus, pretrial discovery not only enhances the fairness of the criminal process but also militates against surprises at trial.

Discovery in the Federal Courts

Discovery in a criminal case is somewhat more limited in federal courts than in state courts. Under the provisions of 18 U.S.C.A. § 3500, a federal criminal defendant is not entitled to inspect a statement or report prepared by a government witness "until said witness has testified on direct examination in the trial of the case." After a witness testifies, the government, on proper request of the defense, must produce that portion of any statement or report that relates to the subject matter on which the witness has testified. The federal statute is commonly referred to as the **Jencks Act** because its effect was first recognized in *Jencks v. United States,* 353 U.S. 657, 77 S.Ct. 1007, 1 L.Ed.2d 1103 (1957). In *Jencks,* a defendant was allowed to obtain for impeachment purposes previous statements made to government agents by prosecution witnesses. Courts have indicated that the principal purpose of the *Jencks* Act is to aid a defendant's right to cross-examination. In some instances the trial judge must make an *in camera* **inspection** of documents where the government asserts that the documents contain statements not relevant to the subject matter to which the witness has testified. The government is not required under the *Jencks* Act to turn over victims' statements to defendants during a pretrial suppression hearing. *United States v. Williams,* 10 F.3d 1070 (4th Cir. 1993).

---

exculpatory evidence That which exonerates or tends to exonerate a person from fault or guilt.

pretrial discovery The process by which the defense and prosecution interrogate witnesses for the opposing party and gain access to the evidence possessed by the opposing party prior to trial.

***Jencks* Act** The common name for a federal statute that permits a defendant to review a witness's prior written or recorded statement, but only after the witness has testified on direct examination for the government.

***in camera* inspection** A trial judge's private consideration of evidence.

CASE-IN-POINT

The Government's Failure to Preserve Evidence

Police obtained a warrant to search Barton's home based on an officer's affidavit that he had smelled marijuana during a prior consensual entry of the home. At a pretrial suppression hearing, Barton claimed that the officer could not have smelled the marijuana plants that were seized because they had no odor. But by the time of the suppression hearing, the plants had rotted because the police had not ventilated the bag in which they stashed the plants. The court recognized that the destruction by the government of evidence that tends to impeach allegations in an affidavit demonstrating probable cause for a search warrant may violate due process principles. Nevertheless, the defendant did not prevail. Rather, the U.S. Court of Appeals for the Ninth Circuit court relied upon the principle declared by the U.S. Supreme Court in *Arizona v. Youngblood*, 488 U.S. 51, 109 S.Ct. 333, 102 L.Ed.2d 281 (1988). There, the Court held that the failure of law enforcement officers through mere negligence and not in bad faith to preserve evidence that might have been helpful to the defendant does not violate a defendant's right to due process of law.

United States v. Barton, 995 F.2d 931 (9th Cir. 1993).

The Right to a Speedy Trial

right to a speedy trial
Constitutional right to have an open public trial conducted without unreasonable delay.

Speedy Trial Act of 1974 This federal statute provides specific time limits for pretrial and trial procedures in the federal courts. For example, an indictment must be filed within thirty days of arrest, and trial must commence within seventy days after the indictment.

The Sixth Amendment to the Constitution guarantees the defendant the **right to a speedy trial**. In *Barker v. Wingo*, 407 U.S. 514, 92 S.Ct. 2182, 33 L.Ed.2d 101 (1972), the Supreme Court refused to mandate a specific time limit between the filing of charges and the commencement of trial but did adopt a balancing test to determine whether a defendant was denied the right to a speedy trial. Under this test, courts must consider (1) the length of the delay, (2) the reasons for the delay, (3) the defendant's assertion of the right, and (4) prejudice to the defendant.

In response to the Court's decision in *Barker v. Wingo*, Congress enacted the **Speedy Trial Act of 1974,** 18 U.S.C.A. § 3161. The act provides specific time limits for pretrial and trial procedures in the federal courts. For example, an indictment must be filed within thirty days of arrest, and trial must commence within seventy days after the indictment. If the defendant's trial does not begin within the time limitations and the defendant enters a motion—before the trial's start or entry of a guilty plea—to dismiss the charges, the district court must dismiss the charges. There are a number of exceptions to the time limits, especially where delays are caused by defendants' motions. Questions have arisen in the lower federal courts as to whether a defendant can simply waive the application of the Speedy Trial Act. In *Zedner v. United States*, 547 U.S. 489, 126 S.Ct. 1976, 164 L.Ed.2d 749 (2006), the Supreme Court ruled that a defendant's prospective waiver of the application of the Speedy Trial Act was ineffective.

The Speedy Trial Clause of the Sixth Amendment applies to the states through the Fourteenth Amendment. *Klopfer v. North Carolina*, 386 U.S. 213, 87 S.Ct. 988, 18 L.Ed.2d 1 (1967). Most states have adopted legislation or court rules similar to the federal speedy trial law. See, e.g., 725 Ill. Comp. Stat. Ann. § 5/103-5. State laws frequently provide that the right to a speedy trial is activated either on the date of the filing of an indictment, information, or other formal accusatorial document or on the date that the accused is taken into custody. In *People v. Hillsman*, 769 N.E.2d 1100 (Ill. App. 2002), the court cites a number of Illinois appellate court decisions holding that an accused is entitled to discharge if his trial begins more than 120 days after he was placed in custody, and that a defendant in such a position is entitled to discharge on the day of his scheduled trial.

Conclusion

The rights afforded by the Fourth, Fifth, Sixth, and Eighth Amendments to the U.S. Constitution (and similar provisions in state constitutions) vitally affect the procedures used in criminal cases. Many of these rights were redefined or enlarged by the courts during the 1960s and 1970s, and they become significant considerations long before a criminal prosecution reaches the trial stage.

Chapter Summary

- LO1

  o Federal and state constitutions require that persons accused of crimes be given fair notice of criminal charges and an adequate opportunity to contest these charges at various stages. The right to counsel is fundamental and includes the right to representation at all critical pretrial stages.

  o Historically the Sixth Amendment to the U.S. Constitution, and similar provisions in state constitutions, were interpreted to allow defendants to retain counsel in criminal prosecutions. Through judicial developments, and eventually by Congressional legislation, counsel was appointed for indigent defendants in federal criminal cases. In 1963, the Supreme Court mandated that states provide counsel to indigent defendants in felony cases; in 1972, it extended the right to defendants sentenced to jail terms for misdemeanors.

  o Today most defendants charged with felonies or serious misdemeanors qualify for representation by a public defender or court-appointed counsel. In addition to representation at trial and sentencing, counsel represent the accused at such preliminary hearings, lineups after charges have been filed, postindictment interrogations, arraignments, and other critical pretrial stages.

  o In 1975, the Supreme Court said a defendant has the constitutional right to elect self-representation if that choice is made "knowingly and intelligently" and that the defendant's legal knowledge or skill has no bearing on the election. Judges sometimes appoint standby counsel to assist *pro se* defendants. In 2008, the Court held that the Constitution does not require a trial judge to allow a minimally competent defendant to elect self-representation at trial.

- LO2

  o In routine traffic violations and minor misdemeanors, police usually issue citations rather than make arrests. Some states have "cite and release statutes." Many persons who are charged with minor offenses waive their right to appear in court and pay a predetermined fine. Those who contest charges receive a summary trial where guilt or innocence is determined according to the reasonable doubt standard.

  o In major misdemeanor and felony cases, pretrial procedure is complex and protracted. Typically, an individual arrested for a felony must promptly be taken before a court for an initial appearance where the charges are read to the accused, who is informed of relevant constitutional rights, including the right to remain silent and the right to counsel, and a determination is made as to whether to grant pretrial release or remand the accused to custody to await the disposition of the case.

o The Federal Rules of Criminal Procedure provide that a person arrested for a federal offense must be taken before a magistrate "without unnecessary delay" for a first appearance. States have similar rules.

o Confessions made during periods of detention that violate the prompt presentment requirement are inadmissible at trial. Congress, however, has provided that a confession made within six hours after arrest is not inadmissible solely because of a delay in bringing the accused before the magistrate.

- LO3

  o Pretrial release can take the form of release on personal recognizance or to the custody of another, or posting a cash or surety bond.

  o The Eighth Amendment states that "excessive bail shall not be required," and the Supreme Court has said that bail is to ensure the accused's appearance of in court, not to inflict punishment: However, the Court has not held the Excessive Bail Clause of the Eighth Amendment to be enforceable against the states, leaving the matter of excessive bail in state criminal cases to the state constitutions, legislatures, and courts.

  o The Federal Bail Reform Act of 1984 allows federal courts to detain arrestees without bail on the ground of the arrestee's danger to the community, as well to ensure future court appearances. Congress has set various factors a court must consider in weighing the appropriateness of pretrial detention, and the government must show that pretrial release will not reasonably ensure the appearance of the accused or the safety of the community. The Act only applies to federal cases, but it suggests the validity of state laws and court decisions that deny bail to persons accused of violent crimes.

  o In many states, a defendant charged with a crime punishable by death or life imprisonment is ineligible for pretrial release if the proof of guilt is evident.

- LO4

  o Prosecutors occupy a unique role in deciding whether to proceed with a criminal case or to negotiate charges. Prosecutorial discretion is very broad, but a prosecutor may not single out a defendant for prosecution on the basis of race, religion, or other impermissible classifications. The Supreme Court has ruled that prosecutors are immune from tort actions for violating a defendant's constitutional rights.

  o When an arrest is made without a warrant, a preliminary hearing is constitutionally required to determine if there is probable cause to bind the accused over to the grand jury or (in the absence of a grand jury requirement) to hold the accused for trial. In many jurisdictions, prosecutors must obtain an indictment or "true bill" from the grand jury in addition to, or instead of, the preliminary hearing.

- LO5

  o The Fifth Amendment to the Constitution states that "[n]o person shall be held to answer for a capital, or otherwise infamous crime, unless on a presentment or indictment of a grand jury." The Supreme Court has held that states are not bound to abide by this requirement. Nevertheless, in about half of the states constitutions or statutes require the use of grand juries in certain types of criminal cases. Other states use grand juries primarily in an investigatory or supervisory capacity, and prosecutors initiate prosecution by filing an information.

o Selection of grand jurors must not systematically exclude certain groups in the community. A majority of jurors must agree to an indictment. Rules of evidence that apply in trials do not bind a grand jury, and although a witness retains Fifth Amendment rights against self-incrimination, a grand jury can override a witness's refusal to answer questions by granting the witness immunity coextensive with the privilege against self-incrimination.

o Under federal law an indictment must be filed within thirty days of arrest, but to claim preindictment delay, a defendant must show actual prejudice and deliberate design by the government. State courts generally take a similar approach.

- LO6

  o The U.S. Constitution provides, "A Person charged in any State with Treason, Felony or any other crime, who shall flee from Justice, and be found in another state, shall on demand of the executive Authority of the State from which he fled, be delivered up, to be removed to the State having Jurisdiction of the crime." Every offense punishable by law of a jurisdiction where it was committed can be subject to extradition, but extradition is usually sought only in serious offenses.

  o Extradition of suspects or convicted criminals between nations is regulated by treaties, which usually provide that the crime involved must be a serious one in both nations and that the penalty for the person extradited will not be disproportionate to the crime.

- LO7

  o Defense counsel and prosecutors file motions seeking to attain certain objectives before trial. Common motions include those seeking severance of defendants and charges and motions to dismiss, to seek continuances, to suppress evidence, to change venue, to require disclosure of a confidential informant, and to determine competency of the accused.

  o Rules governing joinder and severance of parties and of charges against a defendant are usually spelled out in the rules of criminal procedure in each jurisdiction. Courts grant a severance of charges on the motion of either the defense or prosecution if necessary to achieve a fair determination of the defendant's guilt or innocence on each offense. Courts usually grant a severance of defendants when jointly charged defendants pursue inconsistent defenses, when their interests are otherwise antagonistic, or when one defendant chooses to testify and the other does not.

  o Venue refers to the place of the trial, and a federal offense is normally tried in the district where the crime was committed. State criminal cases are tried in the district, county, circuit, and so forth where the offense was committed. Courts exercise considerable discretion and consider many factors in deciding whether to grant a motion for change of venue.

- LO8

  o The arraignment is the first appearance of the accused before a court with the authority to conduct a criminal trial. At this stage, the accused must enter a plea to the charges contained in the indictment or information. The accused may plead not guilty, in which case a trial date is set. Alternatively, the accused may enter a plea of guilty, in which case no trial is necessary. (An *Alford* plea is when a defendant intelligently concludes that his or her interests require the entry of a guilty plea.) Some jurisdictions allow an accused to plead *nolo contendere* (no contest). Although functionally equivalent to a guilty plea, a no-contest plea generally cannot be construed as an admission of guilt in a related civil suit. Before accepting a plea of guilty or no contest, a trial court must determine that a defendant's plea is voluntary and has a factual basis.

○ In a plea bargain, the accused agrees to plead guilty in exchange for a reduction in the number or severity of charges or a promise by the prosecutor not to seek the maximum penalty allowed by law. Usually a plea bargain is arranged by experienced counsel on both sides and is readily approved by the court. Plea negotiations are subject to approval of the trial court, and if the court is unwilling to approve the plea bargain, or modifies it, the defendant may either withdraw the guilty plea and stand trial or accept the plea bargain as modified by the judge.

○ Plea bargaining is controversial, but it is one of the realities of the criminal justice system. Despite constitutional attacks, the Supreme Court has upheld the practice.

- LO9

  ○ The Sixth Amendment to the Constitution guarantees a defendant in a criminal case the right to "have the compulsory process of the law to obtain witnesses in his favor." In 1967, the Supreme Court applied the Compulsory Process clause to the states. This allows a defendant to obtain witnesses and evidence in his or her favor. Most states have adopted liberal rules allowing pretrial discovery in criminal cases. Using appropriate pretrial motions, the defense and prosecution can gain access to the evidence possessed by the opposing party. (The Illinois rule on discovery quoted in the chapter presents a good summary of the type of rules that states allow on pretrial discovery.) Discovery in federal courts is more limited. Federal statutes and the *Jencks* Act provide that a federal criminal defendant is not entitled to inspect a statement or report prepared by a government witness "until said witness has testified on direct examination in the trial of the case."

  ○ In 1963, the Supreme Court stated that "the suppression by the prosecution of evidence favorable to the accused upon request violates due process where the evidence is material either to guilt or punishment, irrespective of the good faith or bad faith of the prosecution." Under this rule defendants are entitled to obtain any exculpatory evidence from the police or prosecutor.

- LO10

  ○ The Sixth Amendment guarantees a defendant the right to a speedy trial. In 1967, the Supreme Court held that the speedy trial requirements apply to the states. In 1972, the Court refused to mandate a specific time limit between the filing of charges and the commencement of trial and adopted a balancing test to consider relevant factors to determine whether a defendant was denied the right to a speedy trial.

○ Congress enacted the Speedy Trial Act of 1974, which provides specific time limits for pretrial and trial procedures in the federal courts. If the defendant's trial does not begin within the time limitations and the defendant enters a motion—before the trial's start or the defendant's entry of a guilty plea—to dismiss the charges, the district court must dismiss the charges. But there are a number of exceptions to the time limits, especially when a defendant's actions are responsible for the delay. States have speedy trial rules roughly patterned after the federal rules.

Key Terms

actual imprisonment standard

Alford plea

arraignment

bail bond

change of venue

citation

cite and release statutes

compulsory process

continuance

criminal procedure

critical pretrial stages

deposition

dispositive motion

excessive bail

exculpatory evidence

extradition

factual basis

Federal Bail Reform Act of 1984

grand jury

in camera inspection

indigency

information

initial appearance

Jencks Act

joinder and severance of parties

joinder of offenses

jurisdiction

motion to dismiss

no-contest plea

petty offenses

plea of guilty

plea of not guilty

preliminary hearing

pretrial detention

pretrial discovery

pretrial motions

pretrial release

prosecutorial discretion

prosecutorial immunity

redaction

release on personal recognizance

right to a speedy trial

right to counsel

self-representation

severance of the charges

skip tracers

Speedy Trial Act of 1974

subpoenas

summary trial

suppression of evidence

surety bond

venue

Key Court Decisions

Scott v. Illinois (1980): There is no constitutional right for an indigent person charged with a misdemeanor to be provided with counsel at public expense unless the charge actually leads to incarceration.

Stack v. Boyle (1951): The Eighth Amendment prohibits bail set at a figure higher than reasonably necessary to ensure the presence of the defendant at future proceedings.

United States v. Salerno (1987): There is no right to bail under the Eighth Amendment; federal courts may detain arrestees without bail on the ground of their danger to the community as well as the need to ensure future court appearances.

United States v. Armstrong (1996): To prevail in a claim of selective prosecution, a party must show that similarly situated individuals of a different race were not prosecuted.

United States v. Calandra (1974): Evidence excluded from trial on Fourth or Fifth Amendment grounds is nevertheless admissible before the grand jury.

Bruton v. United States (1968): Severance of codefendants is required when a one defendant's confession implicates a nontestifying codefendant.

Bordenkircher v. Hayes (1978): It is not a violation of due process for a prosecutor during plea negotiations to threaten to indict the defendant on a more serious charge if the defendant refuses to plead guilty to the crime originally charged.

Questions for Thought and Discussion

1. Have the courts gone too far or not far enough in requiring that indigent defendants be represented by counsel at public expense?

2. What are the arguments for and against allowing defendants without any legal training to represent themselves in felony prosecutions? How far should a trial judge go in advising a defendant of the pitfalls of proceeding without legal counsel?

3. In your opinion, does the Eighth Amendment guarantee the right to pretrial release on bail in a felony case? What about a misdemeanor case? Did the Supreme Court decide the *Salerno* case correctly? Why or why not?

4. How does a magistrate determine how much bail is appropriate and how much is "excessive"? What alternatives, if any, do you see to the traditional bail-bond system to ensure the appearance of the defendant in court?

5. Can you imagine a situation in which a prosecutor would run afoul of the Constitution by engaging in selective prosecution? In your state, can a prosecutor be sued for malicious prosecution? How is this proved?

6. Why does the law insist on a determination of voluntariness and a factual basis when a defendant pleads guilty or *nolo contendere*?

7. Do the courts in your state permit the *nolo contendere* plea? If so, what tactical advantage does the defendant gain by pleading *nolo contendere* rather than guilty?

8. How might a prosecutor persuade a defendant to plead guilty to a criminal charge without running afoul of due process? What prosecutorial tactics are likely to be viewed as fundamentally unfair?

9. Compare the advantages and disadvantages to the defendant of insisting on the right to a speedy trial.

10. Why do you think the U.S. Supreme Court has never held that the Fifth Amendment requirement of indictment by a grand jury applies to the states as well as to the federal government?

11. Does the grand jury still play a viable role in the criminal justice system? Are the criticisms of the grand jury valid? Why or why not?

12. Should plea bargaining be abolished? If not, what modifications may be necessary to protect (a) the defendant and (b) the public?

Problems for Discussion and Solution

1. Lonnie London was cited by police officers for speeding and driving with an expired driver's license, minor offenses punishable only by fines. Appearing in court, Lonnie requests that the judge appoint counsel to represent him on the ground that he is indigent. When the judge refuses, Lonnie exclaims, "I've got a constitutional right to be represented here!" Does Lonnie have a valid constitutional claim?

2. Samuel Penurio was president of a community bank in a small town. He was well thought of in the community, but he was known to drink to excess occasionally. One June evening his bank hosted a cocktail party. About 10:00 P.M., after the party was over, Penurio offered to drive his secretary home. Each had drunk several cocktails. En route to her home, Penurio drove through an intersection controlled by a signal light. His car crashed into a car containing four students who had just left their high school football game. One student, the popular head female cheerleader, died as a result of the injuries she received from the accident. Penurio's blood-alcohol level was 0.10 (which is 0.02 above the legal limit in this state). He was charged with vehicular homicide, which carries a maximum punishment of life imprisonment. Penurio and his secretary claim that he drove through the intersection just as the light was changing and that the car occupied by the students drove through the intersection at an excessive rate of speed. The driver of the students' car had not been drinking, and the surviving students all say Penurio drove through the red light. The local newspaper ran a front-page story with pictures of the students holding a school-wide memorial service for the deceased cheerleader, describing the students' version of the accident, and pointing out that Penurio had been convicted of DWI just a year earlier. Over the next several days, the newspaper and the local radio station carried adverse comments from their readers and listeners about Penurio's conduct. Penurio's counsel has filed a motion for a change of venue. Do you think it likely the court will grant the motion? What, if any, additional information should be sought to support the motion?

3. Willy Doolittle, age thirty-eight, is an unemployed construction worker. He is married with two children in middle school. He has been unable to support his family for the past few weeks because of lack of work. His wife takes care of their rented home, but, in addition to being a high school dropout, she receives Medicaid assistance for a series of physical problems. One night after having a few beers, Doolittle, using a key he had kept from when he had worked in a grocery warehouse, entered the warehouse without permission and stole approximately $1,000 worth of snack foods. The state charged Doolittle with burglary. His bail was set under a standard schedule that calls for $10,000 cash or bond. Doolittle has no means to post cash or a bond. The public defender (PD) was appointed to represent him. Doolittle has no prior criminal record and has lived in the community for three years. He wants to be released, and the PD thinks he may be able to represent him more effectively if Doolittle is released and obtains employment. A social worker reports that the family is in need of support and has offered to assist Doolittle in obtaining employment at a new construction site. The PD asks you to prepare a memorandum to support an application for pretrial release without posting cash or bond. What additional information should you seek? In seeking to obtain Doolittle's release without posting cash or bond, what conditions of release should the PD propose to the court?

4. Lauren L. is an eighteen-year-old woman who has just been arrested and charged with grand theft, possession of cocaine, and resisting arrest. She is being represented by the public defender's office. After being released on bail, Lauren is scheduled to meet with her attorney but fails to show up for the appointment. Minutes before her arraignment, Lauren meets with her lawyer, who informs her that he has made a "good deal" for her. Lauren agrees to take the deal and pleads guilty to misdemeanor theft. The judge asks Lauren if she understands the terms of the plea agreement and she responds in the affirmative. Under the deal, the court withholds adjudication of the drug possession charge on the condition that Lauren successfully complete a residential drug treatment program. Two weeks later, Lauren walks away from the treatment facility without having completed the program. She is arrested several days later and brought back to court, where the judge informs her that she must enter a plea to the cocaine possession charge. In response, Lauren says, "But your honor, nobody ever told me about that part of the deal." How should the judge proceed at this point?

5. Myron Minton, who suffers from schizophrenia, has been institutionalized on several occasions. After being released from a mental health facility, Myron refuses to take his medication and begins wandering the streets aimlessly. He is soon arrested by police on a charge of aggravated battery. According to the police report, Minton has been identified by a homeless man who claims that Minton beat him severely with a pipe. At his first appearance in court, Minton refuses to be represented by the public defender's office. He tells the judge that he intends to represent himself and that he plans to plead not guilty by reason of insanity. How do you think a judge would be likely to handle this situation?

6. Wesley Watson was indicted by a Jefferson County grand jury for solicitation of murder. An undercover police officer posing as a "hit man" testified before the grand jury that Watson had offered him $50,000 to kill Benjamin Bratton, the district attorney. Because Bratton recused himself in the case, a local circuit judge convened the grand jury to investigate the case. After the indictment was handed down, Watson's attorney moved to quash the indictment on the ground that the convening of the grand jury by a member of the judiciary was unlawful and denied his client due process of law. Do you think a criminal court judge would be receptive to this argument? Why or why not?

The Criminal Trial

CHAPTER OUTLINE

JURISPRUDENCE FEATURE BOXES

Williams v. Florida (1970)

Batson v. Kentucky (1986)

Rivera v. Illinois (2009)

Sheppard v. Maxwell (1966)

Nebraska Press Association v. Stuart (1976)

Crawford v. Washington (2004)

LEARNING OBJECTIVES

After reading this chapter, you should be able to explain

1. the constitutional rights that apply to criminal trials

2. how juries are selected and composed

3. what the "death qualification" of a jury in a capital case is

4. the steps judges can take to insulate juries from prejudicial media coverage

5. what powers judges have to maintain order in the courtroom

6. the rules of evidence that apply to criminal trials

7. the role of expert witnesses and the test for admissibility of scientific evidence

8. the mechanics of a criminal trial

9. how and why juries are instructed by judges

10. the rules governing jury deliberations and verdicts

CHAPTER OPENING VIGNETTE

On the evening of December 7, 1993, Jamaican-born Colin Ferguson boarded a commuter train in Long Island, New York, and began shooting passengers at random. Six people were killed and nineteen more were injured in the rampage. When Ferguson paused to reload his handgun, he was subdued by several passengers. Initially, Ferguson was represented by two prominent civil rights lawyers, William Kunstler and Ron Kuby, who undertook the case *pro bono*. But Ferguson disapproved of the defense they intended to put on, namely, that Ferguson was legally insane at the time of the shooting due to an uncontrollable "black rage." Ferguson dismissed Kunstler and Kuby and insisted on representing himself at trial.

The evidence that was produced at trial as to Ferguson's mental state, as well as his bizarre behavior in the courtroom, suggested that an insanity defense might have been effective, but Ferguson's defense amounted to little more than a denial and an insistence that he was a victim of mistaken identity. After hearing from a number of eyewitnesses to the shooting, the jury had little difficulty in convicting Ferguson of six counts of second-degree murder, nineteen counts of attempted second-degree murder, reckless endangerment, and criminal possession of a firearm. Ferguson was sentenced to consecutive prison terms that exceeded two hundred years. Today, he remains confined in New York's Attica prison.

Critics of the trial questioned how the trial judge could find Ferguson competent to stand trial, let alone to represent himself. However, when reviewing the case the Appellate Division of the New York Supreme Court determined that the trial court had properly determined that Ferguson was competent to stand trial. The appellate court held further that the trial court properly allowed Ferguson to represent himself, because a defendant who is deemed competent to stand trial is also competent to waive his right to counsel. *People v. Ferguson*, 248 A.D.2d 725, 670 N.Y.S.2d 327 (N.Y. App. 1998).

Introduction

More than 90 percent of felony charges and an even higher percentage of misdemeanor cases are disposed of before trial. Nevertheless, the criminal trial is the centerpiece of the criminal justice system for several reasons. First, trials are generally held before juries drawn from the community. Second, trials are the most visible aspect of the justice system and often attract widespread media coverage. Finally, cases disposed of by trial often have an important impact on the administration of justice.

Before the invasion of William the Conqueror in England in 1066, criminal trials took the forms of compurgation or ordeal. In a trial by compurgation, a defendant who had denied guilt under oath attempted to recruit a body of men to attest to his or her honor. If a group would swear to the defendant's innocence, the law considered the defendant to be innocent. In a trial by ordeal, the defendant was tortured by fire or water. If the defendant survived the ordeal, people thought that God had intervened to prove the defendant's innocence before the law.

Jury trials as we know them today originated with the Magna Carta, which the English nobles forced King John to sign at Runnymede in 1215. The Magna Carta granted freemen the right of trial by their peers. Early juries were comprised of persons who had knowledge of the facts of a case—it was centuries before trial juries functioned in the role they now perform. The jury became characteristic of the English common law and was a feature that distinguished English law from the law of the European continent, which was based on Roman law.

Constitutional Rights Pertaining to the Criminal Trial

Despite the protections of the common law, English subjects who were accused of crime were not always afforded fair trials. The notorious Star Chamber was established in the fifteenth century to punish offenses outside the common law. Its real purpose was to punish opponents of the monarch. It met in secret, dispensed with jury trials, and offered no legal protections to the accused. Accusation before the Star Chamber was tantamount to conviction. Its punishments were unduly harsh, and often involved torture and disfigurement. Although the Star Chamber was abolished by Parliament in 1641, the framers of the American Bill of Rights wanted to make sure that no such institution would ever be established in this country. Thus, as the Sixth Amendment provides,

> In all criminal prosecutions, the accused shall enjoy the right to a speedy and public trial, by an impartial jury of the State and district wherein the crime shall have been committed, which district shall have been previously ascertained by law, and to be informed of the nature and cause of the accusation; to be confronted with the witnesses against him; to have compulsory process for obtaining witnesses in his favor, and to have the Assistance of Counsel for his defence.

Because they are deemed to be fundamentally important to secure liberty and ensure fairness, the various rights protected by the Sixth Amendment are made applicable to state criminal trials by the Fourteenth Amendment. See, e.g., *Gideon v. Wainwright*, 372 U.S. 335, 344, 83 S.Ct. 792, 796, 9 L.Ed.2d 799, 805 (1963); *Pointer v. Texas*, 380 U.S. 400, 85 S.Ct. 1065, 13 L.Ed.2d 923 (1965); *Duncan v. Louisiana*, 391 U.S. 145, 88 S.Ct. 1444, 20 L.Ed.2d 491 (1968).

The Right to Compulsory Process

The Sixth Amendment guarantees a defendant the right "to have compulsory process for obtaining witnesses in his favor." This affords the defendant the right to obtain court process (a subpoena) to compel witnesses to appear in court. There are some restrictions (for example, a defendant cannot cause numerous witnesses to be subpoenaed simply to give cumulative testimony), but courts allow defendants a fair degree of liberality in causing witnesses to be subpoenaed. Of course, the prosecution can also compel the attendance of witnesses.

The Right to an Open Public Trial

open public trials Trials that are held in public courtrooms that are open to spectators.

The Sixth Amendment guarantees "the right to a speedy and public trial" and the Supreme Court has recognized that **open public trials** are essential to our system of justice. *Richmond Newspapers v. Virginia*, 448 U.S. 555, 100 S.Ct. 2814, 65 L.Ed.2d 973 (1980). But the right to a public trial, even if waived by the defendant, does not allow a defendant to invoke the converse of that right—that is, there is no right to a private trial. *Singer v. United States*, 380 U.S. 24, 34–35, 85 S.Ct. 1783, 790, 13 L.Ed.2d 630, 638 (1965).

The right to an open public trial is not absolute. After pointing out that a public trial is for the benefit of the accused and to ensure that the judge and prosecutor carry out their duties responsibly, the Supreme Court in *Waller v. Georgia*, 467 U.S. 39, 45, 104 S.Ct. 2210, 2215, 81 L.Ed.2d 31, 38 (1984), explained that

> the right to an open trial may give way in certain cases to other rights or interests, such as the defendant's right to a fair trial or the government's interest in inhibiting disclosure of sensitive information. Such circumstances will be rare, however, and the balance of interest must be struck with special care.

The Supreme Court has ruled that the requirement of openness extends to all phases of the trial. Consequently, in 1982 the Court declared invalid a state statute requiring mandatory closing of the courtroom during the testimony of victims of sexual offenses. The Court said the issue of closing should be left to the discretion of the trial judge, who would determine on a case-by-case basis whether the state's legitimate interests in a victim's well-being necessitate closing the courtroom. *Globe Newspaper Company v. Superior Court*, 457 U.S. 596, 102 S.Ct. 2613, 73 L.Ed.2d 248 (1982).

Two years later, the Court held that *voir dire* proceedings (discussed later in this chapter) in criminal trials can be closed only by overcoming the presumption of openness. *Press-Enterprise Company v. Superior Court of California*, 464 U.S. 501, 104 S.Ct. 819, 78 L.Ed.2d 629 (1984). Accordingly, before a trial court orders the closing of court proceedings, it must make specific findings that closure is essential and explain why available alternatives are inadequate. Among the reasons frequently cited by courts for limiting public access to criminal proceedings are the need to protect rape victims or children who have been molested and the need to protect witnesses and jurors from embarrassment, trauma, or intimidation. Based on the *Press-Enterprise* decision, courts now apply a four-prong test for determining the propriety of closing judicial proceedings to spectators. First, the party seeking to close the hearing must advance an overriding interest that is likely to be prejudiced; second, the closure must be no broader than necessary to protect that interest; third, the trial court must consider reasonable alternatives to closing the proceeding; and fourth, it must make findings adequate to support the closure.

Court Upholds Closure of Defendant's Trial during Testimony of Juvenile Witnesses

Robert Morgan was charged with rape, deviate sexual assault, and two counts of aggravated incest committed against his minor stepdaughter. The state moved to close the trial to the public so as to protect the best interests of the minor victim and her brother and stepsister during their testimony against the defendant. Over the defendant's objection, the trial court granted the state's motion, limiting the exclusion order to the three juvenile witnesses. The trial court found that the intimate and embarrassing nature of the testimony warranted the limited closure and did not hamper the public nature of the trial. Morgan was found guilty and appealed, arguing that exclusion of the public during two days of his trial violated his Sixth Amendment right to a public trial. Applying the test developed by the U.S. Supreme Court in *Press-Enterprise v. Superior Court* (1984), the appellate court found that the trial court properly closed the courtroom to spectators during the testimony of the juvenile witnesses, held that the defendant was not denied his constitutional right to a public trial, and affirmed the defendant's conviction.

People v. Morgan, 504 N.E.2d 172 (Ill. App. 1987).

The Right to Counsel

We examined the right to counsel fairly extensively in Chapter 5. However, there are a few specific issues that pertain to the conduct of a trial. In 1976, the Supreme Court ruled that it is a violation of a defendant's Sixth Amendment right to counsel for a trial judge to bar the defendant from conferring with defense counsel during an overnight recess of a trial. *Geders v. United States*, 425 U.S. 80, 96 S.Ct. 1330, 47 L.Ed.2d 592 (1976). More than a decade later, the Court held it was not a denial of the right to counsel for a trial judge to bar a defendant from conferring with counsel during a brief trial recess that occurred after the defendant testified on direct examination but before cross-examination by the prosecutor. *Perry v. Leeke*, 488 U.S. 272, 109 S.Ct. 594, 102 L.Ed.2d 624 (1989). The Court's holdings in these cases acknowledge the importance of a close relationship between attorney and client during a trial but also recognize that the pursuit of truth is the purpose of the in-court examination of witnesses. Thus, there are valid reasons not to allow any witness to confer with counsel between the direct examination and the cross-examination.

Self-Representation

We began the chapter with a vignette based on the infamous Colin Ferguson case, *People v. Ferguson*, 248 A.D.2d 725, 670 N.Y.S.2d 327 (N.Y. App. 1998). That case highlights the danger to defendants, especially defendants of questionable mental competency, of choosing to represent themselves at trial. As we pointed out in Chapter 5, the Supreme Court has held that a defendant has the constitutional right to elect self-representation if that choice is made "knowingly and intelligently" and that the defendant's legal knowledge or skill has no bearing on the election. Any such waiver of counsel must be carefully documented in the court records, and the court, at its option, may appoint **standby counsel** to assist the defendant. *Faretta v. California*, 422 U.S. 806, 95 S.Ct. 2525, 45 L.Ed.2d 562 (1975).

In *State v. Bakalov*, 862 P.2d 1354 (Utah 1993), the Supreme Court of Utah cautioned trial judges to advise a defendant who elects to proceed *pro se* of the risks of presenting a *pro se* defense. A Pennsylvania appellate court has ruled that before the right to counsel may be waived, the trial court is required "to make searching and

standby counsel An attorney appointed to assist an indigent defendant who elects to represent himself or herself at trial.

formal on-the-record inquiry to ascertain (1) whether the defendant is aware of his right to counsel and (2) whether the defendant is aware of the consequences of waiving that right or not." *Commonwealth v. Owens*, 750 A.2d 872, 875 (Pa. Super. 2000). The Supreme Court has now held that the Constitution does not require a trial judge to allow a minimally competent defendant to elect self-representation at trial. *Indiana v. Edwards*, 554 U.S. 164, 128 S.Ct. 2379, 171 L.Ed.2d 345 (2008). At trial, a defense counsel who represents multiple defendants might discover a possible conflict in his or her representation of the defendants. In such an instance, it is the trial court's duty to "either to appoint separate counsel or to take adequate steps to ascertain whether the risk was too remote to warrant separate counsel." *Holloway v. Arkansas*, 435 U.S. 475, 484, 98 S.Ct. 1173, 1178, 55 L.Ed.2d 426, 434 (1978).

The Right to Trial by Jury

In addition, the Sixth Amendment ensures the right to trial by jury. However, the amendment leaves unanswered questions concerning the qualifications of jurors, the method of their selection, and the requirements for a jury to convict a person accused of a crime.

jury trial A judicial proceeding to determine a defendant's guilt or innocence, conducted before a body of people sworn to render a verdict based on the law and the evidence presented.

An accused may waive the right to a **jury trial**. Indeed, many persons who plead not guilty to misdemeanor charges elect a **bench trial**. On the other hand, most defendants who plead not guilty to felony charges choose to be tried by jury. The U.S. Supreme Court has ruled that the constitutional right to a jury trial extends to the class of cases for which an accused was entitled to a jury trial when the Constitution was adopted. This did not include juvenile cases, since there were no such courts at the time; hence, there is no right to a jury trial for juveniles under the federal constitution. *McKeiver v. Pennsylvania*, 403 U.S. 528, 91 S.Ct. 1976, 29 L.Ed.2d 647 (1971). Furthermore, the right to trial by jury is not applicable to military tribunals. *Ex parte Quirin*, 317 U.S. 1, 63S.Ct. 1, 87 L.Ed. 3 (1942).

bench trial A trial held before a judge without a jury present.

The constitutional requirement of a jury trial applies to the states, thereby guaranteeing a defendant a right to a jury trial in a state criminal prosecution if such a right would exist in a federal prosecution. *Duncan v. Louisiana*, supra. Interestingly, the Sixth Amendment right to a jury trial does not afford a defendant the corresponding right to be tried before a judge without a jury. *Singer v. United States*, 380 U.S. 24, 85 S.Ct. 783, 13 L.Ed.2d 630 (1965).

As now interpreted, the Sixth Amendment guarantees an accused the right to a jury trial in criminal cases where a penalty of more than six months' imprisonment can be imposed. *Codispoti v. Pennsylvania*, 418 U.S. 506, 94 S.Ct. 2687, 41 L.Ed.2d 912 (1974). Offenses that carry a possible penalty of no more than six months' imprisonment are generally termed "petty offenses," and a jury trial is not required under the Constitution. *Baldwin v. New York*, 399 U.S. 66, 90 S.Ct. 1886, 26 L.Ed.2d 437 (1970).

In *Blanton v. City of North Las Vegas*, 489 U.S. 538, 109 S.Ct. 1289, 103 L.Ed. 2d 550 (1989), the Supreme Court observed that a defendant might be entitled to a jury trial even if the penalty was no more than six months' imprisonment. The Court said this could occur where additional statutory penalties, in conjunction with the maximum authorized period of incarceration, are so severe as to clearly reflect a legislative determination that the offense is a "serious" one. But the Court held that the prospect of a $1,000 fine, attendance at an alcohol abuse clinic, and the loss of a driver's license for ninety days were not sufficient to make the offense of driving while intoxicated so "serious" as to require a jury trial.

In 1996, in a 5–4 decision, the Supreme Court ruled that a defendant charged with multiple petty offenses is not entitled to a jury trial under the federal constitution, even though the possible sentence may add up to more than six months in prison. *Lewis v. United States*, 518 U.S. 322, 116 S.Ct. 2163, 135 L.Ed.2d 590 (1996).

Notwithstanding the federal constitutional requirements, under some states' constitutions or statutory laws, an accused has the right to a jury trial for certain offenses even though they may be classified as "petty offenses" from a federal constitutional standpoint. In Florida, for example, a defendant is entitled to a jury trial under the state constitution for any offense that was *malum in se* (from the Latin, meaning "evil in itself") and indictable at common law even though the maximum punishment is less than six months' imprisonment. *Reed v. State*, 470 So.2d 1382 (Fla. 1985).

Selection and Composition of the Jury

At common law, a jury consisted of twelve men. Rule 23(b), Federal Rules of Criminal Procedure, requires a twelve-member jury in criminal cases in federal courts unless the defendant stipulates to fewer in writing. If the court finds it necessary to excuse a juror after the jury has retired to consider its verdict, at the discretion of the court, a valid verdict may be returned by the remaining eleven jurors. All states require twelve-member juries in capital cases. Most require the same number for all felony prosecutions. However, many states now use fewer than twelve jurors in misdemeanor cases. Florida uses six-person juries for all but capital felonies. Fla. R. Crim. P. 3.270. In *Williams v. Florida*, 399 U.S. 78, 90 S.Ct. 1893, 26 L.Ed.2d 446 (1970), the Supreme Court upheld the use of six-person juries in the trial of felony offenses in Florida. Subsequently, in *Ballew v. Georgia*, 435 U.S. 223, 98 S.Ct. 1029, 55 L.Ed.2d 234 (1978), the Court held that a jury of only five persons was not acceptable under the Sixth Amendment.

State and federal laws prescribe certain basic qualifications for jurors. Statutes commonly require that jurors be at least eighteen years of age and registered voters in the state or district from which they are to be selected. In contrast with past practices, laws prescribing qualifications cannot discriminate to prevent women as a class from serving as jurors. *Taylor v. Louisiana*, 419 U.S. 522, 95 S.Ct. 692, 42 L.Ed.2d 690 (1975). Convicted felons whose civil rights have not been restored are

---

JURISPRUDENCE

Williams v. Florida, 399 U.S. 78, 90 S.Ct. 1893, 26 L.Ed.2d 446 (1970)

Williams was convicted of armed robbery and was sentenced to life imprisonment. On appeal, one of Williams' arguments was that he had been tried by a jury composed of only six members. The Florida appellate courts rejected all of Williams' claims and sustained his conviction and sentence. In reviewing the case, the U.S. Supreme Court framed the issue as "whether the constitutional guarantee of a trial by 'jury' necessarily requires a trial by exactly 12 persons." The Court held that a jury of twelve is not a requirement under the Sixth Amendment as it applies to the states via the Fourteenth Amendment. Writing for the Court, Justice Byron White concluded that "neither currently available evidence nor theory suggests that the 12-man jury is necessarily more advantageous to the defendant than a jury composed of fewer members." Justice John M. Harlan, one of three dissenters in the case, observed that "before today, it would have been unthinkable to suggest that the Sixth Amendment's right to a trial by jury is satisfied by a jury of six, or less...."

usually excluded from serving on juries. Beyond this, statutes frequently carve out exemptions for expectant mothers and mothers with young children; for persons over seventy years of age; and for physicians, dentists, attorneys, judges, teachers, elected officials, police, firefighters, and emergency personnel. The trend, however, has been for states to restrict exemptions from jury duty so that the pool of prospective jurors will reflect a representative cross-section of the community.

The Jury Selection and Service Act of 1968, 28 U.S.C.A. § 1861ff, was enacted to ensure that jury panels in federal courts are selected at random from a fair cross-section of the community. States also have statutes prescribing the process of selection. Local officials compile a list of persons qualified to serve as jurors, generally from the rolls of registered voters, driver's license lists, or some combination thereof. From this list, prospective jurors are randomly selected and summoned to court. Compensation paid to trial jurors ranges from meager to modest amounts for travel and per diem expenses. Most states prohibit an employer from discharging an employee who has been summoned for jury duty.

Anonymous Juries

Ordinarily, the identities of members of a jury are a matter of public information. But in some cases courts find it necessary to impanel an anonymous jury, where information about the jurors such as their names, residences, employment information, and so forth is not disclosed to the public. Anonymous juries were unknown at common law; the first one was impaneled in the United States in 1979. Courts now employ anonymous juries where necessary to protect potential jurors and their families from threats, harassment, or intimidation, which can occur from organized crime, gang activity, or other sources. In *United States v. Paccione*, 949 F.2d 1183 (2d Cir. 1991), the court said a trial court "should not order the empanelling of an anonymous jury without (a) concluding that there is strong reason to believe the jury needs protection, and (b) taking reasonable precautions to minimize any prejudicial effects on the defendant and to ensure that his fundamental rights are protected." 949 F.2d at 1192.

In *United States v. Krout*, 66 F.3d 1420 (5th Cir. 1995), defendants were convicted in a federal district court of participating in a continuing criminal enterprise of murder, drug distribution, and firearms offenses. One ground that was asserted in their appeal was that they were denied a fair trial because the identities of the jurors who found them guilty were not publicly revealed. The U.S. Court of Appeals for the Fifth Circuit rejected their challenge and held that the trial court did not abuse its discretion in impaneling an anonymous jury. The appellate court mentioned that one of the objectives of the defendants' criminal organization was to interfere with potential witnesses. *United States v. Krout*, 66 F.3d 1420 (5th Cir. 1995).

In *State v. Ivy*, 188 S.W.3d 132 (Tenn. 2006), the Tennessee Supreme Court reviewed a defendant's murder conviction. Among other issues on appeal, the defendant argued that the trial court erred in impaneling an anonymous jury. The issue of impaneling anonymous juries was a matter of first impression with the court. The court upheld the trial court's finding that strong reasons existed to protect the jury, as one of the defendant's apparent motives in committing the charged offense included the defendant's desire to prevent the victim from going to the police. Following the rationale of federal appellate court decisions, the court approved the use of an anonymous jury where there is a strong reason to believe the jury needs protection and where reasonable precautions are taken to ensure that the defendant's fundamental rights are protected.

The *Voir Dire*

The body of persons summoned to be jurors is referred to as the **venire**. After outlining the case to be tried and reciting the names of those expected to participate, the judge may excuse those whose physical disabilities or obvious conflicts of interest based on family relationships or business connections disqualify them from serving. After excusing those who do not qualify, the judge swears in the remaining members of the venire to answer questions that will be put to them by the court and counsel. Then six or twelve of these prospective jurors are called at random to take their seats in the jury box, where either the judge or counsel for each side may ask further questions. This process is called the ***voir dire***.

Lawyers for the prosecution and the defense are permitted to challenge prospective jurors either for cause or peremptorily. A challenge is a request that a juror be excused from serving. Challenges are customarily asserted at the *voir dire* (from the medieval French, meaning "to tell the truth"). The function of the *voir dire* is to enable the court and counsel to obtain the information necessary to ensure the selection of a fair and impartial jury. To assist in obtaining background information and thereby expedite the *voir dire* process, it is not uncommon for courts to submit a series of written questions to be answered by prospective jurors in advance of their appearance in court. In some courts, the *voir dire* examination is conducted by the trial judge, who may invite the lawyers to suggest questions to ask the prospective jurors. In others, lawyers for each side conduct the *voir dire*. In either event, the presiding judge exercises broad discretion to keep the questioning within proper bounds. A *voir dire* examination is generally conducted before the six or twelve prospective jurors initially selected; however, under certain circumstances some courts have allowed the examination of individual jurors apart from the collective group.

The objective of the *voir dire* examination is to select jurors who can render a verdict fairly and impartially. However, it would be naive to expect that the prosecutor and defense counsel are both striving to seat a wholly objective panel of jurors. Obviously, each trial lawyer wants jurors who will be sympathetic to the cause he or she advocates. To accomplish this, trial lawyers must be well versed in the facts of the case and the relevant law. They must also display ingenuity in questioning the prospective jurors to determine whether to exercise their right to challenge jurors' qualifications to serve. Lawyers must be conversant with local court practices because judges have broad discretion in conducting the *voir dire*. Trial lawyers have various theories on how to conduct a *voir dire* examination, but most would agree that a practical knowledge of psychology is helpful. In recent years, some have even retained social scientists for advice and assistance in the jury selection process. The process of excusing prospective jurors is accomplished by counsel exercising challenges, either "for cause" or "peremptorily"—that is, without assigning a reason.

Challenges for Cause

Challenges for cause may be directed to the venire on the basis of the panel having been improperly selected. An example is when the defense counsel contends that the selection procedures exclude minority members. More commonly, challenges for cause are directed to a prospective juror individually concerning some fact or characteristic that would disqualify that person from serving on the particular case. Among the more common reasons for disqualification are having a close relationship with counsel, being significantly involved in the case as a witness or in some other capacity, or having formed a definite opinion about the case. However, it is not expected that the jurors be totally ignorant of the facts and issues involved in the case. Justice Tom C. Clark, writing for the Supreme Court, observed:

> In these days of swift, widespread and diverse methods of communication, an important case can be expected to arouse the interest of the public in the vicinity, and scarcely any of those best qualified to serve as jurors will not have formed some impression or opinion as to the merits of the case. *Irvin v. Dowd*, 366 U.S. 717, 722, 81 S.Ct. 1639, 1642, 6 L.Ed.2d 751, 756 (1961).

With our widespread access to television and the Internet, Justice Clark's observation is even more compelling today than in 1961. Nevertheless, prospective jurors who acknowledge that they have formed an opinion on the merits of the case and cannot disregard this opinion are generally excused for cause. Absent unusual circumstances concerning the parties involved in a case, a person will not be excused for cause because of religious or political affiliations.

Peremptory Challenges of Prospective Jurors

peremptory challenges
Objections to the selection of prospective jurors in which the attorney making the challenges is not required to state the reasons for the objections.

It is not always possible to articulate a basis for dismissing a juror who appears to be biased. Therefore, each side in a criminal trial is also allowed a limited number of **peremptory challenges** that may be exercised on *voir dire* to excuse prospective jurors without stating any reason. The number of peremptory challenges is usually provided by statute or court rules.

In federal courts, each party in a criminal case where the offense is punishable by death is allowed twenty peremptory challenges. If the offense is punishable by more than one year in prison, the government is allowed six, and the defendant is allowed ten. The reason for the discrepancy is to give the defendant every opportunity for a fair trial. Each side is allowed three peremptory challenges where the offense carries a punishment of less than one year in prison. Fed. R. Crim. P. 24(b).

States vary in the number of peremptory challenges allowed in criminal trials. Rather typical is Article 35.15 of Vernon's Annotated Texas Code of Criminal Procedure, which allows the state and the defendant fifteen peremptory challenges each in capital cases where the state seeks the death penalty. Where two or more defendants are tried together, the state is entitled to eight peremptory challenges for each defendant, and each defendant is entitled to eight as well. In noncapital felony cases and in capital cases where the state does not seek the death penalty, the state and defendant

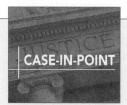

When Should a Juror Be Excused for Cause?

CASE-IN-POINT

The defendant was tried by jury for rape, sodomy, and some weapons offenses. Prospective jurors were not asked during the *voir dire* if they had ever been raped or had a family member or friend who had been raped. After the jury had been selected, a female juror suggested to the court that she should be excused because her daughter had been raped five years earlier. After being closely questioned by the judge and defense lawyer, she expressed convincingly that she and her daughter had effectively recovered from the trauma of the rape and that she could be a fair and impartial juror. The court refused to excuse her from the jury panel. The defendant was convicted and appealed. The Georgia Court of Appeals affirmed the defendant's conviction. In rejecting the defendant's argument that the trial court erred in not excusing the juror for cause, the court said that the trial court had an ample basis upon which to believe the juror would perform her duty justly.

Jamison v. State, 295 S.E.2d 203 (Ga. App. 1982).

are each entitled to ten peremptory challenges. Where two or more defendants are tried together, each defendant is entitled to six peremptory challenges, and the state is likewise entitled to six for each defendant. In misdemeanor cases, each side is allowed either three or five peremptory challenges, depending on the level of court where the defendant is tried.

To determine whether to exercise a peremptory challenge, an attorney conducting a *voir dire* examination attempts to determine the attitudes, backgrounds, and personalities of prospective jurors. Trial courts limit the questions that may be asked of prospective jurors, depending on the nature of the case. Some areas of questioning are considered very delicate and usually will not be permitted. For example, in *Alderman v. State*, 327 S.E.2d 168 (Ga. 1985), the Supreme Court of Georgia upheld a trial judge's refusal to allow a defendant to ask prospective jurors questions concerning the kinds of books and magazines they read, whether they were members of any political organizations, and what kinds of bumper stickers they had on their vehicles.

Racially Based Peremptory Challenges

racially based peremptory challenges Peremptory challenges to prospective jurors that are based solely on racial animus or racial stereotypes.

To reduce the potential for racial discrimination in the exercise of **racially based peremptory challenges**, courts have recently reassessed the historic freedom accorded counsel in exercising peremptory challenges. In 1965, in *Swain v. Alabama*, 380 U.S. 202, 85 S.Ct. 824, 13 L.Ed.2d 759, the Supreme Court said that it was a violation of the Equal Protection Clause of the Fifth Amendment to systematically exclude someone from serving on a jury because of the person's race. To make a *prima facie* case of purposeful discrimination, the defendant faced the formidable task of proving that the peremptory challenge system as a whole was being perverted. There was considerable criticism of the Court's ruling in *Swain v. Alabama*, and the Court again addressed the problem in *Batson v. Kentucky* , 476 U.S. 79, 106 S.Ct. 1712, 90 L.Ed.2d 69 (1986).

In *Batson*, the Supreme Court held that a prosecutor's peremptory challenges to exclude African Americans from a jury trying African-American defendants was ground for a defendant to claim discrimination under the Equal Protection Clause of the Fourteenth Amendment to the Constitution. *Batson* became the basis for trial courts to deny the prosecution's use of a peremptory challenge for exclusion of an African-American juror from a trial of a person of that race if the court was

---

JURISPRUDENCE

Batson v. Kentucky, 476 U.S. 79, 106 S.Ct. 1712, 90 L.Ed.2d 69 (1986)

Batson, an African-American man, was on trial for burglary and receiving stolen goods. The prosecutor used his peremptory challenges to strike all four blacks from the venire, which led to an all-white jury being impaneled. The judge denied the defendant's motion to discharge the jury. Batson was convicted on both counts and the state supreme court affirmed. In a 7–2 decision, the U.S. Supreme Court reversed, holding that Batson had been denied a fair trial due to the purposeful exclusion of blacks from the jury. The Court said that, henceforth, a trial judge must deny a prosecutor's peremptory challenge to an African-American juror where the defendant is also black if the judge is persuaded that the challenge is racially motivated. Justice Lewis Powell concluded his opinion for the Court by predicting that "public respect for our criminal justice system and the rule of law will be strengthened if we ensure that no citizen is disqualified from jury service because of his race."

persuaded the challenge was racially motivated. In 1991, the Supreme Court broadened the rule so that the racial motivation of the prosecutor became subject to challenge irrespective of the defendant and prospective juror being of the same race. *Powers v. Ohio*, 499 U.S. 400, 111 S.Ct. 1364, 113 L.Ed.2d 411 (1991).

In 1992, the Court revisited this area of the law and extended the *Batson* rule by holding that a defendant's exercise of peremptory challenges was state action and that the Equal Protection Clause also prohibits defendants from engaging in purposeful discrimination on the ground of race. *Georgia v. McCollum*, 505 U.S. 42, 112 S.Ct. 2348, 120 L.Ed.2d 33 (1992). And in 2000, the Court suggested that the *Batson* rule applies to ethnicity as well as race. *United States v. Martinez-Salazar*, 528 U.S. 304, 120 S.Ct. 774, 145 L.Ed.2d 792 (2000). In *Rico v. Leftridge-Byrd* , 340 F.3d 178 (3d Cir. 2003), the U.S. Court of Appeals for the Third Circuit relied on that dictum in holding that peremptory challenges to Italian-American prospective jurors are within the scope of the *Batson* rule.

Gender-Based Peremptory Challenges

gender-based peremptory challenges Challenges to a prospective juror's competency to serve that are based solely on the prospective juror's gender.

In the late 1980s and early 1990s, courts moved to restrict **gender-based peremptory challenges**. By 1993, federal appellate courts had issued disparate rulings on the issue. Finally, in *J.E.B. v. Alabama ex rel. T.B.*, 511 U.S. 127, 114 S.Ct. 1419, 128 L.Ed.2d 89 (1994), the U.S. Supreme Court resolved that conflict and held that the Equal Protection Clause of the Fourteenth Amendment also prohibits gender-based peremptory challenges. Writing for the majority, Justice Harry Blackmun emphasized the relationship between racially based and gender-based peremptory challenges: "Failing to provide jurors the same protection against gender discrimination as race discrimination could frustrate the purpose of *Batson* itself." 511 U.S. at 148, 114 S.Ct. at 1430, 128 L.Ed.2d at 107. Now that peremptory challenges based on race, ethnicity, and gender have been invalidated as violations of equal protection, some observers wonder whether the peremptory challenge itself is on the way out.

"Death-Qualified" Juries

In 1970, the Supreme Court expressed concern about some courts automatically excluding from juries trying capital cases persons who oppose or who have

---

JURISPRUDENCE

Rivera v. Illinois, 556 U.S. 148, 129 S.Ct. 1446, 173 L.Ed.2d 320 (2009)

Michael Rivera was tried on two counts of first-degree murder. During *voir dire*, his lawyer sought to use a peremptory challenge against a prospective juror. The judge disallowed the challenge without explaining why. The prospective juror was seated, and Rivera was convicted and sentenced to eighty-five years in prison. On appeal, the Illinois Supreme Court remanded the case to the trial court, demanding that the trial judge explain why he overruled the peremptory challenge. The trial judge indicated that gender discrimination

was the reason. The Illinois Supreme Court rejected this submission and held that the peremptory challenge had been wrongly denied. Nevertheless, the Illinois high court held that this mistake was a harmless error and upheld Rivera's conviction. In 2009, the U.S. Supreme Court unanimously agreed, holding that a trial judge's erroneous denial of a defendant's peremptory challenge to a prospective juror does not automatically require reversal of the defendant's conviction on appeal, as long the judge's ruling was made in good faith and all members of the jury were qualified and unbiased.

conscientious scruples against capital punishment. The Court held that opponents of capital punishment could not be excluded from juries impaneled to hear cases where the death penalty could be imposed unless the prospective jurors indicated that they could not make an impartial decision on the issue of guilt or could never vote to impose the death penalty. *Witherspoon v. Illinois*, 391 U.S. 510, 88 S.Ct. 1770, 20 L.Ed.2d 776 (1968).

In *Wainwright v. Witt*, 469 U.S. 412, 424, 105 S.Ct. 844, 852, 83 L.Ed.2d 841, 851–852 (1985), the Court articulated the proper standard for determining when a prospective juror may be excluded for cause because of views on capital punishment. The test, the Court said, is whether the juror's views would "prevent or substantially impair the performance of his duties as a juror in accordance with his instructions and oath." Justice William J. Brennan, with whom Justice Thurgood Marshall joined in dissent, observed that "basic justice demands that juries with the power to decide whether a capital defendant lives or dies not be poisoned against the defendant." 469 U.S. at 439, 105 S.Ct. at 860, 83 L.Ed.2d at 861. In capital cases, the jury first hears the evidence bearing on the defendant's guilt or innocence; then, only if a guilty verdict is rendered, the jury receives evidence on whether the death penalty should be imposed. This practice is referred to as a bifurcated trial (see Chapter 7).

death qualification of a jury Questioning of prospective jurors in a death penalty case to ensure that the jury is composed of people who do not entertain scruples against imposing capital punishment.

The Supreme Court has said that the **death qualification of a jury** (that is, the exclusion of prospective jurors who will not under any circumstances vote for imposition of the death penalty) is designed to obtain a jury that can properly and impartially apply the law to the facts at both the guilt and sentencing phases of a capital trial. On this rationale, the Court held that removal before the guilt phase in a capital trial of prospective jurors whose opposition to the death penalty would impair or prevent performance of their duties at the sentencing phase is not unconstitutional. *Lockhart v. McCree*, 476 U.S. 162, 106 S.Ct. 1758, 90 L.Ed.2d 137 (1986).

Impaneling of the Jury

If the court anticipates that a trial might be protracted, it may have one or more alternate jurors selected to serve in case any juror becomes ill or has to respond to an emergency. An alternate juror sits with the jury, but unless substituted for a regular juror, the alternate is excused just before the jury retires to deliberate. After selection of the jury is complete, it is sworn as a body by the judge or the clerk of the court to carry out its duties and is admonished not to discuss the case until instructed by the court to deliberate.

Proposals for Jury Reform

In the nationally televised O. J. Simpson case in 1995, the public witnessed considerable bickering between counsel and long delays in impaneling a jury. A protracted jury trial with many delays ensued. Thus, the Simpson trial became a catalyst for reform in the jury processes. Polls taken after that trial revealed a great decline in interest in serving on juries. Many who have been called to serve complain of "just sitting around the courthouse and wasting time" with no explanation for the delay. They are demanding that court officials show them more concern and respect. Although some progress has been made in allowing jurors to remain on call until needed, there remains room for improvement in many jurisdictions.

What Happens When a Juror Becomes Emotionally Disabled?

Fred Mills was convicted of aggravated robbery in Dallas County, Texas. On the morning of his trial, one of the jurors impaneled to hear the case requested permission to attend a memorial service for his grandfather, who had died the previous evening. The trial judge found the juror was "emotionally disabled" and would not be able to concentrate if not allowed to attend the memorial service. Attempts to postpone the trial disclosed conflicts for other jurors and schedules for other docketed cases, so over Mills's objection, the judge proceeded with the trial with the remaining eleven jurors. On federal habeas corpus review, the U.S. Court of Appeals for the Fifth Circuit noted that Article 36.29 of the Texas Code of Criminal Procedure specifies a norm of twelve jurors in felony cases, yet it provides that if one juror becomes "disabled," the remaining eleven can render a verdict. The court declined to review the Texas court's finding that the juror was emotionally disabled due to death of a relative. Citing *Williams v. Florida*, 399 U.S. 78, 90 S.Ct. 1893, 26 L.Ed.2d 446 (1970), the court denied Mills's petition. The court observed that "since Texas provided Mills with a jury possessing the fundamental attributes of the jury guaranteed by the Sixth and Fourteenth Amendments, Mills has no claim for relief."

Mills v. Collins, 924 F.2d 89 (5th Cir. 1991).

Many who have served on juries feel that the jury selection process has become too competitive, with little focus on the goal of obtaining a fair and impartial jury. Others emphasize the need not only to expedite the process of impaneling a jury but also for jurors to be given a greater role during the trial. Suggestions for reform have included limiting the number of peremptory challenges by counsel, allowing jurors to take written notes as a trial proceeds, and permitting questioning of witnesses by jurors. Over the last decade, courts have been increasingly willing to allow jurors to play a more active role in the trial.

Free Press versus Fair Trial

First Amendment guarantees of freedom of the press often collide with a defendant's right to a fair trial before an impartial jury. This is particularly true when heightened public interest results in mass media coverage of a trial, with potential prejudicial effects on witnesses and jurors. When this occurs, the trial court must protect the defendant's right to a fair trial by taking steps to prevent these influences from affecting the rights of the defendant. Failure to do so can result in a verdict of guilty being overturned by an appellate tribunal. The classic example of this is the Dr. Sam Sheppard Case, where the U.S. Supreme Court held that a defendant had been denied a fair trial in a sensational murder case because the trial judge failed to guard against pervasive and prejudicial media coverage. *Sheppard v. Maxwell*, 384 U.S. 333, 86 S.Ct. 1507, 16 L.Ed.2d 600 (1966).

Although the media cannot "take over" the courtroom, it is equally clear that because of First Amendment rights, the public and the press cannot ordinarily be excluded from criminal trials. In 1980, Chief Justice Warren Burger, writing for the Supreme Court, traced the history of criminal trials in Anglo-American jurisprudence; he concluded that public access is an indispensable element of criminal trials. Therefore, the Court concluded that trials may not be closed without findings sufficient to overcome the presumption of openness. *Richmond Newspapers, Inc. v. Virginia*, 448 U.S. 555, 100 S.Ct. 2814, 65 L.Ed.2d 973 (1980).

Sheppard v. Maxwell, 384 U.S. 333, 86 S.Ct. 1507, 16 L.Ed.2d 600 (1966)

In a high-profile homicide case, a jury found Dr. Sam Sheppard guilty of the 1954 murder of his wife, Marilyn. His conviction was affirmed on appeal. But in 1966 the Supreme Court reversed a federal appeals court's denial of Sheppard's petition for habeas corpus. Observing that jurors at Sheppard's trial were constantly exposed to intense media coverage until their deliberations and that the "newsmen took over practically the entire courtroom," the Court found that the highly prejudicial publicity contributed to the denial of due process of law to the defendant. Acknowledging that nothing proscribes the press from reporting events in the courtroom, the Court suggested that trial courts can combat the problem through such measures as (1) proscribing out-of-court statements by lawyers, parties, witnesses, or court officials concerning matters that could be prejudicial to the accused; and (2) insulating the witnesses and sequestering the jury to prevent exposure to reports by the media. The prosecution was given a reasonable time to retry Sheppard. On retrial in 1966, he was acquitted. Sheppard died in 1970, but his son, Sam Reese Sheppard, brought a civil suit against the state of Ohio claiming that his father was wrongfully imprisoned for the crime for which he was later acquitted. In an attempt to clear Sheppard's reputation, counsel attempted to establish that the DNA of a third person—not Sheppard or his wife—was present at the crime scene. On April 10, 2000, a jury in Cuyahoga County, Ohio, unanimously rejected the claim.

Cameras in the Courtroom

In 1965, in a 5–4 decision, the Supreme Court held that the defendant, Billy Sol Estes, was denied due process of law because the proceedings of his criminal trial were televised over his objection. *Estes v. Texas*, 381 U.S. 532, 85 S.Ct. 1628, 14 L.Ed.2d 543 (1965). This was consistent with the longtime ban that courts had imposed on allowing cameras in the courtroom. During the 1970s, many state courts began to allow radio, television, and still-camera coverage of court proceedings subject to limitations that were necessary to preserve the essential dignity of a trial (for example, equipment must be noiseless, and strong lights are not permitted). Also, judges may limit coverage by requiring pooling of media equipment. Nevertheless, Rule 53 of the Federal Rules of Criminal Procedure still prohibits the taking of photographs in the courtroom during the progress of judicial proceedings in federal courts.

Florida is among the states that began permitting televising of trials in the late 1970s. *In re Post-Newsweek Stations, Florida, Inc.*, 370 So.2d 764 (Fla. 1979). Thereafter, Noel Chandler and another defendant, who were charged with several offenses, requested the trial court to exclude live television coverage from their jury trial. The court denied their request, and they were found guilty. A state appellate court affirmed their convictions. *Chandler v. State*, 366 So.2d 64 (Fla. App. 1978). The U.S. Supreme Court granted review. At the outset, the Court acknowledged that it had no supervisory jurisdiction over state courts. Therefore, it confined its review to evaluating the constitutionality of Florida's program permitting radio, television, and photographic coverage of criminal proceedings over an accused's objection. The Court declined to prohibit television cameras from state courts but said that defendants have a right to show that such use prejudiced them in obtaining a fair trial. Finding that Chandler and his codefendant had not shown they were prejudiced in any way by the televising of their trials, the Court denied them any relief. *Chandler v. Florida*, 449 U.S. 560, 101 S.Ct. 802, 66 L.Ed.2d 740 (1981).

Today, cameras are allowed in the courtrooms of almost all state courts. And although there has been some backlash following the O. J. Simpson case, most observers believe that cameras in the courtroom have enhanced the public's awareness of the judicial process. However, it is probably a fair generalization to conclude that, depending on the particular case, judges should be more assertive in exercising control over the televising of criminal proceedings.

The federal ban on cameras in the courtroom came to the forefront in March and April 1993, when four police officers, who had previously been acquitted of criminal charges in a state court trial, were tried in a federal district court in Los Angeles on charges of violating the Fourth Amendment rights of Rodney King. Because this trial attracted widespread interest, the media voiced displeasure at their inability to bring live camera coverage to the public. Nevertheless, in 1994 the Judicial Conference of the United States voted to maintain the ban on television cameras in federal courts. There is less resistance to allowing television and still photography coverage of appellate proceedings, which are inherently much less dramatic. In March 1996, the U.S. Judicial Conference voted 14–12 to allow federal appeals courts to permit television, radio, and still photography in civil, but not criminal, appeals.

Almost all state courts now permit television and photographic coverage of court proceedings. In most states, the consent of the presiding judge is required, and judges generally have considerable discretion to control the coverage. Coverage of jurors is either prohibited or restricted, and most states prohibit coverage of cases involving juveniles and victims of sex crimes. Some states have such restrictive policies that television coverage of trials almost never takes place. However, in many states, television cameras that are permanent fixtures of the courtroom record court proceedings. Television stations and networks can simply pick up the signals, which they can edit or present live to their viewers.

JURISPRUDENCE

Nebraska Press Association v. Stuart, 427 U.S. 539, 96 S.Ct. 2791, 49 L.Ed.2d 683 (1976)

This case stems from the brutal murder of six members of the Henry Kelly family in Sutherland, Nebraska, on the night of October 18, 1975. Erwin Simants, an unemployed handyman, was accused of the crime. Evidence indicated that the victims died as a result of wounds inflicted with a .22-caliber rifle and that some of the victims had been sexually assaulted after the wounds had been inflicted. The grisly crime generated widespread publicity, much of which was prejudicial to the accused. Three days after Simants was arrested, attorneys for the state and the defense asked the local court to issue an order restricting media coverage of the case. The court complied and issued an order prohibiting reportage of certain aspects of the case until a trial jury could

be empaneled. The Nebraska Press Association then filed a civil suit challenging the constitutionality of the gag order. After the Nebraska Supreme Court upheld the lower court's order, the Nebraska Press Association took the case to the U.S. Supreme Court on a writ of certiorari. The Supreme Court held that the gag order entered by the trial judge was an unconstitutional prior restraint on the press. Before the Supreme Court handed down its decision, Erwin Simants was convicted and sentenced to death. Ultimately, however, his conviction was reversed by the Nebraska Supreme Court after it was found that the local sheriff had visited the trial jurors at the motel where they were sequestered during the course of the trial. After a second trial, Simants was found not guilty by reason of insanity and was committed to a mental institution.

The O. J. Simpson case, tried in California in 1995, shows how a sensational criminal trial can draw the mass media's attention. In that case, CNN and Court TV featured live coverage of many of the courtroom activities; other television networks carried daily "O. J. Updates" in their evening news programs.

Gag Orders

gag order A court order prohibiting attorneys, witnesses, jurors, and other persons associated with a trial from talking to the press about the case.

In order to keep the prosecutor and the defense counsel from "trying a case in the media," a judge can issue a gag order prohibiting the attorneys from talking to the press about the case. However, the U.S. Supreme Court has made it very difficult, if not impossible, for judges to extend gag orders to media members. *Nebraska Press Association v. Stuart*, 427 U.S. 539, 96 S.Ct. 2791, 49 L.Ed.2d 683 (1976). Once the media finds out information about a trial, courts cannot restrict reportage of that information.

"Order in the Court"

Occasionally a trial judge is confronted with a defendant or others in attendance at a trial whose disruptive behavior impedes the court from conducting a trial in a proper judicial atmosphere. As Justice Hugo Black observed, "The flagrant disregard in the courtroom of elementary standards of proper conduct should not and cannot be tolerated." *Illinois v. Allen*, 397 U.S. 337, 343, 90 S.Ct. 1057, 1061, 25 L.Ed.2d 353, 359 (1970).

This problem is more likely encountered in a so-called political trial, where there may be support for the cause the defendant claims to represent. One such highly publicized instance of courtroom disruption occurred in the 1969–1970 "Chicago Seven" conspiracy trial in federal court in Chicago. The seven defendants, including antiwar activist David T. Dellinger, were prosecuted under the Federal Anti-Riot Statute (18 U.S.C.A. §§ 2101–2102) for their actions at the August 1968 Democratic National Convention in Chicago. An eighth defendant, Black Panther party leader Bobby G. Seale, was tried separately on similar charges. Considerable antagonism developed among the trial judge, the defendants, and their counsel. As a result of their actions during their trials, all defendants and two of their attorneys were found guilty of contempt of court. Despite the number of unruly and disrespectful actions that took place, the contempt convictions were reversed because of procedural irregularities. *United States v. Seale*, 461 F.2d 345 (7th Cir. 1972); *In re Dellinger*, 461 F.2d 389 (7th Cir. 1972). Subsequently, the defendants' convictions were also reversed by the same federal court of appeals on the basis of judicial error. In this latter opinion the appellate court criticized the trial judge for his own antagonistic behavior during the trial. *United States v. Dellinger*, 472 F.2d 340 (7th Cir. 1972).

Unruly Defendants

power of contempt The authority of a court of law to punish someone who insults the court or flouts its authority.

It is not too difficult for judges to exercise control over members of the public who attend court trials. The problem that does confront judges is a defendant who becomes unruly. In most instances, judges control disruption and defiance by defendants and others through exercise of the **power of contempt**. Yet, in recent years, some courts have had to go further. In *Illinois v. Allen*, supra, the Supreme Court recognized that there is no one formula for maintaining the appropriate courtroom atmosphere, but indicated that

> there are at least three constitutionally permissible ways for a trial judge to handle an obstreperous defendant . . . : (1) bind and gag him, thereby keeping him present; (2) cite him for contempt; (3) take him out of the courtroom until he promises to conduct himself properly. 397 U.S. at 343–344, 90 S.Ct. at 1061, 25 L.Ed.2d at 359.

The Sixth Amendment protects the defendant's right to be present at every critical stage of criminal proceedings. *Snyder v. Massachusetts*, 291 U.S. 97, 54 S.Ct. 330, 78 L.Ed. 674 (1934). The right to be present at trial is fundamental; however, it may be forfeited if the defendant is disruptive or refuses to comply with reasonable standards of the court. For example, in New York a defendant repeatedly insisted on appearing in court while wearing only his underwear covered by a sheet. After warning him of the consequences of not wearing proper attire to court, the trial court allowed the trial to proceed in the defendant's absence. On appeal, the trial court's action was affirmed. *People v. Hinton*, 550 N.Y.S.2d 438 (N.Y. App. Div. 1990).

The Supreme Court in *Illinois v. Allen*, 397 U.S. 337, 90 S.Ct. 1057, 25 L.Ed.2d 353 (1970), explained that a trial judge is justified in employing necessary security measures to control a disruptive defendant. Accordingly, all courts insist that a defendant not disrupt courtroom proceedings. Thus, if there is a real threat of serious disruption by a defendant, or where threats of escape or danger to those in and around the courtroom exist, a defendant may be shackled. Federal and state courts are reluctant to shackle a defendant unless it becomes imperative because, in addition to concerns over the jury's perception of a shackled defendant, shackling may have a prejudicial effect on a defendant's decision to testify at trial. See, e.g., *People v. Duran*, 545 P.2d 1322 (Cal. 1976). Moreover, in some cases such restraints "may . . . impair [the defendant's] ability to confer with counsel, and significantly affect the trial strategy he chooses to follow." *Zygadlo v. Wainwright*, 720 F.2d 1221, 1223 (11th Cir. 1983).

Most state courts probably take the view of the Missouri Supreme Court. In 1996 that court observed that the use of restraints for courtroom security purposes is a matter within the discretion of the trial court. *State v. Kinder*, 942 S.W.2d 313 (Mo. 1996). In 1999, the Illinois Supreme Court, citing one of its earlier decisions, enumerated the following factors a trial judge should consider in determining whether to shackle a defendant:

> . . . the seriousness of the present charge against the defendant; defendant's temperament and character; his age and physical attributes; his past record; past escapes or attempted escapes, and evidence of a present plan to escape; threats to harm others or cause a disturbance; self-destructive tendencies; the risk of mob violence or of attempted revenge by others; the possibility of rescue by other offenders still at large; the size and mood of the audience; the nature and physical security of the courtroom; and the adequacy and availability of alternative remedies. *People v. Buss*, 718 N.E.2d 1, 40 (Ill. 1999).

Behavior of Counsel

Dramatic, fictional presentations of courtroom proceedings now occupy a considerable part of television entertainment. A viewer is quite likely to gain an erroneous impression of courtroom proceedings, particularly in respect to the standards of conduct enforced against lawyers in criminal trials. Lawyers are seen asking inflammatory questions of a witness and expressing personal opinions concerning facts at issue. Others persist in interrogating a witness after the court has sustained an objection to such a line of questioning. It is not uncommon to see a lawyer continuing to press a point of law after the trial judge has made a ruling. Some actually appear to practice deceptive tactics on behalf of a client, justifying the means by the ultimate goal of helping a client. In viewing such tactics, a prospective criminal justice professional could misapprehend the proper role of a prosecutor or defense lawyer. Moreover, a prospective client who sees lawyers on television dramatically pursue such flagrant tactics may gain a false expectation of what a lawyer's role is in the courtroom, and as a result may someday expect his or her own lawyer to pursue such tactics.

In federal and state courts lawyers are subject to rather strict legal and ethical rules in presenting evidence, following trial procedures, and courtroom decorum. When making an opening statement, a lawyer must not express personal knowledge or opinion concerning facts in issue. Lawyers must avoid misstating a fact or point of law; must address their arguments to the court, not to opposing counsel; and must avoid disparaging remarks toward opposing counsel. They are expected to refer to adult witnesses by their surnames and refrain from any gestures of approval or disapproval during a witness's testimony. A lawyer is not permitted to express a personal opinion as to the guilt or innocence of a defendant, but may argue whether the evidence shows guilt or innocence. Furthermore, a lawyer should abstain from flattery or other comments designed to curry favor with a juror. And it goes without saying that a trial judge must maintain a position of dignity and neutrality during the course of a trial.

It is understandable that emotions can run high during a trial, but trial judges generally insist on proper decorum in the courtroom. The court may discipline a lawyer who fails to abide by these rules. An offending lawyer may be found in contempt of court and fined or even jailed in instances of egregious misconduct. However, because of the possible adverse effect on a case, trial judges are hesitant to reprimand a lawyer, particularly defense counsel, in the presence of a jury. Other forms of disciplinary action may be initiated by a bar association and can range from public reprimands to suspension or even disbarment where a lawyer intentionally deceives the court, knowingly makes a false statement or submits a false document, or improperly withholds material information that causes serious injury to a party or a significant adverse effect on a legal proceeding.

The Rules of Evidence

In our adversary system, the purpose of a trial is to search for the truth. Guilt or innocence is determined based on the evidence produced at a trial. This evidence consists of verbal statements, writings, documents, photographs, and tangible items that tend to prove or disprove some fact in issue. Certain rules govern the introduction of evidence in a court of law. Sometimes a judge will tend to relax these rules in a nonjury trial because the judge is trained to "sort out" the probative evidence from the nonprobative. However, in a jury trial in a criminal case, the rules of evidence are strictly enforced.

The subject of evidence is complex. The rules of evidence prescribed by Congress for use in federal courts are known as the Federal Rules of Evidence; they are found in Title 28 of the U.S. Code Annotated. Some states have legislatively or judicially adopted codes of evidence; in other states, the rules of evidence must be gleaned from a study of the decisional law of the state. Volumes have been written on the subject, and thousands of court decisions address its various aspects and refinements of general rules. From a basic text on criminal procedure, the reader can expect to gain only a very basic grasp of the principles involved.

Judicial Notice

judicial notice The act of a court recognizing, without proof, the existence of certain facts that are commonly known.

Commonly known facts are accepted by courts without formal proof, a process known as the court taking **judicial notice** of certain established facts. Usually there is a request by counsel, but in some instances courts take judicial notice without request. The rationale for the doctrine of judicial notice is that courts should not exclude consideration of matters of general knowledge that are well known to informed members of the public. For instance, courts take judicial notice of who is president of the United States, that a particular date in a given month was on a certain day of the week, or that whiskey is an intoxicating liquor. In some instances it may be necessary to bring such commonly accepted facts to the court's attention by presentation of a calendar or an almanac. Courts in a particular area may be asked to take judicial notice of certain facts within the geographic area of the court's jurisdiction. However, judicial notice of a fact must never be used as a substitute for proof of an essential element of a crime. *State v. Welch*, 363 A.2d 1356 (R.I. 1976). Taking judicial notice is not conclusive, because a party can always offer proof to the contrary.

Courts also take judicial notice of the law. All courts take judicial notice of the U.S. Constitution and general acts of Congress, and federal courts take judicial notice of the federal laws and the laws of each state, including statutes or judicial opinions. *Lamar v. Micou*, 114 U.S. 218, 5 S.Ct. 857, 29 L.Ed. 94 (1885). State courts take judicial notice of their own state constitutions and state laws. Municipal ordinances and the laws of other states generally must be established by formal proof, but attorneys frequently stipulate as to the text of these laws. This simply means that counsel will acknowledge the validity of these texts without the need for formal proof. Of course, courts can require counsel to submit memoranda relative to the status of laws and judicial opinions to be judicially noticed.

Proof beyond a Reasonable Doubt

proof beyond a reasonable doubt The standard of proof in a criminal trial or a juvenile delinquency hearing.

Historically, the requirement for **proof beyond a reasonable doubt** in a criminal trial has required proof whereby the fact finder would have "an abiding conviction, to a moral certainty, of the truth of the charge." *Commonwealth v. Webster*, 59 Mass. (5 Cush.) 295, 320 (1850). The historical requirement was elevated to a constitutional mandate in *In re Winship*, 397 U.S. 358, 90 S.Ct. 1068, 25 L.Ed.2d 368 (1970). There, the Supreme Court held that the Due Process Clause of the Fourteenth Amendment requires the prosecution to establish the elements of a charged crime beyond a reasonable doubt. Judges have defined "beyond a reasonable doubt" in a variety of ways. In *Victor v. Nebraska*, 511 U.S. 1, 114 S.Ct. 1239, 127 L.Ed.2d 583 (1994), the Supreme Court held that the Constitution does not require that any one particular form of words be employed. Instead, judges have wide discretion in instructing juries on the meaning of the reasonable doubt standard. In evaluating jury instructions on this issue, the question is whether the court's instruction, taken as a whole, conveys a correct sense of the concept of reasonable doubt. In *Victor*, the Court avoided defining reasonable doubt directly but said that trial courts must avoid definitions of reasonable doubt that permit juries to convict a person on a standard that is less than what is required by due process of law.

Evidentiary Presumptions

evidentiary presumptions Establishment of one fact allows inference of another fact or circumstance.

This standard of requiring proof beyond a reasonable doubt is central to judicial consideration of the validity of **evidentiary presumptions**. At common law, a child younger than seven years old was conclusively presumed to be incapable of committing a crime. A legal presumption of this type is called an irrebuttable presumption. In other words, no evidence can be introduced in court to overcome it. In criminal law, an irrebuttable presumption that provides, based on proof of one fact, that the fact finder (judge or jury) must conclusively find the existence of another fact is problematic. This is because it encroaches on a defendant's due process right to have the prosecution prove the defendant guilty beyond a reasonable doubt.

Today, most presumptions in criminal law are permissive. These are evidentiary devices designed to aid a party who has the burden of proof. For example, under this type of presumption, once evidence establishes a fact, the jury may infer that something else is true, provided there is a rational connection between the basic fact and the presumed fact.

In *County Court of Ulster County, New York v. Allen*, 442 U.S. 140, 99 S.Ct. 2213, 60 L.Ed.2d 777 (1979), the Supreme Court upheld the application of a New York statutory presumption that occupants of a car in which firearms were present are in illegal possession of them, as applied to a case in which three adults and a juvenile were tried for illegal possession of handguns. When the police stopped the vehicle in which the suspects were riding, they saw the handguns located crosswise in an open handbag. The juvenile admitted ownership of the bag. At the conclusion of the ztrial, the judge instructed the jury, in part, that "you may infer and draw a conclusion that such prohibited weapon was possessed by each of the defendants who occupied the automobile at the time when such instruments were found. The presumption, or presumptions, is effective only so long as there is no substantial evidence contradicting the conclusion flowing from the presumption, and the presumption is said to disappear when such contradictory evidence is adduced." The Supreme Court pointed out that "the presumption was merely a part of the prosecution's case, that it gave rise to a permissive inference available only in certain circumstances, rather than a mandatory conclusion of possession, and that it could be ignored by the jury even if there was no affirmative proof offered by defendants in rebuttal." 442 U.S. at 160–161, 99 S.Ct. at 2213, 60 L.Ed.2d at 794.

Shortly thereafter, in *Sandstrom v. Montana*, 442 U.S. 510, 99 S.Ct. 2450, 61 L.Ed.2d 39 (1979), the Court reviewed a case in which the State of Montana charged the defendant, David Sandstrom, with a homicidal crime where intent was a necessary element of the offense. The trial court instructed the jury that "the law presumes that a person intends the ordinary consequences of his voluntary act." Historically, many trial courts commonly instructed juries substantially as quoted. But in *Sandstrom*, the Supreme Court noted that because the jury was not told that the presumption could be rebutted, it may have interpreted the presumption as being conclusive or as shifting to the defendant the burden of persuasion on the element of intent. Thus, the Court viewed the issue to be whether such an instruction relieved the state of its burden to prove the defendant guilty beyond any reasonable doubt. The Court found that the instruction mandated a conclusive presumption that removed the need to prove the essential element of intent and ruled that such a presumption violated the defendant's due process rights under the Fourteenth Amendment.

A decade later, the Court reiterated the principle announced in *Sandstrom*. A defendant had been prosecuted for violating a statute that provided as follows: "Whenever any person who has . . . rented a vehicle willfully and intentionally fails to return the vehicle to its owner within 5 days after the . . . rental agreement has

Constitutionality of a Statute That Creates a Permissive Inference

CASE-IN-POINT The state of Florida charged John Henry Rygwelski with violating Florida Statutes, § 812.155(4)(b), which provides that the failure to redeliver property within five days after receipt of, or within five days after return receipt from, the certified mailing of the demand for return "is prima facie evidence of fraudulent intent." The trial court found that the statute creates a mandatory presumption that relieves the state of its burden to prove an essential element of the offense, in violation of the Due Process Clauses of the federal and Florida constitutions. The appellate court granted the state's petition for review and held that under Florida Supreme Court precedents the statute creates a permissive inference, not a mandatory presumption. Therefore, a party challenging the law is required to demonstrate its invalidity *as applied to him or her*. The court said, "Rygwelski must make an as-applied challenge [of the statute] to its application under the facts of his case for the trial court to determine whether the presumed fact (fraudulent intent) is rationally connected to the proven fact (failure to return property within five days of receipt of demand for return). Given the procedural posture of this case—the only action taken was the ruling on the motion to dismiss; the parties have not submitted evidence as to the alleged violation—any consideration of an as-applied challenge is premature pending further factual development." The appellate court quashed the order under review and remanded this case for further proceedings consistent with its opinion.

State v. Rygwelski, 899 So.2d 498 (Fla. App. 2005).

expired . . . shall be presumed to have embezzled the vehicle." The Court held that the jury instruction that included the mandatory presumption of the statute violated the defendant's due process rights. *Carella v. California*, 491 U.S. 263, 109 S.Ct. 2419, 105 L.Ed.2d 218 (1989).

Requirements of Admissibility

As we pointed out in previous chapters, a defendant has certain constitutional protections concerning the prosecution's use of forced admissions and confessions and of other evidence that has been illegally obtained. In addition, before evidence, whether real or testimonial and whether direct or circumstantial, may be admitted in court, it must meet specific legal requirements. All evidence must be relevant (that is, it must tend to prove or disprove a material fact in issue). For example, assume that a defendant is charged with armed robbery. It would be relevant to show where the defendant and victim were located when the offense occurred, the money or other articles stolen, the force applied by the defendant, details of any weapon used, the victim's resistance, and the defendant's fingerprints. Flight by the defendant when the police sought to make an arrest and, of course, any admissions or confessions of the defendant material to the crime would also be relevant. But offenses committed by the defendant completely that were unrelated to the crime of robbery would be irrelevant, as would be the defendant's individual likes, dislikes, and lifestyle.

Similar Fact Evidence

similar fact evidence
Refers to evidence of facts similar to the facts alleged in the crime charged.

So-called **similar fact evidence** consists of facts similar to the facts in the crime charged. Such evidence might reveal the commission of a collateral crime. The test of admissibility is whether such evidence is relevant and has a probative value in establishing a material issue. Thus, under some limited circumstances, evidence of other crimes or conduct similar to that charged against the defendant may be admitted in evidence in a criminal prosecution. Although such evidence cannot be admitted to prove the defendant's bad character or propensity to commit a crime, in some instances it may be admitted to show motive, identity, or absence of mistake or accident. See, e.g., *Williams v. State*, 110 So.2d 654 (Fla. 1959). This is a very technical area of the law of evidence and is subject to varying interpretations by federal and state courts.

The trend is to admit similar fact evidence in cases that involve prosecutions for sexual abuse of children. In these cases, it often becomes important to establish opportunity, motive, intent, identity, or the absence of a mistake or accident or even to establish a child's credibility as a witness if such credibility is attacked by the defendant. This last point is illustrated by *Gezzi v. State*, 780 P.2d 972 (Wyo. 1989). There, the Wyoming Supreme Court reviewed a defendant's conviction on two counts of committing indecent acts with the younger of his two daughters. During the defendant's trial, the older sister testified to a course of sexual misconduct occurring between her and the defendant similar to the molestation that occurred between the defendant and the younger sister. Admission of this testimony was upheld because the younger sister's credibility was attacked and the evidence admitted at trial was inconclusive as to the cause of the younger sister's physical symptoms. In affirming the defendant's conviction, the court included an exhaustive footnote showing that about half of state courts now liberally recognize the admissibility of prior bad acts (similar acts) as evidence for various purposes in sexual offense cases.

Classifications of Evidence

There are several classifications of evidence. First, evidence may be real or testimonial. **Real evidence** consists of maps, blood samples, X-rays, photographs, stolen goods, fingerprints, knives, guns, and other tangible items. **Testimonial evidence** consists of sworn statements of witnesses. Watching a television drama might give the impression that a criminal trial consists largely of real evidence, but the great majority of evidence presented in criminal trials comes from the mouths of the witnesses, both lay and expert.

Next, evidence may be direct or indirect. **Direct evidence** includes **eyewitness testimony**, whereas **indirect evidence** usually consists of circumstantial evidence—that is, attendant facts from which inferences can be drawn to establish other facts in issue at the trial. To illustrate, a person who testifies to having seen the defendant enter the victim's house is giving direct evidence. Testimony that reveals that the defendant's fingerprints were found on a windowpane of that house shortly after it was broken into is **circumstantial evidence** from which, depending on the circumstances, it may be inferred that the defendant entered the house through that window. The admissibility of circumstantial evidence in criminal trials is well established in American law. *Tot v. United States*, 319 U.S. 463, 63 S.Ct. 1241, 87 L.Ed. 1519 (1943).

The same evidence can be direct regarding one fact and circumstantial regarding another. The witness who testifies that the defendant had possession of a pistol is giving direct evidence of that fact. Depending on other circumstances, it might be inferable from proof of that fact that the defendant attacked the victim.

Actually, there is no real difference in the weight given to circumstantial as opposed to real evidence. Circumstantial evidence may once have been suspect, yet lawyers and judges can point to many instances where circumstantial evidence has proven to be more reliable than testimonial evidence. As the Supreme Court has observed:

real evidence Refers to maps, blood samples, X-rays, photographs, stolen goods, fingerprints, knives, guns, and other tangible items introduced into evidence.

testimonial evidence Evidence received by a court from witnesses who have testified under oath.

direct evidence Evidence that applies directly to proof of a fact or proposition. For example, a witness who testifies to having seen an act done or heard a statement made is giving direct evidence.

eyewitness testimony Testimony given by a person based on personal observation of an event.

indirect evidence Inferences and presumptions that are probative of various facts in issue.

circumstantial evidence Indirect evidence from which the existence of certain facts may be inferred.

Conviction Based Solely on Circumstantial Evidence Must Exclude Every Reasonable Hypothesis of a Defendant's Innocence

A Florida jury found John William Jackson guilty of first-degree murder and armed burglary based entirely on circumstantial evidence. On appeal, Jackson argued that the trial court erred in denying his motion for a judgment of acquittal.

The evidence revealed that on December 19, 1983, around 4:30 A.M., the victim was raped and stabbed in her house trailer. She sought help from a neighbor and described her assailant as "an orange picker, Michigan tag." Shortly thereafter she died from multiple stab wounds to her neck. The police arrived at the scene later that day and collected blood, semen, and saliva stains; fingerprints; and hair samples. Jackson later gave the police his fingerprints, impressions of his teeth, and samples of his pubic and head hair and his blood. An autopsy revealed that a bruise on the victim's right wrist was a bite mark. Jackson, a thirty-one-year-old Caucasian male, had lived in the vicinity of the victim's trailer from approximately July 1983 until a few days before the crime, when he moved a few miles away.

Dr. Richard Souviron, a forensic odontologist, testified that the bite mark on the victim's wrist was consistent with Jackson's teeth impressions. On January 31, 1984, Jackson had a conversation with Charles and Patricia Fuller, on whose property he had lived during the latter part of 1983. Jackson mentioned to them that when the police interrogated him, he learned that the victim had been raped, stabbed, and bitten. This occurred before the police had released the information that the victim had been bitten. Mrs. Fuller acknowledged that Jackson had told her that he had been picking oranges. Mr. Fuller testified that during the time he knew him, the defendant had worked as a heavy equipment operator. FBI Agent Michael Malone, an expert in hair and fiber analysis, identified two head hairs found on the victim's pajama top as being indistinguishable from Jackson's hair sample. Agent Malone also said that "Negroid hairs" were found in a window screen and in the combed pubic hair of the victim.

The appellate court found that the prosecution presented three items of crucial evidence: first, the consistent bite mark; second, Jackson's statement to the Fullers that the victim had been bitten; and third,

the strands of hair matching Jackson's hair found on the victim. The court noted that although Dr. Souviron concluded that the bite marks on the victim's wrist were consistent with Jackson's teeth impression, he added, "this was not a positive bite.... I certainly hope [the detective] didn't arrest John Jackson on this bite." The court found that the fact that Jackson knew the victim had been bitten was not probative of his guilt. The court pointed out that prior to Jackson's conversation with the Fullers, the police had taken impressions of his teeth, an event that would be a strong indication to anyone that a bite mark was involved. The only other significant evidence against Jackson, the court noted, was Agent Malone's testimony that two strands of hair found on the victim's pajamas matched the defendant's hair samples. But Agent Malone also agreed that hair comparisons do not constitute a basis for positive personal identification and added, "It's not a fingerprint, no. I cannot say that that hair came from John Jackson and nobody else."

"Jackson's conviction," the court concluded, "hinges on two hairs found on the victim's clothing which match his hair sample. Hair comparison testimony, while admissible, does not result in identifications of absolute certainty. There was no evidence placing the defendant at the scene of the crime, no indication of a relationship of any kind between the defendant and the victim, or that they even knew each other. The victim's dying words pointed to an 'orange picker, Michigan tag.' Jackson's car, however, had a Florida tag. None of the fingerprints found at the scene of the crime matched Jackson's. This, plus the presence of Negroid pubic hair in the victim's pubic hair combings, adds support to a reasonable hypothesis that someone else committed the crime." Finally, the court explained, "[w]here the only proof of guilt is circumstantial, no matter how strongly the evidence may suggest guilt a conviction cannot be sustained unless the evidence is inconsistent with any reasonable hypothesis of innocence." Because the state failed to present evidence sufficient to enable the jury to exclude every reasonable hypothesis of the defendant's innocence, the court vacated the defendant's convictions.

Jackson v. State, 511 So.2d 1047 (Fla. App. 1987).

[C]ircumstantial evidence may in some cases point to a wholly incorrect result. Yet this is equally true of testimonial evidence. In both instances, a jury is asked to weigh the chances that the evidence correctly points to guilt against the possibility of inaccuracy or ambiguous inference. In both the jury must use its experience with people and events in weighing the probabilities. *Holland v. United States*, 348 U.S. 121, 140, 75 S.Ct. 127, 137–138, 99 L.Ed. 150, 166–167 (1954).

The Requirement of Competency

competent to testify
Having the legal capacity to offer evidence under oath in court.

To be admissible in court, evidence must also be competent. In determining whether a witness is **competent to testify**, the trial judge must consider the ability of the witness to receive and recollect impressions, to understand questions, and to appreciate the moral duty to tell the truth. A very young child may or may not be competent to testify. This depends on the court's finding regarding the child's ability to understand the meaning of telling the truth. No precise rule can be set forth about when a young child may be competent to testify. Rather, it is a matter for determination in the sound discretion of the trial judge. Considerations include the child's age, intelligence, and capacity to appreciate the requirement to tell the truth. See, e.g., *Wheeler v. United States*, 159 U.S. 523, 16 S.Ct. 93, 40 L.Ed. 244 (1895). A determination that a child is competent to testify will generally not be overturned by an appellate court unless the trial court's judgment is clearly erroneous. *Trujillo v. State*, 880 P.2d 575 (Wyo. 1994). Persons of unsound mind may not be competent to testify, but again, a judge must determine this. The presiding judge and members of the jury would not be competent to testify at a trial where they serve.

Expert Witnesses

forensic experts Persons qualified in the application of scientific knowledge to legal principles; usually applied to those who participate in discourse or who testify in court.

Today, **forensic experts** in nearly every field make a specialty of testifying in court. To qualify as an expert, a witness must present proper credentials and be received by the trial court as an expert. A court may call experts on its own motion, but usually the prosecution or defense produces experts. After one side offers a witness as an expert, opposing counsel may cross-examine the prospective witness about his or her qualifications. For example, a physician who is to give evidence as to the cause of death of someone is first asked to relate his or her educational background and experience in the specialized area of medical practice in question. In many cases, attorneys for the prosecution and defense will stipulate that a particular witness is an expert in the field. The trial judge has considerable discretion in determining whether a witness is to be received as an expert.

hypothetical questions Questions based on an assumed set of facts. Hypothetical questions may be asked of expert witnesses in criminal trials.

Unlike lay witnesses, an expert witness may respond to **hypothetical questions** and may express opinions within the realm of his or her expertise. Fingerprint identification, ballistics tests, handwriting exemplars, and medical tests have been prominent among areas where expert evidence is commonly received in criminal cases. More recently, evidence from speed-detection devices as well as breathalyzers and other devices to test blood-alcohol content has become commonplace. Judges and jurors are not necessarily scientists. Indeed, it is unlikely that many of them have more than a basic knowledge of scientific principles. Yet, courts must make rational judgments about new scientific advances to determine their admissibility in court. To accomplish this, courts must depend on experts in the field.

An expert who has knowledge from personal observation may testify on that basis. For example, a psychiatrist who has examined the accused may offer an opinion as to the accused's sanity. If the expert is not acquainted with the subject from personal observation, the expert's opinion can be based on hypothetical questions that assume the existence of facts the evidence tends to establish. Medical experts and handwriting experts frequently are asked hypothetical questions in court, and experts on the subject of accident reconstruction frequently offer testimony about speed, braking, and other factors relevant to determining fault in cases involving auto accidents.

Scientific Evidence in the Courtroom

scientific evidence
Evidence obtained through scientific and technological innovations.

Evidence obtained through scientific and technological innovations can be both relevant and probative in a criminal case. Yet, care must be taken to ensure that a new principle or technique is well supported by research and is generally accepted by the scientific community. The basic issue the courts face is whether the expert **scientific evidence** is reliable. In *Frye v. United States*, 293 F. 1013 (D.C. Cir. 1923), the court said that "in admitting expert testimony deduced from a well-recognized scientific principle or discovery, the thing from which the deduction is made must be sufficiently established to have gained general acceptance in the particular field in which it belongs." 293 F. at 1014.

general acceptance test Also known as the *Frye* test, this test requires that the scientific principle from which the expert's deduction is made has gained general acceptance in its field.

For seventy years the *Frye* test, or **general acceptance test**, was commonly applied in federal courts and in most state courts faced with the issue of whether new scientific tests should be admitted into evidence in criminal trials. In 1993, however, in *Daubert v. Merrell Dow Pharmaceuticals, Inc.*, 509 U.S. 579, 113 S.Ct. 2786, 125 L.Ed.2d 469, the U.S. Supreme Court rejected the general acceptance test. Rather, the Court ruled that the Federal Rules of Evidence supersede *Frye*. The Court held that admissibility of scientific evidence must be based on several factors, including whether the evidence can be tested and whether it can be subjected to peer review. Under *Daubert*, the trial judge must make a preliminary assessment of whether the reasoning or methodology underlying the expert's testimony is scientifically valid and whether that reasoning or methodology can be applied to the facts in issue. Once the court determines admissibility, the jury determines the weight to give to such evidence. Because the Court's ruling in *Daubert* is not one of constitutional dimension, state courts are not required to follow it.

In *Kumho Tire Co. v. Carmichael*, 526 U.S. 137, 119 S.Ct. 1167, 143 L.Ed.2d 238 (1999), the Court extended its *Daubert* reliability requirement beyond scientific testimony to include technical and other specialized expert testimony. State courts are now divided on whether to accept the newer *Daubert* standard or remain with the classic standard announced in 1923 in *Frye v. United States*.

Hypnotically Enhanced Testimony

hypnotically enhanced testimony Testimony offered by a witness whose memory has been refreshed through hypnosis.

One controversial area of expert testimony concerns whether **hypnotically enhanced testimony** is admissible in a criminal trial. After examining extensive scientific literature, research, and testimony on the reliability of hypnotically refreshed memory and determining that the scientific community was divided on the subject, the California Supreme Court determined that hypnotically refreshed memory should not be admitted in judicial proceedings. *People v. Shirley*, 723 P.2d 1354 (Cal. 1982). In earlier years, some courts tended to admit such evidence—see, e.g., *Harding v. State*, 246

A.2d 302 (Md. App. 1968). However, the trend seems to have moved in the direction of not allowing such evidence. The majority of courts in the last decade have held that hypnotically enhanced testimony is not sufficiently reliable to be admissible. In *State v. Tuttle*, 780 P.2d 1203 (Utah 1989), the Utah Supreme Court published an exhaustive opinion analyzing the status of the law in this area and held that hypnotically enhanced testimony, as well as testimony regarding anything first recalled from the time of a hypnotic session forward, is inadmissible as evidence.

In *Rock v. Arkansas*, 483 U.S. 44, 107 S.Ct. 2704, 97 L.Ed.2d 37 (1987), the U.S. Supreme Court held that excluding hypnotically enhanced testimony, when applied to prevent an accused from testifying to his or her own posthypnotic recall, violated her constitutional right to testify on her own behalf. Accordingly, the position of the majority of courts to exclude all hypnotically induced testimony should not prevent an accused from testifying to his or her own posthypnotic recall. Recently some state and federal courts have allowed hypnotically enhanced testimony, but only after first conducting a determination of reliability.

Polygraph Evidence

Known in the vernacular as a lie detector, a polygraph records a subject's respiration, blood pressure, and heartbeat as the subject is questioned by an examiner. The examiner poses certain questions and records the subject's responses. The premise of the polygraph is that deception is accompanied by stress that is manifested in increased respiration, pulse, and blood pressure. The use of a polygraph is controversial. Polygraph operators argue that a properly administered polygraph test is effective in detecting deception, and they cite impressive figures attesting to the accuracy of results. However, some critics argue that an individual can so control physiological responses as to distort the findings.

polygraph evidence
Results of lie detector tests (generally inadmissible into evidence).

Historically, federal and state courts have declined to admit **polygraph evidence.** As late as 1989, the Minnesota Supreme Court held that the results of polygraph tests, as well as any direct or indirect references to the taking of or refusal to take such tests, are inadmissible. *State v. Fenney*, 448 N.W.2d 54 (Minn. 1989). Most state courts agree and hold that the reliability of polygraph testing has not been scientifically demonstrated to such a degree of certainty as to permit its use in evidence. However, some courts allow the results of polygraph testing to be admitted in court on stipulation of the prosecution and the defense. See, e.g., *State v. Souel*, 372 N.E.2d 1318 (Ohio 1978); *State v. Valdez*, 371 P.2d 894 (Ariz. 1962). Of course, such an agreement must be entered into prior to the administration of the polygraph test. Other state supreme courts have held that polygraph evidence is not admissible in a criminal trial even when the parties stipulate to its admissibility. See, e.g., *People v. Baynes*, 430 N.E.2d 1070 (Ill. 1981).

The prognosis for the use of polygraph evidence remains uncertain. Advocates of polygraph evidence were heartened in 1989 when the Eleventh Circuit Court of Appeals observed that polygraph testing has gained increasingly widespread acceptance as a useful and reliable scientific tool: "We agree with those courts which have found that a per se rule disallowing polygraph evidence is no longer warranted." *United States v. Piccinonna*, 885 F.2d 1529, 1535 (11th Cir. 1989). But on March 31, 1998, the U.S. Supreme Court upheld a ban on the use of polygraph evidence in military courts. *United States v. Scheffer*, 523 U.S. 303, 118 S.Ct. 1261, 140 L.Ed.2d 413 (1998). A military appeals court had ruled that an airman should not have been barred from introducing lie-detector evidence during his court-martial on charges of using drugs and writing bad checks. In reversing that decision, the Court, in an opinion by Justice Clarence Thomas, observed that there was no consensus that such evidence is reliable and ruled that the military ban on the use of such evidence did not unconstitutionally abridge the airman's right to present a defense. However, four of the justices in the court's eight-member majority recognized that in some future case, the polygraph test might be so crucial that its results should be allowed.

Battered Woman Syndrome

Expert testimony concerning the battered woman syndrome has gained substantial scientific acceptance, and in the past several years such testimony has been received in many courts in cases where women claim to have acted in self-defense. In 1989, the Ohio Supreme Court departed from its 1981 decision declaring such evidence inadmissible. The court took a fresh look at the literature published in this area since 1981 and said that "expert testimony on the battered woman syndrome would help dispel the ordinary lay person's perception that a woman in a battering relationship is free to leave at any time. Popular misconceptions about battered women should be put to rest, including beliefs that the women are masochistic." *State v. Koss*, 551 N.E.2d 970, 971 (Ohio 1990). To some extent, a woman's reliance on evidence of the battered woman syndrome depends on whether state law imposes a duty to retreat before defending oneself with deadly force.

On May 15, 2006, the Supreme Court of New Jersey held that "It is beyond debate that battered women's syndrome has gained general acceptance as a scientific doctrine within the professional community." Recognizing that the ramifications of a battering relationship are beyond the knowledge of the average juror, the court noted that expert testimony is admissible "because it has been determined to be useful in explaining conduct exhibited by battered women toward their abusers." *State v. Townsend*, 897 A.2d 316, 327 (N. J. 2006).

DNA Evidence

DNA testing Laboratory tests that compare DNA molecules extracted from a suspect's specimen with DNA molecules extracted from specimens found at a crime scene to determine whether the samples match.

Since its introduction in the late 1980s, **DNA testing** has had a profound impact on law enforcement and criminal procedure. DNA is an abbreviation of deoxyribonucleic acid, the chemical that carries an individual's genetic information. DNA is extracted from a biological specimen (for example, white blood cells, semen, body hair, or tissue). Through sophisticated testing results, DNA printing tests compare DNA molecules extracted from a suspect's specimen with DNA molecules extracted from specimens found at a crime scene to determine whether the samples match. Scientists and law enforcement officers attempt to develop what a layperson might call "genetic fingerprints."

In one of the first uses of DNA evidence in a criminal trial in the United States, Tommy Lee Andrews was convicted of rape by a Florida court in 1987 after his DNA was matched to that of semen traces obtained from the victim's body. *Andrews v. State*, 533 So.2d 841, 842–843 (Fla. App. 1989). Since then the use of DNA printing has proliferated, especially in rape and homicide cases.

When it was introduced, DNA profiling was widely heralded by prosecutors. Defense counsel usually accepted the validity of the evidence without presenting their own experts to challenge it. Courts, too, were extremely impressed with this new form of evidence. One federal court referred to the reliability and accuracy of DNA profiling as justifying "an aura of amazement." See, e.g., *United States v. Jakobetz*,

747 F. Supp. 250, 258 (D. Vt. 1990). During the 1990s, defense counsel began to challenge DNA evidence principally on the basis of the test results. Courts became increasingly concerned over the issue of reliability of test results due to documented instances of false positive and false negative entries by DNA laboratories. See, e.g., *State v. Cauthron*, 846 P.2d 502 (Wash. 1993); *People v. Barney*, 10 Cal.Rptr.2d 731 (Cal. App. 1992). There are ways in which DNA test results can be manipulated or misinterpreted.

Introduction of DNA evidence must satisfy the tests for scientific evidence. As previously noted, federal and several state courts follow *Daubert v. Merrell Dow Pharmaceuticals, Inc.*, supra, where the trial judge assesses whether the reasoning or methodology underlying an expert's testimony is scientifically valid and can be applied to the facts in issue. Many state courts continue to follow the *Frye* "general acceptance test." Irrespective of the test courts follow for admission of DNA evidence, the trend has been to take a more rigorous approach.

In *Turner v. State*, 746 So.2d 355 (Ala. 1998), the Alabama Supreme Court stated that although the *Frye* test remains the standard of admissibility for scientific evidence generally, trial courts must follow additional specific requirements in determining the admissibility of DNA evidence. The court noted that evidence concerning the use of genetic markers contained in or derived from DNA for identification purposes is admissible provided "the trial court shall be satisfied that the expert testimony or evidence meets the criteria for admissibility as set forth by the U.S. Supreme Court in *Daubert v. Merrell Dow Pharmaceuticals, Inc.*" *Id*. at 360. The court cautioned, "Trial courts should use the flexible *Daubert* analysis in making the 'reliability' (scientific validity) assessment. In making that assessment, the courts should employ the following factors: (1) testing; (2) peer review; (3) rate of error; and (4) general acceptance admissibility standard established in *Daubert*." *Id*. at 361.

The Florida Supreme Court continues to follow the *Frye* standard for admissibility of scientific evidence but now requires proof of a two-step DNA testing process.

> The first step relies on principles of molecular biology and chemistry to determine that two DNA samples match, while a second statistical step is needed to give significance to the match. The second step relies on principles of statistics and population genetics, and the calculation techniques used in determining and reporting DNA population frequencies must also satisfy the *Frye* test. *Brim v. State*, 695 So.2d 268, 269 (Fla. 1997).

In January 2005, the Supreme Judicial Court of Massachusetts, citing recent judicial authorities, explained that

> A determination of the reliability of the [DNA] testing process entails a fact-based inquiry, including questions of credibility. . . . The analysis calls on a judge to determine whether testing was properly performed . . . and whether an expert's conclusions based on clinical experience and observations were sufficiently reliable. The judge's decision under the reliability prong is reviewed under the abuse of discretion standard. *Commonwealth v. Gaynor*, 820 N.E.2d 233, 250 (Mass. 2005).

Although courts' requirements for the introduction of DNA evidence vary, no court has rejected DNA evidence on the ground that it is invalid from a scientific standpoint. But the admissibility of DNA evidence must satisfy the requirements for courts to receive scientific evidence. One current legal issue concerns the extent to which defense attorneys are entitled to discover the underlying data necessary to challenge the reliability of methods used in gathering, testing, and processing DNA evidence.

"Your Honor, I Object"

Anyone who has observed a criminal trial, or even a television drama depicting one, is familiar with the advocates frequently addressing the court: "Your honor, I object." To this, the objecting lawyer might add "on the ground that the testimony is irrelevant." This is called a **general objection**. Or the lawyer might make a **specific objection** and add "because the testimony sought would be hearsay," "because the answer calls for an opinion of the witness which the witness is not qualified to give," or another specific reason. There are numerous other grounds for specific objections. We consider some of the more common objections in the following sections.

On the Ground of Hearsay

Hearsay evidence refers to an oral or written statement by a person other than the one testifying in court. The general rule is often stated as follows: A witness may not testify as to a statement made by another if that statement is offered as proof of the matter asserted. Thus, a witness who testifies, "I know the defendant was home on the night of the offense because my sister told me so" would be giving hearsay testimony. The real test of hearsay is whether a lawyer can cross-examine the person responsible for the contents of a statement.

The hearsay rule has many exceptions. Sometimes a hearsay statement is admissible to prove something other than the truth of the statement itself. Spontaneous or excited utterances, a person's dying declaration, evidence of a person's reputation, matters contained in old family records, and certain business and public records are among the most common exceptions recognized by courts. Likewise, a defendant's out-of-court statement generally may be used if it is an admission, confession, or some other statement against the defendant's interest. But the use of hearsay evidence in criminal trials presents some unique constitutional issues. When a hearsay declarant is not present for cross-examination, the declarant's statement can be admitted in evidence if it bears what courts refer to as "adequate indicia of reliability." Courts have usually taken the view that the Confrontation Clause of the Sixth Amendment to the U.S. Constitution is met as long as the court found the hearsay statements reliable even though the defendant had no opportunity to cross-examine the declarant. This view was espoused by the U.S. Supreme Court in *Ohio v. Roberts*, 448 U.S. 56, 100 S.Ct. 2531, 65 L.Ed.2d 597 (1980). But in *Crawford v. Washington*,

general objection An objection raised against a witness's testimony or introduction of evidence when the objecting party does not recite a specific ground for the objection.

specific objection Counsel's objection to a question posed to a witness by opposing trial counsel where a specific reason is given for the objection—for example, that the question calls for hearsay evidence.

hearsay evidence Testimony by a witness as to facts the witness has heard from others that is offered in evidence at a trial or hearing to prove the truth of the matter asserted.

JURISPRUDENCE

Crawford v. Washington, 541 U.S. 36, 124 S.Ct. 1354, 158 L.Ed.2d 177 (2004)

In 1999, Michael D. Crawford was charged with assault and attempted murder for the alleged stabbing of Kenneth Lee. Sylvia Crawford, the defendant's wife, witnessed the incident. In a tape-recorded statement to a police officer, she indicated that Crawford's actions were not in self-defense. Under the state's marital privilege, Ms. Crawford was not permitted to testify against her husband. When the State sought to introduce Ms. Crawford's recorded statement to the

police as an exception to the hearsay rule, the defendant objected on the ground that admitting her statement would violate his constitutional right to confront witnesses against him. Eventually this issue reached the Supreme Court. In an opinion by Justice Antonin Scalia, the Court held that admission of Ms. Crawford's out-of-court recorded statement to police officers regarding the incident violated the Confrontation Clause, which provides that "[i]n all criminal prosecutions, the accused shall enjoy the right . . . to be confronted with the witnesses against him."

541 U.S. 36, 124 S.Ct. 1354, 158 L.Ed.2d 177 (2004), the Court overturned *Ohio v. Roberts* and effectively barred out-of-court testimonial statements by a witness unless the witness is unavailable and the defendant has had a prior opportunity to cross-examine the witness.

The Court's *Crawford* decision left unanswered the precise meaning of *testimonial statements*, thereby creating considerable uncertainty. On June 19, 2006, in another opinion by Justice Scalia, the Supreme Court attempted to clarify its holding in *Crawford*. The Court in *Davis v. Washington*, 547 U.S. 813, 126 S.Ct. 2266, 165 L.Ed.2d 224 (2006), held that statements in response to a 911 operator are nontestimonial unless the circumstances objectively indicate that there is no such emergency. The Court went on to explain that if interrogation is intended primarily to "establish or prove past events," the resulting statements are testimonial and subject to the requirements of the Confrontation Clause. Confrontation issues frequently arise regarding out-of-court statements in cases involving charges of sexual abuse of children, and the dichotomy between testimonial and nontestimonial will be the subject of further litigation in the lower courts.

On the Ground of the Best Evidence Rule

best evidence Primary evidence used to prove a fact—usually an original written document that evidences a communication or transaction.

Ordinarily, the **best evidence** of a transaction must be offered in court. This rule applies to writings and means that an original document must be offered unless the party who offers a copy can present a plausible explanation of why the original is not available. For example, historically the original check allegedly forged by the defendant had to be produced rather than a photocopy of it. But the Federal Check Clearing for the 21st Century Act, PL 108-100 (Check 21 Law) became effective on October 28, 2004. Among its many provisions, the act provides that a substitute check is the legal equivalent of the original check.

On the Ground that the Question Calls for an Opinion from the Witness

A lay witness is supposed to testify regarding facts of which he or she has personal knowledge. In addition, lay witnesses are generally permitted to testify about matters perceived through their physical senses and matters that are within the common knowledge of most people, such as the speed of a vehicle, sizes, distances, or the appearance of a person. They cannot give opinions on matters beyond the common experience and understanding of laypersons. To illustrate, a driver can give an estimate of the speed of a vehicle he or she observed traveling on the street, but a witness must be qualified as an expert to be permitted to testify as to the speed of a car based on observation of the car's skid marks on the pavement. Such an opinion must generally be based on facts perceived by the witness and not on hearsay statements. Rule 701 of the Federal Rules of Evidence limits lay witnesses to testifying to those opinions rationally based on the perception of the witness and helpful to an understanding of the testimony or determination of a fact in issue. States have similar rules of evidence.

opinion evidence Testimony in which the witness expresses an opinion, as distinct from expressing knowledge of specific facts.

A trial judge has considerable discretion to determine whether to admit **opinion evidence** from a lay witness. Although it is difficult to formulate precise rules, two illustrations shed light on the views of appellate courts. In *State v. Anderson*, 390 So.2d 878 (La. 1980), the Louisiana Supreme Court held that it was an error for the trial court to have allowed a police detective to give his opinion regarding the reasons he received an anonymous call in a homicide case; however, the court found the error harmless under the circumstances of the case. In *State v. Lagasse*, 410 A.2d 537 (Me. 1980), the court held that a lay witness's opinion testimony that a girl "looked like she had been slapped" was admissible.

Privileged Communications

privileges Rights extended to persons by virtue of law—for example, the right accorded a spouse to not be required to testify against the other spouse.

The rules of evidence also recognize certain **privileges** that limit testifying. Privileges raise difficult issues by requiring the law, in the search for truth, to choose between protecting a person's confidentiality and allowing testimony that can result in full disclosure of all relevant evidence.

At common law, individuals who were in certain close relationships were privileged not to testify about certain matters. Today, statutes, court rules of evidence, and judicial decisions protect parties in certain relationships from being required to testify. These protections are known as privileges, and a person who asserts a privilege must establish the existence of the required relationship. We discuss the most common evidentiary privileges, which protect communications between attorney and client, husband and wife, and clergy and penitent.

Attorney–client Privilege

attorney–client privilege The right of a person (client) not to testify about matters discussed in confidence with an attorney in the course of the attorney's representation.

The **attorney–client privilege** can be claimed either by the client or by the attorney on behalf of the client regarding communications between them in the course of the attorney's legal representation. The privilege belongs to the client, and if the client waives that privilege, the attorney can be required to disclose the communication. *Hunt v. Blackburn*, 128 U.S. 464, 9 S.Ct. 125, 32 L.Ed. 488 (1888). Several state supreme courts have ruled that the privilege survives the client's death. There was doubt as to whether this prevailed at the federal level; however, in a 1998 case involving activities of the Independent Counsel Kenneth Starr, the U.S. Supreme Court in a 7–2 decision ruled that the attorney–client privilege does survive the client's death. *Swidler & Berlin v. United States*, 524 U.S. 399, 118 S.Ct. 2081, 1421 L.Ed.2d 379 (1998).

In 2003, the North Carolina Supreme Court recognized an exception to the principle that attorney–client privilege survives the client's death. The court held that in the context of a pretrial criminal investigation, if a trial court "determines that some or all of the communications between a client and an attorney do not relate to a matter that affected the client at the time the statements were made, about which the attorney was professionally consulted . . . , such communications are not privileged and may be disclosed." *In re Death of Eric Miller*, 565 S.E.2d 663 (N.C. 2003).

Marital Privilege

marital privilege The privilege of married persons not to be compelled to testify against each other.

A husband and wife enjoy a privilege as to confidential communications between them during their marriage. This **marital privilege** emanates from the common law but has been codified by statutes and court rules in most jurisdictions. The privilege is based on the policy of promoting and preserving domestic harmony and the repugnance of convicting one person through the testimony of another who shares intimate secrets of domestic life. Either spouse may assert the privilege to avoid disclosing privileged matters; either may assert it to prevent the other spouse from testifying about privileged matters. Federal and state courts recognize the privilege, although the ramifications of it vary somewhat in different jurisdictions. The privilege does not preclude a spouse from testifying as to observations of the other's criminal activities and generally does not apply where one spouse is charged with a crime against the other or against a child of either.

A number of appellate court decisions recognize that the marital privilege survives the termination of a marriage by death or divorce. Some states have enacted statutes to so provide. See, for example, § 57-3-4 of the West Virginia Code, which states:

Neither husband nor wife shall, without the consent of the other, be examined in any case as to any confidential communication made by one to the other while married, nor shall either be permitted, without such consent, to reveal in testimony after the marriage relation ceases any such communication made while the marriage existed.

The spousal privilege can apply to confidential communications between parties to a valid common-law marriage where such marriage is recognized by law, but numerous appellate courts have held the privilege does not extend to unmarried cohabitants. See, e.g., *People v. Delph*, 156 Cal.Rptr. (Cal. App. 1979). But under Vermont's civil union law, which became effective July 1, 2000, same-sex couples registered under the law have the benefit of "laws relating to immunity from compelled testimony and the marital communication privilege." 15 Vt. Stat. Ann. § 1204(e)(15).

Clergy–Penitent Privilege

clergy–penitent privilege The exemption of a clergyperson and a penitent from disclosing communications made in confidence by the penitent.

Generally priests, ministers, and rabbis are prohibited from testifying about matters related to them by the penitent in confidence. This is known as the **clergy–penitent privilege**, and the clergyperson can assert the privilege on behalf of the penitent. This privilege is rooted in the English common law but is recognized by federal statute and by statutes in all fifty states. It is not based on the Religion Clauses of the First Amendment. In *Commonwealth v. Kane*, 445 N.E.2d 598 (Mass. 1983), the Massachusetts Supreme Judicial Court held that the privilege could be asserted only by the defendant and that a cleric may not refuse to answer questions where the defendant has waived the privilege. In that case, a defendant maintained that he had confessed nothing that was incriminating and wanted his priest to corroborate that position. The priest refused and was held in contempt by the trial court.

Other Privileges

Some jurisdictions also recognize testimonial privileges between a physician and a patient, between a psychotherapist and a patient, and between an accountant and a client. These expand the common-law concept of testimonial privilege, so the statutes and judicial decisions of a particular jurisdiction must be consulted.

The common law did not provide any testimonial privilege for confidential communications between a parent and a child, and most courts have rejected such a privilege. In a few states the legislature has provided that a parent or the parent's minor child may not be examined as to any communication made in confidence by the minor to the minor's parent. See, e.g., Minn. Stat. Ann. § 595.02.

The Trial Process

The trial is the centerpiece of the criminal justice system, and in American courts the trial judge is the person most responsible for ensuring that the system operates in a fair, efficient, and impartial manner. Trial judges come into office through election or appointment. Ideally, they are selected because of their scholarship, integrity, and the patience and compassion the public associates with the fair and impartial administration of justice. To those appearing before the court and to the jurors and court personnel, the black-robed judge stands as a symbol of justice. In previous chapters, we have pointed out that judges perform numerous functions in the pretrial phases of the criminal justice system, but the most visible aspects of the judge's work are presiding at trials and, when convictions result, setting punishments.

In many respects, the judge serves as an umpire during a trial. The judge rules on the questions that may be asked of potential jurors, determines whether witnesses are competent to testify, controls the scope of interrogation of lay and expert witnesses, and instructs the jury on the law applicable to the particular case. The judge also determines all important judicial and administrative matters concerning the trial. Trial judges are held accountable by appellate courts sitting to review judgments and sentences and to correct harmful errors. Yet, in numerous administrative and procedural areas (for example, whether to grant a postponement of a trial or to limit the number of expert witnesses), a judge's actions are discretionary, and appellate review in such areas is limited to determining whether the trial judge abused that discretion. "In discharging his responsibilities, the trial judge may properly caution, correct, advise, admonish, and, to a certain extent, criticize counsel during the case, provided it is done in such manner as not to subject counsel to contempt or ridicule, or to prejudice the accused in the minds of the jurors." *M.T. v. State*, 677 So.2d 1223, 1229 (Ala. Cr. App. 1995). Nevertheless, trial judges must be very cautious of being critical of attorneys, especially in a jury trial, because jurors place great importance on the judge's attitude. A trial judge who is critical of a defendant's attorney might hold that attorney up to ridicule in the eyes of the jury and thereby impede the fairness of the trial. In *Earl v. State*, 904 P.2d 1029 (1995), the trial judge made many derogatory remarks before the jury concerning the defense counsel's capacity as a lawyer. The appellate court reversed the defendant's conviction and remanded the case for a new trial, noting that the trial judge's comments toward the defense attorney cumulatively prejudiced the defendant's case. In *State v. Jenkins*, 445 S.E.2d 622 (N.C. App. 1994), the court reversed a defendant's convictions because the judge turned his back to the defendant and the jury during the defendant's testimony. The appellate court was concerned that the jury may have interpreted the judge's action to mean that he did not believe the defendant's testimony to be credible.

Usually, either or both sides in a criminal trial request the court to invoke the traditional rule that requires all witnesses, except the defendant, to remain outside the courtroom except when testifying. The purpose of **putting witnesses under the rule**, as lawyers commonly refer to it, is to prevent witnesses from matching narratives. Whether witnesses should be excluded from the courtroom is a matter within the sound discretion of the trial court, *Witt v. United States*, 196 F.2d 285 (9th Cir. 1952); however, the request is generally granted.

Witnesses are interrogated by counsel in the adversary system of American justice; however, it is the right, and sometimes becomes the duty, of a judge to interrogate a witness. This is another delicate area, and appellate courts have emphasized that questioning from the bench should not show bias or feeling and should not be protracted. *Commonwealth v. Hammer*, 494 A.2d 1054, 1060 (Pa. 1985).

putting witnesses under the rule Placing witnesses under the traditional rule that requires them to remain outside the courtroom except when testifying.

The Opening Statements

Once the jury is in place, the trial is ready to begin. The prosecution and the defense are each allowed to make an **opening statement** outlining their respective theories of the case and the evidence to be presented. These opening statements must not be argumentative, nor may counsel make disparaging remarks against one another. Often a defense lawyer defers making an opening statement until the prosecution rests its case. Opening statements are designed to orient the jury; therefore, if the defendant elects a bench trial, they are frequently waived.

opening statement A prosecutor's or defense lawyer's initial statement to the judge or jury in a trial.

If not waived, opening statements of counsel are usually very brief in bench trials. After the opening statements have been presented, the prosecution calls its first witness to take the stand.

The Case for the Prosecution

Prosecutors are ever mindful that when a defendant pleads not guilty, the government must establish the defendant's guilt beyond any reasonable doubt. In presenting the government's case, the prosecuting attorney usually calls as witnesses police officers, the victim, and any other available witnesses whose testimony can support the charge against the defendant. The government's witnesses may also include experts. For example, in a homicide prosecution the prosecutor usually calls a physician; in a drug trafficking case, a chemist; in a forgery prosecution, a handwriting expert. In a DUI case the prosecution often calls the technician who performed a breath test on the defendant. A scientist who has conducted laboratory tests on DNA samples is often called to testify in homicide and sexual battery cases.

The Right to Confrontation and Cross-Examination

The Sixth Amendment to the Constitution guarantees the defendant the right to be confronted with the witnesses who offer evidence against the defendant. This means that the defendant has the right to be present at trial, *Illinois v. Allen*, supra, and to cross-examine each witness. As explained in *California v. Green*, this right of confrontation

1. insures that the witness will give his statements under oath. . . .
2. forces the witness to submit to cross examination, the "greatest legal engine ever invented for the discovery of truth" [and]
3. permits the jury . . . to observe the demeanor of the witness . . . thus aiding the jury in assessing his credibility. 399 U.S. 149, 158, 90 S.Ct. 1930, 1935, 26 L.Ed.2d 489, 497 (1970).

right of cross-examination The right to question witnesses for the opposing side in a criminal trial.

The **right of cross-examination** of an adversary's witness is absolute. *Alford v. United States*, 282 U.S. 687, 51 S.Ct. 218, 75 L.Ed. 624 (1931). However, the permissible scope of cross-examination varies somewhat in different jurisdictions and is a matter largely within the discretion of the trial court. *Smith v. Illinois*, 390 U.S. 129, 88 S.Ct. 748, 19 L.Ed.2d 956 (1968). Courts generally agree that the right of cross-examination is limited to (1) questioning the witness about matters he or she testified to on direct examination; and (2) asking any questions that might tend to impeach the witness's credibility or demonstrate any bias, interest, or hostility of the witness.

leading questions A question that suggests an answer. Leading questions are permitted at a criminal trial on cross-examination of witnesses and in other limited instances.

The right of cross-examination is available to both the prosecutor and the defense counsel and is extremely valuable in criminal trials. Although in most instances it is objectionable for a lawyer who is examining a witness to ask **leading questions** on direct examination, the rules of evidence permit a cross-examiner to ask leading questions. When skillfully employed, cross-examination often develops facts favorable to the cross-examiner's side of the case. Frequently, a cross-examiner is successful in bringing out inconsistencies, contradictions, and any bias or hostility of the witness. A witness may also be subject to **impeachment**—that is, having his or her credibility attacked on cross-examination. A witness's credibility may be attacked in the following ways:

impeachment Impugning the credibility of a witness by introducing contradictory evidence or proving his or her bad character.

- Showing the witness's inability to have viewed or heard the matters the witness has testified to, or inability to recall the event testified to
- Demonstrating that the witness has made prior conflicting statements on an important point
- Showing the witness has been convicted of a crime
- Establishing that the witness bears a bad reputation for truthfulness in the community
- Showing bias, prejudice, or motive to misrepresent the facts, or that the witness has a definite interest in the result of the trial

right of confrontation The right to face one's accusers in a criminal case.

The defendant's **right of confrontation** guaranteeing a face-to-face meeting with witnesses appearing before the judge or jury is not absolute. It must occasionally give way to considerations of public policy and the necessities of the case. *Thomas v. People*, 803 P.2d 144 (Colo. 1990).

The constitutional right of confrontation came into sharp focus in 1988, when the Supreme Court held that a defendant's Sixth Amendment right to confront witnesses was violated in a sexual abuse case in which the trial judge, pursuant to an Iowa law, allowed a screen to be erected between the defendant and the two thirteen-year-old girls that he was accused of assaulting. The two children were situated so they could not see the defendant during their testimony. *Coy v. Iowa*, 487 U.S. 1012, 108 S.Ct. 2798, 101 L.Ed.2d 857 (1988). The Court left open the question of whether a procedure that shields a child sex abuse victim maybe constitutionally acceptable if there is an individualized finding that the witness is in need of such protection. Two years later, in *Maryland v. Craig*, 497 U.S. 836, 110 S.Ct. 3157, 111 L.Ed.2d 666 (1990), the Court held that the Confrontation Clause of the Sixth Amendment does not absolutely prohibit states from using one-way closed circuit television to receive a child's testimony in a case involving child abuse.

child shield statutes Laws that allow a screen to be placed between a child victim of sexual abuse and a defendant while the child testifies in court.

Since the Supreme Court's decision in *Coy*, several states have refined their **child shield statutes** affecting children who are victims of sexual abuse. These revised statutes have met with varying reactions from state appellate courts. However, one thing seems clear: to avoid the constitutional requirements of the Confrontation Clause, the prosecution must show and the trial judge must make particularized findings that a child victim of sexual abuse would suffer unreasonable and unnecessary mental or emotional harm if the child were to testify in the presence of the defendant. In view of the Supreme Court's March 8, 2004, decision in *Crawford v. Washington*, supra, requiring testimonial evidence to comport with the Sixth Amendment right of confrontation, the validity of child protective statutes may be subject to further review. Of course, *Crawford* focuses on out-of-court statements and arguably might not affect the in-court procedures addressed by child shield statutes.

directed verdict A verdict rendered by a jury by direction of the presiding judge.

It must be remembered that all evidence, whether from the prosecution or defense, must comport with the rules of evidence as previously outlined. When the prosecution rests its case, the next move is up to the defense.

The Defense Strategy in Moving for a Judgment of Acquittal

judgment of acquittal In a nonjury trial, a judge's order exonerating a defendant based on a finding that the defendant is not guilty. In a case heard by a jury that finds a defendant guilty, a judge's order exonerating the defendant on the ground that the evidence was not legally sufficient to support the jury's finding of guilt.

At the close of the prosecution's evidence, the defense counsel will frequently move the court to grant a **directed verdict** or, as it is called in federal courts and some state courts, a **judgment of acquittal**. The purpose of such a motion is to have the trial judge determine whether the evidence presented by the prosecution is legally sufficient to support a verdict of guilty. For the purpose of ruling on the motion, the trial judge must view the prosecution's evidence in the light most favorable to the government. The trial judge's authority to direct a verdict has long been recognized. *France v. United States*, 164 U.S. 676, 17 S.Ct. 219, 41 L.Ed. 595 (1897).

Should the motion be granted, the defendant is discharged. If, as in most cases, the motion is denied, defense counsel proceeds with the case on behalf of the defendant, and if additional evidence is offered, defense counsel may renew the motion at the close of the evidence. Federal appellate courts will not review the sufficiency of the evidence to support a verdict unless a motion for a judgment of acquittal was made at the close of all the evidence in the trial court. See, e.g., *Corbin v. United States*, 253 F.2d 646 (10th Cir. 1958). This principle also prevails in many state appellate courts.

The Defense Case: Will the Defendant Take the Stand?

Under the Fifth Amendment, the defendant does not have to testify in a criminal case, and often defendants choose to rely simply on cross-examination of the government's witnesses in an effort to obtain an acquittal. Or the defendant may present witnesses in support of an alibi, to contradict the prosecution's witnesses, or to establish an affirmative defense.

Perhaps the major tactical decision a defendant and defense counsel must make at trial is whether the defendant will take the stand and testify on his or her OWN behalf. The Fifth Amendment privilege against self-incrimination, which applies to the states through the Fourteenth Amendment, *Malloy v. Hogan*, 378 U.S. 1, 84 S.Ct. 1489, 12 L.Ed.2d 653 (1964), protects the defendant from being required to testify, absent a grant of immunity. Moreover, it also forbids any direct or indirect comment by the prosecution on the accused's failure to testify. *Griffin v. California*, 380 U.S. 609, 85 S.Ct. 1229, 14 L.Ed.2d 106 (1965).

When an accused chooses to testify on his or her own behalf, the prosecution may cross-examine the accused about his or her testimony with the same latitude as with any other witness. *Fitzpatrick v. United States*, 178 U.S. 304, 20 S.Ct. 944, 44 L.Ed. 1078 (1900). Moreover, even though illegally obtained evidence cannot be used to prove the government's case, in recent years it has been held that there is no federal constitutional prohibition that prevents the prosecution from using such evidence to impeach statements made by the defendant on cross-examination. *United States v. Havens*, 446 U.S. 620, 100 S.Ct. 1912, 64 L.Ed.2d 559 (1980); *Harris v. New York*, 401 U.S. 222, 91 S.Ct. 643, 28 L.Ed.2d 1 (1971). These realities must weigh heavily in a defendant's decision whether to testify, because the threat of contradiction and impeachment always exists in cross-examination. Regardless of whether the defendant testifies, any witnesses presented by the defendant are subject to cross-examination by the prosecution.

The Rebuttals

rebuttal witnesses
Witnesses called to dispute the testimony of the opposing party's witnesses.

At the conclusion of the defendant's case, the prosecution is entitled to present **rebuttal witnesses** to dispute the testimony of the defendant's witnesses. After examination by the prosecution and cross-examination by the defense counsel, the defense may present its own rebuttal witnesses. They, in turn, are subject to examination by the defense counsel and to cross-examination by the prosecutor. This usually concludes the evidentiary phase of the trial.

Conduct of the Jury during the Trial

The traditional role of the juror has been to listen attentively to the evidence as presented by the prosecution and defense, to avoid any outside influences, and to withhold judgment until all the evidence has been presented and the jury retires to deliberate. Most trial judges today allow jurors to take notes. In recent years trial courts have increasingly allowed jurors to submit questions to witnesses.

Historically judges have been reluctant to allow jurors to question witnesses in criminal trials. One principal concern has been that the questions may be improper, yet counsel may hesitate to object to a juror's question. In *United States v. Witt*, 215 F.2d 580 (2nd Cir. 1954), the court said it was within the discretion of the trial judge to permit jurors to put questions to witnesses and receive answers. Other federal courts have allowed jurors to ask questions, but the practice has never been encouraged. In *United States v. Land*, 877 F.2d 17, 19 (8th Cir. 1989), the court noted that the practice of allowing jurors to submit questions to witnesses is "fraught with dangers which can undermine the orderly progress of the trial to verdict." Nevertheless, every federal circuit court and virtually every state appellate court that has considered this practice has permitted it. In *United States v. Richardson*, 233 F.3d 1285 (11th Cir. 2000), the U.S. Court of Appeals for the Eleventh Circuit rejected an appellant's claim that the trial judge's decision to allow jurors to submit questions to witnesses violated her right to a fair trial. The court, however, cautioned that "jurors should not be permitted to directly question a witness but rather should be required to submit their questions in writing to the trial judge, who should pose the questions to the witness in a neutral manner." 233 F.3d at 1290.

Based on the premise that allowing juror questions in criminal cases would impact juror impartiality and relieve the prosecution of its burden of proof, the Minnesota Supreme Court recently held that no court shall permit jurors to question witnesses in a criminal trial. *State v. Costello*, 646 N.W.2d 204 (Minn. 2002). During the 1990s, the Mississippi and Nebraska Supreme Courts and the Texas Court of Criminal Appeals made similar rulings prohibiting jurors from interrogating witnesses.

In *Coates v. State*, 855 So.2d 223 (Fla. App. 2003), the appellant contended the trial court abused its discretion in allowing any jury questioning. He argued that allowing jurors to ask questions compels them to become advocates, rather than neutral finders of fact. The appellate court, however, pointed out that the trial judge instructed the jurors to write out their questions and hand them to the bailiff. Jurors were then asked to leave the courtroom while the judge ruled on any objections by attorneys. Thereafter, the jury was returned to the courtroom and the judge asked the question of the witness, with each attorney afforded an opportunity to ask follow-up questions. The court found the trial court had not abused its discretion in handling the questioning in such a controlled manner.

There is a definite trend in state courts to allow some form of questioning of witnesses by jurors. In a recent scholarly article, Jehle and Miller noted:

> Some states have implemented pilot projects and produced reports recommending juror questioning. The results of the reports influenced Hawaii, New Jersey, Colorado, Washington, and Tennessee to implement procedural rules for allowing the jury innovation. In addition, the Massachusetts and Ohio courts have ruled in favor of the practice after their states' pilot projects, although they used precedent for their reasoning and do not mention the projects in their decisions. Alayna Jehle and Monica K. Miller, Controversy in the Courtroom: Implications of Allowing Jurors to Question Witnesses. 32 *Wm. Mitchell L. Rev.* 27, 53 (2005).

In 2009 a Massachusetts appellate court reiterated that the decision whether to allow juror questioning and the manner of questioning rests in the sound discretion of the trial judge. *Commonwealth v. Reeder*, 901 N.E.2d 701 (Mass. App.).

The Jury Instructions Conference

jury instructions A judge's explanation of the law applicable to a case being heard by a jury.

After all evidence has been presented in a jury trial, the trial judge customarily confers with counsel outside the presence of the jury concerning the instructions on the law that the judge will give to the jury. The prosecutor and defense counsel may be asked to present proposed instructions for the court to consider. More commonly, the trial judge announces that the court will give certain standard instructions and offers to supplement them with specific instructions to be chosen from those submitted by counsel. A defendant is entitled to have the jury instructed on the law applicable to any legitimate theory of defense that is supported by the evidence presented. See, e.g., *United States v. Creamer*, 555 F.2d 612 (7th Cir. 1977). **Jury instructions** are settled in advance of closing arguments by counsel so that the prosecutor and defense counsel can present their arguments knowing how the judge will instruct the jury.

The Closing Arguments of Counsel

closing arguments Arguments presented at trial by counsel at the conclusion of the presentation of evidence.

The Sixth Amendment guarantee of the right to assistance of counsel has been interpreted to include the right to present **closing arguments** in a criminal case, regardless of whether the case is tried before a jury or before a judge. *Herring v. New York*, 422 U.S. 853, 95 S.Ct. 2550, 45 L.Ed.2d 593 (1975). A defendant represented by counsel has no right to share the closing argument with his or her counsel, but if the defendant is pro se—that is, representing him- or herself—the court must allow the defendant to make a closing argument. *State v. Plaskonka*, 577 A.2d 729 (Conn. App. 1990). Although the constitutional guarantee accords the right of closing arguments to the defendant, by statute or rules of court the government and the defendant are each accorded the right to have counsel to make closing arguments. The order of the arguments may be set by statute or court rule, but the trial judge retains control of the extent of the argument. The prosecutor usually argues first, followed by the defense counsel, with the prosecutor having an opportunity for a brief rebuttal.

Closing arguments are designed to assist the jury in recalling and evaluating the evidence and in drawing inferences therefrom. Many lawyers begin by recapitulating the evidence in the light most favorable to their client. After that, the arguments frequently become emotional, with each side entreating the jury to "do its duty" by either convicting or acquitting the defendant, arguing why the jury should by its interpretation of the evidence thereby either convict or acquit.

In closing arguments, counsel may comment on the weight of the evidence and the credibility of the witnesses, but it is improper for either the prosecutor or defense counsel to state a personal belief about the guilt or innocence of the accused. Likewise, it is improper for counsel to refer to any matters—other than those of common, everyday knowledge—that have not been introduced in evidence. Because a judge is trained in evaluating evidence, counsel in nonjury cases frequently waive their right to make closing arguments; otherwise, the arguments are generally quite brief.

Although prosecutors may use every legitimate method to obtain a conviction, a legion of appellate court opinions admonishes them to be fair and objective in their presentations to a jury. Characteristically, the Wisconsin Supreme Court observed that the prosecutor's role should be "to analyze the evidence and present

Improper Argument by a Prosecutor

Defendant Larry Witted was charged with attempted murder and armed robbery. At his jury trial, the chief issue was whether the victim had correctly identified the defendant as the person who robbed him. While the victim's testimony was positive, it was uncorroborated by any other evidence. During closing arguments, the defense counsel argued that the process used to identify the defendant as the perpetrator was unduly suggestive. In rebuttal, the prosecutor implied that witnesses for the defense had perjured themselves at the request of defense counsel and that the defendant had a criminal background that the defense was hiding from the jury. Because the prosecutor's remarks were made during his rebuttal closing argument, the defense had no opportunity to challenge the inferences that were made. Witted was convicted, but the court awarded him a new trial, citing the prosecutor's misconduct during closing arguments.

People v. Witted, 398 N.E.2d 68 (Ill. App. 1979).

facts with a reasonable interpretation to aid the jury in calmly and reasonably drawing just inferences and arriving at a just conclusion. . . ." *State v. Genova*, 8 N.W.2d 260, 263 (Wis. 1943).

Prosecutors are prohibited from making inflammatory remarks to the jury. If a prosecutor does make inflammatory remarks or statements that have no basis in the evidence or that can be interpreted as a comment on the defendant's failure to testify, the judge may admonish the prosecutor. Usually this is followed by a cautionary instruction directing the jury to disregard such remarks. If the defendant objects and the trial judge fails to take appropriate action, or if the prosecutor's remarks are so prejudicial that they cannot be erased from the minds of the jurors, the defendant may be able to obtain a mistrial or, if convicted, win a new trial from an appellate court.

Perhaps because the government cannot ordinarily appeal on the basis of improper comments by a defense counsel, the law seems to indulge a defendant in a somewhat wider latitude in jury arguments. Nevertheless, there are restraints, and sanctions for violations may take the form of an admonition by the trial judge or even disciplinary action where a defense lawyer's performance is egregious. Despite the fact that counsel must strive for acquittal of a client in our adversary system of justice, courts frequently remind defense lawyers that they, too, are officers of the court. Accordingly, they must aid in the administration of justice to the end that the lawful rights and privileges of the defendant are not violated. See, e.g., *State v. Leaks*, 10 A.2d 281 (N.J. 1940).

The Judge Instructs the Jury

Typically, at the conclusion of the closing arguments the judge either reads the indictment or information or explains the charges against the defendant to the jury. This is followed by an admonition that the defendant is presumed innocent unless and until the government proves the defendant guilty of each element of the crime beyond a reasonable doubt. The judge defines the elements of any crime charged and explains any technical legal terms. Where applicable, the court generally instructs on the offense of attempt as well. Where the jury may convict the defendant of a lesser offense, the judge must go further than merely defining the crime charged. For example, if the defendant is charged with first-degree murder, the judge must describe the lesser degrees of murder as well as manslaughter and excusable and justifiable homicide.

These instructions on the crimes may be followed by an explanation of any defenses pled by the defendant and the burden of proof, if any, on the defendant to sustain such defenses. A defendant is entitled to an instruction about any defense sustained by the evidence. At the request of the defendant, the judge usually informs the jury that it should not consider any inference of guilt because the defendant exercised the right not to testify. However, many defense lawyers prefer not to have the judge give this instruction.

The trial judge always explains to the jury that its role is to be the sole judge of the facts and advises the jury about some of the things it should consider in evaluating the credibility of the evidence presented. If expert witnesses have testified, the judge explains their role and informs the jury that it is free to accept or reject their opinions. In America, in contrast with the English practice, the trial judge generally is not permitted to summarize the evidence or express an opinion on the weight of that evidence or the credibility of the witnesses. Rule 31(c) of the Federal Rules of Criminal Procedure provides,

> The defendant may be found guilty of an offense necessarily included in the offense charged or of an attempt to commit either the offense charged or of an offense necessarily included therein if the attempt is an offense in its own right.

A defendant is entitled to have the jury instructed on any lesser included offense whenever (1) the elements of the lesser offense are a subset of elements of the charged offense and (2) the evidence at trial is such that a jury could rationally find the defendant guilty of the lesser offense yet acquit the defendant of the greater offense. *Schmuck v. United States*, 489 U.S. 705, 109 S.Ct. 1443, 103 L.Ed.2d 734 (1989).

Practices in state courts vary in the extent to which the trial judge must instruct a jury on offenses that are lesser than the offense charged against a defendant. Some courts distinguish between those offenses that are necessarily included in the offense charged and those that may be included based on the allegations of the offense charged and the evidence presented at trial. In state courts, a defendant is generally entitled to an instruction of an offense of a less serious nature than the one charged if the elements of the charged offense can constitute the lesser crime. If the evidence is such that no rational jury could conclude the lesser offense was proper, however, the trial court's refusal to give the lesser offense instruction is not necessarily considered a reversible error by most appellate courts. See, e.g., *People v. Tucker*, 542 N.E.2d 804 (Ill. App. 1989).

In a few states, juries determine sentences. In these jurisdictions, the judge must also instruct the jury on the range of sentences permitted. In most states that have the death penalty, a jury trial in a capital case is bifurcated, with the jury first determining guilt or innocence. If the jury finds the defendant guilty, a second phase ensues, during which the jury hears evidence of aggravating and mitigating circumstances and determines whether the death penalty should be imposed (see Chapter 7).

The judge's instructions are given orally, and in some instances the jury is given a copy of the instructions. The clerk furnishes the jury forms of verdicts so they may find the defendant not guilty, guilty as charged, or guilty of some degree of the offense charged or of a lesser included offense. In federal criminal trials and in most state courts, the judge explains the requirement of a unanimous verdict. In some states, the judge is required to inform the jury of the penalties that can be imposed

foreperson The person selected by fellow jurors to chair deliberations and report the jury's verdict.

for the offense charged. Finally, the jury is directed to retire, select one of its members as **foreperson**, and deliberate on its verdict. Usually a jury is allowed to take with it to the jury room all exhibits received in evidence.

The Jury Deliberates and Returns Its Verdict

sequestration Holding jurors incommunicado during trial and deliberations.

When directed to deliberate, the jurors are escorted to their quarters by a court bailiff. In some cases, the judge orders the jury sequestered, which means the jury must remain together until it reaches its verdict. **Sequestration** often requires the bailiff to escort the jurors to a hotel and to be present with them during meals to ensure that no outside influences are brought to bear on their judgment. Once in the jury room, the jurors' first order of business is to elect a foreperson. Then they are ready to commence their deliberations.

Because jury deliberations are secret, we can only speculate about the reasoning processes of jurors. However, we do know that juries usually take a preliminary vote shortly after electing a foreperson. In most cases, the jury probably arrives at its verdict without much discussion. In the famous "Monkey Trial" of John Scopes in Dayton, Tennessee, in 1925, the jury deliberated only eight minutes before convicting Scopes of unlawfully teaching the theory of evolution in his high school biology class. More recently, in the O. J. Simpson case the jury returned its verdict of not guilty after only four hours. In other instances, jurors may deliberate for hours or days, and many votes may be taken. In the murder trial of Charles Manson in 1971, the jury deliberated about forty-two hours.

In federal criminal trials, a jury verdict must be unanimous. *Andres v. United States*, 333 U.S. 740, 68 S.Ct. 880, 92 L.Ed. 1055 (1948); see also Fed. R. Crim. P. 31(a). The same is true in most states; however, a few states accept less-than-unanimous verdicts. The Supreme Court has approved nonunanimous verdicts rendered by twelve-person juries. *Johnson v. Louisiana*, 406 U.S. 356, 92 S.Ct. 1620, 32 L.Ed.2d 152 (1972); *Apodaca v. Oregon*, 406 U.S. 404, 92 S.Ct. 1628, 32 L.Ed.2d 184 (1972). But the Court has held that a conviction by a nonunanimous six-person jury in a state trial for a nonpetty offense violates the right to trial by jury guaranteed by the Sixth and Fourteenth Amendments. *Burch v. Louisiana*, 441 U.S. 130, 99 S.Ct. 1623, 60 L.Ed.2d 96 (1979).

The Deadlocked Jury

deadlocked jury A jury whose members cannot agree on a verdict. Often referred to as a "hung jury."

Sometimes juries become "hung"—that is, they cannot agree on a verdict. This was illustrated in 1988, when a young man was tried in New York City for allegedly strangling a young woman in Central Park. The so-called yuppie murder case drew national attention, partly because the testimony revealed that the victim's death resulted from "a rough sexual encounter" between the defendant and the victim. After a twelve-week trial, a panel of eight men and four women deliberated for nine days. They then sent a note to the judge saying they had reached an impasse. At that point, in a desire to conclude the proceedings—and perhaps rather than risk another trial—the defendant entered a negotiated plea of guilty to manslaughter, a lesser offense than that charged.

***Allen* charge** A judge's instruction to jurors who are deadlocked, encouraging them to listen to one another's arguments and reappraise their own positions in an effort to arrive at a verdict.

If a jury reports that it is a **deadlocked jury**, the trial judge can either declare a mistrial or urge the jury to make further attempts to arrive at a verdict. One tool that both federal and state trial judges sometimes employ is to give the jury a supplemental instruction called an ***Allen* charge**. The instruction takes its name from an

Factors Considered in Approving a Trial Court's Use of the *Allen* Charge Where the Jury Is Deadlocked

Defendant Lindel and others were charged in U.S. District Court with thirty-five counts of various crimes stemming from a marijuana importation scheme. They were convicted on several counts and then appealed. Among their points on appeal, the defendants contended that when the jury sent notes that it was hopelessly deadlocked, the trial court should have declared a mistrial instead of giving an *Allen* charge to the jury. In rejecting the defendants' challenge, the U.S. Court of Appeals for the Fifth Circuit first noted that the language in the judge's charge to the jury comported with the modified *Allen* charge

language repeatedly approved. Then the court pointed out that the trial lasted for three weeks, that the verdict was a discriminating one returning both guilty and not guilty verdicts on the various counts, that in giving the *Allen* charge the judge did not set a deadline on deliberations, and that the verdict was not returned until two days after the *Allen* charge was given. Considering these factors, the court found no abuse of discretion in the trial judge's having given the charge, and after rejecting other points raised by the defendants, the court of appeals affirmed the defendants' convictions.

United States v. Lindel, 881 F.2d 1313 (5th Cir. 1989).

opinion issued by the Supreme Court at the turn of the twentieth century, *Allen v. United States*, 164 U.S. 492, 17 S.Ct. 154, 41 L.Ed. 528 (1896). A number of modifications have been made to the original *Allen* charge, but the basic thrust remains to urge "that if much the larger number were for conviction, a dissenting juror should consider whether his doubt was a reasonable one. . . . If, upon the other hand, the majority were for acquittal, the minority ought to ask themselves whether they might not reasonably doubt the correctness of a judgment that was not concurred in by the majority." 164 U.S. at 501, 17 S.Ct. at 157, 41 L.Ed. at 531.

In Colorado the *Allen* charge is called "the third-degree instruction," and New Mexico courts have referred to it as the "shotgun instruction." *Leech v. People*, 146 P.2d 346, 347 (Colo. 1944); *State v. Nelson*, 321 P.2d 202, 204 (N.M. 1958).

The use of the *Allen* charge in its original form or in its many modified forms has been criticized as having a coercive effect for implying that the majority view is the correct one and for importuning the minority to change their views. In a few states, the state supreme court has banned its use. See, e.g., *State v. Randall*, 353 P.2d 1054 (Mont. 1960). Nevertheless, federal and most state courts have generally approved the use of some version of the instruction when it has been cautiously given. See, e.g., *Benscoter v. United States*, 376 F.2d 49 (10th Cir. 1967).

Jury Pardons

jury nullification The fact of a jury disregarding the court's instructions and rendering a verdict on the basis of the consciences of the jurors.

jury pardon An action taken by a jury, despite the quality of the evidence, acquitting a defendant or convicting the defendant of a lesser crime than charged.

At times, juries disregard the evidence and the judge's instructions on the law and acquit a defendant or convict the defendant of a lesser offense than charged. This is referred to as **jury nullification** or as granting the defendant a **jury pardon**. Jurors, of course, take an oath to follow the law as charged by the judge and are expected to do so. *United States v. Powell*, 469 U.S. 57, 105 S.Ct. 471, 83 L.Ed.2d 461 (1984). But it is also recognized that a jury has the prerogative to exercise its judgment and bring in a verdict of not guilty or guilty of a lesser offense.

In death penalty cases, there has been explicit recognition of the principle. For instance, in *Beck v. Alabama*, 447 U.S. 625, 100 S.Ct. 2382, 65 L.Ed.2d 392 (1980), the Supreme Court held that the death penalty may not be imposed if the jury is not permitted to consider a verdict of guilty of a lesser included noncapital offense when the evidence would have supported such a verdict. The Court explained that "the nearly universal acceptance of the rule in state and federal courts establishes the value to the defendant of this procedural safeguard." 447 U.S. at 637, 100 S.Ct. at 2389, 65 L.Ed.2d at 402.

In trials for noncapital offenses, the reality of jury nullification exists, but there is no requirement for a judge to inform the jury of that power. See, e.g., *United States v. Dougherty*, 473 F.2d 1113 (D.C. Cir. 1972). Acquittals by juries are not subject to appeal, so it is difficult to know when jury nullification occurs, but undoubtedly some defendants are acquitted or convicted of lesser offenses as a result of a jury pardon. In *United States v. Dougherty*, the court in footnote 33 cites a number of examples taken from a study undertaken at the University of Chicago Law School of the types of cases in which a jury voted to acquit because of its empathy with the defendant. The examples mentioned include sale of liquor to a minor who is a member of the armed forces and violence erupting after domestic strife.

The Verdict

verdict The formal decision rendered by a jury in a civil or criminal trial.

When a jury has concluded its deliberations, it returns to the courtroom and delivers its written **verdict**. The verdict is usually first handed to the judge, who reviews it to determine whether it is in proper form. If it is, the judge hands the verdict to the clerk or jury foreperson to be read aloud in open court. A defendant who is acquitted by a jury is immediately discharged. If a jury finds the defendant guilty, the defendant is generally taken into custody to await sentencing. In some instances, the defendant may be continued on bail, pending application for a new trial or an appeal. We discuss sentencing and appellate procedures in Chapters 7 and 8, respectively.

polling the jury Practice in which a trial judge asks each member of the jury whether he or she supports the jury's verdict.

After a verdict has been read, the court or any party may have the jury polled individually. The clerk or judge handles **polling the jury** by asking each juror, "Is this your verdict?" or words to that effect. In most cases, each juror responds affirmatively and the jury is discharged. If, on the other hand, a juror expresses dissent from the verdict, the trial judge may either direct the jury to retire for further deliberation or discharge the jury. See, e.g., *People v. Kellogg*, 397 N.E.2d 835 (Ill. 1979).

Posttrial Motions

motion for a new trial A formal request made to a trial court to hold a new trial in a particular case that has already been adjudicated.

A convicted defendant may, and frequently does, file a **motion for a new trial**, alleging that errors were committed at trial. This type of motion affords the trial judge an opportunity to rectify errors by awarding the defendant a new trial. In most instances, however, it is a *pro forma* prelude to an appeal and is denied by the trial court. A defendant may also seek bail pending appeal (see Chapter 8). When the court disposes of these motions, the process moves into sentencing (see Chapter 7).

Conclusion

Despite the relatively small proportion of criminal cases that go to trial, the criminal trial remains a vital part of the criminal justice system. Adjudications at trial set the overall tone for the administration of the criminal law in the community. Jury verdicts become weather vanes of the public's attitude on the enforcement of the law.

Criminal trials also have an important bearing on the reshaping of both the statutory and decisional law in light of contemporary community values. With counsel now available to indigent defendants to handle their appeals as well as to represent them at trial, appellate courts have the opportunity to update precedents and refine trial court procedures based on current constitutional standards.

Court procedures are slow to change, but changes are occurring and will continue into the future. Despite changes, the basic function of the criminal trial by a jury of one's peers will remain. It must because it is not only each citizen's protection against overzealous law enforcement and prosecutions; it also ensures the public that no defendant will gain preferred status by virtue of prominence or be dealt with unfairly because of lowly status.

Chapter Summary

- LO1

  - Trial by jury has historic roots in the English common law.

  - The Sixth Amendment to the U.S. Constitution, which is applicable to state criminal trials by the Fourteenth Amendment, grants a defendant the right to a speedy and public trial by an impartial jury, the right to be informed of the nature and cause of the accusation, the right to confront prosecution witnesses, the right to subpoena defense witnesses, and the right to have the assistance of counsel.

  - A defendant is entitled to an open and public trial, but not to a private trial. Courts can close trials to protect rape victims, molested children, and witnesses and jurors from embarrassment or intimidation. The Supreme Court has said that closing a trial to the public is left to the trial judge's discretion on a case-by-case basis.

  - The Supreme Court has ruled that the right to a jury trial extends to cases where a defendant is subject to more than six months' imprisonment. Some states opt to be more liberal. In 1996, the Court ruled that a defendant who is charged with multiple petty offenses is not entitled to a jury trial, even though the possible sentences may add up to more than six months in prison. Juveniles and defendants in military tribunals do not have a right to a jury trial.

  - The right to counsel in a criminal case is well established; a defendant also has the right of self-representation, no matter what the defendant's knowledge of legal procedures, as long as the defendant's election is exercised voluntarily and intelligently. But in 2008, the Supreme Court held that a trial judge is not required to allow a minimally competent defendant to elect self-representation at trial.

- LO2

  - A common-law jury consisted of twelve men. Federal courts require a twelve-member jury unless the defendant stipulates to fewer in writing. States require twelve-member juries in capital cases; most require twelve in felony prosecutions. Many use fewer in misdemeanor cases. In 1970, the Supreme Court upheld six-person juries in felony trials; three years later it said that a jury of only five was not acceptable.

- Statutes commonly require jurors to be at least eighteen years old and registered voters. Statutes frequently exempt expectant mothers, mothers with young children, persons over seventy, physicians, dentists, attorneys, judges, teachers, elected officials, and police, fire, and emergency personnel. The trend, however, is to limit exceptions.

- The Jury Selection and Service Act of 1968 requires that jurors in federal courts be selected at random from a fair cross-section of the community. States have similar statutes. Where necessary to protect potential jurors and their families, courts can employ anonymous juries.

- Those summoned to be jurors constitute the "venire." The judge excuses those with physical disabilities, close family relationships, or business conflicts. After the remaining members have been sworn in, prospective jurors answer questions from the court and counsel (the *voir dire*.)

- Challenges for cause may be directed to prospective jurors concerning any matters that would disqualify them from serving. The prosecution and defense may exercise a limited number of peremptory challenges to excuse prospective jurors without stating any reason. In 1986, the Supreme Court held that the Equal Protection Clause prohibits racially-based peremptory challenges, in 1994 it prohibited gender-based peremptory challenges, and in 2000 it suggested that this rule applies to ethnicity as well.

- After selection, the jury is sworn and is admonished not to discuss the case until instructed by the court to deliberate. Increasingly courts allow jurors to take written notes and to question witnesses.

- An alternate juror sometimes sits with the jury but, unless substituted for a regular juror, is excused before the jury deliberates.

- LO3

  - "Death qualification" of a jury is meant to ensure that the views of prospective jurors in a capital case would not prevent them from voting for the death penalty.

  - The Supreme Court has said that death qualification is designed to obtain a jury that can properly and impartially apply the law to the facts at both the guilt and sentencing phases of a capital trial. The Court has held that removal before the guilt phase in a capital trial of prospective jurors whose opposition to the death penalty would impair or prevent performance of their duties at the sentencing phase is not unconstitutional

- LO4

  - Members of the media have a First Amendment right to monitor and report trials, but the trial judge must make sure that media coverage does not disrupt a trial and must take steps to ensure that the defendant receives a fair trial.

  - In order to keep the prosecutor and the defense counsel from "trying a case in the media," a judge can issue a gag order prohibiting the attorneys from talking to the press about the case. However, the U.S. Supreme Court has made it very difficult, if not impossible, for judges to extend gag orders to media members.

  - The Federal Rules of Criminal Procedure prohibit photography of judicial proceedings, but cameras are now allowed in most state courts.

- o Judges exercise discretion and usually prohibit or restrict coverage of jurors and prohibit coverage of juveniles and victims of sex crimes.

- LO5

  - o A defendant has the right to be present at every critical stage of criminal proceedings; however, a defendant who disrupts proceedings or fails to comply with court standards forfeits that right.

  - o Judges can control order in court by attendees (and usually defendants) by excising the power of contempt.

  - o In 1970, the Supreme Court indicated that in addition to contempt, judges may have an unruly defendant removed from the courtroom or bound and gagged until the defendant agrees to proper decorum.

  - o Trial judges must maintain dignity and neutrality and recognize that adverse comments toward the defense attorney can prejudice the case.

  - o Lawyers must observe courtroom decorum and ethical rules. Offending lawyers may be disciplined by a bar association, found in contempt and fined, or even jailed in for egregious misconduct.

- LO6

  - o In 1970, the Supreme Court elevated to a constitutional mandate the historic rule that to convict a defendant the evidence must show the defendant guilty "beyond a reasonable doubt." The burden of proof is on the prosecution, not the defendant.

  - o The Federal Rules of Evidence are in the U.S. Code. Some states have legislatively or judicially adopted codes of evidence; in others the rules must be gleaned from the decisional law.

  - o Courts take "judicial notice" of commonly known facts without formal proof, but a party can offer proof to the contrary. Courts also take judicial notice of constitutions, statutes, and judicial opinions.

  - o Evidentiary presumptions are devices to aid a party who has the burden of proof and are subject to refutation. Presumptions must be permissive, as conclusive presumptions violate due process of law.

  - o Evidence of crimes or conduct similar to that charged against the defendant may be admitted in evidence to show motive, identity, or absence of mistake or accident, but not to prove the defendant's bad character or propensity to commit a crime.

  - o Real evidence consists of such tangible items such as maps, blood samples, X-rays, photographs, stolen goods, fingerprints, knives, and guns. Testimonial evidence consists of sworn statements of witnesses.

  - o Direct evidence includes eyewitness testimony; indirect evidence usually consists of circumstantial evidence—that is, attendant facts from which inferences can be drawn to establish other facts in issue.

  - o Whether real or testimonial, direct or circumstantial, evidence must be relevant—that is, it must tend to prove or disprove a material fact in issue.

- Trial lawyers make general objections on grounds that the evidence proffered is not relevant. They make specific objections on grounds that proffered evidence violates rules against hearsay testimony (there are many exceptions) or the rule that requires production of the best evidence of written transactions, or that questions call for an opinion that a lay witness is not competent to give.

- In determining whether a witness is competent to testify, the trial judge considers the witness's ability to receive and recollect impressions, to understand questions, and to appreciate the moral duty to tell the truth. A very young child may or may not be competent to testify.

- Evidentiary privileges limit testifying by not allowing testimony that is protected by the attorney–client privilege, the marital privilege, or the privilege for communications related by a penitent in confidence to a clergyperson.

- LO7

  - A witness with proper credentials can be received as an expert, may testify based on personal knowledge, and may respond to hypothetical questions that assume the existence of facts the evidence tends to establish.

  - Historically federal and most state courts applied the general acceptance (*Frye*) test in determining admissibility of new scientific tests. But in 1993, the Supreme Court ruled that the federal rules of evidence supersede the *Frye* test and that admissibility of scientific evidence must be based on several factors, including whether the evidence can be tested and be subjected to peer review (the *Daubert* standard). In 1999, the Court extended its *Daubert* reliability requirement to nonscientific expert testimony.

  - The majority of courts hold that hypnotically enhanced testimony is not sufficiently reliable to be admissible and that the reliability of polygraph testing has not been scientifically demonstrated to such a degree of certainty as to permit its use in evidence. However, some courts allow the results of polygraph testing to be admitted on stipulation of the prosecution and the defense.

  - Expert testimony concerning the battered woman syndrome has gained substantial scientific acceptance, and some courts now receive such testimony when a woman claims to have acted in self-defense against a spouse or cohabitant.

  - DNA is extracted from biological specimens such as white blood cells, semen, body hair, and tissue. DNA printing tests attempt to develop "genetic fingerprints" and compare DNA molecules extracted from a suspect's specimen with DNA molecules extracted from specimens found at a crime scene to determine whether the samples match. DNA evidence must satisfy the tests for scientific evidence.

- LO8

  - The trial judge exercises discretion in determining judicial and administrative matters at trial, including whether to exclude witnesses from the courtroom while other witnesses are testifying. Witnesses are interrogated by counsel, but the judge can allow narrative testimony.

- The prosecution and the defense are each allowed to make a non-argumentative opening statement outlining their theories and the evidence to be presented. (In a bench trial, counsel often waive opening statements or make only limited remarks.)

- The prosecution presents its witnesses first—typically, the victim, police officers, and other lay and expert witnesses.

- The Sixth Amendment guarantees a defendant the right to confront and cross-examine prosecution witnesses. Cross-examination is available to both the prosecutor and the defense counsel, but the trial judge regulates the scope of cross-examination, which is generally limited to matters that a witness has testified to on direct examination and questions that tend to impeach the witness's credibility.

- A witness's credibility may be attacked by showing the witness's inability to recall events; by prior conflicting statements; by showing the witness has an interest in the result of the trial; or by establishing that the witness has been convicted of a crime, bears a bad reputation for truthfulness, or is biased, prejudiced, or has motives to misrepresent the facts.

- In 1990, the Supreme Court held that the Sixth Amendment's Confrontation Clause does not absolutely prohibit states from using one-way closed circuit television to receive a child's testimony in a child abuse case, but the trial judge must make particularized findings that a child victim of sexual abuse would suffer unreasonable and unnecessary mental or emotional harm if required to testify in the defendant's presence.

- At the close of the prosecution's evidence, defense counsel frequently moves for a judgment of acquittal (directed verdict). In ruling, the trial judge views the prosecution's evidence in the light most favorable to the government. If the motion is denied, the defense must decide if the defendant will testify and be subject to cross-examination.

- The Fifth Amendment privilege against self-incrimination protects the defendant from being required to testify, absent a grant of immunity, and forbids any direct or indirect comment by the prosecution on the defendant's failure to testify.

- After the defendant's case has been presented, the prosecution and defense may present rebuttal witnesses.

- Jurors are directed to withhold judgment until all the evidence has been presented and the jury retires to deliberate. Most trial judges now allow jurors to take notes, and in recent years courts have increasingly allowed jurors to submit questions to witnesses.

- LO9

  - At the conclusion of a jury trial, the judge confers with counsel outside the presence of the jury and formulates the instructions to be given to the jury.

  - A defendant is entitled to have the jury instructed on the law applicable to any legitimate theory of defense supported by the evidence.

  - The prosecution and defense are each afforded the right to make closing arguments and may comment on the weight of the evidence and credibility of the witnesses. However, neither may state a personal belief about the defendant's guilt or innocence or refer to matters not in evidence, except for matters of common knowledge. (In nonjury cases, counsel frequently waive their right to make closing arguments.)

○ If the trial judge fails to take appropriate action when the prosecutor makes improper remarks, or if the prosecutor's remarks are too prejudicial to be erased from the minds of the jurors, the defendant may be able to obtain a mistrial or, if subsequently convicted, a new trial.

○ After closing arguments, the judge reads the charges against the defendant to the jury and admonishes the jury that the defendant is presumed innocent unless and until the prosecution proves the defendant guilty of each element of the crime beyond a reasonable doubt. The judge defines the elements of any crime charged and any lesser offenses and, where applicable, instructs on the offense of attempt to commit any crime charged. A defendant is entitled to have the jury instructed on any lesser included offense when the jury could rationally find the defendant guilty of the lesser offense.

○ The trial judge is not permitted to summarize the evidence or express an opinion on the weight of the evidence or the credibility of the witnesses.

- LO10

  ○ After being instructed by the judge, the members of the jury retire to the jury room, select one of their number as foreperson, and deliberate on a verdict.

  ○ Usually a jury is allowed to take with it to the jury room all exhibits received in evidence.

  ○ In some cases, the judge orders the jury to be sequestered until it reaches its verdict.

  ○ In federal (and most state) criminal trials, a jury verdict must be unanimous. A few states, however, accept less-than-unanimous verdicts. The Supreme Court has approved nonunanimous verdicts by twelve-person juries, but has held that a conviction by a nonunanimous six-person jury in a state trial for a nonpetty offense violates the Sixth Amendment.

  ○ If the jury is deadlocked, the trial judge can either declare a mistrial, or by giving a supplemental instruction (*Allen* charge) the judge may urge the jury to make further attempts to arrive at a verdict.

  ○ A jury nullification or jury pardon occurs when a jury disregards the evidence and the judge's instructions and goes ahead to acquit the defendant or convict the defendant of a lesser offense.

  ○ The court or any party may have the jury polled individually, asking each juror, "Is this your verdict?" If any juror expresses dissent from the verdict, the trial judge may either direct the jury to retire for further deliberation or discharge the jury.

  ○ The defendant may be continued on bail, pending application for a new trial or an appeal. A motion for a new trial affords the trial judge an opportunity to rectify errors by awarding the defendant a new trial, but in most instances it is a *pro forma* prelude to an appeal and is denied.

Key Terms

Allen charge

attorney–client privilege

bench trial

best evidence

challenges for cause

child shield statutes

circumstantial evidence

clergy–penitent privilege

closing arguments

competent to testify

deadlocked jury

death qualification of a jury

direct evidence

directed verdict

DNA testing

evidentiary presumptions

eyewitness testimony

forensic experts

foreperson

gag order

gender-based peremptory challenges

general acceptance test

general objection

hearsay evidence

hypnotically enhanced testimony

hypothetical questions

impeachment

indirect evidence

judgment of acquittal

judicial notice

jury instructions

jury nullification

jury pardon

jury trial

leading questions

marital privilege

motion for a new trial

open public trials

opening statement

opinion evidence

peremptory challenges

polling the jury

polygraph evidence

power of contempt

privileges

proof beyond a reasonable doubt

putting witnesses under the rule

racially based peremptory challenges

real evidence

rebuttal witnesses

right of confrontation

right of cross-examination

scientific evidence

sequestration

similar fact evidence

specific objection

standby counsel

testimonial evidence

venire

verdict

voir dire

Key Court Decisions

Williams v. Florida (1970): The Sixth Amendment as it applies to the states via the Fourteenth Amendment does not require a jury of twelve persons in a state criminal trial; a six-person jury is constitutionally permissible.

Batson v. Kentucky (1986): A prosecutor's use of peremptory challenges to exclude African Americans from a jury trying an African-American defendant solely on the basis of the race the prospective jurors is impermissible discrimination under the Equal Protection Clause of the Fourteenth Amendment.

Rivera v. Illinois (2009): A trial judge's erroneous denial of a defendant's peremptory challenge to a prospective juror does not automatically require reversal of the defendant's conviction on appeal, as long the judge's ruling was made in good faith and all members of the jury were qualified and unbiased.

Sheppard v. Maxwell (1966): A defendant is denied due process of law if the trial judge fails to guard against pervasive and prejudicial media coverage that result in an unfair trial.

Nebraska Press Association v. Stuart (1976): Absent extraordinary circumstances in which a judge has no other means to protect a defendant's right to a fair trial, trial courts may not imposed gag orders to limit media coverage of criminal trials.

Crawford v. Washington (2004): Out-of-court testimonial statements are inadmissible in a criminal trial unless the witness is unavailable and the defendant has had a prior opportunity to cross-examine the witness.

Questions for Thought and Discussion

1. Jurors are generally selected from among those citizens who have registered to vote or who have registered motor vehicles. Do these methods produce juries drawn from a "representative cross-section of the community"? Can you suggest a better way of selecting jurors?

2. In England, the *voir dire* process is conducted by the trial judge and is extremely limited. Do you think the American system of criminal justice would have more credibility if *voir dire* were conducted exclusively by the judge, with only challenges for cause permitted? Explain your view.

3. What factors should a defense attorney consider in deciding whether to advise a client to testify on his or her own behalf at trial?

4. In 1965, Justice Tom Clark, writing for the Supreme Court in *Estes v. Texas*, observed that "[t]rial by television is . . . foreign to our system." Evaluate Justice Clark's statement in view of contemporary attitudes toward communications technology.

5. Many rules of evidence applied in jury trials are derived from the early common law, when jurors were largely uneducated. These rules were designed to prevent jurors from hearing evidence that might prejudice their judgment about the case. Given the educational standards in the United States, should these rules be made less restrictive regarding evidence that can be presented in court? What constitutional problems would arise if hearsay evidence were allowed to be presented against a defendant?

6. What testimonial privileges are available to witnesses in your state? What is the rationale for each?

7. Do you think a trial judge should be allowed to summarize the evidence for the jury's benefit before the jurors retire to deliberate? What advantages and disadvantages can you see in such a practice? Would it be constitutional?

8. In some jurisdictions, a judge instructs the jury about its general duties and responsibilities at the beginning of the trial rather than waiting until the evidence has been presented. Do you favor this approach? Why or why not?

9. Do you think that the trial judge should inform a jury that it has the power to issue a jury pardon despite the evidence of the defendant's guilt when the jury feels that in "good conscience" the defendant should not be convicted of the crime charged or any lesser crime supported by the evidence at trial? Give reasons for your view.

10. The Supreme Court has said that state criminal trial juries need not observe the unanimity principle that prevails in the federal courts. Could it not be argued that the reasonable doubt standard necessarily entails the unanimity principle, as the doubt of one juror is sufficient to suggest a reasonable doubt about the guilt of the accused?

Problems for Discussion and Solution

1. A defendant is tried before a jury on a DWI charge. At the conclusion of the trial, the judge instructs the jury: "If you find from the evidence that the defendant had a blood-alcohol content of .10, you must presume she was intoxicated." On what basis should the defendant's attorney object to this instruction?

2. A defendant is being tried for first-degree murder. The prosecutor presents an eyewitness to the victim's being shot. After asking the witness some preliminary questions, the prosecutor begins a question with "When the defendant shot and killed the victim . . ." Should the defense attorney pose an objection to this question? On what ground?

3. In response to the prosecutor's questions, a lay witness who is a high school graduate testifies as follows:

   "I measured the defendant's skid marks, and I believe he was driving at least sixty-five miles per hour."

   "In my opinion, anyone who drinks two beers becomes intoxicated."

   "When I saw the defendant right after the accident, his face appeared flushed and he staggered as he walked."

   "My sister told me that the defendant did a lot of drinking at the nearby bar."

   What, if any, objections should the defense make to each one of the witness's statements?

4. Luke Lumberjack is being tried for raping a woman he has known for a year. The state's evidence disclosed that Lumberjack, age twenty-three, had spent an evening with the female complainant, age twenty-one. Afterward, at his invitation, they went to his apartment and had a few beers. The complainant testified that Lumberjack, a large, husky male, forced her to have sex with him, despite her stated unwillingness. During cross-examination, the complainant admitted having once before had a consensual sexual relationship with the defendant. During the state's closing argument, in referring to the defendant, the prosecutor told the jury, "This big hunk of cruelty is an animal, one who must be put away to protect the young women of this community. It's important to do your duty by convicting him and send a message to the community." Defense counsel objected on the ground that the prosecutor's comments were inflammatory, prejudicial, and unfair. He requested that the trial judge strike the prosecutor's comments, inform the jury that they should be disregarded, and admonish the prosecutor for having made such statements. How should the trial judge rule?

5. Lawrence Liverless is being tried before a jury for armed robbery and murder of a convenience store clerk. The indictment alleges that Liverless shot and killed the clerk before prying open the cash register and stealing the $451 contained therein. Because the video surveillance camera was not working at the time of the robbery, the prosecution is relying heavily on the testimony of Officer Dusty Broome, who arrived at the scene of the robbery in response to a silent alarm triggered by the convenience store clerk before he was fatally shot. Officer

Broome testified that he did not see the perpetrator, but that before he died the clerk told him that the robber had a tattoo of a dragon on his arm. The defendant, Liverless, has a large tattoo of a dragon on his right arm. On what ground might the defense object to this testimony? How should the judge rule on the objection? If the judge upholds the objection, does this constitute a basis for declaring a mistrial?

CHAPTER **7**

Sentencing and Punishment

CHAPTER OUTLINE

JURISPRUDENCE FEATURE BOXES

Kansas v. Hendricks (1997)
Furman v. Georgia (1972)
Gregg v. Georgia (1976)
Ford v. Wainwright (1986)
Payne v. Tennessee (1991)
Bearden v. Georgia (1983)
Cunningham v. California (2007)
Ewing v. California (2003)
Apprendi v. New Jersey (2000)

LEARNING OBJECTIVES

After reading this chapter, you should be able to explain

1. the historical antecedents and philosophical underpinnings of the forms of criminal punishment used today

2. how and why criminal penalties are controlled by statutes as well as by constitutional provisions

3. how and why judges grant and revoke probation in lieu of incarceration

4. why courts have allowed violent sexual predators who have completed their prison terms to be confined via civil commitment

5. how the death penalty has evolved and why it remains controversial

6. how the sentencing process works and why sentencing in capital cases is unique

7. the different statutory approaches to incarceration

8. why the federal government and some states have adopted sentencing guidelines

9. what constitutional rights are retained by people in prison

10. what rights are afforded to victims of crimes

CHAPTER OPENING VIGNETTE

In November 1999, 14-year-old Kuntrell Jackson and two other teenage boys decided to commit a robbery at a video store in Arkansas. When Jackson learned that one of the boys was carrying a concealed firearm, he remained outside the store while the other two went inside, confronted the clerk and demanded money. Jackson then entered the store and said something, though what he said was in dispute at trial. The defense claimed that Jackson said to his friends, "I thought you all was playin'." The prosecution claimed that Jackson told the clerk, "We ain't playin'." In any event, when the clerk refused to give up the money, one of the other teenagers shot and killed her. The three then fled the scene empty-handed. Jackson was tried as an adult, convicted of aggravated robbery and felony murder, and sentenced to life in prison without possibility of parole in accordance with Arkansas law. In reviewing the case, the U.S. Supreme Court struck down the law under which Jackson was sentenced. The Court also struck down a similar Alabama statute. Speaking for the Court, Justice Elena Kagan opined that "by requiring that all children convicted of homicide receive lifetime incarceration without possibility of parole, regardless of their age and age-related characteristics and the nature of their crimes, the mandatory sentencing schemes before us violate [the] principle of proportionality, and so the Eighth Amendment's ban on cruel and unusual punishment." *Miller v. Alabama*, 567 U.S. ___, 132 S.Ct. 2455, 183 L.Ed.2d 407 (2012). As you will see throughout this chapter, The Cruel and Unusual Punishments Clause of the Eighth Amendment figures prominently in the law affecting sentencing and punishment.

Introduction

retribution Something demanded as payment or revenge from one who has committed a criminal offense; the theory of punishment that stresses just deserts.

The concept of criminal punishment is an ancient one. The Code of Hammurabi, promulgated in Babylonia circa 1800 B.C., contained a detailed schedule of crimes and punishments and first codified the notion of "an eye for an eye." In a similar vein, the Mosaic Law mandated severe but proportionate punishment based on this principle of **retribution**.

While it is sometimes equated with legalized vengeance, the concept of retribution was a great leap forward in the evolution of criminal punishment. It replaced the personal or familial (and often excessive) acts of vengeance that frequently followed injuries to persons or property. Moreover, retribution carried with it a sense of **proportionality**, which continues to have relevance in criminal sentencing today.

proportionality The degree to which a particular punishment matches the seriousness of a crime or matches the penalty other offenders have received for the same crime.

Most ancient legal systems prescribed severe punishments for those who committed the kinds of acts we now consider *mala in se* (from the Latin, meaning "evil in itself"). Execution, torture, mutilation, and banishment from the community were not uncommon. But ancient legal systems also employed economic sanctions such as forfeiture of property, especially when members of the upper classes committed transgressions against members of the lower classes.

The Common-Law Background

By contemporary standards, the English common law was quite severe—the death penalty was prescribed for most felonies. In the early days of the common law, nobles who committed **capital crimes** were shown mercy by simply being beheaded. Commoners who were sentenced to death were often subjected to more grisly forms of punishment—they were "broken on the wheel" (where the condemned was strapped to a wagon wheel and his limbs broken with an iron rod), "drawn and quartered" (where the condemned, after being disemboweled, was cut into four pieces), or "burned at the stake" (where the condemned was tied to a post and burned alive). Eventually, the comparatively humane method of hanging was adopted as the principal means of execution in England.

capital crimes Crime for which death is a permissible punishment.

Persons convicted of misdemeanors were generally subjected to nonlethal **corporal punishment** such as flogging. The misdemeanant was taken into the public square, bound to the whipping post, and administered as many lashes as were prescribed by law for the offense.

corporal punishment Punishment that inflicts pain or injury on a person's body.

In England—indeed, throughout Europe—the administration of punishment was intentionally a matter of public spectacle. The idea was that public display of painful and humiliating punishment would deter others from engaging in criminal acts. This theory, known as **general deterrence**, is still prevalent today.

general deterrence The theory that punishment serves to deter others from committing crimes.

During the colonization of the New World, English subjects convicted of misdemeanors were often sent to penal colonies in America to do hard labor. After the American Revolution, they were sent to Australia.

The American Experience

In colonial America, criminal punishment followed common-law practice, although the Massachusetts Code of 1648 mandated capital punishment in cases of idolatry, witchcraft, blasphemy, sodomy, and adultery, as well as for the common-law capital crimes. At the time of the American Revolution, the death penalty was in wide use for a variety of felonies. And corporal punishment, primarily flogging, was widely used for a variety of crimes, including many misdemeanors.

The American Bill of Rights, ratified in 1791, prohibited the imposition of "cruel and unusual punishments." The framers of the Bill of Rights sought to prevent the use of torture, which had been common in Europe as late as the eighteenth century. However, they did not intend to outlaw the death penalty, nor did they intend to abolish all forms of corporal punishment.

During the nineteenth century, reformers introduced the concept of the penitentiary—literally, "a place to do penance." The idea was that criminals could be reformed through isolation, Bible study, and hard labor. This gave rise to the notion

rehabilitation Restoring someone or something to its former status; a justification for punishment emphasizing reform rather than retribution.

incarceration Another term for imprisonment.

death penalty Capital punishment; a sentence to death for the commission of a crime.

incapacitation Punishment making it impossible for an offender to reoffend.

of **rehabilitation**: the idea that the criminal justice system could reform criminals and reintegrate them into society. Many of the educational, occupational training and psychological programs found in modern prisons are based on this theory.

By the twentieth century, **incarceration** had replaced corporal punishment as the mainstay of criminal sentencing. All states, as well as the federal government, constructed prisons to house persons convicted of felonies. Even cities and counties constructed jails to confine persons convicted of misdemeanors. The **death penalty** remained in wide use for the most serious violent felonies. But it was rendered more "humane" as the gallows were replaced by the firing squad, the gas chamber, the electric chair, and, eventually, lethal injection. The death penalty remains in effect today in more than half the states, as well as in the federal system, although its use is now limited to the most aggravated cases of first-degree murder. It remains one of the most intensely controversial aspects of the American system of criminal justice.

Today the focus of criminal punishment is on the goal of **incapacitation**. Incapacitation means that offenders are prevented from committing further criminal acts. In ancient societies, banishment was sometimes used to protect the community from those whose presence was regarded as unduly threatening. Contemporary American society resorts to imprisonment or, in extreme cases, execution to rid itself of seriously threatening behavior. Although nearly everyone favors incapacitation of violent offenders, in practice incapacitation extends beyond execution or incarceration. When a state revokes a person's driver's license for driving while intoxicated, the purpose is primarily incapacitation. Similarly, some states have laws offering convicted rapists the option of taking a drug to render them incapable of committing rape. Other forms of incapacitation can be extremely controversial. For example, may a judge order a convicted child abuser to refrain from having any more children to prevent future child abuse?

Those who favor incapacitation to the exclusion of the other purposes of punishment are likely to favor harsh sentences, even for relatively minor crimes. They prefer to "lock 'em up and throw away the key." Again, we must consider the issue of proportionality: Crime control is not the only goal of the criminal justice system—dispensing justice is equally important.

Legal Constraints on Sentencing and Punishment

There are procedural as well as substantive issues in the area of sentencing and punishment. Sharp disagreements exist regarding the roles that legislatures, judges, and corrections officials should play in determining punishments. Generally, judges are required to impose sentences that fall within the parameters of appropriate punishment specified by statute, yet within these parameters, courts exercise substantial discretion. Recent concern about sentencing disparities has resulted in a variety of measures aimed at reducing the range of judicial discretion in sentencing.

Just as judges' sentencing decisions are constrained by statutes, statutory penalties must comport with substantive and procedural requirements imposed by the federal and state constitutions. Specifically, criminal punishment is limited by the Eighth Amendment prohibition of cruel and unusual punishments, the Due Process Clauses of the Fifth and Fourteenth Amendments, and similar provisions in all fifty state constitutions. Recent judicial activity in the areas of sentencing and punishment has focused on the need for procedural regularity in sentencing and proportionality in punishment.

Contemporary Forms of Criminal Punishment

Today, the criminal law provides for a variety of criminal punishments, including monetary fines, incarceration, probation, community service, and, of course, the death penalty. Although most people agree about the propriety of punishing criminal behavior, they disagree about the legality, morality, and efficacy of specific modes of criminal punishment. The death penalty in particular remains a hotly debated issue.

Fines

monetary fine A sum of money that offenders are required to pay as punishment for the commission of crimes.

By far the most common form of criminal punishment today is the **monetary fine**. Most misdemeanors carry monetary fines, especially for first offenses. Some felonies, especially serious economic crimes defined by federal law, carry heavy monetary fines as penalties. For example, offenses against federal banking laws and securities and exchange laws are punishable by fines reaching into the millions of dollars. Increasingly, drug trafficking offenders are being punished by large fines.

In many states, a court can sentence a defendant to pay a fine in addition to serving a sentence of imprisonment or probation. In New Jersey, for example, such fines may range from $500 to $200,000, depending on the nature and degree of the offense. N.J. Stat. Ann. § 2C:43-3. Fines may be appropriate devices of retribution and deterrence for economic crimes, but they hardly seem suitable as punishments for criminal acts of violence. And many have questioned the fairness and effectiveness of established minimum and maximum fines that do not consider the economic circumstances of individual defendants.

Forfeiture of Property

forfeiture Sacrifice of ownership or some right (usually in property) as a penalty.

Federal law provides for **forfeiture** of the proceeds of a variety of criminal activities. See, generally, 18 U.S.C.A. §§ 981–982. More controversial are the federal law provisions allowing forfeiture of property used in illicit drug activity. Under federal law, a "conveyance," which includes aircraft, motor vehicles, and vessels, is subject to forfeiture if it is used to transport controlled substances. 21 U.S.C.A. § 881(a)(4). Real estate may be forfeited if it is used to commit or facilitate the commission of a drug-related felony. 21 U.S.C.A. § 881(a)(7). Many states have similar statutes. See, e.g., Oklahoma's Uniform Controlled Dangerous Substances Act, 63 Okl. Stat. Ann. § 2-503.

State courts dealing with forfeiture under state law generally review forfeitures under the "excessive fines" provisions of their state constitutions. See, e.g., *In re King Properties*, 635 A.2d 128 (Pa. 1993), where the court found that forfeiture of a house used as a base of operations in an ongoing drug business was not excessive. Where a state constitutional provision exempts a homestead from forced sale, courts generally hold that it also prohibits civil or criminal forfeiture of homestead property. See, e.g., *Butterworth v. Caggiano*, 605 So.2d 56 (Fla. 1992). However, a federal appeals court has ruled that federal law preempts—that is, overrides—state homestead exemptions when federal crimes have been committed. *United States v. Lot 5, Fox Grove, Alachua County, Fla.*, 23 F.3d 359 (11th Cir. 1994).

Under federal and state laws, asset forfeiture may be accomplished through civil or criminal proceedings. In *Austin v. United States*, 509 U.S. 602, 113 S.Ct. 2801, 125 L.Ed.2d 488 (1993), the Supreme Court said that civil forfeiture "constitutes 'payment to a sovereign as punishment for some offense' . . . and, as such, is subject to the limitations of the Eighth Amendment's Excessive Fines Clause." 509 U.S. at 622, 113 S.Ct. at 2812, 125 L.Ed.2d at 505. However, the Court left it to state and lower federal courts to determine the tests of "excessiveness" in the context of forfeiture. In 1994, the Illinois Supreme Court said that three factors should be considered in this regard: (1) the gravity of the offense relative to the value of the forfeiture, (2) whether the property was an integral part of the illicit activity, and (3) whether illicit activity involving the property was extensive. *Waller v. 1989 Ford F350 Truck* (*Kusumoto*), 642 N.E.2d 460 (Ill. 1994).

Incarceration

Confinement is generally regarded as the only effective way to deal with violent offenders. Although some question the efficacy of the prison, regarding it as little more than a factory for producing future criminals, incarceration does protect society from dangerous offenders. Prison is an effective incapacitator; it is rarely an effective rehabilitator. In fact, serving time in prison often reinforces criminal tendencies.

Today more than 1.5 million inmates are housed in federal or state prisons. See U.S. Department of Justice, Bureau of Justice Statistics, "Correctional Population in the United States, 2010," December 2011, NCJ 236319. Although the increase in the national incarceration rate has slowed somewhat since 2004, most state prisons are operating at or just below capacity. The federal system continues to operate well above its designed capacity. This problem has led to judicial intervention in many instances, but society appears reluctant to provide additional resources to expand prison capacity. Imprisonment is expensive, costing taxpayers roughly $20 billion per year.

As criminologists have become increasingly dissatisfied with the effects of the prison system, judges have responded by imposing limits on prison populations and by scrutinizing the conditions of confinement. Meanwhile, fiscal pressures prevent legislatures from appropriating the funds necessary to construct more prisons. Accordingly, attention has shifted to alternatives to incarceration, especially for less dangerous offenders. One of the most serious criticisms of all such alternatives emphasizes the difficulty of determining who should be eligible for an alternative form of punishment. In an age of overcrowded prisons, alternative punishments carry the real possibility that truly dangerous offenders will not be sufficiently controlled.

The Boot Camp: An Alternative to Prison?

boot camp An institution that provides systematic discipline in a military-like environment designed to rehabilitate an offender; employed as a sentencing alternative.

One alternative to the traditional prison setting is the **boot camp**, a program designed to employ a system of discipline much like the one the military uses to instill discipline in its recruits. Boot camps were designed to rehabilitate young, nonviolent offenders who have committed theft, burglary, forgery, and other nonviolent offenses, often brought about by their drug abuse. Although boot camps produced some short-term changes in behavior, they did little to reduce recidivism, in part because of insufficient focus on the offender's reentry into the community. In January 2006, a fourteen-year-old boy died after being roughed up by guards at a sheriff's boot camp in Panama City, Florida. The boy's death led to the dismantling of the Florida boot camp program. After a lengthy investigation, in November 2006 the state charged seven former guards and a nurse at the facility with manslaughter arising out of the incident. Although the defendants were ultimately acquitted, the incident gave more impetus to criticism of boot camps nationwide, and it now appears that the national boot camp experiment is coming to an end.

Probation

probation Conditional release of a convicted criminal in lieu of incarceration.

Of the various alternatives to incarceration, **probation** is by far the most common. According to the Bureau of Justice Statistics, at the end of 2010, roughly 4.9 million adult men and women were under federal, state, or local probation or parole jurisdiction. U.S. Department of Justice, Bureau of Justice Statistics, "Correctional Population in the United States, 2010," supra.

An outgrowth of nineteenth- and twentieth-century developments in criminal justice, probation is the conditional release of a convicted offender by a trial court. If prisons have become little more than factories for producing future criminals, probation seems to be a viable alternative to prison terms, especially for nonviolent first-time offenders. The primary purpose of probation is to rehabilitate the defendant. Thus, the defendant is released under the supervision of a probation officer, who is responsible to the court for making sure that the offender abides by the **conditions of probation**.

conditions of probation A set of rules that must be observed by a person placed on probation.

The mandatory and discretionary conditions for probation for federal offenses are set out in 18 U.S.C.A. § 3563. By 1967, all states provided for probation, often varying in the offenses and defendants eligible. State laws generally provide for certain mandatory conditions. A sentencing judge is afforded broad discretion in formulating additional conditions of a defendant's probation. Certain conditions are relatively standard—for example, that the probationer will not commit further crimes, will avoid certain persons or places, will maintain gainful employment and support any dependents, and will not travel outside the court's jurisdiction without permission of the court or probation officer. The sentencing judge, however, can tailor additional conditions to the defendant's rehabilitation, even to the extent of imposing conditions that infringe a probationer's constitutional rights, including First Amendment rights of free speech and association, as long as those conditions are related to the goal of rehabilitation. *Malone v. United States*, 502 F.2d 554 (9th Cir. 1974); *Porth v. Templar*, 453 F.2d 330 (10th Cir. 1971).

The U.S. Supreme Court has had little to say on the subject of probation since stating in 1932 that probation conditions must serve "the ends of justice and the best interest of both the public and the defendant." *Burns v. United States*, 287 U.S. 216, 220, 53 S.Ct. 154, 156, 77 L.Ed. 266, 268 (1932). In *Higdon v. United States*, 627 F.2d 893 (9th Cir. 1980), a leading federal decision, the court noted, "The only factors which the trial judge should consider when deciding whether to grant probation are the appropriateness and attainability of rehabilitation and the need to protect the public by imposing conditions which control the probationer's activities." *Id*. at 897. The court fashioned a two-step process for reviewing conditions of probation. The court first determines whether the conditions are permissible; if so, it then looks to whether there is a reasonable relationship between the conditions imposed and the purpose of the probation.

Most probationary sentences are imposed by state courts, which frequently cite *People v. Dominguez*, 64 Cal.Rptr. 290 (Cal. App. 1967), as the standard for judging the reasonableness of conditions of probation. There the court established that a condition of probation that (1) has no relationship to the crime of which the offender was convicted, (2) relates to conduct which is not in itself criminal, and (3) requires or forbids conduct which is not reasonably related to future criminality does not serve the ends of probation and is invalid. *Id*. at 293. In *Dominguez*, the court reasoned that a condition that the probationer not become pregnant without being married was unrelated to her offense or to future criminality and thus was invalid.

CASE-IN-POINT

Conditions of Probation

In 1990 the Supreme Court of Ohio reviewed the conviction of a defendant on a charge of contributing to the delinquency of a child by furnishing alcohol to three young boys. The court focused on a single point: whether the trial court abused its discretion in imposing a condition of probation stipulating that the defendant "have no association or communication, direct or indirect, with anyone under the age of 18 years not a member of his immediate family." The court noted that while a trial judge is granted broad discretion in setting conditions of probation, that discretion is not limitless, and courts must guard against overly broad conditions that impinge upon the probationer's liberty. Nevertheless, the court found the restriction imposed against the defendant "reasonably related to rehabilitating [the defendant] without being unduly restrictive." Citing various state and federal authorities, the court said that in setting conditions of probation, trial judges should consider whether a condition to be imposed (1) is reasonably related to rehabilitating the offender, (2) has some relationship to the crime for which the offender was convicted, and (3) relates to conduct that is criminal or reasonably related to future criminality.

State v. Jones, 550 N.E.2d 469 (Ohio 1990).

Because most probationers are grateful to receive a probationary sentence and avoid incarceration, constitutional challenges to conditions are not too common. Nevertheless, some courts that have reviewed such conditions have ruled there are limits to probation conditions. In *Biller v. State,* 618 So.2d 734 (Fla. 1993), the Florida Supreme Court invalidated a probation order that required the probationer to refrain from using or possessing alcoholic beverages. The court pointed out that nothing in the record showed any connection between alcohol consumption and the weapons violation of which the probationer had been convicted.

In *Commonwealth v. LaFrance,* 525 N.E.2d 379 (Mass. 1988), the Supreme Judicial Court of Massachusetts invalidated a condition of probation that required the defendant to submit to a search of herself, her possessions, and any place where she may be, with or without a search warrant, on request of a probation officer. Although the court determined that condition violated the defendant's rights, the court suggested that the following condition could be substituted: "On the basis of a reasonable suspicion that a condition of the probationer's probation has been violated, a probation officer, or any law enforcement officer acting on the request of the probation office, may search the probationer, her property, her residence, and any place where she may be living, and may do so with or without a search warrant depending on the requirements of law." *Id.* at 383.

Courts tend to scrutinize conditions that restrict such fundamental rights as procreation. A Florida appellate court held that although a condition of probation prohibiting custody of children had a clear relationship to the crime of child abuse and was valid, conditions prohibiting marriage and pregnancy added nothing to decrease the possibility of further child abuse and were found to be invalid. *Rodriguez v. State,* 378 So.2d 7 (Fla. App. 1979). Three years later, the same court struck down a condition of probation that required that the defendant "must not father any children during [the] probation period." *Burchell v. State,* 419 So.2d 358 (Fla. App. 1982). In *State v. Mosburg,* 768 P.2d 313 (Kan. App. 1989), the court held that a probation condition requiring a defendant who was convicted of endangering a child to refrain from becoming pregnant during the term of probation unduly intruded on the defendant's right to privacy. At a time when some in society equated long hair with unacceptable behavior, in *Inman v. State,* 183 S.E.2d 413 (Ga. App. 1971), a Georgia appellate court held invalid a condition of probation that required a male defendant to maintain a short haircut as not related to his rehabilitation and therefore unconstitutionally invasive of his right of self-expression.

Different factual scenarios can result in different judicial approaches and reach different conclusions. Consider the approach of the Wisconsin Supreme Court. In *State v. Oakley*, 629 N.W.2d 200 (Wis. 2001), David Oakley, the father of nine children, pled no contest to intentionally refusing to provide child support. The trial judge placed him on probation to enable him to make meaningful payments of support that would not be possible if he was incarcerated. As a condition of Oakley's probation, the judge stipulated, "Oakley cannot father any additional children unless he can demonstrate that he has the financial ability to support them, and that he is supporting the children he has." *Id.* at 203. In rejecting his challenge based on his constitutional right to procreate, the court pointed out that Wisconsin law grants judges broad discretion in fashioning probation conditions and concluded, "[B]ecause Oakley can satisfy this condition by not intentionally refusing to support his current nine children and any future children required by the law, we find that the condition is narrowly tailored to serve the State's compelling interest of having parents support their children." *Id.* at 212.

Conditions of probation imposed on offenders convicted of child pornography offenses have included some innovative approaches. In *United States v. Zinn*, 321 F.3d 1084 (11th Cir. 2003), the court ruled that it was not an abuse of discretion for the district court to require the defendant to submit to polygraph testing reasonably related to his child pornography offense and his personal history.

In imposing conditions of probation, other courts have noted the strong link between child pornographers and their use of the Internet, and the need to protect children from sex offenders. For example, in *United States v. Rearden*, 349 F.3d 608, 620 (9th Cir. 2003), the defendant was convicted of shipping child pornography (over the Internet) in violation of 18 U.S.C.A. § 2253(a)(1)(A). The appellate court said the district court did not err in imposing conditions of supervised release that prohibited him from possessing or using a computer with Internet access without prior approval of his probation officer.

In *State v. Ehli*, 681 N.W.2d 808 (N.D. 2004), the defendant pleaded guilty to sexual abuse of a young child. He had used pornography from the Internet to "instruct" the child on certain adult sexual acts. The state supreme court rejected the defendant's challenge to the suspended part of his sentence that included conditions of probation that prohibited him from having access to the Internet.

In *People v. Harrisson*, 134 Cal.App.4th 637 (2005), the defendant pleaded no contest to possession of child pornography after having used his computer to send pornographic images to an undercover police officer. The court rejected his contention that the probationary part of his sentence that prohibited him access to the Internet violated his constitutional rights.

Community Service

community service A sentence or condition of probation requiring that the criminal perform some specific service to the community for some specified period of time.

Another alternative to incarceration, **community service**, is growing in popularity. Community service refers to sentences whereby offenders are required to perform a specified number of hours of service to the community doing specified tasks. Often, community service is required as one of several conditions of probation.

Community service has the virtues of keeping the offender out of the undesirable prison environment and exacting a penalty that is useful to the community. Ideally, it seems like an excellent way to instill in the offender a sense of responsibility to the community for having committed criminal actions, but community service also has its drawbacks. It is difficult for the community to reap any real benefit without providing a degree of training to and supervision of the offender. Training and supervision can be costly and can, in many instances, exceed the value of the community service to be performed.

Community Control

community control A sentence imposed on a person found guilty of a crime that requires that the offender be placed in an individualized program of noninstitutional confinement.

Another alternative to incarceration is **community control**, a neologism for an ancient practice known as **house arrest**. Under this alternative, an offender is allowed to leave home only for employment and approved community service activities. Increasingly, house arrest is monitored electronically by requiring persons to wear bracelets that permit officials to track their whereabouts. Community control is generally employed when incarceration is not warranted but probation is not considered sufficiently restrictive. Community control requires intensive surveillance and supervision and may not be practical in many cases. For example, consider a convicted rapist whose occupation is plumbing. To allow this offender to carry on his trade may pose a significant risk to householders. Comparable risks often militate against placing offenders under community control.

house arrest A sentencing alternative to incarceration where the offender is allowed to leave home only for employment and approved community service activities.

Creative Alternatives to Confinement

Judges seeking alternatives to jail or prison have become increasingly creative recently. One judge in Houston, Texas, has been known to require offenders to clean out the police department stables as part of their "community service." Some juvenile courts require offenders to make public apologies to their victims. In a few cities, billboards have been erected bearing the names of persons convicted for driving while under the influence of intoxicating substances. Some jurisdictions even publish the names of persons who patronize prostitutes. These actions are intended to shame offenders by drawing public attention to their misconduct. In seventeenth-century Massachusetts, women found guilty of adultery were required to wear a scarlet "A." The idea that offenders need to experience shame appears to be making a comeback.

In 1987, a convicted child molester was sentenced by an Oregon court to five years' probation on the condition that he display on his front door and automobile a warning sign: DANGEROUS SEX OFFENDER: NO CHILDREN ALLOWED. Although the unusual sentence drew praise from prosecutors and many citizens' groups, civil libertarians objected.

One county judge in Sarasota, Florida, made national news in 1986 by requiring that DWI offenders—as a condition of probation—place bumper stickers on their cars to alert the driving public to their convictions. On appeal, the practice was upheld against an Eighth Amendment attack. As the appellate court said, "The mere requirement that a defendant display a 'scarlet letter' as part of his punishment is not necessarily offensive to the Constitution." *Goldschmitt v. State*, 490 So.2d 123, 125 (Fla. App. 1986). On the other hand, the New York Court of Appeals invalidated a condition of probation that ordered the defendant to attach a CONVICTED DWI sign to the license plate of any car driven by the defendant on the ground that it bore no relationship to the goal of rehabilitation. *People v. Letterlough*, 655 N.E.2d 146 (N.Y. 1995). Obviously, there is room for judicial disagreement on such matters.

JURISPRUDENCE

Kansas v. Hendricks, 521 U.S. 346, 117 S.Ct. 2072, 138 L.Ed.2d 501 (1997)

Leroy Hendricks, an inmate with a history of sexually molesting children, was scheduled for release from prison soon after the act became effective. The state invoked the act to commit him to custody. After hearing testimony, which included Hendricks's own testimony that when he gets "stressed" he continues to be unable to control his sexual desires for children, a jury determined he was a sexually violent predator. The court ordered him confined. On appeal, the Kansas Supreme Court invalidated the act, and the State of Kansas sought review in the U.S. Supreme Court.

In a 5–4 decision, the U.S. Supreme Court held that the act does not offend the constitutional prohibitions against *ex post facto* laws and double jeopardy because it does not criminalize conduct that was legal before its enactment and because it does not constitute punishment. Writing for the majority, Justice Clarence Thomas stated that "[t]he State may take measures to restrict the freedom of the dangerously mentally ill. This is a legitimate nonpunitive governmental objective." Dissenting justices argued that the act was not simply an effort to commit Hendricks civilly but rather an effort to inflict further punishment upon him for crimes committed prior to enactment of the act.

Civil Commitment of Violent Sexual Predators

In 1994, Kansas enacted the Sexually Violent Predator Act. The act establishes procedures for the civil commitment of persons who, because of mental abnormality or personality disorder, are likely to engage in "predatory acts of sexual violence." The Act allows for the continued confinement of sexual predators who already have completed their prison sentences. In 1997, the U.S. Supreme Court upheld this statute against the arguments that it represented "double jeopardy" and amounted to an "*ex post facto* law." *Kansas v. Hendricks*, 521 U.S. 346, 117 S.Ct. 2072, 138 L.Ed.2d 501 (1997).

A similar federal statute enacted in 2006, codified at 18 U.S.C. § 4248, permits a federal district court to order the continued confinement of sexually violent offenders who have completed their prison sentences. In 2010, the Supreme Court upheld this statute against a challenge based on the argument that Congress had exceeded its implied powers under the Necessary and Proper Clause of Article I, Section 8 of the U.S. Constitution. Writing for the Court, Justice Stephen Breyer concluded that "the statute is a 'necessary and proper' means of exercising the federal authority that permits Congress to create federal criminal laws, to punish their violation, to imprison violators, to provide appropriately for those imprisoned, and to maintain the security of those who are not imprisoned but who may be affected by the federal imprisonment of others." *United States v. Comstock*, 560 U.S. 126, 147, 130 S.Ct. 1949, 1965, 176 L.Ed.2d 878, 899 (2010).

The Death Penalty

The death penalty remains the single most controversial issue in the realm of criminal punishment. Although the death penalty has deep roots in religious and legal traditions, the twentieth century witnessed widespread abolition of capital punishment. At present, the United States is the only Western democracy that retains the death penalty. Thirty-eight states currently authorize capital punishment for first-degree murder or other types of aggravated homicide.

Historical Background

capital punishment The death penalty.

The framers of the Bill of Rights did not intend for the Cruel and Unusual Punishments Clause of the Eighth Amendment to abolish the death penalty. The Bill of Rights assumes the existence of **capital punishment**. Indeed, the Fifth Amendment refers specifically to "capital" crimes and the deprivation of life. A reform movement in the nineteenth century succeeded in limiting public executions and reducing the range of capital offenses. The movement to eliminate the death penalty achieved its first victory in 1847, when Michigan abolished capital punishment. This movement grew steadily throughout the twentieth century. By the 1960s, it appeared that the death penalty was on the way out. Public opinion no longer favored it; many states abolished it. In those that did not, the courts began to impose restrictions on its use. In 1967, two persons were executed in the United States. Ten years passed before another person was put to death. When the Supreme Court declared Georgia's death penalty law unconstitutional in *Furman v. Georgia*, 408 U.S. 238, 92 S.Ct. 2726, 33 L.Ed.2d 346 (1972), some observers thought it signaled the abolition of the death penalty in America.

Revival of the Death Penalty

The Supreme Court's 1972 decision striking down the Georgia death penalty concentrated on the virtually unlimited discretion the state placed in trial juries that were empowered to impose death sentences. According to Justice Potter Stewart's concurring opinion in *Furman*, Georgia's administration of the death penalty was unpredictable to the point of being "freakishly imposed." 408 U.S. 238, 310, 92 S.Ct. 2726, 2763, 33 L.Ed.2d 346, 390 (1972). In the wake of the *Furman* decision, Georgia and most other states revised their death penalty laws to address the concerns raised by the Court.

bifurcated trial A capital trial with separate phases for determining guilt and punishment.

Under the revised Georgia statute, a **bifurcated trial** is held in cases where the state seeks the death penalty. In the first stage, guilt is determined according to the usual procedures, rules of evidence, and standard of proof. If the jury finds the defendant guilty, the same jury considers the appropriateness of the death sentence in a separate proceeding where additional evidence is received to determine

---

JURISPRUDENCE

Furman v. Georgia, 408 U.S. 238, 92 S.Ct. 2726, 33 L.Ed.2d 346 (1972)

In this landmark decision the Supreme Court invalidated Georgia's death penalty statute. The decision represents three death penalty cases that were consolidated on appeal. All three defendants were African American. One of them was convicted for murder; two were found guilty of rape. All three were sentenced to death by juries in Georgia. In a 5–4 decision, the Supreme Court struck down Georgia's death penalty. There was, however, only a brief *per curiam* opinion announcing the judgment of the Court. For the majority's rationale, one has to look at

five separate concurring opinions. Only two of the five justices—Brennan and Marshall—held that the death penalty itself was cruel and unusual punishment, given the "evolving standards of decency." Of the five justices who voted to invalidate the death penalty, Justice Stewart's opinion seems to have been the most influential. For Stewart the problem with the death penalty was not the punishment itself but the manner in which it was being administered. Trial juries were being left with virtually unfettered discretion in deciding when to impose capital punishment. The result, according to Stewart, was that the death penalty was "wantonly and … freakishly imposed."

aggravation or mitigation of the punishment. To impose the death penalty, the jury must find at least one of several **aggravating factors** specified in the statute. The purpose of requiring aggravating factors before imposing the death penalty is to narrow the range of offenders and persons eligible for capital punishment and make the imposition of the death penalty more predictable.

aggravating factors
Factors attending the commission of a crime that make the crime or its consequences worse.

Under Georgia law, the specific aggravating factors to be considered by the jury are whether

1. The offense . . . was committed by a person with a prior record of conviction for a capital felony;
2. The offense . . . was committed while the offender was engaged in . . . another capital felony or aggravated battery, or the offense of murder was committed while the offender was engaged in the commission of burglary or arson in the first degree;
3. The offender . . . knowingly created a great risk of death to more than one person in a public place by means of a weapon or device which would normally be hazardous to the lives of more than one person;
4. The offender committed the offense of murder for himself or another for the purpose of receiving money or any other thing of monetary value;
5. The murder of a judicial officer, former judicial officer, a district attorney or solicitor-general, or former district attorney, solicitor or solicitor-general was committed during or because of the exercise of his or her official duties;
6. The offender caused or directed another to commit murder or committed murder as an agent or employee of another person;
7. The offense . . . was outrageously or wantonly vile, horrible or inhuman in that it involved torture, depravity of mind or an aggravated battery to the victim;
8. The offense of murder was committed against any peace officer, corrections employee, or fireman while engaged in the performance of his official duties;
9. The offense of murder was committed by a person in, or who has escaped from, the lawful custody of a peace officer or place of lawful confinement; or
10. The murder was committed for the purpose of avoiding, interfering with, or preventing a lawful arrest or custody in a place of lawful confinement, of himself or another; or
11. The offense of murder, rape, or kidnapping was committed by a person previously convicted of rape, aggravated sodomy, aggravated child molestation, or aggravated sexual battery.

Official Ga. Code Ann. § 17-10-30(b).

To hand down a death sentence, a Georgia jury must find that at least one of these aggravating circumstances was present in the crime. The jury must then weigh the aggravating factors against any **mitigating factors** presented by the defense. See Official Ga. Code Ann. § 17-10-31. Should the jury make this finding and opt for the death penalty, the statute provides for automatic appeal to the state supreme court.

mitigating factors
Circumstances or factors that tend to lessen culpability.

That court is required to consider

1. Whether the sentence of death was imposed under the influence of passion, prejudice or any other arbitrary factor; and
2. Whether . . . the evidence supports the jury's or judge's finding of a statutory aggravating circumstance . . ., and
3. Whether the sentence of death is excessive or disproportionate to the penalty imposed in similar cases, considering both the crime and the defendant.

Gregg v. Georgia, 428 U.S. 153, 96 S.Ct. 2909, 49 L.Ed.2d 859 (1976)

Troy Gregg, was convicted of armed robbery and murder and was sentenced to death. In accordance with Georgia's death penalty law revised after *Furman v. Georgia*, the trial was conducted in two stages, a guilt stage and a sentencing stage. For the jury to impose the death penalty, it has to find at least one of several statutorily prescribed aggravating factors. Automatic appeal to the state supreme court is also provided. The appellate review must consider not only the procedural regularity of the trial, but whether the evidence supports the finding of the aggravating factor and whether the death sentence is disproportionate to the penalty imposed in similar cases. The Court had little difficulty upholding the new Georgia statute, with only Justices Brennan and Marshall dissenting. Justice Stewart's opinion announcing the judgment stated: "The new Georgia sentencing procedures ... focus the jury's attention on the particularized nature of the crime and the particularized characteristics of the individual defendant.... In this way the jury's discretion is channeled. No longer can a jury wantonly and freakishly impose the death sentence, it is always circumscribed by the legislative guidelines." Thus, after a hiatus of four years, the death penalty was reinstated.

Official Code Ga. Ann. § 17-10-35(c).

In *Gregg v. Georgia*, 428 U.S. 153, 96 S.Ct. 2909, 49 L.Ed.2d 859 (1976), the Supreme Court upheld Georgia's revised death penalty statute by a vote of 7–2. Apparently, the Court was satisfied that this scheme had sufficiently addressed the evils identified in *Furman*. Thirty-eight states now have death penalty statutes modeled along the lines of the law upheld in *Gregg*.

Shortly after the death penalty was effectively reinstated by the Supreme Court's *Gregg* decision, executions in the United States began anew. On January 17, 1977, the state of Utah executed convicted murderer Gary Gilmore by firing squad. Between the date of the Gilmore execution and the end of 2005, a total of 1,004 prisoners were executed in the United States. At the end of 2005, there were 3,254 persons under sentence of death in thirty-eight jurisdictions (thirty-six states, the U.S. military, and the federal government). U.S. Department of Justice, Bureau of Justice Statistics, *Capital Punishment 2005,* December 2006, NCJ 21508.

The Federal Death Penalty

In August 1997, Timothy McVeigh was sentenced to death by lethal injection for his role in the bombing of the federal office building in Oklahoma City in 1995. In his federal trial, McVeigh was convicted of twenty-eight counts of murder of a federal law enforcement agent on active duty. See 18 U.S.C.A. § 1114. Under federal law, executions are carried out in the state where the defendant was sentenced unless that state has no death penalty, in which case the prisoner is transferred to another state for execution. 18 U.S.C.A. § 3596. McVeigh was executed at the federal prison in Terre Haute, Indiana, in June 2001. Prior to the McVeigh execution, the federal government had not put anyone to death since 1963.

The Anti-Drug Abuse Act of 1988, 21 U.S.C.A. § 848(e), allows the death penalty for so-called drug kingpins who control "continuing criminal enterprises" whose members intentionally kill or procure others to kill in furtherance of the enterprise. In 1993, Juan Raul Garza was sentenced to death under this statute for three murders committed as head of a Texas-based drug trafficking organization. The conviction and sentence were affirmed by the U.S. Court of Appeals for the Fifth Circuit. *United*

States v. Flores & Garza, 63 F.3d 1342 (5th Cir. 1995). A federal district judge set Garza's execution for August 5, 2000, but in July of that year President Bill Clinton ordered the execution delayed to allow Garza to request executive clemency under new rules promulgated by the Justice Department. After President George W. Bush denied his plea for clemency, Garza was finally put to death in June 2001.

In 1994, Congress enacted the **Federal Death Penalty Act (FDPA)**, 18 U.S.C.A. §§ 3591 *et seq.* Section 3592 lists the mitigating and aggravating factors affecting a decision of whether to impose the death penalty. Section 3593 provides for a special hearing to determine whether a sentence of death is justified in a particular case. The FDPA dramatically increased the number of federal crimes eligible for the death penalty. Capital punishment is now authorized for dozens of federal crimes, including nonhomicidal offenses such as treason and large-scale drug trafficking. It remains to be seen whether the federal courts will permit the death penalty for nonhomicidal crimes. *Coker v. Georgia*, 433 U.S. 584, 97 S.Ct. 2861, 53 L.Ed.2d 982 (1977), the Supreme Court prohibited capital punishment for the crime of rape. *Coker* suggests that the death penalty is an inappropriate punishment for any crime that does not involve the taking of a human life.

Federal Death Penalty Act (FDPA) Federal legislation that (1) lists the mitigating and aggravating factors affecting a decision of whether to impose the death penalty and (2) provides for a special hearing to determine whether a sentence of death is justified in a particular federal case.

Death, Deterrence, Retribution, and Incapacitation

One of the most intense battles among academicians in the field of criminal justice has been waged over the alleged deterrent value of the death penalty. At this point, the evidence appears to be mixed, making firm conclusions impossible. Whatever the possible deterrent value of the death penalty, its actual deterrent effect is reduced by the years of delay between sentencing and execution. Obviously, the death penalty has no value as a means of rehabilitation. Therefore, if the death penalty is to be justified, it must be primarily on grounds of retribution and incapacitation. Supporters of the death penalty argue, perhaps ironically, that the value of human life is underscored by imposing the severest of sanctions on those who commit murder. Certainly the death penalty is proportionate to the crime of murder. Indeed, the Supreme Court has made it clear that murder is the only crime for which the death penalty is permissible. *Coker v. Georgia*, supra.

Advocates of capital punishment also stress the incapacitation of the offender, and it is difficult to argue that death is not a complete incapacitator. But are retribution and incapacitation sufficient justifications for the death penalty?

Is the Death Penalty Racially Discriminatory?

Whether the Court achieved the evenhandedness in the administration of capital punishment it sought through its decisions in *Furman* and *Gregg* is questionable. Critics have long charged that the death penalty is racially discriminatory. During the 1970s, criminologist David Baldus collected data on more than 1,000 murder cases in Georgia and found significant disparities in the imposition of the death penalty based primarily on the race of the murder victims and, to a lesser extent, on the race of the defendants. The data reveal that blacks who killed whites were more than seven times more likely to receive the death sentence than were whites who killed blacks.

In April 1987, the Supreme Court reviewed the death sentence of a black man convicted of killing a white police officer in Georgia. The Court refused to accept statistical evidence derived from the Baldus study as a basis for reversing the death sentence. In the Court's view, even if there is statistical evidence of race discrimination, a defendant sentenced to death cannot prevail on appeal unless the defendant can show that the death sentence was imposed because of race discrimination in this case. *McCleskey v. Kemp*, 481 U.S. 279, 107 S.Ct. 1756, 95 L.Ed.2d 262 (1987). Obviously, this would be difficult, although certainly not impossible, for a defendant to demonstrate.

In a 1990 report, the U.S. General Accounting Office concluded that available research demonstrated "a pattern of evidence indicating racial disparities in the charging, sentencing, and imposition of the death penalty." Similarly, in 1994 the U.S. House of Representatives Subcommittee on Civil and Constitutional Rights concluded that members of racial minorities were being disproportionately prosecuted under the federal death penalty law. According to the Death Penalty Information Center, of the 133 defendants authorized for death penalty prosecution from 1988 to 1998, 76 percent were members of racial minorities. Of the 3,254 death row inmates in the United States at the end of 2005, 42 percent were African American. U.S. Department of Justice, Bureau of Justice Statistics, *Capital Punishment 2005*, December 2006, NCJ 215083. Certainly these statistics provide a basis for concern about the fairness with which the death penalty has been administered in this country.

Capital Punishment of Juvenile Offenders

One very difficult issue that the Supreme Court faced during the 1980s was whether, and under what circumstances, a juvenile may be executed when convicted of a capital crime. The Court responded in three decisions. In *Thompson v. Oklahoma*, 487 U.S. 815, 108 S.Ct. 2687, 101 L.Ed.2d 702 (1988), the Court ruled in a 6–3 decision that the Constitution forbids executing a juvenile who was fifteen years of age or younger at the time of commission of a capital crime. The following year, in *Stanford v. Kentucky*, 492 U.S. 361, 109 S.Ct. 2969, 106 L.Ed.2d 306 (1989), the Supreme Court split 5–4 in holding that a juvenile sixteen or older at the time of the crime may be sentenced to death.

Concurring in *Stanford*, Justice Sandra Day O'Connor commented that "it is sufficiently clear that no national consensus forbids the imposition of capital punishment on 16- or 17-year-old capital murderers." 492 U.S. at 381, 109 S.Ct. at 2981, 106 L.Ed.2d at 325. In both *Thompson* and *Stanford*, the Court referred to "evolving standards of decency" as the proper test for judging the constitutionality of whether a juvenile may be executed. Applying that test, the Court in *Roper v. Simmons*, 543 U.S. 551, 125 S.Ct. 1183, 161 L.Ed.2d 1 (2005), forbade the execution of anyone who was under eighteen at the time of his or her offense.

Writing for the Court in *Roper*, Justice Anthony Kennedy noted the decreasing frequency with which juvenile offenders were being sentenced to death as evidence of an emerging national consensus against capital punishment for juveniles. At the time of the *Roper* decision, only twenty states still allowed juveniles to be executed, and since 1995 only three states (Oklahoma, Texas, and Virginia) had actually executed inmates for crimes committed as juveniles. In any event, the Supreme Court's decision in *Roper* effectively ended the execution of juveniles in the United States.

Execution of Prisoners Who Have Become Insane

The rate of mental illness is abnormally high among prisoners and especially high among those on death row. Should a death row inmate whose mental illness has become so severe as to meet the legal definition of insanity be put to death? For

JURISPRUDENCE

Ford v. Wainwright, 477 U.S. 399, 106 S.Ct. 2595, 91 L.Ed.2d 335 (1986)

In 1974 Alvin Ford was convicted of murder and sentenced to death by a Florida court. There was no indication that he was mentally incompetent at the time of the trial. However, while in prison awaiting execution, Ford began to exhibit profound changes in behavior and to experience bizarre delusions. In 1983 a prison psychiatrist diagnosed Ford as suffering from a severe and uncontrollable mental disease closely resembling paranoid schizophrenia. Ford's attorney then invoked procedures under Florida law governing the determination of competency of a condemned prisoner. A panel of psychiatrists examined Ford, and although they differed in their specific diagnoses, all agreed that Ford was not insane under Florida law. On April 30, 1984,

Governor Bob Graham signed Ford's death warrant. Ford's attorney then filed a petition for habeas corpus in the U.S. District Court, seeking an evidentiary hearing on his client's sanity. The district court denied relief, and the court of appeals affirmed. The U.S. Supreme Court agreed to review the case to resolve the issue of whether the Eighth Amendment prohibits the execution of a person who is insane. On June 26, 1986, the Supreme Court announced its decision in *Ford v. Wainwright* holding that the Eighth Amendment bars the execution of a person who is insane. The Court also held that Florida's procedures for determining the sanity of a death row prisoner violated due process standards. The Court ruled that Ford was entitled to a *de novo* evidentiary hearing in the district court on the question of his competence to be executed.

those who view capital punishment solely as a means of incapacitation, analogous to "putting down" a rabid dog, the mental health of the prisoner to be executed makes little difference. But in *Ford v. Wainwright*, 477 U.S. 399, 106 S.Ct. 2595, 91 L.Ed.2d 335 (1986), the Supreme Court held that the Constitution forbids the execution of someone who is legally insane. Writing for a plurality of justices, Justice Thurgood Marshall declared: "It is no less abhorrent today than it has been for centuries to exact in penance the life of one whose mental illness prevents him from comprehending the reasons for the penalty or its implications." 477 U.S. at 417, 106 S.Ct. at 2606, 91 L.Ed.2d at 351. In 2007, the Court ruled that once a prisoner makes a preliminary showing that his current mental state would bar his execution, he is entitled to a hearing to determine his condition. *Panetti v. Quarterman*, 551 U.S. 930, 127 S.Ct. 2842, 168 L.Ed.2d 662 (2007). Today it is not uncommon for executions to be delayed pending the outcome of such hearings.

Execution of Mentally Retarded Persons

Like mental illness, mental retardation is unusually prevalent among people who commit the sorts of grisly murders that lead to sentences of capital punishment. In *Penry v. Lynaugh*, 492 U.S. 302, 109 S.Ct. 2934, 106 L.Ed.2d 256 (1989), the U.S. Supreme Court held that execution of a mentally retarded prisoner does not necessarily violate the Cruel and Unusual Punishments Clause. However, the Court held that juries must be allowed to consider evidence of mental retardation as a mitigating factor in the sentencing phase of a capital trial. By 2001, eighteen of the thirty-eight states that allowed the death penalty had, either by statute or judicial decision, outlawed the execution of retarded prisoners. In *Atkins v. Virginia*, 536 U.S. 304, 122 S.Ct. 2242, 153 L.Ed.2d 335 (2002), the U.S. Supreme Court reconsidered the issue and held that there was a sufficient national consensus for the Court to prohibit the execution of mentally retarded persons via the Eighth Amendment. Writing for a majority of six justices, Justice John Paul Stevens concluded that mentally retarded persons who meet the law's requirements for criminal responsibility should be tried and punished when they commit crimes. Because of their disabilities in areas of reasoning, judgment and control of their impulses, however, they do not act with the level of moral culpability that characterizes the most serious adult criminal conduct. 536 U.S. at 306, 122 S.Ct. at 2244, 153 L.Ed.2d at 341.

Writing for the three dissenters, Justice Antonin Scalia argued that the decision had "no support in the text or history of the Eighth Amendment." Justice Scalia accused the majority of making policy rather than law, saying, "Seldom has an opinion of this Court rested so obviously upon nothing but the personal views of its members." 536 U.S. at 338, 122 S.Ct. at 2259, 153 L.Ed.2d at 363.

Should Child Rapists Be Subject to the Death Penalty?

We noted that in *Coker v. Georgia*, supra, the Supreme Court said that capital punishment is disproportionate to the crime of rape. In *Kennedy v. Louisiana*, 554 U.S. 407, 128 S.Ct. 2641, 171 L.Ed.2d 525 (2008), the Court continued to narrow the scope of offenses for which the death penalty may be given by striking down a state law allowing child rapists to be sentenced to death. Writing for a sharply divided bench, Justice Anthony Kennedy held that the Eighth Amendment "bars [imposing] the death penalty for the rape of a child where the crime did not result, and was not intended to result, in death of the victim." 554 U.S. at 413, 128 S.Ct. at 2646, 171 L.Ed.2d at 534. Citing "a consensus against the death penalty for child rape," Kennedy observed: "Difficulties in administering the penalty to ensure against its arbitrary and capricious application require adherence to a rule reserving its use, at this stage of evolving standards and in cases of crimes against individuals, for crimes that take the life of the victim." 554 U.S. at 446–447, 128 S.Ct. at 2665, 171 L.Ed.2d at 555. Joined by three of his colleagues, Justice Samuel Alito dissented vigorously, arguing that

> (1) This holding is not supported by the original meaning of the Eighth Amendment; (2) neither *Coker* nor any other prior precedent commands this result; (3) there are no reliable "objective indicia" of a "national consensus" in support of the Court's position; (4) sustaining the constitutionality of the state law before us would not "extend" or "expand" the death penalty; (5) this Court has previously rejected the proposition that the Eighth Amendment is a one-way ratchet that prohibits legislatures from adopting new capital punishment statutes to meet new problems; (6) the worst child rapists exhibit the epitome of moral depravity; and (7) child rape inflicts grievous injury on victims and on society in general. 554 U.S. at 469, 128 S.Ct. at 2677, 171 L.Ed.2d at 569.

Methods of Execution

Until recently, there were five methods of execution in the United States: the electric chair, the gas chamber, the firing squad, hanging, and lethal injection. As a result of litigation invoking the Cruel and Unusual Punishment Clause, as well as changes in state laws, lethal injection has now become the standard means of execution.

Although lethal injection is hailed by many as a more humane alternative to the electric chair and the gas chamber, death penalty opponents are now attacking lethal injection as cruel and unusual punishment. In particular, they claim that the paralyzing agent used as part of the lethal combination of drugs masks the pain and suffering of the person being executed.

In *Baze v. Rees*, 553 U.S. 35, 128 S.Ct. 1520, 170 L.Ed.2d 420 (2008), the Supreme Court upheld Kentucky's protocol for lethal injection, a protocol used by most states that employ lethal injection to administer the death penalty. Had that decision gone the other way, it might well have signaled the demise of the death penalty in America. Despite the Court's decision in *Baze v. Rees*, litigation over lethal injection continues, as lawyers for death row inmates continue to challenge protocols that differ somewhat from Kentucky's.

Critics of lethal injection also point to cases where technicians have struggled to find veins, thus subjecting the condemned inmates to unnecessary stress and discomfort. In one noteworthy case in 2006, the execution of Angel Díaz in Florida was botched when the needle missed the vein. An additional injection was required, and it took more than a half hour for Díaz to die. Of course, defenders of the death penalty tend to dismiss such concerns. For most of them, the fact that capital punishment entails stress and pain is not a serious problem.

The Sentencing Stage of the Criminal Process

presentence investigation An investigation held to aid the court in determining the appropriate punishment before sentencing a convicted criminal.

Every jurisdiction requires that criminal sentences for adults be imposed in open court, although in many instances juvenile offenders may be sentenced *in camera*. In misdemeanor cases, sentencing usually occurs immediately on conviction. In felony cases, where penalties are greater, sentencing may be postponed to allow the court to conduct a **presentence investigation**.

The Presentence Report

presentence report A report containing the results of a presentence investigation.

In many states, as well as in the federal system, the court is required to order a **presentence report** when the offender to be sentenced is a first offender or is under a certain age. In other state jurisdictions, the sentencing judge is accorded discretion in this area. For example, rule 702 of the Pennsylvania Rules of Criminal Procedure provides as follows:

A. Presentence Investigation Report.

1. The sentencing judge may, in the judge's discretion, order a presentence investigation report in any case.

2. The sentencing judge shall place on the record the reasons for dispensing with the presentence investigation report if the judge fails to order a presentence report in any of the following instances:

(a) when incarceration for one year or more is a possible disposition under the applicable sentencing statutes; or

(1) when the defendant is less than twenty-one years old at the time of conviction or entry of a plea of guilty; or

(2) when a defendant is a first offender in that he or she has not heretofore been sentenced as an adult.

3. The presentence investigation report shall include information regarding the circumstances of the offense and the character of the defendant sufficient to assist the judge in determining sentence.

4. The presentence investigation report shall also include a victim impact statement as provided by law.

Rule 703 makes the reports confidential and available only to the sentencing judge, counsel for the state and the defense, and experts appointed by the court to assist the court in sentencing.

In some states, statutes, court rules, or judicial interpretations mandate that courts release a presentence report to the defendant or defendant's counsel, usually allowing some exemptions for sensitive material. In other states, courts have ruled that this is a matter within the discretion of the sentencing judge. In some instances, courts will reveal factual material such as police reports but decline to disclose statements made in confidence to investigators. Often the judicial interpretation depends on the language of the statute or court rule. The Supreme Court requires the release of presentence reports to defendants who may be sentenced to death.

The presentence report sets forth the defendant's history of delinquency or criminality, medical history, family background, economic status, education, employment history, and other information. Much of this information is obtained by probation officers, who interview individuals such as the defendant's family members, friends, and employers. In addition, most jurisdictions allow courts to order physical or mental examinations of defendants. This information can be very useful to a judge who must determine a sentence that is at once fair, humane, and meaningful.

The Sentencing Hearing

sentencing hearing A hearing held by a trial court before the sentence is pronounced.

After the presentence report is completed, a **sentencing hearing** is held. At this hearing, the court considers the evidence received at trial, the presentence report, any evidence offered by either party in aggravation or mitigation of sentence, and any statement the defendant wishes to make. In addition, most jurisdictions require judges to hear arguments concerning various sentencing alternatives. Sentencing is a critical stage of the criminal process, and counsel must be supplied to indigent defendants. *Mempa v. Rhay*, 389 U.S. 128, 88 S.Ct. 254, 19 L.Ed.2d 336 (1967).

Pronouncement of Sentence

pronouncement of sentence Formal announcement of a criminal punishment by a trial judge.

After the judge has digested the sentencing report, heard arguments from counsel and the defendant's statement, and considered the relevant provisions of law, the sentence is pronounced in open court. The **pronouncement of sentence** is the stage when the trial court imposes a penalty on a defendant for the offense of which the defendant has been adjudged guilty. Sentences are usually pronounced by the judge who presided at the defendant's trial or the entry of plea. In misdemeanor cases, sentencing often occurs immediately after the entry of a plea or a finding of guilty by the judge or jury. In felony cases, the pronouncement is often delayed until the court has received a presentence investigation report or until the prosecutor and defense counsel have had an opportunity to prepare a presentation. The procedure at the pronouncement stage is generally outlined in the criminal procedure rules of each jurisdiction. See, e.g., Rule 704 of the Pennsylvania Rules of Criminal Procedure.

right of allocution The right of a criminal defendant to make a statement on his or her own behalf before the sentence is pronounced.

The rules of evidence are relaxed during a sentencing proceeding. Traditionally, a defendant has been afforded an opportunity to make a statement on his or her own behalf, a procedure often referred to as the **right of allocution**. Generally, special rules govern the sentencing of a defendant who is insane, and often sentencing must be deferred for a female defendant who is pregnant.

Suspended Sentences and Credit for Time Served

When the trial court sentences a defendant to incarceration, it generally allows the defendant credit against any term of incarceration for all time spent in custody as a result of the charge for which the sentence is imposed. In most instances where defendants are convicted of **noncapital crimes**, courts are authorized to suspend the imposition of the sentence and place defendants on probation or under community control for some determinate period. Statutes often require courts to impose certain conditions (similar to probation conditions) on a defendant whose sentence is suspended. See, e.g., N.J. Stat. Ann. § 2C:45–1. Of course, if the defendant violates conditions set by the court, the original sentence may be imposed. A **suspended sentence** is most often used for first offenses or nonviolent offenses. Authority to suspend a felony conviction is generally limited to a first conviction. See, e.g., La. C. Cr. P. Art. 83.

Concurrent and Consecutive Sentences

A defendant who is convicted of multiple crimes must be given separate sentences for each offense. These sentences may run consecutively or concurrently, usually at the discretion of the sentencing judge. See, e.g., Pa. R. Crim. P. 705. **Concurrent sentencing** in a given case may simply reflect the court's view that **consecutive sentencing** would result in a punishment that is too harsh for the crime. In *Oregon v. Ice*, 555 U.S. 160, 129 S.Ct. 711, 172 L.Ed.2d 517 (2009), Justice Ruth Bader Ginsburg observed:

> Most States continue the common-law tradition: They entrust to judges' unfettered discretion the decision whether sentences for discrete offenses shall be served consecutively or concurrently. In some States, sentences for multiple offenses are presumed to run consecutively, but sentencing judges may order concurrent sentences upon finding cause therefor. Other States, including Oregon, constrain judges' discretion by requiring them to find certain facts before imposing consecutive, rather than concurrent, sentences. 555 U.S. at 163–164, 129 S.Ct. at 714, 172 L.Ed.2d at 522.

Sentencing in Capital Cases

In those cases where the prosecution is permitted by law to seek the death penalty, the sentencing procedure is considerably more complex. As we noted in the discussion of the death penalty, a bifurcated trial is employed. Following the conviction of a defendant for a capital crime, the jury hears testimony in aggravation or mitigation of the sentence. For the jury to hand down the death penalty, it must find beyond a reasonable doubt that the aggravating factors outweigh the mitigating ones. The aggravating factors are specified by law; the mitigating factors are those characteristics of the defendant or the crime that suggest that leniency might be appropriate. Quite often the defense attorney will put the defendant's relatives on the stand to testify about the defendant's redeeming qualities or to generally plead for mercy.

Victim Impact Evidence

Prosecutors counter emotional pleas on the defendant's behalf by presenting **victim impact evidence**. This evidence takes the form of testimony addressing the impact

---

noncapital crimes Crimes that do not carry the ultimate penalty, whether death or life in prison with no possibility of parole.

suspended sentence Trial court's decision to place a defendant on probation or under community control instead of imposing an announced sentence on the condition that the original sentence may be imposed if the defendant violates the conditions of the suspended sentence.

concurrent sentencing The practice by which a trial court imposes separate sentences to be served at the same time.

consecutive sentencing The practice by which a trial court imposes a sentence or sentences to be served following completion of a prior sentence or sentences.

victim impact evidence Evidence relating to the physical, economic, and psychological impact that a crime has on the victim or victim's family.

Payne v. Tennessee, 501 U.S. 808, 111 S.Ct. 2597, 115 L.Ed.2d 720 (1991)

After drinking beer and injecting cocaine, Pervis Tyrone Payne entered an apartment occupied by twenty-eight-year-old Charisse Christopher, her two-year-old daughter Lacie, and her three-year-old son Nicholas. After Charisse resisted Payne's sexual advances, Payne became enraged and repeatedly stabbed the woman and her two children with a kitchen knife. Only the three-year old boy survived the attack. Payne was convicted by a jury on two counts of first-degree murder and one count of assault with intent to commit murder in the first degree. During the penalty phase of Payne's trial, the State presented the testimony of Charisse's mother, who talked about how the little boy who survived the attack still cried for his mother. In his closing argument to the jury, the prosecutor commented at some length on this "victim impact evidence." Payne was sentenced to death for each of the murders and to 30 years in prison for the assault. The Tennessee Supreme Court upheld Payne's convictions and sentence. On certiorari, the U.S. Supreme Court, splitting 6–3, affirmed the judgment, thereby receding from its holdings in prior cases. Writing for the Court, Chief Justice Rehnquist opined that the "State may legitimately conclude that evidence about the victim and about the impact of the murder on the victim's family is relevant to the jury's decision as to whether or not the death penalty should be imposed." Dissenting, Justice John Paul Stevens observed, "Until today our capital punishment jurisprudence has required that any decision to impose the death penalty be based solely on evidence that tends to inform the jury about the character of the offense and the character of the defendant. Evidence that serves no purpose other than to appeal to the sympathies or emotions of the jurors has never been considered admissible."

of the murder on the victim and the victim's family, including the physical, economic, and psychological effects of the crime. For example, the victim's surviving spouse might be called to testify to the toll the homicide has taken on the family. Needless to say, such testimony is often fraught with emotion and can have a powerful impact on the jury.

In 1987, the U.S. Supreme Court struck down a Maryland statute requiring that a **victim impact statement** be considered during the penalty phase of capital cases. *Booth v. Maryland*, 482 U.S. 496, 107 S.Ct. 2529, 96 L.Ed.2d 440 (1987). The Court said that such statements raised the real possibility that death sentences would be based on irrelevant considerations. Four years later, however, in *Payne v. Tennessee*, 501 U.S. 808, 111 S.Ct. 2597, 115 L.Ed.2d 720 (1991), the Court overruled its decision in *Booth*. According to Chief Justice William Rehnquist, who wrote the majority opinion in *Payne*, the *Booth* decision "deprives the State of the full moral force of its evidence and may prevent the jury from having before it all the information necessary to determine the proper punishment for a first-degree murder." 501 U.S. at 825, 111 S.Ct. at 2608, 115 L.Ed.2d at 735. Notwithstanding the Supreme Court's decision in *Payne v. Tennessee*, appellate courts may still find that a particular victim impact statement has impermissibly injected too much emotionalism into the jury's sentencing deliberations.

victim impact statement Statement read into the record during the sentencing phase of a criminal trial to inform the court about the impact of the crime on the victim or victim's family.

What Are Juries Entitled to Know about the Defendant?

In 1994, the Supreme Court also decided two important cases dealing with the information that juries may consider in deciding whether to impose the death penalty. In *Romano v. Oklahoma*, 512 U.S. 1, 114 S.Ct. 2004, 129 L.Ed.2d 1

(1994), the Court held that neither the Eighth Amendment nor the Due Process Clause of the Fourteenth Amendment prohibits capital-sentencing juries from being informed that the defendant is already under sentence of death for another crime. Petitioner John Romano had already been sentenced to death for robbing and murdering one man when he was tried for another robbery-murder. During the sentencing phase, the prosecution sought to introduce evidence of the former crime and sentence. Romano's attorney objected, claiming that the jury knowledge of the previous death sentence would diminish its sense of responsibility in imposing another death sentence. The trial judge overruled the objection, and Romano was sentenced to death. Writing for the Supreme Court, Chief Justice Rehnquist observed that although the prior death sentence was irrelevant, the Constitution "does not establish a federal code of evidence to supersede state evidentiary rules in capital sentencing proceedings." 512 U.S. at 12, 114 S.Ct. at 2011, 129 L.Ed.2d at 13.

Chief Justice Rehnquist's observation in *Romano* notwithstanding, the Court in *Simmons v. South Carolina*, 512 U.S. 154, 114 S.Ct. 2187, 129 L.Ed.2d 133 (1994), held that defendants facing the death penalty have a right to tell juries if the only alternative to a death sentence is life imprisonment without the possibility of parole. Jonathan Simmons was convicted of murdering a seventy-nine-year-old woman in her home. Because Simmons had been convicted twice before of sexually assaulting elderly women, South Carolina law provided that he would be ineligible for parole if sentenced to prison. Over defense counsel's objection, the trial judge granted the prosecution's motion to exclude any mention of parole during the trial. During the sentencing phase, the court denied the defense counsel's request to explain to the jury that a life sentence carried no possibility of parole. Finally, during deliberations the judge told the jury not to consider whether Simmons could be paroled if he was sentenced to life imprisonment. Simmons was sentenced to death. The Supreme Court remanded the case for resentencing, saying that the trial judge's refusal to provide the requested instruction constituted a denial of due process. In dissent, Justice Scalia accused the Court of trying to impose "Federal Rules of Death Penalty Evidence" on the states. 512 U.S. at 185, 114 S.Ct. at 2205, 129 L.Ed.2d at 156.

The Role of the Judge in Capital Sentencing

States vary as to the role of the trial judge in determining death sentences. Under the capital sentencing procedures in Georgia, where the jury finds at least one statutory aggravating circumstance and recommends the death penalty, the trial judge must sentence the defendant to death. Official Ga. Code Ann. § 17-10-31. In other states, a different method is employed. For example, in Florida the trial court decides whether to accept a jury's recommendation of death or life imprisonment. See *Spaziano v. Florida*, 468 U.S. 447, 104 S.Ct. 3154, 82 L.Ed.2d 340 (1984). Where a jury recommends life imprisonment and the trial court overrides that recommendation and imposes the death penalty, the decision is carefully scrutinized by the Florida Supreme Court. For the trial court's override to be sustained, the life imprisonment recommendation by the jury must have been unreasonable. If the state supreme court's review finds there was a reasonable basis for the jury's recommendation, it reverses the court's imposition of the death penalty and remands the case for a sentence as recommended by the jury. *Buford v. State*, 570 So.2d 923 (Fla. 1990).

What Happens When a Capital Jury Is Deadlocked on the Sentence?

When the jury in a capital case cannot agree on the appropriate sentence, sentencing normally reverts to the judge. As we have seen, in some jurisdictions, the judge is barred from imposing the death penalty without a jury recommendation. In such instances, the judge must sentence the defendant to any lesser sentence authorized by law. The judge is not required to instruct the jury with regard to the consequences of deadlock, however. *Jones v. United States*, 527 U.S. 373, 119 S.Ct. 2090, 144 L.Ed.2d 370 (1999).

Granting and Revoking Probation

Probation is a sentencing option in the federal courts and in most state courts. Under federal law, a defendant who has been found guilty of an offense may be sentenced to a term of probation unless (1) the offense is a felony where the maximum term of imprisonment authorized is twenty-five years or more, life imprisonment, or death; (2) the offense is one for which probation has been expressly precluded; or (3) the defendant is sentenced at the same time to a term of imprisonment for the same or a different offense. A defendant who has been convicted for the first time of a domestic violence crime must be sentenced to a term of probation if not sentenced to a term of imprisonment. 18 U.S.C.A. § 3561. Probation terms for a felony must not be less than one nor more than five years and for a misdemeanor not more than five years. 18 U.S.C.A. § 3561. Certain conditions of probation are mandatory, and others are discretionary with the federal judge who imposes probation. 18 U.S.C.A. § 3563.

In most states, the term of probation is limited to the maximum statutory term of confinement for the particular offense. As in federal cases, probation is subject to mandatory and special conditions. Probation is often combined with a fine, restitution to the victim, or a short term of incarceration to give the probationer "a taste of jail." Because the procedures in state courts vary widely, it is difficult to generalize; however, it is important for the probationer to receive a written order incorporating the terms of probation and outlining his or her responsibilities to the probation officer and the court. Courts must guard against imposing vague conditions of probation or delegating overly broad authority to probation officers.

Revocation of Probation

In every jurisdiction, the commission of a felony while on probation is grounds for revocation. In many jurisdictions, certain misdemeanors likewise qualify as grounds for revocation. In addition, the violation of any substantive condition of probation is grounds for revocation. Typically, a probation officer is vested with broad discretion in determining when to seek revocation of probation.

In August 2006, the South Carolina Supreme Court upheld revocation of probation where the probationer violated a condition "that probationer not associate with people who had criminal records." The court found the condition was not so overly broad that it violated due process. The court, however, explained that the evidence must show that the probationer knew about the person's criminal record during the period of association before the condition may be applied to revoke probation. *State v. Allen*, 634 S.E.2d 653 (S.C. 2006).

A probationer facing the loss of freedom is entitled to a fair hearing. At this hearing the probationer has the right to call favorable witnesses, to confront hostile witnesses, and to be represented by counsel. *Gagnon v. Scarpelli*, 411 U.S. 778, 93 S.Ct. 1756, 36 L.Ed.2d 656 (1973). In *Gagnon*, the Supreme Court said that indigent probationers may have a constitutional right to have counsel appointed at revocation hearings, depending on the complexity of the issues involved, and that if counsel is not provided, the judge must state the reason. In practice, counsel is usually provided. There is a statutory right to appointment of counsel for those financially unable to obtain counsel in federal probation revocation proceedings. 18 U.S.C.A. § 3006A.

The Federal Rules of Criminal Procedure require a two-step process before probation can be revoked: a preliminary hearing to determine if there is probable cause to believe that a violation occurred and, if so, a revocation hearing. Fed. R. Crim. P. 32.1(b).

The rules of evidence applicable at criminal trials are relaxed at probation-revocation hearings. For example, in federal courts hearsay evidence may be received over a probationer's objection because a probation revocation hearing is not a criminal trial. *United States v. Miller*, 514 F.2d 41 (9th Cir. 1975). In most state courts, "reliable" hearsay evidence is admissible in probation revocation proceedings. This most commonly applies to laboratory reports and other documentation. Nevertheless, a legion of state appellate court decisions hold that probation cannot be revoked solely on the basis of hearsay evidence. See *Turner v. State*, 293 So.2d 771 (Fla. App. 1974). Thus, an appellate court found insufficient evidence that a defendant had violated a condition of his probation prohibiting changing residence without permission where the only evidence of violation was hearsay testimony from the defendant's probation officer that the probationer's mother stated that she did not know where he was. *Cito v. State*, 721 So.2d 1192 (Fla. App. 1998). Some state courts hold hearsay evidence to be inadmissible in probation revocation proceedings. See, for example, *Wolcott v. State*, 604 S.E.2d 478 (Ga. 2004), where the Georgia Supreme Court held that hearsay evidence is inadmissible but found it harmless in the particular case because it was cumulative to other admissible evidence that established the defendant had committed an offense that constituted a probation violation.

As noted, a large number of state appellate court decisions make it clear that hearsay evidence alone is not sufficient to revoke probation. See *Nadeau v. State*, 920 So.2d 206 (Fla. App. 2006). Most revocation cases do not reach the highest state courts, but in 1993 the Tennessee Supreme Court held that probation could not be revoked based solely on a lab test indicating that the probationer had used illicit drugs where the technician who performed the drug test was not available to be cross-examined at the revocation hearing. *State v. Wade*, 863 S.W.2d 406 (Tenn. 1993).

Courts have frequently articulated that the standard to be applied at revocation hearings is not "reasonable doubt" or "preponderance of evidence," but whether from the evidence presented the court is reasonably satisfied of the probationer's violation. Nor is there any requirement that a probationer be granted a jury trial in revocation proceedings, even when those proceedings are predicated on a violation of a criminal law. *United States v. Czajak*, 909 F.2d 20 (1st Cir. 1990). Often a court will modify rather than revoke a defendant's probation, but if the court does revoke probation, statutory and decisional law generally permit it to sentence the defendant to any term that would have been appropriate for the underlying offense. And although a probationer may not be sentenced on revocation for the conduct that constituted the probation violation, it is proper for the trial court to consider the probationer's conduct while on probation to assess a potential for rehabilitation. See, e.g., *People v. Vilces*, 542 N.E.2d 1269 (Ill. App. 1989).

Bearden v. Georgia, 461 U.S. 660, 103 S.Ct. 2064, 76 L.Ed.2d 221 (1983)

Danny Bearden pled guilty to charges of burglary and theft. Pursuant to Georgia's First Offenders Act, Official Code Ga. Ann. § 27-2727 *et seq.*, current version at § 42-8-60, he was placed on three years' probation and was required to pay a $500 fine and make restitution of $250. After making some payments, Bearden was laid off from work and became unable to continue making payments. As a result, the trial court revoked his probation and sentenced him to serve the remaining portion of his term of probation in prison. The U.S. Supreme Court reversed the revocation of probation because the trial court had made no finding that Bearden was responsible for his failure to make the required payments. Nevertheless, the Court said, "If the probationer willfully refused to pay or failed to make sufficient bona fide efforts legally to acquire the resources to pay, the court may revoke probation."

The violation of any valid substantive condition is grounds for revocation of probation, but in practice courts may hold that a minor or technical violation, such as a probationer's being a day late in filing a monthly report, is not sufficient for a court to revoke probation.

Statutory Approaches to Incarceration

Once it has been determined that a defendant is to be incarcerated, several variations of the type and extent of the defendant's sentence may be available. The legislative trend has been to limit judicial discretion in imposing incarceration by statutorily providing whether the defendant is subject to an indeterminate or determinate sentence and whether a minimum mandatory term is to be imposed. In recent years, in an attempt to cope with the problem of recidivism, legislatures have enacted laws providing for enhanced terms of incarceration.

Indeterminate Sentencing

For much of the twentieth century, legislatures commonly allowed judges to sentence criminals to imprisonment for indeterminate periods. This was designed to assist corrections officials in rehabilitating offenders. Officials were permitted to hold a criminal in custody until they determined that he or she was rehabilitated. Under this system, release from prison took the form of parole. Abuses of the system, combined with the decline of popular support for rehabilitation, have led most jurisdictions to abandon the concept of **indeterminate sentencing**.

indeterminate sentencing Form of criminal sentencing where criminals are sentenced to prison for indeterminate periods until corrections officials determine that rehabilitation has been accomplished.

Notwithstanding the trend away from indeterminate sentencing, a number of state laws retain indeterminate sentencing for youthful offenders. For example, New Jersey law specifies the following:

Any person who, at time of sentencing, is less than 16 years of age and who has been convicted of a crime may be sentenced to an indeterminate term at the Youth Correctional Institution Complex, . . . in the case of men, and to the Correctional Institute for Women, . . . in the case of women, instead of the sentences otherwise authorized by the code. N.J. Stat. Ann. § 2C:43-5.

In *State v. Styker*, 619 A.2d 1016 (N.J. Super. 1993), the court pointed out that while the youthful offender law offers the benefits of rehabilitation in certain instances, "its application is now merely an option, the exercise of which is reserved solely for those limited cases where the sentencing court, in its sound discretion, deems it to be appropriate." *Id.* at 1024.

Definite and Determinate Sentencing

definite sentencing
Legislatively determined sentencing with no discretion given to judges or corrections officials to individualize punishment.

At the opposite extreme from indeterminate sentencing is **definite sentencing**. The concept here is to eliminate discretion and ensure that offenders who commit the same crimes are punished equally. The definite sentence is set by the legislature, with no leeway for judges or corrections officials to individualize punishment. Under **determinate sentencing**, a variation of the definite sentence, the judge sets a fixed term of years within statutory parameters, and the offender is required to serve that term without the possibility of early release. Although the sentence is for a fixed term, these laws often allow the trial court to increase the term if it finds one or more aggravating circumstances.

determinate sentencing The process of sentencing whereby the judge sets a fixed term of years within statutory parameters and the offender must serve that term without possibility of early release.

Indefinite Sentencing

indefinite sentencing Form of criminal sentencing whereby a judge imposes a term of incarceration within statutory parameters and corrections officials determine actual time served through parole or other means.

The most common statutory approach to sentencing is referred to as **indefinite sentencing**. Here, there is judicial discretion to impose sentences within a range of prescribed minimum and maximum penalties for specific offenses. What distinguishes indefinite from determinate sentencing is that indefinite sentencing allows early release from prison on parole. This example of a statute that permits indefinite sentencing is drawn from the New Jersey Code:

> Except as otherwise provided, a person who has been convicted of a crime may be sentenced to imprisonment, as follows: (1) In the case of a crime of the first degree, for a specific term of years which shall be fixed by the court and shall be between 10 years and 20 years; (2) In the case of a crime of the second degree, for a specific term of years which shall be fixed by the court and shall be between 5 years and 10 years; (3) In the case of a crime of the third degree, for a specific term of years which shall be fixed by the court and shall be between 3 years and 5 years; (4) In the case of a crime of the fourth degree, for a specific term which shall be fixed by the court and shall not exceed 18 months. N.J. Stat. Ann. § 2C:43-6(a).

JURISPRUDENCE

Cunningham v. California, 549 U.S. 270, 127 S.Ct. 856, 166 L.Ed.2d 856 (2007)

John Cunningham was tried by jury and convicted in a California court of continuous sexual abuse of a child under the age of fourteen. The jury found him guilty but made no factual findings. The California determinate sentencing law required the trial court to sentence Cunningham to twelve years unless it found one or more additional facts in aggravation. The trial court found several aggravating factors and sentenced Cunningham to an additional four years' imprisonment. The sentence was affirmed by the state courts. The U.S. Supreme Court granted review and on January 22, 2007, held that California's determinate sentencing law, which authorized a judge, not a jury, to find facts exposing a convicted defendant to an elevated sentence, violated a defendant's right to trial by jury. Writing for a 6–3 majority, Justice Ruth Bader Ginsburg observed that the jury's verdict alone limited the permissible sentence to twelve years and that by sentencing Cunningham to an additional four years based on the trial court's fact finding, the trial court deprived him of his right to a jury trial under the Sixth Amendment.

Except for certain offenses where a mandatory minimum sentence applies, New Jersey judges retain discretion to impose probation, fines, or other alternatives to incarceration. N.J. Stat. Ann. § 2C:43-2. If the judge opts for imprisonment, the judge's discretion is channeled as indicated earlier. The New Jersey scheme qualifies as indefinite sentencing because in most cases the law allows offenders to be released on parole before the completion of their prison terms.

Mandatory Minimum Sentencing

Mandatory sentences result from legislative mandates that offenders who commit certain crimes must be sentenced to prison terms for minimum periods. Under mandatory minimum sentencing, judges have no option to place offenders on probation. Most often, mandatory sentences are required for violent crimes, especially those involving the use of firearms. For example, Iowa law mandates that persons who use firearms in the commission of "forcible felonies" must be sentenced to a five-year minimum prison term with no eligibility for parole until the person has served the minimum sentence of confinement. Iowa Code Ann. § 902.7.

As a result of the "war on drugs" launched in the 1980s, federal law now mandates minimum prison terms for serious drug crimes prosecuted in federal courts. For example, a person charged with possession with the intent to distribute more than five kilograms of cocaine is subject to a mandatory minimum sentence of ten years in prison. See 21 U.S.C.A. § 841(b)(1)(A). In *Melendez v. United States*, 518 U.S. 120, 116 S.Ct. 2057, 135 L.Ed.2d 427 (1996), the U.S. Supreme Court made it clear in a unanimous decision that federal courts have no authority to impose lesser sentences than those mandated by Congress unless prosecutors specifically request such departures. This, of course, provides federal prosecutors substantial leverage in persuading defendants to provide evidence against other suspects, which is particularly useful in prosecuting drug distribution conspiracies.

Mandatory minimum sentences for federal drug crimes have contributed to prison overcrowding. Moreover, a difference in how the law treated crack and powder cocaine contributed to the racial imbalance in the federal prisons. Under the Anti-Drug Abuse Act of 1986, 21 U.S.C.A. § 841, possession of "crack" cocaine was subject to the same prison term as one hundred times more powder cocaine. Because crack tends to be used more among African Americans and powder tends to be favored by white users, African Americans were being punished much more severely for essentially the same offense. A chorus of criticism of this policy led to the enactment of the Fair Sentencing Act of 2010, Pub. L. 111-220. The new law reduced the ratio between powder and crack cocaine from 100:1 to 18:1. It also eliminated the mandatory five-year minimum sentence that formerly applied to the simple possession of crack cocaine.

Habitual Offender Statutes

In an effort to incapacitate habitual offenders, the laws of many states require automatic increased penalties for persons convicted of repeated felonies. For example, an Iowa law states,

An habitual offender is any person convicted of a class "C" or a class "D" felony, who has twice before been convicted of any felony in a court of this or any other state, or of the United States. An offense is a felony if, by the law under which the person was convicted, it is so classified at the time of the person's conviction. A person sentenced as an habitual offender shall not be eligible for parole until he or she has served the minimum sentence of confinement of three years. Iowa Code Ann. § 902.8.

Most courts hold that habitual offender status is not established if a defendant committed the present offense before having been convicted of a prior offense. Courts have struggled with the issue of whether multiple convictions entered on one day are to be treated as separate or as one conviction, but they usually treat these multiple convictions as one irrespective of whether they arise from one or multiple criminal transactions.

In *Rummel v. Estelle*, 445 U.S. 263, 100 S.Ct. 1133, 63 L.Ed.2d 382 (1980), the U.S. Supreme Court upheld a life sentence imposed under the Texas habitual offender statute mandating life terms for persons convicted of three felonies. Rummel was convicted of obtaining $120.75 under false pretenses after previously being convicted of the fraudulent use of a credit card to obtain $80.00 worth of goods and passing a forged check for $28.36. After his third felony conviction, Rummel was sentenced to life imprisonment.

Solem v. Helm, 463 U.S. 277, 103 S.Ct. 3001, 77 L.Ed.2d 637 (1983), the Court vacated a life sentence without parole under a South Dakota **habitual-offender statute**. Because the defendant's convictions involved nonviolent felonies, the Court found the life sentence to be "significantly disproportionate" and thus invalid under the Eighth Amendment.

habitual offender statute A law that imposes an additional punishment on a criminal who has previously been convicted of crimes.

"Three Strikes and You're Out"

three strikes and you're out Popular term for a statute that provides for mandatory life imprisonment for a convicted felon who has been previously convicted of two or more serious felonies.

A variation on the habitual offender law is known colloquially as **three strikes and you're out**. In 1994, California voters overwhelmingly approved a ballot initiative under which persons convicted of a third violent or "serious" felony would be incarcerated for twenty-five years to life. Prosecutors immediately availed themselves of this new weapon, but in many instances the new law led to controversial results. In one well-known case, a man received twenty-five years to life after being convicted of robbery stemming from an incident where he stole a slice of pizza. *People v. Romero*, 917 P.2d 628 (Cal. 1996). In reversing the sentence, the California Supreme Court said that judges must retain the power to set sentences in furtherance of justice.

The 1994 Federal Crime Bill provided for mandatory life sentences for persons convicted in federal court of a "serious violent felony" after having been previously convicted, in federal or state court, of two "serious violent felonies" or "one or more serious violent felonies and one or more serious drug offenses; and each serious violent felony or serious drug offense used as a basis for sentencing under this subsection, other than the first, was committed after the defendant's conviction of the preceding serious violent felony or serious drug offense." 18 U.S.C.A. § 3559. Currently, the federal government and most states have some form of habitual offender or "three-strikes" statute. In most states, prosecutions under these statutes are relatively infrequent. In 2003, the U.S. Supreme Court upheld California's three-strikes law against constitutional challenges based on the Eighth Amendment's Cruel and Unusual Punishments Clause. *Ewing v. California*, 538 U.S. 11, 123 S.Ct. 1179, 155 L.Ed.2d 108 (2003); *Lockyer v. Andrade*, 538 U.S. 63, 123 S.Ct. 1166, 155 L.Ed.2d 144 (2003).

Ewing v. California, 538 U.S. 11, 123 S.Ct. 1179, 155 L.Ed.2d 108 (2003)

Gary Ewing was convicted of grand theft for stealing several golf clubs worth nearly $1,000. In 2000, when Ewing committed this crime, he was on parole after having served six years in prison for robbery and burglary committed in the fall of 1993. Aptly described by the Supreme Court as "no stranger to the criminal justice system," Ewing had previously been convicted of grand theft auto (1988), petit theft (1990), battery (1992), burglary (January 1993), possession of drug paraphernalia (February 1993), appropriating lost property (July 1993), and unlawful possession of a firearm and trespassing (September 1993). After being convicted of grand theft for stealing the golf clubs, Ewing was sentenced under the three-strikes law to twenty-five years to life. In a 5–4

decision, the Supreme Court upheld Ewing's sentence and the three-strikes statute on which it was based. However, the Court failed to produce a majority opinion. Writing for a plurality of three justices, Justice O'Connor concluded that Ewing's sentence was constitutionally permissible as it was not "grossly disproportionate" to his offenses. The remaining members of the majority, Justices Thomas and Scalia, rejected the approach taken by Justice O'Connor. In their view, the Eighth Amendment "was aimed at excluding only certain *modes* of punishment, and was not a 'guarantee against disproportionate sentences.'" Writing for the four dissenters, Justice Stephen Breyer concluded that Ewing's sentence was "grossly disproportionate" inasmuch as it was "2 to 3 times the length of sentences that other jurisdictions would impose in similar circumstances."

Truth in Sentencing

truth in sentencing Laws requiring that people sentenced to prison serve a specified proportion of their sentences.

Federal Sentencing Reform Act of 1984 A federal act directing the promulgation of sentencing guidelines.

good-time credit Credit toward early release from prison based on good behavior during confinement.

Truth in sentencing refers to a movement that began in the 1980s to close the gap between the sentences imposed by courts and the time actually served in prison. Prior to the enactment of truth-in-sentencing laws, the average prisoner served less than half the sentence in prison before being paroled. The **Federal Sentencing Reform Act of 1984** dramatically toughened federal sentencing policies by abolishing parole, ending **good-time credit** (time off for good behavior in prison), and prohibiting judges from imposing suspended sentences. Of course, these reforms applied only to the federal justice system. In 1994, Congress provided a strong financial incentive to the states to change their sentencing laws. The Violent Crime Control and Law Enforcement Act of 1994 provided federal grants to states that conform to the federal truth-in-sentencing guideline, which mandates actual confinement for at least 85 percent of the court-imposed prison sentence. By 2001, more than two-thirds of the states had adopted truth-in-sentencing laws to comply with the federal guideline. Since then, budgetary pressures have led some states to repeal or liberalize these laws.

Penalty Enhancement

Another approach to sentencing that has gained popularity in recent years is enhancing or extending penalties based on characteristics of the crime or the victim. For example, in an effort to strengthen law enforcement in the war on drugs, the Violent Crime Control and Law Enforcement Act of 1994 included several provisions for enhanced penalties. Drug trafficking in prisons and "drug-free" zones, and illegal drug use in or smuggling drugs into federal prisons, are now subject to enhanced penalties. See 42 U.S.C.A. §§ 14051, 14052.

Enhanced Penalties for Hate Crimes

Throughout the United States, recent years have seen growing concern over "hate crimes," crimes where victims are targeted on the basis of race, gender, or other characteristics. The federal government and many states currently have laws increasing the severity of punishment in hate crime cases. In 1993, the U.S. Supreme Court upheld a Wisconsin statute of this type. *Wisconsin v. Mitchell,* 508 U.S. 476, 113 S. Ct. 2194, 124 L.Ed.2d 436 (1993). Stressing that the statute was aimed at conduct rather than belief, the Court held that increasing punishment because the defendant targeted the victim on the basis of his race does not infringe the defendant's freedom of conscience as protected by the First Amendment.

penalty enhancement statutes Sentencing laws that provide for increased penalties when certain conditions were present in crimes—for example, the racial motivations of the perpetrator.

Typically, **penalty enhancement statutes** require that a judge find by a preponderance of the evidence that a crime was racially motivated before applying penalty enhancement during sentencing. In a decision with far-reaching implications, the U.S. Supreme Court in June 2000 ruled that any fact that increases criminal punishment beyond the statutory maximum (other than a prior conviction) must be submitted to a jury and proved beyond a reasonable doubt. *Apprendi v. New Jersey,* 530 U.S. 466, 120 S.Ct. 2348, 147 L.Ed.2d 435 (2000). This 5–4 decision raises questions about numerous statutory sentencing schemes under which particular sentencing determinations are based on facts found by judges during sentencing rather than by juries as part of the trial. In a later 5–4 decision, *Oregon v. Ice,* 555 U.S. 160, 129 S.Ct. 711, 172 L.Ed.2d 517 (2009), the Court, in an opinion by Justice Ginsburg, ruled that the Sixth Amendment, as construed in *Apprendi,* does not prohibit judges from finding facts necessary to the imposition of consecutive, rather than concurrent, sentences for multiple offenses. Writing for four dissenting justices, Justice Scalia argued that to permit judges to increase the presumed sentence based on facts found by the judge rather than a jury violates the Sixth Amendment as interpreted in *Apprendi.*

JURISPRUDENCE

Apprendi v. New Jersey, 530 U.S. 466, 120 S.Ct. 2348, 147 L.Ed.2d 435 (2000)

Charles Apprendi fired several gunshots into a house occupied by an African-American family and also made a statement that he did not want that family in his neighborhood. Apprendi was charged with second-degree possession of a firearm for an unlawful purpose. After Apprendi pleaded guilty, the prosecutor filed a motion to enhance the sentence, due to race being an underlying motivation of the offense. The trial court found that the shooting was racially motivated and sentenced Apprendi to twelve years in prison on the firearms charge. Apprendi appealed the sentence on the grounds that the Due Process Clause of the Fourteenth Amendment requires that a finding used to enhance a penalty must be proved to a jury beyond a reasonable doubt. The state appellate courts affirmed the sentence holding that a judge's finding based on a preponderance of the evidence was sufficient for penalty enhancement. The U.S. Supreme Court reversed, holding that the Constitution "requires that any fact that increases the penalty for a crime beyond the prescribed statutory maximum, other than the fact of a prior conviction, must be submitted to a jury and proved beyond a reasonable doubt." Justice Stevens, speaking for the majority, stated that the "Fourteenth Amendment right to due process and the Sixth Amendment right to trial by jury, taken together, entitle a criminal defendant to a jury determination that he is guilty of every element of the crime with which he is charged, beyond a reasonable doubt." As a result, Apprendi's sentence was overturned and the case remanded for further proceedings.

Sentencing Guidelines

Facing considerable criticism of judicial discretion, which often resulted in great disparities in sentences, Congress and a number of state legislatures adopted **sentencing guidelines**. Some states have adopted voluntary guidelines; others have mandated that sentencing conform to guidelines absent a compelling reason for departing from them.

sentencing guidelines Legislative guidelines mandating that sentencing conform to guidelines absent a compelling reason for departing from them.

The Sentencing Reform Act of 1984

The federal guidelines came into being with the enactment of the Sentencing Reform Act of 1984, now codified at 18 U.S.C.A. §§ 3551 *et seq.* 28 U.S.C.A. §§ 991–998. The new act applies to all crimes committed after November 1, 1987. Its stated purpose was "to establish sentencing policies and practices for the federal criminal justice system that will assure the ends of justice by promulgating detailed guidelines prescribing the appropriate sentences for offenders convicted of federal crimes." To accomplish this, the act created the **United States Sentencing Commission** to establish sentencing guidelines. The commission promulgated guidelines that drastically reduced the discretion of federal judges by establishing a narrow sentencing range, with the requirement that judges who depart from these ranges state in writing their reasons for doing so. In addition, the new act provides for appellate review for sentences and abolishes the U.S. Parole Commission.

United States Sentencing Commission A federal body that proposes guideline sentences for defendants convicted of federal crimes.

In *United States v. Scroggins*, 880 F.2d 1204 (11th Cir. 1989), the Eleventh Circuit Court of Appeals discussed the mechanics of sentencing under the new federal guidelines:

> [T]he district court begins the guidelines sentencing process by determining the circumstances of the defendant's offense conduct, the defendant's criminal history, and any other facts deemed relevant by the guidelines. The court then proceeds to assess the severity of the defendant's offense by applying the guidelines to the facts and circumstances of the defendant's offense conduct. . . . This process yields a numeric "total offense level" that consists of three elements: a "base offense level," which reflects the seriousness of the average offense sentenced under that particular guideline; "specific offense characteristics," which increase or decrease the base offense level in light of various factors considered relevant to the defendant's offense conduct; and "adjustments," which increase or decrease the offense level in light of certain factors considered generally relevant for sentencing purposes. The resulting total offense level can range from 1 (least serious) to 43 (most serious).
>
> Having determined the total offense level, the court next surveys the criminal history of the offender. . . . This inquiry places the defendant within a "criminal history category" that evaluates the need to increase his sentence incrementally to deter him from further criminal activity. By correlating the offense level with the offender's criminal history category on the sentencing table developed by the Sentencing Commission, the court then identifies the "guideline range" for the offender's sentence. . . . In general, the district court must sentence the offender within this range.

Departure from the Guidelines

The sentences prescribed by the guidelines were not intended to be absolute. The sentencing court is permitted to depart from the guidelines if it "finds that there exists an aggravating or mitigating circumstance of a kind, or to a degree, not adequately taken into consideration . . . in formulating the guidelines that should result in a sentence different from that described." *United States v. Aguilar-Pena,*

887 F.2d 347, 349 (1st Cir. 1989). Of course, it is impermissible to depart from the guidelines on the basis of the defendant's race, sex, national origin, religion, or socioeconomic status. *United States v. Burch*, 873 F.2d 765 (5th Cir. 1989). Other factors not ordinarily deemed relevant in determining whether to depart include the defendant's age, education, mental and physical condition, employment history, and family and community ties. *United States v. Lira-Barraza*, 897 F.2d 981 (9th Cir. 1990), n. 5.

In *Nichols v. United States*, 511 U.S. 738, 114 S.Ct. 1921, 128 L.Ed.2d 745 (1994), the Supreme Court overruled precedent and held that a prior misdemeanor conviction in which the defendant was not represented by counsel could form the basis for a two-year sentence enhancement under the federal sentencing guidelines. Acting without counsel, Kenneth Nichols had pleaded no contest to a DUI charge in 1983. In 1990, then represented by counsel, Nichols was convicted of a federal drug conspiracy offense. The judge gave Nichols an enhanced sentence based on the prior DUI conviction. The Supreme Court upheld the enhanced sentence, saying that the sentencing process is a broad inquiry that may bring in information regarding the defendant's past misconduct even if it had not resulted in a criminal conviction. The Court thus went well beyond the facts of the case to permit federal judges broad discretion in handing down enhanced sentences under the sentencing guidelines. Critics of the Court's decision in *Nichols* pointed out that the reason the guidelines were adopted was to reduce judicial discretion in sentencing.

Blakely v. Washington, 542 U.S. 296, 124 S.Ct. 2531, 159 L.Ed.2d 403 (2004), involved a challenge to the Washington sentencing guidelines, which, like the federal guidelines, permitted the trial court to enhance a defendant's sentence based on facts that were not found by a jury. The Supreme Court held that the state trial court's sentencing of a defendant to a prison term above the statutory maximum of the standard range for his offense, on the basis of the sentencing judge's finding that the defendant acted with deliberate cruelty, violated the defendant's Sixth Amendment right to a trial by jury.

Although Congress intended the federal sentencing guidelines to be mandatory, the U.S. Supreme Court's decision in *United States v. Booker*, 543 U.S. 220, 125 S.Ct. 738, 160 L.Ed.2d 621 (2005), effectively relegated the guidelines to an advisory position. Relying on its 2000 decisions in *Apprendi v. New Jersey*, supra, and its 2004 decision in *Blakely v. Washington*, supra, the Court in *Booker* held that, as originally constituted, the guidelines violated the Sixth Amendment right to trial by jury inasmuch as they authorized judges to increase sentences based on factual determinations not made by juries. Rather than invalidate the guidelines altogether, the *Booker* Court chose to strike down the provisions making them mandatory.

In *Booker* the Court held: "Any fact (other than a prior conviction) which is necessary to support a sentence exceeding the maximum authorized by the facts established by a plea of guilty or a jury verdict must be admitted by the defendant or proved to a jury beyond a reasonable doubt." *Booker* at 523 U.S. at 244, 125 S.Ct. at 756, 160 L.Ed.2d at 650. After *Booker* a district court's authority to determine sentencing factors by a preponderance of the evidence endures and does not violate the Due Process Clause of the Fifth Amendment. *United States v. Vaughn,* 430 F.3d 518 (2d Cir. 2005). *Booker,* however, forbids use of a judge's finding of fact, based on a preponderance of the evidence, to increase a defendant's maximum or mandatory punishment. Thus, in *United States v. Mickens,* 453 F.3d 668, 673 (6th Cir. 2006), the court explained that post-*Booker,* the district court retains the ability to make findings of fact based on a preponderance of evidence as long as the court appreciates that the guidelines are advisory, not binding.

In the wake of *Booker*, federal judges are not required to use the sentencing guidelines, but many still do use them on an "advisory" basis. Many cases from the lower federal courts reflected uncertainty with respect to application of the sentencing guidelines. The Supreme Court recognized this and in *Rita v. United States*, 551 U.S. 338, 127 S.Ct. 2456, 168 L.Ed.2d 203 (2007), it held that federal appeals courts hearing challenges of a defendant's sentence may presume that a sentence imposed within properly calculated sentencing guidelines is reasonable.

The State Experience

States have experimented with sentencing guidelines with varying results. Minnesota, which in 1970 was the first state to adopt presumptive sentencing guidelines, has a relatively simple system that has proven to be workable, although it has resulted in a higher incarceration rate. Washington's sentencing guidelines worked reasonably well until the state legislature began to mandate increased penalties overall as well as harsher minimum sentences for particular crimes. This has necessitated that the guidelines be revised. In Tennessee, the commission that established sentencing guidelines was terminated, although the guidelines themselves remain in effect. In Wisconsin, one of the early states to adopt sentencing guidelines, the sentencing commission as well as the guidelines it promulgated have been abolished by the state legislature because of political forces and fiscal pressures.

In 1990, the North Carolina legislature created the Sentencing and Policy Advisory Commission to study and repair a system of sentencing that had become dysfunctional. Due to prison overcrowding, felons were being paroled to the point that the system had become a revolving door. Thus, sentencing guidelines in North Carolina originated not so much from concern for sentencing disparity but from a desire to rationalize a system that had become chaotic. The commission followed the example of states such as Washington and Minnesota in adopting a simplified model of sentencing guidelines. Whereas the federal sentencing guidelines contain forty-three levels of felony offenses, the North Carolina guidelines contain ten levels. Thus far, the system seems to have worked reasonably well. However, it should be noted that North Carolina has eased pressure on the prison system by adopting intermediate measures such as house arrest and electronic monitoring for less serious offenders.

There is still considerable uncertainty about the efficacy of sentencing guidelines. There is evidence that they have reduced sentencing disparities, but they clearly have not eliminated this problem altogether. There is also concern that sentencing guidelines have generally promoted higher incarceration rates and have thus contributed to the problem of prison overcrowding. It is fair to say that to be successful, sentencing guidelines must be accompanied by policies designed to effectively manage prison populations.

Finally, state sentencing guidelines must now be viewed in the wake of the U.S. Supreme Court's decision in *Blakely v. Washington*, supra. There the Court held the State of Washington's sentencing guidelines violated the defendant's Sixth Amendment right to trial by jury to the extent that they allowed a judge to enhance a defendant's criminal sentences beyond the statutory maximum based on facts other than those decided by a jury or confessed to by a defendant.

minimum security facilities Prisons and jails that offer inmates the most freedom of movement within the least secure environment.

maximum security prisons Prisons designed to minimize the movement and maximize the surveillance and control of inmates.

The Rights of Prisoners

Contrary to popular mythology, America's prisons are not country clubs. Although some **minimum security facilities** (like the military base where the Watergate conspirators were confined) are reasonably comfortable, **maximum security prisons** are another story. They are sometimes unsanitary; they are almost all overcrowded. All are violent, dangerous places to live.

The federal courts have made it clear that the Eighth Amendment's prohibition of cruel and unusual punishments imposes obligations on prison administrators to maintain certain standards of confinement. A sizable number of state prison systems have been or are currently under court orders to improve conditions of confinement or reduce overcrowding. Recently, some state courts have begun to focus their attention on the deplorable conditions existing in many city and county jails.

Historically, courts were quite unreceptive to claims brought by prisoners. They essentially adopted a "hands-off" policy, allowing prison officials free rein. In the late 1960s, that began to change as federal and state tribunals examined prison conditions and policies. As the courts signaled their willingness to scrutinize the prisons, litigation in this area mushroomed.

conditions of confinement The conditions under which inmates are held in jails and prisons. These conditions are subject to challenge under the Eighth Amendment's Cruel and Unusual Punishments Clause.

In one dramatic case involving prison conditions, Federal District Judge Frank M. Johnson, Jr. found that the **conditions of confinement** in the Alabama system were barbarous and inhumane, thus violating the Eighth Amendment. Judge Johnson issued a detailed set of requirements to remedy the situation and appointed a special committee to oversee implementation of the order. Moreover, he threatened to close down the prison system unless his requirements were met. *Pugh v. Locke*, 406 F. Supp. 318 (M.D. Ala. 1976), aff'd sub nom. *Newman v. Alabama*, 559 F.2d 283 (5th Cir. 1977).

Perhaps the most notorious story of prison conditions is that of the Arkansas prison system, which was scrutinized in a series of federal lawsuits beginning in 1969 with *Holt v. Sarver*, 309 F. Supp. 362 (E.D. Ark. 1970), aff'd, 442 F.2d 304 (8th Cir. 1971). The most egregious conditions occurred at prison farms run largely by "trusties," senior prisoners entrusted with the job of controlling their fellow inmates. It should be noted that the trusty system is widely condemned by penologists. Under the Arkansas system, trusties smuggled in weapons, liquor, and drugs and sold them to the other inmates. Trusties hoarded food purchased with taxpayers' money and forced the other inmates to pay for their meals. Violence and even torture were commonly used by the trusties in maintaining their grip over the other prisoners. Medical care was almost totally lacking, and conditions of sanitation were miserable. Some prisoners were held in punitive isolation cells for months at a time. Overall, the penal farms were characterized by pervasive filth, disease, and violence.

In a series of decisions handed down during the 1970s, the federal district court issued detailed orders aimed at remedying the conditions in the Arkansas prison system. Especially controversial was an order placing a maximum limit of thirty days on the use of punitive isolation. The Supreme Court had little difficulty upholding this measure on appeal. *Hutto v. Finney*, 437 U.S. 678, 98 S.Ct. 2565, 57 L.Ed.2d 522 (1978).

As currently interpreted, the Eighth Amendment requires that prisoners must be provided with reasonably adequate food, clothing, shelter, medical care, and sanitation. There must also be a reasonable assurance of their personal safety. Nevertheless, the Eighth Amendment does not require that prisoners be furnished everything they deem essential to their physical or psychological well-being. *Newman v. Alabama*, supra. Air conditioning, television, weightlifting equipment, and other nonessential items can be provided or removed at the discretion of prison authorities.

In 1992, the Supreme Court held that a prisoner who is beaten maliciously by guards may bring a civil action for damages based on a claim of cruel and unusual punishment, even if the prisoner does not suffer "significant injuries." *Hudson v. McMillian*, 503 U.S. 1, 112 S.Ct. 995, 117 L.Ed.2d 156 (1992). During the 1990s, prisoners began litigating the question of whether being subjected to environmental tobacco smoke (ETS) amounts to a violation of a prisoner's right to be free from cruel and unusual punishment under the Eighth Amendment. Lower federal courts recognized that the government has a duty to provide a safe environment for those incarcerated in its institutions but had disagreed as to whether exposure to ETS in a penitentiary setting constituted cruel and unusual punishment.

In 1993, the Supreme Court in *Helling v. McKinney*, 509 U.S. 25, 113 S.Ct. 2475, 125 L.Ed.2d 22, squarely faced the issue of whether the health risk posed by involuntary exposure of a prison inmate to ETS can be the basis of a claim for relief under the Eighth Amendment. In its landmark decision, the Court held that a prisoner who alleged that the prison system had, with "deliberate indifference," exposed him to levels of environmental tobacco smoke that posed an unreasonable risk of serious damage to his future health stated an actionable claim under the Eighth Amendment against his custodians.

The Overcrowding Issue

Much of the current litigation challenging conditions of criminal confinement focuses on the problem of prison overcrowding. During the 1980s, the prison population in the United States nearly doubled. Rising crime rates and an increasingly punitive posture adopted by legislatures and courts, combined with fiscal stress, led to an overcrowding crisis in many prison systems. As mandatory sentence laws and sentencing guidelines have required judges to imprison larger numbers of convicted criminals, the number of prisoners has far outstripped the capacity of prisons in the United States. Today most state prisons are filled well beyond design capacity.

Throughout the 1980s, litigation in the federal courts by prisoners increased dramatically. Although the Supreme Court has said that "the Constitution does not mandate comfortable prisons," *Rhodes v. Chapman*, 452 U.S. 337, 101 S.Ct. 2392, 69 L.Ed.2d 59 (1981), lower federal courts have intervened to limit the number of inmates who can be housed in some prisons. The public is relatively unconcerned about prison overcrowding, but prison officials often welcome judicial intervention. Prison overcrowding makes it considerably more difficult to control inmate populations.

The Problem of Prison Rape

One of the most serious problems that a prison inmate can encounter is rape by a fellow inmate. Prison officials have not succeeded in eliminating this brutal aspect of prison life. Smaller, weaker inmates, especially those not aligned with a particular gang, are the most vulnerable to such attack. In recent years the problem has gained national attention, and in July 2003 Congress enacted the Prison Rape Reduction Act. The new act created a commission to examine all issues relating to the problem and requires the Department of Justice to provide assistance to federal, state, and local officials. It envisions the development of national standards applicable to the federal prisons with provisions for grants to encourage the states and local authorities to adopt such standards.

constitutional rights of prison inmates Under modern interpretation of the federal and state constitutions, prisoners retain those constitutional rights that are not inconsistent with the fact that they are confined in a secure environment.

Other Rights of Prisoners

In addition to Eighth Amendment challenges to prison conditions, numerous lawsuits have sought to persuade the courts to recognize other **constitutional**

rights of prison inmates. Traditionally, convicted felons were viewed as having forfeited most, if not all, of their constitutional rights. Thus, even reform-minded judges have been cautious in this area. For the most part they have deferred to prison officials, stressing the traditional view that "lawful incarceration brings about the necessary withdrawal or limitation of many privileges and rights, a retraction justified by the considerations underlying our penal system." *Price v. Johnston*, 334 U.S. 266, 285, 68 S.Ct. 1049, 92 L.Ed. 1356, 1369 (1948). Nevertheless, certain constitutional rights have been recognized. The Supreme Court has held that a prison inmate retains those First Amendment rights "that are not inconsistent with his status as a prisoner or with the legitimate penological objectives of the corrections system." *Pell v. Procunier*, 417 U.S. 817, 822, 94 S.Ct. 2800, 2804, 41 L.Ed.2d 495, 501 (1974).

For example, consider rights arising under the free exercise of religion clause of the First Amendment. Courts are generally receptive to prisoners' rights to possess Bibles, prayer books, and other religious materials, as well as inmates' rights to be visited by the clergy. On the other hand, courts have generally upheld restrictions on religious exercises if they disrupt prison order or routine. See, e.g., *O'Lone v. Estate of Shabazz*, 482 U.S. 342, 107 S.Ct. 2400, 96 L.Ed.2d 282 (1987). If prison officials allow inmates who belong to mainstream religious denominations to attend worship services, however, then members of other religious sects must be given a reasonable opportunity to exercise their religious beliefs as well. *Cruz v. Beto*, 405 U.S. 319, 92 S.Ct. 1079, 31 L.Ed.2d 263 (1972).

One of the most firmly established rights of prisoners is the right of access to the courts. The Supreme Court made it clear decades ago that prison officials may not deny inmates access to the courts or penalize them for using that access. *Ex parte Hull*, 312 U.S. 546, 61 S.Ct. 640, 85 L.Ed. 1034 (1941). Similarly, courts have held that indigent inmates must be furnished writing materials and notary services to assist them in filing petitions and seeking writs from courts. Courts have generally upheld the right of prisoners to meet with counsel in privacy and, in the absence of other forms of legal assistance, to have access to law libraries. See *Bounds v. Smith*, 430 U.S. 817, 97 S.Ct. 1491, 52 L.Ed.2d 72 (1977).

The courts have also recognized that prisoners are entitled to limited rights of expression. For example, prisoners retain a limited right to communicate with the outside world via the mails, although prison officials may limit and censor the mail prisoners send and receive, provided there is no interference with attorney–client relationships. *Lee v. Tahash*, 352 F.2d 970 (8th Cir. 1965).

Prison officials also have broad latitude to restrict visitation privileges if there is reason to believe that an inmate is receiving contraband smuggled into the prison by visitors. *Kentucky Department of Corrections v. Thompson*, 490 U.S. 454, 109 S.Ct. 1904, 104 L.Ed.2d 506 (1989). Likewise, prison regulations impinging on inmates' interests in free assembly and association have been consistently upheld. See, for example, *Jones v. North Carolina Prisoners' Labor Union, Inc.*, 433 U.S. 119, 97 S.Ct. 2532, 53 L.Ed.2d 629 (1977), where the Supreme Court refused to extend First Amendment protection to an effort to organize a labor union among prisoners. Obviously, prison is by definition antithetical to the ideas of freedom of assembly and freedom of association. Congress enacted the Ensign Amendment as part of the Omnibus Consolidated Appropriations Act of 1997. Pub. L. No. 104-208, § 614, 109 Stat. 3009-66 (1996). The Ensign Amendment prohibits prisons from using federal funds to distribute any information or material that is sexually explicit or features nudity. The law exempts any nudity featured for purposes of medical, educational, or anthropological content.

Prison Disciplinary Measures

prison disciplinary measures Steps taken by prison officials to punish prisoners for misconduct, largely accomplished by removing good-time credits that prisoners earn for exemplary behavior in prison.

The federal courts have imposed limits on **prison disciplinary measures** such as corporal punishment and the extended use of **punitive isolation**. Today, at least in most state prisons, discipline is largely accomplished by granting and removing good-time credit—that is, early release for good behavior. If officials pursue this policy, then due process demands that certain procedural requirements be observed before good time credit is removed for disciplinary purposes. Specifically, there must be written notice of the disciplinary action, and the inmate has the right to an administrative hearing with a written record. The inmate must be accorded the right to produce evidence refuting the charges of misconduct and may even call witnesses on his or her behalf. *Wolff v. McDonnell*, 418 U.S. 539, 94 S.Ct. 2963, 41 L.Ed.2d 935 (1974). These rights have not been extended to allow an inmate to have counsel present at such a hearing. *Baxter v. Palmigiano*, 425 U.S. 308, 96 S.Ct. 1551, 47 L.Ed.2d 810 (1976).

punitive isolation Solitary confinement of a person who is incarcerated.

Parole and Its Revocation

parole Conditional release from jail or prison of a person who has served part of his or her sentence.

Historically, the federal government and most states provided for early release from prison on **parole** for those inmates who could demonstrate to the parole board's satisfaction their willingness to conform their conduct to the requirements of the law. In recent years, parole has been abolished or restricted greatly in many jurisdictions. This generally corresponds to the "truth-in-sentencing" movement described above. Naturally, there are also provisions by which parole can be revoked if the offender violates the conditions of release. As with internal prison disciplinary actions, the revocation of parole is affected by due process considerations. Essentially, before parole can be revoked, the parolee has the right to a hearing within a reasonable time after being retaken into custody. *Morrissey v. Brewer*, 408 U.S. 471, 92 S.Ct. 2593, 33 L.Ed.2d 484 (1972). However, the Supreme Court has stressed the informality of this hearing, saying that "the process should be flexible enough to consider evidence including letters, affidavits, and other material that would not be admissible in an adversary criminal trial." 408 U.S. at 489, 92 S.Ct. at 2604, 33 L.Ed.2d at 499. In practice, courts generally admit any relevant evidence that is not privileged, but as previously pointed out in respect to revocation of probation, courts generally do not allow revocation of parole based solely on hearsay evidence. See, e.g., *Grello v. Commonwealth*, 477 A.2d 45 (Pa. Cmwlth. 1984). A year after its decision in *Morrissey v. Brewer*, the Supreme Court held that the right to counsel may apply to **parole revocation hearings**, depending on the complexity of the issues involved. *Gagnon v. Scarpelli*, supra.

parole revocation hearings Administrative hearings held for the purpose of determining whether an offender's parole should be revoked.

The Rights of Crime Victims

victims' rights Refers to the various rights possessed by victims of crimes.

Although crime is by definition an injury to society as a whole, we must not forget that most serious crimes injure individual victims, often quite severely. The injury may transcend physical or economic injury to include emotional hardship. During the 1960s, the dominant concern of the criminal law was for the rights of the accused. In the 1990s, the trend was to recognize the rights of crime victims. Most states have adopted constitutional amendments specifically recognizing **victims' rights**, while others have adopted statutes along these lines. See, e.g., West's Ann. Cal. Penal Code § 679 *et seq*. During the 1990s, a proposal to add a victims' rights amendment to the

U.S. Constitution surfaced in Congress. Although that measure did not pass, it provided the impetus for Congress to enact legislation in this area.

In 2004, Congress enacted the **Crimes Victims' Rights Act (CVRA)**. Title 18 U.S.C.A. 3771 provides eight basic rights:

Crime victims' rights.

Crime Victims' Rights Act (CVRA) Federal legislation that provides eight basic rights for crime victims where crimes are prosecuted in the federal system.

(a) A crime victim has the following rights:

(1) The right to be reasonably protected from the accused.

(2) The right to reasonable, accurate, and timely notice of any public court proceeding, or any parole proceeding, involving the crime or of any release or escape of the accused.

(3) The right not to be excluded from any such public court proceeding, unless the court, after receiving clear and convincing evidence, determines that testimony by the victim would be materially altered if the victim heard other testimony at that proceeding.

(4) The right to be reasonably heard at any public proceeding in the district court involving release, plea, sentencing, or any parole proceeding.

(5) The reasonable right to confer with the attorney for the Government in the case.

(6) The right to full and timely restitution as provided in law.

(7) The right to proceedings free from unreasonable delay.

(8) The right to be treated with fairness and with respect for the victim's dignity and privacy.

18 U.S.C.A. 3771(b) provides that "the court shall ensure that the crime victim is afforded the rights described in subsection (a)."

The federal Crime Victims' Rights Act has become an important component in the federal criminal justice system. It not only assists victims of federal crimes, but it also provides an impetus to states to update their victims' rights laws. Most crimes are prosecuted under state laws, and each state has now adopted constitutional amendments or has enacted laws providing crime victims with rights in the criminal justice process. The National Crime Victims Law Institute, organized in 1997, is a "national resource for crime victim lawyers and victims to support the assertion and enforcement of victims' rights in criminal and civil processes." Its website, www.ncvli.org, includes a wealth of information on rights of crime victims, including a listing of victims' rights laws in each state.

The Uniform Victims of Crime Act

Uniform Victims of Crime Act (UVCA) A law proposed by the Uniform Law Commission designed to provide uniform rights and procedures concerning crime victims.

The **Uniform Victims of Crime Act (UVCA)** is an attempt to lend uniformity to the patchwork of victims' rights laws that now exists at the state level. The UVCA was developed by the Uniform Law Commission, a voluntary association representing the legal profession. Like the Model Penal Code developed by the American Law Institute, the UVCA has no status as law unless and until it is adopted by a state legislature. Under the UVCA, prosecutors or court personnel must notify victims of their rights under the act, as well as the times of any court proceedings involving the person or persons who allegedly victimized them. A crime victim has the right to be present at any court proceeding that the defendant has the right to attend. If the defendant is convicted, the victim has the right to make an impact statement during the sentencing hearing and assert an opinion as to the proper sentence. Finally, the UVCA provides for victims to be compensated by the state, up to $25,000, for any physical or emotional injuries suffered as the result of the victimization. However, this amount may be denied or reduced if the victim receives compensation through insurance or restitution from the defendant.

Restitution

restitution The act of compensating someone for losses suffered.

Restitution is a time-honored means of protecting the interests of crime victims. Restitution refers to "the return of a sum of money, an object, or the value of an object that the defendant wrongfully obtained in the course of committing the crime." *State v. Stalheim*, 552 P.2d 829, 832 (Or. 1976). Although restitution was practiced under the early common law, it was eventually abandoned as a remedy in criminal cases in favor of fines payable to the Crown. In modern America, however, restitution is making a comeback in the criminal law. Several states have enacted laws allowing trial courts to require restitution as a condition of probation in lieu of sentencing offenders to prison. In states that have adopted restitution laws, courts have held that (1) restitution is not necessarily incompatible with incarceration, *State v. Murray*, 621 P.2d 334 (Hawaii 1980); (2) restitution may be ordered for damages caused by the defendant during a criminal episode, irrespective of whether the loss is directly related to a specific conviction, *People v. Gallagher*, 223 N.W.2d 92 (Mich. App. 1974); and (3) a defendant may be ordered to pay restitution to a party other than the victim, *Shenah v. Henderson*, 476 P.2d 854 (Ariz. 1970).

Restitution is not practical in many criminal cases. Many offenders are not suited to probation, and even among those who are, there is no guarantee that they will be able to make payments to the victim. Recognizing this problem, several states have established victims' compensation commissions. For example, the Florida Crimes Compensation Act of 1977 makes victims and certain relatives eligible for compensation from a state commission where a crime results in injuries and is reported within seventy-two hours. Awards are limited to meeting the victims' actual needs. West's Fla. Stat. Ann. §§ 960.001-960.298.

Conclusion

The various forms of punishment meted out to convicted criminals rest on differing assumptions about crime and human nature. These assumptions lead to differing philosophies of punishment that stress retribution, deterrence, incapacitation, or rehabilitation. A great debate continues regarding both the propriety of these goals and the efficacy of the measures designed to achieve them. In particular, the deterrent value of the death penalty and the rehabilitative value of incarceration have been seriously questioned.

Courts of law tend to avoid the philosophical, theoretical, and empirical questions that surround the various forms of criminal punishment. Rather, they focus on the substantive and procedural limitations that the federal and state constitutions impose on the criminal justice system. In so doing, they tend to reflect the dominant values of the society.

Chapter Summary

- LO1
  - Early forms of criminal punishment were based on the concept of retribution, which carried a sense of proportionality. Colonial America followed the

English common law, which prescribed the death penalty for most felonies and corporal punishment for misdemeanors.

o Nineteenth-century reforms introduced the penitentiary and the concept of rehabilitation. By the twentieth century, incarceration had replaced corporal punishment, and state and the federal governments housed convicted felons in prisons.

o In contemporary America incarceration is imposed for most serious offenses, although the death penalty remains in effect in more than half the states for aggravated cases of murder.

o With federal and state prisons at or in excess of capacity, attention has shifted to alternative forms of punishment.

- LO2

  o Congress provides for penalties for persons convicted of violating federal laws. State legislatures do likewise for state offenders. Sentences meted out by courts must comport with these statutory provisions.

  o The Eighth Amendment to the U.S. Constitution, ratified in 1791, prohibits "cruel and unusual punishments." The Supreme Court has said that the Amendment applies to the states and must draw its meaning from "evolving standards of decency."

  o The process by which offenders are sentenced and punishments carried out must also comport with the Due Process Clauses of the Fifth and Fourteenth Amendments, and with similar provisions in all fifty state constitutions.

- LO3

  o Where judges consider it appropriate, they increasingly grant probation for nonviolent first-time offenders. Probation is the conditional release of a convicted offender under the supervision of a probation officer.

  o Statutes prescribe certain mandatory conditions on the probationer's activities and judges impose additional conditions that have a relationship to the defendant's offense.

  o Courts have held that probation conditions may infringe a probationer's constitutional rights, including First Amendment rights of free speech and association, as long as the conditions are related to the goal of rehabilitation. Appellate courts have invalidated conditions that restrict such fundamental rights as marriage, procreation, and the right of self-expression, but have upheld conditions restricting a probationer's use of the Internet by a defendant convicted of sexual and child abuse offenses.

  o Community service is sometimes imposed as a condition of probation.

  o Courts increasingly impose community control (house arrest), where an offender is allowed to leave home only for employment and approved community service activities. House arrest is often monitored by requiring persons to wear bracelets that permit officials to track their whereabouts. Some courts have imposed forms of creative punishment, for example, bumper stickers and signs indicating a person's status as an offender.

- LO4

  - In 1997, the U.S. Supreme Court, in a 5–4 decision, upheld the constitutionality of a Kansas law that establishes procedures for the civil commitment of persons who, due to a "mental abnormality" or a "personality disorder," are likely to engage in "predatory acts of sexual violence."

  - In 2010, the Supreme Court upheld the federal statute that allows for civil commitment of violent sexual predators who have completed their prison sentences.

- LO5

  - By the 1960s, many states had abolished the death penalty. In 1972, the Supreme Court declared Georgia's death penalty law unconstitutional because it allowed juries virtually unlimited discretion. Georgia revised its laws to make the death penalty more predictable. In 1976, the Court upheld Georgia's revised death penalty statute. Thirty-eight states with death penalty laws have modeled their statutes along the lines of the revised Georgia statute.

  - Federal crimes subject to the death penalty now include dozens of nonhomicidal offenses including treason and large-scale drug trafficking. It remains to be seen whether the federal courts will permit the death penalty for nonhomicidal crimes.

  - Since the 1980s, the Supreme Court has rendered several significant decisions in appeals involving the death penalty: In 1986, the Court held that the Eighth Amendment bars the execution of a person who is insane. In 1989, it said that execution of a mentally retarded prisoner does not necessarily violate the Eighth Amendment. In 2002, the Court ruled that there was a sufficient national consensus to prohibit execution of mentally retarded persons. And in 2005, the Court prohibited execution of anyone who was under eighteen at the time of their offense.

  - In the modern era executions have been carried out using the electric chair, the gas chamber, the firing squad, hanging, and lethal injection. In 2008, the U.S. Supreme Court upheld Kentucky's protocol for lethal injection, which is used by most states that employ lethal injection to administer the death penalty.

- LO6

  - Every jurisdiction requires that adults be sentenced in open court; in many instances juvenile offenders are sentenced *in camera*. For misdemeanors, sentencing usually occurs immediately on conviction. In felony cases, sentencing may be postponed to allow for a presentence investigation (PSI).

  - Sentencing is a critical stage of the criminal process, and counsel must be supplied to indigent defendants.

  - At the sentencing hearing, the court considers the evidence received at trial, any presentence report, evidence offered by the prosecution and defense relevant to sentencing, and any statement the defendant wishes to make.

  - Upon pronouncement of the sentence, a defendant to be incarcerated is given credit for time served since arrest. A defendant convicted of multiple crimes must be given separate sentences for each offense. Sentences may run consecutively or concurrently, usually at the discretion of the judge.

o Where the prosecution seeks the death penalty, the jury hears the evidence of mitigating and aggravating circumstances. To hand down a death sentence, the jury must find beyond a reasonable doubt that the aggravating factors outweigh the mitigating ones.

o In 1991, receding from its previous position, the Supreme Court ruled that the prosecution may submit a victim impact statement to be considered by a jury in determining whether to impose the death penalty.

o In 1994, the Court held that defendants facing the death penalty have a right to tell juries if the only alternative to a death sentence is life imprisonment without the possibility of parole.

- LO7

o Formerly, legislatures commonly allowed judges to sentence criminals to imprisonment for indeterminate periods—that is, until corrections officials decided the convict was sufficiently rehabilitated. Abuses of the system, combined with the decline of popular support for rehabilitation, have led most jurisdictions to abandon the concept of indeterminate sentencing.

o Under determinate sentencing, the judge sets a fixed term of years within statutory parameters, and the offender is required to serve that term without the possibility of early release.

o Many states now require mandatory minimum sentences for violent crimes and offenses involving firearms. Federal law now mandates minimum prison terms for serious drug crimes prosecuted in federal courts.

o In many states, "habitual offender" laws require increased penalties for persons convicted of repeated felonies. Currently, the federal government and most states have some form of habitual offender or "three-strikes-and-you're-out" statute. In most states, prosecutions under the "three-strikes" statutes are infrequent. In 2003, the Supreme Court upheld California's three-strikes law against a constitutional challenge based on the Eighth Amendment's Cruel and Unusual Punishments Clause.

o Truth in sentencing refers to movement seeking to close the gap between the sentences imposed and time actually served in prison. By 2001, more than two-thirds of the states had adopted "truth-in-sentencing" laws. Since then budgetary pressures and prison overcrowding have caused some states to repeal or liberalize these laws.

- LO8

o To eliminate the disparities in sentencing, Congress and a number of states adopted sentencing guidelines; some mandatory, others advisory. The federal guidelines resulted from the Sentencing Reform Act of 1984. State sentencing guidelines came about before and after that date.

o The guidelines provide a matrix of various factors to be considered in setting a defendant's sentence. Courts have leeway to depart from the guidelines for exceptional reasons. The guidelines have reduced, but not eliminated, unwarranted sentencing disparities. They have increased rates of incarceration, thereby contributing to the overcrowding in prisons.

○ In 2004, the Supreme Court held that a state trial court's sentencing of a defendant to a prison term above the statutory maximum on the basis of the judge's finding that the defendant acted with deliberate cruelty violated the defendant's Sixth Amendment right to a trial by jury.

○ Although Congress intended the federal sentencing guidelines to be mandatory, in 2005 the Supreme Court effectively relegated the guidelines to an advisory position.

- LO9

  ○ Historically, courts allowed prison officials free rein in running prisons and dealing with prisoners. In the late 1960s, as federal and state tribunals examined prison conditions and policies, litigation mushroomed.

  ○ As currently interpreted, the Eighth Amendment requires that prisoners must be provided with reasonably adequate food, clothing, shelter, medical care, sanitation, and a reasonable assurance of their personal safety. Nevertheless, the Eighth Amendment does not require that prisoners be furnished everything they deem essential to their physical or psychological well-being.

  ○ Although the Supreme Court has said that "the Constitution does not mandate comfortable prisons," lower federal courts have intervened to limit the number of inmates who can be housed in some prisons.

  ○ The Supreme Court has held that a prison inmate retains those First Amendment rights "that are not inconsistent with his status as a prisoner or with the legitimate penological objectives of the corrections system." Courts say that prisoners may possess Bibles, prayer books, and other religious materials, and be visited by the clergy. On the other hand, courts have generally upheld restrictions on religious exercises that disrupt the prison routine.

  ○ Prisoners retain a limited right to communicate via the mails, although prison officials may limit and censor the mail prisoners send and receive, provided there is no interference with attorney–client relationships.

  ○ Prison officials also have broad latitude to restrict the visitation privileges of an inmate who is receiving contraband smuggled into the prison by visitors.

  ○ Courts have consistently upheld prison regulations restricting free assembly and association.

  ○ The Supreme Court has long held that prison officials may not deny inmates access to the courts or penalize them for using courts. More recently courts have held that inmates must be furnished writing materials and notary services to assist them in filing petitions and seeking writs from courts. Courts have generally upheld the right of prisoners to meet with counsel in private and, in absence of other forms of legal assistance, to have access to law libraries.

  ○ Courts have said that there must be written notice of disciplinary actions, and that an inmate has the right to an administrative hearing with a written record and the right to produce evidence refuting the charges of misconduct, and may even call witnesses on his or her behalf. Likewise, revocation of parole is subject to minimal due process considerations.

- LO10

  - The Uniform Victims of Crime Act (UVCA) provides for notification to victims of court proceedings involving the persons who allegedly victimized them, and the right to be present at any court proceeding that the defendant has the right to attend. If the defendant is convicted, the victim has the right to make an impact statement during the sentencing hearing and assert an opinion as to the proper sentence. Finally, the Uniform Act recognizes that many offenders are not suited to probation, and even among those who are, there is no guarantee they will be able to make restitution to the victim and certain relatives.

  - Where a crime results in injuries and is promptly reported, UVCA provides for victims to be compensated by the state for any physical or emotional injuries suffered as the result of the victimization and provides for funding to state agencies that have established compensation programs to reimburse crime victims.

  - In 2004, Congress enacted the Federal Crimes Victims Act, which provides eight basic rights to crime victims where crimes are prosecuted in the federal system. Importantly, the Act stipulates that the court shall ensure that crime victims are afforded these rights.

Key Terms

aggravating factors

bifurcated trial

boot camp

capital crimes

capital punishment

community control

community service

concurrent sentencing

conditions of confinement

conditions of probation

consecutive sentencing

constitutional rights of prison inmates

corporal punishment

Crime Victims' Rights Act (CVRA)

death penalty

definite sentencing

determinate sentencing

Federal Death Penalty Act (FDPA)

Federal Sentencing Reform Act of 1984

forfeiture

general deterrence

good-time credit

habitual offender statute

house arrest

incapacitation

incarceration

indefinite sentencing

indeterminate sentencing

maximum security prisons

minimum security facilities

mitigating factors

monetary fine

noncapital crimes

parole

parole revocation hearings

penalty enhancement statutes

presentence investigation

presentence report

prison disciplinary measures

probation

pronouncement of sentence

proportionality

punitive isolation

rehabilitation

restitution

retribution

right of allocution

sentencing guidelines

sentencing hearing

suspended sentence

three strikes and you're out

truth in sentencing

Uniform Victims of Crime
Act (UVCA)

United States Sentencing Commission

victim impact evidence

victim impact statement

victims' rights

Key Court Decisions

Kansas v. Hendricks (1997): Laws that allow for the continued confinement of sexual predators who already have completed their prison sentences do not constitute "double jeopardy" or amount to "*ex post facto* laws.

Furman v. Georgia (1972): Georgia's death penalty statute is struck down as cruel and unusual punishment in violation of the Eighth Amendment.

Gregg v. Georgia (1976): Georgia's new sentencing procedures in death penalty cases are upheld as they "focus the jury's attention on the particularized nature of the crime and the particularized characteristics of the individual defendant."

Ford v. Wainwright (1986): The Eighth Amendment bars the execution of a person who is insane.

Payne v. Tennessee (1991): Victim impact statements are permissible during the sentencing phase of death penalty cases.

Bearden v. Georgia (1983): Probation can be revoked where a probationer willfully refuses to pay or fails to make sufficient efforts to pay fines and/or restitution.

Cunningham v. California (2007): Where a defendant was convicted by a jury, the jury must find the additional facts required for the judge to impose a longer prison sentence.

Ewing v. California (2003): California's "three strikes" law is determined not to violate the Eight Amendment prohibition of cruel and unusual punishments.

Apprendi v. New Jersey (2000): Where a defendant was convicted by a jury, the judge may not enhance the sentence beyond the statutory maximum based on facts not found by the jury.

Questions for Thought and Discussion

1. Why have the courts generally viewed corporal punishment as "cruel and unusual" yet been unwilling to take the same view of capital punishment?

2. How could a prisoner on death row establish that his or her death sentence was the result of racial discrimination?

3. Does your state impose the death penalty? If so, what does the state law provide with respect to juries considering aggravating and mitigating factors? Do you think your state's law governing the death penalty should be amended? If so, explain why and how.

4. What alternatives to imprisonment exist to deal with violent criminals who are repeat offenders? What alternatives, if any, would you propose? What legal problems are implicit in these alternatives to incarceration?

5. Discuss the pros and cons of mandatory sentences. Do mandatory sentences remove discretion from the sentencing judge and vest discretion in the

prosecutor, who may elect to charge a defendant with a lesser offense to avoid imposition of a mandatory sentence?

6. Suppose you were a probation officer and a judge asked you to recommend probation conditions for a first-time offender convicted of the sale and possession of cocaine. What specific conditions would you propose?

7. Should a defendant always be permitted to view the contents of a presentence report? What are the arguments for and against this?

8. What implications do the U.S. Supreme Court's decisions in *Apprendi v. New Jersey* (2000), *Blakely v. Washington* (2004), and *United States v. Booker* (2005) have for future use of sentencing guidelines?

9. What is the rationale for granting only minimal due process rights to parolees and probationers and to prisoners in disciplinary proceedings?

10. To what extent have the legal rights of prisoners been expanded since the 1960s? Have the courts been unduly solicitous in entertaining lawsuits brought by prison inmates?

11. Do you think that the introduction of a victim impact statement during the sentencing phase of a capital trial is appropriate, or do you think it might inject too much emotionalism into the process?

12. Should the government be permitted to require continued custodial supervision of sexual predators who have served their sentence for sexual abuse of children? Support your views.

13. What are the merits of granting or denying "good-time credit" to prisoners?

Problems for Discussion and Solution

1. Inmate Jay Leburd has brought suit in federal court challenging the conditions of his confinement in the Intensive Management Unit (IMU) of a maximum security state prison. Specifically, Leburd argues that the lack of any opportunity for outdoor exercise, total lack of reading materials, and absence of radio and television amount to "cruel and unusual punishment" in violation of the Eighth Amendment. Responding to the suit, the state prison system has conceded that the conditions in the IMU are "substantially as described by plaintiff." Nevertheless, the state has asked the court to dismiss the suit on the ground that "the Eighth Amendment does not guarantee fresh air and sunshine to inmates in solitary confinement, nor does it require that they be entertained." What is the federal judge likely to do? What do you think the judge should do?

2. In 1987, Douglas Deville was convicted in a state court for felonious possession of cocaine. He received probation for that offense. Three years later, Deville was found guilty of another drug-related felony in the same state. For that offense, he served five years in state prison. Three months after being released from prison, Deville was arrested for possession of 100 grams of cocaine base and 400 grams of marijuana. This time the case was prosecuted in federal court, where Deville was convicted of felony possession with intent to distribute. Because this was his third drug-related felony, Deville was sentenced to life imprisonment without parole under 21 U.S.C.A. § 841(b)(1)(A) (1994). On appeal, Deville claims that this sentence is "utterly disproportionate to his offense" and that, accordingly, it constitutes a violation of the Eighth Amendment's Cruel and Unusual Punishments Clause. Deville is relying on the U.S. Supreme Court's opinion in *Solem v. Helm* (1983). Does Deville have a case? Is he likely to prevail? In your opinion, is Deville's sentence fair and just? Is it constitutional?

3. Megan Mortensen was convicted of kidnapping and first-degree murder stemming from an incident in which she and her boyfriend, Vigo Stern, kidnapped, tortured, and killed an off-duty police officer. In a separate trial, Stern has been found guilty of the same offenses and sentenced to death by lethal injection. Upon what additional facts would a jury be likely to sentence Megan to death? Upon what facts would the jury be likely to choose a lesser punishment? If you were representing Megan in this case, what would you want to know about her beyond the facts of the case?

CHAPTER 8

Appeal and Postconviction Relief

CHAPTER OUTLINE

JURISPRUDENCE FEATURE BOXES

Chapman v. California (1967)
Douglas v. California (1963)
Felker v. Turpin (1996)
O'Sullivan v. Boerckel (1999)
Wiggins v. Smith (2003)

LEARNING OBJECTIVES

After reading this chapter, you should be able to explain

1. the different mechanisms by which appellate courts review criminal convictions and sentences

2. what defendants may challenge on appeal and the limited circumstances under which the prosecution can appeal

3. the error correction and lawmaking functions of appellate courts

4. the circumstances under which persons appealing their convictions may obtain pretrial release while their appeals are being adjudicated

5. the extent to which indigent persons convicted of crimes are entitled to representation at public expense to pursue appeals

6. the procedural steps followed by appellate courts in reviewing criminal cases

7. how and why the writ of habeas corpus is an important component of the modern appeals process

8. how states have adopted postconviction remedies that do not rely on habeas corpus

9. why DNA evidence can play an important role in postconviction relief

10. the nonjudicial remedies available to persons convicted of crimes

CHAPTER OPENING VIGNETTE

In the overwhelming majority of criminal cases there is no appeal. This is because most defendants are induced to plead guilty and in so doing bring closure to the judicial process. Death penalty cases are different. Most states that retain the death penalty provide for automatic appeals of death sentences. Many death penalty cases also involve some form of postconviction relief after the ordinary appeals process has concluded. Contemporary death penalty cases often highlight the complex character of modern judicial federalism. For example, consider the case of Robert Glen Coe.

In 1979, eight-year-old Cary Ann Medlin was abducted a few blocks from her home in Greenfield, Tennessee. Her body was found in a field the next day; she had been raped and stabbed to death. Three days later police arrested twenty-three-year-old Robert Glen Coe as he prepared to board a bus for Georgia. In 1981, Coe was sentenced to death for first-degree murder and given life sentences for aggravated rape and aggravated kidnapping. In 1983, the Tennessee Supreme Court affirmed Coe's conviction and sentence. The following year, the U.S. Supreme Court denied Coe's petition for discretionary review. Coe then filed a petition for postconviction relief in the state court where he had been tried, arguing that he had been denied a fair trial because his lawyers had not put on an adequate defense. In 1986, that petition was denied, and the denial was affirmed by a state appellate court. Coe then filed a petition for habeas corpus in federal district court. In 1989, that petition was denied on the grounds that Coe had failed to exhaust his remedies in the state courts. Coe then filed a second petition for postconviction relief in the state courts. That petition was denied, the denial affirmed on appeal, and review denied by the state supreme court. Coe then returned to federal court with a second petition for habeas corpus. In 1996, a federal district court judge overturned Coe's conviction and sentence on the basis of improper jury instructions and other errors in his trial. Two years later, a three-judge panel of the U.S. Circuit Court of Appeals for the Sixth Circuit reversed that ruling and reinstated Coe's conviction and sentence. The following year, the Sixth Circuit denied Coe's petition to have the case reconsidered by a full bench. The U.S. Supreme Court denied review. While Coe's second federal habeas petition was being litigated, his third petition for

trial *de novo* "New trial." Refers to trial court review of convictions for minor offenses by courts of limited jurisdiction by conducting a new trial instead of merely reviewing the record of the initial trial.

appeal of right An appeal that a defendant is entitled to make as a matter of law.

postconviction relief was being considered, and ultimately was denied, by the Tennessee courts. In early 2000, Coe made his last effort to avoid execution by asking the state trial court to find him mentally incompetent. When that failed, Coe's case was reviewed once more by the Tennessee Supreme Court, which approved his execution. Coe was put to death by lethal injection in April of 2000, more than twenty years after the murder of Cary Ann Medlin.

Introduction

Society's commitment to standards of fairness and procedural regularity is reflected in the opportunities that exist for defendants in criminal cases to seek judicial review of adverse court decisions. These opportunities have increased in recent decades, largely through judicial interpretation of various constitutional and statutory provisions.

discretionary review Form of appellate court review of lower court decisions that is not mandatory but occurs at the discretion of the appellate court.

postconviction relief Term applied to various mechanisms a defendant may use to challenge a conviction after other routes of appeal have been exhausted.

writ of habeas corpus A judicial writ requiring that a party be brought before a court. The primary function of habeas corpus is to release a person from unlawful confinement.

Forms of review in criminal cases include **trial *de novo***, **appeal of right**, **discretionary review**, and **postconviction relief**. Trial *de novo* occurs when a trial court of general jurisdiction reviews a conviction rendered by a court of limited jurisdiction. Appeal of right, the most common form of appeal, refers to an appellate court's review of a criminal conviction rendered by a trial court of general jurisdiction. A defendant whose conviction is affirmed on appeal may seek further review by a higher court by petitioning for discretionary review. Finally, a defendant confined to prison may seek additional review of his or her conviction or sentence by applying for a **writ of habeas corpus** or seeking another form of postconviction relief. The writ of habeas corpus allows a court of competent jurisdiction to review the legality of a prisoner's confinement. This device permits prisoners to raise a variety of legal issues in attacking their convictions and sentences. Each mechanism plays an important part in determining cases that move beyond the trial stage of the criminal process. In addition to correcting errors made by lower courts, appeals allow higher courts to refine and standardize both the substantive and procedural law.

Error Correction and Lawmaking Functions of Appellate Courts

error correction The function of appellate courts in reviewing routine appeals and correcting the errors of trial courts.

lawmaking One of the principal functions of an appellate court; often referred to as the law development function.

Appellate courts perform dual functions in the criminal process: **error correction** and **lawmaking**. Most criminal appeals are reviewed by intermediate federal or state appellate courts, although in the less populous states, routine appeals are handled by the highest court of the state (see Figure 8.1). In these routine appeals, the primary function of appellate courts is correcting errors made by trial courts. Appellate review is designed to ensure that substantive justice has been accomplished under constitutional standards of due process of law. Because of gaps in the statutory law and the inevitable need to interpret both statutory and constitutional provisions, appellate courts in effect must "make law." This lawmaking function is more characteristic of the highest levels of courts than of intermediate appellate tribunals.

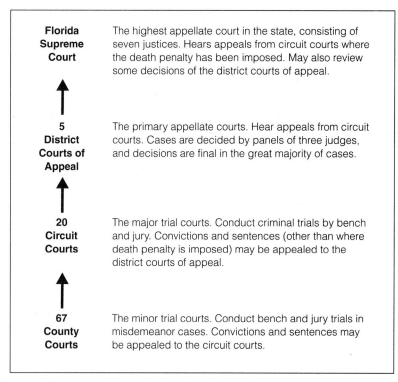

FIGURE 8.1 Criminal Appeals in the Florida Court System.
Source: Based on West's Fla. Stat. Ann. Const. Art. V. §§ 1–6; West's Fla. Stat. Ann. chs. 26, 34, 35.

The Common-Law Background

Before the eighteenth century, there was no common-law right to appeal from a criminal conviction. On rare occasions, the Crown issued a writ of error to require a new trial, but there was no appeal in the modern sense. Indeed, the term "appeal" at common law had a very different usage from ours. At common law, appeal referred to an effort by a person convicted of treason to obtain a pardon from the Crown by accusing others of being accomplices to the treasonable act.

In a landmark decision in 1705, the Court of King's Bench ruled that a **writ of error** had to be issued where a person convicted of a misdemeanor made proper application for the writ. *Paty's Case*, 91 Eng. Rep. 431 (K.B. 1705). In cases of felony and treason, the writ of error continued to be discretionary, although after 1700 the courts became more liberal in their issuance of the writ. The writ of error was finally abolished when Parliament enacted the Criminal Appeal Act of 1907, giving defendants the right to appeal their convictions.

writ of error A writ issued by an appellate court for the purpose of correcting an error revealed in the record of a lower court proceeding.

Appeal of Right

The federal constitution makes no mention of the right to appeal from a criminal conviction, although some might argue that the right to appeal is implicit in the Due Process Clauses of the Fifth and Fourteenth Amendments. In 1894, the U.S. Supreme Court held that the federal constitution provides no right to appeal from a criminal conviction. *McKane v. Durston*, 153 U.S. 684, 14 S.Ct. 913, 38 L.Ed. 867 (1894). Referring to the 1894 decision, Justice (later Chief Justice) Rehnquist observed: "While no one would agree that the State may simply dispense with the trial stage of proceedings without a criminal defendant's consent, it is clear that the State need not provide any appeal at all." *Ross v. Moffitt*, 417 U.S. 600, 611, 94 S.Ct. 2437, 2444, 41 L.Ed.2d 341, 351 (1974). Given the recent expansion of the concept of due process, the Court might reconsider this holding but for the fact that federal and state statutes now allow criminal defendants to appeal their convictions and seek other forms of postconviction relief. Defendants convicted after entering a plea of not guilty are entitled under federal and state law to one appeal as a matter of right.

Appeals of right in federal criminal cases are heard by the U.S. Courts of Appeals (circuit courts). State criminal appeals are heard by state supreme courts, by intermediate appellate courts, and—in Alabama, Oklahoma, Tennessee, and Texas—by specialized appellate courts that hear only criminal appeals. Beyond these appeals of right, opportunities exist for defendants to have their cases reviewed by the highest state courts and the U.S. Supreme Court, which may review convictions by issuing **writs of certiorari**.

Most states that allow the death penalty provide for automatic appeals of death sentences to their highest court. In such cases the defendant does not have to file an appeal; the process begins automatically.

A party who takes an appeal of right is called the **appellant**; the party against whom the appeal is taken is the **appellee**. A party who seeks further review is referred to as the **petitioner**; the other party is designated the **respondent**.

What Defendants May Challenge on Appeal

In a direct appeal from a criminal conviction, a defendant may challenge any act of the trial court objected to by the defendant during the pretrial, trial, or posttrial phases of the defendant's case. Irrespective of whether an objection was made in the trial court, a defendant may challenge the trial court's jurisdiction and those trial court actions or rulings considered to be **fundamental errors**. Appellate courts take different approaches to how serious an error must be to be classified as fundamental. Essentially, the courts will deem an error to be fundamental if it undermines confidence in the integrity of the criminal proceeding. When the defendant has been convicted of a capital crime, courts are more liberal in reviewing errors first challenged at the appellate stage. Indeed, the U.S. Supreme Court has said that those fundamental errors not specifically challenged by the appellant should be corrected when a person's life is at stake. *Fisher v. United States*, 328 U.S. 463, 66 S.Ct. 1318, 90 L.Ed. 1382 (1946).

In practice, a defendant usually raises from one to six major points on appeal as a basis for reversal of the trial court's judgment or sentence. Often these points are referred to as **assignments of error**. The most common assignments of error on direct appeal are claims that the trial court erred in its ruling in one or more of the following areas:

1. pretrial violations of the defendant's rights, particularly those rights guaranteed by the Fourth, Fifth, and Sixth Amendments to the federal constitution
2. procedural matters, especially trial court rulings admitting or excluding evidence
3. irregularities in the impaneling or conduct of the jury
4. failure to give jury instructions requested by the defendant, or giving instructions objected to by the defendant
5. prosecutorial misconduct such as improper remarks or arguments

writs of certiorari Order issued by an appellate court to grant discretionary review of a case decided by a lower court.

appellant The party that takes an appeal to a higher court.

appellee The party against whom an appeal is taken.

petitioner A party who brings a petition before a court of law.

respondent A party asked to respond to a lawsuit or writ.

fundamental errors Errors in a judicial proceeding that adversely affect the substantial rights of the accused.

assignments of error A written presentation to an appellate court identifying the points that the appellant claims constitute errors made by the lower tribunal.

6. sufficiency of the evidence to support a finding of the defendant's guilt beyond a reasonable doubt
7. interpretations of statutes or ordinances
8. the legality and, in some jurisdictions, the reasonableness of the sentence imposed
9. jury selection, deliberation, and misconduct
10. the voluntariness of a guilty plea

The Doctrine of Harmless Error

Although appellate review is designed to correct errors that occur before, during, or after trial, not all errors necessitate reversal. To obtain reversal of a judgment, the appellant must generally show that some prejudice resulted from the error and that the outcome of the trial or the sentence imposed would probably have been different in the absence of the error. Although specific standards vary among jurisdictions, all appellate courts operate on the principle that reversal is required only when substantial, as distinct from merely technical, errors are found in the record. This approach is illustrated by a provision of the California constitution that permits reversal on appeal only to prevent a **miscarriage of justice**. The California Supreme Court has interpreted this standard as follows: "[A] 'miscarriage of justice' should be declared only when the court, after an examination of the entire cause, including the evidence, is of the opinion that it is reasonably probable that a result more favorable to the appealing party would have been reached in the absence of the error." *People v. Watson*, 299 P.2d 243, 254 (Cal. 1956).

miscarriage of justice Decision of a court that is inconsistent with the substantial rights of a party to a case.

Appellate courts frequently find that technical errors cited by appellants are harmless and do not merit a reversal; however, the U.S. Supreme Court has imposed a strict standard on the finding of harmless error. Where an error at trial involves provisions of the federal constitution, the Supreme Court has said that appellate courts must find beyond a reasonable doubt that the error was harmless if they are to affirm the trial court. *Chapman v. California*, 386 U.S. 18, 87 S.Ct. 824, 17 L.Ed.2d 705 (1967).

JURISPRUDENCE

Chapman v. California, 386 U.S. 18, 87 S.Ct. 824, 17 L.Ed.2d 705 (1967)

Ruth Elizabeth Chapman and Thomas LeRoy Teale were convicted of robbery, kidnapping and murder. Chapman was sentenced to life in prison; Teale received a death sentence. Neither Chapman nor Teale testified at their trials. California law at that time allowed the prosecutor to comment on a defendant's decision not to testify. When Chapman refused to testify at her trial, the prosecutor commented extensively on that fact to the jury. The judge presiding over the trial informed members of the jury that they were free to draw their own conclusions from Chapman's decision not to take the stand. After Chapman's trial, but prior to her appeal, the U.S. Supreme Court

invalidated the law allowing prosecutors to comment on a defendant's decision not to testify. Nevertheless, the California Supreme Court upheld Chapman's conviction on the basis of the harmless error doctrine. The U.S. Supreme Court reversed Chapman's conviction. The Court, speaking through Justice Black, held in order for an error to be harmless, the state "must be able to demonstrate beyond a reasonable doubt" that the error was in fact harmless. In this particular case, the Court held the state was unable to establish beyond a reasonable doubt that the prosecutor's "repetitive comments to the jury, and the trial court's instruction ... did not contribute to the convictions." As a result, Chapman's conviction was vacated and the case was remanded for a new trial.

doctrine of harmless error An error that does not affect a party's substantive rights or the case's outcome.

The **doctrine of harmless error** is subject to certain qualifications. For example, appellate courts generally do not consider each error at trial in isolation. Rather, they often consider the cumulative effect of a series of errors. Thus, an appellant might secure reversal of a conviction where the trial was replete with error, even though each particular error might be considered harmless by itself.

When an Appeal May Be Taken by a Defendant

Generally, only a defendant who has pled not guilty has the right to appeal, and that appeal must wait until the defendant has been convicted and sentenced. However, there are some instances in which courts permit other appeals by defendants. For example, an order modifying or revoking probation is usually appealable.

Typically, a defendant who pleads guilty may raise on appeal only those issues relating to the trial court jurisdiction, the voluntariness of the guilty plea, and the legality of the sentence imposed. Even then, an appellate court may refuse to review these aspects of a case, other than the issue of jurisdiction, unless the trial court has refused the defendant's request to withdraw the plea of guilty.

Federal Rule of Criminal Procedure 11(a)(2) provides, "With the consent of the court and the government, a defendant may enter a conditional plea of guilty or *nolo contendere*, reserving in writing the right to have an appellate court review an adverse determination of a specified pretrial motion. A defendant who prevails on appeal may then withdraw the plea."

Some state jurisdictions also permit a defendant to plead *nolo contendere* or guilty and reserve the right to appeal a specific ruling of the trial court. See, for example, Fla. Stat. § 924.051. Defendants who unsuccessfully employ a constitutional defense frequently rely on this procedure. For instance, a defendant may file a pretrial motion to suppress certain evidence on the ground that it was obtained in violation of the Fourth Amendment, or a motion challenging the legal sufficiency of the charging document or constitutionality of a controlling statute. If the trial judge denies the motion, the defendant can plead *nolo contendere*, reserving the right to appeal that specific point of law. Generally the point reserved must be one that would be dispositive of the appeal.

Appeals by the Prosecution

Early rulings by American state courts uniformly denied state governments the right to appeal acquittals of criminal defendants. The U.S. Supreme Court adopted this position in 1892, when it ruled that the federal government had no right to appeal an acquittal. *United States v. Sanges*, 144 U.S. 310, 12 S.Ct. 609, 36 L.Ed. 445 (1892). This prohibition is sensible inasmuch as the Double Jeopardy Clause of the Fifth Amendment (applicable to the states through the Fourteenth Amendment) prohibits a defendant who has been acquitted from being tried again for the same offense.

Texas law makes the following provisions regarding the prosecution's right to appeal:

(a) The state is entitled to appeal an order of a court in a criminal case if the order:

(1) dismisses an indictment, information, or complaint or any portion of an indictment, information, or complaint;

(2) arrests or modifies a judgment;

(3) grants a new trial;

    (4) sustains a claim of former jeopardy;

    (5) grants a motion to suppress evidence, a confession, or an admission, if jeopardy has not attached in the case and if the prosecuting attorney certifies to the trial court that the appeal is not taken for the purpose of delay and that the evidence, confession, or admission is of substantial importance in the case;

    (6) is issued under Chapter 64 [refers to orders concerning DNA testing].

(b) The state is entitled to appeal a sentence in a case on the ground that the sentence is illegal.

(c) The state is entitled to appeal a ruling on a question of law if the defendant is convicted in the case and appeals the judgment. . . .

(d) The state is entitled to appeal an order granting relief to an applicant for a writ of habeas corpus. . . .

Source: From http://www.statutes.legis.state.tx.us/Docs/CR/htm/CR.44.htm

Vernon's Tex. Code Crim. Proc. Art. 44.01.

Either by statute or rule of court, most states afford similar opportunities for appeals by the prosecution. Similarly, 18 U.S.C.A. § 3731 permits the federal government to appeal an order of a federal district court (a) dismissing an indictment, (b) granting a new trial after judgment or verdict, (c) releasing a defendant before trial or after conviction, or (d) suppressing evidence or requiring the return of seized property before the time that the defendant is put in jeopardy. Both the government and the defendant have the right to appeal from a sentence imposed in violation of law, one that results from an erroneous application of a sentencing guideline, or one that is imposed by the court in violation of the terms of a plea agreement. In federal case, appeals by the prosecution from sentencing require prior approval by the office of the Attorney General or Solicitor General. 18 U.S.C.A. §§ 3742(a) and (b).

The constitutional proscription of double jeopardy does not prevent appeals by the prosecutor of pretrial orders because jeopardy does not apply before the impaneling of a jury or the taking of evidence in a nonjury trial. *Crist v. Bretz*, 437 U.S. 28, 98 S.Ct. 2156, 57 L.Ed.2d 24 (1978); *Serfass v. United States*, 420 U.S. 377, 95 S.Ct. 1055, 43 L.Ed.2d 265 (1975).

Trial *de Novo* in Minor Misdemeanor Cases

Most criminal appeals are heard "on the record." This means that the appellate court is asked to scrutinize the official record of the pretrial, trial, and posttrial proceedings for procedural errors that would require reversal of the judgment. Many misdemeanor cases are tried in local courts that are not courts of record; therefore, no record of the proceedings is available for review. Most of these involve summary justice. Trial is before a judge or magistrate without a jury in what is commonly called a bench trial. Counsel is rarely present, and frequently the only witnesses for the prosecution are police officers. The defendant may or may not choose to testify. Yet, persons convicted of misdemeanors are generally entitled to an appeal by law. Where no record has been made of the proceedings, a trial *de novo* (literally, a "new trial") is held in a trial court of superior jurisdiction. In many instances, persons convicted at trial *de novo* may take an appeal to a higher court, but further review of such cases is generally discretionary.

Discretionary Review

A defendant whose conviction has been sustained by an intermediate appellate court may petition a court of last resort for discretionary review. In the U.S. Supreme Court and most state supreme courts, discretionary review occurs through the grant of a writ of certiorari. Rule 13 of the Rules of the U.S. Supreme Court states that a "petition for a writ of certiorari . . . shall be in time when it is filed . . . within 90 days after the entry of the judgment" of the lower court. The highest court in each state (usually the state supreme court) may entertain petitions if they are filed within the time prescribed by the court's rules, usually thirty days after the intermediate appellate court enters its decision.

substantial federal question A significant legal question pertaining to the U.S. Constitution or a federal statute, treaty, regulation, or judicial interpretation of any of the foregoing.

"Cert petitions," as they are commonly called, are granted at the discretion of the reviewing court. In deciding whether to exercise its discretion, the U.S. Supreme Court evaluates whether a **substantial federal question** is involved. If so, the Court is then interested in whether the petitioner has exhausted all other remedies available. In deciding whether to grant certiorari, the Court follows the **rule of four**, meaning that at least four of the nine justices must vote to place a case on the docket.

rule of four U.S. Supreme Court rule whereby the Court grants certiorari only on the agreement of at least four justices.

In determining whether to grant review, the high state appellate tribunals usually have unlimited discretion. The U.S. Supreme Court's rule of four serves as a model for some state supreme courts; however, others are guided by formal or informal rules in determining whether to "grant cert." Among the criteria frequently employed are whether the intermediate appellate court's decision conflicts with a decision of another intermediate court or the supreme court, is without authoritative precedent, or departs from the essential requirements of the law.

The Appellate Process

To the layperson, the jurisdictional requirements and procedures of appellate courts appear complex. Although these procedures vary in detail, they essentially follow the same basic path. In some instances the defendant must file a motion for a new trial before making an appeal. This is often *a pro forma* measure, but it affords the trial judge an opportunity to review the defendant's claim of error and award a new trial if necessary.

Release of Defendant on Bail Pending Appeal

Federal and state statutes and rules of court usually specify criteria for the release of a convicted defendant pending appeal. Admission to bail after conviction is not a matter of right, but instead is at the discretion of the trial court. A defendant wanting to appeal is not aided by a presumption in favor of release on bail. Principally, the trial judge attempts to determine whether an appeal is taken in good faith and whether it presents a debatable point of law for appellate review. An appeal must not be frivolous or taken for the purpose of delay. *Birge v. State*, 230 S.E.2d 895 (Ga. 1976).

Trial judges typically consider several factors in exercising their discretion to grant or deny bail pending appeal. Among those factors are the defendant's habits and respect for the law, family and community ties, and the severity of punishment imposed. If the term of imprisonment imposed is relatively short, the court may also consider whether the denial of bail would render the defendant's right to appeal meaningless. Rules of criminal procedure generally provide for prompt appellate review of a decision denying bail to a convicted defendant or setting that bail unreasonably high. Absent such procedures, a defendant may seek a writ of habeas corpus.

pendency of the appeal The period after an appeal is filed but before the appeal is adjudicated.

If the state takes an appeal, the defendant is often released on personal recognizance during the **pendency of the appeal**—that is, while the appeal is being decided. Most states provide for the release of defendants pending an appeal by the prosecution. In Illinois, for example, "a defendant shall not be held in jail or to bail during the pendency of an appeal by the State . . . unless there are compelling reasons for his continued detention or being held to bail." Ill. Sup. Ct. Rule 604(a)(3).

Release of the Defendant in Federal Appeals

Bail Reform Act of 1984 An act that provides that a defendant charged with a federal crime may be denied bail if the prosecution can show that the defendant poses a threat to public safety.

Under the Federal Bail Reform Act of 1966 (repealed in 1984), the defendant in a federal court was entitled to bail unless there was "reason to believe that no one or more conditions of release will reasonably assure that the person will not flee, or pose a danger to any other person or any other community." The **Bail Reform Act of 1984**, 18 U.S.C.A. §§ 3141–3150, reversed that presumption of entitlement and allows federal judges to detain a criminal defendant without bail if the defendant poses a special threat to community safety or a high risk of flight.

Under the Bail Reform Act, the defendant has the burden of proving an entitlement to bail based on criteria specified in the law. Before granting bail pending appeal, the court must find:

1. that the defendant is not likely to flee or pose a danger to the safety of any other person or the community if released;
2. that the appeal is not for the purpose of delay;
3. that the appeal raises a substantial question of law or fact; and
4. that if that substantial question is determined favorably to defendant on appeal, that decision is likely to result in reversal or an order for a new trial of all counts on which imprisonment has been imposed. *United States v. Miller*, 753 F.2d 19, 24 (3rd Cir. 1985).

In an earlier topic, we pointed out that the federal government can take an appeal from certain pretrial orders under 18 U.S.C.A. § 3731 or from sentencing or plea agreement violations under 18 U.S.C.A. § 3742(b). Where an appeal is taken under § 3731, the Bail Reform Act ordinarily governs release of the defendant pending the appeal. If the government's appeal is taken under § 3742 and the defendant has been sentenced to imprisonment, the defendant is ordinarily not released pending the appeal.

Right to Counsel on Appeal

As we pointed out in previous chapters, the U.S. Supreme Court has interpreted the Constitution to require that indigent defendants be furnished assistance of counsel in criminal prosecutions. To what extent does the Constitution require the appointment of counsel for indigent defendants who appeal their convictions to higher courts? In *Douglas v. California*, 372 U.S. 353, 83 S.Ct. 814, 9 L.Ed.2d 811 (1963), the Supreme Court said that states must provide counsel to indigent persons convicted of felonies who exercise their statutory right to appeal. In *Ross v. Moffitt*, 417 U.S. 600, 94 S.Ct. 2437, 41 L.Ed.2d 341 (1974), however, the Supreme Court held that a state's failure to provide counsel to an indigent

---

SIDEBAR   **Steps in the Appellate Process**

Usually the appellate process in a criminal appeal will take between nine and twelve months, depending on whether counsel must seek extensions of permitted times for record preparation and briefing, whether the case is orally argued, and the court's caseload. The following describes the usual steps in a direct appeal of right to a state or federal appellate court.

1. *Filing a notice of appeal by appellant*, usually with the clerk of a lower court, with a copy served on the opposing party.
2. *Filing a record of lower court proceedings*, and, where there has been a trial, evidentiary exhibits, transcript of trial testimony, and the judge's instructions to the jury. Although this is a function of the court reporter and clerk of the lower court, the appellant is responsible for ensuring that the record is properly completed and filed in the appellate court.
3. *Filing by the appellant of an initial brief* raising the issues to be argued, supported by citations to the record on appeal and relevant constitutional provisions, statutes, and judicial decisions.
4. *Filing of motions* by the appellant (and sometimes the appellee) seeking interim forms of relief such as bail reductions, stay orders, extensions of time requirements for filing briefs, continuances of oral arguments, supplementing the record on appeal, striking sections of briefs, and so forth.
5. *Rulings* by the appellate court on motions.
6. *Filing by the appellant of an application for oral argument*, if desired.
7. *Filing by the appellee of an answer brief* refuting the appellant's arguments, likewise supported by citations to the record on appeal and relevant constitutional provisions, statutes, and judicial decisions.

8. *Filing by the appellee of an application for oral argument*, if desired and if not already requested by the appellant.
9. *Filing by the appellant of a brief in reply* to the appellee's answer brief.
10. *Review of the record and briefs* by the judges who are assigned to hear and decide the appeal.
11. *Oral argument by counsel*, where requested by counsel and granted by the court.
12. *Conference of judges* assigned to decide the case, often resulting in a tentative decision and assignment of a judge to prepare the court's decision.
13. *Additional research* by the appellate court's staff attorneys, where necessary.
14. *Drafting of proposed decision* by the assigned judge and circulation of it to remaining judges who have participated in the case, followed by their agreement with the proposed decision or by their offering a dissenting opinion.
15. *Issuance of the court's decision* by the clerk of the appellate court and circulation of that decision to counsel for the parties.
16. *Motion by the losing party for a rehearing* or issuance of a clarifying decision, usually based on an allegation of the court's having overlooked some significant fact or point of law, followed by the court's ruling on the motion.
17. *Motion for* en banc *rehearing*, assuming the case was heard by fewer than all judges on the court.
18. *Ruling on motion for* en banc *review*. If granted, the court proceeds to rehear the case *en banc* and issues a decision by all judges who participate.
19. *Issuance of mandate.* After time for motions for rehearing to be filed, and, if granted, disposed of, the appellate court issues a mandate commanding the court's decision be followed. This is served on counsel and filed in the lower court.

---

defendant seeking discretionary review in the state and federal supreme courts did not violate due process or equal protection. Thus, the government must provide counsel as a matter of course when defendants have a statutory right to be heard in an appellate court. At later stages of the appeals process, there is no such requirement.

The Supreme Court's decision in *Douglas v. California* produced a tremendous increase in appellate caseloads. Providing counsel at public expense aggravated the

JURISPRUDENCE

Douglas v. California, 372 U.S. 353, 83 S.Ct. 814, 9 L.Ed.2d 811 (1963)

William Douglas and his codefendant, Bennie Will Meyes, were tried jointly and convicted on thirteen various felonies. At trial they were represented by the public defender's office. Douglas requested appointed counsel for his appeal by right to the state appellate court. The trial court, in accordance with the relevant state rule of criminal procedure, reviewed the record and concluded that the appointment of counsel would neither serve the Douglas's interests nor be "helpful to the appellate court." As a result, Douglas's appeal was heard without the assistance of counsel, and his conviction was affirmed. The U.S. Supreme Court held that "where the merits of the one and only appeal an indigent has as of right [are] decided without [the] benefit of counsel in a state criminal case, there has been a discrimination between the rich and the poor which violates the Fourteenth Amendment." As a result, the judgment was vacated and the case remanded to the lower court.

---

frivolous appeals Appeals wholly lacking in legal merit.

problem of **frivolous appeals** (that is, appeals lacking any arguable basis for reversal). In such cases, appointed counsel often attempt to withdraw.

In *Anders v. California*, 386 U.S. 738, 87 S.Ct. 1396, 18 L.Ed.2d 493 (1967), the Supreme Court invalidated a state rule that allowed appointed counsel to withdraw by merely stating that an appeal had no merit. Reasoning that the right to counsel meant the right to have an effective advocate on appeal, the Court held that appointed counsel could withdraw only after submitting a brief claiming that the appeal was wholly frivolous and referring to any arguable issues. Recently, California developed a new procedure for handling criminal appeals by indigents. An appointed attorney may now write a "no-merit brief" summarizing the procedural and factual history of the case. The court orders a briefing by counsel only if it finds arguable issues. Therefore, before rejecting the appeal, both counsel and the court have to find the appeal lacking in arguable issues. In January 2000, in *Smith v. Robbins*, 528 U.S. 259, 120 S.Ct. 746, 145 L.Ed.2d 756, the U.S. Supreme Court ruled that such "no-merit brief" procedure satisfies the requirements of *Anders v. California*. The basic *Anders* approach is followed in most jurisdictions, and when an appellate court accepts an ***Anders* brief**, it usually notifies the defendant of the appointed counsel's withdrawal and permits the defendant to file a memorandum pointing to any claim of error. With the proliferation of criminal appeals by indigent defendants, the *Anders* brief has become a commonplace element of appellate procedure.

***Anders* brief** A law brief submitted to an appellate court by publicly appointed defense counsel in which counsel explains that the defendant's appeal is nonmeritorious and requests release from further representation of the defendant.

Self-Representation on Appeal

In Chapter 5, we pointed out that it is incumbent on a trial judge to allow self-representation by a defendant who voluntarily and intelligently elects to proceed in the trial court without counsel. *Faretta v. California*, 422 U.S. 806, 95 S.Ct. 2525, 45 L.Ed.2d 562 (1975). We also pointed out in Chapter 6 that in 2008 the Supreme Court held that a trial judge is not required to allow a minimally competent defendant to elect self-representation at trial. *Indiana v. Edwards*, 554 U.S. 164, 128 S.Ct. 2379, 171 L.Ed.2d 345 (2008).

Many appellate courts allow convicted defendants to file *pro se* petitions for habeas corpus but generally do not allow defendants to handle direct appeals on a *pro se* basis. After Salvador Martinez represented himself before a trial court, the California courts denied him the right to represent himself before the California Court of Appeal. He obtained review in the U.S. Supreme Court, and on January 12,

2000, the Court upheld California's denial of his right to handle his appeal without counsel. The Court observed that although the Sixth Amendment to the Constitution provides a basis for self-representation at the trial level, it does not include any right to appeal. The Court pointed to significant differences between the trial and appellate stages of a criminal proceeding and emphasized the need for a defendant to have counsel when attempting to overturn a criminal conviction. The Court recognized that states are free to determine whether to allow a defendant to proceed in an appellate court without counsel; nevertheless, it held that a criminal defendant does not have the right under the U.S. Constitution to elect self-representation on a direct appeal from a judgment of conviction. *Martinez v. California Court of Appeal*, 528 U.S. 152, 120 S.Ct. 684, 145 L.Ed.2d 597 (2000).

Filing the Appeal

Once the appellant has determined the correct forum for an appeal or a petition for discretionary review, the process is governed by federal or state rules of appellate procedure. The notice of appeal or petition for review must be filed in the appropriate court within a specified period of time. The time requirement tends to be strictly enforced because this notice or petition confers jurisdiction on the appellate court to act on the case.

Federal Rules of Appellate Procedure Rules of procedure governing the practice of law before the U.S. courts of appeals.

Rule 4(b) of the **Federal Rules of Appellate Procedure** provides that an appeal by a defendant from a judgment and sentence in a federal district court must be filed within ten days after the entry of the judgment or the filing of the government's notice of appeal. Under certain circumstances the time period may be extended, but the extension cannot exceed an additional thirty days. If a defendant makes a timely motion for judgment of acquittal for a new trial or for arrest of a judgment, then the **notice of appeal** must be filed within ten days after the trial court enters an order disposing of such motion(s). When an appeal by the government is authorized by statute, the notice of appeal must be filed within thirty days after the entry of judgment.

notice of appeal Document filed notifying an appellate court of an appeal from a judgment of a lower court.

In state courts, an aggrieved party usually has thirty days after entry of judgment and sentence to file an appeal. For example, Maryland requires that the notice of appeal must be filed within thirty days after the trial court has entered its judgment or denied a motion for a new trial. Md. Rules, Rule 8-202(a)(b). The filing of a notice of appeal must be accompanied by the payment of a required filing fee, unless the appellant is represented by the public defender's office or other counsel assigned by any other legal services organization that accepts as clients only those persons meeting the financial eligibility criteria established by the Federal Legal Services Corporation or other appropriate governmental agency. Md. Rules, Rule 8-201(b).

Motions

During the early stages of the appellate process, counsel for both parties frequently file motions in the appellate court. Some motions address substantive issues—for example, a motion asserting legal grounds to dismiss the appeal. More commonly, counsel use motions to draw the court's immediate attention to procedural matters outside the routine of the appellate process. For example, counsel may request additional time to meet deadlines for filing petitions and briefs. Occasionally, counsel will move for expedited consideration of an appeal. By appropriate motions, separate appeals may be consolidated and multiple appeals may be severed. Ordinarily, filing an appeal does not stay the judgment or sentence. However, on a showing of good cause, an appellate court may stay a judgment or sentence pending resolution of the appeal.

After a notice of appeal or a petition for discretionary review has been filed, a series of procedural steps are set in motion. It is incumbent on the appellant or petitioner to have the clerk of the trial court forward to the appellate tribunal certified copies of pertinent records and transcripts of testimony relevant to the issues to be raised on appeal. Beyond this, procedures vary somewhat, depending largely on whether the appeal is one of right or whether the defendant is seeking discretionary relief.

Submission of Briefs by Counsel

brief A document filed by a party to a lawsuit to convince the court of the merits of that party's case.

In an appeal of right, the appellant files a **brief** summarizing the legal posture and the factual background of the case in the lower tribunal, the issues on appeal, and the legal authorities that support a reversal of the trial court's rulings. Briefs are the principal instruments used to persuade the appellate court to reverse, affirm, or modify the decision being appealed. They are usually heavily laden with citations to constitutional provisions, statutes, and court decisions that are regarded as persuasive by the advocates. The extent of background information contained in the briefs depends on the points to be presented to the appellate court. The appellee is permitted to respond to the appellant's contentions by filing an **answer brief**, and the appellant is usually permitted a **reply brief**. The whole process resembles the order of a classroom debate, where the affirmative presents its case, followed by the negative, and then by a rebuttal by the affirmative.

answer brief The appellee's written response to the appellant's law brief filed in an appellate court.

reply brief A brief submitted by an appellant in response to an appellee's answer brief.

Where a petitioner seeks discretionary review, the appellate court must first decide whether to accept or deny the request to take jurisdiction. If the court determines to proceed on the petition, it will order all affected parties to furnish the court a written response. As in an appeal of right, often the petitioner is permitted to file a reply to that response. The petition and response may be supplemented by such briefs as the court requires.

The format and submission of briefs must adhere closely to the requirements of the particular jurisdiction. Counsel must always furnish copies of briefs and other materials to their adversaries.

Oral Argument

oral argument Verbal presentation made to an appellate court in an attempt to persuade the court to affirm, reverse, or modify a lower court decision.

After briefs have been submitted and reviewed by the appellate court, an **oral argument** may be held where counsel for both parties appear. Typically, appellate courts conduct oral arguments in about half the cases they decide. (In the federal courts, the rate may be closer to 25 percent.) During oral arguments, counsel for both parties summarize their positions orally and then respond to questions from the bench. The trend is for oral argument to be less structured and more of a dialogue between court and counsel.

The appellate rules of courts in many jurisdictions set out the time allowed for oral argument. For example, as Rule 24 of the Rhode Island Rules of Appellate Procedure stipulates, "Counsel on each side will be allowed a period not in excess of thirty minutes for presentation of argument, and a period not in excess of ten minutes will be allowed the moving party for reply." Rule 28 of the U.S. Supreme Court provides, "Oral argument should emphasize and clarify the written arguments in the briefs on the merits. Counsel should assume that all Justices have read the briefs before oral argument." It further states, "Unless the Court directs otherwise, each side is allowed one-half hour for argument." Rule 34(d) of the U.S. Court of Appeals for the Fourth Circuit allows either fifteen or twenty minutes, depending on the type of appeal. Rather than stipulating a specific time, rules in some federal and state jurisdictions provide that the appellate court will specify the times for oral argument on the court calendar. Most state appellate courts allow twenty or thirty minutes for oral argument, but the court always reserves the right to shorten or lengthen the time allocated.

The Judicial Conference

judicial conference A meeting of judges to deliberate on the disposition of a case.

Appellate judges customarily confer about the disposition of appeals. The **judicial conference** is regarded as an essential part of the collegial process that distinguishes the appellate role from that of the trial court. If there has been oral argument, it is common for the panel of judges that heard the case to confer shortly thereafter. At that time the panel frequently attempts to determine the disposition of the appeal but, in some instances, finds it necessary to further canvass the record or call on counsel or the court's own staff lawyers for additional legal research. Where there has been no oral argument, the panel of judges assigned to the case usually confers after each judge has reviewed the briefs, pertinent records, and results of any research assignments given to the court's legal staff.

Judgment of the Court

affirm To uphold, ratify, or approve.

reverse To set aside a decision on appeal.

remand To send back, usually with instructions.

Essentially, an appellate court has three options in addressing a case before it. First, it may dismiss the appeal. This is uncommon in appeals of right unless the appeal is untimely. Dismissal is more common in cases of discretionary review. For example, the U.S. Supreme Court will sometimes dismiss a petition for certiorari as having been improvidently granted even after the case has been fully argued. When an appeal or cert petition is dismissed, the judgment of the lower court remains undisturbed. The second option of the appellate court is to **affirm** the decision being reviewed, which preserves the judgment of the lower court. The third option is to **reverse** the judgment of the lower court. A reversal is usually accompanied by an order to **remand** the case to the lower court for further proceedings consistent with the higher court's opinion. In the criminal context, this may mean the defendant receives a new trial or new sentencing hearing. When a court of last resort remands a case to an intermediate appellate court, the latter must reconsider the case based on the higher court's decision.

Appellate Court Opinions

After an appellate court has arrived at a decision, the court will issue an opinion announcing its decision. Some opinions simply announce the court's decision; others are quite lengthy in considering the arguments of counsel and articulating the reasons for the court's decision. Opinions are generally prepared by an individual judge or justice. If responsibility for the preparation of an opinion has not been previously given to one judge, that responsibility is usually assigned at conference by the senior judge or the senior judge voting with the majority of the panel.

per curiam opinion An opinion rendered "by the court," as distinct from one attributed to one or more judges.

opinion of the court The opinion expressing the judgment and reasoning of the court, representing the views of at least a majority of the judges participating in a decision.

dissenting opinion An opinion rendered by a judge disavowing or disagreeing with the decision of a collegial court.

concurring opinion An opinion handed down by a judge that supports the judgment of the court but often does so through different reasoning.

concurring in the judgment Issuance of an opinion by a judge or justice that agrees with the judgment of an appellate court without agreeing with the court's reasoning process.

reporters Books containing judicial decisions and accompanying opinions.

motion for rehearing A formal request made to a court of law to convene another hearing in a case in which the court has already ruled.

There are two basic types of appellate court opinions: *per curiam* and signed. A *per curiam* opinion represents the appellate court as a whole; it is not attributed to any individual judge or group of judges on the court. More commonly the decision of the appellate court is announced in an **opinion of the court** authored by one judge and joined by other judges constituting a majority. A judge who disagrees with the decision of the court may write a **dissenting opinion**. A judge who agrees with the court's decision but wants to address or emphasize certain arguments not addressed or emphasized in the opinion of the court may write a separate **concurring opinion**. Sometimes, a separate opinion is listed as **concurring in the judgment** only, meaning that it supports the decision of the court but for reasons other than those articulated in the court's opinion.

Publication of Appellate Decisions

Most decisions of appellate courts in America are published in books known as **reporters**. The publication of appellate decisions plays an important role in developing the law because judges and lawyers regularly consult the case reporters for guidance in pending cases. Today, it is common for appellate opinions to become immediately available via the Internet. The U.S. Supreme Court, each of the federal circuits, and most state appellate courts maintain websites from which opinions are downloadable at no cost. (Access to published opinions, through both electronic and traditional means, is discussed in some detail in Appendix A.)

Motions for Rehearing

Rules of appellate procedure uniformly permit the filing of a motion asking the appellate court to reconsider its decision in a given case. A **motion for rehearing** is designed to address some misstatement of material fact in the court's opinion or to direct the court's attention to an overlooked or misapprehended proposition of law. In the U.S. Courts of Appeals and in many state appellate courts, where cases are decided by panels of judges, a party may request that all judges (or a majority of the judges in appellate courts consisting of a large number of judges) of the court participate in **an en banc rehearing**. The likelihood of an appellate court's granting a motion for *en banc* rehearing is greater when there are conflicting opinions between or among panels of judges within the court. Appellate courts view many motions for rehearing as little more than attempts by dissatisfied parties to have another chance to persuade the court of their position. Accordingly, motions for rehearing are seldom granted.

Postconviction Relief

en banc rehearing A hearing in an appellate court in which all or a substantial number of the judges assigned to that court participate.

Normally, an appeal of a lower court decision must be made in a timely manner, usually within thirty days after that court's judgment or sentence. Petitions for certiorari (or other forms of discretionary review) are also subject to time limits. Yet, incarcerated criminals may seek review of their convictions long after their rights to appeal have been exhausted or expired by means of a mechanism known as the writ of habeas corpus. It is available in the federal courts and in all fifty state judicial systems.

"Habeas corpus" is a Latin term meaning "that you have the body." In law, it refers to a writ issued by a court to a person who is holding another in custody, requiring that the former show cause for holding the latter. Habeas corpus has roots deep in the common law. William Blackstone, the foremost English jurist of the eighteenth century, called it "the most celebrated writ in the English law." 3 W. Blackstone, *Commentaries* 129. The framers of the American Constitution explicitly recognized habeas corpus as a fundamental right of citizens by declaring: "The Privilege of the Writ of Habeas Corpus shall not be suspended unless when in Cases of Rebellion or Invasion the public Safety may require it." U.S. Const., Art. 1, Sec. 9. Only once in our history, during the Civil War, was the writ of habeas corpus suspended throughout the federal courts. This was accomplished via an executive order issued by President Lincoln in November 1862 and a subsequent act of Congress in March 1863. After hostilities had ceased, this thoroughgoing suspension of habeas corpus was declared unconstitutional by the Supreme Court. *Ex parte Milligan*, 71 U.S. (4 Wall.) 2, 18 L.Ed. 281 (1866).

Challenging State Court Convictions in Federal Court

federal habeas corpus review Review of a state criminal trial by a federal district court on a writ of habeas corpus after the defendant has been convicted, has been incarcerated, and has exhausted appellate remedies in the state courts.

The U.S. Supreme Court can review only a minute proportion of the thousands of petitions for certiorari through which persons convicted in state courts challenge their convictions on federal constitutional grounds. In recent decades, **federal habeas corpus review** of state criminal convictions has become a common form of appellate procedure. It has also greatly multiplied the opportunities for persons convicted of state offenses to obtain relief. Consequently, it has become the focus of considerable controversy.

The Judiciary Act of 1789, 1 Stat. 82 (1789), recognized the power of federal courts to issue writs of habeas corpus for federal prisoners only. In 1867, federal law was amended, 14 Stat. 385, 386, to allow federal courts to entertain habeas corpus petitions from state prisoners who allege that their incarceration violates provisions of the U.S. Constitution or federal statutes or treaties. The federal law on habeas corpus currently provides the following:

> The Supreme Court, a Justice thereof, a circuit judge, or a district court shall entertain an application for a writ of habeas corpus in behalf of a person in custody pursuant to the judgment of a State court only on the ground that he is in custody in violation of the Constitution or laws or treaties of the United States. 28 U.S.C.A. § 2254(a).

Before the twentieth century, the federal habeas corpus jurisdiction was seldom used to review state criminal convictions. When habeas corpus was granted, it was merely to ascertain that the state trial court had jurisdiction over the person being tried. In *Frank v. Mangum*, 237 U.S. 309, 35 S.Ct. 582, 59 L.Ed. 969 (1915), the Supreme Court broadened federal habeas corpus review to ensure that states supplied some "corrective process" whereby criminal defendants could seek to vindicate their federal constitutional rights. In 1953, the Court held that federal courts could use habeas corpus review to readjudicate federal constitutional issues that had been addressed in state court proceedings. *Brown v. Allen*, 344 U.S. 443, 73 S.Ct. 397, 97 L.Ed. 469 (1953).

Federal law had long provided that federal habeas corpus relief was available only to state prisoners who had exhausted all available remedies in the state courts. In 1963, the Supreme Court under Chief Justice Earl Warren held that a state prisoner did not have to take a direct appeal to the state supreme court to seek federal habeas corpus review. Nor was the prisoner barred from raising constitutional issues in federal court merely because the issues had not been raised on direct appeal in state courts. *Fay v. Noia*, 372 U.S. 391, 83 S.Ct. 822, 9 L.Ed.2d 837 (1963). The Warren Court also held that a petitioner could challenge a state conviction despite a failure to develop a material fact in state proceedings unless it was determined that the petitioner deliberately bypassed the opportunity to develop the fact in the state courts. *Townsend v. Sain*, 372 U.S. 293, 83 S.Ct. 745, 9 L.Ed.2d 770 (1963).

The Warren Court's efforts to broaden the availability of federal habeas corpus review coincided with its expansion of the constitutional rights of the accused. No doubt, the Court was initially reluctant to depend on state courts to implement these expanded rights, so it broadened the power of the federal district courts to review state criminal convictions. This resulted in numerous state convictions being overturned by the federal courts, often on Fourth or Fifth Amendment grounds. Indeed, many observers came to see state criminal trials merely as precursors to inevitable federal intervention.

The Supreme Court Restricts Access to Federal Habeas Corpus

Growing criticism of federal court intervention, coupled with the increasing professionalism of the state judiciaries, led the Supreme Court to restrict access to federal habeas corpus relief during the 1970s, '80s, and '90s. The following are synopses of the most significant decisions of that period:

- *Stone v. Powell*, 428 U.S. 465, 96 S.Ct. 3037, 49 L.Ed.2d 1067 (1976). The Court held that state prisoners could not use federal habeas corpus hearings to challenge searches and seizures where they had been provided an opportunity for full and fair litigation of a Fourth Amendment claim in the state courts.
- *Engle v. Isaac*, 456 U.S. 107, 102 S.Ct. 1558, 71 L.Ed.2d 783 (1982). The Court refused to allow a state prisoner to use federal habeas corpus to challenge a questionable jury instruction to which he had failed to object during trial.
- *McCleskey v. Zant*, 499 U.S. 467, 111 S.Ct. 1454, 113 L.Ed.2d 517 (1991). The Court said that a death row inmate abused the writ of habeas corpus when he filed a second federal habeas corpus petition. The Court held that a state need not prove that a petitioner deliberately abandoned a constitutional claim in his or her first habeas corpus petition for the petitioner to be barred from raising the claim in a subsequent petition.
- *Keeney v. Tamayo-Reyes*, 504 U.S. 1, 112 S.Ct. 1715, 118 L.Ed.2d 318 (1992). The Court overturned precedent (*Townsend v. Sain*, supra) and held that a petitioner's failure to develop a claim in state court proceedings should be excused only if he or she can show that a fundamental miscarriage of justice would result from failure to hold a federal evidentiary hearing.
- *Brecht v. Abrahamson*, 507 U.S. 619, 113 S.Ct. 1710, 123 L.Ed.2d 353 (1993). The Court ruled that federal district courts may not overturn state convictions unless the petitioner can show "actual prejudice" from the errors cited in the habeas corpus petition. Previously, the state carried the burden of proving beyond a reasonable doubt that any constitutional error committed during or before trial was "harmless"—that is, not prejudicial to the defendant. *Brecht v. Abrahamson* had the effect of shifting the burden of proof from the state to the petitioner in a federal habeas corpus hearing.

The Supreme Court's decisions in *McCleskey v. Zant*, *Engle v. Isaac*, *Keeney v. Tamayo-Reyes*, and *Brecht v. Abrahamson* came when many in Congress were calling for legislative restrictions on federal habeas corpus. Both the Supreme Court and Congress were responding to a widespread perception that state prisoners were being afforded excessive opportunities to challenge their convictions in federal courts. Indeed, some commentators questioned the need for federal postconviction review of state criminal cases altogether.

Congress Modifies the Federal Habeas Corpus Procedure

On April 24, 1996, President Clinton signed into law the Antiterrorism and Effective Death Penalty Act of 1996. One provision of this statute curtails second habeas corpus petitions by state prisoners who have already filed such petitions in federal court. Under the new statute, any second or subsequent habeas petition must meet a particularly high standard and must pass through a gatekeeping procedure exercised by the U.S. Courts of Appeals. The grant or denial of an authorization by a court of appeals for an inmate to file a second or successive petition for habeas corpus in the district court is not appealable and is not subject to a petition for rehearing or for a writ of certiorari. 28 U.S.C.A. § 2244(b)(3).

In *Felker v. Turpin*, 518 U.S. 651, 116 S.Ct. 2333, 135 L.Ed.2d 827 (1996), an inmate awaiting execution in Georgia challenged the constitutionality of this provision, posing two constitutional objections: (1) that the new law amounted to an unconstitutional "suspension" of the writ of habeas corpus and (2) that the prohibition against Supreme Court review of a circuit court's denial of permission to file a subsequent habeas petition is an unconstitutional interference with the Supreme

---

JURISPRUDENCE

Felker v. Turpin, 518 U.S. 651, 116 S.Ct. 2333, 135 L.Ed.2d 827 (1996)

Ellis Wayne Felker was convicted of murder and sentenced to death in a Georgia state court. Felker appealed his conviction on a direct appeal, but was denied relief. Felker also sought and was denied relief in a federal habeas corpus proceeding. While Felker was awaiting execution, the Antiterrorism and Effective Death Penalty Act of 1996 was signed into law. The Act require requires "dismissal of a claim presented in a state prisoner's second or successive federal habeas application if the claim was also presented in a prior application." The Act also compels dismissal of a claim that was not presented in a prior federal application, unless certain conditions apply. The Act also functions as a "gatekeeping mechanism, whereby the prospective applicant files in the court of appeals a motion for leave to file a second or successive habeas application in the district court, and a three-judge panel determines whether the application makes a prima facie showing that it satisfies" the Act's requirements.

Lastly, the Act declares that a panel's grant or denial of authorization to file "shall not be appealable and shall not be the subject of a petition for . . . writ of certiorari." As a result of these provisions, Felker filed a motion in a federal appeals court for leave to file a second federal habeas petition," which was denied based on the premise that "the grounds raised had not been presented in his first petition." After the appellate court's denial, Felker filed a petition before the Supreme Court for a writ of habeas corpus and certiorari. The Supreme Court held that the Act "does not violate the Constitution's Suspension Clause, which provides that '[t]he Privilege of the Writ of Habeas Corpus shall not be suspended.'" The Court held that "the new restrictions on successive habeas petitions constituted a restraint on what is called … 'abuse of the writ.'" Because Felker did not comply with the Act's requirements nor did he show "exceptional circumstances" in "justifying the issuance of the writ" of habeas corpus, the Court denied Felker's petition.

Court's jurisdiction as defined in Article III of the Constitution. In a unanimous decision rendered less than one month after the case was argued, the Supreme Court rejected these challenges and upheld the statute. In a "saving construction" of the statute, the Court interpreted the law in such a way as to preserve the right of state prisoners to file habeas corpus petitions directly in the Supreme Court. However, the Court stated that it would exercise this jurisdiction only in "exceptional circumstances."

Claims of Actual Innocence

In *Herrera v. Collins*, 506 U.S. 390, 113 S.Ct. 853, 122 L.Ed.2d 203 (1993), the Supreme Court held that a belated claim of innocence does not entitle a state prisoner on death row to a federal district court hearing before being executed. But two years later, in *Schlup v. Delo*, 513 U.S. 298, 115 S.Ct. 851, 130 L.Ed.2d 808 (1995), the Court mitigated somewhat the harshness of *Herrera v. Collins*. In *Schlup* the Court held that where claims of actual innocence are coupled with assertions of constitutional violations, in order to prevent a miscarriage of justice a federal court may grant habeas corpus relief that would normally be procedurally barred.

Assistance of Counsel in Federal Habeas Corpus Cases

As we have seen, there is no federal constitutional right to counsel beyond the appeal of right. Congress has provided for representation of federal prisoners seeking habeas corpus relief in federal court, see 18 U.S.C.A. § 3006A, but has not provided for counsel for state prisoners seeking federal habeas corpus review. Representation in such cases is sometimes provided *pro bono* by groups such as the American Civil Liberties Union or the Legal Aid Society. In some instances, prisoners write their own petitions for federal habeas corpus review or get fellow inmates to do this for them.

Ineffective Counsel as a Basis for Postconviction Relief

The Supreme Court has recognized that the right to counsel means little unless counsel provides a defendant with effective representation. *McMann v. Richardson*,

JURISPRUDENCE

O'Sullivan v. Boerckel, 526 U.S. 838, 119 S.Ct. 1728, 144 L.Ed.2d 1 (1999)

Darren Boerckel was convicted in an Illinois court of rape, burglary, and aggravated battery. The Illinois Appellate Court affirmed the conviction, and the Illinois Supreme Court denied Boerckel's petition for discretionary review. Boerckel then initiated a federal habeas corpus action in which he raised six federal constitutional claims. The federal district court denied the petition, finding that Boerckel had "procedurally defaulted" his first three claims by failing to include them in his petition for discretionary review to the

Illinois Supreme Court. On appeal, the Seventh Circuit reversed, holding that filing for discretionary review by the state's highest court is not necessary to exhaust one's state court remedies for purposes of the federal habeas corpus statute. Reviewing the case on certiorari, the Supreme Court reversed again, holding that a state prisoner must present his claims to a state supreme court in a petition for discretionary review when such review is part of the State's "ordinary appellate review procedure." Failure to do so constitutes procedural default and precludes these issues from being raised on federal habeas corpus review.

397 U.S. 759, 90 S.Ct. 1441, 25 L.Ed.2d 763 (1970). Failure of counsel, whether appointed or retained, to be an effective advocate for the defendant constitutes a basis to award a defendant a new trial. *Cuyler v. Sullivan*, 446 U.S. 335, 100 S.Ct. 1708, 64 L.Ed.2d 333 (1980). Some examples of ineffective representation where relief might well be afforded include failure of counsel to present evidence favorable to the accused, failure to challenge the admissibility of evidence presented by the prosecution, and failure to challenge prosecutorial misconduct.

ineffective assistance of counsel Deficient performance by a lawyer representing a defendant that results in serious errors that prejudice the right of a defendant to a fair trial.

The requirement to furnish counsel to indigent defendants has probably contributed to a rise in claims of **ineffective assistance of counsel**. Indigent defendants are sometimes distrustful of public defenders and other appointed counsel. If convicted, these defendants may be more likely to feel that their representation was ineffective compared with that provided by privately retained attorneys.

A defendant's claim of error or deficiency in counsel's performance is rarely challenged in the trial court, so it is not generally subject to being raised on direct appeal. But in some instances where the record of the trial shows on its face that counsel was ineffective, an appellate court will consider the issue on direct appeal. For example, in *Eure v. State*, 764 So.2d 798 (Fla. App. 2000), on a direct appeal from the defendant's conviction for possession and sale of cocaine, a Florida appellate court reversed the defendant's conviction because it found the defendant's counsel was ineffective for failing to object to a series of improper arguments by the prosecutor.

In *Strickland v. Washington*, 466 U.S. 668, 104 S.Ct. 2052, 80 L.Ed.2d 674 (1984), the Supreme Court articulated a uniform constitutional standard for determining the issue of ineffective counsel:

> First, the defendant must show that counsel's performance was deficient. This requires showing that counsel made errors so serious that counsel was not functioning as the "counsel" guaranteed the defendant by the Sixth Amendment. Second, the defendant must show that the deficient performance prejudiced the defense. This requires showing that counsel's errors were so serious as to deprive the defendant of a fair trial, a trial whose result is reliable. Unless a defendant makes both showings, it cannot be said that the conviction . . . resulted from a breakdown in the adversary process that renders the result unreliable. 466 U.S. at 687, 104 S.Ct. at 2063, 80 L.Ed.2d at 693.

The standard announced in *Strickland v. Washington* has been criticized by numerous commentators as being too lax. Only twice since 1984 has the Supreme Court upheld a claim of ineffective assistance on the basis of the *Strickland* test. In the first of these decisions, *Williams v. Taylor*, 529 U.S. 362, 120 S.Ct. 1495, 146 L.Ed.2d 389 (2000), the Court upheld a lower court determination that the attorneys representing Terry Williams in a capital murder case failed to provide effective assistance during the sentencing phase and that it was reasonably probable that Williams would not have received the death penalty if his attorneys had presented and fully explained to the jury all of the available evidence pertaining to mitigating factors. More recently, in *Wiggins v. Smith*, 539 U.S. 510, 123 S.Ct. 2527, 156 L.Ed.2d 471 (2003), the Court noted that the failure of the assistant public defenders to discover and present powerful mitigating evidence in the sentencing phase of a capital murder trial was constitutionally deficient. Writing for a majority of five justices, Justice Sandra Day O'Connor noted, "Had the jury been able to place petitioner's excruciating life history on the mitigating side of the scale, there is a reasonable probability that at least one juror would have struck a different balance." 539 U.S. at 536, 123 S.Ct. at 2543, 156 L.Ed.2d at 495.

JURISPRUDENCE

Wiggins v. Smith, 539 U.S. 510, 123 S.Ct. 2527,156 L.Ed.2d 471 (2003)

Kevin Wiggins was convicted of capital murder and sentenced to death in a Maryland court. At the sentencing phase, Wiggins's public defender stated in his opening statement that the jury would hear evidence regarding Wiggins's "difficult life," but no evidence was actually submitted to the jury for their consideration. The only mitigating evidence presented at sentencing was that Wiggins had no prior criminal history. At a subsequent postconviction relief hearing, Wiggins's new counsel argued "that his trial counsel had rendered ineffective assistance by failing to investigate and present mitigating evidence of his dysfunctional background." Expert testimony revealed "the severe physical and sexual abuse [Wiggins] had suffered at the hands of his mother and while under the care of a series of foster parents." Trial counsel testified at the hearing that while funds were available for such expert testimony, "he did not remember retaining a forensic social worker to prepare a social history before sentencing." The trial court denied Wiggins's petition for postconviction relief, and the state court of appeals affirmed. However, the U.S. District Court "granted Wiggins relief on his federal habeas petition, holding that the Maryland court's rejection of his ineffective assistance claim involved an unreasonable application of clearly established federal law." The Fourth Circuit Court of Appeals reversed. The Supreme Court agreed with the District Court, holding: "The performance of Wiggins' attorney at sentencing violated his Sixth Amendment right to effective assistance of counsel." In writing for the majority, Justice O'Connor noted that Wiggins's trial counsel failed to conduct "a reasonable investigation," which "fell short of the professional standards." Also, Justice O'Connor observed that "in light of the facts counsel discovered in the DSS records concerning Wiggins's alcoholic mother and his problems in foster care, counsel's decision to cease investigating when he did was unreasonable." O'Connor wrote: "Any reasonably competent attorney would have realized that pursuing such leads was necessary to making an informed choice among possible defenses, particularly given the apparent absence of aggravating factors from Wiggins's background." As a result of the inadequate representation at sentencing, the Court held "counsel's failures prejudiced Wiggins's defense." Given, Wiggins's sufficiently satisfied the two-prong test in *Strickland*, the Court reversed the death sentence and remanded the case for further proceedings.

The Court's decisions in the *Williams* and *Wiggins* cases suggest the Court's willingness to scrutinize the performance of counsel at sentencing as well as in the trial stage in cases where defendants' lives are at stake.

Collateral Attack in State Court

At one time federal habeas corpus review was the only real means of postconviction relief available to state prisoners who had exhausted their appeals of right in the state courts. Today, most states have statutes or court rules that permit state prisoners, under appropriate circumstances, to challenge illegal convictions or sentences even after their ordinary appeals have been exhausted. These procedures, known as **collateral attack** or postconviction relief, provide for state-level judicial review of judgments and sentences imposed in violation of the federal or state constitutions. As access to federal habeas corpus relief has been constricted by Congress and the Supreme Court, these state-level mechanisms take on even greater importance.

North Carolina statutes that provide opportunities for collateral relief to convicted defendants appear typical of the grounds for postconviction relief available to defendants convicted in state courts. The grounds that a defendant may assert by a motion for collateral relief include the following:

collateral attack The attempt to defeat the outcome of a judicial proceeding by challenging it in a different proceeding or court.

The trial court lacked jurisdiction over the defendant.

The defendant's conviction was obtained in violation of the U.S. or North Carolina constitutions.

A significant change has occurred in the law applied in the proceedings leading to the defendant's conviction or sentence, and such changed law must be applied retroactively.

The defendant's sentence is illegal; or the defendant is entitled to release for having fully served the sentence imposed.

In addition, within a reasonable time after discovery, a defendant may assert that evidence is available that was unknown or unavailable to the defendant at trial and that has a direct and material bearing on the defendant's eligibility for the death penalty or the defendant's guilt or innocence. West's N.C.G.S.A. § 15A-1415. This is particularly significant in light of the Supreme Court's decision in *Herrera v. Collins*, supra, that federal habeas corpus review is not the proper mechanism for litigation of belated claims of actual innocence brought by persons convicted in state courts. The other states have similar provisions for postconviction relief.

DNA Evidence as a Basis for Postconviction Relief

As we pointed out in Chapter 6, the introduction of DNA testing has had an enormous impact on criminal trials, especially in rape and homicide prosecutions. But DNA evidence is not only useful to prosecutors seeking convictions, it is also extremely valuable as a mean of proving the actual innocence of persons who were convicted of rape or homicide on the basis of eyewitness testimony or circumstantial evidence. According to research conducted by the Innocence Project, there have been more than 180 DNA exonerations in the United States since the first one in 1989. Fourteen of these exonerees were death-row inmates wrongly convicted of murder. See www.innocenceproject.org/docs/DNAExonerationFacts_WEB.pdf.

Most states now recognize newly discovered evidence as a basis for postconviction relief. In the case of DNA evidence, though, testing of genetic material is required before such evidence can be obtained. In most cases, a convicted person needs to gain access to evidence through a sort of postconviction discovery process. Yet many jurisdictions have not established standards or procedures to govern such discovery. In some states, courts have formulated standards and procedures based on norms of due process, which are expressed through judicial opinions. In other states, prisoners seeking to demonstrate their innocence on the basis of DNA evidence must apply for executive clemency. A few states now have statutes addressing this problem. For example, New York law provides that

> in cases of convictions . . . where the defendant's motion requests the performance of a forensic DNA test on specified evidence, and upon the court's determination that any evidence containing deoxyribonucleic acid (DNA) was secured in connection with the trial resulting in the judgment, the court shall grant the application for forensic DNA testing of such evidence upon its determination that if a DNA test had been conducted on such evidence, and if the results had been admitted in the trial resulting in the judgment, there exists a reasonable probability that the verdict would have been more favorable to the defendant. McKinney's N.Y. Crim. Proc. Law § 440.30 (1-a)(a).

Unlike New York, some states, through legislation or rules of court, impose time limits on applications for postconviction DNA testing. Florida Rule of

Criminal Procedure 3.853 originally imposed a deadline, but, after several extensions the Supreme Court of Florida, in 2007, revised Rule 3.853 to provide: "The motion for postconviction DNA testing may be filed or considered at any time following the date that the judgment and sentence in the case becomes final." *Amendments to Florida Rules of Criminal Procedure,* 953 So.2d 513 (Fla. 2007). Likewise the requirements for seeking DNA testing are different under various state statutes and rules of court. Florida Rule of Criminal Procedure 3.853(b), as recently amended, requires that a motion for postconviction DNA testing must be under oath and must include:

1. a statement of the facts relied on in support of the motion, including a description of the physical evidence containing DNA to be tested and, if known, the present location or last known location of the evidence and how it originally was obtained;

2. a statement that the evidence was not tested previously for DNA, or a statement that the results of previous DNA testing were inconclusive and that subsequent scientific developments in DNA testing techniques likely would produce a definitive result establishing that the movant is not the person who committed the crime;

3. a statement that the movant is innocent and how the DNA testing requested by the motion will exonerate the movant of the crime for which the movant was sentenced, or a statement of how the DNA testing will mitigate the sentence received by the movant for that crime;

4. a statement that identification of the movant is a genuinely disputed issue in the case and why it is an issue, or an explanation of how the DNA evidence would either exonerate the defendant or mitigate the sentence that the movant received;

5. a statement of any other facts relevant to the motion; and

6. a certificate that a copy of the motion has been served on the prosecuting authority.

Advocates of expanding prisoners' access to postconviction relief based on DNA evidence believe that prosecutors should be required to maintain biological evidence used to secure a conviction as long as that person is incarcerated. They also argue that statutes of limitations on convicted persons seeking postconviction relief should be abolished (as Florida recently did) and that funding should be provided so that prisoners seeking postconviction relief can have adequate legal representation throughout the process.

Exonerations of convicted persons, especially those on death row, based on DNA testing have received enormous media coverage and have shocked the conscience of the public. While prosecutors often resist efforts to undo convictions through DNA testing, there is growing public sentiment that the need for finality in the judicial process must give way to the search for truth when such powerful scientific means of seeking the truth are now available.

The U.S. Supreme Court Grants Relief Based on Newly Discovered DNA Evidence

In *House v. Bell*, 547 U.S. 518, 126 S.Ct. 2064, 165 L.Ed.2d 1 (2006), a case reminiscent of *Schlup v. Delo*, supra, the Supreme Court, in a 5–3 decision, granted Paul Gregory House, a Tennessee death row inmate, a hearing in federal district court to litigate a procedurally defaulted claim of ineffective assistance of counsel on the basis on newly discovered DNA evidence. Writing for the majority, Justice Kennedy summed up the case as follows:

CASE-IN-POINT

DNA Evidence Used to Exonerate a Man Falsely Convicted of Rape

In 1983, Bernard Webster was convicted of rape and sentenced to thirty years in prison by a Maryland court after a schoolteacher identified him as the man who sexually assaulted her in her apartment. Twenty years later, Webster was exonerated after DNA testing was performed on semen residues that had been obtained from the victim shortly after the rape occurred in 1982. In proving his innocence, Webster took advantage of a Maryland statute enacted in 2001 that requires judges to order DNA testing pursuant to motions for postconviction relief in murder and rape cases where there is "reasonable probability" that testing will produce evidence of actual innocence. In securing postconviction relief, Webster was aided by the Innocence Project, a *pro bono* group dedicated to assisting persons who were wrongfully convicted of crimes. According to a study conducted by the Center for Wrongful Convictions at Northwestern University, false identification by eyewitnesses is a leading cause of wrongful convictions.

This is not a case of conclusive exoneration. Some aspects of the State's evidence . . . still support an inference of guilt. Yet the central forensic proof connecting House to the crime . . . has been called into question, and House has put forward substantial evidence pointing to a different suspect. Accordingly, and although the issue is close, we conclude that this is the rare case where—had the jury heard all the conflicting testimony—it is more likely than not that no reasonable juror viewing the record as a whole would lack reasonable doubt. 547 U.S. at 553, 126 S.Ct. at 2086, 165 L.Ed.2d at 63.

By allowing appeals based on newly discovered DNA and other technological developments, courts risk more extended processes with attendant delays and costs. But the risk of affirming convictions based on evidence that is proven to be scientifically unreliable forcefully argues for expansion of the appellate process to accommodate such developments. This is an issue that legislative bodies and courts are now facing as new technologies are being developed and convicted defendants seek the right to ask expansion of the appellate process.

Nonjudicial Remedies Available to Persons Convicted of Crimes

clemency A grant of mercy by an executive official commuting a sentence or pardoning a criminal.

Under the English common law, appeal to the Crown predated appeal to higher courts as the remedy for an unjust conviction or unreasonable sentence. In addition, because a crime was viewed as an offense against the Crown, the monarch possessed the authority to forgive the wrongdoer or grant **clemency**. In contemporary America, the appeal to executive authority remains as a carryover from the common law and as a supplement to judicial review.

Presidential Pardons

pardon An executive action that mitigates or sets aside punishment for a crime.

Article II, Section 2, Clause 1 of the U.S. Constitution states that the president "shall have Power to grant Reprieves and Pardons for Offences against the United States, except in Cases of Impeachment." This broad power includes the right to commute sentences, remit fines and penalties, and even grant conditional pardons. Indeed, the presidential **pardon** may be issued before conviction, as was amply demonstrated in 1974, when President Gerald Ford pardoned former president Richard Nixon for his role in the Watergate scandal. It was demonstrated again in December 1992, when President George H. W. Bush granted a pardon to Caspar Weinberger, the former Secretary of Defense, and five others who allegedly were involved in the much-publicized controversy concerning the trading of arms for hostages. These pardons were politically controversial, but there was no question as to their legality.

Equally if not more controversial was President Clinton's last-minute pardon of Marc Rich, a fugitive from a 1983 indictment for federal income tax evasion. The Rich pardon, which was given without the normal consultation with the Department of Justice, prompted congressional hearings and an investigation by federal prosecutors. Investigators looked into the possibility that Rich purchased a presidential pardon by passing money through his former wife, who made large contributions both to the Clinton presidential library foundation and to Hillary Clinton's 2000 Senate campaign.

The Supreme Court has said that "[t]he plain purpose of the broad power conferred . . . was to allow . . . the President to 'forgive' the convicted person in part or entirely, to reduce a penalty in terms of a specified number of years, or to alter it with conditions which are in themselves constitutionally unobjectionable." *Schick v. Reed*, 419 U.S. 256, 266, 95 S.Ct. 379, 385, 42 L.Ed.2d 430, 438–439 (1974). Therefore, a full presidential pardon totally restores any civil rights the recipient may have lost as a result of conviction. In effect, the full pardon makes an individual as innocent as if the crime had never been committed. *Ex parte Garland*, 71 U.S. (4 Wall.) 333, 18 L.Ed. 366 (1866).

Clemency at the State Level

Either by constitutional or statutory provisions, executive authorities in all fifty states are likewise granted broad powers to pardon and commute sentences of persons convicted of violations of state criminal law. In many states, the pardoning power is vested exclusively in the governor. In a few states, the governor is limited to granting pardons approved by a state commission. In some states, the pardoning power is vested entirely in a state commission.

In recent years, a number of state prisoners convicted of rape and murder have sought executive clemency based on DNA testing that shows their innocence. Increasingly, such claims are handled judicially through motions for postconviction relief, as courts and legislatures recognize the need to allow persons who claim to have been wrongfully convicted of crimes to prove their innocence through DNA testing.

One of the most dramatic uses of executive clemency in American history took place in January 2003, when Governor George Ryan commuted the death sentences of 156 inmates awaiting execution in Illinois. All but three of the inmates had their sentences commuted to life in prison without possibility of parole; the other three were given life sentences with the possibility of seeking parole. Governor Ryan's dramatic and controversial order came three years after he announced a moratorium on the death penalty in Illinois and appointed a commission to study the issue. After receiving the commission's report, which identified various problems with trials, sentencing, and the appeals process, Governor Ryan concluded that the system was "haunted by the demon of error, error in determining guilt, and error in determining who among the guilty deserves to die."

Conclusion

Under the early English common law, the right to appeal was nonexistent. Eventually, through court decisions and statutes, defendants gained the right to appeal criminal convictions. In America, federal and state statutes guarantee at least one appeal of right to defendants who are convicted after entering a plea of not guilty. Beyond these appeals of right, defendants may seek review from higher courts by filing petitions for certiorari or discretionary review. Finally, the historic writ of habeas corpus provides prisoners with an avenue to seek postconviction relief in state and federal tribunals. In many states, postconviction relief has become structured under criteria specified by statute or rules of court. One of the most common issues raised on postconviction review is whether a defendant received effective assistance of counsel at trial. Perhaps the most dramatic recent development in appellate processes has been acceptance of DNA evidence as proof of innocence of persons convicted of rape and homicide crimes on the basis of eyewitness testimony or circumstantial evidence.

There is considerable criticism today of the delays caused by the seemingly inexhaustible routes of appellate review of some cases, but the public is generally unaware of the thousands of appeals that are resolved in a timely manner. In America, where criminal law and procedure are guided by due process values as well as by society's need for crime control, delays in appellate processes must be weighed against society's deep and historic commitment to fundamental fairness.

Chapter Summary

- LO1

  - Until Parliament enacted the Criminal Appeal Act of 1907, the English common law afforded defendants limited review of criminal convictions.

  - In America, review includes trial *de novo*, appeal of right, discretionary review, and postconviction relief. Trial *de novo* occurs when a trial court of general jurisdiction reviews a conviction by a court of limited jurisdiction.

  - Appeal of right refers to an appellate court's review of a criminal conviction from a trial court of general jurisdiction. Appeals of right in federal criminal cases are heard by U.S. Courts of Appeals (circuit courts). Intermediate state appellate courts hear most appeals of right, although in less populous states, the highest court of the state handles routine appeals. In four states, special appellate courts hear only criminal appeals.

  - A defendant whose conviction has been sustained by an intermediate appellate court may petition a court of last resort for a writ of certiorari (discretionary review). The U.S. Supreme Court may review federal and state criminal cases involving federal issues by exercising its certiorari jurisdiction.

  - A defendant in prison may seek additional review of a conviction or sentence by applying for a writ of habeas corpus or another form of postconviction relief.

- LO2

  - On appeal, a defendant may challenge trial court rulings objected to during pretrial, trial, or posttrial phases. Irrespective of an objection, a defendant may challenge the trial court's jurisdiction and any fundamental errors.

- A defendant usually raises from one to six major assignments of error or points as a basis to secure a reversal of the trial court's judgment or sentence.

- Typically, a defendant who pleads guilty may raise on appeal only issues relating to the trial court's jurisdiction, voluntariness of the guilty plea, and legality of the sentence. Even then, an appellate court may refuse to review other than jurisdictional issues unless the trial court has denied the defendant's request to withdraw a plea of guilty.

- The Federal Rules of Criminal Procedure allow defendants to enter conditional pleas of guilty or *nolo contendere*, reserving in writing the right to have an appellate court review an adverse determination of a specified pretrial motion. Some states have similar provisions.

- Most states provide automatic appeals of death sentences to their highest court.

- The federal government has no right to appeal a defendant's acquittal but may appeal dismissal of an indictment, granting a defendant a new trial, releasing a defendant before trial or after conviction, or orders suppressing evidence before the defendant is put in jeopardy. States, in general, limit appeals by the prosecution to similar grounds.

- LO3

  - The primary function of appellate courts is to correct trial court errors. Appellate courts (especially the highest state courts and the U.S. Supreme Court) not only interpret statutory and constitutional provisions, they "fill in gaps" in the law, and effectively "make law."

  - Most criminal appeals are heard "on the record," which appellate courts scrutinize for procedural errors of trial courts. Appellate courts frequently find technical errors to be harmless; however, in 1967 the U.S. Supreme Court ruled that where an error involves provisions of the federal constitution, before affirming a trial court judgment, an appellate court must find beyond a reasonable doubt that the error was harmless.

- LO4

  - The Bail Reform Act of 1984 allows federal judges to detain a criminal defendant without bail if the defendant poses a special threat to community safety or a high risk of flight. A defendant who appeals a conviction has the burden of proving an entitlement to bail based on criteria specified in the law. The Act also governs release pending appeal by the government.

  - In an appeal from a state court conviction, the trial court usually determines whether a defendant can be released by considering the defendant's family and community ties and whether the appeal is taken in good faith and presents a debatable point of law. If the state appeals, the defendant is usually released on personal recognizance.

- LO5

  - In 1963, the Supreme Court held that an indigent defendant is entitled to be furnished counsel to pursue an appeal of right; in 1974 the Court ruled that there is no requirement to furnish counsel to assist an indigent defendant who seeks further discretionary review.

o In 1967, the Court ruled that appointed counsel who finds no merit to a defendant's appeal may withdraw from representation, but only after submitting a brief claiming that the appeal was wholly frivolous and referring to any arguable issues.

- LO6

  o Filing a notice of appeal invokes requirements for the appellant to file pertinent lower court records and briefs on the law. The appellee has the right to respond.

  o Briefs of counsel are the principal instruments used to persuade the appellate court to reverse, affirm, or modify the decision being appealed.

  o In some appeals, courts hear oral arguments by counsel, but appellate court decisions are made in private conferences.

  o Once judges arrive at a decision, the appellate court releases its opinion. A *per curiam* opinion represents the appellate court as a whole; more commonly an opinion is authored by one judge and joined by other judges.

  o A judge who disagrees with the court's decision may write a dissenting opinion.

  o A judge who agrees with the court's decision but wants to write on issues not addressed or emphasized in the court's opinion may write a separate concurring opinion, or may simply concur in the court's judgment.

  o Most appellate court decisions are published in books known as reporters. Published appellate opinions play an important role in developing the law, as judges and lawyers regularly consult the reporters for guidance in pending cases.

  o After the court issues its decision, counsel may seek a rehearing or rehearing *en banc*.

- LO7

  o Long after the right to appeal has expired or appeals have been exhausted, a prisoner may seek a writ of habeas corpus. The U.S. Constitution declares: "The Privilege of the Writ of Habeas Corpus shall not be suspended unless when in Cases of Rebellion or Invasion the public Safety may require it." U.S. Const., Art. 1, Sec. 9.

  o Before the twentieth century, the federal habeas corpus jurisdiction was seldom used to review state criminal convictions except to ascertain that the state trial court had jurisdiction over the person being tried. In 1915, the Supreme Court broadened issuance of the writ to ensure that states supplied some "corrective process" whereby criminal defendants could seek to vindicate their federal constitutional rights.

  o During the 1960s under Chief Justice Earl Warren, the Supreme Court greatly broadened federal habeas corpus to allow a state prisoner to seek the writ without having first taken a direct appeal in state courts. Criticism of federal court intervention, coupled with the increasing professionalism of the state judiciaries, led the Supreme Court to restrict access to federal habeas corpus relief during the 1970s, '80s, and '90s.

- The Antiterrorism and Effective Death Penalty Act of 1996 curtailed second habeas corpus petitions by state prisoners who have already filed such petitions in federal court. The Supreme Court unanimously rejected constitutional challenges to the Act.

- **LO8**

  - Today, most states have statutes or court rules that permit state prisoners, under appropriate circumstances, to challenge illegal convictions or sentences even after their ordinary appeals have been exhausted. These procedures, known as collateral or postconviction relief, provide opportunities for prisoners to seek state-level judicial review of judgments and sentences allegedly issued in violation of federal or state constitutions.

  - States recognize claims of ineffective counsel and newly discovered evidence as a basis for postconviction relief. In 1984, the Supreme Court articulated a uniform constitutional standard for determining the issue of ineffective counsel that requires a defendant to show that counsel's performance was deficient and that such deficiency prejudiced the defense. that such deficiency prejudiced the defense.

- **LO9**

  - In 2006, the Supreme Court granted a death row inmate a hearing in federal district court to litigate a procedurally defaulted claim of ineffective assistance of counsel on the basis of newly discovered DNA evidence. Since then, state legislatures and courts have recognized that DNA evidence may establish the innocence of defendants convicted of rape and homicidal crimes on the basis of eyewitness testimony.

  - In most cases, a convicted person needs to gain access to DNA evidence through a postconviction discovery process.

- **LO10**

  - Article II, Section 2, Clause 1 of the U.S. Constitution states that the president "shall have Power to grant Reprieves and Pardons for Offences against the United States, except in Cases of Impeachment." This broad power includes the right to commute sentences, remit fines and penalties, and even grant conditional pardons. In effect, the full pardon makes an individual as innocent as if the crime had never been committed.

  - Either by constitutional or statutory provisions, executive authorities in all fifty states are granted broad powers to pardon and commute sentences of persons convicted of violations of state criminal laws.

  - In many states, the pardoning power is vested exclusively in the governor. In a few, the governor is limited to granting pardons approved by a state commission. In some states, the pardoning power is vested entirely in a state commission.

Key Terms

affirm

Anders brief

answer brief

appeal of right

appellant

appellee

assignments of error

Bail Reform Act of 1984

brief

clemency

collateral attack

concurring in the judgment

concurring opinion

discretionary review

dissenting opinion

doctrine of harmless error

en banc rehearing

error correction

federal habeas corpus review

Federal Rules of Appellate Procedure

frivolous appeals

fundamental errors

ineffective assistance of counsel

judicial conference

lawmaking

miscarriage of justice

motion for rehearing

notice of appeal

opinion of the court

oral argument

pardon

pendency of the appeal

per curiam opinion

petitioner

postconviction relief

remand

reply brief

reporters

respondent

reverse

rule of four

substantial federal question

trial *de novo*

writ of error

writ of habeas corpus

writs of certiorari

Key Court Decisions

Chapman v. California (1967): Where an error at trial involves provisions of the federal constitution, an appellate court must find beyond a reasonable doubt that the error was harmless.

Douglas v. California (1963): States must provide counsel to indigent persons convicted of felonies who exercise their statutory right to appeal.

Felker v. Turpin (1996): Restrictions on access to federal habeas corpus review brought about by the Antiterrorism and Effective Death Penalty Act of 1996 do not constitute a suspension of the writ of habeas corpus or an impermissible interference with the Supreme Court's jurisdiction.

O'Sullivan v. Boerckel (1999): A state prisoner's failure to present his claims to a state supreme court in a petition for discretionary review when such review is part of the State's ordinary appellate process constitutes procedural default and precludes these issues from being raised on federal habeas corpus review.

Wiggins v. Smith (2003): The failure of assistant public defenders to discover and present powerful mitigating evidence in the sentencing phase of a capital murder trial constitutes ineffective assistance of counsel.

Questions for Thought and Discussion

1. What court or courts in your state have jurisdiction to hear appeals from felony convictions? What changes, if any, would you propose for your state's system of appellate courts?

2. Is the right to appeal a necessary concomitant of due process of law? In the absence of statutory rights to appeal, would the current Supreme Court find a constitutional right to appeal implicit in the due process requirements of the Constitution?

3. What new or revised procedures would expedite the resolution of criminal appeals? Would such procedures detract from the fair and deliberative review essential to determine whether the decision of the trial court in a criminal case was arrived at fairly and accurately?

4. In addition to determining whether a sentence imposed on a convicted defendant is within the statutory bounds, do you think an appellate court is an appropriate forum to reconsider the reasonableness of the sentence imposed by the trial court?

5. How has the "nationalization" of the criminal law that occurred through decisions of the U.S. Supreme Court during the 1960s and 1970s affected the appellate process?

6. The U.S. Supreme Court has recognized a constitutional right to represent oneself in a criminal trial. Could a person who insisted on self-representation at trial later challenge his or her conviction by claiming ineffective assistance of counsel?

7. Where a defendant has had an opportunity for a full and fair review of his or her trial through an appeal, what justifies the availability of additional avenues of review through collateral attack?

8. After studying briefs submitted by counsel and hearing oral arguments in a proceeding open to the public, appellate judges retire to privately discuss and decide the merits of criminal appeals. Should these deliberations be open to the public? Why or why not?

9. In a substantial number of criminal appeals, some state appellate courts routinely issue decisions merely stating, "Judgment Affirmed." When an appellate court rejects a defendant's issues on appeal, should it be required to issue an opinion justifying its decision? In discussing this issue, consider whether such a requirement would (a) require greatly increasing the number of judges and support staff and the additional costs thereof, or (b) detract from the court's ability to direct its efforts to writing opinions on novel questions of law.

10. Do you think the ability of a convicted defendant to secure DNA testing rises to an issue of due process of law? Should there be a statute of limitations on a defendant raising the issue? Does Congress have a role to play in providing a standardized process throughout the country? Should the process be governed by federal statute, or should state legislatures and courts be left free to develop their own procedures?

Problems for Discussion and Solution

1. John Dunnit was convicted of aggravated sexual battery and was sentenced to state prison. After exhausting his appellate remedies in the state courts, Dunnit filed a federal habeas corpus application, which was denied. Dunnit challenged the denial in an appeal to the federal circuit court and was again denied relief. Dunnit filed a second federal habeas corpus petition after President Clinton signed the Antiterrorism and Effective Death Penalty Act of 1996 amending the federal habeas corpus statute. How does this new law affect Dunnit's case? Is Dunnit's second application for a writ of habeas corpus affected by recent Supreme Court decisions mentioned in this chapter?

2. Culp Able was convicted of murder in state court. Central to the state's case was a confession that Able uttered before being given his *Miranda* warnings. The trial judge received the confession in evidence over the defendant's objection, and Able was convicted. On appeal, the intermediate state appellate court and later the state supreme court considered and rejected Able's challenge to the admissibility of the confession. Then Able filed an application for federal habeas corpus relief, citing only the alleged *Miranda* violation as a basis for the reversal of his conviction. Relying on *Stone v. Powell* (1976), the state argues that the petition should be dismissed because Able was afforded "a full and fair opportunity to litigate his Fifth Amendment claim in the state courts." If you were the federal district judge, how would you rule? Should Able get his day in federal court?

3. Imagine that Congress adopted a statute requiring all state and federal courts to consider belated claims of innocence based on newly discovered physical evidence, regardless of the amount of time that has elapsed since conviction. Boris Bonanza, who is currently on death row in the state of Cornucopia, was convicted of first-degree murder seventeen years ago. The victim in the case, Sheila Softmore, had been stabbed repeatedly with a knife. Bonanza was found on the scene, his clothes stained with blood. A bloody kitchen knife was found on the floor nearby. At trial Bonanza claimed that he was innocent and that the blood found on his clothes were not from the victim, but from the real killer, whom he had stabbed after wrestling the knife from him. According to the statement Bonanza gave police, Bonanza arrived on the scene too late to save Softmore and the real killer fled after being stabbed. The crime lab determined that the blood on Bonanza's shirt was the same type as the victim's, O-positive, but no DNA test was performed. The state of Cornucopia has a statute of limitations on the use of newly discovered physical evidence to support belated claims of evidence, and the statute has already tolled in Bonanza's case. In a petition for postconviction relief, Bonanza's attorney is arguing that under the new federal statute, Bonanza is entitled to a DNA comparison between blood residue on his shirt, which remains in storage at the crime lab, and the victim, whose body would have to be exhumed to make the comparison. How might the assistant state attorney general, who is arguing against the petition, argue the state's case? If you were the judge, how would you be inclined to rule? What additional information would you need to make a ruling?

Access to the Law through Legal Research

The Nature of Legal Research

Successful legal research requires a systematic method of finding the law applicable to a particular problem or set of facts. Before beginning research, it is helpful, if not essential, for the criminal justice professional or student to have a basic understanding of the law and the legal system.

After assembling the relevant facts and completing a preliminary analysis of the problem, the researcher must find the applicable constitutional and statutory materials and then search for authoritative interpretations of the law. Interpretations are usually found in appellate court decisions construing the particular constitutional provision or statute in analogous situations. These judicial decisions are referred to as cases in point. Legislative and judicial sources of the law are referred to as primary sources because they are authoritative.

A variety of other legal materials, called secondary sources, are available to the researcher. These consist of legal encyclopedias, textbooks by scholars and practitioners, law reviews published by law schools, and journals and periodicals published by various legal organizations. These secondary sources are extremely helpful to the researcher, especially to one unfamiliar with the law in a given area.

Getting Started in Legal Research

Once you become knowledgeable about the sources of the law and the process of its development by courts and you develop the skill of analyzing a problem, you can get started in legal research. Here is a suggestion that can help. If you attend a college at or near a law school, a law librarian might help you in the use of law books or electronic sources. Or you might get assistance from law students, as they usually take a course in legal research in their first year. If you are working from home, do not overlook the fact that in many communities, local governments, courthouses, and bar associations have established law libraries that are usually available to the public; some of these may even offer the free use of legal research databases and other electronic sources.

Legal research has changed rapidly due to the Internet, and more information is becoming available online every day. But before undertaking online research, it is essential that the legal researcher become knowledgeable about the sources that are the traditional professional tools for legal research, when books are the best sources to use, and when to go online instead.

Primary Legal Sources

Federal and state constitutions are often the beginning points in legal research in the criminal justice area because they provide the framework for our government and guarantee certain basic rights to the accused. As explained in this text, the rights of an accused are protected by several provisions of the federal constitution and the Bill of Rights. Most state constitutions afford criminal defendants similar protections. Thus, a person concerned about the legality of an arrest, search, or seizure would examine the relevant federal and state constitutional provisions and then seek to determine how the courts have construed the law in analogous situations.

Federal offenses are defined in statutes enacted by the U.S. Congress, and state offenses are defined in statutes enacted by state legislatures. Federal statutes (in sequence of their adoption) are published annually in the *United States Statutes at Large*. Most states have similar volumes, called session laws, which incorporate the laws enacted during a given session of the legislature. These federal and state laws are initially compiled in sequence of their adoption and are generally consulted to find the history of a law. Later they are merged into legal codes that systematically arrange the statutes by subject and provide an index. Of far greater assistance to the criminal justice researcher are commercially prepared versions of these codes that classify all federal and state laws of a general and permanent nature by subject and include reference materials and exhaustive indexes. These volumes are kept current by periodic supplements and revised volumes.

The United States Code Annotated

One popular compilation of the federal law widely used by lawyers, judges, and criminal justice professionals is the *United States Code Annotated*. The "U.S.C.A.," as it is known, is published by Thomson/West. The U.S.C.A. consists of fifty separate titles that conform to the text of the Official Code of the Laws of the United States (the official name for the U.S. Code). For instance, Title 18 is titled "Crimes and Criminal Procedure" and is of particular interest to the criminal justice researcher. Each statute in the U.S.C.A. is followed by a series of annotations consisting of court decisions interpreting the particular statute, along with historical notes, cross-references, and other editorial features. The U.S.C.A. also has a General Index, printed annually, that will guide the researcher to a particular title and section number by subject. If the researcher knows only the popular name of a federal statute, the corresponding U.S. Code title and section number can be found in the Popular Name Table. The U.S.C.A. is kept up to date by the use of "pocket parts," annual updates with the latest laws and amendments, which are slipped into the back pockets of the individual volumes so that the researcher can easily find the latest versions of the laws.

Annotated State Codes

Most states have annotated statutes published by either the state or a private publisher. For example, West's *Annotated California Codes* follows the same general format as the U.S.C.A. Annotated statutes are popular aids to legal research and can save the researcher valuable time in locating cases in point. They are especially effective tools for locating interpretations of criminal statutes.

The National Reporter System

Volumes containing appellate court decisions are referred to as reporters. The National Reporter System, by Thomson/West, includes decisions from the U.S. Supreme Court, the lower federal courts, and the state appellate courts. Reported cases are available in bound volumes and online through Westlaw and various Internet sites.

Decisions of the U.S. Supreme Court are officially published in the *United States Reports* (abbreviated U.S.). Two private organizations also report these decisions in hardcover volumes. The *Supreme Court Reporter* (abbreviated S.Ct.) is published by Thomson/West, and *Lawyers Edition,* now in its second series (abbreviated L.Ed.2d), is published by West/Lawyers Cooperative. Although the three reporters have somewhat different editorial features, the actual opinions of the Supreme Court are reproduced identically in all three reporters.

References to judicial decisions found in the reporters are called citations. U.S. Supreme Court decisions are often cited to all three publications—for example, *Miranda v. Arizona,* 384 U.S. 436, 86 S.Ct. 1602, 16 L.Ed.2d 694 (1966). For each of these publications, the citation tells you exactly where the case is published. For example, "384 U.S. 436" means that the *Miranda* case is in volume 384 of the United States Reports on page 436.

Since 1889, the decisions of the U.S. courts of appeals have been published in *West's Federal Reporter,* now in its third series (abbreviated F.3d). Decisions of federal district (trial) courts are published in *West's Federal Supplement,* which is now in its second series (abbreviated F. Supp. 2d). A citation to a case in *Federal Reporter* will read, for example, *Newman v. United States,* 817 F.2d 635 (10th Cir. 1987). This refers to a 1987 case reported in volume 817, page 635 of the *Federal Reporter,* second series, decided by the United States Court of Appeals for the Tenth Circuit. A citation to *United States v. Klopfenstine,* 673 F. Supp. 356 (W.D. Mo. 1987), refers to a 1987 federal district court decision from the Western District of Missouri, reported in volume 673, page 356 of the *Federal Supplement.*

Additional federal reporters publish the decisions from other federal courts (for example, bankruptcy and military appeals), but the federal reporters referred to earlier are those most frequently used by criminal justice professionals.

The Regional Reporters

The decisions of the highest state courts (usually but not always called supreme courts) and the decisions of other state appellate courts (usually referred to as intermediate appellate courts) are found in seven regional reporters, West's *California Reporter,* and the *New York Supplement.* Regional reporters, with their abbreviations in parentheses, include decisions from the following states:

- *Atlantic Reporter* (A. and A.2d): Maine, Vermont, New Hampshire, Connecticut, Rhode Island, Pennsylvania, New Jersey, Maryland, Delaware, and the District of Columbia
- *North Eastern Reporter* (N.E. and N.E.2d): Illinois, Indiana, Massachusetts, New York (court of last resort only—other New York appellate courts have their opinions in the New York Supplement), and Ohio
- *North Western Reporter* (N.W. and N.W.2d): North Dakota, South Dakota, Nebraska, Minnesota, Iowa, Michigan, and Wisconsin

- *Pacific Reporter* (P., P.2d and P.3d): Washington, Oregon, California, Montana, Idaho, Nevada, Utah, Arizona, Wyoming, Colorado, New Mexico, Kansas, Oklahoma, Alaska, and Hawaii
- *Southern Reporter* (So., So.2d and So.3d): Florida, Alabama, Mississippi, and Louisiana
- *South Eastern Reporter* (S.E. and S.E.2d): Virginia, West Virginia, North Carolina, South Carolina, and Georgia
- *South Western Reporter* (S.W., S.W.2d and S.W.3d): Texas, Missouri, Arkansas, Kentucky, and Tennessee

For many states (in addition to New York and California), West publishes separate volumes reporting the decisions as they appear in the regional reporters. *Pennsylvania Reporter* and *Texas Cases* are examples of this.

The following examples of citation forms appear in some of the regional reporters:

- *State v. Hogan*, 480 So.2d 288 (La. 1985). This refers to a 1985 decision of the Louisiana Supreme Court found in volume 480, page 288 of the *Southern Reporter*, second series.
- *State v. Nungesser*, 269 N.W.2d 449 (Iowa 1978). This refers to a 1978 decision of the Iowa Supreme Court found in volume 269, page 449 of the *North Western Reporter*, second series.
- *Henry v. State*, 567 S.W.2d 7 (Tex. Cr. App. 1978). This refers to a 1978 decision of the Texas Court of Criminal Appeals found in volume 567, page 7 of the *South Western Reporter*, second series.

Syllabi, Headnotes, and Key Numbers

The National Reporter System and the regional reporters contain not only the official text of each reported decision but also a brief summary of the decision, called the syllabus, and one or more topically indexed "headnotes." These headnotes briefly describe the principles of law expounded by the court and are indexed by a series of topic "key numbers." West assigns these key numbers to specific points of decisional law. For instance, decisions dealing with first-degree murder are classified under the topic "homicide" and a key number is assigned for each particular aspect of that crime. Thus, a homicide case dealing with the intent requirement in first-degree murder may be classified as "Homicide 9—Intent and design to effect death." Using this key number system, a researcher can locate headnotes of various appellate decisions on this aspect of homicide and is, in turn, led to other relevant cases.

In addition, each of these volumes contains a table of statutes construed in the cases reported in that volume, with reference also to the American Bar Association's *Standards for Criminal Justice*.

United States Law Week

United States Law Week, published by the Bureau of National Affairs, Inc., Washington, D.C., presents a weekly survey of American law. *Law Week* includes all the latest decisions from the U.S. Supreme Court as well as significant current decisions from other federal and state courts.

Criminal Law Reporter

Also published by the Bureau of National Affairs, Inc., the weekly *Criminal Law Reporter* reviews contemporary developments in the criminal law. It is an excellent source of commentaries on current state and federal court decisions in the criminal law area.

Digests

Digests are tools that enable the researcher to locate cases in point through topics and key numbers. By finding a particular topic and key number and looking it up in the pertinent digest, the researcher can locate other cases on the narrow point of law covered by that key number. West publishes the *Decennial Digests*, which topically index all the appellate court decisions from the state and federal courts. The *Decennial Digests* are kept current by a set called the *General Digests* so that the researcher can always find the latest cases.

A series of federal digests contains key number headnotes for decisions of the federal courts. The current series published by West is *Federal Practice Digest 4th*. In addition, separate digests are published for some states as well as for the Atlantic, North Western, Pacific, and South Eastern reporters.

The index at the beginning of each topic identifies the various points of law by numerically arranged key numbers. In addition to the basic topic of criminal law, many topics in the field of criminal law are listed by specific crimes (such as homicide, forgery, and bribery). Procedural topics such as arrest and search and seizure are also included. The digests contain a descriptive word index and a table of cases sorted by name, listing the key numbers corresponding to the decisions. Thus, the researcher can find, by key number, topics that relate to the principles set out in the headnotes prepared for each judicial decision. A researcher who locates a topic and key number has access to all reported decisions on this point of law.

Shepard's Citations

Shepard's Citations is a series that provides the judicial history of cases by reference to the volume and page number of the cases in the particular reporters. Because the law is constantly changing and new laws and decisions come out all the time, it is essential that a researcher keep up to date and know if there are new cases or what might have happened to a case the researcher has found. By using the symbols explained in *Shepard's Citations*, the researcher can determine whether a particular decision has been affirmed, followed, distinguished, modified, or reversed by subsequent court decisions. Most attorneys "Shepardize" the cases they cite in their law briefs to support various principles of law. There is a separate set of *Shepard's Citations* for the U.S. Supreme Court reports, for the federal appellate and district courts, for each regional reporter, and for each state that has an official reporter. *Shepard's* can also be found on Lexis.

KeyCite

Another source that is used for updating a case history, and locating cases that refer to it, is KeyCite, available online as part of Westlaw. Like *Shepard's* (both print and computer versions), KeyCite gives the history of a case and subsequent cases that have cited it. Among other useful features that KeyCite has is a ranking system for the later cases, which shows which cases have discussed or explained the original one in detail and which give a mere mention of the case. This is of great help to the researcher who might otherwise be faced with a long list of cases to read and no way to differentiate their value.

Secondary Sources

Legal authorities other than constitutions, statutes, ordinances, regulations, and court decisions are called secondary sources. Secondary sources explain the law and provide background and analysis of it. They help you understand the law and its applications and also will help you locate even more authorities, such as other cases and statutes.

A basic necessity for any legal researcher's work is a good law dictionary. Several are published, and *Black's Law Dictionary* (9th ed.), published by Thomson/West, is one of the best known. *Black's* is available both in print and on Westlaw.

Legal Encyclopedias

Beyond dictionaries, the most commonly used secondary legal authorities are legal encyclopedias. These are arranged alphabetically by subject and are used much like any standard encyclopedia.

There are two principal national encyclopedias of the law: *Corpus Juris Secundum* (C.J.S.), published by West, and *American Jurisprudence,* second edition (Am.Jur.2d), published by West /Lawyers Cooperative. Appellate courts frequently include citations to these encyclopedias, as well as to cases in the reporters, to document the rules and interpretations contained in their opinions.

Each of these encyclopedias is an excellent set of reference books; one significant difference is that *Corpus Juris Secundum* cites more court decisions, whereas *American Jurisprudence 2d* limits footnote references to the leading cases pertinent to the principles of law in the text. *Corpus Juris Secundum* includes valuable cross-references to West topic key numbers and other secondary sources, including forms. *American Jurisprudence 2d* includes valuable footnote references to another of the company's publications, *American Law Reports,* now in its sixth series. These volumes (cited as A.L.R.) include annotations to the decisional law on selected topics. For example, a 1987 annotation from A.L.R. entitled "Snowmobile Operation as D.W.I. or D.U.I." appears in 56 A.L.R.4th 1092. Both *Corpus Juris Secundum* and *American Jurisprudence 2d* are supplemented annually by cumulative pocket parts and are exceptionally well indexed. They serve as an excellent starting point for a researcher because they provide a general overview of topics. A general index for each set is published annually, and researchers should use this first to find their specific subjects and section numbers.

For example, a person researching the defenses available to a defendant charged with forgery would find a good discussion of the law in this area in either of these encyclopedias. A citation to the text on defenses to forgery found in *Corpus Juris Secundum* would read as follows: 37 C.J.S. Forgery § 41; in *American Jurisprudence 2d* it would read like this: 36 Am.Jur.2d Forgery § 42. In addition to these major national encyclopedias, some states have encyclopedias for the jurisprudence of their state—for example, *Pennsylvania Law Encyclopedia* and *Texas Jurisprudence.* Like the volumes of *Corpus Juris Secundum* and *American Jurisprudence 2d,* most encyclopedias of state law are annually supplemented with cumulative pocket parts.

Textbooks

Textbooks and other treatises on legal subjects often read much like encyclopedias; however, most address specific subjects in greater depth. One of the better-known textbooks is LaFave and Scott, *Criminal Law*, published by Thomson/West.

Law Reviews, Journals, and Professional Publications

Most leading law schools publish law reviews that contain articles, commentaries, and notes by academics, judges, lawyers, and law students who exhaustively research topics. Law review articles can be excellent sources of in-depth analysis and background information on specific legal topics. A citation for a law review article in the criminal justice field, "Consequences of Refusing Consent to a Search and Seizure," 75 S. Cal. L. Rev. 901 (2002), refers to a scholarly article published in volume 75 at page 901 of the *Southern California Law Review*.

An example of a professional publication is the *Criminal Law Bulletin*, published bimonthly by Warren, Gorham & Lamont of Boston. It contains many valuable articles of contemporary interest. For instance, "Probable Cause and the Fourth Amendment" was published in the September 2003 issue. The American Bar Association and most state bar associations publish numerous professional articles in their journals and reports. Some of these present contemporary views on the administration of justice; often they talk more about how the law is actually applied, not just the theory behind it that law review articles sometimes focus on.

The *Index to Legal Periodicals*, published by H. W. Wilson Company of the Bronx, New York, indexes articles from leading legal publications by subject and author. Another index for legal articles is the *Current Law Index*, published by Gale/Cengage in cooperation with the American Association of Law Libraries. These valuable research tools are found in many law libraries and are kept current by periodic supplements. Many college and law school libraries also have these available online. Periodicals published by law schools, bar associations, and other professional organizations can be valuable both in doing research and in gaining a perspective on many contemporary problems in the criminal justice field. The federal government also publishes numerous studies of value to the criminal justice professional and student.

Words and Phrases

Words and Phrases, another West publication, consists of numerous volumes alphabetically arranged in dictionary form. Hundreds of thousands of legal terms are defined with citations to appellate court decisions. The volumes are kept current by annual pocket part supplements.

Computerized Legal Research

Increasingly, legal research is being done electronically using computerized legal databases such as Westlaw. Westlaw operates from a central computer system at the West headquarters in St. Paul, Minnesota, and has databases for state and federal statutes, appellate decisions, attorney general opinions, and certain legal periodicals. For example, the law review article referred to earlier, "Consequences of Refusing Consent to a Search and Seizure," 75 S. Cal. L. Rev. 901 (2002), is available on West-law in the ScALR database and can be quickly retrieved by typing the citation—75 S. Cal. L. Rev. 901—into the "find this document" box on the welcome page. Subscribers can access Westlaw through the Internet. Westlaw users enter queries into the system to begin research, using connectors recognized by the system. A properly formulated query pinpoints the legal issue to be researched and instructs Westlaw to retrieve all data relevant to the query.

Westlaw also has a searching method that uses natural language, which allows queries to be entered in plain English without special terms or connectors. The statutes, cases, and other research results found on Westlaw can be printed, downloaded, or e-mailed. One of the most useful features of Westlaw is the ability to check the history of cases using KeyCite. When the researcher needs to update a large number of cases, Westlaw can save a tremendous amount of time and substantially reduce the possibility of error.

Westlaw is constantly adding new features and new types of materials, such as court documents and practice guides. Westlaw provides tutorials on how to use its new features when they are added.

Lexis is an excellent competing system. As with Westlaw, researchers can use Lexis to find cases and statutes, search for items either by forming queries or using natural language, and find cases by typing in their citations. Unlike Westlaw, which has KeyCite to check citation history, Lexis has an electronic version of *Shepard's* to check cites. It is a bit easier to use and more up-to-date than the printed *Shepard's* volumes. Lexis also has tutorials available to help you find out a about new features or ways to search.

Legal Research Using the Internet

The phenomenal growth of the Internet makes it impossible to firmly state what legal sources or sites currently are available, because new things are being added constantly. The federal and state governments are among those rapidly adding data to the Internet, and for that reason a person looking for government information, or statutes and codes is likely to find it on the Internet. Among the best ways to search for legal information is to use a comprehensive legal site such as ALSO!—American Law Sources On-line (www.lawsource.com)—which has a detailed listing of law websites for each state and for federal sources. ALSO! provides links to official sites such as those of government agencies, courts, and codes as well as other helpful sites such as state bar associations and legal aid groups. Another major site is Findlaw (www.findlaw.com), which uses categories to neatly divide legal information so that a user can search for the appropriate category and then find the information available on that topic or issue. Among Findlaw's categories are state law (further divided into categories for each individual state) and international law (indeed, the Internet is currently the best source for locating law from other countries). Another excellent source for federal information is Thomas (thomas.loc.gov), the Library of Congress website, which contains pending bills, federal laws, and links to other federal sites.

Findlaw's Supreme Court category offers U.S. Supreme Court opinions dating back to 1893 in a searchable format. In addition, the Legal Information Institute (LII) at Cornell University (www.law.cornell.edu/supct/) offers downloadable Supreme Court opinions. The LII archive now contains all opinions of the Court issued since May 1990 as well as hundreds of the most important historical decisions of the Court. The Supreme Court itself now has its own website, useful for finding information about pending or recently decided cases, at www.supremecourtus.gov.

More and more lower courts, both at the federal and state levels, are putting up their own websites, and often very recently decided cases can be found on them. ALSO! is a good place to begin in trying to locate these sites, as its listing for each state includes links to courts of that state. (The researcher may notice that many states have websites that cover all of their courts; for example, www.flcourts.org, the Florida courts website, has links to extensive information from all Florida appellate courts and many of the trial-level courts, too.) Findlaw also can help the researcher find the statutes, court decisions, and court rules of most states, almost all of which are now on the Internet. Regular search engines such as Google and Yahoo can be very helpful in locating court sites and other legal information. When using one of these search engines to locate a particular court decision, it is important to be very specific. One might try a docket number or an obscure or unique term that is found in the case. Most search engines also have advanced search features that let a researcher narrow the search to a particular web domain (for example, only government websites), or format (such as .pdf files), or date. These can be extremely helpful to use.

One of the most helpful sites for finding case law and even secondary sources on the Internet is Google Scholar (scholar.google.com). By going to this and clicking on "legal opinions," the researcher can then do a search for federal and state cases; using the advanced search features, the researcher can specify what courts or dates to look through. While Google Scholar does not offer the wide variety of searching methods that are available on Westlaw, it is a free resource to use when looking for cases.

Although the Internet is convenient and low in cost, there are limitations to consider in doing research there. The Internet is a solid source for finding up-to-date information, such as current state statutes and some recent court decisions; it is also a good source for finding factual material, such as statistics and background information. Because most legal research involves finding more than just the latest cases and laws, however, a researcher may need to use other print or computer resources in addition to the Internet. When that is the case, the researcher will need to fall back on traditional methods of research.

How to Research a Specific Point of Law

The following example demonstrates how a legal researcher might employ the research tools discussed earlier to find the law applicable to a given set of facts. Consider this hypothetical scenario:

> Mary Jones, a student at a Florida college, filed a complaint accusing Jay Grabbo of taking her purse while she was walking across campus on the afternoon of November 20, 2008. In her statement to the police, Jones was vague on whether Grabbo had used any force in taking the purse and whether she had offered any resistance. She stated that she had recently purchased the purse for $49 and that it contained $22 in cash plus a few loose coins and personal articles of little value. Further inquiry by the police revealed that Grabbo was unarmed.

A researcher who needs to gain a general background on the offense of robbery and how it differs from theft can profitably consult one of the legal encyclopedias mentioned earlier. Someone with a general knowledge of criminal offenses might still need to review the offense of robbery from the standpoint of state law. If so, *Florida Jurisprudence 2d* or some similar text should be consulted.

Given a general knowledge of the crimes of theft and robbery, a likely starting point would be the state statutes. In this instance, reference could be made to the official Florida Statutes. But from a research standpoint, it might be more productive to locate the statutes proscribing theft and robbery in the index to *West's Florida Statutes Annotated* and review the statutes and pertinent annotations in both the principal volume and the pocket part. The researcher would quickly find the offense of theft defined in § 812.014 and the offense of robbery defined in § 812.13.

Research of the statutory law would disclose that under Florida law, the theft of Jones's purse would be petit theft in the second degree if the total value was less than $100. West's Fla. Stat. Ann. § 812.014. This offense is a misdemeanor for which the maximum penalty is sixty days in jail and a $500 fine. West's Fla. Stat. Ann. § 775.082 and § 775.083. Unarmed robbery, on the other hand, is defined in West's Fla. Stat. Ann. § 812.13(1) as

> the taking of money or other property which may be the subject of larceny from the person or custody of another, with intent to either permanently or temporarily deprive the person or the owner of the money or other property, when in the course of the taking there is the use of force, violence, assault, or putting in fear.

If in the course of committing the robbery the offender carried no firearm, deadly weapon, or other weapon, then the robbery is a felony of the second degree, punishable by fifteen years' imprisonment and a maximum fine of $10,000 as provided in §§ 775.082, 775.083, or 775.084. (The latter statute refers to sentences for habitual offenders.) Therefore, it becomes very important to determine whether Grabbo should be charged with petit theft or robbery.

The researcher would then proceed to references noted under the topics of "force" and "resistance" that follow the text of the robbery statute. The annotated statutes would identify pertinent Florida appellate decisions on these points. For example, the researcher would find a note to *Mims v. State,* 342 So.2d 116 (Fla. App. 1977), indicating that purse snatching is not robbery if no more force is used than is necessary to physically remove the property from a person who does not resist. If the victim does resist and that resistance is overcome by the force of the perpetrator, however, the crime of robbery is complete. Another reference points the researcher to *Goldsmith v. State,* 573 So.2d 445 (Fla. App. 1991), which held that the slight force used in snatching a $10 bill from a person's hand without touching the person was insufficient to constitute robbery and instead constituted petit theft. Additional decisions refer to these and related points of law. For example, *Robinson v. State,* 680 So.2d 481 (Fla. App. 1999), indicates that while a stealthful taking may be petit theft, the force required to take someone's purse can make the offense robbery.

A further check into *West's Florida Statutes Annotated* reveals that the legislature enacted a new statute called "Robbery by Sudden Snatching" effective October 1, 1999. The new statute has been indexed as § 812.131 and provides,

> (1) "Robbery by sudden snatching" means the taking of money or other property from the victim's person, with intent to permanently or temporarily deprive the victim or the owner of the money or other property, when, in the course of the taking, the victim was or became aware of the taking. In order to satisfy this definition, it is not necessary to show that:
>
> > (a) The offender used any amount of force beyond that effort necessary to obtain possession of the money or other property; or

(b) There was any resistance offered by the victim to the offender or that there was injury to the victim's person.

This offense is a third-degree felony, punishable by a maximum of five years' imprisonment and a fine of $5,000. West's Fla. Stat. Ann. § 775.082 and § 775.083.

Annotations to Fla. Stat. § 775.082 reveal that in *Brown v. State,* 848 So.2d 361 (Fla. App. 2003), the court reversed a defendant's conviction for robbery by sudden snatching where the victim herself was unaware of the snatching of her purse at the time it was taken. The court noted that the offense requires that property be taken from the victim's actual, physical possession, and that because the evidence at the defendant's trial revealed that the victim was unaware of the snatching until after it had been accomplished, the defendant should be acquitted of the charge of robbery by sudden snatching.

In *Walker v. State*, 933 So.2d 1236 (Fla. App. 2006), the appellate court agreed with *Brown v. State* and reversed a defendant's conviction because the State failed to prove beyond a reasonable doubt that the victim knew that her property was being taken during the course of the taking. Finally, on April 18, 2008, in *Walls v. State*, 977 So.2d 802 (Fla. App. 2008), the court of appeals found that because the state presented no testimony or other evidence indicating that the defendant took the purse by snatching it from the victim's person, the court correctly reduced the defendant's conviction to petit theft.

After locating these and other pertinent references, the researcher should go to the *Southern Reporter 2d* and *3d* to read the located cases. After concluding the search, the researcher should "Shepardize" or "KeyCite" the decisions to determine whether they have been subsequently commented on, distinguished, or even reversed.

In view of the newer statute and the recent appellate court interpretation, before arriving at a conclusion, the researcher will likely need additional information from the victim as to her awareness of Grabbo's taking her purse and what, if any, force was involved. If the research is undertaken for the prosecutors or the police, they can determine whether any further factual investigation is necessary. They can then decide the charge to place against Grabbo and the proof required to sustain that charge. On the other hand, if the research is undertaken for a defense attorney, once charges are placed against the accused the defense attorney can obtain more precise information from the victim's testimony through discovery procedures. That, along with the results of the legal research, would assist counsel in advising Grabbo, assuming he is charged with a crime, on how to plead and what defenses may be available.

The steps outlined here are basic and are designed to illustrate rudimentary principles of gaining access to the criminal law on a particular subject. As previously indicated, another method might involve using digests with the key number system of research. Moreover, there will often be issues of interest still undecided by courts in a particular state. If so, then research into the statutes and court decisions of other states may be undertaken. The methodology and level of research pursued will often depend on the researcher's objectives, knowledge of the subject, and experience in conducting legal research.

Conclusion

Understanding how to gain access to the primary and secondary sources of the criminal law is tremendously important to students and practitioners of criminal justice. The ability to assemble relevant facts, analyze a problem, and conduct a systematic search for applicable authoritative statements of constitutional, statutory, and decisional law is a skill to be acquired by both the criminal justice student and the working professional. Professionally trained lawyers, who must make the critical judgments concerning the prosecution and defense of criminal actions, increasingly assign basic legal research to paralegals and criminal justice personnel. The ability to access the law through traditional as well as computerized methods will assist the student and professional in becoming better acquainted with the dynamics of the criminal law. Moreover, the honing of such skill will enhance a person's ability to carry out specific research assignments and to support his or her recommendations with relevant legal authorities.

The Constitution of the United States of America

We the People of the United States, in Order to form a more perfect Union, establish Justice, insure domestic Tranquility, provide for the common defense, promote the general Welfare, and secure the Blessings of Liberty to ourselves and our Posterity, do ordain and establish this Constitution for the United States of America.

Article I

Section 1. All legislative Powers herein granted shall be vested in a Congress of the United States, which shall consist of a Senate and House of Representatives.

Section 2. (1) The House of Representatives shall be composed of Members chosen every second Year by the People of the several States, and the Electors in each State shall have the Qualifications requisite for Electors of the most numerous Branch of the State Legislature.

(2) No Person shall be a Representative who shall not have attained to the age of twenty-five Years, and been seven Years a Citizen of the United States, and who shall not, when elected, be an Inhabitant of that State in which he shall be chosen.

(3) Representatives and direct Taxes shall be apportioned among the several States which may be included within this Union, according to their respective Numbers, which shall be determined by adding to the whole Number of free Persons, including those bound to Service for a Term of Years, and excluding Indians not taxed, three fifths of all other Persons. The actual Enumeration shall be made within three Years after the first Meeting of the Congress of the United States, and within every subsequent Term of ten Years, in such Manner as they shall by Law direct. The Number of Representatives shall not exceed one for every thirty Thousand, but each State shall have at Least one Representative; and until such enumeration shall be made, the State of New Hampshire shall be entitled to choose three, Massachusetts eight, Rhode Island and Providence Plantations one, Connecticut five, New York six, New Jersey four, Pennsylvania eight, Delaware one, Maryland six, Virginia ten, North Carolina five, South Carolina five, and Georgia three.

(4) When vacancies happen in the Representation from any State, the Executive Authority thereof shall issue Writs of Election to fill such Vacancies.

(5) The House of Representatives shall choose their Speaker and other Officers; and shall have the sole Power of Impeachment.

Section 3. (1) The Senate of the United States shall be composed of two Senators from each State, chosen by the Legislature thereof, for six Years; and each Senator shall have one Vote.

(2) Immediately after they shall be assembled in Consequence of the first Election, they shall be divided as equally as may be into three Classes. The Seats of the Senators of the first Class shall be vacated at the Expiration of the second Year, of the second Class at the Expiration of the fourth Year, and of the third Class at the Expiration of the sixth Year, so that one third may be chosen every second Year; and if Vacancies happen by Resignation, or otherwise, during the Recess of the Legislature of any State, the Executive thereof may make temporary Appointments until the next Meeting of the Legislature, which shall then fill such Vacancies.

(3) No Person shall be a Senator who shall not have attained, to the Age of thirty Years, and been nine Years a Citizen of the United States, and who shall not, when elected, be an Inhabitant of that State for which he shall be chosen.

(4) The Vice President of the United States shall be President of the Senate, but shall have no Vote, unless they be equally divided.

(5) The Senate shall choose their other Officers, and also a President pro tempore, in the Absence of the Vice President, or when he shall exercise the Office of the President of the United States.

(6) The Senate shall have the sole Power to try all Impeachments. When sitting for that Purpose, they shall be on Oath or Affirmation. When the President of the United States is tried, the Chief Justice shall preside: And no Person shall be convicted without the Concurrence of two thirds of the Members present.

(7) Judgment in Cases of Impeachment shall not extend further than to removal from Office, and disqualification to hold and enjoy any Office of honor, Trust or Profit under the United States: but the Party convicted shall nevertheless be liable and subject to Indictment, Trial, Judgment and Punishment, according to Law.

Section 4. (1) The Times, Places and Manner of holding Elections for Senators and Representatives, shall be prescribed in each State by the Legislature thereof; but the Congress may at any time by Law make or alter such Regulations, except as to the Places of choosing Senators.

(2) The Congress shall assemble at least once in every Year, and such Meeting shall be on the first Monday in December, unless they shall by Law appoint a different Day.

Section 5. (1) Each House shall be the Judge of the Elections, Returns and Qualifications of its own Members, and a Majority of each shall constitute a Quorum to do Business; but a smaller Number may adjourn from day to day, and may be authorized to compel the Attendance of absent Members, in such Manner, and under such Penalties as each House may provide.

(2) Each House may determine the Rules of its Proceedings, punish its Members for disorderly Behavior, and, with the Concurrence of two thirds, expel a Member.

(3) Each House shall keep a Journal of its Proceedings, and from time to time publish the same, excepting such Parts as may in their Judgment require Secrecy; and the Yeas and Nays of the Members of either House on any question shall, at the Desire of one fifth of those Present, be entered on the Journal.

(4) Neither House, during the Session of Congress, shall, without the Consent of the other, adjourn for more than three days, nor to any other Place than that in which the two Houses shall be sitting.

Section 6. (1) The Senators and Representatives shall receive a Compensation for their Services, to be ascertained by Law, and paid out of the Treasury of the United States. They shall in all Cases, except Treason, Felony and Breach of the Peace, be privileged from Arrest during their Attendance at the Session of their respective Houses, and in going to and returning from the same; and for any Speech or Debate in either House, they shall not be questioned in any other Place.

(2) No Senator or Representative shall, during the Time for which he was elected, be appointed to any civil Office under the Authority of the United States, which shall have been created, or the Emoluments whereof shall have been increased during such time; and no Person holding any Office under the United States, shall be a Member of either House during his Continuance in Office.

Section 7. (1) All Bills for raising Revenue shall originate in the House of Representatives; but the Senate may propose or concur with Amendments as on other Bills.

(2) Every Bill which shall have passed the House of Representatives and the Senate, shall, before it become a Law, be presented to the President of the United States; If he approve he shall sign it, but if not he shall return it, with his Objections to that House in which it shall have originated, who shall enter the Objections at large on their Journal, and proceed to reconsider it. If after such Reconsideration two thirds of that House shall agree to pass the Bill, it shall be sent, together with the Objections, to the other House, by which it shall likewise be reconsidered, and if approved by two thirds of that House, it shall become a Law. But in all such Cases the Votes of both Houses shall be determined by Yeas and Nays, and the Names of the Persons voting for and against the Bill shall be entered on the Journal of each House respectively. If any Bill shall not be returned by the President within ten Days (Sunday excepted) after it shall have been presented to him, the Same shall be a Law, in like Manner as if he had signed it, unless the Congress by their Adjournment prevent its Return, in which Case it shall not be a Law.

(3) Every Order, Resolution, or Vote to which the Concurrence of the Senate and House of Representatives may be necessary (except on a question of Adjournment) shall be presented to the President of the United States; and before the Same shall take Effect, shall be approved by him, or being disapproved by him, shall be re-passed by two thirds of the Senate and House of Representatives, according to the Rules and Limitations prescribed in the Case of a Bill.

Section 8. (1) The Congress shall have Power To lay and collect Taxes, Duties, Imposts and Excises, to pay the Debts and provide for the common Defense and general Welfare of the United States; but all Duties, Imposts and Excises shall be uniform throughout the United States;

(2) To borrow Money on the credit of the United States;

(3) To regulate Commerce with foreign Nations, and among the several States, and with the Indian Tribes;

(4) To establish an uniform Rule of Naturalization, and uniform Laws on the subject of Bankruptcies throughout the United States;

(5) To coin Money, regulate the Value thereof, and of foreign Coin, and to fix the Standard of Weights and Measures;

(6) To provide for the Punishment of counterfeiting the Securities and current Coin of the United States;

(7) To establish Post Offices and post Roads;

(8) To promote the Progress of Science and useful Arts, by securing for limited Times to Authors and Inventors the exclusive Right to their respective Writings and Discoveries;

(9) To constitute Tribunals inferior to the supreme Court;

(10) To define and punish Piracies and Felonies committed on the high Seas, and Offenses against the Law of Nations;

(11) To declare War, grant Letters of Marque and Reprisal, and make Rules concerning Captures on Land and Water;

(12) To raise and support Armies, but no Appropriation of Money to that Use shall be for a longer Term than two Years;

(13) To provide and maintain a Navy;

(14) To make Rules for the Government and Regulation of the land and naval Forces;

(15) To provide for calling forth the Militia to execute the Laws of the Union, suppress Insurrections and repel Invasions;

(16) To provide for organizing, arming, and disciplining, the Militia, and for governing such Part of them as may be employed in the Service of the United States, reserving to the States respectively, the Appointment of the Officers, and the Authority of training the Militia according to the discipline prescribed by Congress;

(17) To exercise exclusive Legislation in all Cases whatsoever, over such District (not exceeding ten Miles square) as may, by Cession of particular States, and the Acceptance of Congress, become the Seat of the Government of the United States, and to exercise like Authority over all Places purchased by the Consent of the Legislature of the State in which the Same shall be, for the Erection of Forts, Magazines, Arsenals, dock-Yards, and other needful Buildings;—And

(18) To make all Laws which shall be necessary and proper for carrying into Execution the foregoing Powers, and all other Powers vested by this Constitution in the Government of the United States, or in any Department or Officer thereof.

Section 9. (1) The Migration or Importation of such Persons as any of the States now existing shall think proper to admit, shall not be prohibited by the Congress prior to the Year one thousand eight hundred and eight, but a Tax or Duty may be imposed on such Importation, not exceeding ten dollars for each Person.

(2) The Privilege of the Writ of Habeas Corpus shall not be suspended unless when in Cases of Rebellion or Invasion the public Safety may require it.

(3) No Bill of Attainder or ex post facto Law shall be passed.

(4) No Capitation, or other direct, Tax shall be laid, unless in Proportion to the Census or Enumeration herein before directed to be taken.

(5) No Tax or Duty shall be laid on Articles exported from any State.

(6) No Preference shall be given by any Regulation of Commerce or Revenue to the Ports of one State over those of another; nor shall Vessels bound to, or from, one State, be obliged to enter, clear or pay Duties in another.

(7) No Money shall be drawn from the Treasury, but in Consequence of Appropriations made by Law; and a regular Statement and Account of the Receipts and Expenditures of all public Money shall be published from time to time.

(8) No Title of Nobility shall be granted by the United States: And no Person holding any Office of Profit or Trust under them, shall, without the Consent of the Congress, accept of any present, Emolument, Office, or Title, of any kind whatever, from any King, Prince or foreign State.

Section 10. (1) No State shall enter into any Treaty, Alliance, or Confederation; grant Letters of Marque and Reprisal; coin Money; emit Bills of Credit; make any Thing but gold and silver Coin a Tender in Payment of Debts; pass any Bill of Attainder, ex post facto Law, or Law impairing the Obligation of Contracts, or grant any Title of Nobility.

(2) No State shall, without the Consent of Congress, lay any Imposts or Duties on Imports or Exports, except what may be absolutely necessary for executing its inspection Laws: and the net Produce of all Duties and Imposts, laid by any State on Imports or Exports, shall be for the Use of the Treasury of the United States; and all such Laws shall be subject to the Revision and Control of the Congress.

(3) No State shall, without the Consent of Congress, lay any Duty of Tonnage, keep Troops, or Ships of War in time of Peace, enter into any Agreement or Compact

with another State, or with a foreign Power, or engage in War, unless actually invaded, or in such imminent Danger as will not admit of Delay.

Article II

Section 1. (1) The executive Power shall be vested in a President of the United States of America. He shall hold his Office during the Term of four Years, and, together with the Vice President, chosen for the same Term, be elected, as follows:

(2) Each State shall appoint, in such Manner as the Legislature thereof may direct, a Number of Electors, equal to the whole Number of Senators and Representatives to which the State may be entitled in the Congress: but no Senator or Representative, or Person holding an Office of Trust or Profit under the United States, shall be appointed an Elector.

The Electors shall meet in their respective States, and vote by Ballot for two Persons, of whom one at least shall not be an Inhabitant of the same State with themselves. And they shall make a List of all the Persons voted for, and of the Number of Votes for each; which List they shall sign and certify, and transmit sealed to the Seat of the Government of the United States, directed to the President of the Senate. The President of the Senate shall, in the presence of the Senate and House of Representatives, open all the Certificates, and the Votes shall then be counted. The Person having the greatest Number of Votes shall be the President, if such Number be a Majority of the whole Number of Electors appointed; and if there be more than one who have such Majority, and have an equal Number of Votes, then the House of Representatives shall immediately choose by Ballot one of them for President; and if no Person have a Majority, then from the five highest on the List the said House shall in like Manner choose the President. But in choosing the President, the Votes shall be taken by States, the Representation from each State having one Vote; a quorum for this Purpose shall consist of a Member or Members from two thirds of the States, and a Majority of all the States shall be necessary to a Choice. In every Case, after the Choice of the President, the Person having the greatest Number of Votes of the Electors shall be the Vice President. But if there should remain two or more who have equal Votes, the Senate shall choose from them by Ballot the Vice President.

(3) The Congress may determine the Time of choosing the Electors, and the Day on which they shall give their Votes; which Day shall be the same throughout the United States.

(4) No Person except a natural born Citizen, or a Citizen of the United States, at the time of the Adoption of this Constitution, shall be eligible to the Office of President; neither shall any Person be eligible to that Office who shall not have attained to the Age of thirty five Years, and been fourteen Years a Resident within the United States.

(5) In Case of the Removal of the President from Office, or of his Death, Resignation, or Inability to discharge the Powers and Duties of the said Office, the Same shall devolve on the Vice President, and the Congress may by Law provide for the Case of Removal, Death, Resignation or Inability, both of the President and Vice President, declaring what Officer shall then act as President, and such Officer shall act accordingly, until the Disability be removed, or a President shall be elected.

(6) The President shall, at stated Times, receive for his Services, a Compensation, which shall neither be increased nor diminished during the Period for which he shall have been elected, and he shall not receive within that Period any other Emolument from the United States, or any of them.

(7) Before he enter on the Execution of his Office, he shall take the following Oath or Affirmation:—"I do solemnly swear (or affirm) that I will faithfully execute the Office of President of the United States, and will to the best of my Ability, preserve, protect and defend the Constitution of the United States."

Section 2. (1) The President shall be Commander in Chief of the Army and Navy of the United States, and of the Militia of the several States, when called into the actual Service of the United States; he may require the Opinion, in writing, of the principal Officer in each of the executive Departments, upon any Subject relating to the Duties of their respective Offices, and he shall have Power to grant Reprieves and Pardons for Offenses against the United States, except in Cases of Impeachment.

(2) He shall have Power, by and with the Advice and Consent of the Senate, to make Treaties, provided two thirds of the Senators present concur; and he shall nominate, and by and with the Advice and Consent of the Senate, shall appoint Ambassadors, other public Ministers and Consuls, Judges of the supreme Court, and all other Officers of the United States, whose Appointments are not herein otherwise provided for, and which shall be established by Law: but the Congress may by Law vest the Appointment of such inferior Officers, as they think proper, in the President alone, in the Courts of Law, or in the Heads of Departments.

(3) The President shall have Power to fill up all Vacancies that may happen during the Recess of the Senate, by granting Commissions which shall expire at the End of their next Session.

Section 3. He shall from time to time give to the Congress Information of the State of the Union, and recommend to their Consideration such Measures as he shall judge necessary and expedient; he may, on extraordinary Occasions, convene both Houses, or either of them, and in Case of Disagreement between them, with Respect to the Time of Adjournment, he may adjourn them to such Time as he shall think proper; he shall receive Ambassadors and other public Ministers; he shall take Care that the Laws be faithfully executed, and shall Commission all the Officers of the United States.

Section 4. The President, Vice President and all Civil Officers of the United States, shall be removed from Office on Impeachment for, and Conviction of, Treason, Bribery, or other high Crimes and Misdemeanors.

Article III

Section 1. The judicial Power of the United States, shall be vested in one supreme Court, and in such inferior Courts as the Congress may from time to time ordain and establish. The Judges, both of the supreme and inferior Courts, shall hold their Offices during good Behavior, and shall, at stated Times, receive for their Services, a Compensation, which shall not be diminished during their Continuance in Office.

Section 2. (1) The judicial Power shall extend to all Cases, in Law and Equity, arising under this Constitution, the Laws of the United States, and Treaties made, or which shall be made, under their Authority;—to all Cases affecting Ambassadors, other public Ministers and Consuls;—to all Cases of admiralty and maritime Jurisdiction;—to Controversies to which the United States shall be a party;—to Controversies between two or more States;—between a State and Citizens of another State;—between Citizens of different States;—between Citizens of the same State claiming Lands under Grants of different States, and between a State, or the Citizens thereof, and foreign States, Citizens or Subjects.

(2) In all Cases affecting Ambassadors, other public Ministers and Consuls, and those in which a State shall be Party, the supreme Court shall have original

Jurisdiction. In all the other Cases before mentioned, the supreme Court shall have appellate Jurisdiction, both as to Law and Fact, with such Exceptions, and under such Regulations as the Congress shall make.

(3) The Trial of all Crimes, except in Cases of Impeachment, shall be by Jury; and such Trial shall be held in the State where the said Crimes shall have been committed; but when not committed within any State, the Trial shall be at such Place or Places as the Congress may by Law have directed.

Section 3. (1) Treason against the United States, shall consist only in levying War against them, or in adhering to their Enemies, giving them Aid and Comfort. No Person shall be convicted of Treason unless on the Testimony of two Witnesses to the same overt Act, or on Confession in open Court.

(2) The Congress shall have Power to declare the Punishment of Treason, but no Attainder of Treason shall work Corruption of Blood, or Forfeiture except during the Life of the Person attainted.

Article IV

Section 1. Full Faith and Credit shall be given in each State to the public Acts, Records, and judicial Proceedings of every other State. And the Congress may by general Laws prescribe the Manner in which such Acts, Records and Proceedings shall be proved, and the Effect thereof.

Section 2. (1) The Citizens of each State shall be entitled to all privileges and Immunities of Citizens in the several States.

(2) A Person charged in any State with Treason, Felony, or other Crime, who shall flee from Justice, and be found in another State, shall on Demand of the executive Authority of the State from which he fled, be delivered up, to be removed to the State having Jurisdiction of the Crime.

(3) No Person held to Service of Labor in one State, under the Laws thereof, escaping into another, shall, in Consequence of any Law or Regulation therein, be discharged from such Service or Labor, but shall be delivered up on Claim of the Party to whom such Service or Labor may be due.

Section 3. (1) New States may be admitted by the Congress into this Union; but no new State shall be formed or erected within the Jurisdiction of any other State; nor any State be formed by the Junction of two or more States, or Parts of States, without the Consent of the Legislatures of the States concerned as well as of the Congress.

(2) The Congress shall have power to dispose of and make all needful Rules and Regulations respecting the Territory or other Property belonging to the United States; and nothing in this Constitution shall be so construed as to Prejudice any Claims of the United States, or of any particular State.

Section 4. The United States shall guarantee to every State in this Union a Republican Form of Government, and shall protect each of them against Invasion; and on Application of the Legislature, or of the Executive (when the Legislature cannot be convened) against domestic Violence.

Article V

The Congress, whenever two thirds of both Houses shall deem it necessary, shall propose Amendments to this Constitution, or, on the Application of the Legislatures of two thirds of the several States, shall call a Convention for proposing Amendments, which, in either Case, shall be valid to all Intents and Purposes, as Part of this Constitution, when ratified by the Legislatures of three fourths of the several States, or by Conventions in three fourths thereof, as the one or the other Mode of Ratification may be proposed by the Congress; Provided that no Amendment which may be made prior to the Year One thousand eight hundred and eight shall in any Manner affect the first and fourth Clauses in the Ninth Section of the first Article; and that no State, without its Consent, shall be deprived of its equal Suffrage in the Senate.

Article VI

(1) All Debts contracted and Engagements entered into, before the Adoption of this Constitution, shall be as valid against the United States under this Constitution, as under the Confederation.

(2) This Constitution, and the Laws of the United States which shall be made in Pursuance thereof; and all Treaties made, or which shall be made, under the Authority of the United States, shall be the supreme Law of the Land; and the Judges in every State shall be bound thereby, any Thing in the Constitution or Laws of any State to the Contrary notwithstanding.

(3) The Senators and Representatives before mentioned, and the Members of the several State Legislatures, and all executive and judicial Officers, both of the United States and of the several States, shall be bound by Oath or Affirmation, to support this Constitution; but no religious Test shall ever be required as a Qualification to any Office or public Trust under the United States.

Article VII

The Ratification of the Conventions of nine States, shall be sufficient for the Establishment of this Constitution between the States so ratifying the Same.

Articles in Addition to, and Amendment of, the Constitution of the United States of America, Proposed by Congress, and Ratified by the Several States, Pursuant to the Fifth Article of the Original Constitution.

Amendment I (1791)

Congress shall make no law respecting an establishment of religion, or prohibiting the free exercise thereof; or abridging the freedom of speech, or of the press; or the right of the people peaceably to assemble, and to petition the Government for a redress of grievances.

Amendment II (1791)

A well regulated Militia, being necessary to the security of a free state, the right of the people to keep and bear Arms, shall not be infringed.

Amendment III (1791)

No Soldier shall, in time of peace be quartered in any house, without the consent of the Owner, nor in time of war, but in a manner to be prescribed by law.

Amendment IV (1791)

The right of the people to be secure in their persons, houses, papers, and effects, against unreasonable searches and seizures, shall not be violated, and no Warrants shall issue, but upon probable cause, supported by Oath or affirmation, and particularly describing the place to be searched, and the persons or things to be seized.

Amendment V (1791)

No person shall be held to answer for a capital, or otherwise infamous crime, unless on a presentment or indictment of a Grand Jury, except in cases arising in the land or naval forces, or in the Militia, when in actual service in time of War or public danger; nor shall any person be subject for the same offence to be twice put in jeopardy of life or limb; nor shall be compelled in any criminal case to be a witness against himself, nor be deprived of life, liberty, or property, without due process of law; nor shall private property be taken for public use, without just compensation.

Amendment VI (1791)

In all criminal prosecutions, the accused shall enjoy the right to a speedy and public trial, by an impartial jury of the State and district wherein the crime shall have been committed, which district shall have been previously ascertained by law, and to be informed of the nature and cause of the accusation; to be confronted with the witnesses against him; to have compulsory process for obtaining witnesses in his favor, and to have the Assistance of Counsel for his defense.

Amendment VII (1791)

In Suits at common law, where the value in controversy shall exceed twenty dollars, the right of trial by jury shall be preserved, and no fact tried by a jury, shall be otherwise re-examined in any Court of the United States, than according to the rules of the common law.

Amendment VIII (1791)

Excessive bail shall not be required, nor excessive fines imposed, nor cruel and unusual punishments inflicted.

Amendment IX (1791)

The enumeration in the Constitution, of certain rights, shall not be construed to deny or disparage others retained by the people.

Amendment X (1791)

The powers not delegated to the United States by the Constitution, nor prohibited by it to the States, are reserved to the States respectively, or to the people.

Amendment XI (1798)

The Judicial power of the United States shall not be construed to extend to any suit in law or equity, commenced or prosecuted against one of the United States by Citizens of another State, or by Citizens or Subjects of any Foreign State.

Amendment XII (1804)

The Electors shall meet in their respective states and vote by ballot for President and Vice-President, one of whom, at least, shall not be an inhabitant of the same state with themselves; they shall name in their ballots the person voted for as President, and in distinct ballots the person voted for as Vice-President, and they shall make distinct lists of all persons voted for as President, and of all persons voted for as Vice-President, and of the number of votes for each, which lists they shall sign and certify, and transmit sealed to the seat of the government of the United States, directed to the President of the Senate;—The President of the Senate shall, in the presence of the Senate and House of Representatives, open all the certificates and the votes shall then be counted;—The person having the greatest number of votes for President, shall be the President, if such number be a majority of the whole number of Electors appointed; and if no person have such majority, then from the persons having the highest numbers not exceeding three on the list of those voted for as President, the House of Representatives shall choose immediately, by ballot, the President. But in choosing the President, the votes shall be taken by states, the representation from each state having one vote; a quorum for this purpose shall consist of a member or members from two-thirds of the states, and a majority of all the states shall be necessary to a choice. And if the House of Representatives shall not choose a President whenever the right of choice shall devolve upon them, before the fourth day of March next following, then the Vice-President shall act as President, as in the case of the death or other constitutional disability of the President—The person having the greatest number of votes as Vice-President, shall be the Vice-President, if such number be a majority of the whole number of Electors appointed, and if no person have a majority, then from the two highest numbers on the list, the Senate shall choose the Vice-President; A quorum for the purpose shall consist of two-thirds of the whole number of Senators, and a majority of the whole number shall be necessary to a choice. But no person constitutionally ineligible to the office of President shall be eligible to that of Vice-President of the United States.

Amendment XIII (1865)

Section 1. Neither slavery nor involuntary servitude, except as a punishment for crime whereof the party shall have been duly convicted, shall exist within the United States, or any place subject to their jurisdiction.
Section 2. Congress shall have power to enforce this article by appropriate legislation.

Amendment XIV (1868)

Section 1. All persons born or naturalized in the United States and subject to the jurisdiction thereof, are citizens of the United States and of the State wherein they reside. No State shall make or enforce any law which shall abridge the privileges or immunities of citizens of the United States; nor shall any State deprive any person of life, liberty, or property, without due process of law; nor deny to any person within its jurisdiction the equal protection of the laws.

Section 2. Representatives shall be apportioned among the several States according to their respective numbers, counting the whole number of persons in each State, excluding Indians not taxed. But when the right to vote at any election for the choice of electors for President and Vice-President of the United States, Representatives in Congress, the Executive and Judicial officers of a State, or the members of the Legislature thereof, is denied to any of the male inhabitants of such State, being twenty-one years of age, and citizens of the United States, or in any way abridged, except for participation in rebellion, or other crime, the basis of representation therein shall be reduced in the proportion which the number of such male citizens shall bear to the whole number of male citizens twenty-one years of age in such State.

Section 3. No person shall be a Senator or Representative in Congress, or elector of President and Vice-President, or hold any office, civil or military, under the United States, or under any State, who, having previously taken an oath, as a member of Congress, or as an officer of the United States, or as a member of any State legislature, or as an executive or judicial officer of any State, to support the Constitution of the United States, shall have engaged in insurrection or rebellion against the same, or given aid or comfort to the enemies thereof. But Congress may by a vote of two-thirds of each House, remove such disability.

Section 4. The validity of the public debt of the United States, authorized by law, including debts incurred for payment of pensions and bounties for services in suppressing insurrection or rebellion, shall not be questioned. But neither the United States nor any State shall assume or pay any debt or obligation incurred in aid of insurrection or rebellion against the United States, or any claim for the loss or emancipation of any slave; but all such debts, obligations and claims shall be held illegal and void.

Section 5. The Congress shall have power to enforce, by appropriate legislation, the provisions of this article.

Amendment XV (1870)

Section 1. The right of citizens of the United States to vote shall not be denied or abridged by the United States or by any State on account of race, color, or previous condition of servitude.

Section 2. The Congress shall have power to enforce this article by appropriate legislation.

Amendment XVI (1913)

The Congress shall have power to lay and collect taxes on incomes, from whatever source derived, without apportionment among the several States, and without regard to any census or enumeration.

Amendment XVII (1913)

The Senate of the United States shall be composed of two Senators from each State, elected by the people thereof, for six years; and each Senator shall have one vote. The electors in each State shall have the qualifications requisite for electors of the most numerous branch of the State legislatures.

When vacancies happen in the representation of any State in the Senate, the executive authority of such State shall issue writs of election to fill such vacancies: Provided, That the legislature of any State may empower the executive thereof to make temporary appointments until the people fill the vacancies by election as the legislature may direct.

This amendment shall not be so construed as to affect the election or term of any Senator chosen before it becomes valid as part of the Constitution.

Amendment XVIII (1919)

Section 1. After one year from the ratification of this article the manufacture, sale, or transportation of intoxicating liquors within, the importation thereof into, or the exportation thereof from the United States and all territory subject to the jurisdiction thereof for beverage purposes is hereby prohibited.

Section 2. The Congress and the several States shall have concurrent power to enforce this article by appropriate legislation.

Section 3. This article shall be inoperative unless it shall have been ratified as an amendment to the Constitution by the legislatures of the several States, as provided in the Constitution, within seven years from the date of the submission hereof to the States by the Congress.

Amendment XIX (1920)

The right of citizens of the United States to vote shall not be denied or abridged by the United States or by any State on account of sex.

Congress shall have power to enforce this article by appropriate legislation.

Amendment XX (1933)

Section 1. The terms of the President and Vice President shall end at noon on the 20th day of January, and the terms of Senators and Representatives at noon on the 3rd day of January, of the years in which such terms would have ended if this article had not been ratified; and the terms of their successors shall then begin.

Section 2. The Congress shall assemble at least once in every year, and such meeting shall begin at noon on the 3rd day of January, unless they shall by law appoint a different day.

Section 3. If, at the time fixed for the beginning of the term of the President, the President elect shall have died, the Vice President elect shall become President. If a President shall not have been chosen before the time fixed for the beginning of his term, or if the President elect shall have failed to qualify, then the Vice President elect shall act as President until a President shall have qualified; and the Congress may by law provide for the case wherein neither a President elect nor a Vice President elect shall have qualified, declaring who shall then act as President, or the manner in which one who is to act shall be selected, and such person shall act accordingly until a President or Vice President shall have qualified.

Section 4. The Congress may by law provide for the case of the death of any of the persons from whom the House of Representatives may choose a President whenever the right of choice shall have devolved upon them, and for the case of the death of any of the persons from whom the Senate may choose a Vice President whenever the right of choice shall have devolved upon them.

Section 5. Sections 1 and 2 shall take effect on the 15th day of October following the ratification of this article.

Section 6. This article shall be inoperative unless it shall have been ratified as an amendment to the Constitution by the legislatures of three-fourths of the several States within seven years from the date of its submission.

Amendment XXI (1933)

Section 1. The eighteenth article of amendment to the Constitution of the United States is hereby repealed.

Section 2. The transportation or importation into any State, Territory or possession of the United States for delivery or use therein of intoxicating liquors, in violation of the laws thereof, is hereby prohibited.

Section 3. This article shall be inoperative unless it shall have been ratified as an amendment to the Constitution by conventions in the several States, as provided in the Constitution, within seven years from the date of the submission hereof to the States by the Congress.

Amendment XXII (1951)

Section 1. No person shall be elected to the office of the President more than twice, and no person who has held the office of President, or acted as President, for more than two years of a term to which some other person was elected President shall be elected to the office of the President more than once. But this Article shall not apply to any person holding the office of President when this Article was proposed by the Congress, and shall not prevent any person who may be holding the office of President, or acting as President, during the term within which this Article becomes operative from holding the office of President or acting as President during the remainder of such term.

Section 2. This Article shall be inoperative unless it shall have been ratified as an amendment to the Constitution by the legislatures of three-fourths of the several States within seven years from the date of its submission to the States by the Congress.

Amendment XXIII (1961)

Section 1. The District constituting the seat of Government of the United States shall appoint in such manner as the Congress may direct:

A number of electors of President and Vice President equal to the whole number of Senators and Representatives in Congress to which the District would be entitled if it were a State, but in no event more than the least populous State; they shall be in addition to those appointed by the States, but they shall be considered, for the purposes of the election of President and Vice President, to be electors appointed by a State; and they shall meet in the District and perform such duties as provided by the twelfth article of amendment.

Section 2. The Congress shall have power to enforce this article by appropriate legislation.

Amendment XXIV (1964)

Section 1. The right of citizens of the United States to vote in any primary or other election for President or Vice President, for electors for President or Vice President, or for Senator or Representative in Congress, shall not be denied or abridged by the United States or any State by reason of failure to pay any poll tax or other tax.

Section 2. The Congress shall have power to enforce this article by appropriate legislation.

Amendment XXV (1967)

Section 1. In case of the removal of the President from office or of his death or resignation, the Vice President shall become President.

Section 2. Whenever there is a vacancy in the office of the Vice President, the President shall nominate a Vice President who shall take office upon confirmation by a majority vote of both Houses of Congress.

Section 3. Whenever the President transmits to the President pro tempore of the Senate and the Speaker of the House of Representatives his written declaration that he is unable to discharge the powers and duties of his office, and until he transmits to them a written declaration to the contrary, such powers and duties shall be discharged by the Vice President as Acting President.

Section 4. Whenever the Vice President and a majority of either the principal officers of the executive departments or of such other body as Congress may by law provide, transmit to the President pro tempore of the Senate and the Speaker of the House of Representatives their written declaration that the President is unable to discharge the powers and duties of his office, the Vice President shall immediately assume the powers and duties of the office as Acting President.

Thereafter, when the President transmits to the President pro tempore of the Senate and the Speaker of the House of Representatives his written declaration that no inability exists, he shall resume the powers and duties of his office unless the Vice President and a majority of either the principal officers of the executive department or of such other body as Congress may by law provide, transmit within four days to the President pro tempore of the Senate and the Speaker of the House of Representatives their written declaration that the President is unable to discharge the powers and duties of his office. Thereupon Congress shall decide the issue, assembling within forty-eight hours for that purpose if not in session. If the Congress, within twenty-one days after receipt of the latter written declaration, or, if Congress is not in session, within twenty-one days after Congress is required to assemble, determines by two-thirds vote of both Houses that the President is unable to discharge the powers and duties of his office, the Vice President shall continue to discharge the same as Acting President; otherwise, the President shall resume the powers and duties of his office.

Amendment XXVI (1971)

Section 1. The right of citizens of the United States, who are eighteen years of age or older, to vote shall not be denied or abridged by the United States or by any State on account of age.

Section 2. The Congress shall have power to enforce this article by appropriate legislation.

Amendment XXVII (1992)

No law, varying the compensation for the services of the Senators and Representatives, shall take effect, until an election of Representatives shall have intervened.

Glossary

abandoned property Property over which the former owner has relinquished any claim of ownership.

actual imprisonment standard The standard governing the applicability of the federal constitutional right of an indigent person to have counsel appointed in a misdemeanor case. For the right to be violated, the indigent defendant must actually be sentenced to jail or prison after having been tried without appointed counsel.

actus reus A "wrongful act" which, combined with other necessary elements of crime, constitutes criminal liability.

affiant A person who makes an affidavit.

affidavit A written document attesting to specific facts of which the affiant has knowledge, and sworn to or affirmed by the affiant.

affirm To uphold, ratify, or approve.

aggravating factors Factors attending the commission of a crime that make the crime or its consequences worse.

***Alford* plea** A plea of guilty with a protestation of innocence.

***Allen* charge** A judge's instruction to jurors who are deadlocked, encouraging them to listen to one another's arguments and reappraise their own positions in an effort to arrive at a verdict.

***Anders* brief** A law brief submitted to an appellate court by publicly appointed defense counsel in which counsel explains that the defendant's appeal is nonmeritorious and requests release from further representation of the defendant.

anonymous tip Information given to the police by an unknown individual.

answer brief The appellee's written response to the appellant's law brief filed in an appellate court.

anticipatory search warrant A search warrant issued based on an affidavit that at a future time evidence of a crime will be at a specific place.

appeal of right An appeal that a defendant is entitled to make as a matter of law.

appellant The party that takes an appeal to a higher court.

appellate courts Judicial tribunals that review decisions from lower tribunals.

appellee The party against whom an appeal is taken.

arraignment An appearance before a court of law for the purpose of pleading to a criminal charge.

arrest To take someone into custody or otherwise deprive that person of freedom of movement.

arrest warrant A document issued by a magistrate or judge directing that a named person be taken into custody for allegedly having committed an offense.

assignments of error A written presentation to an appellate court identifying the points that the appellant claims constitute errors made by the lower tribunal.

attorney–client privilege The right of a person (client) not to testify about matters discussed in confidence with an attorney in the course of the attorney's representation.

Attorney General The highest legal officer of a state or of the United States.

automobile exception Exception to the Fourth Amendment warrant requirement. The exception allows the warrantless search of a vehicle by police who have probable cause to search but because of exigent circumstances are unable to secure a warrant.

bail bond Sum of money posted to ensure a defendant's subsequent appearance in court.

Bail Reform Act of 1984 An act that provides that a defendant charged with a federal crime may be denied bail if the prosecution can show that the defendant poses a threat to public safety.

bench trial A trial held before a judge without a jury present.

best evidence Primary evidence used to prove a fact—usually an original written document that evidences a communication or transaction.

bifurcated trial A capital trial with separate phases for determining guilt and punishment.

Bill of Rights A written enumeration of basic rights, usually part of a written constitution—for example, the first ten amendments to the U.S. Constitution.

boot camp An institution that provides systematic discipline in a military-like environment designed to rehabilitate an offender; employed as a sentencing alternative.

border searches Searches of persons entering the borders of the United States.

brief A document filed by a party to a lawsuit to convince the court of the merits of that party's case.

canons of construction Rules governing the judicial interpretation of constitutions, statutes, and other written instruments.

capias "You are to take." A general term for various court orders requiring that some named person be taken into custody.

capital crimes Crime for which death is a permissible punishment.

capital punishment The death penalty.

challenges for cause Objections to a prospective juror on some specified ground (for example, a close relationship to a party in the case).

change of venue The removal of a legal proceeding, usually a trial, to a new location.

child shield statutes Laws that allow a screen to be placed between a child victim of sexual abuse and a defendant while the child testifies in court.

circumstantial evidence Indirect evidence from which the existence of certain facts may be inferred.

citation A summons to appear in court, often used in traffic violations and other minor offenses.

cite and release statutes Laws permitting or requiring police officers to issue citations instead of making arrests for traffic violations or other minor misdemeanors or infractions.

citizen's arrest An arrest made by a person who is not a law enforcement officer.

clemency A grant of mercy by an executive official commuting a sentence or pardoning a criminal.

clergy–penitent privilege The exemption of a clergyperson and a penitent from disclosing communications made in confidence by the penitent.

closing arguments Arguments presented at trial by counsel at the conclusion of the presentation of evidence.

coerced confession A confession or other incriminating statements obtained from a suspect by police through force, violence, threats, intimidation, or undue psychological pressure.

collateral attack The attempt to defeat the outcome of a judicial proceeding by challenging it in a different proceeding or court.

community control A sentence imposed on a person found guilty of a crime that requires that the offender be placed in an individualized program of noninstitutional confinement.

community policing Style of police work that stresses development of close ties between police officers and the communities they serve.

community service A sentence or condition of probation requiring that the criminal perform some specific service to the community for some specified period of time.

competent to testify Having the legal capacity to offer evidence under oath in court.

compulsory process The power to subpoena witnesses to appear in court.

concurrent sentencing The practice by which a trial court imposes separate sentences to be served at the same time.

concurring in the judgment Issuance of an opinion by a judge or justice that agrees with the judgment of an appellate court without agreeing with the court's reasoning process.

concurring opinion An opinion handed down by a judge that supports the judgment of the court but often does so through different reasoning.

conditions of confinement The conditions under which inmates are held in jails and prisons. These conditions are subject to challenge under the Eighth Amendment's Cruel and Unusual Punishments Clause.

conditions of probation A set of rules that must be observed by a person placed on probation.

confidential informants An informant known to the police but whose identity is held in confidence.

consecutive sentencing The practice by which a trial court imposes a sentence or sentences to be served following completion of a prior sentence or sentences.

consent to a search The act of a person voluntarily permitting police to conduct a search of person or property.

constitutional rights of prison inmates Under modern interpretation of the federal and state constitutions, prisoners retain those constitutional rights that are not inconsistent with the fact that they are confined in a secure environment.

constitutional supremacy The doctrine that the Constitution is the supreme law of the land and that all actions and policies of government must be consistent with it.

continuance Delay of a judicial proceeding on the motion of one of the parties.

corporal punishment Punishment that inflicts pain or injury on a person's body.

corrections system The system of prisons, jails, and other penal and correctional institutions.

Court of Appeals for the Armed Forces The court (formerly known as the Court of Military Appeals), consisting of five civilian judges, that reviews sentences affecting a general or flag officer or imposing the death penalty and cases certified for review by the judge advocate general of a branch of service. It may grant review of convictions and sentences on petitions by service members.

court-martial A military tribunal convened by a commander of a military unit to try a person subject to the Uniform Code of Military Justice who is accused of violating a provision of that code.

courts of general jurisdiction Courts that conduct trials in felony and major misdemeanor cases. Also refers to courts that have jurisdiction to hear civil as well as criminal cases.

courts of limited jurisdiction Courts that handle pretrial matters and conduct trials in minor misdemeanor cases.

Crime Victims' Rights Act (CVRA) Federal legislation that provides eight basic rights for crime victims where crimes are prosecuted in the federal system.

criminal procedure The rules of law governing the procedures by which crimes are investigated, prosecuted, adjudicated, and punished.

criminal trial A trial in a court of law to determine the guilt or innocence of a person charged with a crime.

critical pretrial stages Significant procedural steps that occur before a criminal trial. A defendant has the right to counsel at these critical stages.

cruel and unusual punishments Criminal penalties that shock the moral conscience of the community—for example, torture and other extreme forms of corporal punishment. Prohibited by the Eighth Amendment to the U.S. Constitution.

curtilage The enclosed space of ground surrounding a dwelling.

cybersecurity Security measures designed to protect computers and computer networks from unauthorized access.

deadlocked jury A jury whose members cannot agree on a verdict. Often referred to as a "hung jury."

death penalty Capital punishment; a sentence to death for the commission of a crime.

death qualification of a jury Questioning of prospective jurors in a death penalty case to ensure that the jury is composed of people who do not entertain scruples against imposing capital punishment.

decisional law Law declared by appellate courts in their written decisions and opinions.

defense attorney A lawyer who represents defendants in criminal cases.

definite sentencing Legislatively determined sentencing with no discretion given to judges or corrections officials to individualize punishment.

Department of Justice (DOJ) The department within the executive branch of the federal government that is headed by the Attorney General and staffed by U.S. Attorneys.

deposition The recorded sworn testimony of a witness; not given in open court.

derivative evidence Evidence that is derived from or obtained only as a result of other evidence.

determinate sentencing The process of sentencing whereby the judge sets a fixed term of years within statutory parameters and the offender must serve that term without possibility of early release.

direct evidence Evidence that applies directly to proof of a fact or proposition. For example, a witness who testifies to having seen an act done or heard a statement made is giving direct evidence.

directed verdict A verdict rendered by a jury by direction of the presiding judge.

discretionary review Form of appellate court review of lower court decisions that is not mandatory but occurs at the discretion of the appellate court.

dispositive motion A motion made to a court where the ruling on the motion will determine the outcome of the case.

dissenting opinion An opinion rendered by a judge disavowing or disagreeing with the decision of a collegial court.

DNA testing Laboratory tests that compare DNA molecules extracted from a suspect's specimen with DNA molecules extracted from specimens found at a crime scene to determine whether the samples match.

doctrine of harmless error An error that does not affect a party's substantive rights or the case's outcome.

doctrine of incorporation The doctrine under which provisions of the Bill of Rights are held to be incorporated within the Due Process Clause of the Fourteenth Amendment and are thereby made applicable to actions of the state and local governments.

drug courier profiles Sets of characteristics that are believed to typify drug couriers.

drug testing Procedures, usually involving urinalysis, designed to test for the presence of illegal drugs in the body.

due process of law Procedural and substantive rights of citizens against government actions that threaten the denial of life, liberty, or property.

electronic eavesdropping Covert listening to or recording of a person's conversations or messages by electronic means.

emergency searches Searches by law enforcement officers in response to an emergency. In such an instance, police can seize evidence in plain view despite not having a search warrant.

en banc **hearing** A hearing in an appellate court in which all or a substantial number of the judges assigned to that court participate.

English common law The body of law based largely on custom as declared by English judges beginning in the medieval period.

enumerated powers Powers explicitly granted to a government by its constitutions.

error correction function The function of appellate courts in reviewing routine appeals and correcting the errors of trial courts.

evanescent evidence Evidence that tends to disappear or be destroyed. Often, police seek to justify a warrantless search on the ground that destruction of the evidence is imminent.

evidentiary presumptions Establishment of one fact allows inference of another fact or circumstance.

excessive bail Where a court requires a defendant to post an unreasonably large amount or imposes unreasonable conditions as a prerequisite for a defendant to be released before trial. The Eighth Amendment to the U.S. Constitution prohibits courts from requiring "excessive bail."

exclusionary rule Judicial doctrine forbidding the use of evidence in a criminal trial where the evidence was obtained in violation of the defendant's constitutional rights.

exculpatory evidence That which exonerates or tends to exonerate a person from fault or guilt.

exigent circumstances Unforeseen situations that demand unusual or immediate action.

extradition The surrender of a person by one jurisdiction to another for the purpose of criminal prosecution.

eyewitness testimony Testimony given by a person based on personal observation of an event.

factual basis When a defendant pleads guilty to an offense, the court requires a recitation of facts (usually by counsel) to establish that proof is available to show the defendant's guilt of the elements of the offense.

fair hearing A hearing in which both parties have a reasonable opportunity to be heard—to present evidence and make arguments.

fair notice The requirement, stemming from due process, that government provide adequate notice to a person before it deprives that person of life, liberty, or property.

Federal Bail Reform Act of 1984 An act that provides that a defendant charged with a federal crime may be denied bail if the prosecution can show that the defendant poses a threat to public safety.

Federal Bureau of Investigation (FBI) The primary federal agency charged with investigating violations of federal criminal laws.

Federal Death Penalty Act (FDPA) Federal legislation that (1) lists the mitigating and aggravating factors affecting a decision of whether to impose the death penalty and (2) provides for a special hearing to determine whether a sentence of death is justified in a particular federal case.

federal habeas corpus review Review of a state criminal trial by a federal district court on a writ of habeas corpus after the defendant has been convicted, has been incarcerated, and has exhausted appellate remedies in the state courts.

Federal Rules of Appellate Procedure Rules of procedure governing the practice of law before the U.S. courts of appeals.

Federal Sentencing Reform Act of 1984 A federal act directing the promulgation of sentencing guidelines.

federalism The constitutional distribution of government power and responsibility between the national government and the states.

felonies Serious crimes for which a person may be imprisoned for more than one year.

forensic evidence Evidence obtained through scientific techniques of analyzing physical evidence.

forensic experts Persons qualified in the application of scientific knowledge to legal principles; usually applied to those who participate in discourse or who testify in court.

foreperson The person selected by fellow jurors to chair deliberations and report the jury's verdict.

forfeiture Sacrifice of ownership or some right (usually in property) as a penalty.

***Franks* hearing** A pretrial proceeding that allows a defendant to challenge the veracity of an affiant's statements in the affidavit that supports the issuance of a search warrant.

frivolous appeals Appeals wholly lacking in legal merit.

fruit of the poisonous tree doctrine A doctrine based on the judicial interpretation of the Fourth Amendment that holds that evidence derived from other, illegally seized evidence cannot be used by the prosecution.

fundamental errors Errors in a judicial proceeding that adversely affect the substantial rights of the accused.

gag order A court order prohibiting attorneys, witnesses, jurors, and other persons associated with a trial from talking to the press about the case.

gender-based peremptory challenges Challenges to a prospective juror's competency to serve that are based solely on the prospective juror's gender.

general acceptance test Also known as the *Frye* test, this test requires that the scientific principle from which the expert's deduction is made has gained general acceptance in its field.

general deterrence The theory that punishment serves to deter others from committing crimes.

general objection An objection raised against a witness's testimony or introduction of evidence when the objecting party does not recite a specific ground for the objection.

general warrant A search or arrest warrant that is not particular as to the person to be arrested, place to be searched, or property to be seized.

good-faith exception An exception to the exclusionary rule (which bars the use of evidence obtained by a search warrant found to be invalid). The exception allows use of the evidence if the police relied in good faith on the search warrant, even though the warrant is subsequently held to be invalid.

good-time credit Credit toward early release from prison based on good behavior during confinement.

grand jury A group of citizens who are convened either to conduct an investigation or to determine whether there is sufficient evidence to warrant the prosecution of an accused.

habitual offender statute A law that imposes an additional punishment on a criminal who has previously been convicted of crimes.

handwriting exemplar A sample of a suspect's handwriting.

hearsay evidence Testimony by a witness as to facts the witness has heard from others that is offered in evidence at a trial or hearing to prove the truth of the matter asserted.

hot pursuit (1) The right of police to cross jurisdictional lines to apprehend a suspect or criminal; (2) The Fourth Amendment doctrine allowing warrantless searches and arrests where police pursue a fleeing suspect into a protected area.

house arrest A sentencing alternative to incarceration where the offender is allowed to leave home only for employment and approved community service activities.

hypnotically enhanced testimony Testimony offered by a witness whose memory has been refreshed through hypnosis.

hypothetical questions Questions based on an assumed set of facts. Hypothetical questions may be asked of expert witnesses in criminal trials.

identification procedures Scientific and nonscientific procedures employed by police to assist in the identification of suspects.

impeachment Impugning the credibility of a witness by introducing contradictory evidence or proving his or her bad character.

implied consent An agreement or acquiescence manifested by a person's actions or inaction.

implied exception An exclusion that can reasonably be inferred or assumed based on the purpose and intent of an ordinance, statute, or contract.

implied powers Powers not expressly granted to government by a constitution but fairly implied by the document.

in camera **inspection** A trial judge's private consideration of evidence.

incapacitation Punishment making it impossible for an offender to reoffend.

incarceration Another term for imprisonment.

incriminating statements Statements, typically made to police, that increase the likelihood that one will be found guilty of a crime.

indefinite sentencing Form of criminal sentencing whereby a judge imposes a term of incarceration within statutory parameters and corrections officials determine actual time served through parole or other means.

independent counsel A special prosecutor appointed to investigate and, if warranted, prosecute official misconduct.

independent source doctrine The doctrine that permits evidence to be admitted at trial as long as it was obtained independently from illegally obtained evidence.

indeterminate sentencing Form of criminal sentencing where criminals are sentenced to prison for indeterminate periods until corrections officials determine that rehabilitation has been accomplished.

indictment A formal document handed down by a grand jury accusing one or more persons of the commission of a crime or crimes.

indigency Poverty: in context, the inability to afford an attorney.

indigent defendants Persons accused of crimes who cannot afford to retain private legal counsel and are therefore entitled to be represented by a public defender or a court-appointed lawyer.

indirect evidence Inferences and presumptions that are probative of various facts in issue.

ineffective assistance of counsel Deficient performance by a lawyer representing a defendant that results in serious errors that prejudice the right of a defendant to a fair trial.

inevitable discovery doctrine The doctrine that holds that evidence derived from inadmissible evidence is admissible if it inevitably would have been discovered independently by lawful means.

information An accusatorial document filed under oath by a prosecutor charging a person with one or more violations of the criminal law; similar to an indictment issued by a grand jury.

initial appearance After arrest, the first appearance of the accused before a judge or magistrate, at which the charges against a defendant are read and the defendant is advised of his or her constitutional rights. Sometimes referred to as the "first appearance."

intermediate appellate courts Judicial tribunals consisting of three or more judges that review decisions of trial courts but that are subordinate to the final appellate tribunals.

interrogation Questioning of a suspect by police or questioning of a witness by counsel.

inventory search An exception to the warrant requirement that allows police who legally impound a vehicle to conduct a routine inventory of the contents of the vehicle.

investigatory detention Brief detention of a suspect by a police officer who has reasonable suspicion that criminal activity is afoot.

Jencks **Act** The common name for a federal statute that permits a defendant to review a witness's prior written or recorded statement, but only after the witness has testified on direct examination for the government.

joinder and severance of parties The uniting or severing of two or more parties charged with a crime or crimes.

joinder of offenses The uniting of different charges or counts alleged in an information or indictment into one case for trial.

judgment of acquittal In a nonjury trial, a judge's order exonerating a defendant based on a finding that the defendant is not guilty. In a case heard by a jury that finds a defendant guilty, a judge's order exonerating the defendant on the ground that the evidence was not legally sufficient to support the jury's finding of guilt.

judicial conference A meeting of judges to deliberate on the disposition of a case.

judicial notice The act of a court recognizing, without proof, the existence of certain facts that are commonly known.

judicial review The power of courts of law to review governmental acts and declare them null and void if they are found to be unconstitutional.

jurisdiction The authority of a court to hear and decide certain categories of legal disputes. Jurisdiction relates to the authority of a court over the person, subject matter, and geographical area.

jury A group of citizens convened for the purpose of deciding factual questions relevant to a civil or criminal case.

jury instructions A judge's explanation of the law applicable to a case being heard by a jury.

jury nullification The fact of a jury disregarding the court's instructions and rendering a verdict on the basis of the consciences of the jurors.

jury pardon An action taken by a jury, despite the quality of the evidence, acquitting a defendant or convicting the defendant of a lesser crime than charged.

jury trial A judicial proceeding to determine a defendant's guilt or innocence, conducted before a body of people sworn to render a verdict based on the law and the evidence presented.

juvenile courts Judicial tribunals having jurisdiction over minors defined as juveniles who are alleged to be status offenders or to have committed acts of delinquency.

juvenile delinquency Actions of a juvenile in violation of the criminal law.

knock and announce The provision under federal and most state laws that requires a law enforcement officer to first knock and announce his or her presence and purpose before entering a person's home to serve a search or arrest warrant.

lawmaking function One of the principal functions of an appellate court; often referred to as the law development function.

leading questions A question that suggests an answer. Leading questions are permitted at a criminal trial on cross-examination of witnesses and in other limited instances.

legislative intent The purpose the legislature sought to achieve in enacting a particular provision of law.

legislature An elected lawmaking body such as the Congress of the United States or a state assembly.

lineups Police identification procedure where suspects are included in a group with other persons and the group is exhibited to victims.

marital privilege The privilege of married persons not to be compelled to testify against each other.

maximum security prisons Prisons designed to minimize the movement and maximize the surveillance and control of inmates.

mens rea "Guilty mind"; criminal intent.

minimum security facilities Prisons and jails that offer inmates the most freedom of movement within the least secure environment.

Miranda **warnings** Based on the Supreme Court's decision in *Miranda v. Arizona* (1966), these warnings are given by police to individuals who are taken into custody before they are interrogated. The warnings inform persons in custody that they have the right to remain silent and to have a lawyer present during questioning and that anything they say can and will be used against them in a court of law.

miscarriage of justice Decision of a court that is inconsistent with the substantial rights of a party to a case.

misdemeanors Minor offenses, usually punishable by fine or imprisonment for less than one year.

mitigating factors Circumstances or factors that tend to lessen culpability.

monetary fines Sums of money that offenders are required to pay as punishment for the commission of crimes.

motion for a new trial A formal request made to a trial court to hold a new trial in a particular case that has already been adjudicated.

motion for rehearing A formal request made to a court of law to convene another hearing in a case in which the court has already ruled.

motion to dismiss A formal request to a trial court to dismiss the criminal charges against the defendant.

no bill Decision of a grand jury not to return an indictment.

no-contest plea Also called *nolo contendere*, a defendant's plea to a criminal charge that, although it is not an admission of guilt, generally has the same effect as a plea of guilty. A no-contest plea is usually not admissible in evidence in a subsequent civil suit.

nolle prosequi A formal entry by a prosecutor who declines to proceed further in the prosecution of an offense; commonly called a *nol pros.*

noncapital crimes Crimes that do not carry the ultimate penalty, whether death or life in prison with no possibility of parole.

notice of appeal Document filed notifying an appellate court of an appeal from a judgment of a lower court.

nullum crimen, nulla poena, sine lege "There is no crime, there is no punishment, without law." Refers to the doctrine that one cannot be found guilty of a crime unless there is a violation of an existing provision of law defining the applicable criminal conduct.

open fields doctrine The doctrine that the Fourth Amendment does not apply to the open fields around a home, even if these open fields are private property.

open public trials Trials that are held in public courtrooms that are open to spectators.

opening statement A prosecutor's or defense lawyer's initial statement to the judge or jury in a trial.

opinion evidence Testimony in which the witness expresses an opinion, as distinct from expressing knowledge of specific facts.

opinion of the court The opinion expressing the judgment and reasoning of the court, representing the views of at least a majority of the judges participating in a decision.

oral argument Verbal presentation made to an appellate court in an attempt to persuade the court to affirm, reverse, or modify a lower court decision.

order maintenance The police officer's function of keeping the peace, as distinct from enforcement of the law.

pardon An executive action that mitigates or sets aside punishment for a crime.

parens patriae "The parent of the country." Refers to the role of the state as the guardian of minors, mentally ill individuals, and other legally disabled persons.

parole Conditional release from jail or prison of a person who has served part of his or her sentence.

parole revocation hearings Administrative hearings held for the purpose of determining whether an offender's parole should be revoked.

pat-down search A manual search by a police officer of the exterior of a suspect's outer garments.

pen register Device that enables law enforcement to obtain the numbers that have been dialed by use of a specific telephone instrument.

penalty enhancement statutes Sentencing laws that provide for increased penalties when certain conditions were present in crimes—for example, the racial motivations of the perpetrator.

pendency of the appeal The period after an appeal is filed but before the appeal is adjudicated.

penitentiary A synonym for prison. Literally, a place for doing penance.

per curiam **opinion** An opinion rendered "by the court," as distinct from one attributed to one or more judges.

peremptory challenges Objections to the selection of prospective jurors in which the attorney making the challenges is not required to state the reasons for the objections.

petit (trial) jury A trial jury, usually composed of either six or twelve persons.

petitioner A party who brings a petition before a court of law.

petty offenses Minor crimes for which fines or short jail terms are the only prescribed modes of punishment.

photo packs Collections of "mug shots" exhibited to a victim or witness in an attempt to identify the perpetrator of a crime.

plain meaning rule The judicial doctrine holding that if the meaning of a text is plain, a court may not interpret it but must simply apply it as written.

plain view Readily visible to the naked eye.

plain-view doctrine The Fourth Amendment doctrine under which a police officer may seize evidence of a crime that is readily visible to the officer's naked eye as long as the officer is legally in the place where the evidence becomes visible.

plea bargaining Negotiations between a defendant and a prosecutor whereby the defendant agrees to plead guilty in exchange for some concession (such as a reduction in the number of charges brought).

plea of guilty A formal answer to a criminal charge in which the accused acknowledges guilt and waives the right to a trial.

plea of not guilty A formal answer to a criminal charge in which the accused denies guilt and thus exercises the right to a trial.

police deception Intentional deception by police in order to elicit incriminating statements from a suspect.

police departments Agencies, established by municipalities and sometimes states, whose function is to enforce the criminal laws within their respective jurisdictions

polling the jury Practice in which a trial judge asks each member of the jury whether he or she supports the jury's verdict.

polygraph evidence Results of lie detector tests (generally inadmissible into evidence).

postconviction relief Term applied to various mechanisms a defendant may use to challenge a conviction after other routes of appeal have been exhausted.

power of contempt The authority of a court of law to punish someone who insults the court or flouts its authority.

preliminary hearing A hearing held to determine whether there is sufficient evidence to hold an accused for trial.

presentence investigation An investigation held to aid the court in determining the appropriate punishment before sentencing a convicted criminal.

presentence report A report containing the results of a presentence investigation.

presumption of innocence In a criminal trial, the accused is presumed innocent until proven guilty.

pretextual stops An incident in which police stop a suspicious vehicle on the pretext of a motor vehicle infraction.

pretrial detention Holding a defendant in jail pending trial.

pretrial discovery The process by which the defense and prosecution interrogate witnesses for the opposing party and gain access to the evidence possessed by the opposing party prior to trial.

pretrial diversion A program in which a first-time offender is afforded the opportunity to avoid criminal prosecution by participating in some specified treatment, counseling, or community service.

pretrial motions Requests for rulings or orders before the commencement of a trial.

pretrial release Release of a defendant on bail or personal recognizance pending adjudication of criminal charges.

prison disciplinary measures Steps taken by prison officials to punish prisoners for misconduct, largely accomplished by removing good-time credits that prisoners earn for exemplary behavior in prison.

privileges Rights extended to persons by virtue of law—for example, the right accorded a spouse to not be required to testify against the other spouse.

probable cause A reasonable ground for belief in certain alleged facts.

probation Conditional release of a convicted criminal in lieu of incarceration.

procedural criminal law The branch of the criminal law that deals with the processes by which crimes are investigated, prosecuted, and punished.

pronouncement of sentence Formal announcement of a criminal punishment by a trial judge.

proof beyond a reasonable doubt The standard of proof in a criminal trial or a juvenile delinquency hearing.

proportionality The degree to which a particular punishment matches the seriousness of a crime or matches the penalty other offenders have received for the same crime.

prosecutor A public official empowered to initiate criminal charges and conduct prosecutions.

prosecutorial discretion The leeway afforded prosecutors in deciding whether or not to bring charges and to engage in plea bargaining.

prosecutorial immunity A prosecutor's legal shield against civil suits stemming from his or her official actions

public defenders Public officials who are attorneys and are responsible for defending indigent persons charged with crimes.

public safety exception Exception to the requirement that police officers promptly inform suspects taken into custody of their rights to remain silent and have an attorney present during questioning. Under the public safety exception, police may ask suspects questions motivated by a desire to protect public safety without jeopardizing the admissibility of suspects' answers to those questions or subsequent statements.

punitive isolation Solitary confinement of a person who is incarcerated.

putting witnesses under the rule Placing witnesses under the traditional rule that requires them to remain outside the courtroom except when testifying.

racial profiling Practice of singling out members of minority groups by law-enforcement officers for purposes of investigation.

racially based peremptory challenges Peremptory challenges to prospective jurors that are based solely on racial animus or racial stereotypes.

real evidence Refers to maps, blood samples, X-rays, photographs, stolen goods, fingerprints, knives, guns, and other tangible items introduced into evidence.

reasonable doubt standard The requirement in a criminal trial that the prosecution prove the defendant's guilt beyond a reasonable doubt.

reasonable expectation of privacy Doctrine holding that the Fourth Amendment protects persons from official intrusions as long as they have a subjective expectation of privacy that society is prepared to accept.

reasonable suspicion A police officer's belief based on all relevant circumstances that criminal activity is afoot.

rebuttal witnesses Witnesses called to dispute the testimony of the opposing party's witnesses.

redaction Editing out portions of a transcript in order to maintain secrecy of someone's identity or other information.

rehabilitation Restoring someone or something to its former status; a justification for punishment emphasizing reform rather than retribution.

release on personal recognizance Pretrial release of a defendant based solely on the defendant's promise to appear for future court dates.

remand To send back, usually with instructions.

reply brief A brief submitted by an appellant in response to an appellee's answer brief.

reporters Books containing judicial decisions and accompanying opinions.

respondent A party asked to respond to a lawsuit or writ.

restitution The act of compensating someone for losses suffered.

retribution Something demanded as payment or revenge from one who has committed a criminal offense; the theory of punishment that stresses just deserts.

reverse To set aside a decision on appeal.

right of allocution The right of a criminal defendant to make a statement on his or her own behalf before the sentence is pronounced.

right of confrontation The right to face one's accusers in a criminal case.

right of cross-examination The right to question witnesses for the opposing side in a criminal trial.

right to a speedy trial Constitutional right to have an open public trial conducted without unreasonable delay.

right to counsel (1) The right to retain an attorney to represent oneself in court. (2) The right of an indigent person to have an attorney provided at public expense.

roadblocks Barriers set up by police to stop motorists.

rule of four U.S. Supreme Court rule whereby the Court grants certiorari only on the agreement of at least four justices.

rule of law The idea that law, not the discretion of officials, should govern public affairs.

rules of evidence Legal rules governing the admissibility of evidence at trial.

rules of procedure Rules promulgated by courts of law under constitutional or statutory authority governing procedures for trials and other judicial proceedings.

rules of statutory interpretation Rules developed by courts to determine the meaning of legislative acts.

scientific evidence Evidence obtained through scientific and technological innovations.

search Inspection; attempt to locate a particular person or object.

search incident to a lawful arrest Search of a person placed under arrest and the area within the arrestee's grasp and control.

seizure Action of police in taking possession or control of property or persons.

self-representation Also known as a *pro se* defense, representing oneself in a criminal case.

sentencing guidelines Legislative guidelines mandating that sentencing conform to guidelines absent a compelling reason for departing from them.

sentencing hearing A hearing held by a trial court before the sentence is pronounced.

separation of powers Constitutional assignment of legislative, executive, and judicial powers to different branches of government.

sequestration Holding jurors incommunicado during trial and deliberations.

session laws Collection of laws enacted during a particular legislative session.

severance of the charges Conducting multiple trials for multiple charges, as distinct from joinder, which refers to trying all charged offenses at once. Where two or more related offenses are charged in a single indictment or information, the trial judge often grants a severance of the charges on the motion of either the defense or the prosecution.

sheriff The chief law enforcement officer of a county.

showups Events in which victims are taken to see suspects to make an identification.

similar fact evidence Refers to evidence of facts similar to the facts alleged in the crime charged.

skip tracers People who track down alleged offenders who have fled to avoid prosecution. Also known as bounty hunters.

sobriety checkpoints Roadblocks set up for the purpose of administering field sobriety tests to motorists who appear to be intoxicated.

special agents Officers of the FBI with the power to make arrests and use force in the enforcement of federal law.

specific objection Counsel's objection to a question posed to a witness by opposing trial counsel where a specific reason is given for the objection—for example, that the question calls for hearsay evidence.

speedy and public trial An open and public criminal trial held without unreasonable delay as required by the Sixth Amendment to the U.S. Constitution.

Speedy Trial Act of 1974 This federal statute provides specific time limits for pretrial and trial procedures in the federal courts. For example, an indictment must be filed within thirty days of arrest, and trial must commence within seventy days after the indictment.

standby counsel An attorney appointed to assist an indigent defendant who elects to represent himself or herself at trial.

standing The right to initiate a legal action or challenge based on the fact that one has suffered or is likely to suffer a real and substantial injury.

state supreme court The highest appellate court of a state.

state's attorneys State prosecutors.

status offenses Noncriminal conduct on the part of juveniles that may subject them to the authority of a juvenile court.

statutes Generally applicable laws enacted by legislatures.

stop-and-frisk An encounter between a police officer and a suspect during which the latter is temporarily detained and subjected to a pat-down search for weapons.

strict liability offenses Crimes that do not require proof of the defendant's intent.

strip searches Searches of suspects' or prisoners' private parts.

subpoenas Judicial orders to appear at a certain place and time to give testimony.

substantial federal question A significant legal question pertaining to the U.S. Constitution or a federal statute, treaty, regulation, or judicial interpretation of any of the foregoing.

substantive criminal law That branch of the criminal law that defines criminal offenses and defenses and specifies criminal punishments.

summary trial A trial that is conducted by a trial court to determine guilt or innocence in minor misdemeanor cases where defendants plead not guilty.

suppression of evidence Judicial rule forbidding the use of evidence in a criminal trial where the evidence was obtained in violation of the defendant's constitutional rights. See **exclusionary rule**.

surety bond A sum of money or property that is posted or guaranteed by a party, usually an insurer, to ensure the future court appearance of another person.

suspended sentence Trial court's decision to place a defendant on probation or under community control instead of imposing an announced sentence on the condition that the original sentence may be imposed if the defendant violates the conditions of the suspended sentence.

sworn officers Law enforcement officers sworn to uphold the Constitution and laws of the United States and of their own states.

***Terry* stop** An encounter between a police officer and a suspect during which the latter is temporarily detained and subjected to a pat-down search for weapons.

testimonial evidence Evidence received by a court from witnesses who have testified under oath.

third-party consent Consent, usually to a search, given by a person on behalf of another—for example, a college roommate who allows the police to search a roommate's effects.

three strikes and you're out Popular term for a statute that provides for mandatory life imprisonment for a convicted felon who has been previously convicted of two or more serious felonies.

totality of circumstances Circumstances considered in the aggregate as opposed to individually.

trap-and-trace devices Devices that capture incoming electronic impulses that identify the originating number of a device from which an electronic communication was transmitted.

treatment programs Programs designed to rehabilitate offenders. The term is most commonly used in connection with alcohol or drug abuse rehabilitation.

trial courts Judicial tribunals usually presided over by one judge who conducts proceedings and trials in civil and criminal cases with or without a jury.

trial *de novo* "New trial." Refers to trial court review of convictions for minor offenses by courts of limited jurisdiction by conducting a new trial instead of merely reviewing the record of the initial trial.

true bill An indictment handed down by a grand jury in a criminal case.

truth in sentencing Laws requiring that people sentenced to prison serve a specified proportion of their sentences.

U.S. Code The comprehensive and systematic collection of federal laws currently in effect.

Uniform Code of Military Justice (UCMJ) A code of laws enacted by Congress that governs military service personnel and defines the procedural and evidentiary requirements in military law and the substantive criminal offenses and punishments.

Uniform Victims of Crime Act (UVCA) A law proposed by the Uniform Law Commission designed to provide uniform rights and procedures concerning crime victims.

United States Attorneys Lawyers appointed by the president with consent of the U.S. Senate to prosecute federal crimes in federal judicial districts.

United States Code Annotated (U.S.C.A.) An annotated version of the United States Code. The annotations include references to court decisions and other legal authorities.

United States Congress The national legislature of the United States, consisting of the Senate and the House of Representatives.

United States Courts of Appeals The twelve intermediate appellate courts of appeals in the federal system that sit in specified geographical areas of the United States and in which panels of appellate judges hear appeals in civil and criminal cases, primarily from the U.S. District Courts.

United States District Courts The principal trial courts in the federal judicial system, these courts sit in ninety-four geographical districts throughout the United States.

United States Marshals Service Law enforcement officers of the U.S. Department of Justice who are responsible for enforcing federal laws, enforcing federal court decisions, and effecting the transfer of federal prisoners.

United States Sentencing Commission A federal body that proposes guideline sentences for defendants convicted of federal crimes.

United States Supreme Court The highest court in the United States, consisting of nine justices, that has jurisdiction to review, by appeal or writ of certiorari, the decisions of lower federal courts and many decisions of the highest courts of each state.

USA PATRIOT Act Controversial act of Congress enacted in 2001 to strengthen the federal government's efforts to combat terrorism.

venire The group of citizens from whom a jury is chosen in a given case.

venue The location of a trial or hearing.

verdict The formal decision rendered by a jury in a civil or criminal trial.

victim A person who is the object of a crime or tort.

victim impact evidence Evidence relating to the physical, economic, and psychological impact that a crime has on the victim or victim's family.

victim impact statement Statement read into the record during the sentencing phase of a criminal trial to inform the court about the impact of the crime on the victim or victim's family.

victims' rights Refers to the various rights possessed by victims of crimes.

voice exemplar A sample of a person's voice, usually taken by police for the purpose of identifying a suspect.

void for vagueness Doctrine of constitutional law holding unconstitutional (as a violation of due process) legislation that fails to clearly inform the person of what is required or proscribed.

voir dire "To speak the truth." The process by which prospective jurors are questioned by counsel and/or the court before being selected to serve on a jury.

voluntariness of a confession The quality of a confession having been freely given.

waiver of *Miranda* rights A known relinquishment of the right to remain silent and/or have counsel present during police interrogation.

warrant A judicial writ or order directed to a law enforcement officer authorizing the doing of a specified act, such as an arrest or a search.

warrantless arrest An arrest made by police who do not possess an arrest warrant.

warrantless searches Searches made by police who do not possess search warrants.

wiretap orders Court orders permitting electronic surveillance for a limited period.

wiretapping The use of electronic devices to intercept telephonic communications.

writ of certiorari Order issued by an appellate court to grant discretionary review of a case decided by a lower court.

writ of error A writ issued by an appellate court for the purpose of correcting an error revealed in the record of a lower court proceeding.

writ of habeas corpus A judicial writ requiring that a party be brought before a court. The primary function of habeas corpus is to release a person from unlawful confinement.

writs of certiorari Order issued by an appellate court to grant discretionary review of a case decided by a lower court.

Case Index

Subject Index